Managerial Economics

Managerial Economics
Markets and the Firm

SECOND EDITION

WILLIAM BOYES
The W.P. Carey School of Business at Arizona State University

SOUTH-WESTERN
CENGAGE Learning

Australia • Brazil • Japan • Korea • Mexico • Singapore • Spain • United Kingdom • United States

SOUTH-WESTERN
CENGAGE Learning

**Managerial Economics,
Second Edition**

William Boyes

Vice President of Editorial, Business: Jack W. Calhoun

Sr. Acquisitions Editor: Steve Scoble

Supervising Developmental Editor: Katie Trotta

Editorial Assistant: Allyn Bissmeyer

Marketing Manager: Nate Anderson

Sr. Content Project Manager: Holly Henjum

Media Editor: Sharon Morgan

Sr. Buyer: Kevin Kluck

Sr. Marketing Communications Manager: Sarah Greber

Marketing Coordinator: Suellen Ruttkay

Production Service: Cadmus Communications Company

Sr. Art Director: Michelle Kunkler

Internal Design: Juli Cook, Plan-It-Publishing, Inc.

Cover Design: Kathy Heming

Cover Image: © Tom Bonaventure/Getty Images, Inc.

For product information and technology assistance, contact us at
Cengage Learning Customer & Sales Support, 1-800-354-9706

For permission to use material from this text or product,
submit all requests online at **www.cengage.com/permissions**

Further permissions questions can be emailed to
permissionrequest@cengage.com

Library of Congress Control Number: 2010940367

Student Edition ISBN-13: 978-0-618-98862-4

Student Edition ISBN-10: 0-618-98862-9

South-Western

5191 Natorp Boulevard

Mason, OH 45040

USA

Cengage Learning products are represented in Canada by Nelson Education, Ltd.

For your course and learning solutions, visit **www.cengage.com**

Purchase any of our products at your local college store or at our preferred online store **www.CengageBrain.com**

Printed in the United States of America
1 2 3 4 5 6 7 14 13 12 11 10

Brief Contents

Contents

PART I Introduction and Foundation

PART II   Seeking Competitive Advantage

PART III   Sustaining Competitive Advantage

PART IV   Analytic Problem-Solving Tools

PART V   Looking Outside the Firm

PART VI   Putting It All Together

Preface

It is quite amazing to look around the world today and see the huge differences in wealth from one nation to another. A person in Malawi may have less than $1 a day to live on, while the average person in the United States has more than $40,000 per year. In 1800 it would be hard to know whether you were living in Latin America, North America, or Europe; standards of living were not very different. By 1900, a differential between wealthy and poor nations was being created. Today the differences are huge. According to the United Nations' Food and Agriculture Organization, there are over 800 million people in the world who don't get enough to eat. Thirty percent of children in Malawi are malnourished, and more than two of every ten will die before their fifth birthday. Why have some countries become so wealthy while others remain mired in poverty? Although development economists have studied this issue since prior to Adam Smith's *The Wealth of Nations* in 1776, the answer is relatively simple. It is economic freedom and private property. How does this apply to firms? There is a direct analogy between this answer and the answer to the question of which firms are successful and which fail? And there are direct implications for firm policy and strategy.

What I try to do in this text is to rely on the similarities between the development of economies and the emergence of firms, on the similarities between the factors that are necessary for a system of markets to develop and the internal workings of the firm, and on the analogy between the success and failure of nation-states and the success and failure of firms. In so many economics texts, particularly managerial texts, the emphasis is on optimization with constraints, solving for some algebraic formula or some optimal solution. But, this emphasis brings up the age old problem of getting lost in the trees without seeing the forest. Without understanding where firms come from, what their role is and what drives success or failure, the optimization problems provide few insights. In this text I provide an intuitive tour of managerial economics. I minimize use of graphs and math and rely instead on the verbal tradition. It is my belief that if you can understand and explain how business problems develop, what the problems are, and how they can be resolved, you can be a successful manager. You need not solve an algebraic problem.

Until the 1960s, economists looked at the firm as a black box into which went inputs and out of which came the output. What went on inside the firm was not a subject of interest. Since the 1970s, in particular, the black box has been broken into. The structure of a firm, its organization or architecture, its culture, its compensation structure and personnel policies are now subjects of interest to economists. The roles of the entrepreneur, the manager, the owners, and employees are being examined. The typical structure of a managerial economics text is to introduce demand and supply, derive production and cost functions and discuss demand prior to looking at any issues internal to the firm. I think this is backward, putting the emphasis, as I say, on optimization under constraints rather than understanding and intuition. In this text the emergence of firms, their organization, structure, personnel policies, and internal workings are considered even before the production and costs typically covered in the first part of a managerial course, especially when the firm is treated as a "black box."

In addition to considering the firm as a black box, economists have generally ignored the role of the entrepreneur. The economy is usually viewed as being in equilibrium or as changing from one equilibrium to another while the firm is typically seen as arriving at an equilibrium position defined by the market structure in which the firm operates. There is, therefore, no explicit role for innovation and recognition of profit opportunities, in other words, no role for the entrepreneur. Only those economists referred to as Austrian economists (because their initial founders came from Austria) have explicitly provided a role for entrepreneurs, but until very recently their focus has been on the macro economy, not the individual firm. The Austrians looked upon the economy as always being in motion and the entrepreneur's role as both driving innovation and equilibrating markets via competition. The entrepreneur plays an important role in the economy in innovating, creating new firms, discovering profitable opportunities even if those opportunities consist of getting the government to transfer resources from others to the entrepreneur. So, in this text, the entrepreneur is discussed and the role of the entrepreneur examined.

Tour of the Text

Chapter 1 is an introduction, indicating what will be and won't be done in the remainder of the text. The idea of "how to think like an economist", opportunity costs and scarcity, tradeoffs and thinking at the margin are discussed. In Chapter 2 the power of markets, the market process, efficiency, competition and barriers to entry are discussed. In Chapter 3 the material of Chapter 2 is carried over and market issues such as market failures are examined. The role of government in the economy is discussed as is the structure and organization of government. Then in Chapters 4 and 5, the knowledge from Chapters 2 and 3 are applied to the firm. Why firms emerge and their structure and organization are examined. In Chapter 6 the examination of market failures and government's role in the economy is applied to structures and activities inside the firm.

Chapters 7–10 are devoted to strategy. Chapter 7 is devoted to how the firm behaves when other firms do not react to whatever the first firm does? In Chapter 8 the firm's behavior is examined when its rivals do react to what it does. Chapter 9 discusses strategy with respect to the government. Chapter 10 is devoted to the entrepreneur.

In Chapter 11 the question "what should the firm do" is discussed. Should the firm maximize profit, maximize stockholder return, ensure a safe environment for customers and employees, contribute to charitable organizations or all of the above?

Chapters 12–14 contain the standard cost, demand, and profit material presented in most managerial texts.

Chapter 16 is devoted to what has become known as "the knowledge" economy. Do firms act differently when they are high-tech or do employees act differently when their productivity is based primarily on what is in their minds? Is everything now different? The answer is generally no and the explanation is presented in the Chapter.

Chapter 17 contains information about the cost of capital and the corporate form. The use of the cost of capital in allocating resources internally is discussed. In Chapter 18, this is extended to the idea of using markets as decision tools for internal allocation. Chapter 19 is focused on measuring economic profit. How accountants measure profit and how this measure is not particularly useful is discussed. Then the accounting definition is adjusted so that the measure of profit is of use in determining resource flows.

In Chapter 20 the firm is discussed in the setting of a national economy and in a global economy. The following questions are discussed. What do cycles in business activity mean for firms? What causes fluctuations in business activity? What policies does the government use to attempt to control business cycles and are these successful? What do exchange rate changes mean for a firm? Can a firm be affected by currency changes in another country?

In Chapter 21, some commonly assumed topics in strategy and business are discussed. For instance the idea that a firm has to grow to be successful is examined. Also, topics such as diversification, repressed technologies, and leadership are discussed.

In Chapter 22 several interesting cases are presented. These cases are written along the lines of the opening chapter cases.

Pedagogical Features

The opening case in each chapter presents an issue that is answered in the chapter. At the end of the chapter, a discussion of the case is presented. Each chapter contains summaries and exercises as well as key terms, margin notes, and business insight vignettes.

Ancillary Package

- Instructor's Manual guides instructors through every chapter with a Chapter Summary, Teaching Objectives, and Important Terms. For classroom help, Topics and Teaching Suggestions and Answers are offered.
- Test Bank, available in ExamView and Word formats, allows instructors to generate and edit tests easily. For ease of use, answers, level of difficulty, and topic section appear with each individual question.
- PowerPoint Slides contain key lecture points and exhibits from the text. Instructors can use these PPT slides as is, or they can edit, delete, and add them to suit specific class needs.
- Student CourseMate provides an extended learning environment for students where materials are carefully developed to complement and supplement each chapter. Students will find numerous opportunities to test their mastery of chapter content—including electronic flashcards, key term crossword puzzles, videos, practice quizzes, and Internet Exercises that are linked to the text. To access additional course materials, including CourseMate, please visit www.cengagebrain.com. At the CengageBrain.com home page, search for the ISBN of your title.

Acknowledgements

I want to thank my colleagues and others who have read the manuscript, offered suggestions and criticisms, and provided ideas, especially William S. Mounts of Mercer University, Jonathon Eyer, and Alexia Shonteff of Arizona State University.

I would also like to thank the following reviewers who provided valuable comments at various stages:

Ryan Amacher, University of Texas, Arlington

Anthony Paul Andrews, Governors State University

Javed Ashraf, University of St. Thomas

Hamid Bastin, Shippensburg University

Michael Becraft, Austin Peay State University

Barry Blecherman, New York University-Polytechnic

Robert F. Brooker, Gannon University

Paul Burgess, Arizona State University

Jeffrey Cohen, University of Hartford

Damian S. Damianov, University of Texas - Pan American

Berna Demiralp-Foreman, Old Dominion University

David Eaton, Murray State University

Harold W. Elder, University of Alabama

Kenneth C. Fah, Ohio Dominican University

Brendan P. Finucane, Shippensburg University

Yoshi Fukasawa, Midwestern State University

Mark Funk, University of Arkansas at Little Rock

Satyajit Ghosh, University of Scranton

Animesh Ghoshal, DePaul University

Stephan F. Gohmann, University of Louisville

William A. Hamlen, Jr., SUNY Buffalo

Richard Hawkins, University of West Florida

John Hayfron, Western Washington University

Stella Hofrenning, Augsburg College

Tim James, Arizona State University

Jonatan Jelen, The City College of New York

Raja Kali, University of Arkansas

Raja Kali, University of Arkansas

David Kalist, Shippensburg University

Robert Knox, Arizona State University

James Leady, University of Notre Dame

Daniel Lee, Shippensburg University

David Lehr, Longwood University

David Levy, University of Baltimore

Carl B. Linvill, University of Arkansas

Vince Marra, University of Delaware

Martin Milkman, Murray State University

Martin Milkman, Murray State University

Kathryn Nantz, Fairfield University

Andrew Narwold, University of San Diego

Michael Nieswiadomy, University of North Texas

Nitin Paranjpe, Oakland University

Abdul Qayum, Portland State University

Ken Slaysman, York College of Pennsylvania

Gary L. Stone, Winthrop University

Elizabeth J. Wark, Worcester State College

Introduction and Foundation

PART 1

CHAPTER **1**

Economics and Management

Hans Brinker or the Silver Skates

The Dodd–Frank financial regulation law (enacted in 2010 in reaction to the 2008–2010 financial crisis) establishes tighter requirements for capital and restricts risk-taking. It also contains a significant consumer watchdog component and seeks to prohibit banks from becoming too big to fail. The so-called Volcker Rule—named after White House economic adviser and former Federal Reserve chairman Paul Volcker—restricts to 3 percent of Tier 1 capital the amount banks can hedge or put into private equity. Any financial entity that is deemed "too big to fail" is subject to regulation by the Federal Reserve.

The costs of complying with the law are considerable. Many financial firms took write-downs in 2010 in anticipation of the effects of the law on their earnings.

1. What is the significance of the title, "Hans Brinker or the Silver Skates"?
2. How do firms subject to serious government regulation succeed?

What Makes a Firm Successful?

Restaurants seem to pop up suddenly and then rapidly disappear. It is not unusual to see a single corner as home first to a Mexican food restaurant, then a Chinese restaurant, followed by a new-age sandwich shop. If you look around, you see new businesses springing up all the time and at the same time existing businesses quitting. On average each year, about 7 percent of all firms in the United States are new and 1 percent go out of business. In 1917, *Forbes* published its first list of the 100 largest American companies. By 1987, that original group of 100 had been dramatically changed. Of the original group, 61 had ceased to exist; of the 39 that remained in business, 18 had managed to stay in the top 100; and of the 18 that stayed in the top 100, only 2 performed better than market average—Kodak and GE and, of course, Kodak has since fallen.[1] The speed with which firms arise, grow to be one of the largest, and then fade or become acquired by another firm is astounding. Fewer than 25 percent of today's major corporations will exist in 25 years!

Why do some firms succeed while many others fail? Why do some firms succeed for a longer period of time than others?

Is It Just Luck?

Luck plays a role in a firm's performance. There are many cases throughout history where luck defined success as much as, if not more than, skill. Consider the Philadelphia pharmacist on his honeymoon in 1875 who tasted tea made from an innkeeper's old family recipe. The pharmacist acquired the recipe and created a solid concentrate of the drink that could be made for home consumption. The pharmacist was Charles Hires, a devout Quaker, who intended to sell "Hires Herb Tea" as a nonalcoholic alternative to beer and whiskey.[2] A friend suggested that miners would not drink anything called "tea" and recommended that he call his drink "root beer." Or how about the luck of a sanitarium handyman named Will Kellogg who was helping his older brother prepare wheat meal to serve to patients in the dining room. The two men would boil wheat dough and then run it through rollers to produce thin sheets of meal. One day they left a batch of the dough out overnight. The next day, when the dough was run through the rollers, it broke into flakes instead of forming a sheet. These wheat flakes were an immediate success.[3]

Regardless of these and other examples, luck is typically not the primary factor in a firm's performance. If a company relied on luck as its primary strategy, how would the company do? Most business scholars would not expect success from a strategy of waiting for a random draw.

Is Quality Necessary?

In the 1970s, many Japanese companies followed the advice of management consultant W. Edwards Deming, focusing their efforts on producing quality products; they succeeded—and succeeded wildly—in entering the U.S. marketplace. Is a focus on quality the key to success? A study of 450 firms undertaken in the late 1980s concluded that the single most important factor influencing a business unit's profitability is the quality of its products and services relative to those of rivals.[4] Yet this does not mean that any or all attempts to improve quality will be worthwhile. Consumers may not be willing to pay more just to have a small improvement in quality. SAS Airlines pursued a philosophy of "quality only" in the late 1980s only to find that its costs escalated unchecked. In 1989 then-CEO Jan Carlzon pronounced: "We have to identify and evaluate the business traveler's total service needs … our mission is to take care of all their practical details." Two years later, Carlzon's philosophy had changed: "Everything that does not further the competitiveness of our airline activities must be removed, sold or turned into separate entities."[5] From Ford Motor Company we heard that "at Ford quality is job one," but we also saw the problems associated with the quality of the Ford Explorer.

Sir Stelios Haji-Ioannou has created an empire based on the idea that quality is not necessarily the most important thing to consumers. He owns easyGroup, which in turn owns a portfolio of companies called "easy companies". The business plan is to take the price down as low as possible by decreasing the amenities. There is a clear connection between offering services without the frills and offering lower quality services. Most people would consider a cruise line to have low quality if there was no swimming pool, casino, or window in the room (not to mention having to pay extra if you want your linens changed). Stelios has found that some people do not value the increased quality of the experience enough to pay extra. easyGroup has expanded the concept of selling lower quality products to those who are not willing to pay more for the increased quality to include easyJet, easyCar (rentals), all the way to easyPizza. For his efforts Stelios Haji-Ioannou is the 49th richest person in the United Kingdom.[6]

The Early Bird Gets the Worm but It Is the Second Mouse Who Gets the Cheese[7]

Most people believe that first movers—the first firms to bring out new products—are often the most successful.[8] Standard Oil, Bayer, Kodak, Xerox, IBM, Coca-Cola, Microsoft, Amazon.com, and Intel are examples of first movers that now have or once had well-known brand names and substantial market advantages due to being the first firm to develop a market or introduce a new product or innovation. Yet VF Corporation, a clothing supplier, has made itself a success by moving second. It allows others to take the risks, and then it jumps in with better distribution and service to take over the market. Most people believe Procter & Gamble invented the disposable diaper business when it launched Pampers in 1961. In fact, the now-defunct Chux had already been going for a quarter-century. Pampers was not a new product; it was just cheaper and aimed at a wider market. The same story can be told about video recorders. An American firm, Ampex, pioneered the product in 1956 but was swept out of the way 20 years later by cheaper models from Japanese manufacturers such as Matsushita and Sony. One study finds that the pioneers in more than 50 markets are leaders in only 10 percent of the markets examined and that, on average, the current leaders in the market entered the market 13 years after the first mover.[9]

Business Insight

First Mover Disadvantage

Being the first to stake a claim in new territory can confer certain advantages, such as setting industry standards or gaining economies of scale. But there are costs. A market has to be created, and consumers have to be educated as to the new product. In many cases, entrepreneurs are better off building the second or third version of the better mousetrap. Visicalc was the first desktop spreadsheet program. It lost out to Lotus 1-2-3, which, in turn, gave way to Microsoft's Excel. TiVo may have suffered from a first mover disadvantage. Although people now say "tivo it" for "record a television show" the market is still not huge. TiVo hit the market in 1999 and had only 800,000 subscribers by the end of 2003.[10]

Do You Have to Be Large to Be Successful?[11]

Does size mean success? Are large, dominant firms more successful than smaller firms? On average, as a business's **market share** has risen, its profit rate has also tended to increase.[12] The profit rate does not rise as fast as market share, however. Having a market share of about 10 percent yields a profit rate of about 10 percent, whereas a market share of 60 percent yields a profit rate of about 38 percent.[13] This does not mean that an emphasis on size and market share is necessarily a route to success. Acer Computer Company focused so much on market share that it lost sight of profits and very nearly went bankrupt. It has since organized into about 20 separate companies operating under a loose umbrella. Striving for market share may be a mistake. Simply being big or having a large share of the market does not necessarily mean success.

Regardless of the weak relationship between market share and profitability, most executives want increased market share for their firms. A survey by the consulting company KPMG asking what a company's motive was in launching mergers or takeovers found that over 50 percent said the reason was to raise market share.[14] Yet, achieving mass has virtually no effect on long-term company survival. In 1912 US Steel was the largest industrial company in the world; US Steel no longer has that honor. In fact, US Steel no longer exists. It was transformed into a different company, USX, after US Steel nearly went bankrupt. USX exemplifies the typical history of large firms. They rarely just close up shop and disappear. Their normal fate is to disappear from the scene when, after a period of attrition, they are acquired by more vibrant successors.

In many cases, rather than celebrating their size, large companies seem to hide it, imitating smaller rivals by shrinking headquarters, slashing layers of management, and subdividing into smaller units. Both AT&T, America's biggest telephone company, and International Telephone and Telegraph (ITT), split themselves into three parts in 1995. The movement away from size as a panacea has been applauded by two management gurus who have gone so far as to claim that the age of size is finished. The late management scholar, Peter Drucker, announced that "the Fortune 500 is over." A management consultant, Tom Peters, argued that "smaller firms are gaining in almost every market."[15] The average size of companies and workplaces has been falling since the 1970s. This does not mean, however, that size is a guarantee of failure. While Kmart and Sears have experienced serious losses and even bankruptcy while attempting to grow larger, McDonald's, Marks and Spencer, Wal-Mart, Disney, Starbucks, and Toyota have prospered while growing larger.[16] It is important to know when size is important for success and when it is a detriment.

Focus on Core Competency or Diversify?

Mergers and acquisitions by industry is provided at

www.allcountries. org/uscensus/883_ mergers_and_ acquisitions_by _industry.html

Many analysts have argued that success hinges not on acquiring a diverse set of businesses but on divesting unrelated businesses to focus on a single line of business—a core competency.[17] But here again, counterexamples are easily found. You could look at the success of GE Capital and argue against the view that a business must focus on doing just one thing. Some firms have achieved success by combining the entire production line, or "value chain," in one firm, but others have been better off outsourcing as many activities as possible to other firms.[18] Nike, for instance, does not manufacture its products itself. Instead, it uses independent contractors for producing its goods and focuses on marketing the products.

In contrast to a single focus, some firms have found success by merging or combining companies. Typically, one firm acquires another or two firms merge into a single firm. The justifications managers give for a merger or acquisition vary from case to case. General Electric acquired many unrelated firms as an attempt to diversify the risk of focusing on one product—avoiding having all one's eggs in one basket. Rowntree's brands were well known and successful in the United Kingdom (UK) but not in the rest of Europe. The acquisition of Rowntree by Nestlé, a Swiss company, enabled the company to have a presence in the UK and continental Europe. Philip Morris acquired Miller, a brewery, because it believed that its marketing. knowledge could be applied to other products. Sony acquired Columbia Pictures in order to have access to Columbia's film library; Sony had created a certain format for its HDTV and believed that control over the most important films could ensure that other studios would adopt the Sony format. WMX acquired hundreds of firms throughout the world in the 1980s in order to become the largest waste management firm in the world. Quaker Oats, a food company, acquired Snapple, a drink company, in 1994 in order to enhance its product line. Price Club and Costco Wholesale, two discount retailers, merged in order to gain further market share. American Airlines and TWA merged in 2001 in order to become more efficient. Exxon and Mobil merged in 2001 and Chevron and Texaco merged in 2002 to "leverage synergies." Hewlett-Packard acquired Compaq in 2002 in order to broaden the product base.

The number and dollar amounts of mergers and acquisitions rose dramatically between 1990 and 2001, slowed a little with the recession of 2001–2002, and then picked up steam again in 2002 and continued to rise through 2007. Yet, evidence shows that mergers and acquisitions typically do not increase the profitability of the resulting firm. For instance, Quaker sold Snapple for a loss, and Price Club and Costco were in disarray less than a year after their merger, and these were far from the only failed marriages. Some studies have shown that about 60 percent of the merged firms lagged behind their industries in terms of total returns to shareholders for three to five years after a merger. The long-run failure rate is even higher. Over a 25-year period, about half of acquisitions are subsequently divested (split up), and merged companies tend to do worse in terms of stock prices than the market as a whole.[19]

Globalization

For an interesting perspective on globalization, visit

news.bbc.co.uk/1/hi/special_report/1999/02/99/e-cyclopedia/711906.stm

Visit the World Trade Organization's website at

www.wto.org.

Globalization has been touted as a key strategy for success. Go into the business section of any bookstore, and you will see the word "global" emblazoned on almost every other book. Talk to the executives of almost any company, and globalization will soon dominate the conversation. The growth of world trade has been tremendous in recent decades. Governments have lowered trade barriers through the GATT (General Agreement on Tariffs and Trade), or what is now known as the World Trade Organization (WTO), and through regional trade agreements such as the European Union (EU), the North American Free Trade Agreement (NAFTA), and Latin America's Mercosur. Over the past decade, foreign direct investment (investment made to acquire lasting interest in enterprises operating outside of the economy of the investor) grew four times as fast as world output and three times faster than world trade.

According to the United Nations, there are close to 40,000 transnational companies—companies doing business in more than one nation, three times the figure 25 years ago. Together these companies control about a third of all private-sector assets.

Many people look on globalization as the homogenizing of markets, whereby all markets become identical. Some fear this so much that they protest at international trade meetings or even vandalize McDonald's or other firms that seem to be everywhere. But while goods and services may flow more freely among nations than ever before, markets are not homogeneous. Only a few truly global brands—brands such as Coca-Cola, McDonald's, and Marlboro—are recognized worldwide. Yet, a close look at Coca-Cola's strategy shows that even with such a well-known product, national differences are not ignored. The Coke recipe changes from country to country. The southern Japanese like their Coca-Cola slightly sweeter than do people in Tokyo, and the company obliges.

Two-thirds of Coca-Cola's Japanese products are made specifically for the local market: "Georgia Coffee," for example, can be seen everywhere in Tokyo but is unknown in Atlanta.[20]

In Japan, McDonald's stumbled until it allowed a local entrepreneur to set up small snack bars in the center of Tokyo, rather than the large suburban eateries used in the United States, and the company began using burgers made with local meat, which is much fattier than that used in America. Moreover, the hamburgers come with optional teriyaki sauce. In Mexico, the burgers come with chili peppers. PepsiCo also adjusts from country to country. It had to rename 7-Up in Shanghai because in the local dialect the phrase means "death through drinking."[21]

Leadership

Some management gurus argue that the secret of success is the person in charge. Jack Welch is credited with the success of General Electric; Bill Gates of Microsoft is looked upon as a visionary. Kenneth Lay was counted among these visionary leaders until the collapse of Enron in 2002.[22] Case studies[23] often emphasize the importance of a single person, like Herb Kelleher of Southwest Airlines, Thomas Watson of IBM, Andy Grove of Intel, Jack Welch of GE, and Michael Marks of Marks and Spencer.[24] Most of these case studies spend considerable time on the CEO's personality and background. They often feature an isolated CEO, struggling to resolve the fundamental issues of the company's strategic direction. These cases present the reasoning behind attributing a firm's success to a leader. Is success due to a charismatic personality or a visionary leader, or does it occur independently of the person in charge?

Recent studies have found that the lives of CEOs can influence the performance of their companies. For instance, traumatic events in the lives of CEOs can affect the companies' profitability. A firm's performance fell on average about 15 percent two years after the death of a CEO's child, and by about 15 percent after the death of a spouse. Another study found that the stocks of companies run by leaders who buy or build mega-mansions sharply underperform the market. Other studies have found underperformance, in both profits and stock prices, at companies led by executives who received awards such as best-manager kudos from the business press. The idea is that once they become stars, some CEOs may pay more attention to writing memoirs and sitting on outside boards and a little less to running their companies.[25]

There is no doubt that in a few instances the success of a company derives from the personality of the entrepreneur. But no research has been able to identify a set of characteristics of the people in charge that defines success.[26] Can someone be taught to be an enlightened leader?[27]

The Role of Economics

The point of the preceding discussion is that there is no formula that guarantees success. If there were, then no firm would have an advantage, since all would use the formula. Moreover, it is no more possible to teach someone to be a successful manager than it is to teach someone to be a visionary leader. However, it is possible to provide people with approaches and knowledge that aid them in thinking about business issues and making business decisions—how to identify what is important, to determine which strategies make sense when, and to deal with change.

In the 1990s, the management gurus' advice was to flatten the pyramid, become a horizontal organization, eliminate hierarchy from the company, empower the people, open the environment, transform the culture, listen to customers, create a customer-focused organization, and commit to total customer satisfaction. In addition, the leader was to increase value and price for value, write a mission statement, put together a strategic plan, continuously improve, shift the paradigm, think out of the box, reengineer the corporation, and create order out of chaos. The main problem with this advice is that there are costs involved in adopting any of it. But none of the gurus point out the costs. This is where economics is valuable. One of the basic principles of economics is that there are costs involved in any action or decision. In other words, by undertaking one action, benefits from other actions that were not undertaken are forgone. Consider, for instance, the advice "know your customer."

Know Your Customer

Knowing your customer is not some esoteric management term; it is basic economics. It simply says: Understand the demand for your firm's goods and services. A manager must know whether customers and/or rivals respond to price changes and understand when price and/or strategies not focused on price make sense. Consider Figure 1.1, which shows two standard-looking demand curves. One is very steep and the other quite flat. What difference would it make which demand represents a firm's customers? At price P_1 the quantity the customer's demand according to both demand curves is Q_1. If the firm lowers the price to P_2, notice that the quantity customers demand is quite different depending on which demand curve is correct. Similarly, whether the firm should advertise, offer guarantees or warranties, improve service or quality, focus on packaging, devote resources to ensuring distribution channels, or introduce new or different products are all decisions that require an understanding of the demand for a firm's goods and services. Do these things affect the quantities customers will buy at any given price?

Trade-offs

Economics tempers the enthusiasm of a manager to jump on some management fad or bandwagon by pointing out the costs of undertaking a particular strategy. For instance, consultants often call on the firm to be customer-focused. Yet, while paying attention to the customer makes sense, focusing solely on the customer may result in ignoring other important players in the game of business. Suppliers may be important, as may also firms that provide a complementary product. For example, Microsoft benefits when Intel develops a faster chip, and Intel benefits when Microsoft develops new software that strains the limits of existing hardware.

The reason there are **trade-offs** is scarcity: There is not enough, even at a zero price, for everyone to have everything they want. To get more of an item, something has to be

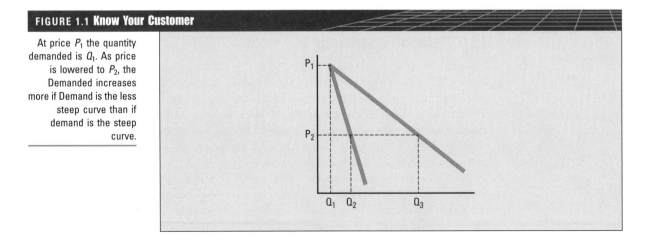

FIGURE 1.1 Know Your Customer

At price P_1 the quantity demanded is Q_1. As price is lowered to P_2, the Demanded increases more if Demand is the less steep curve than if demand is the steep curve.

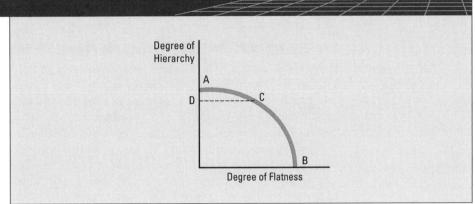

FIGURE 1.2 Trade-offs

As the firm gets flatter, from point *A* to point *C*, it gives up some hierarchy.

given up. This principle is typically illustrated in a diagram such as 1.2, which is often called a trade-off curve. Consider the organization of a firm; a choice between hierarchy or flatness exists. Along the vertical axis is the amount of hierarchy in a firm; along the horizontal axis is the flatness of the firm. Suppose the manager can select any combination from total hierarchy, point *A*, to total flatness, point *B*. Starting at point *A*, if the manager wants to flatten the hierarchy a little, he or she makes changes to move from point *A* to point *C*. Notice that something is given up—the amount of hierarchy shown in the vertical direction from *A* to *D*—to get an amount of flatness, shown as the horizontal distance from *D* to *C*.

Nothing is free To get more of some valuable thing means that some other valuable item has to be given up. Total quality management, or TQM, was the business buzzword of just a few years ago. Managers were told to increase quality or focus on quality and success would follow. In short, it was claimed that quality was free. But economics teaches that there is no free lunch—a lesson business quickly learned when it joined the quality revolution. In November 1989, Florida Power and Light became the first U.S. firm to win the Deming Prize—Japan's award for quality. Two months later, on January 11, 1990, the Florida Public Services Commission denied a rate increase request made by Florida Power and Light. Florida Power and Light wanted the higher rates to pay for the quality improvements it had made and the resources devoted to applying for the award. Florida Power and Light is not alone. Wallace Co. Inc., a Houston-based pipe and valve distributor, won a 1990 Baldrige Award, the top quality award given in the United States. In February 1992, Wallace Co. filed for Chapter 11 bankruptcy. Wallace's quality programs increased on-time deliveries from 75 to 82 percent and the company's market share almost doubled, from 10 to 18 percent, but these improvements came with a cost— about $2 million in additional overhead costs.[28]

When the quality revolution first struck the United States around 1990, several academic institutions were pressured into adopting quality practices as well. In a quarterly newsletter, the dean of the engineering school at a major university proclaimed the school's commitment to quality as not allowing a single student to fail. This sounds terrific, but it could be very costly. Consider the student who does not want to pursue the course of study or who decides that, for the time being, college is for fun, not for attending classes and studying. Is the engineering school going to devote faculty time and other support efforts to ensuring that this student succeed? If so, it will probably fail to provide support to other students—unless the school's resources are unlimited.

In short, quality is costly, and whether it is worth pursuing depends on how much the customers value quality. Virtually everyone would agree that the Concorde supersonic airplane was a great way to fly, but not many people chose it over standard flights because its cost was so much higher.

How Management Theory and Economic Principles Relate

There are more than 100 magazines and newspapers devoted to business issues. There are also at least 30,000 business books in print, and about 3,500 new ones are published each year. The advice managers get from the vast and ever expanding supply of business books, articles, gurus, and consultants is inconsistent. Consider the following clashing recommendations: Hire a charismatic CEO; hire a modest CEO. Embrace complexity; strive for simplicity. Become a strategy-focused organization; don't waste time on strategic planning. Business is war; business is what I learned in kindergarten. The demand for quick answers and easy solutions is huge, and many entrepreneurs have responded to the demand. The management "theory industry" is alive and doing very well today. However, good management may involve the opposite of the quick-fix prescriptions.[29] For example, some of the ideas in vogue in recent years include the following:

Activity-based accounting
Benchmarking
Cash cows, stars, question markets, and dogs
Change management
Codes of ethics
Core competencies
Corporate culture
Empowerment
Experience curves
Generic strategies
Hypercompetition
Intrapreneurship
Just-in-time inventory control
Lean manufacturing
Management by objectives
Market-driven and close-to-customers
Matrix management
Portfolio management
Reengineering
Relationship marketing
Self-managed teams
Skunk works
Strategic alliances and networks
Theory Z
Time-based competition
Total quality management
Zero-based budgeting

The following website is devoted to buzzwords:

www.buzzwhack.com.

Many of these terms will be discussed throughout the text. In most cases, we find that the term is simply an exotic way of referring to some basic economic rule or principle. The exotic turn of phrase is as much a marketing ploy to enhance a consultant's reputation as anything. But because the term is advertised as a quick fix to business problems, it may become attractive to managers looking for a solution to their woes. However, as is usually the case, when something seems too good or too easy to be true, it usually is—or, as the economists say, "There's no free lunch." Look at the list of management fads and ask how many are actually relied on today. Typically after a brief flurry, we don't hear about a management fad.

Many of the prescriptions offered by the management consultants are thought-provoking. The problem is that typically these ideas are adopted without an understanding of what their implementation involves or of whether the situation is appropriate for their adoption.

The essence of good management is to determine whether the implementation of a practice increases the value of a firm: Does it make money? When does a customer-only or total quality strategy make sense? When does reengineering make sense, and in what types of firms? Does just-in-time inventory control improve performance? Does downsizing or reengineering improve productivity? Understanding economics enables the manager to answer these questions. Rather than simply grabbing any hand-hold offered, the manager, having knowledge of economics, is more able to choose one that is firmly rooted.

Our Study of Managerial Economics: How Do We Proceed?

In this book we use economics to study business. This means we rely on the logic of economics to examine the way businesses compete and cooperate, their approach to structuring themselves, their compensation plans, their treatment of employees, their governance and behavior, their culture, and so on and so forth. The basis of our analysis is economic reasoning or decision making. What is economic decision making? It is what we have been talking about in this chapter—recognizing that something cannot be acquired without giving up something else. Economists refer to such decision making as comparing costs and benefits and evaluating trade-offs.

An economic adviser to an executive would require the executive to list his or her goals, to list the options available for achieving those goals, and then to select the option or options needed to reach those goals. The executive would then be required to calculate the costs and benefits of each option. A strategy such as "we want to be the best at everything" would simply be unacceptable—it is impossible. Executives must evaluate each feasible option by comparing its value and its cost, and that cost is what must be sacrificed in order to attain something. Trade-offs—giving up something in order to get something else—lie at the heart of the executive's job. And this is what economics is about.

Marginal Analysis

In the early 1950s, steelmaking was changed by the oxygen furnace. The furnace reduced milling time to 40 minutes as compared with the 6 to 8 hours needed with the open-hearth (OH) furnace that had been the industry standard since World War I. Despite the apparent superiority of the oxygen furnace, U.S. steelmakers added nearly 50 million additional tons of the old furnace (OH) capacity during the 1950s and 1960s. Meanwhile, steelmakers in the rest of the world were building new plants incorporating state-of-the-art technology. The cost advantage afforded by this new technology was a key reason why Japanese and Korean steelmakers were able to penetrate and take over the American domestic market.

Why did American steelmakers continue to invest in a seemingly inefficient technology? American steel firms had developed a considerable amount of specific know-how related to the old technology and thought that since so much had been invested it was necessary to continue investing in that same technology. But this was like throwing good

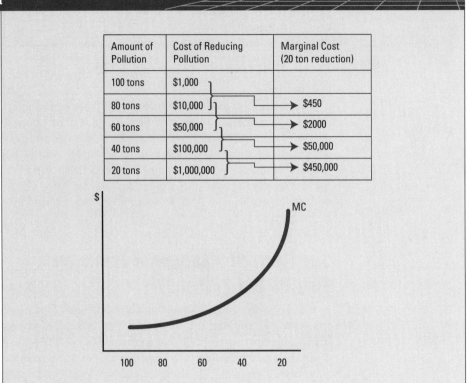

FIGURE 1.3 Marginal Cost

The change in total cost divided by the change in output is marginal cost.

Amount of Pollution	Cost of Reducing Pollution	Marginal Cost (20 ton reduction)
100 tons	$1,000	
80 tons	$10,000	$450
60 tons	$50,000	$2000
40 tons	$100,000	$50,000
20 tons	$1,000,000	$450,000

money after bad. The real decision was whether the next dollar invested would generate a greater return if it was used in the old technology or if it was used to move toward the new technology. The next dollar—the **marginal** dollar—not all previously spent dollars—was what mattered. Economics focuses on the margin—the incremental benefit or incremental cost. The focus is placed on the margin because it yields the best understanding of behavior. People allocate their budgets to all kinds of goods and services. They have to decide whether to purchase another box of cookies or dish detergent or gas for the car or clothes for the kids and on and on. So to make themselves as happy as possible, they will choose to spend that next dollar, that incremental or marginal dollar on the item that they will most enjoy.

Consider the data in. 1.3, which present a hypothetical list of the cost of reducing air pollution. The marginal cost is derived by taking the change in costs and dividing that by the corresponding change in quantity of pollution. So going from 100 tons of pollution to 80 tons is an increment of 20 tons. The cost of limiting pollution to 100 tons is $1,000, while the cost of limiting it to 80 tons is $10,000. The increment in costs is $9,000. So, dividing $9,000 by 20 tons is $450. This is marginal cost, $450 per 20 additional tons.

Now consider the data in Figure 1.4, which is the benefit side of Figure 1.3. As with marginal cost, marginal benefit is calculated as the incremental benefits that come with a 20-ton reduction in the quantity of pollution. As pollution is reduced, the initial benefits are large because health is improved and life is made easier. As more and more pollution is reduced, the additional benefits are smaller and smaller. Going from 90 percent clean to 92 percent clean adds miniscule benefits.

Figure 1.4 shows that marginal cost and marginal benefit intersect at some point. This point is the maximum *net benefits*—the point at which benefits exceed costs by

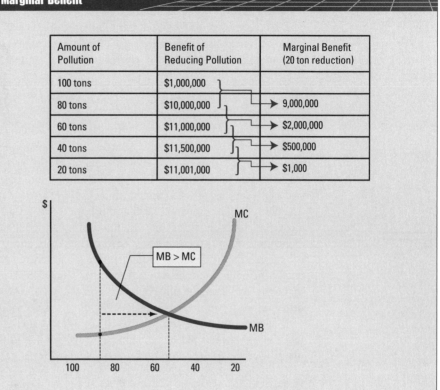

FIGURE 1.4 Marginal Cost and Marginal Benefit

The marginal cost of Figure 1.3 is combined with the marginal benefit. As long as marginal benefit exceeds marginal cost, the total net benefits increase; when marginal benefit is less than marginal cost, the net benefits decrease.

Amount of Pollution	Benefit of Reducing Pollution	Marginal Benefit (20 ton reduction)
100 tons	$1,000,000	
80 tons	$10,000,000	9,000,000
60 tons	$11,000,000	$2,000,000
40 tons	$11,500,000	$500,000
20 tons	$11,001,000	$1,000

the greatest amount. At any quantity of pollution reduction smaller than the intersection point there are additional net benefits to be had by reducing pollution more. At any quantity of pollution reduction larger than the intersection point there are additional net benefits to be had by increasing pollution. Economists focus on the margin because the margins can identify the optimal amount—in this case the optimal amount of pollution reduction. Notice that the optimal amount is not zero because at that point costs would far, far exceed benefits.

Costs and Benefits

Economics is the comparison of costs and benefits of choices. For instance, the environment and global warming is a major issue of concern; Al Gore's documentary, *An Inconvenient Truth*, tells us that climate change is the most important issue we face today. The question becomes how much should human-created greenhouse gases be reduced in order to reduce global warming.

According to *Newsweek*,

There are ominous signs that the Earth's weather patterns have begun to change dramatically and that these changes may portend a drastic decline in food product—with serious political implications for just about every nation on Earth. The drop in food output could begin quite soon, perhaps only 10 years from now.

The evidence in support of these predictions has now begun to accumulate so massively that meteorologists are hard-pressed to keep up with it. In England, farmers have seen their growing season decline by about two weeks since 1950, with a resultant overall loss in grain production estimated at up to 100,000 tons annually. During the same time, the average temperature around the equator has risen by a fraction of a degree—a fraction that in some areas can mean drought and desolation. Last April, in the most devastating outbreak of tornadoes ever recorded, 148 twisters killed more than 300 people and caused half a billion dollars' worth of damage in 13 U.S. states.

To scientists, these seemingly disparate incidents represent the advance signs of fundamental changes in the world's weather.

This sounds like the global warming stories we are accustomed to today, but it is actually a story from 1975 entitled "The Cooling World."[30] Today we worry that global warming will increase the outreach of malaria, but in 1975, we worried about freezing effects on flora and fauna, but we did not appreciate what cooling would mean for the spread of malaria. If we worried about a shortening of growing seasons in a cooling world, we should be glad that global warming lengthens the growing season. More heat in the United States or the United Kingdom will cause more heat deaths, but this will be greatly outweighed by fewer cold deaths, which in the United States are about twice as frequent. The point of this comparison is that there are costs and benefits to each situation, and it is a comparison of the costs and benefits that we undertake to make a decision.

Economists call the practice of comparing costs and benefits **rational self-interest**. It is assumed that individuals are inherently self-interested. Not necessarily selfish and definitely including sacrifice or what many call altruism, it is the assumption of economics that people will use the information they have at hand to determine whether they will be better or worse off undertaking some action than not undertaking that action.

Decisions involve a comparison of costs and benefits. Do we go to college or get a job? Do we get married or remain single? Do we live in the dorm, a house, or an apartment? Decisions, decisions, decisions! Don't we ever get a break from the pressure of making choices? Not unless scarcity disappears will we be freed from having to make choices. As the trade-off curve illustrates, to get more of one item means some amount of other items has to be given up. What is given up is the cost of the item gained.

With every choice, a marginal benefit and a marginal cost calculation take place. That does not mean we all walk around with a calculator and actually measure the costs of benefits of every decision and action. But we act as if we do. We choose to do something because we think it will provide marginal benefits that exceed the marginal costs.

Although scarcity and choice are pervasive, how people make decisions is a question that has eluded scientific explanation. Some decisions seem to be based on feelings or to come from the heart, whereas others seem more calculated. Some are quick and impulsive, whereas others take months or years of research. Is it the appeal of the book cover that makes you decide to buy one book rather than another? Does a television commercial affect your decision? The answers to these questions depend on your values, on your personality, on where you were raised, on how others might react to your decision, and on many other factors.

Although the important factors in a decision may vary from person to person, everyone makes decisions in much the same way. People tend to compare the perceived costs and benefits of alternatives and to select those that they believe will give them the greatest relative benefits. Typically, economists have little to say about why some people prefer country and western music and others classical music, although the issue is interesting. The usual assumption is that tastes and preferences are given, and those given tastes and preferences are used to describe the process of decision making.[31]

The rationality assumption is not all that restrictive. Since the 1700s, economists have assumed that people are rational—that they compare costs and benefits before undertaking any action. This assumption makes humans seem more like robots than like thinking, feeling beings. But the appearance is not correct. People are emotional, and they definitely don't have all the facts when they make decisions. People make decisions that in hindsight might look irrational, but in reality are the rational results of a brain that is economizing—finding shortcuts and easier ways to make decisions. This is one of the basic building blocks of economic analysis.

What Is to Come

Economic principles apply to problems whenever and wherever they exist, no matter the setting. The reason is that economics is based on the fact that people have to make choices. Because time, resources, and other things are not unlimited, choices always have to be made. It does not matter whether we are examining individuals, a division in a firm, a firm, or nations, choices have to be made and the principles of economics focus on how these choices are made.

Perhaps the most important part of studying economics is developing the intuition that is called economic thinking. Economics might reasonably be termed the study of unintended consequences because the logic of economics leads to results that so-called common sense might not have considered. For example, it is very common for people to argue that we will help the poor by restricting access to something such as food items or apartments or jobs. In many large cities, rents are limited by law. Not allowing rents on apartments to rise appears on the surface to be beneficial to lower income people. However, the restriction limits the number of apartments available for rent and reduces access to apartments. Often, the people acquiring the apartments are not the poor but those with connections or those with whom the landlord associates. Several states have recently restricted the business of payday check cashing, where people could get a short-term loan to carry them over until the next payday. The argument is that these loans charge excessively high interest rates. Not allowing people to get high-interest loans from payday companies would appear to benefit those people paying 30 percent or more for an advance on their paychecks. However, if they cannot have access to the funds from the payday shop, they will seek access elsewhere. Is that better?

These are just simple examples illustrating that the consequences of good intentions are often not what they were intended to be. This principle carries over to very important issues such as why some nations are wealthy and others dirt poor. In fact, the policies put in place to help the poor nations become wealthier often have unintended consequences that do more harm than good. Understanding these issues will help one understand business issues. It will enhance one's ability to solve business problems and manage companies. In fact, it is worthwhile to examine these big issues to develop the intuition necessary to understand issues regarding nations, firms, and individuals. In the next two chapters we are going to examine why some nations are wealthy and others poor because this will provide great insights into business.

Hans Brinker or the Silver Skates

The Dodd–Frank financial regulation law (enacted in 2010) establishes tighter requirements for capital and restricts risk-taking. It also contains a significant consumer watchdog component and seeks to prohibit banks from becoming too big to fail. But, as is always the case, industry executives will show that they're smarter than the regulators. For instance, the so-called Volcker Rule—named after White House economic adviser and former Federal Reserve Chairman Paul Volcker—restricts to 3 percent of Tier 1 capital the amount banks can hedge or put into private equity. But banks like Goldman Sachs can sell private equity funds to a third party and then establish a management contract in which Goldman would run those funds and take a percentage of the increase in value.

Foreign banks don't have to abide by the U.S. rules, and U.S. banks doing business overseas also can skirt the financial regulations in certain instances. Because the United

States is the world's largest economy and has the largest and deepest capital markets, there's no way for any big bank to avoid the United States, but banks will examine more closely what business they do here and what business they do elsewhere. Under the new rules, you run the risk of the Federal Reserve saying, "we're going to regulate you, or you can create a consolidated subsidiary in Switzerland which since nobody sees it, there's no regulation."

Also, many of the increased costs caused by the law will simply be passed onto customers. Free checking will not exist anymore, and customers likely will have to pay $10 to $12 a month to maintain their accounts, he said, meaning some on lower incomes may be forced to close their accounts.

Perhaps the greatest irony is that a bill designed to prevent banks from becoming too big to fail almost ensures the future of behemoth banks. Banks that lack the capital to survive will be absorbed by larger firms. For instance, JPMorgan Chase swallowed Bear Stearns and Washington Mutual; Bank of America took in Merrill Lynch; Wells Fargo ate up Wachovia. Banks are actually much bigger than they were five years ago. Rather than being broken apart, they're bigger and stronger. What it leaves is a situation where you have six huge banks, a bunch of regional banks and thousands of small banks.

What is the meaning of the title, "Hans Brinker or the Silver Skates"? The story of Hans Brinker is that of a 15-year-old Dutch boy who kept plugging holes in the dike with his thumb. Of course once one gets plugged, leaks appear elsewhere. It is like the search for profit—making it more costly to do business one way induces those firms to change their procedures and seek profits in another way.

Summary

1. Managerial economics is the study of business decision making and strategy. The economist should be able to provide valuable insights to managers on topics such as costs, prices, markets, mergers, divestitures, globalization, and personnel, since these are the topics of economics.
2. Managers have to make choices. Since economics is the study of decision making, it should provide benefits to managers.
3. There is no single formula for success. If there were, it could be taught and learned, and everyone would have it. The formula would then have no value.
4. Choice is selecting one thing or one use of resources over other things or other uses. This means that something must be forgone, or given up, in order to do something else. These are called trade-offs.
5. There is no quick and easy solution to business problems. If there were, everyone would do it and it would have no value. The study of economics can provide useful approaches to solving business problems.
6. Economics is the study of choice. Because everything is scarce, choices have to be made. So economics can be useful to understanding the behavior of individuals, organizations including firms, and governments and nations.
7. The basic assumption is that individuals are rational. This means they compare costs and benefits.
8. Economics focuses attention on the margin—the incremental dollar spent or the next dollar received, and so on.

Key Terms

Market share
Trade-offs

Marginal
Rational self-interest

Exercises

1. When would being first be a valuable strategy?
2. Would a focus on gaining market share make sense?
3. Look up the latest *Business Week* list of best-selling business books. What are five of the quick fixes suggested there?
4. You are to decide whether to implement teams in this course. Describe the costs and benefits of having teams of students work together on papers, exams, and homework. Would you implement teams? Why or why not?
5. What does it mean to say that economics focuses on the margin? What is the difference between average and marginal?
6. In the following table, total cost is listed. Calculate marginal cost.

Total Cost	10	20	40	80	130	200
Quantity	1	2	3	4	5	6

7. In the following table, total revenue is listed. Calculate marginal revenue.

Total Revenue	200	350	450	520	580	630
Quantity	5	10	15	20	25	30

8. If economics assumes people are self-interested, then according to economics, why would executives, experienced in business and exposed to business practices over many years, be so quick to grab hold of a management fad?

9. What does the phrase "there is no free lunch" mean?
10. China is the world's most populous nation with 1.25 billion people. Firms look at that population as a huge customer base and are rushing to establish themselves in China. Is this appropriate for all firms? Why or why not?
11. What is meant by the statement that "quality is not free"?
12. How would you describe globalization? Thomas Friedman wrote a book called *The World Is Flat* that was published in April 2005. From the title, what would you suggest is his main thesis?
13. Suppose the marginal cost of solving the global warming problem and the marginal benefit of doing so are listed below. How many degrees of temperature to be reduced are best for society to implement? Explain why?

Marginal Cost	10	15	22	30	50	100	500
Marginal Benefit	400	200	50	30	5	0	0
Degrees Reduced	.001	.007	.01	.015	.017	.019	.019

14. An entrepreneur quits a job where she was earning $60,000 per year and starts her own business. In this business she is earning $20,000. What is the cost of the business? Suppose the entrepreneur is so happy being on her own that she thinks it gives her the same joy that a $100,000 job would. What is the cost of the business?

CHAPTER NOTES

1. David Armstrong, Monte Burke, Emily Lambert, Nathan Vardi, and Rob Wherry, "85 Innovations 1917–1938," *Forbes*, December 23, 2002, www.forbes.com/free_forbes/2002/1223/124.html; *Creative Destruction: Why Companies That Are Built to Last Underperform the Market—And How to Successfully Transform Them*, by Richard Foster, Sarah Kaplan, New York: Random House, 2001; 5th Business, www.5thbusiness.com/page.aspx?_id=5Infeb0705.htm.
2. *Hire's Root Beer Extract a Success Story*, American Druggist and Pharmaceutical Record, October 1911, www.bottlebooks.com/hires.htm.
3. Patricia Zacharias, "Snap, Crackle and Profit—The Story behind a Cereal Empire," *The Detroit News* info.detnews.com/redesign/history/story/historytemplate.cfm?id=146&CFID=10687760&CFTOKEN=63149870.
4. R. Buzzell and B. Gale, *The PIMS Principles Linking Strategy to Performance* (New York: Free Press, 1987).
5. Thomas S. Robertson, "Corporate Graffiti," *Business Strategy Review,* 6, no. 1 (Spring 1995): 27–44.
6. www.easy.com/stelios, February 6, 2008.
7. www.quotelady.com/writings/early-bird.html, February 5, 2008
8. See, for example, Alfred D. Chandler, "The Enduring Logic of Industrial Success," in C. A. Montgomery and M. E. Porter, eds., *Strategy: Seeking and Securing Competitive Advantage* (Boston: Harvard Business School Publishing Division, 1991).
9. Gerard Tellis and Peter Golder, "First to Market, First to Fail: Real Causes of Enduring Market Leadership," *Sloan Management Review,* 37, no. 2 (Winter 1996): 65–75.

10. For more on first mover disadvantages, see: A. Gary Shilling, *First-Mover Disadvantage*, June 18, 2007, www.forbes.com/free_forbes/2007/0618/154.html.

11. For an interesting discussion of market share as a strategy, see www.buseco.monash.edu.au/depts/ ebs/pubs/wpapers/ "Competitor-oriented Objectives: The Myth of Market Share" by J. Scott Armstrong and Kesten C. Green.

12. See F. M. Scherer and D. Ross *Industrial Market Structure and Economic Performance* (Boston: Houghton Mifflin, 1990), p. 429; and Richard Miniter, *The Myth of Market Share: Why Market Share Is the Fool's Gold of Business* (New York: Crown Publishers, 2003), pp. 21–34.

13. Miniter, *The Myth of Market Share,* note 5.

14. Peter Bartram, "Why Addition Won't Add Up" *Accountancy Age,* February 3, 2000, p. 1; David Henry, "The Urge to Merge," *USA Today,* July 16, 1998, Business Section.

15. As noted in John Micklethwait and Adrian Wooldridge, *The Witch Doctors: Making Sense of Management Gurus* (New York: Random House, 1996), p. 100.

16. In late 2002 McDonald's had to slow down its rate of growth. Its size was becoming too costly.

17. See C. K. Prahalad and Gary Hamel, "The Core Competence of the Corporation," in Cynthia Montgomery and Michael Porter, eds., *Strategy* (Boston: Harvard Business School Publishing Division, 1991), pp. 277–300.

18. See James Brian Quinn, Thomas L. Doorley, and Penny C. Paquette, "Beyond Products: Services-Based Strategy," in Montgomery and Porter, *Strategy,* pp. 301–314.

19. John Kay, *Why Firms Succeed* (New York: Oxford University Press, 1995), pp. 148–151. Note the following conclusions. "At the same time, the success rate of M&As has been poor—some estimates put failure rates as high as 60%. The stats on M&A failure, in fact, might be gloomier than the American divorce rate. Depending on whether success is defined by shareholder value, customer satisfaction, or some other measure, most research places the merger failure rate somewhere between 50% and 80%."

20. In contrast to the idea that the world is flat and everything is homogenized, Pankaj Ghemawatb, *Redefining Global Strategy: Crossing Borders in a World Where Differences Still Matter* (Cambridge, MA: Harvard Business Press, September 2007), shows many differences across borders.

21. Micklethwait and Wooldridge, *The Witch Doctors,* p. 220.

22. Kurt Eichenwald, *Conspiracy of Fools* (New York: Random House, Broadway Books, 2005).

23. Case studies, such as the Harvard Business School cases, typically focus on a specific decision or series of decisions made by a firm at some point in the past. A significant part of the discussion usually focuses on the people in charge.

24. Marks and Spencer is a UK–based retail department store.

25. Summarized in *Wall Street Journal,* Online, September 5, 2007, online.wsj.com/article/SB1188397 67564312197.html; Crocker H. Liu and David Yermack, "Where Are the Shareholders' Mansions? CEOs' Home Purchases, Stock Sales, and Subsequent Company Performance" (October 17, 2007). Available at SSRN: ssrn.com/abstract=970413.

26. Rakesh Khurana, *Searching for a Corporate Savior: The Irrational Quest for Charismatic CEOs* (Englewood Cliffs, NJ: Princeton University Press, 2002).

27. Perhaps not, but perhaps a drug will be developed to help. Recent research on oxytocin indicates that it can reduce shyness and anxiety without any ill effects. brainethics.wordpress.com/2007/03/ 13/oxytocin-is-the-window-to-the-soul, accessed June 23, 2008.

28. Eileen C. Shapiro, *Fad Surfing in the Boardroom* (Cambridge, MA: Perseus Publishing, 1996), p. 175.

29. Shapiro, *Fad Surfing in the Boardroom*; and Micklethwait and Wooldridge, *The Witch Doctors.*

30. "The Cooling World," *Newsweek*, April 28, 1975, www.denisdutton.com/cooling_world.htm, February 6, 2008.

31. Recent research has relaxed that assumption and started looking into the factors that create tastes and preferences. This line of research is called neuroeconomics.

CHAPTER 2

The Power of Markets and the Wealth of Nations

Land Titling in Argentina[1]

In 1981, about 1,800 families took over a piece of wasteland in San Francisco Solano in the Province of Buenos Aires, Argentina. The occupants were landless citizens organized by a Catholic chapel. The Church and squatters believed the land belonged to the state. Once situated, the squatters had to resist several attempts of eviction, but eventually, the military government lost track of them.

Then once the military government was replaced by a democracy, the squatters brought the issue of ownership to the attention of the government. It was discovered that the land was not state property; the area was composed of different tracts of land, each with a different legal owner. So the Congress of the Province of Buenos Aires ordered the transfer of the land from the original owners to the state in exchange for a monetary compensation. About 60 percent of the land was sold to the government, and these parcels were deeded to the squatters; legal titles secured the property of the parcels. The other original owners refused to give up the land, arguing that the compensation was too low. They contested the government compensation in the Argentine courts, a contest that continued for more than 20 years.

As a result, there are two divisions of land in the occupied region: Some of the squatters obtained formal land rights, while others are living in the occupied parcels without paying rent but without legal titles. Although the groups shared the same household characteristics before the ownership and although they lived next to each other for 20 years, the outcome of their ownership arrangements has been dramatically different. Those with title invested in their properties, whereas those without title did not. As a result, there is a significant difference in the quality of housing on the untitled and titled properties. The titled properties have been upgraded, expanded, and improved; the untitled properties remain run-down, deteriorated, crumbling shanties. Not only is the housing different, those with title behaved differently than those without title: They had fewer children, and the children acquired more education and had better health.

1. Why does the title to property matter?
2. Why would those with titles behave differently than those without titles?

Why Are Some Countries Rich and Others Dirt Poor?

There are successful firms and firms that fail. Similarly, there are nations that are successful and nations that fail. It is quite amazing to look around the world today and see the huge differences in wealth. A person in Malawi may have less than $1 a day to live on, while the average person in the United States has more than $40,000 per year. Why have some countries become so wealthy while others remain mired in poverty? The answer might provide some insights into why some firms succeed and others fail.

In 1800 it would be hard to know whether you were living in Latin America, North America, or Europe; standards of living were not very different. By 1900, a differential between wealthy and poor nations was being created. Today the differences are huge. According to the United Nations' Food and Agriculture Organization, there are over 800 million people in the world who don't get enough to eat. Thirty percent of children in Malawi are malnourished, and more than two of every ten will die before their fifth birthday.

Ownership

In 1978 in Xiaogang, Anhui Province—the heart of China's rice-growing region—20 families held a secret meeting to find ways to combat starvation. The system that the communists had in place all over China was leading to a breakdown in food production. Under this system, everybody was collectively responsible for tilling the land and everybody had a share in the land's output. You got your rice share whether or not you worked hard and, as a result, people hardly worked.

The villagers of Xiaogang decided they would divide up the land and farm it individually, with each person keeping the output of his own land. They had to keep this arrangement secret out of fear of the communist authorities. But as rice production in Xiaogang continued to rise, the secret became known. Neighboring villages discovered the secret and implemented their own arrangements. It was not long until the communist authorities found out. In 1982 the Communist Party decided to allow some individual farming.[2]

The colonies first established in North America, Jamestown and the Virginia colony in 1607 and 1609, respectively, failed miserably. In each case, within a year at least half of the settlers had starved to death. The colonies were established by profit-seeking entities, and the settlers were indentured servants recruited on the streets of London from the homeless and unemployed. The settlers had no financial stake in the outcome of the colony. Working harder or longer was of no benefit to them; having been given free passage to the New World, these settlers were supposed to compensate the Virginia Company through their labor. The investors wanted everything produced to go to a company store and then sent back to England.

When representatives of the government and investors arrived in the colonies to find out why there were problems, it quickly became evident what the basic issue was. People were not working. Why should they? The produce they raised would not keep them alive; instead it had to go to the company store. As a result, settlers did not devote their efforts to planting and producing. Once the problem was identified, the solution seemed simple: Each settler was given title to a few acres of land, and only a small payment was required from them to provide returns to investors. The colonies prospered from that point on.

These historical anecdotes suggest that a primary reason that some nations are rich and others poor is private ownership. It is pretty clear that systems without private ownership don't fare as well as those with such ownership. Look at Figure 2.1, which lists

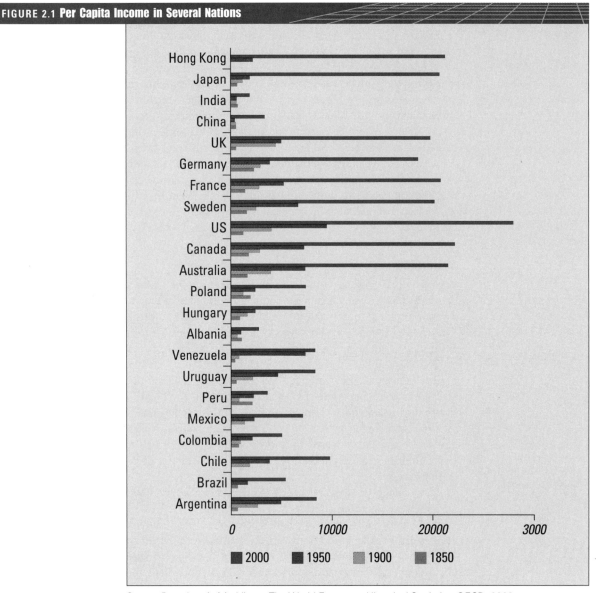

FIGURE 2.1 **Per Capita Income in Several Nations**

Source: Based on A. Maddison, *The World Economy: Historical Statistics*, OECD, 2003.

several countries along with their per capita incomes in 1850, 1900, 1950, and 2000. You can see, looking at the gray bars, that the incomes do not differ all that much in 1850. But in 2000, the differences are staggering.

In the wealthy nations, when you own something, that something is yours to do with as you want—at least as long as you do not harm others. This seems like such a simple idea. Think about renting a house or renting a car. You don't take care of it in the same way you do when you own the house or own the car. You have no incentive, other than avoiding a fee for damages, because if you spend the time, effort, and money to maintain the house or car or improve it, you get nothing in return. When you own it, you can expect to get something back on any improvements you make.

This situation goes by the phrase **private property rights**. Private property rights mean that people can own things and they can pretty much do what they want with what they own. Others cannot steal private property or damage it. In the richest nations private property rights exist and are enforced. People or governments cannot take your property without just compensation. In the poor nations either there are no private property rights or what private property rights that do exist are not enforced by government. People can steal or take property and assault you without penalty. Corruption and bribes are necessary to carry out trades or to otherwise use so-called private property.

When private property rights are not secure, people are unlikely to be able to sell the things they own or to use them for collateral on a loan or pass them along to family. And they have much less incentive to improve the property because they are not assured of a return on any investments they make.

Until just recently in China, everything was owned by government; in Pakistan, no one could be sure that whatever they claimed as theirs would remain theirs; in much of Latin America, the security of private property has not been established over lengthy periods of time. Beginning in 2006, the governments of Venezuela and Bolivia started to confiscate private property. And for much of the poor in Latin America, there is no legal ownership or titling of property.

When private property rights are not universal among citizens, or when enforcement is not wide scale, a nation will not prosper. An abundance of a natural resource such as oil may distort this fact for awhile, but the abundance cannot carry over to all citizens unless private property exists. In most oil-producing nations the oil is owned by government, and only a very few benefit from the resource. But when private property rights prevail, nations prosper even without abundant resources. Hong Kong had nothing, no natural resources except a harbor, and it emerged as one of the wealthiest countries in the world in just a few decades (Hong Kong is not actually a country as it was never independent, having been part of the British Empire for 150 years and now part of China). The wealthiest nations have a system of private property rights where people can own property and be secure in their ownership. The poorest nations do not.

Private property may seem like something just for the rich, but it is crucial for the poor. If people have no title to property, they cannot rent it to others, subdivide it, sell it, use it for collateral, or pass it on to family. Peruvian economist Hernando de Soto[3] has argued that in the developing world, the value of property owned but not legally titled is worth about $10 trillion. That is a lot of collateral—just think if it was a 20 percent down payment how much additional liquidity could be created and how that liquidity might lead to increased investments and wealth.

The farmers in Xiaogong who agreed to divide up the land for cultivation could not sell their land or even pass it along to family. The amount of rice raised on the so-called private plots was significantly greater than when everything was communal, but there was a limit on what could be done with the property and thus a limit to possible returns on that land.

Incentives

Incentives matter. When you own something you have the incentive to take care of it, that is, you have the incentive to increase its value and to invest in it. If farmers can raise corn and that corn is theirs, they can take the corn to market and sell it. They will invest in ways to provide better quality and ensure that they have seeds remaining to grow more corn next year. Similarly, when we offer to work, we are taking our own labor, something we own, and exchanging it for pay. The higher the quality of our work, the more productive we are and the more we can earn.

When no one owns something, no one has an incentive to take care of it. Forced to work in shipbuilding factories in Gdansk, Poland during the communist regime, workers would show up and then loaf. They had no incentives to be productive as they received the same pay no matter what they did. When you own your own labor or property, you have the incentive to make it as valuable as possible because then you can trade for other things you want.

Trade

Abraham Lincoln argued that the United States should not buy cheap iron rails from Britain to finish the transcontinental railroad. He said, "It seems to me that if we buy the rails from England, then we've got the rails and they've got the money. But if we build the rails here, we've got our rails and we've got our money."[4]

Think about Lincoln's logic for a moment. If you want beef, following Lincoln's logic, you should raise the cow in your backyard since then you have both the beef and your money. Why don't we raise our own beef? We don't because it would take too much of our time and resources. We can be better off to let ranchers raise the beef and focus on what we do best. If we do what we are best at and rely on others to do what they do best, we can all gain by exchanging what we create.

This works for nations as well. The United States can do a lot of things better than any other nation. It is the most productive agricultural producing country in the world, while it is also the greatest technological country. Bangladesh, on the other hand, is a very poor country, unable to create or produce anything that matches what the United States can do. So what can a poor country like Bangladesh offer the United States? Bangladesh has a huge supply of unskilled labor that enables it to assemble things, especially clothing, tremendously less expensively than the United States can. A t-shirt can be put together in Bangladesh for a fraction of the cost of making that t-shirt in the United States. So if the consumers in the United States want t-shirts, are they better off making them in the United States or allowing Bangladesh to make the t-shirts and trade them to the United States for food or products? Rather than giving up a few hours to create a t-shirt, a U.S. engineer can simply take what he earns for working 10 minutes and purchase several t-shirts that were made in Bangladesh.

The fact that voluntary trade benefits the traders is often counterintuitive, as illustrated by Lincoln's statement. To clarify how people gain from trade, let's consider a simple numerical example. Suppose that if the United States devoted all its resources to agriculture, it would be able to produce 10 units. Conversely, if all U.S. resources were devoted to high-tech products, 10 units of such products and equipment could be produced. China, on the other hand, could produce 4 units of high-tech products and equipment by devoting all its resources to high technology or could produce 8 units of agricultural products by devoting all its resources to agriculture. The United States is able to produce more of everything than China but is relatively more efficient at producing high-tech products and equipment. We say that the United States has an **absolute advantage** in high technology and agriculture but a **comparative advantage** in high-tech production. China has no absolute advantage. However, it does have a comparative advantage in agricultural production: It gives up 1/2 unit of high technology for each unit of agriculture, while the United States gives up 1 unit of high technology for each unit of agriculture. In other words, it costs the United States more to produce a unit of agricultural products than it does China, even though the United States is able to produce more of everything. One unit of agricultural products costs the United States one unit of high-tech products; in China, one unit of agricultural products costs just ½ unit of high-tech products.

Suppose each country completely specializes in areas where each has a comparative advantage—the United States produces 10 units of high technology and China, 8 units of agriculture—they can then trade to get what they want. For instance, suppose China agrees to give up 6 units of agricultural products in return for the 4 units of high-tech products and equipment. Then the United States ends up with 6 units of agricultural products and 6 units of high-tech products and equipment, while China gets 2 units of agricultural products and 4 units of high-tech products and equipment. The United States could have produced only 5 units of agricultural products and 5 units of high-tech products and equipment on its own, so it gains 1 unit of agricultural products and 1 unit of high-tech products with the trade. China by itself could have produced only 4 units of high-tech products and equipment; it gains 2 units of agricultural products with the trade. Each country can get more by specializing and trading than by being self-sufficient.

When everyone does what they do at the least cost and then trades, everything is getting produced at the least cost. This means it will take less to get everything—in essence, everyone's income has risen. This is referred to as **gains from trade**.

Tiger Woods is the best golfer in the world and generates millions of dollars in income a year. He did study accounting at Stanford University for a year or so and probably could handle his own money management and accounting. He does not; he hires a money manager. Why? Because he uses his time to improve his golf, which generates more income than he would save by doing his own money management.

Once people specialize in what they do at relatively lower costs than others, they have to trade for everything else they want and need. How does trade occur—how are the specialized producers to get together or to know who specializes in what? The answer depends on how we decide who gets the goods and services and who produces them.

Allocation Mechanisms

Every good is **scarce**; if not, it would be free or it would be bad, something we would pay to have less of. Scarcity of a good means some people will acquire that good and others won't; scarcity of resources means some activities will be selected and others won't. Scarcity would not exist if everyone had everything they wanted. Who or what gets the resources or products depends on the way the resources and products are allocated.

An allocation mechanism is the system by which scarce goods are distributed. Allocation mechanisms in use today include the price or market system, first-come-first-served, government-determined allocation, and even luck. Does it matter? The answer is yes, as you can see by completing the following survey.

For each of the following situations, indicate what you think of each of the following means of distributing the water to the hikers by responding to each allocation approach with one of these five responses:

    a. Completely Agree
    b. Agree
    c. Slightly Disagree
    d. Disagree Strongly
    e. Totally Unacceptable

Scenario I: At a sightseeing point, reachable only after a strenuous hike, a firm has established a stand where bottled water is sold. The water, carried in by the employees of the firm, is sold to thirsty hikers in 6-ounce bottles. The price is $1 per bottle. Typically only 100 bottles of the water are sold each day. On a particularly hot day, 200 hikers want to buy at least one bottle of water.

1. Increasing the price until the quantity of bottles hikers are willing and able to purchase exactly equals the number of bottles available for sale.
2. Selling the water for $1 per bottle on a first-come-first-served basis.

3. Having the local authority (government) buy the water for $1 per bottle and distributing it according to its own judgment.
4. Selling the water at $1 per bottle following a random selection procedure or lottery.

Scenario II: The following is a similar situation but involves a different product. A physician has been providing medical services at a fee of $100 per patient and is unable to see more than 30 patients per day. One day the flu bug has been so vicious that the number of patients attempting to visit the physician exceeds 60. Indicate what you think of each of the following means of distributing the physician's services to the sick patients by responding with one of the five answers shown above.

1. Raising the price until the number of patients the doctor sees is exactly equal to the number of patients willing and able to pay the doctor's fee.
2. Selling the services at $100 per patient on a first-come-first-served basis.
3. Having the local authority (government) pay the physician $100 per patient and choosing who is to receive the services according to its own judgment.
4. Selling the physician's services for $100 per patient following a random selection procedure or lottery.

Scenario III: The following describes an all too familiar situation of shortage. The number of people needing new kidneys far exceeds the number of kidneys being donated for transplant. Evaluate the various methods for determining who gets a new kidney.

1. Raising the price until the number of patients willing and able to purchase a kidney is exactly equal to the number of people willing and able to sell a kidney.
2. Providing the kidneys on a first-come-first-served basis.
3. Having the government choose who is to receive the kidneys.
4. Starting a lottery-determined allocation—kidney patients are put into a lottery and the winning names receive kidneys.

Figure 2.2 illustrates the results of an expanded version of the questionnaire administered to several hundred people. The allocation mechanism (first-come-first-served, government, price, random) is noted along the horizontal axis, and the percentage of respondents selecting either A:"Strongly Agree" or B:"Acceptable" is shown along the vertical axis. Each bar then represents the percentage of survey respondents who

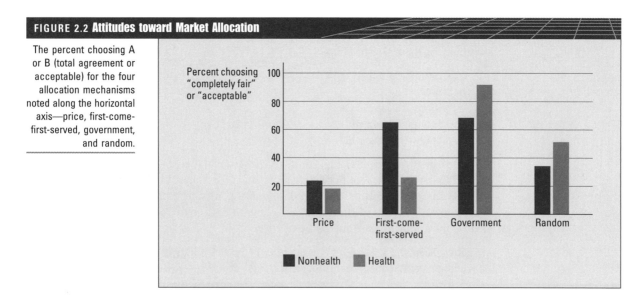

FIGURE 2.2 Attitudes toward Market Allocation

The percent choosing A or B (total agreement or acceptable) for the four allocation mechanisms noted along the horizontal axis—price, first-come-first-served, government, and random.

Percent choosing "completely fair" or "acceptable"

Nonhealth ■ Health

essentially agree with the allocation mechanism indicated for nonhealth items (blue) and for health items (gray).

The general public does not particularly care for the price system and agrees more with government allocation. Why? Many say that the market system is unfair because only the rich get things. But each allocation mechanism is unfair in the sense that someone gets the good or service and someone doesn't. With the price system, it is those without income or wealth who must do without. Under the first-come-first-served system, it is those who arrive later who do without. Under the government scheme, it is those not in favor or those who do not match up with the government's rules who do without. And with a random procedure, it is those who do not have the lucky tickets who are left out.

Business Insight

Price Controls on Energy in China

Price controls on hundreds of items remain in force in China, even though many were lifted when China entered the World Trade Organization in 2001. The Chinese government continues to set prices on fuel, for instance, and government allocation does not necessarily provide fuel where it is most needed. With oil prices reaching record-high levels worldwide in 2005–2007, China had difficulty allocating the scarce resource. Dozens of service stations in cities near Hong Kong ran out of fuel just as officials in Beijing were debating requests from domestic oil companies to charge more for diesel and gasoline. The result was long lines of angry motorists at gas stations and freight shipments that were disrupted because trucks could not make trips.[5]

Since each allocation mechanism is in a sense unfair, how do we decide which to use? Once again, incentives matter. With the price system, the incentive is to acquire purchasing ability. This means you must provide goods and services that have high value to others and provide resources that have high value to producers—to enhance your worth as an employee by acquiring education or training, to enhance the value of the resources you own—in order to obtain income and wealth. The price system also provides incentives for quantities of scarce goods to increase. In the case of the bottled-water stand described earlier, if the price of the bottles increases and the owner of the stand is earning significant profits, others may carry water to the sightseeing point and sell it to thirsty hikers—the amount of water available thus increases. In the case of the doctor, other doctors may think that opening an office near the first might be a way to earn more—the amount of physician services available thus increases. The price system creates the incentive for the amount supplied to increase. In the case of kidneys, more and more people offer to provide kidneys.

But, you say, what will happen is that people will jump you and steal your kidney. This might happen on a rare occasion.[6] It depends on whether you have ownership of your body. You own your car. Are you afraid to drive it down the street for fear that someone will jump you and take the car? It does happen but not much—it is illegal. Similarly, it is illegal for someone to steal your organs. So, it is not valid to argue against a market in human organs because of the fear of theft, any more than it is to argue against a market in bottles of water for fear of theft.

The incentives of the market system ensure that economies grow and expand and that standards of living improve. The price system also ensures that resources are allocated to where they are most highly valued. If the price of an item rises, consumers may switch over to another item or another good or service that can serve about the same purpose.

When consumers switch, production of the alternative good rises and thus resources used in its production must increase as well. The resources then are reallocated from lower-valued uses to higher-valued uses.

With the first-come-first-served allocation scheme, the incentive is to be first. You have no reason to acquire an education or improve the quality of your products. Your only incentive is to be first. Yet, first for what? No one will produce anything. Supply will not increase; growth and standards of living will not rise. A society based on first-come-first-served would die a quick death.

A government scheme provides an incentive either to be a member of government and thus help determine the allocation rules or to perform according to government dictates. There are no incentives to improve production and efficiency, or to improve quantities supplied, and thus no reason for the economy to grow.

Random allocation provides no incentives at all—simply hope that manna from heaven will fall on you.

Business Insight

Attitudes toward Free Markets

Throughout the Western world people's attitudes toward the virtues of free markets vary widely. According to the World Value Survey, only 22 percent of French people believe that owners should run their businesses and appoint their managers, while about 58 percent of Americans do believe owners should run their business and appoint managers. Of the richest 18 countries, Iceland, the United States, Canada, and Australia are most supportive of the free market while Belgium, Japan, France, and the Netherlands are the least supportive. The ranking of these nations on the belief that competition is good (on a scale of 10 where 10 is the strongest agreement with this belief) is as follows:

Iceland	7.2	Germany	6.6
Australia	6.8	New Zealand	6.5
Austria	6.8	Finland	6.1
United States	6.7	Denmark	6.0
Switzerland	6.7	United Kingdom	6.0
Sweden	6.7	Belgium	5.6
Norway	6.6	Japan	5.6
Singapore	6.6	France	5.5
Canada	6.6	Netherlands	5.5

Source: Augustin Landler, David Thesmar, and Mathia Thoenig, "What Accounts for Europe's and America's Different Attitudes toward the Free Market?" Sternbusiness, Fall/Winter 2007. w4.stern.nyu.edu/sternbusiness/fall_2007/comparative Capitalism.html; www.worldvaluessurvey.org/

Efficiency

It is the incentives created by allocation mechanisms that make the market system "better" than the others. A system of markets and prices is generally the most **efficient** means of coordinating and organizing activities, where efficiency means you get the same amount at a lower cost. Individuals offer to sell goods and services at various prices, and other individuals offer to buy goods and services at various prices. Without having anyone coordinating the buyers and sellers, the market determines a price for each traded good at which the quantities that people are willing and able to sell are equal to the quantities that people are willing and able to buy. But not just this. The market does this using fewer resources than other allocation mechanisms as well.

In his television special, "Greed,"[7] John Stossel wonders how beef gets to New York from the farms in Iowa. Economist Walt Williams responds: "If it was all compassion and caring about your fellow man, I feel sorry for New Yorkers in terms of beef. Not a single cow would end up in New York." Somehow the right amount of beef makes its way from a field in Iowa to a restaurant in Manhattan. Similarly, a neighborhood flower vendor has exactly what customers want every morning, even though the plants may come from half way around the world; the baker has the bread his customers desire; the chef has the exact ingredients desired by patrons. An economy involves billions of transactions every day that take place without any central planning or government dictate.

We have the things we desire when we desire them because of the market. We can purchase nearly anything 24 hours a day from the comfort of our own homes. What we purchase is not only much better than the same type of thing was just a few years ago but we are able to purchase more of it. We see this in constantly rising standards of living, which means improvement in every aspect of life: Life expectancy has nearly doubled in a century, and diseases such as polio, tuberculosis, typhoid, and whooping cough have essentially been wiped out.

This result occurs because the market encourages people to do what they do best and to improve themselves. And everyone acting to improve and increase their own living standards leads to a thriving and ever improving standard of living for society.

Exchange and Markets

Of course, specialization means you are not producing all the things you need to survive, let alone to prosper. So to get what you want, you must exchange what you produce for those things you actually want, and this requires some form of coordination. In a market system, that coordination is carried out not by some centralized bureaucrat but by individuals pursuing their self-interests. The farmer raises cattle in order to sell the cattle and be able then to purchase whatever else the farmer wants. The butcher packages and sells the beef in order that he can have money to purchase a car, house, and so on. The truck driver delivers the beef in order that he can earn the money necessary to purchase whatever he desires. The supermarket sells the beef to customers. The beef makes its way from Iowa to New York via hundreds, if not hundreds of thousands, of transactions wherein individuals are seeking not beef, but something else.

Prices inform buyers and sellers about what they must give up to acquire a unit of the good (what economists call their **opportunity costs**), and prices let them know whether their activities have value. Day in and day out, without any conscious central direction, the price system induces people to employ their talents and resources in the most effective manner.

People do not have to be fooled or forced to do their part in a market system but instead pursue their own objectives as they see fit. Workers, attempting to maximize their own individual happiness and well-being, select the training, careers, and jobs where their talents and energy are most valuable. Producers, pursuing only private profits, develop the goods and services on which consumers put the highest value and produce these goods and services at the lowest possible costs. Owners of resources and capital assets, seeking only to increase their own wealth, deploy these assets in socially desirable ways.

This sounds good, but it can't possibly be true, can it? Don't many people simply have no choice—they simply have to work in terrible conditions or what we would call sweatshops? Clearly these poor people who have been exploited by the market system are not better off than they would be without the market system. Actually they are better off. People take jobs in unpleasant, low-wage facilities voluntarily. They do so because it is the best employment option they have. What would happen if every sweatshop was eliminated and wages and working conditions improved to match the standards in wealthy nations? All those who had jobs in the sweatshops would be without jobs.[8]

When trade is not voluntary, it is a different matter. When people are forced to work in occupations not of their choosing, when citizens are forced through threat of violence to pay tribute or taxes, then the trade is not making people better off. People engage in voluntary trade or exchange because they are able to get more for less, to make themselves better off. This is one of the essential assumptions of economics—that people try to make themselves as well off as possible. Different people have different preferences and so behave somewhat differently. People who are wealthy may choose different things than people who are not, and nations that are wealthy may select different options from those who are not. These are simple facts. The complexity comes when we ask whether the preferences of the wealthy should dictate what the poor can do? Should the preferences of the wealthy nations be imposed on the poor nations? Economists, in general, answer no. But policymakers do it all the time. Think about the declining populations of rhinos in sub-Saharan Africa. Poachers kill the animals for their tusks; a single rhino tusk could reap as much as $30,000.[9] The wealthy nations have attempted to stop the practice by banning the tusks, and wealthy individuals don't understand how poachers could kill these and other wild animals. But put yourself in the shoes of someone who is starving or whose children are at risk of dying of malaria. If a skin or tusk could ensure life for a year, would you hesitate to shoot the rhino?

Competition

When the Mazda Miata was introduced in the United States in 1990, the little sports roadster was an especially desired product in Southern California. Its suggested retail price was $13,996, the price at which it was selling in Detroit. In Los Angeles, however, the purchase price was nearly $25,000. The identical product, the Miata, was selling for different prices in different markets—the Detroit auto market and the Los Angeles auto market. Stories were circulating at several colleges that students could be paid to go to Detroit to pick up a Miata and drive it back to L.A. There must have been some truth in the stories because within a reasonably short time, the price differential between Detroit and L.A. was reduced. The increased sales in Detroit drove the price there up, while the increased number of Miatas being sold in Los Angeles reduced the price there. The price differential continued to decline until it was less than the cost of shipping the cars from Detroit to Los Angeles.

The process of buying identical products in one market and selling them in another at virtually the same time is referred to as **arbitrage**. Arbitrage is the market process in operation. It ensures that resources are allocated to their highest valued uses—that inefficient transactions, inefficient organizations, and inefficiency of any sort wither away. Arbitrage need not just be dealing with price. The idea that people will search for the greatest return, everything else being the same, works on other dimensions as well. If two products are differentiated only by quality, arbitrage will involve buying the higher-quality product and selling the lower-quality one. This forces the lower quality product to increase its quality, or prices will change to reflect quality differences.

Arbitrage is a search for gains. By buying in a low-priced market and selling in a higher-priced market, you come away with a gain or a profit. In fact, the search for profit is what drives each person and each firm to innovate, to do things better, to do things cheaper. If you make a better mousetrap, the world will beat a path to your door; if you make the same old mousetrap, you better offer it for less or it is time to start firing people.

Wal-Mart made a better mousetrap. As a result, it is the largest retailer in the world and one of the best performing firms over the past 30 years. Its success has been based on a simple strategy of low prices. Although communities fight the openings of the big box warehouses, whenever they do open, customers flock to them. They flock to Wal-Mart because the store offers an amazing range of products cheaper than can be purchased anywhere else. Obviously, customers think this is a very good thing. They can spend $100 for items that would cost $150 without Wal-Mart. This allows people to spend that $50 to acquire something else; being able to buy goods cheaper is essentially the same thing as having more income.

The search for profit is the market in action—it is competition. Competition drives out inefficiency and ensures that resources are allocated to their highest valued uses. Think what would occur if a firm were not using resources efficiently or in their highest valued use. When Wal-Mart enters a community, it offers products at much lower prices than the mom and pop stores that exist in that community. Customers buy from Wal-Mart rather than mom and pop. This means that the mom and pop store has to offer low prices as well, but it can't do that unless it can become as efficient as Wal-Mart. In communities where the mom and pop stores fail to match Wal-Mart's prices, many end up going out of business. The resources previously employed in the mom and pop are let go and must find use in other endeavors.

Wal-Mart seems to be the ultimate nightmare for Joe's Hardware store and for mom and pop stores everywhere.[10] This nightmare is competition in operation; it is progress. We can look back and see the amazing technological breakthroughs of the past 300 years, bringing to the public the steam engine, spinning wheel, telephone, and vaccines against measles, mumps, polio, and others. At the same time, those advances eradicated whole industries—telegraph operators, blacksmiths, and bloodletters. In 1900 half of all Americans worked in farming or ranching; today less than 2 percent of the population is involved in these industries.

Although entire industries have been destroyed by competition, many more have been created. We have more and better foodstuffs, and 48 percent of the population is not unemployed. The people who would have been farming had things not changed are instead designing computer software, playing professional sports, and producing movies. This process of resources moving to where their value is the greatest as a result of competition is called creative destruction.

Creative destruction is a tremendous positive force in the long run; the problem is that in the short run people lose jobs and ways of life. When a steel plant in Gary, Indiana closes, hundreds of workers are idled. They can't pay their mortgages, buy groceries, or send their kids to school. A few years later many will have left Gary for other cities and jobs; others will have taken jobs with new companies moving into the area; and others will have retired. For some it is extremely difficult and sad. But in the long run, more wealth is created, better products are provided, and standards of living rise.

Why does competition work this way? It stems from the basic assumption that individuals want to make themselves as well off as possible. So, people will try to sell the use of their resources for the highest value possible. Given a choice among occupations, people will choose the one that provides them the best quality of life. If that particular occupation no longer provides the best quality of life, people will move, or acquire training, or pursue other occupations. Similarly, people will rent their land to the highest valued use for that land and will put their savings/investments into those activities that they expect to generate the greatest return for any given risk. If nothing changed, then the resources would remain where they are doing exactly what they are doing. But because people want to make themselves as well off as possible, they are always looking for ways to create greater returns—higher pay, better investments, higher rents. They come up with better ways of doing things. Bill Gates devised a computer operating system for the PC; Intel came up with faster and faster computer chips; Wal-Mart created an inventory control system that enabled it to sell items for less than other retailers could. These innovations occurred because of competition—people are continually looking for ways to excel, to earn more and live better.

Competition drives prices ever closer to the costs of production. If it costs $0.70 to produce a cup of coffee and I sell it for $1.50, someone is going to come along and sell it for $1.00. Then someone else will sell it for $0.90. Eventually, it will be selling for something very near $0.70. Competition requires that resources be used as efficiently as possible. Anyone not being as efficient as possible will not last long in the market. If you can't produce that coffee for $0.90, then you will not be in business when the price drops below $0.90.

Moreover, being efficient at one point in time does not mean you will remain there forever. Just look at the performance of firms over time. You not only have to build a better mousetrap, but you have to continually improve it. There is no resting on one's laurels when competition is prevalent. In 2006 and 2007, Wal-Mart stumbled as other retailers were able to introduce comparable efficiencies and match the low prices. It is very difficult for a firm to sustain its success over many years.

Barriers to Entry

The competitive market provides a kind of consumer heaven. We get what we want, when we want it, and at the lowest possible prices. Yet, at the same time, it seems to be a problem for sellers. Prices are driven down lower and lower as rivals attempt to solicit customers. As long as a rival can begin selling what you are selling, you are limited in what you can earn. To earn more than what the competitive market would allow, a business has to acquire some type of monopoly—a way to limit the competition they face. Although coffee costs about $0.70 per cup, Starbucks charges $1.65 for a small (called "tall") cup of coffee. Starbucks charges more than most other coffee shops and makes good money while charging more; it does this because it has acquired a sort of **monopoly**—a unique place in the market.

How is a firm able to maintain its monopoly, that is, to limit competition? Starbucks has done it by creating a well-known name and reputation. People know they will get the same taste and ambience no matter which Starbucks they enter. Coca-Cola has done it by convincing people that its combination of corn syrup and water is different from any other combination; it is Coke, not just soda. A **brand name** is a form of monopoly—a market niche in which competition is limited. A firm with a strong brand name can charge more for the same item than a firm with a generic name. In these cases, consumers choose to purchase from these companies. Consumers are not forced or required to purchase from them but choose to do so and to pay high prices because they perceive a benefit.

A more formidable barrier to competition is the government. Government-granted monopolies, regulations, restrictions, market controls, and on and on, all alter or restrict competition. The market cannot work to create the incentives necessary to raise standards of living or to solve shortages and surpluses if economic freedom does not prevail. Economic freedom refers to the degree to which private individuals are able to carry out voluntary exchange without government involvement and, thus, provides an indication of what trade without corruption means.

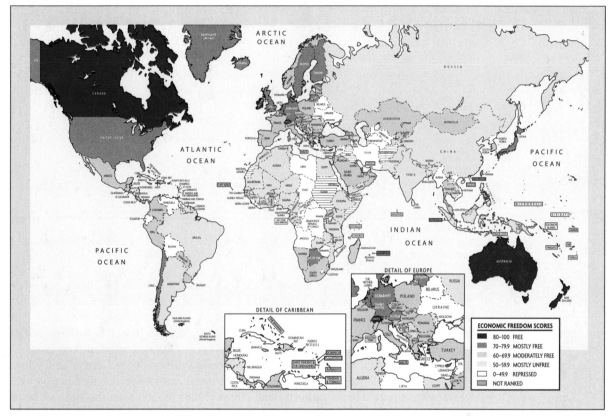

FIGURE 2.3 2010 Index of Economic Freedom

Each year, the Heritage Foundation and *The Wall Street Journal* calculate the list of the most and least economically free nations.

Source: The Heritage Foundation

The *Wall Street Journal* and the Heritage Foundation coauthor an annual measure of economic freedom called the Index of Economic Freedom (see Figure 2.3). According to the Index of Economic Freedom, the United States is only about the tenth freest economy in the world. Nations such as Luxembourg, Ireland, New Zealand, Ukraine, and even Hong Kong are rated as being freer than the United States. What this means is that government is more involved in the economy in the United States than it is in these other nations. Higher taxes mean less economic freedom, more rules and regulations mean less economic freedom, restrictions on travel mean less economic freedom, restrictions on international trade mean less economic freedom, the paperwork necessary to comply with government rules and regulations means less economic freedom, and so on.

In general, the greater a nation's economic freedom, the higher its standard of living. The freest nations average more than $30,000 per capita income, the mainly free economies average about $14,000, and the mainly unfree and repressed economies average just over $4,000, little more than one-eighth that of the freest nations.[11]

Lessons

So what are the steps necessary for the success of nations? First, private property rights must exist and people must be secure in these; that is, they must be able to ensure that

Table 2.1			
Ten Economically Freest Countries	Each year, the Heritage Foundation and the *Wall Street Journal* calculate the list of the most and least economically free nations.		

RANK	COUNTRY	OVERALL INDEX
1	Hong Kong	89.7
2	Singapore	86.1
3	Australia	82.6
4	New Zealand	82.1
5	Ireland	81.3
6	Switzerland	81.1
7	Canada	80.4
8	United States	78.0
9	Denmark	77.9
10	Chile	77.2

Definition: Free 80–100
Mostly Free 60–79.9
Source: Based on data from *The Wall Street Journal* and the Heritage Foundation.

others cannot take away their ownership. People must be able to own things and know they can do what they want with these things as long as it does not harm others. Second, people must have economic freedom. They must be able to voluntarily trade what they own for what they want to own. Private property rights and economic freedom enable people to specialize in those activities they do at relatively low costs and then trade for what they want. With everyone doing that, all goods and services are created at the lowest possible costs. Finally, barriers to entry and to exit must be minimal. Whenever entrepreneurs cannot open a business and compete with others, resources are not being used efficiently. Similarly, if inefficient firms are unable to exit and their resources reallocated to where they are more highly valued, then society loses.

Land Titling in Argentina

Why does a title make a difference? If someone simply claims ownership without title, such as the squatters in Argentina did, why would it change their behavior? The answer is that the title is the legal claim; it is what allows the owners to leverage their property, to gain from its value increase or to lose from a value decrease. Without that legal title, ownership is not secure. Increasing the value of the property could mean that the value accrues to someone else. So, why would anyone invest in the property?

This is the problem with a lack of property rights or a system in which property rights are not secure and established. Korea provides another natural experiment, not dissimilar to the Argentine titling case mentioned at the beginning of the chapter. Korea was occupied by Japan from 1905 until it was divided into two countries following World War II. North Korea retained a strong version of communism and totalitarianism, while the South slowly moved in the direction of private property rights and, eventually, political democracy. The differences in economic growth and changes in standards of living during the past 30 years are astounding. North Korea is mired in poverty, unable to feed its population. The economy is in such shambles that over 2 million people have starved to death and more than 60 percent of the children are malnourished. South Koreans enjoy a standard of living far in excess of North Korea.

In Argentina, those who received title to property have prospered relative to those who did not. In Korea, those who have lived under private property rights and economic freedom have prospered relative to those grinding out tough lives under a despotic regime which allows no freedom and no private property.

Summary

1. Ownership or private property rights are a precursor to economic growth and prosperity.
2. With ownership, people have an incentive to do what they can do relatively less expensively than others and to trade for what they want.
3. Specialization according to comparative advantage and then trade enables all parties to gain.
4. Efficiency is the situation in which the most goods and services are produced at the lowest costs and the allocation of goods, services, and resources could not be changed without making someone worse off.
5. Allocation mechanisms are used to distribute scarce goods, services, and resources. Allocation mechanisms in use today include the price system, government schemes, first-come-first-served, and random allocation (luck). The price system is the predominant mechanism because it is the most efficient. Nonetheless, other mechanisms are used. In some cases, other mechanisms are used because the outcome of the price system is disliked. In other cases, the price system may not be the most efficient; there may be market failures, or transaction costs may be high.
6. Arbitrage is the market process in operation. It forces identical goods to sell for virtually identical prices in different markets. Arbitrage is the process of buying where price is low and selling where price is high.
7. Economic freedom refers to the ability of individuals to engage in voluntary trade without restrictions or interventions.

Key Terms

Private property rights	Efficient
Absolute advantage	Opportunity costs
Comparative advantage	Arbitrage
Gains from trade	Monopoly
Scarce	Brand name

Exercises

1. What are gains from trade? What is the primary benefit of trade? Why is the idea that trade is beneficial counterintuitive?
2. What is the difference between absolute advantage and comparative advantage? How can a less developed country like Mexico have a comparative advantage relative to the United States?
3. What is the difference between rich and poor nations? How did they become rich or poor?
4. It has been argued that climate is a predominant explanatory variable in income distribution in the sense that nations along the equator are poor while those in cooler climates are rich. Can you explain why this might make sense?
5. Another argument is that the dominance of Catholicism explains economic development. A third argument is that the form of colonialism is what matters. Try to explain these positions using private property rights.
6. Why might a policy that simply forgives $40 billion of debt not benefit those nations whose debt is forgiven? Would this policy and the incentives created say anything about the policy response to the "subprime mortgage" crisis experienced in the United States in 2007 and 2008;

the government enacted legislation "forgiving" the debt of some debtors.

7. What are private property rights? Why are private property rights necessary for markets to function?

8. Hernando de Soto argues that property rights are even more important in the developing world than in rich nations. What is his argument? How could the absence of well-defined property rights affect economic development? What might the absence of well-defined property rights mean for illegal immigration? De Soto has argued that the less developed countries fail to grow primarily because of a lack of private property rights. How does that analysis apply to the Native American?

9. What does the following statement mean? "Indeed, every decision we make involves some kind of trade-off." Under what condition would the statement not be true?

10. It has been said that "prices are like giant neon billboards that flash important information." Describe the types of information that market prices provide.

11. It has been said that "profit opportunities attract firms like sharks to blood." Explain

12. Wheelan (in *Naked Economics,* p. 20) states that "the problem with Asian sweatshops is that there are not enough of them." How is Wheelan's statement illustrative of the concept that every market transaction makes all parties better off?

13. What incentives are created by each of the following allocation mechanisms? Market, first-come-first served, government.

14. Why does market allocation lead to an increased supply whenever a shortage situation exists?

15. The following data represent the production possibilities of two people in solving math and economics problems. If they devote their total effort and time to math, A can solve 10 math problems and B can solve 10 math problems. If they devote their total effort and time to economics, A can solve 10 economics problems and B 5 economics problems.

Percent of Resources Devoted to:		A		B	
Math	**Economics**	**Math**	**Economics**	**Math**	**Economics**
100	0	10	0	10	0
0	100	0	10	0	5

a. Who has the absolute advantage?
b. Who has the comparative advantage?
c. Assume that each will be self-sufficient and devote half their resources to math and half to economics.

The outcome follows.

	A Math	A Economics	B Math	B Economics
Alone—no trade	5	5	5	2.5

Now assume that they specialize according to comparative advantage. How much math and economics will they produce together? What are the gains from trade?

CHAPTER NOTES

1. Based on Sebastian Galiani and Ernesto Schargrodsky, "Property Rights for the Poor: Effects of Land Titling," Coase Institute Working Paper, August 9, 2005.
2. William Easterly, *The White Man's Burde*n (New York: Penguin Press, 2006), p. 108.
3. *The Mystery of Capital: Why Capitalism Triumphs in the West and Fails Everywhere Else* (*New York: Basic Books and London: Bantam Press/Random House,* 2000).
4. Charles Wheelan, *Naked Economics* (New York: W. W. Norton, 2002), p. 190; McKillen, Elizabeth, "Economic Nationalism: Bashing Foreigners in Iowa," *The Economist*, September 21, 1991.
5. "China Says Price Controls Will Not Distort Market," Reuters, January 16, 2008 www.cnbc .com/id/22699523.
6. In January 2008, an Indian doctor was arrested for taking the kidneys of poor people and selling them to wealthy Indians and foreigners. "Indian Gang Accused of Stealing Human Kidneys: Police uncover racket that tricked or forced poor to give up organs." abcnews.go.com/Story?id=4201900 &page=1
7. ABC News, Home Video, "Greed," by John Stossel, March 11, 1999.
8. The Independent Institute found that the typical sweatshop worker is paid above the national average (for workers) in six of the nine countries for which they compiled data. Benjamin Powell and David Skarbek, Working Paper 53. "Sweatshops and Third World Living Standards: Are the Jobs Worth the Sweat," September 27, 2004, www.independent.org/pdf/working_papers/53_ sweatshop.pdf.

9. Wheelan, *Naked Economics,* p. 23.
10. Andrea M. Dean and Russell S. Sobel, "Has Wal-Mart Buried Mom and Pop?" *Regulation* (Spring 2008): 38–45, argue that "Wal-Mart has had no significant impact on the overall size and growth of U.S. small business activity," p. 45.
11. The average Index of Economic Freedom (IEF) score for a country with GDP growth of over 10 percent is 10 percent higher than the IEF score for the countries with GDP growth of 3 percent or less. These numbers are for 2005. Libya, which had the lowest score where reliable GDP growth figures are available, had a growth rate of 3.5 percent in a year that the average growth rate was almost 5 percent. Zimbabwe, which had the second lowest IEF score, had a 6.5 percent GDP decline.

CHAPTER **3**
Spontaneous Order,[1] Markets, and Market Failure

CASE

Wal-Mart in Germany

Wal-Mart began in 1962 when Sam Walton and his brother Bud set up the first store in Rogers, Arkansas. Continuous double-digit growth turned it into the world's largest retailer. In the late 1980s Wal-Mart embarked on an ambitious internationalization drive. Its goal was to have foreign operations contribute a third of Wal-Mart's total profits by 2005. On the international scene Wal-Mart's proven U.S. success formula—everyday low prices due to the extensive use of advanced IT, sophisticated logistics and inventory management techniques, a strong emphasis on customer service, and highly motivated personnel—paid off in Latin America and Canada. Wal-Mart expanded into Germany in late 1997. This move was a disaster. Wal-Mart pulled out of the German market in 2006 without having made a profit in part because it was unable to fight off competition from local discount retailers Aldi and Lidl. In addition, it seemed unable to convince German executives to enforce American-style management practices. Many analysts and Wal-Mart's CEO argued that it was a clash of cultures. Does this explanation make any sense? If there were cultural differences, wouldn't initial failure have led Wal-Mart to change what was necessary and continue with its low prices and high value? Wouldn't the market lead to some sort of arbitrage where cultural differences did not matter in offering lower prices and higher value?

1. How could Wal-Mart be so successful in the United States and elsewhere but fail so miserably in German?
2. Does arbitrage function along cultural lines as it does for price differences?

The Prime Directive: Look to the Market

In the *Star Trek* television and movie stories, the Prime Directive is the guiding principle of the United Federation of Planets. The Prime Directive dictates that no primitive culture can be given or exposed to any information regarding advanced technology or alien races, even if that exposure is well intentioned. The Prime Directive was violated on many occasions intentionally and unintentionally. In one episode, an early Federation ship visited a primitive planet and left behind the book *Chicago Mobs of the Twenties*, which the inhabitants quickly seized upon as a blueprint for their entire society.

The Prime Directive in economics might be: *to look to the market first*. If a transaction is occurring outside of the market, ask why. If the market does not seem to be allocating resources efficiently, find out what is interfering with the market process. If institutions exist to carry out or help carry out voluntary transactions, ask what purpose these institutions have in the market.

Relying on the Prime Directive as a guiding principle is a big undertaking because in even the most market oriented of economies, the vast bulk of economic activity occurs within formal, managed organizations rather than through market exchanges. Only a small percentage of all the transactions in the U.S. economy occur through markets. Most importantly, the firm constitutes about 75 percent of all transactions.[2] The Prime Directive demands that we ask why. If the market is so efficient, why do firms exist? If the market is so efficient, why do so many transactions take place outside of a market? Why, for instance, is first-come-first-served the allocating mechanism for many medical services, most college classes, and the use of highways or roadways? Why are government schemes used to allocate airline routes, radio and television broadcast bands, land use (zoning), and rights-of-way at intersections; and why does luck—random allocation—play a part in the allocation of some items, such as concert tickets, lottery winnings, and other contest prizes?

If the price system is such an efficient mechanism, why is it not universally relied on? One reason is that for some products some people do not like the outcome of the price system; that is, they don't like creative destruction. When people do not like the outcome, they may expend resources to change the result or to implement some other allocation mechanism. They lobby the government or attempt to convince voters that some other scheme would be preferable. This is called **rent seeking**.

In some situations, the market is unable to efficiently allocate resources or goods and services. These are referred to as **market failures**. So if the market fails, how are resources to be allocated? Some mechanism other than the market must serve as the allocator. Let's begin with a brief overview of what economists refer to as market failures.

Externalities

In 2008 the price of a gallon of gasoline in the United States exceeded $4. This caused a few people to abandon their SUVs and to purchase smaller, gasoline-efficient, or hybrid cars instead. Nevertheless, many people continued to purchase those larger SUVs that get perhaps 8 or 9 miles per gallon. The decision to purchase the SUV affects others. The emissions are larger than a small car or a hybrid battery–gasoline car. In addition, if a collision between an SUV and a small car occurs, the inhabitants of the SUV are much less likely to be injured. Yet, the SUV owners don't have to compensate the small car owners for putting their lives at risk. Nor do they compensate people with breathing problems who are made worse by the emissions created as the SUVs cruise around town. But since these are the costs of driving the less fuel-efficient car, someone has to pay. The problem is that it is the people who are not voluntarily part of the transaction to purchase the SUV who have to pay.

Because costs are imposed on people who are not part of the decision to purchase and drive the SUV, these costs are called **externalities**. The problem created by externalities is that the price does not reflect all the costs. If it did, the price of the SUVs would be higher and fewer would be purchased. This is shown in Figure 3.1. Notice that the higher social costs, the total costs including externalities, would lead to fewer SUVs being purchased as compared to the private marginal costs, the costs to the individual buyer which does not include the externality. This means that *too many* SUVs are driven, *too much* pollution is created, and *too much* risk is created for drivers of smaller vehicles. The too many and too much refer to the quantities that would occur if there were no external costs.

McDonald's sells its drinks in plastic or Styrofoam cups. Customers discard the cups, often simply throwing them out of the car window. Neither McDonald's nor the customers pay for cleaning up the trash. This means society as a whole has to pay the costs of cleaning up the trash; those who threw the trash out the window and the McDonald's outlet that put the food and drinks in the plastic containers pay no more than anyone else.

Externalities can be positive or negative. If they are negative, they impose costs on others; if they are positive, they grant benefits to others. There are 1.5 million cars stolen in the United States each year. An antitheft device called Lojack was first introduced in Boston in 1986 and is now available in most major metropolitan areas. Usually sold to new-car purchasers by car dealers for a one-time fee of about $600, the Lojack system involves a small radio transmitter that is hidden in the car. If the car is reported stolen, the police activate the transmitter by remote control with high-tech equipment provided by the company. About 95 percent of stolen vehicles equipped with Lojack are recovered. By leading police directly to stolen cars, Lojack helps them to shut down "chop shops" that dismantle vehicles for resale of parts. Professional car thieves have no way of knowing whether a car is armed with Lojack. As a result, it is estimated that one auto theft is eliminated annually for every three Lojack systems that are installed. Thus, the benefit to society in terms of less overall auto theft—benefits such as lower insurance costs—exceeds the benefit to the individual owners who install the Lojack system. Society benefits by the sum of the benefits each owner who installs a Lojack system receives and the reduced insurance costs everyone receives.

Another positive externality is created by a vaccination program such as that for measles. It takes time to get a shot. It often costs and it often hurts. As a result, many people

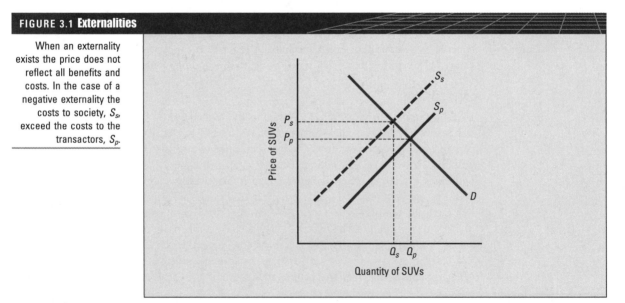

FIGURE 3.1 Externalities

When an externality exists the price does not reflect all benefits and costs. In the case of a negative externality the costs to society, S_s, exceed the costs to the transactors, S_p.

choose not to get the vaccine. As long as enough people get the vaccine, then someone who doesn't is unlikely to come down with the measles. People who do not get the shots benefit from all those who do get the vaccination. In essence, these people have greater benefits without paying for them.

Externalities refer to situations in which not all the costs or benefits of a transaction are included in the transaction. In other words, people not involved in the transaction receive a benefit or a cost from the transaction. As a result, resources may not be allocated to their highest valued uses. In the case of a negative externality, more resources go into the activity than if the external cost was accounted for. For instance, more Styrofoam cups are produced and sold than if McDonald's and/or its customers had to pay the additional cost of cleanup for the discarded cups. In the case of a positive externality, not enough resources go into the activity. If the benefits of the Lojack system were provided only to the individual buyers, the buyers would receive a lower price and more Lojack systems would be installed.

It is argued that smoking creates both negative and positive externalities. Second-hand cigarette smoke is an irritant and bothers some people a great deal—a negative externality. The American Lung Association says that the average smoker dies seven years earlier than the average nonsmoker. This is a positive externality in that these people won't live long enough to enjoy social security or receive society-provided health care. Nonsmokers get to share the funds left by smokers. The net benefit of smoking to the Czech Republic government, including taxes and health benefits, was estimated to be $148 million in 2000.[3]

The existence of externalities is referred to as a market distortion or market failure because resources are not allocated to where they have the highest value. But the world is full of externalities. In fact, it seems that every activity creates positive and negative externalities. So, it might be difficult to know if too much or too little is being supplied or consumed. A simple action such as purchasing milk at a grocery store has many externalities associated with it. By standing in the grocery line, you impose costs on others who have to wait for you to make your transaction. Also, by purchasing the milk, you are expressing to the store your desires for the store to carry that brand of milk; this benefits others who also want to have the milk available. Every innovation and invention creates jobs and new industries. These are positive externalities. At the same time, the innovation and invention replace now obsolete jobs and industries. These are negative externalities.

Externalities are a problem because of a lack of well-defined private property rights. If no one owns the emission coming out of an automobile, then no one has to take care of it. If no one owns the protection people get from someone getting a vaccination, then no one has the incentive to get it. No ownership or common ownership creates problems for the efficient allocation of resources.

Common Ownership

In Chapter 2 we discussed the fact that in the Jamestown colony in America, failure was imminent because of common ownership. Common ownership is another case where the market is not able to efficiently allocate goods and services, as illustrated in this simple story about four people named Everybody, Somebody, Anybody, and Nobody. There was an important job to be done, and Everybody was sure that Somebody would do it. Anybody could have done it, but Nobody did it. Somebody got angry about that because it was Everybody's job. Everybody thought Anybody could do it. But Nobody realized that Everybody wouldn't do it. The end result was that Everybody blamed Somebody when Nobody did what Anybody could have. When nobody owns something nobody takes care of it. When somebody owns something, somebody takes care of it. When everybody owns something, nobody takes care of it.

Business Insight

Ball Marks

Golfers hate ball marks. A ball mark is an indentation caused by a golf ball landing on the putting surface, the green, with some force. A ball mark is easily repaired by pushing the grass and ground in toward the indentation and leveling the result. The problem is that most golfers don't make the repair, thereby leaving an indentation in the ground that will affect another player's putts. A golfer carefully lines up the putt then strikes it and sees it going toward the hole. All of a sudden the ball bounces up and veers sideways, away from the intended target. This is the effect of a ball mark. *Golf Digest* (October 2005, p. 56) carried out a study to see how many people repair their marks. A par three hole was observed on a public course and another on a private course. The results of the *Golf Digest* study can be summarized as follows:

	Public Course	Private Course
Percent of players who hit the green	49.5	42.1
Percent of players who repair their mark	30.1	46.9
Percent of players who repaired more than one	12.5	26.7
Percent of players who missed the green who repaired a mark	0	18.2

Notice that the *Golf Digest* study of ball mark repairs shows that 70 percent of the golfers making ball marks on public courses did not repair their own marks. On private courses, less than 50 percent of golfers repaired their own ball marks. This externality is a curse to golfers. Yet, no rules have been devised to force those creating the marks to repair them. It is left to the individual players to decide. Why? Because it is too costly to form an organization that monitors the ball marking on each green. It is too costly to have a ball mark policy or some other way to require that golfers repair the marks. If the benefits of repaired ball marks were high enough, then it would be beneficial to create some mechanism for enforcing ball mark repair.

On private courses, more people repair the marks; why is this? Perhaps because of the threat of ostracism. If other players see you not repairing ball marks, then perhaps they will develop lower opinions of you. Or perhaps it is because there is a much higher possibility that your ball mark may affect your play tomorrow. Players repeat play on a private course much more than they do on a public course.

Chickens and cows are not on the endangered species list, but elephants and rhinos are. Why? No one owns the elephants and rhinos. The result is that they are *overutilized*—they are becoming extinct. In most nations with elephants, large national parks have been created in which hunting is forbidden. But even in the face of these bans on hunting, the reduction in the number of elephants has continued. A decade ago, Africa's elephant population was more than a million; it has now fallen to less than half of that. In contrast to the common ownership strategy, the governments of Botswana and South Africa created private property rights by allowing individuals to own elephants. These elephant farmers ensure that the elephants breed and reproduce so that they can be sold for their tusks, for hunting in special hunting parks, or to zoos in developed nations. This has led to a revival of the elephant population in these nations.[4]

Common ownership or lack of private property rights means the market cannot work. If you don't own something, you can't sell or trade that item. The creation of private property rights creates the ownership necessary for markets to function.

Some Goods Don't Fit the Market; Public Goods

If something is available for you to use and you don't have to pay for it, why would you pay? That's the problem with what economists call **public goods**: People can get these goods without paying for them. When goods are public, an individual has an incentive to be a **free rider**—a consumer or producer who enjoys the benefits of a good or service without paying for that good or service. As an example, suppose that national defense was not provided by the government and paid for with tax money; instead, you would not be protected by the armed forces unless you paid a fee. A problem would arise because national defense is a public good; you would be protected whether or not you paid for it as long as others paid. No one could actually own the defense—that is, no one could be excluded from enjoying the defense because they did not pay the fee. Of course, because each person has an incentive not to pay for it, few will voluntarily do so, which means the good may not be provided, or, if it is provided, the quantity produced will be "too small" from society's viewpoint.

My car has a GPS that just baffles me. It reports where the car is at any moment—the altitude and the address. It works by sending and receiving a system from a satellite circulating the globe. But I am not the only person using a GPS; there are millions of users. We don't take turns but use the system at the same time. Yet, my reception does not deteriorate simply because someone else is using the system. What would each of us users do if someone offered us a chance to subscribe to a general positioning system? We would laugh—why pay when we get it for free?

The GPS is not the only good where the quantity of the good available to others is not reduced when I use the good. All such goods are called *public goods*. Public goods have two properties that pose problems for markets. The first property is called *nonrivalry* in consumption; the second is called *nonexcludability*. An example of a nonexcludable public good is national defense—if one person in an area receives it, all do. Television broadcasts are an example of a nonrivalrous public good. When one person views a television show, the signal to others does not diminish.

Since one person's purchases are automatically available to all (in the nonexcludable case), there is a temptation to *free ride* on others' contributions. If free riding is extensive, no one has an incentive to offer a good for sale.

What We Don't Know Can Hurt Us: Asymmetric Information

You see a car with a for sale sign on the corner. You contact the owner, ask about the car, drive it, and decide to purchase it. A month later the car fails to work and you find out it is not repairable. You have been taken. Because of such a risk, if you ever purchase a used car, you won't pay much for it. In general, because people don't know much about the used cars offered by private individuals, those cars command very low prices. This means that anyone wanting to sell a used car in premium condition is not going to get what the car is really worth. As a result, the only used cars in the market are *lemons*.

This is called an **adverse selection** problem—bad quality drives good quality out of the market. Another example often suggested exists in lending markets. Lending institutions do not know whether or not a potential borrower is a good risk. If the lender raises the interest rate on the loans provided, low-risk borrowers decide not to take out a loan. It is the high-risk borrowers who remain in the market. The lender is in a quandary: If the interest rate is lowered, all borrowers—low and high risk—seek loans. If the lender increases the interest rate, low-risk borrowers drop out of the market, leaving just the high-risk borrower.

A second form of market problem created by informational asymmetry is called **moral hazard**. Suppose you purchase a new car; you drive safely until you get insurance. Once you have insurance, you drive recklessly because if anything happens to your new car the insurance company pays to repair it. This change in your behavior is called moral hazard. If the insurance company has no information about your driving behavior after selling you insurance, the company is unable to charge you what would be commensurate with your riskier behavior.

Solutions to Market Failure Problems

All of these issues—externalities, common ownership, public goods, asymmetric information—are called market failures because the market fails to allocate resources to their highest value use. Private property rights are necessary for a market to exist and work. When the private property rights are not defined or are ambiguous, goods and services may not be allocated to where they have the highest value. In such situations, there are incentives for a solution to be devised. Theoretically, the solution to market failure problems is straightforward: Assign private property rights. There are two broad approaches to assigning private property rights. One is to allow market participants to come up with an assignment of private property rights. The other is to have a government assign the private property rights. The one that is best is the one that creates the most benefits at the least cost.

Consider the difficulty of getting every golfer to meet and agree on proper ways to fix ball marks and on who will do the repairs. (That might be one reason that you find fewer ball marks on private courses than on public courses. Members of private courses are more likely to know other players.) Or it would be even more difficult to have every motorist meet with everyone affected by automobile emissions to solve the automobile emissions problem.

Many people argue that, owing to the difficulty of arranging private negotiation, it is the government's responsibility to solve the problem. The government could assign ownership. It could then command that market participants behave in certain ways, or it could impose taxes or provide subsidies to ensure that the participants behave appropriately. In some cases, the government takes ownership and then sells rights to use the item in question. An approach taken recently to reduce emissions has been to create a market in the right to pollute. The government defines how much pollution to permit and then assigns ownership to the right to pollute. For example, if the target pollution level in the Los Angeles basin is 400 billion particulates per day, the government could issue a total of 400 permits, each permitting the emission of 1 billion particulates per day. This is shown in Figure 3.2 with a vertical supply curve—400 permits are issued. Then the government could sell the permits. Demanders, typically the polluting firms, would purchase the permits, allowing them to pollute up to the amount specified by the permits they own. If a firm purchased 20 permits, it could emit up to 20 billion particulates per day. If that firm implemented a cleaner technology or for some other reason did not use all of its permits, it could sell them to other firms. The resulting price would be an equilibrium—where traders are comparing the cost of purchasing permits to the costs of implementing cleaner technologies.

If the amount of pollution allowed is reduced, then fewer permits are issued. Figure 3.2 illustrates this with an inward shift of the supply curve. Demanders bid for the now fewer pollution permits, driving the price of the permits up. As the price rises, some firms will decide not to purchase the permits, but instead to purchase new pollution abatement equipment or to reduce the amount they produce.

The higher price gives firms an incentive to adopt more efficient pollution abatement equipment. The permit market also enables others to influence the total amount of pollution created. Anyone can purchase permits. A few people might try to make money by buying and selling permits. If you expect the price of the permits to rise in the future, you might purchase the permits now, hoping to sell them later. If the price does rise, the owners of the permits will be able to sell them for a gain. Others purchase permits in order to control the quantity of pollution. Environmental groups, such as the Nature Conservancy and the Sierra Club, have purchased permits and taken them out of circulation. In this way, they reduce the total number of permits in circulation and thus reduce the total amount of pollution permitted.

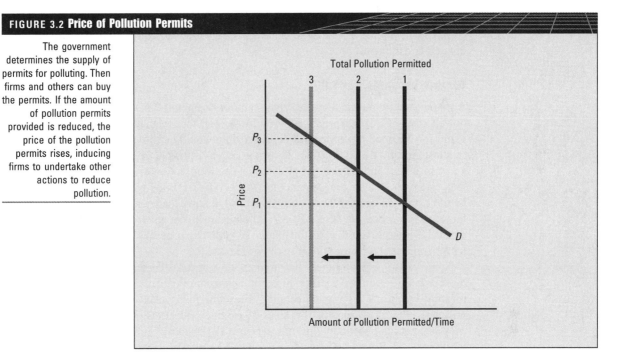

FIGURE 3.2 Price of Pollution Permits

The government determines the supply of permits for polluting. Then firms and others can buy the permits. If the amount of pollution permits provided is reduced, the price of the pollution permits rises, inducing firms to undertake other actions to reduce pollution.

Similarly, if a commonly owned good can be converted to a privately owned one, then overutilization may be eradicated. Thousands of acres of Amazon forest are burned or cut each year to provide land for Brazil's ranchers and subsistence farmers and to extract wood for use elsewhere. No one owns the rain forest, leading it to be overutilized. If the Brazilian government created private property rights to the forest, the forest would be taken care of. Consider what has happened in Sweden and neighboring Finland. Sweden and Finland have more standing forest today than at any time in the past because they converted forest land to privately owned forests. Private owners do not cut at a loss and do not cut to maintain employment levels or for other political reasons. They cut at the rate that yields them the greatest return. If they simply razed their forests, they would have no income in coming years. So they cut or harvest at rates that ensure viable populations.

Building large stadiums around baseball or football fields restricts the viewing of the games from outside of the stadiums—you have to purchase a ticket to see the contest. Without the stadiums, the games would be available for anyone to watch for free and no one would pay to watch.

Adverse selection and moral hazard problems are primarily problems of ambiguous ownership of property rights. Who owns the information that is necessary, and how is that information to be provided in the market? When moral hazard or adverse selection exists, there may be an opportunity for someone to profit from providing information. Carfax provides the history of a car for a fee. Equifax and other credit agencies provide individual credit histories for a fee. When private property rights to missing information can be assigned, the problem of asymmetric information will disappear.

Sometimes a moral hazard problem can be reduced by having the person or firm creating the hazard and the person or firm being taken advantage of share in the costs. This is a reason that insurance companies require a deductible and banks and other lending institutions require a down payment: so that the company and the customer share in the expenses and risks. You are more likely to drive carefully and safeguard your health if you have to pay some of the costs of an accident or illness. Similarly, if you must pay a co-payment, you are less likely to behave in a way that causes you to bear a large number of such co-payments.

The Market Does Not Fail

A market failure means that the "right" amount of a good or service is not produced. If not all costs of a transaction are borne by people making that transaction, then the demand for the good or service will be larger than would be the case if all costs were borne by those making the transaction. Thus, too much of the good or service will be produced and consumed. Similarly, if not all benefits of a transaction are borne by people making that transaction, then the demand for the good or service will be smaller than would be the case if all benefits were borne by those making the transaction. Thus, too little of the good or service will be produced and consumed. But why would the market not self-correct if price is too low or too high? Wouldn't this be like an arbitrage opportunity where some profitable opportunity presented itself?

Some economists do argue that markets do not fail.[5] They point out that a so-called market failure requires a static or stationary economy. For instance, suppose that in roasting the beans for my coffee shop, the odor floats next door making people who walk there ill. The cause of the illness becomes well known. The fact that my coffee shop is creating a cost that I do not bear is an externality. In a static economy, that is a market failure. But what if someone opens an identical coffee shop nearby that does not create the foul odor? If customers leave me and go to my competitor, I have to either eliminate the odor or shut down the business. In a dynamic economy, one in which individuals are continually evaluating costs and benefits, it is not likely that an externality will remain a problem for long. Similar arguments are made for other market failures. If private property rights are not well defined and this increases costs to someone, then there will be a move to define the private property rights. Regardless of these types of arguments, the majority of economists believe that markets do sometimes fail.

Governance and Government Failure

A market system requires the existence of private property rights and the enforcement of those rights. A governance system that enhances efficiency must be one that supports private property rights. A governance system that inhibits voluntary trade and ignores private property rights creates inefficiencies. Let's turn now to discuss governance.

Rules and regulations can enhance the functioning of markets. When I got in my car to go to work today, it never dawned on me to drive on the left side of the road. In most Western countries, a light switch usually turns a light on when it is up. Common practices such as these make life easier—you don't have to figure out which side to drive on or learn a light switch rule for each light switch. Think what it would mean if every time you got in the car you had to decide whether to drive on the right or left, or read an English-language book from top to bottom or bottom to top. Every single activity involving driving or reading would be more difficult. The purpose of common practices is to enable gains from trade, to ensure that resources are not wasted in communication and action when they could instead improve standards of living. A governance system that codifies these efficient rules enhances gains from trade; a governance system that interferes with efficient rules and practices detracts from gains of trade.

Efficient practices arise because of the opportunity to reduce the costs of trading or transacting. If we began with chaos, it would not take long for people to devise rules by which the chaos would be reduced and gains from trade increased. And even the process of devising rules becomes efficient. Common law is based on precedent and experience and results from practices that are efficient.

When people carry out face-to-face transactions, they can devise trading rules that benefit both traders. When small communities comprise the universe of traders, the communities will devise rules or social norms that enhance trade in the communities. At some stage governments may be devised, and rules and laws created.

Consider the simple situation where we live next door to each other in a setting where there are no rules of property or protection. Suppose each of us has the same amount of money but only two choices as to what to do with it—produce new goods and thus increase our funds in the future, or spend some of our resources on guns, which will enable us to protect our own property and also seize our neighbors' property at gunpoint. If you buy a gun and I don't, then you get my money and your original money less the cost of the gun, and I end up with nothing. If I buy a gun and you don't, then the opposite is true. We would both be better off by not buying guns and just producing. Yet each one of us can do better by buying a gun, whatever the other one does. If you don't buy a gun, I can seize your property and increase my funds more than by production. If you do buy a gun, I can at least defend my property against you. So buying a gun is my best move no matter what you do; the same holds for you, and so we both wind up with less money than if we had both been peaceful.

If we bought guns and didn't produce, we wouldn't last long. And since there would be other neighbors to worry about if we took over the property of our closest neighbor, it makes a lot more sense for us to pool our resources, perhaps hire a sheriff to solve problems between us. Perhaps we agree to put some funds into a pool of money the sheriff holds, and if one of us transgresses on the agreements with the other, the sheriff gives the other the money. This institution, called posting a bond, would be more efficient than always fighting it out; it would enable us to devote a great deal more of our resources to production.

While it might make sense to buy a gun for one year, expecting to be around longer than a year might suggest a better alternative. If no one is producing, no one can last longer than a year. Since we are expecting to have to deal with each other many times over the years, it would be to our mutual benefit to both produce and forgo guns. If we feared a third neighbor taking our product, we might combine resources, producing and purchasing a gun for mutual protection.

If we don't trust each other, we couldn't pool our resources and purchase just one gun. The person with the gun would be able to steal the production of the other person. A trader who cheats won't be carrying out many trades. If you cheat, you won't get repeat business. But creating trust may take several honest transactions. This is why the average business relationship in Africa lasts seven years; lots of time is required to establish the trust. Malagasy grain traders don't grant a client trade credit until after they have done about 10 cash transactions with the client. African manufacturers report that they require 6 to 12 months of repeated interaction with a client until they grant trade credits.

If repeat transactions are not likely to occur without trust, then trades may be limited to small, well-known units. In many countries, companies tend to be family enterprises because family members are the only ones felt to be trustworthy. Ethnic networks may serve as extended families in many nations. In pre-industrial Europe, it was the Jews. In East Africa, it's the Indians. (Indians own almost all businesses in Kenya, although they make up only 1 percent of the population.) In West Africa, it is the Lebanese. In southern Africa, it is whites and Indians. Among indigenous African groups, often one group dominates trading—the Bamileke in Cameroon, the Luba in the Democratic Republic of the Congo, the Hausa in West Africa, the Igbo in Nigeria, and the Serahule in the Gambia.[6]

Corruption

In these types of cultures, what we might call casual governments, it would seem perfectly natural for public officials to exhibit favoritism toward friends and relatives, including persons who purchase their friendship with a generous bribe. Nepotism, clientalism, and bribery become substitutes for contract arrangements when private property rights are not well defined and secure. In short, corruption arises when governments are not efficient enforcers of private property rights.

Corruption might be defined as making a covert payment to those who have the authority to deliver a favor. Transparency International publishes annual rankings of corruption in different countries.[7] It also defines the most corrupt rulers in recent history. Indonesia's Suharto is the most corrupt, having skimmed off about $30 billion, followed by the Philippines' Marcos at $8 billion, Zaire's Mobutu at $5 billion, Nigeria's Abacha at $4 billion, Serbia's Milosevic at $1 billion, Haiti's Duvalier at $800 million, and so on. Interestingly, Suharto presided during a period when Indonesian incomes quadrupled to $1,000 per capita in the 1980s and 1990s, poverty, infant mortality, and fertility plummeted, and literacy soared. By contrast, Mobutu left Zaire poorer and more desperate than ever, as did Abacha in Nigeria and Duvalier in Haiti.

Transparency International's list of 133 countries ranked in order of corruption shows that well-off Western countries are the least corrupt. See Figure 3.3. As you move down the list, the standard of living generally declines. But there are a few fast-growing countries that rank low on the list (i.e., are relatively corrupt). China comes in at 66 and India at 83, and both have been growing at very high rates. Bangladesh, rated as one of the 10 most corrupt countries, has been growing at 5 percent annually for a decade.

Why does corruption exist with both good and bad economic performance? One reason might be the expectation of corruption, that is, its certainty. Businessmen, in

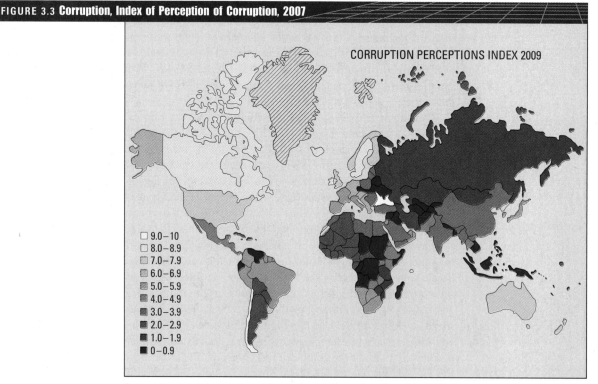

FIGURE 3.3 Corruption, Index of Perception of Corruption, 2007

CORRUPTION PERCEPTIONS INDEX 2009

9.0–10
8.0–8.9
7.0–7.9
6.0–6.9
5.0–5.9
4.0–4.9
3.0–3.9
2.0–2.9
1.0–1.9
0–0.9

Source: Reprinted from Index of Perception of Corruption. Copyright 2009 Transparency International: The Global Coalition Against Corruption. Used with permission. For more information, visit www.transparency.org.

response to a survey by the World Bank, reported that the main problem with corruption was that it increased risks and uncertainties. The risks declined significantly if corruption produced reliable outcomes, as in Indonesia. For instance, if everyone knew they had to pay 15 percent to acquire licenses to operate businesses, but for that 15 percent could be sure of getting their licenses, entrepreneurs could treat this as just one more tax, factor it into their rate of return calculations, and invest with confidence. But if they pay 2 percent one time, 22 percent another time, and in all cases don't know whether they will get the licenses, then they can't carry out investment calculations. Arbitrariness creates problems; some entrepreneurs pay huge sums in vain, while others pay little or nothing and succeed. In Indonesia the Suhartos were known as "10 percenters" because every transaction had to include 10 percent for the Suhartos.

Imagine a dictator who has just taken office. He has to decide whether to take everything from those he controls or to leave enough that they can invest and produce. This is not much different from a lumber company deciding whether to clear-cut the forest or to selectively prune. If there is no expected value in the future, the decision is clear cut. For the dictator, the incentive is to leave nothing, unless he plans on remaining in power next year. A self-interested dictator cannot destroy the economy and starve the people if he plans on sticking around. He would exhaust all resources and have nothing for next year if he purely plundered. As already noted, it is arbitrariness that creates problems. If the dictator decides to steal half of the country's income every year, then a business owner considering an investment of $1,000 that is expected to return $100 knows he will have to pay half of that to the government. So instead of a return of 10 percent, the return is 5 percent. The businessman has to compare the known 5 percent return to other things he could do with the $1,000. But if the dictator is arbitrary and could appear at any time to plunder, the businessman would have to consider the risk of losing everything. The certainty of the 50 percent is likely to be preferable to uncertainty.

A dictator must keep his supporters happy in order to maintain power. In theory, a dictator would impose the least damaging taxes possible in whatever quantity was necessary and distribute the proceeds to his supporters. What happens instead is government-tolerated corruption on a widespread scale. Police spend their time harassing travelers in return for bribes. A four-hour trip takes six hours; travelers carry less money or find ways to carry concealed funds, travel less often or at busier times of the day, and find other ways to help fend off attempts to extract bribes. There's no point investing in a business because the government will not protect you against thieves—so you might as well become a thief yourself. There is no point in paying your phone bill because no court can make you pay, so there is no phone company. There is no point setting up an import business because the customs officials will be the ones to benefit. There is no point getting an education because jobs are not handed out on merit.[8]

Corruption can more easily arise when the governance system impedes market exchange rather than enhances it. For instance, price controls, whose purpose is to lower the price of some good below its market value, create incentives for individuals or groups to bribe officials to maintain the flow of such goods or to acquire an unfair share at the below-market price. Resource-rich economies may be more likely to be subject to corruption than are resource-poor countries if the resources are in government control. In developing countries, the amount of corruption is negatively linked to the level of investment and economic growth—that is to say, the more corruption, the less investment and the less economic growth.[9]

Whenever the government is able to control the allocation of goods and services, the potential for corruption arises. In Cambodia, school teachers supplement their income by soliciting bribes from students, including sale of examination questions and answers. It takes 153 days to start a business in Maputo compared to 2 days in Toronto and an hour in Hong Kong.[10] It costs 126 percent of the debt value to enforce a contract in Jakarta but 5.4 percent in Seoul. It takes 21 procedures to register commercial property in Abuja but 3 in Helsinki. In Mexico, a speeding ticket is simply a means for a local police officer to supplement his salary.

Studies have shown that less corruption occurs in open economies. In other words, countries tend to be less corrupt when their trade is relatively free of government restrictions that officials can abuse. Competition drives inefficiencies away, and corruption is a major inefficiency. Competition and free entry do not enable officials to extract payments for favors from local businesses. Competition in government, that is, political competition, limits corruption.

Form of Government

The problem of corruption underscores the importance of the legal framework to economic development. An honest, incorruptible police, criminal law enforcement machinery, and an honest judiciary can increase economic efficiency. Government institutions, such as courts, judges, and police, improve efficiency by enforcing contracts, protecting property rights, providing security against predators, and punishing lawbreakers. But the problem is that any government powerful enough to protect citizens against predators is also powerful enough to be a predator itself.

Political freedom, an open society with a free press, free speech, freedom of assembly, and political rights for dissidents, provides constraints on those in power to be predators. Free individuals will expose corrupt behavior by elected officials and vote them out of office. If secession or voting with one's feet is available, bad government will be met with the exodus of citizens even if they cannot vote the corrupt politicians out of office. But in most cases, voting with one's feet is not easily done.

The quality of governance is an important factor for growth. Virtually all of the nations that are rich today have democracy with checks and balances, enforcement of the rule of law, and clear rules of the game that prevent the majority from excluding or expropriating a minority. The road to a stable democracy is tenuous. Elections can be and are corrupted. Even without corruption, a natural problem that arises is that the majority may become a tyranny over the minority. The majority often decides to redistribute the income of a minority. In fact, for a long time democracy was viewed as a threat to private property. In the U.S. Constitution, the Fifth Amendment addresses this issue, stating that one cannot be deprived of property without just compensation. But that does not stop a majority from voting for high taxes on a minority.

> *A democracy is always temporary in nature; it simply cannot exist as a permanent form of government. A democracy will continue to exist up until the time that voters discover that they can vote themselves generous gifts from the public treasury. From that moment on, the majority always votes for the candidates who promise the most benefits from the public treasury, with the result that every democracy will finally collapse due to loose fiscal policy, which is always followed by a dictatorship.*
>
> —Alex De Tocqueville, *Democracy in America* (1835–1840)

A democracy is a government form in which no one is the owner—there are no private property rights to the government. This form of government is a commons or public good. The story of the commons is that if someone owns it, someone takes care of it. If everyone or no one owns it, no one takes care of it. Government is the same. If government is a private good, someone will take care of it; if government is a public good, no one will take care of it. Democracy has existed only short times in history—Athenian democracy, Rome during its republican era until 31 B.C., the republics of Venice, Florence, and Genoa during the Renaissance period, the Swiss cantons since 1291, the United Provinces from 1648 until 1673, and England under Cromwell from 1649 until 1660.

Democracy made a strong comeback in the mid-nineteenth century, and by the end of World War I, it was the dominant form of government in Western nations.

Ludwig Von Mises, one of the founders of the Austrian School, rejected a princely state as being incompatible with the protection of private property rights. He argued that democracy and democratic government would serve these functions better than monarchies. Rather than majority rule, to Mises democracy meant "self determination, self government, self rule."[11] To Mises democracy was an essentially voluntary membership organization in that it recognized each of its constituents' unrestricted right to secession. No one was coerced or forced against his will into the structure of the state. Whoever wants to emigrate is not held back. "When a group wants to secede, they are able to do that. The right of self determination in regard to the question of membership in a state thus means: whenever the inhabitants of a particular territory, whether it be a single village, a whole district, or a series of adjacent districts, make it known, by a freely conducted plebiscite, that they no longer wish to remain united to the state to which they belong at the time, their wishes are to be respected and complied with."[12]

A government is a territorial monopolist with coercion—an entity that can engage in violations of private property rights in the forms of taxation, regulation, and expropriation of private property. As a result, it is hard to find many proponents of democracy in the history of political theory. Almost all major thinkers had nothing but contempt for democracy. The Founding Fathers of the United States were strictly opposed to it. Without an exception they thought of democracy as mob rule. They considered themselves to be members of a natural aristocracy, and rather than a democracy they advocated an aristocratic republic.

The problem of democracy is mob rule, the trampling of private property rights via the growth of government. Before the late nineteenth century, government accounted for a very small percentage of gross domestic product in most Western countries, typically no more than 5 percent. But with the twentieth century came the growth of governments across the Western world, to the point where government expenditures are now 40 or 50 percent of gross domestic product. And with an increase in government's role in the economy comes a decrease in economic growth.[13]

Why does government inevitably get larger in democratic nations. The answer is the endemic problem in political economy that nineteenth-century French economist Frederic Bastiat called the "seen and the unseen," which is related to what modern economists call concentrated benefits and diffuse costs. When the benefits of an action or policy are concentrated and the costs are spread out, the action or policy will be undertaken. Since there are a handful of automobile producers and millions of automobile consumers, it makes sense for an automobile company, acting individually, to lobby Congress for tariffs. It doesn't make sense for an individual consumer to lobby Congress in opposition. It will cost an individual thousands of dollars to lobby against the tariff, and preventing the tariff would save him little on his next car purchase.

We know what leads to a nation's success and rising standards of living. It is economic freedom and private property rights. This was the basis of the founding of the United States. The U.S. Constitution, based on the writings of John Locke, ensured property, ownership, and protection from aggression. The American founders intended to design a government that would protect the rights of its citizens, and at that time the most serious threat to people's rights was government. The principle underlying American government was liberty. Thus, whereas the nation's first constitution, the Articles of Confederation, tightly constrained the powers of the federal government, the Constitution relaxed these constraints. Nevertheless, the Republic form of government was intended to keep government small. But even with a Republic, the United States government has only grown. Democracy is simply not an efficient form of government.

In theory, an oligarchy (rule by the few) is more efficient than a democracy.[14] The oligarchy could eliminate the democratic threat to property rights and could induce economic growth. But oligarchy in practice typically infringes on private property rights, confiscating the property of poorer citizens until a revolution occurs.

Transparency

When one party to a transaction has better information than another party, the market may be inefficient. The market has to be transparent to the point that inefficiency does not occur. An important role of governance is transparency. If each party in the governance system has to provide information and if actions are well known, then competition will drive the system to efficient outcomes.

The problem of the oligarch is that transparency does not typically exist. Democracy is usually a move toward more transparency. Of course, parties can make themselves better off in many cases by obscuring information and reducing transparency.

CASE *review*

Wal-Mart's German Failure

The Prime Directive tells us to look to the market first. In the case of Wal-Mart's German failure, we must ask, was the market functioning? If Wal-Mart had been able to provide the relatively low prices it offers in the United States, why wouldn't Wal-Mart have been successful? No one would argue that Germans do not want lower prices and higher value. The problem is that the German market is not allowed to function. In the United States, Wal-Mart is a strictly nonunion employer. In Germany, as in most other parts of Continental Europe, unions wield enormous influence politically and within firms. The unions opposed Wal-Mart's employment practices, and this added to Germany's laws regarding the workplace. The Germans receive generous welfare benefits from government. They said to themselves, why accept a relatively low-paying job at Wal-Mart when without working at all they could receive government benefits equal to what pay would have been. The result was that Wal-Mart had a tough time hiring enough workers to offer its "high-quality service." In addition, Germany's restrictive shopping hour regulations prevented Wal-Mart from offering its customers the usual 24/7 operation. German laws also restricted Wal-Mart from offering low prices. Section 20(4) of the Act Against Restraints of Competition "bans all firms with superior market power from selling a range of goods below cost." Wal-Mart was thus unable to compete in the manner it has in other countries, particularly in the United States. It could not offer loss-leaders; it could not offer goods at prices below the costs of other firms; it could not provide better service.

Summary

1. The Prime Directive refers to the idea that markets are efficient and create the incentives for standards of living to rise more rapidly than any other allocation mechanism. As such, whenever the market is not being relied on, we need to ask why.
2. Some market outcomes are not what people want; they then devote resources to changing the outcome. This is called rent seeking.
3. In some situations, not all costs and benefits of a private voluntary exchange are borne by the exchange participants. If costs are imposed on innocent bystanders, then these are called negative externalities. If benefits are received by innocent bystanders, then these are called positive externalities.

4. Externalities mean that either too much or too little is being produced and consumed because not all costs and benefits are included in the transactions.

5. Common ownership means that there are no private property rights. Without private property rights, the market cannot allocate goods and services.

6. A public good refers to a situation where a good or service is nonexcludable and nonrivalrous. Since anyone can use the good (nonexcludable) if it is provided, then few will pay for it—people will free ride. Since one person's uses does not affect another's, there is no reason for private parties to provide the good.

7. Asymmetric information occurs when one party to a transaction has more information relative to the transaction than other parties.

8. Moral hazard occurs because one party to a transaction knows more about the transaction than the other party. Two people agree to a behavior and then one changes the behavior to the determinant of the other.

9. Adverse selection occurs because parties to a transaction have different information about the transaction. If good quality and bad quality cannot be differentiated, the bad quality will drive the good quality out of the market.

10. Some economists maintain that markets do not fail, that what are called market failures will resolve themselves. In some cases all that is necessary is for private property rights to be assigned.

11. If negotiation between individual parties can occur and if property rights are clear and secure, the outcome will be efficient.

12. It is often argued that the government must step in to resolve a market problem; if private negotiation is not possible or is very costly, then having the government solve the problem may be the preferred outcome.

13. Governance refers to the rules and regulations under which transactions occur. If government is good, creates trust, and enhances exchange, it has a more positive effect on development and standards of living than if government is not trustworthy and increases inefficiency.

14. If government intervention in a market causes more inefficiency, then a government failure has occurred.

15. Governance must be transparent and minimize corruption.

16. Law that evolves, that codifies efficient practices, works better than law that is imposed by authority. Common law is law based on precedent; it evolves. Civil law is imposed by authority.

Key Terms

Rent seeking
Market failures
Externalities
Public goods

Free rider
Adverse selection
Moral hazard

Exercises

1. What does it mean to say that people don't like the market outcome?

2. Give some examples of rent seeking. If rent seeking is inefficient, will it be competed away? Why or why not?

3. What is an "externality"? Why might it create a problem for market allocation?

4. Why is it widely accepted that the government is responsible for dealing with externalities?

5. Give an example of an externality between firms, between customers and firm, and between suppliers and firm?

6. Explain how smoking can simultaneously generate positive and negative externalities. Is there

too much or too little smoking? Explain why smoking bans on bars and restaurants do not efficiently solve an externality problem.

7. Using a tax to correct for an externality means subtracting the private cost of the activity from the social cost. Who should determine /quantify this social cost, and how should they do it? What is the analogous approach to externalities within the firm or between firms?

8. "Anyone who tells you that markets left to their own devices always lead to socially beneficial outcomes is talking utter nonsense." Do you agree with this statement? Defend your position.

9. Is the government provision of interstate highways a productive use of resources? What would have occurred had the government not taken responsibility for building and maintaining highways?

10. What is a public good? Is it necessary for government to provide a public good? Apply your answer to national defense. Also apply your answer to a lighthouse. Could either be privatized?

11. Describe two examples of times when you behaved as a "free rider." For each instance, explain how your behavior may have been different had you had to pay for the good/service involved. How should these specific "free-rider" problems be rectified? Explain.

12. Suppose that a firm has a choice between male and female lawyers and that the two appear to be identical on paper. Why might the choice of the male be an asymmetrical information problem?

13. What is adverse selection? What is moral hazard? Give an example of these two problems arising between a firm and its suppliers.

14. "Markets tend to favor the party that knows more." True or false? So if you think you might know less, how does that change your behavior?

15. Is it necessary to have democracy to have a "free enterprise economy"? Can a free enterprise economy and totalitarianism coexist?

16. We have all experienced the "co-pay" when it comes to health insurance. We also have had to choose how large of a deductible we are willing to live with when we purchase auto insurance. Explain how co-pays and deductibles reduce problems of moral hazard and adverse selection.

17. Why does corruption negatively affect economic growth and standards of living? Why is corruption like a tax on doing business?

18. Why does corruption tend to arise more when government has a larger role in an economy than when government's role is small?

19. A beekeeper, Yung, lives next to an apple orchard. She not only benefits from the bees' honey, which she sells, but she also creates a positive externality for her apple grower neighbor: Yung's bees help pollinate the apple trees so the apple grower can grow more apples. Yung's total cost and benefit for keeping her bees is the following:

Price per 1,000 bees	27	24	23	21	18	15	12
Quantity of bees demanded	1	2	3	4	5	6	7
Quantity of bees supplied	9	8	7	6	5	4	3

a. Ignoring the externality, how many bees will be kept?

b. If the apple grower wants to see 6,000 bees kept, what is the value of the externality? What would have to happen for the socially optimal (including externality) amount of bees to be kept?

20. Suppose that an automobile race track is built several miles from a small town. After the construction is completed, it is discovered that the heavy roar from the cars regularly disturbs the 2,500 local residents between the hours of 10:00 P.M. and 1:00 A.M. on summer nights. Each local resident places a value of $150 on having quiet evenings at home during the summer concert season. The amphitheater owners could install a retractable roof over the track that would eliminate the noise at a cost of $350,000. Local residents could install extra insulation in their homes to soundproof them at a cost of $125 per resident. Suppose that it is easy for the theater owner and the town residents to reach an agreement that makes them all better off. If the amphitheater must provide full monetary compensation for any noise damage imposed on the community, what will the outcome be? If the amphitheater is NOT required to pay any compensation for any noise damage done to the community, what will the outcome be?

CHAPTER NOTES

1. "Good order results spontaneously when things are let alone." The thinkers of the Scottish Enlightenment were the first to seriously develop and inquire into the idea of the market as a 'spontaneous order'. The Austrian School of Economics, led by Carl Menger, Ludwig von Mises and Friedrich Hayek, argued that a market was "a more efficient allocation of societal resources than any design could achieve." They claim this spontaneous order is superior to any order human mind can design due to the specifics of the information required. This is also illustrated in the concept of the *invisible hand* proposed by Adam Smith in *The Wealth of Nations*.

2. John McMillan, *Reinventing The Bazaar* (New York: W.W. Norton, 2002), pp. 168–169.

3. edition.cnn.com/2001/BUSINESS/07/16/czech.morris/study.doc

4. In fact, South Africa has found it necessary to reduce the herds. The elephant population rose from 8,000 in 1995 to 18,000 in 2007 and the elephants are becoming aggressive as they compete with humans for limited forest and water. news.bbc.co.uk/1/hi/world/africa/7262951.stm; BBC, Monday, February 25, 2008.

5. Most of these are of the Austrian School. The Austrian School defines economics as the study of human behavior, or praxeology. Humans are always striving to make themselves happier or better off.

6. William Easterly, *The White Man's Burden* (New York: The Penguin Group, 2006). Douglas North, *Understanding the Process of Economic Change* (Princeton, NJ: Princeton University Press, 2005).

7. *Source:* www.transparency.org/policy_research/surveys_indices/cpi/2009.

8. Tim Harford, "Why Poor Countries Are Poor," *Reason* Magazine, March 2006. www.reason.com/news/show/33258.html.

9. "Why Worry about Corruption?" Paolo Mauro, International Monetary Fund, February 1997.

10. Simeon Djankov, Rafael La Porta, Florencio Lopez-de-Silanes, and Andrei Shleifer, The Regulation of Entry, NBER Working Paper No. W7892 (September 2000).

11. Ludwig Von Mises, *Nation, State, and Economy: Contributions to the Politics and History of Our Time* (New York: New York University Press, 1983), p. 46.

12. Ludwig Von Mises, *Liberalism* (Jena: Gustav Fischer Verlag, 1927 in German; Princeton: Van Nostrand, 1962 in English), pp. 109–101.

13. Heitger (2001) examined the impact of government expenditures in 21 OECD countries from 1960 to 2000. He noted a substantial growth in average government expenditures over that period and a corresponding decline in average economic growth. The larger the scope of government in OECD countries, the more pronounced the decline in economic growth; a 10 percent reduction in government expenditures by OECD countries would boost economic growth by about 0.5 percent on average. Other studies have found a similar negative relationship. Barro (1989) found that "the ratio of real government consumption expenditure to real GDP had a negative association with growth and investment." Sachs and Warner (1995) concluded that "an increase in government spending by 1 percentage point of trend GDP decreases profits as a share of the capital stock by about 1/10 of a percentage point."

14. Daron Acemoglu and James A. Robinson, *Economic Origins of Dictatorship and Democracy* (New York: Cambridge University Press, 2006).

Seeking Competitive Advantage

CHAPTER **4**

Spontaneous Order and the Firm

Governance

Corporate governance, the subject of our conference, has evolved over the past century to more effectively promote the allocation of the nation's savings to its most productive uses. And, generally speaking, the resulting structure of business incentives, reporting, and accountability has served us well. We could not have achieved our current level of national productivity if corporate governance had been deeply flawed.

Yet, our most recent experiences with corporate malfeasance suggest that governance has strayed from the way we think it is supposed to work. By law, shareholders own our corporations, and corporate managers ideally should be working on behalf of shareholders to allocate business resources to their optimum use.

But as our economy has grown and our business units have become ever larger, de facto shareholder control has diminished: Ownership has become more dispersed, and few shareholders have sufficient stakes to individually influence the choice of boards of directors or chief executive officers. The vast majority of corporate share ownership is for investment, not for operating control of a company. Thus, corporate officers, especially chief executive officers, have increasingly shouldered the responsibility for guiding businesses in what one hopes they perceive to be the best interests of shareholders. Not all CEOs have appropriately discharged their responsibilities and lived up to the trust placed in them, as the events that led to the passage of the Sarbanes-Oxley Act demonstrated. In too many instances, some CEOs, under pressure to meet elevated short-term expectations for earnings, employed accounting devices for the sole purpose of obscuring adverse results.

A change in behavior, however, may already be in train. The sharp decline in stock and bond prices after the collapse of Enron and WorldCom has chastened many of those responsible for questionable business practices. Corporate reputation is emerging out of the ashes of the debacle as a significant economic value. I hope that we will return to the earlier practices of firms competing for the reputation of having the most conservative and transparent set of books.

* * *

It is hard to overstate the importance of reputation in a market economy. To be sure, a market economy requires a structure of formal rules—a law of contracts, bankruptcy statutes, a code of shareholder rights—to name but a few.

continues

But rules cannot substitute for character. In virtually all transactions, whether with customers or with colleagues, we rely on the word of those with whom we do business. If we could not do so, goods and services could not be exchanged efficiently. Even when followed to the letter, rules guide only a small number of the day-to-day decisions required of corporate management. The rest are governed by whatever personal code of values corporate managers bring to the table.

Market transactions are inhibited if counterparties cannot rely on the accuracy of information. The ability to trust the word of a stranger still is an integral part of any sophisticated economy. A reputation for honest dealings within a corporation is critical for effective corporate governance. Even more important is the reputation of the corporation itself as seen through the eyes of outsiders. It is an exceptionally important market value that in principle is capitalized on a balance sheet as goodwill.

1. Why does Greenspan note the growth of firms and the separation of shareholders and corporate officers?
2. What is the role of a governance system?
3. Does a good governance system replace the role of a market in guiding CEO behavior?

Remarks by Chairman Alan Greenspan, *Corporate Governance,* at the 2003 Conference on Bank Structure and Competition, Chicago, Illinois (via satellite), May 8, 2003.[1]

Hayek and Spontaneous Order

F. A. Hayek argued that the failure of a socialist or totalitarian system was inevitable because such a system could not organize and allocate resources like the free market does. It is a "fatal concept," said Hayek, for anyone to believe that he could determine prices, quantities, resource allocations, and the like, exactly like a free market would. As we know, in a free, unfettered market system, resources would be allocated to their highest valued use, people would get what they want and are willing and able to pay for, and everything would be produced at the lowest possible price. This occurs not because of some dictator or government decree. Instead, it occurs because of the self-interest of individuals being able to enter into voluntary transactions. People get others to purchase what they produce by serving the buyers—giving them what they want at a value they are willing to pay. People don't have to like each other; they just have to serve each other. This result of a free, unfettered market occurs spontaneously. There is a spontaneous order as opposed to an order created by a dictator or government.

The Prime Directive says that to understand why the world is the way it is, we should first look to the market because individuals, allowed to own property and be secure in their ownership, and allowed to voluntarily carry out exchange, will create results that are most beneficial to society. So, if something other than market exchange occurs, we would have to believe that either the market has not been allowed to work or that there is a market problem.

In looking at the developed world, we note that most exchanges are not carried out in open, free, unfettered markets. Most are carried out through or in institutions such as firms. People trade their labor services to a firm in return for compensation, and owners of land and capital trade the services of their resources for compensation. Resources are allocated within a firm. These exchanges are not made in a market but rather occur in an organization that looks more like a centrally planned government than a market. There is a leader—chief executive officer or president—telling people what to do and when to do it, allocating resources, and even setting prices. But since firms exist, they must be doing something that is beneficial in a market system, mustn't they?

The Existence of the Firm

Consider a very simple thought experiment. Suppose the world consists of individuals who are all self-sufficient, producing what they need to sustain themselves. Some are better at raising foods, others at making clothes, creating candles, or other activities, but everyone does a little of everything. At some point, a few would come up with the idea of specializing so as to gain from trade. The problem is that this specializing could be risky. If a farmer does well one year with his crops and then experiences terrible weather and a bad crop, he might prefer not to specialize. If a sheep herder is able to produce healthy coats and lots of wool one year but experiences reduced supplies another year, he might prefer not to specialize. The result is that no one specializes and thus there are no gains from trade.

To be able to gain, several individuals might decide to form a team in order to be able to specialize and also avoid the risk of specialization. Before forming the team, they would have to agree how to divide the output after they have each produced. In other words, they need to know who is to get what before they spend time and resources to produce. If they did not do this ahead of time, they would create a mess once output is produced: It would be a mad scramble to gather as much as possible before the others grabbed it. So they create a set of contracts that specify who gets what and they agree to these contracts before they actually join forces. This system of cooperation, based on contracts, enables the team to reduce risk and gain from specialization and trade.

Part of what enables people to gain from cooperating is their different attitudes toward risk. Most people are risk averse, but some less so than others. By pooling activities and forming a team in return for a salary, people reduce the risk involved in being a sole proprietor. Revenues created by the team are used to pay the agreed upon salaries and what is left goes to the owners. Thus, the risk is shifted to the owners who are compensated with **residual income**, the income left after all costs have been paid. Thus, the firm allows risk-averse people to shift some of their risk to the owners and allows those who are not as risk-averse to gain from taking on some risk.

But all this could be done with contracts that laid out the exchanges that were to occur. People could agree to work for someone, others could agree to take the risk, and so on. A firm would not have to exist if every contingency could be accounted for in a contract—called **complete contracts.** With complete contracts, each individual would act as an independent contractor, joining with one group to complete a job and then moving on to another group to carry out the next job. This does not occur because there is no way that every possible event can be contracted for. A team can set up contracts for everything the members can think of but will still not be able to account for every possibility. And think of the costs (transaction costs) of trying to create all these contracts. It would be prohibitive. The world is one of **incomplete contracts,** and incomplete contracts provide a role for firms.

The Monitor or Boss

A firm may enable people to specialize and gain from trade; it may allow people to reduce their risk; and it may be more efficient than attempting to write a set of complete contracts. But this view of a firm makes the firm a "team," and teams create incentive problems. Teams create incentives for individual members to "free ride." The farmer becomes a member of the firm but decides to loaf and still enjoy his share of output once everyone else has produced.

To reduce this incentive for free riding, the members have to assign someone the role of monitor, ensuring that each member is accountable to the organization. The monitor role is given to the manager, someone who has a comparative advantage in this activity. The manager is supposed to measure the contributions of each member of the team, ensure that each contributes appropriately, and fire or discipline members when necessary.

This structure is shown in Figure 4.1, with the monitor pictured as being "above" the employees. Although each member has voluntarily entered into an agreement and no one member is superior to any other, the impression is that the manager is at the top of a command and control system, giving orders to an army of workers. This is a misleading impression. The manager and workers are all team members who voluntarily agree to perform certain functions.

"A firm replaces a market." This statement means that transactions that could be carried out bilaterally—between individuals through a market—are instead carried out under the umbrella of an organization wherein individuals interact contractually. The accountant provides cash flow statements to the managers; an assembly-line worker fulfills a certain function so the product can move to the next station; and so on and so forth. A firm is a system of voluntarily entered into contracts. As such, it is itself a market system. By entering freely into an association, an individual agrees not only to sell his services, but also to cooperate with others according to some specific rules.

The Prime Directive suggests that firms exist because they are more efficient than the individual bilateral transactions would be. Firms exist because of:

1. *Incomplete contracts.* If contracts could be written that would account for every possible contingency, there would be no reason for firms. But asymmetric information means that not all contingencies can be contracted for and the transactions costs involved in trying to account for them would be prohibitive.
2. *Team product.* Forming a team to reduce risk and enable gains from specialization and trade leads to free riding.
3. *Incentives.* A hierarchical form minimizes free riding; compensation based on residual income ensures that managers appropriately monitor employees.

Democracy versus Dictator   As noted in the previous chapter, democracy is not necessarily the most efficient form of governance. In fact, the founders of the United States

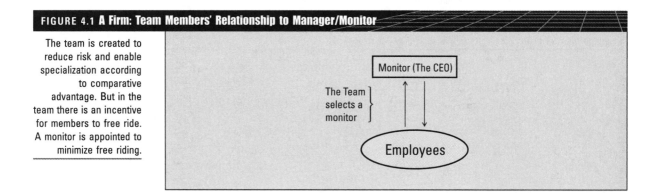

FIGURE 4.1 A Firm: Team Members' Relationship to Manager/Monitor

The team is created to reduce risk and enable specialization according to comparative advantage. But in the team there is an incentive for members to free ride. A monitor is appointed to minimize free riding.

Monitor (The CEO)

The Team selects a monitor

Employees

attempted to limit the weaknesses of democracy as much as possible while still relying on citizens to determine the policies and the functioning of government by placing governance in a Republic. Yet, even so, the Constitution has been bent, molded, and perhaps broken by extensive use of the Commerce Clause and the Welfare Clause.[2]

The inefficiency of democracy as a governing system suggests that firms would not rely on democratic management and instead would select a "benevolent" dictator.[3] But note that the firm's dictator is subject to a market test, something different than national dictators. First, the firm's dictator is monitored by the Board of Directors. Second, if the firm's dictator does not add value to the firm, the dictator is driven out of office. While a national dictator can run a country inefficiently, wasting or confiscating resources, up to the point that a revolution occurs, a CEO must run the firm efficiently or be relieved of his or her position because of the market test of the CEO's actions. See the analogy between a country and a firm in Figure 4.2.

Whereas the state can coerce individuals to behave as dictated, a firm has to provide incentives and induce people to voluntarily behave as desired. Whereas a state is not subject to a market test and need not be run efficiently, a firm has to be run efficiently or it will disappear. A state need not be of a size that is efficient, but a firm must take on only those transactions that contribute to efficiency. The size of a firm is referred to as the boundaries of the firm.

Boundaries of the Firm

A firm is deep—vertical structure—and wide—horizontal structure—and has an organizational platform or architecture that supports these structures—the internal organization including compensation, reporting lines, and so on. This entire set of features is referred to as the firm's architecture, that is, its internal organization. How deep the firm is depends on how much of the supply chain a firm includes in-house. How wide the firm is depends on how many different activities the firm includes in-house, the firm's scope.

Vertical Boundaries   The process that begins with the acquisition of raw material and ends with the distribution and sale of finished goods is known as the value or supply chain.[4] The vertical boundaries of a firm define the supply chain activities that the firm performs itself instead of purchasing from other firms via the market. We might think of each step in the supply chain as a distinct market. Then whether to use the market at each step depends on whether the market is more efficient than carrying out the activity in-house.

FIGURE 4.2 Analogy between a Country and a Firm

In a simple view, the beginning and structure of a country and a firm are similar. In a state, citizens voluntarily agree to contract with a state, that is, a government. The form of government may be some type of democracy or some version of a totalitarian system. In a firm, individual sole proprietors voluntary agree to specialize and share output. They contract with a monitor, someone who is chosen to minimize free riding. The monitor or CEO is subject to a market test.

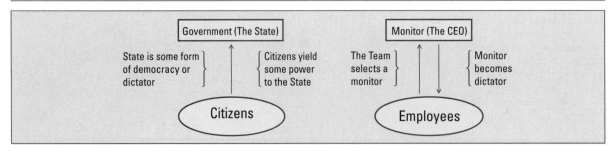

Although many firms have been successful in producing their own supportive activities or inputs, others prefer to obtain these from specialized providers in the market. When a firm buys activities or inputs from other firms, we say that it is using the market; when a firm carries out more than one step in the vertical chain itself, we say that it is **vertically integrated** in those activities. General Motors is a vertically integrated firm: Fisher Body is the manufacturer of automobile frames for General Motors, and Fisher Body is part of General Motors. Many manufacturing companies prefer to contract with independent salespeople, called manufacturers' representatives, rather than maintaining their own sales force. These manufacturers' reps specialize in providing the products and services customers desire and typically earn a commission on sales. They are not part of the manufacturing company and don't receive insurance, retirement, or other benefits from the manufacturing company. A vertically integrated manufacturing company would include the sales force in-house.

One firm's relationship to another is often described as being upstream or downstream in the supply chain. The terms are relative—a firm may be upstream from some firms and downstream from others. Intel is downstream from Corning but upstream from PC makers such as IBM and Dell. IBM is downstream from Intel but upstream from Procter & Gamble. If Intel acquired Corning, that would be a vertical acquisition; if Intel acquired IBM or Dell, that also would be a vertical acquisition.

A firm's decision to perform an upstream or downstream activity itself or purchase it from an independent firm is called a **make-or-buy** decision. Consider the distribution of finished goods from a manufacturer to retailers. The manufacturer could distribute the goods itself or use an independent distributor. Choosing to buy rather than make does not eliminate the expenses of the activity because the capital used to purchase has an opportunity cost. Suppose that it costs a distributor $100,000 to run the distribution business, for which it expects to generate $110,000 in net revenues. It appears that the distributor is realizing a profit margin of 10 percent that the manufacturer could gain for itself if it distributed the goods itself. If the manufacturer does its own distribution, it would be investing $100,000 of its own funds. The manufacturer thus faces an opportunity cost—it could use those funds elsewhere. If the manufacturer could invest the money in an equally risky venture and generate more than a 10 percent increase in net revenues, then it would lose money by tying up $100,000 in distribution. A firm must compare the costs and benefits of using the market rather than performing the activity in-house. In May 2002, Sears offered to purchase Lands' End. Sears could have simply contracted with Lands' End to provide Lands' End clothing in its stores; instead, it decided to integrate the firm into the Sears Company.

If the firm has some special competence in carrying out a supply activity, then it makes sense to do the activity in-house. But if those who specialize in the activity are more proficient than those within the firm, outsourcing (using the market) is the most efficient organization. Another circumstance is when one firm has control over an essential good or resource. Dealing with that firm could be like dealing with a monopolist who could arbitrarily limit or withhold supply at a crucial time—the hold-up problem. How would a firm avoid the possibility of being held up? It could own the necessary assets and supply the good in-house. If the monopoly inefficiency was greater than the cost of owning assets in-house, then the vertically integrated firm would make sense.

Another rationale in favor of making rather than buying is to keep information private. Relying on internal provision may be the most efficient way to protect sensitive knowledge from misappropriation by suppliers. Thus, the market may be replaced by the firm because of the inefficiency of protecting intellectual property in the market.

Horizontal Boundaries　The firm's horizontal boundaries are the varieties of products and services that the firm produces—the scope of the firm. A horizontal boundary refers to activities carried out by the firm at one specific level on the value chain. Quaker Oats, for example, produces drinks (Snapple, Gatorade) and cereals, both of which are at the same level on the value chain. Tomorrow International Holdings, which has a core business manufacturing electronic timing and weather-monitoring devices, has been acquiring pharmaceutical projects. Microsoft has been diversifying for some time into areas such as Internet service provision, enterprise software, mobile computing, and games consoles. For decades, diversification was the watchword at TRW, Inc. At one time, the company made parts for everything from blue jeans, refrigerators, automobiles, aircraft, and satellites to intercontinental ballistic missiles.

Just as with the vertical boundary, the horizontal boundary of the firm is defined by efficiency. Is it more efficient to produce multiple products in-house or to narrow production to one or a few goods and use the market for others? Rationales for horizontal expansion include economies of scope and transactions costs. Economies of scope exist if the per-unit cost declines as a firm increases the variety of activities it performs, such as the variety of goods it produces. In business jargon, the exploitation of economies of scope is referred to as "leveraging core competencies," "synergies," "competing on capabilities," and "mobilizing invisible assets."[5] Economies of scope may arise at any point in the value chain, from acquisition and use of raw materials to distribution and retailing.

An example of economies of scope in distribution arises in a number of industries in which goods and services are routed to and from several markets. In these industries, which include airlines, railroads, and telecommunications, distribution is often organized around hub-and-spoke networks. In an airline hub-and-spoke network, an airline flies passengers from a "spoke" city through a central "hub," where passengers then change planes and fly from the hub to their outbound spoke destination. Thus, a passenger flying from Indianapolis to Salt Lake City on American Airlines—whose hub is Chicago—would fly from Indianapolis to Chicago, change planes, and then fly from Chicago to Salt Lake City. American Airlines is able to offer travel to many pairs of cities less expensively by going through Chicago than by offering direct flights between them, such as Indianapolis to Salt Lake City.

Firms that sell a variety of products or that sell in many markets may enjoy scope economies in advertising. Economies of scope may also result from R&D spillovers—where ideas that arise in one research project are of help in another project.

If a firm exists in a market system to enable specialization and gains from trade, why isn't there just one big firm? The limits to the size of a firm are referred to as the **boundaries** of the firm. The boundaries of the firm occur in both vertical and horizontal directions. The vertical direction of a firm likens the production of a good or service to a river. One activity is upstream relative to another downstream activity. If Intel purchases raw materials from a supplier, the supplier is upstream to Intel. If Intel sells chips to Apple, then Apple is downstream to Intel. The entire vertical process from raw materials to final consumer good is called the **supply chain.** The production of any good or service usually requires a wide range of activities organized in the supply chain. Production activities are said to flow from upstream suppliers of raw inputs to downstream manufacturers, distributors, and retailers. The vertical boundary refers to bringing upstream and downstream transactions under the umbrella of the firm. When it is more efficient to leave the transaction in the market rather than have it occur inside the firm, that defines the vertical boundary of the firm.

A supply chain for a pharmaceutical firm is shown in Figure 4.3. It illustrates how the raw materials end up in your medicine cabinet.

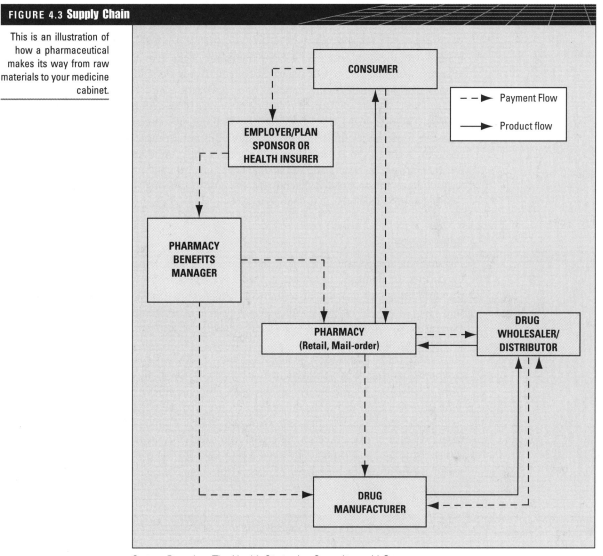

FIGURE 4.3 Supply Chain

This is an illustration of how a pharmaceutical makes its way from raw materials to your medicine cabinet.

Source: Based on The Health Strategies Consultancy LLC.

The horizontal boundaries of the firm refer to the firm's market share and its scope. The firm's market share is how much of the total product market the firm serves. If the total market size is $400 billion and the firm sells $40 billion, the firm's market share is 10 percent. The firm's **scope** is the variety of products and services the firm produces or provides for sale. GE has a wide scope; it owns Universal Pictures, Universal parks, NBC stations, Telemundo stations, aircraft engines, commercial finance, consumer products, industrial systems, insurance, medical systems, plastics, power systems, specialty materials, transportation systems, and other businesses. Texas Pacific owns Scottish & Newcastle, Debenhams, Burger King, Seagate Technology, Punch Taverns, Del Monte Foods, and the Ducati motorbike business.

As with the vertical boundaries, the decision as to whether to bring a transaction inside the firm or have it occur in the market depends on costs and benefits. If it is more efficient to have the firm increase market share or increase its scope than to leave those to the market, then the firm grows horizontally.

The make-or-buy decision depends on comparison of the marginal cost and marginal benefit of the transaction inside the firm, as illustrated in Figure 4.4. If bringing one more activity in-house costs more than the benefits it creates, then that is the limit or boundary of the firm. In Figure 4.4, the boundary of the firm occurs at point *B*, the point at which marginal cost equals marginal benefit. The marginal benefits of bringing transactions in-house include the benefits of specialization and reductions in transactions costs. These additional benefits decline as more transactions are made rather than bought. The marginal cost of bringing transactions in-house rises as additional transactions are made rather than bought. As more and more transactions are occurring within the firm, managers lose control over the transactions; there are too many, and they are too diverse.[6] As a result, additional managers are brought on board and a larger and larger bureaucracy is created. Eventually, the cost of carrying out another transaction inside the firm exceeds the marginal benefit.

Governance

For markets to exist and function, people have to be secure that what they own won't be confiscated or damaged by others. Governance refers to the ways in which rights and responsibilities are distributed and define the decision-making systems and structure that enforce private property rights. A governance system can be good—enforcing private property rights efficiently—or it can be bad—interfering with private property rights or enforcing them inefficiently.

A governance system for a firm plays the same role in defining, protecting, and enforcing property rights as a governance system does for a society. Most publicly traded firms are headed by the Board of Directors and the chief executive officer, the CEO. When the CEO can direct the company according to the CEO's preferences as opposed to those of shareholders, then governance is faulty. Think of Enron, Tyco, and other cases where a firm's officers confiscated resources for personal gain. It is similar to Robert Mugabe confiscating Zimbabwe's resources for his own uses or Putin and Medveded confiscating the resources of Russia for their uses. Corruption can occur when

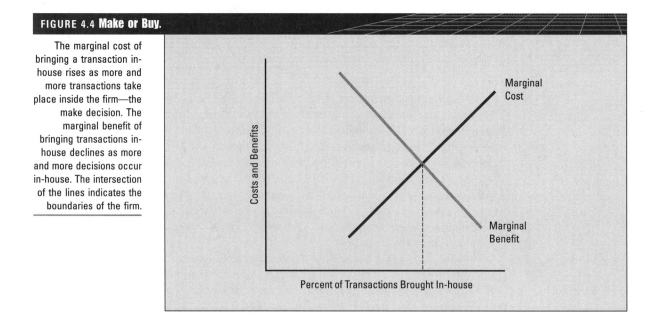

FIGURE 4.4 Make or Buy.

The marginal cost of bringing a transaction in-house rises as more and more transactions take place inside the firm—the make decision. The marginal benefit of bringing transactions in-house declines as more and more decisions occur in-house. The intersection of the lines indicates the boundaries of the firm.

Costs and Benefits

Marginal Cost

Marginal Benefit

Percent of Transactions Brought In-house

governance is not transparent and information is asymmetrically distributed. In other words, if the CEO can behave as he wishes without the scrutiny of others and if the CEO has better or more information than others, then corruption occurs. This situation is typically called a **principal-agent problem**.

Principal-Agent Issues and Revolution

What assurance is there that the monitor carries out the actions necessary to create maximum team performance and to ensure that the owners will earn the most "residual income"? The monitor may have objectives that differ from those of the owners. Perhaps the monitor just wants to have an easy job, and not have to fight battles and evaluate people. If so, it is unlikely that the team's performance will be very good. When a principal and his agent have differing objectives, a principal-agent problem arises. The monitor was hired to ensure that the team maximizes performance, but the monitor has different objectives. If paid a fixed salary, the monitor would have little incentive to act in the owner's best interests. But if the monitor is compensated based on what is left over after all team members have been given their agreed upon pay—that is, if the monitor is made an owner and receives residual income—the monitor will be more likely to ensure the team is productive.

Originally, the CEO and owner were the same person; businesses were sole proprietorships. But with the industrial revolution came the necessity for the owner to hire a professional manager to run the company. This development meant a separation of ownership and control. The hired managers controlled the company, while the owners, shareholders, paid little attention to the company. Moreover, ownership became widely dispersed, so that in most corporations it is rare that a shareholder will have a sufficient stake to individually influence the corporation.

The fact that the owners of corporations are not the managers means there may be a conflict of interest—a principal-agent problem. Owners may have different goals and objectives than the manager. A manager will raise capital from financiers to produce goods in a firm. The financiers expect the manager to generate returns on the capital they have provided, but a manager could use the capital for personal gain at the expense of owners or could direct the firm in activities that don't generate the greatest possible gain.

In a world of complete contracts, a contract that would specify how the manager should perform in every state of the world would perfectly tie management and ownership interests together. But because not every possible contingency can be predicted and/or it would be prohibitively costly to anticipate every contingency, such a perfect link is not feasible. The next best scheme is to make the manager an owner, reducing his incentive to act in ways that harm owners. In addition, a monitor of the monitor is created. The Board of Directors is supposed to be the monitor of the manager or CEO. If the Board is perfectly tuned to the goals and objectives of the owners, then the principal-agent problem is minimized. However, there is no reason to think that the Board's incentives would necessarily be identical to those of the owners. The Board may align more closely with the CEO and not work for the benefits of the owners. This is why a good governance system must exist. A good governance system ensures that the actions of the Board and managers are transparent to the owners. Transparency reduces the costs of monitoring and thus helps ensure that the interests of Board, managers, and owners are more closely aligned.

When the government of a nation is bad, what happens? Resource use is inefficient and performance is poor. Often the only way for things to improve is for a revolution to take place. An external revolution is one in which one country takes over another and imposes a government. An internal revolution is one in which citizens rise up and institute a new government. The same occurs with firms: Firms may be taken over, or leaders may be changed.

The takeover boom of the 1980s was a response to faulty governance. The mergers, acquisitions, leveraged buyouts (LBOs), and other restructurings represented a revolution against the entrenched authority of incumbent managers. Control of the corporation was transformed from an internal, secretive arrangement into a marketplace where the highest bidder made certain that the owners' interests would prevail. During the 1980s, a steady increase in the size of deals took place until it finally ended in the $25 billion buyout of RJR Nabisco by Kohlberg, Kravis, and Roberts (KKR). KKR was a firm organized as a partnership with fewer than 60 employees.[7] RJR Nabisco was huge, having around 79,000 employees.

Barbarians at the Gate, the best-selling account of the RJR Nabisco transaction, focused on the greed and tricks that occurred in some of the Wall Street deals during the time.[8] But what the book failed to note was clear evidence of the inefficient way in which RJR Nabisco was being run. By 1995, the RJR takeover and subsequent actions by KKR had provided $15 billion in added value. The takeover had returned resources to the owners. In short, it took an external revolution to resolve RJR's massive failure of governance.

The role of takeovers in curbing corporate inefficiency reflects a lack of quality governance. Managers were able to run the companies in the way they wanted without considering whether it was in the interests of owners. From 1976 to 1994 over 45,000 control transactions occurred, including mergers, tender offers, divestitures, and LBOs, totaling over $3 billion.[9]

The market for control of corporations disciplined managers and aligned the interests of owners and managers, when the governance failed to do so. But the market for corporate control came under pressure by politicians in 1989; the government nearly eliminated hostile takeovers. This left more responsibility with a company's governance system. Corporate governance has to secure private property rights, and it needs to be transparent in order to minimize monitoring costs. It defines the rules that guide the company, and it details the checks and balances and roles played by CEO, Boards of Directors, shareholders, and creditors.[10] Problems arise when the governance system is faulty.

Examples of faulty governance abound. General Motors failed to make major changes in its strategy for years. The losses continued to mount until the company reported losses of $6.5 billion in 1990 and 1991. The Board finally acted to remove the CEO. IBM failed to adjust to the substitution away from its mainframe business following the changes in the workstation and personal computer market. Only after reporting losses of about $3 billion in 1991 and a loss of about 65 percent of its value did the Board finally change the CEO. Of course, we know that this change did not help; GM was taken over by the U.S. government in 2008. Eastman Kodak, another major company formerly dominant in its market, failed to adjust to competition and took a decade to respond; it is struggling even in 2010. BP's oil well blowout in the Gulf of Mexico in 2010 led to heavy cash outlays and a struggle for BP to survive. The internal revolution was a replacement of the CEO at that time.

The wasting of resources became serious enough after about 2002 that another form of revolution occurred, the private equity takeover. The private equity firms are groups of private investors whose objective is to purchase companies and make them more efficient, essentially to fix them, grow them, and then sell them in three to five years following acquisition. The eventual buyer could be another company in the portfolio company's industry, another private equity firm, or the public. Private equity firms own a growing stable of America's most famous companies—Hertz, Neiman Marcus, and

Toys "R" Us, among others. The private equity market has improved the efficiency of many firms just as the takeover revolution did during the 1980s.

Revolutions can reduce the confiscation of private property by the governing group, but they are costly. It would be better if governance was of high quality and revolution was not necessary. Shareholders individually don't have much incentive to monitor managers because doing so is too costly for a single shareholder. However, monitoring is more likely if the managers' actions are transparent. Good governance requires transparency. If CEOs can hide actions from the Board of Directors and from investors, then resources can be confiscated from the shareholders by the CEO.

Firm governance must enhance efficiency. If not, it will be changed or the firm will disappear. Consider the Enron experience. The company was highly successful for a few years as it moved from a pipeline company to an energy trading company. But when officers began to see a slowdown in profit growth and began to undertake unethical behaviors, its governance system failed for awhile. It soon was discovered that Enron executives were carrying out illegal and unethical behaviors. The market penalized the company as investors sold shares and abandoned the firm.[11] The company went into bankruptcy in 2001, and officials were thrown into jail.

Governance systems also failed, leading to the 2008 housing bubble collapse. Major Wall Street firms were caught in the housing bubble and collapse because the actions of some divisions were not transparent to the rest of the company. Goldman Sachs, Lehman, J.P.Morgan, Merrill Lynch, and large banks such as Bank of America, Wachovia, and HBS all found themselves too leveraged and overloaded with "toxic" assets. As a result, they were forced to merge with others, to acquire huge government bailouts, or to go bankrupt in 2008. Much of the problem could be ascribed to each company's poor governance and lack of transparency.[12]

The Analogy between Markets and Firms

If a market is to function, private property rights must exist and be secure. People will not enter into voluntary exchange if they are not assured that they can do as they want with what they own. When private property rights do not exist or are not well defined and secure, then exchange will not occur or will occur inefficiently. The same has to be true for the firm. For people to enter into voluntary transactions, they must be secure in what they own. This applies to transactions within a firm as well. For transactions to occur within the firm, the private property rights of decision makers must be secure. Who owns what must be clear. A firm in which no one is sure who makes what decisions and allocates what resources is one that surely will be inefficient.

The firm is an enhancement of market exchange or an umbrella encompassing many market transactions. Thus, we should expect the issues that arise in market exchange to crop up inside firms as well. For instance, so-called market failures in the form of externalities, public goods, and asymmetric information ought to arise within the firm. This means that part of the success of a firm's management and governance systems is how well it deals with these issues, as we will discover in the coming chapters.

Property Rights in the Firm

Who owns what in a firm, and what ensures that these ownership rights are secure? The firm's owners do not actually have private property rights to the land, labor, and capital. People own their own bodies and intellects. When they agree to go to work for a firm, they don't give up that ownership. What they "sell" the firm is the right to use their labor and intellectual services. When a landowner rents her land to the firm, the landowner retains ownership of the land. The firm owns the use of that land, as specified in the contract. A capital owner sells the right to use that capital. Thus the property rights in a firm are the rights to the services of the resources and the rights to make decisions regarding the use of those resources.

The firm's owners may purchase the assets or land they use, in which case they would own both the assets and the services of those assets, but such ownership is not possible in the case of labor. So, a firm could not function if the property rights to resource services could not be separated from the owners of the assets. An owner of an asset used in a specific situation for which there are no substitutes could "hold up" the firm and demand additional payment. Property rights to resource uses are assigned to owners of the firm to avoid **hold-up problems**. These are the private property rights necessary for the firm to function.

It is unlikely that anyone, ever, has washed his rental car. Since the renter does not own the car, the renter does not take care of it. Ownership is necessary if people are to take care of an item. Similarly, ownership of one's job and tasks is necessary if one is to take care of the job or tasks. If an employee takes ownership of his job, then he will take care of it and attempt to improve its value.

Central planning does not work. Similarly, the top-down structure of a firm wherein employees are nothing but robots without responsibilities, ownership of tasks, and jobs, and decision rights will fail, especially in a world of "knowledge" workers. In an industrial system where management was designed from the top down (a system called scientific management devised by Frederick Winslow Taylor in the 1880s and 1890s) and all decisions were made by the top, the centrally planned system was not as obviously inefficient as it is today when innovation, creativity, and risk taking are necessary for success.

Each employee needs to know exactly what he "owns"—what he is responsible for and what decisions he has the right to make without checking with a boss. Ownership induces employees to take care of their assignment, tasks, and jobs. This, in turn, enables people to specialize where they have a comparative advantage and for the firm to gain from trade among these employees, all in a form of spontaneous order. In most firms, jobs or tasks are assigned, but a great deal of leeway exists on exactly how the tasks or jobs are to be accomplished. The choice is for the manager to micromanage every activity or to assign ownership and allow the system to function.

Governance

Alan Greenspan notes that as the economy has grown and business units have become ever larger, ownership has become more dispersed. Moreover, few shareholders have sufficient stakes to individually influence the choice of Boards of Directors or chief executive officers. Thus, corporate officers have the responsibility for guiding businesses in what one hopes they perceive to be the best interests of shareholders. We know Greenspan is talking about a principal agent issue here. But why would it matter whether the company is small or large when it comes to principal-agent problems? It would be transparency—the cost of monitoring the behavior of the agent. So would transparency, that is, a good governance system, solve the problem? Greenspan suggests perhaps not. He notes that not all CEOs have appropriately discharged their responsibilities and lived up to the trust placed in them. Greenspan goes on to note that more than governance is required. The firm is a market system and operates in a market system. As such, it must be trusted by those working for the firm and for those dealing with it outside. Greenspan says that a "market economy requires a structure of formal rules—a law of contracts, bankruptcy statutes, a code of shareholder rights—to name but a few. But rules cannot substitute for character." "Even when followed to the letter, rules guide only a small number of the day-to-day decisions required of corporate management." A good reputation is crucial. Reputation enhances efficiency; the market will drive those without a good reputation out of business.

Summary

1. A firm is an extension of markets. It exists so that individual members can specialize and gain from trade as well as minimize the risk of being a sole proprietor.
2. A firm exists as an efficient market result when not all contingencies can be anticipated ahead of time and contracted for.
3. A firm is a voluntarily entered into team. As such, there are incentives for free riding. The creation of a monitor or manager is a means of minimizing free riding.
4. The manager and owners may not have the same interests. This is called the principal agent problem. Making the manager an owner by compensating him with residual income minimizes the principal agent problem.
5. A set of private property rights exist within a firm. The rights are ownership to the uses of resource services.
6. The private property rights that are assigned within the firm must be secure, that is, enforced by a governance system.
7. Corporate governance refers to the rules and regulations that guide the firm. The governance system for most firms in the United States consists of a Board of Directors, CEO, and shareholders.
8. Governance must assure transparency and ensure that the property of the owners is not confiscated or misused.
9. The necessity for employees to claim property rights to tasks, jobs, and decisions implies that micromanagement is not efficient.

Key Terms

residual income
complete contracts
incomplete contracts
vertically integrated
boundaries

supply chain
scope
make-or-buy
principal-agent problem
hold-up problems

Exercises

1. Why do firms exist? Why is there not just one large firm?
2. Would there be a reason for firms to exist in a world where there were complete contracts? Why or why not?
3. If investors are reluctant to invest in companies whose CEOs have unsavory reputations or companies that despoil the environment, then we might expect (explain)

   a. the value of a company to reflect the reputation of the CEO.
   b. the price of a share of stock of the company to rise or fall depending on who is CEO.

   c. the value of a company to decline when a company fails to devote resources to protecting the environment.
   d. the price of a share of stock of a company to fall if investors suspect a company is polluting the groundwater.

4. If investors are reluctant to invest in companies whose CEOs have unsavory reputations or companies that despoil the environment, but information about CEOs and about activities with regard to the environment are difficult for a typical investor to obtain, then we might expect (explain)

a. the value of a company not to reflect the reputation of the CEO.

b. the price of a share of stock of the company not to rise or fall depending on who is CEO.

c. the value of a company not to decline when a company fails to devote resources to protecting the environment.

d. the price of a share of stock of a company not to fall if investors suspect a company is polluting the groundwater.

e. a company to begin offering such information to investors as a profit-seeking activity.

5. Are there private property rights within a firm? Who owns what? What is not owned? Can trade and exchange occur within the firm without the existence of private property rights?

6. What are the "boundaries" of a firm? What determines the extent of vertical boundaries—vertical integration? What determines the extent of horizontal integration—scope? Use a cost-benefit analysis to describe the optimal boundaries of a firm.

7. What is the purpose of a revolution? What forms do revolutions take—in countries, in firms?

8. Why did the evolution of large firms lead to a principal-agent problem? How can the principal-agent problem between owners and managers be minimized?

9. What is the purpose of corporate governance?

10. If corporate governance is lax, then how might the interests of managers and owners be made to coincide.

11. Confiscation of private property in nations occurs because of faulty governance. What does faulty governance mean for a firm?

12. What is the role of the Board of Directors? Should the Board's interests be aligned with the interests of managers or owners? Explain.

13. In 2010, an explosion on an oil rig in the Gulf of Mexico led to the largest environmental catastrophe in the United States. Is it possible that BP's governance was at fault? Why or why not?

14. Explain how a focus on core competency could be compatible with an expanding vertical boundary; with an expanding horizontal boundary.

15. What is meant by "supply chain"? Explain when a firm should bring its supply chain in-house. Explain when a firm should let its supply chain remain external.

16. In Chapter 1 it was noted that economics examines issues "at the margin." Explain how this would apply to the decision to make or buy.

CHAPTER NOTES

1. www.federalreserve.gov/boarddocs/speeches/2003/20030508/default.htm

2. Article I, Section 8 of the Constitution reads: "The Congress shall have Power To lay and collect Taxes, Duties, Imposts, and Excises, to pay the Debts and provide for the common Defence and general Welfare of the United States; …" and then, "To regulate Commerce with foreign Nations and among the several States." The Supreme Court has expanded the Commerce Clause to mean virtually any business in any state. Similarly, the Welfare Clause has been used to justify any action that supposedly benefits the general public.

3. A management movement developed in recent years, called organizational democracy or workplace democracy, is different than having each decision made by a vote. Yet it is also not the strict top-down organization. We will discuss this movement in the next chapter.

4. The term *value chain* was introduced by Michael Porter, *Competitive Advantage* (New York: Free Press, 1985).

5. C. K. Prahalad and G. Hamel, "The Core Competence of the Corporation," *Harvard Business Review,* 68 (May/June 1990): 79–91; G. Stalk, P. Evans, and L. Shulman, "Competing on Capabilities: The New Rules of Corporate Strategy," *Harvard Business Review,* 70 (March/April 1992): 57–69; and H. Itami, *Mobilizing Indivisible Assets* (Cambridge, MA: Harvard University Press, 1987).

6. In the management literature this is referred to as the manager's span of control.

7. For more on governance and buyouts, see *A Theory of the Firm* by Michael C. Jensen (Cambridge, MA: Harvard University Press, 2000), Chapter 1.

8. Bryan Burrough and John Helyar, *Barbarians at the Gate: The Fall of RJR Nabisco* (New York: Harper and Row, 1990)

9. Michael C. Jensen, *Theory of the Firm,* pp. 12–13. In a recent takeover attempt, the firm Lions Gate used financial maneuvering to protect executives from Carl Icahn's hostile takeover. Icahn filed suit against Lions Gate Entertainment, Inc., over what he called a "reprehensible" debt-to-equity deal, in an ongoing fight between the investor and the film company. Lions Gate helped shield itself from a hostile takeover attempt by Mr. Icahn through a complex financial maneuver that put newly issued shares in the hands of its second-biggest shareholder, and board member, Mark Rachesky. Mr. Icahn filed suit in New York state court against Lions Gate; its board; Mr. Rachesky and his investment fund; and Kornitzer Capital Management LLC, with whom the exchange of notes was conducted, and its principal John C. Kornitzer. The suit seeks damages, an injunction rescinding the debt-to-equity move and the prohibition of the defendants from voting their shares to elect any directors. Wall Street Journal Online, JULY 26, 2010, 10:12 A.M. ET, "Icahn Sues Lions Gate over Equity Swap" by Nathan Becker.

10. Merritt B. Fox and Michael A. Heller, "What Is Good Governance?," *Corporate Governance Lessons from Transition Economy Reforms* (Princeton, NJ: Princeton University Press, 2006), pp. 3–31.

11. See Kurt Eichenwald, *Conspiracy of Fools* (New York: Random House, 2005).

12. Michael Lewis's *The Big Short* (New York: W.W. Norton, 2010) is an interesting read on this period.

CHAPTER 5

Organization of the Firm

Intelligence Failure

Between 1947 and 2004, the U.S. intelligence system consisted of 15 separate agencies, including several that were run within the Department of Defense and dedicated to obtaining intelligence data through technical means such as spy satellites. An official appointed by the president of the United States—the director of Central Intelligence—was responsible for coordinating all the agencies concerned with foreign intelligence. Following September 11, 2001, a number of official investigations concluded that lack of coordination among intelligence agencies was one reason that the U.S. government did not foresee and forestall the attacks. Per the recommendations of the 9/11 Commission, Congress passed the Intelligence Reform and Terrorism Prevention Act of 2004, which President George W. Bush signed into law on December 17, 2004. The director of National Intelligence is the chief of all 16 U.S. intelligence agencies and is supposed to coordinate their work and analytic product. The head of the Central Intelligence Agency reports to him.

In the run-up to the U.S.-led invasion of Iraq in 2003, virtually the entire intelligence system of the United States (and the world) held the mistaken belief that Saddam Hussein possessed weapons of mass destruction. In the 12 years preceding the invasion, "the Intelligence Community did not produce a single analytical product that examined the possibility that Saddam Hussein's desire to escape sanctions … would cause him to destroy his WMD" (WMD Commission, 2005, pp. 155–156).

The intelligence agencies relied heavily on information supplied by Iraqi exiles, some of whose reports came through the Iraqi National Congress, an umbrella Iraqi opposition group organized in the early 1990s that attempted to coordinate the actions of all the anti-Hussein groups. The reports contained similar findings, and this appearance of corroboration made them persuasive.

In 2007, the U.S. intelligence agency produced the National Intelligence Estimate. This document stated that U.S. agencies "judge with high confidence that in fall 2003, Tehran halted its nuclear weapons program" and that "the halt lasted at least several years." But in 2009 that opinion was reversed.

1. Does a hierarchical system make sense for collection of intelligence?
2. Is the new hierarchical organization working for U.S. intelligence agencies?

Organizing for Performance

The way in which a firm—or a church, university, government, or other institution for that matter—is organized depends on the exchange or transaction issues inherent in the activities of that organization. Consider how the communists had to alter their organization to carry out their successful revolution in Vietnam. The problem the communists faced was free riding. They had to get the population involved in the revolution.[1] When the communists took over villages, they redistributed land, giving peasants private property. The peasants then commonly went out of their way to warn Viet Minh cadres that French soldiers or agents were in the area. Even though communism abhors private property, the Viet Minh used it to solve their public goods problem.

In military organizations or spy networks, a hierarchical system seems to work best. The information and control has to be in the hands of just a few. By having virtually everyone reporting to someone above them in the hierarchy, the superiors obtain all information and those lower on the scale receive only what they need. Terror organizations, however, do not utilize this structure. Their problem is not the flow of information but, instead, individual initiative and empowerment. Terror organizations such as Al Qaeda appear to be semi-independent cells connected in a very loose network. This makes it easier for individuals to show initiative and be empowered but harder for those at the top to communicate orders or strategic thinking or to exercise control. Al Qaeda offset this problem with video and audio tapes broadcast on Al Jazeera and the Internet.

"Our organization is paralyzed by the smiling dead hand of middle management," complained the general manager. "Whenever I want to take an initiative, do something different, rock the boat, I see the smiles and nods of agreement … but nothing happens. What do I do?" The management consultant's answer: "Flatten the structure."[2]

This advice was rampant in the 1990s. Hierarchy had been branded as "the devil we know." Accordingly, many firms set out to obliterate hierarchy and change reporting relationships and titles. In the resulting organization, the pyramid was flattened, turned upside down, or even recast as a horizontal organization. Instead of subordinates and superiors or bosses and underlings, people referred to associates, colleagues, sponsors, or advisers. The work unit became the team, not the individual.[3] But teams don't work well for all firms. They create problems that can be greater than their benefits.

Institutions, organizations, and organizational structures will not exist in a market system in the long run unless they are efficient. When a firm is able to create a more efficient architecture than other firms, it has a competitive advantage over these firms. **Architecture** refers to the organization or structure of the firm. As long as the firm is able to sustain the advantage, it can earn above-normal profits. It is logical, then, that firms will search for competitive advantage not only in their relations with each other and vis-à-vis customers but also internally in their architecture.

The Evolution of the Firm

Before 1840, most businesses were family owned and operated, and were typically sole proprietorships. The dominance of the family-run business was a direct consequence of the limitations in transportation, communications, and finance of the time. Transportation was either by waterway or wagon; the primary mode of long-distance communication in 1840 was the public mail via pony express; and financing was local and cumbersome. Most businesses found it difficult to obtain external financing. Public ownership (shares of stock) was virtually nonexistent, and most loans were made on the basis of personal relationships.

Between 1840 and 1910, developments in transportation, communications, and finance meant that larger firms could be more efficient than smaller ones. The owner-operator's responsibilities in functional areas of business—purchasing, sales, distribution, and finance—rose tremendously. Because a single owner-operator could not be involved in every aspect of business, owners increasingly turned to professional managers. The professional manager created a central office or headquarters to ensure that production runs went smoothly and finished goods found their way to market. As the business grew, it was organized into semiautonomous divisions, each of which made the principal operating decisions for itself, while decisions that affected the entire corporation were made at headquarters. For example, the divisions of General Motors would make operating decisions for each car line, while corporate management would make decisions regarding corporate finance and research and development.

By the mid-twentieth century, continued market growth had caused many firms difficulty in coordinating production processes across different customer groups and market areas. Firms such as Dow Corning, Amoco, Citibank, and Pepsi-Co reorganized according to two or more different types of divisions—geographic and client, product groups and functional departments, or geographic and functional lines. The market growth also meant that specialization in various activities became feasible. Firms could purchase from others many activities they had previously performed in-house.

In the 1990s, firms moved to reduce, or "flatten," their hierarchical structure, to downsize, and to focus on core competencies. Firms reduced the number of managers and administrative staff; they chose to keep fewer activities in-house and thus purchased more from other firms. Enron captured the essence of what many thought was the ideal structure in 2002 for many companies—the corporation without fixed assets. All activities requiring fixed assets were outsourced. Outside firms would then specialize in providing the services associated with a particular fixed asset, while the assetless company would focus on trading. Of course, when Enron imploded and then the dot-com bubble burst and later the housing bubble burst, firms began seeking more efficient organizations.

While the historical evolution of the firm applies generally across all firms at any given point, it does not mean that every firm will have the same architecture. Firms seek the most efficient way to do what they do; they want to be as cost effective as they can.

The flattening of the hierarchy is supposed to reduce costs by increasing productivity. One way to increase the productivity of a resource is to reduce the quantity of that resource without changing sales. This is what downsizing was supposed to accomplish—a reduction in labor, in particular, without a reduction in output. So, downsizing accompanied an attempt to flatten the organization.

Labor costs are not the only costs that are emphasized. The supply chain—the acquisition of resources—has been a recent point of focus for many businesses because a more efficient supply chain can increase resource productivity. Wal-Mart was able to create a system by which it could control inventory, thereby devoting less capital to supplies and the management of supplies. Manufacturing firms have implemented just-in-time inventory control (JIT) with the objective of minimizing the costs of holding inventories. Improved communication and IT can improve resource productivity. While these and other steps may reduce costs, they may lead to inefficiencies in other areas. The job of management is to find the architecture that enables the firm to be efficient.

At any point in time, different firms will be organized differently, depending on which structure managers believe works best for the firm and whether managers are pursuing a strategy of cost effectiveness, growth, or performance. Johnson & Johnson is composed of over 150 semi-independent companies that carry out their own product development, marketing, and sales, and pay dividends to the parent; the firms compete with each other. British Petroleum is the opposite of J&J, organized through a hierarchical matrix structure.[4] Nike is responsible for the product design, marketing, and distribution to retailers but does not produce. Benetton outsources the basic design work and most of the manufacturing for its products and relies on retail outlets that are independently owned. The electronics industry as a whole has adopted a decentralized structure that is not too dissimilar from Nike's. Many firms outsource almost all manufacturing to electronic manufacturing services (EMS) companies such as Solectron and Flextronic. At many companies, profit centers are established, and the various profit centers operate almost like independent firms. At Chevron, the procurement division, called Supplier Management & Integration, provides services to the other divisions, and at Intel the commodity management division is the middleman between the factory and buyer. W.L. Gore did away with titles, has workers join in teams to accomplish tasks, and is organized in what the company calls a flat lattice organization.

Why do firms have such different architectures? Each has to be as efficient as possible; the inefficient won't last. Perhaps it is what each firm is attempting to accomplish that dictates the structure. Some firms focus on performance, others on growth or market share, still others on serving a niche, and, most likely, the most efficient structure for doing each of these is different.

Hierarchy versus Flat Organization

Consider a situation where the firm's output necessitates inputs from each employee. For instance, each employee is a specialist in a part of production that must be shared with other employees. In general, the number of potential interactions among n independent individuals is $n(n-1)/2$, since each individual must interact with the $(n-1)$ other individuals. In contrast, the number of interactions among n individuals, one of whom supervises the others, is $(n-1)$, since each of the $(n-1)$ individuals has to interact with just the one boss. Hence, as n increases, it becomes increasingly more efficient in terms of number of interactions to have bosses or managers. Here, a *hierarchical* form minimizes transactions costs.

Complex hierarchy arises when employees must interact with a group of employees quite often, but not with all employees. It is efficient to organize individuals into groups and then organize those groups into larger groups. *Departmentalization* is a grouping along dimensions such as a common task or function, input, output, geographic location, or time of work. Examples of departments organized around common tasks or functions include accounting, marketing, and production. Examples of input- and output-based groupings include the Pepsi Bottling Group and Fountain Beverage Division. Examples of departments organized around location include regional sales offices of publishing companies such as Houghton Mifflin and McGraw-Hill. An example of time-based groupings would be multiple shifts within a manufacturing firm: 8:00 A.M. to 4:00 P.M., 4:00 P.M. to midnight, and midnight to 8:00 A.M. Departmentalization is efficient when there are economies of scale in specific activities. However, departmentalization can be inefficient when problems overlap divisions or departments.

U-Form   In the late nineteenth century, most larger firms were characterized by loose combinations of formerly independent firms, often still run by their founders. US Steel looked this way when it became the first billion-dollar firm in 1901. But at this time, developments in technology and market infrastructures created opportunities for achieving unprecedented benefits from being larger in industries. Firms responded to these opportunities by investing in large-scale production facilities and internalizing activities, such as sales and distribution, which had previously been performed for them by independent companies. The organizational structure that evolved in these early firms is called the U-form. The **U-form**, also called **unitary form**, refers to the case in which a single department is responsible for a single basic business function: finance, marketing, production, purchasing, and so on. This structure allowed firms to develop a specialization of labor that facilitated the achievement of economies of scale in manufacturing, marketing, and distribution. The first firms to adopt the U-form generated above-normal profits; as a result, imitation proceeded rapidly.

An illustration of the U-form is shown in Figure 5.1. Each general manager of a department reports to the staff vice presidents in the corporate headquarters. Within each department are staff and employees.

M-Form   The firms that were the first in their industries to invest in large-scale production facilities and develop managerial hierarchies expanded rapidly and were often able to dominate their industries. But most of the early growth of these firms occurred within a single line of business or within a single market. For example, as late as 1913 only 3 percent of DuPont's sales came from outside its core business of gunpowder, and nearly all of its gunpowder was sold in the United States. As markets grew, firms moved away from a focus on a single line of business or a single market to continue to exploit economies of scale and scope. Firms such as Singer and International Harvester expanded overseas. Other firms, such as DuPont and Procter & Gamble, expanded by diversifying their product lines.

This shift in strategy from a focus on a single business or market to product-line diversification was a problem for the U-form of organization. The attempt by the top management of the firms to monitor functional departments led to administrative overload, or—to use the jargon of organizational management—to exceeding the manager's "span of control."

The multidivisional structure, or M-form, that emerged in the United States after 1920 was a response to the limitations of the functional organization in diversified firms. The M-form removed top managers from involvement in the operational details of functional departments, allowing them to specialize in strategic decision making and long-range planning. Division managers would monitor the operational activities of the functional departments that reported to them and would be rewarded on the basis of divisional performance.

The **M-form,** or **multidivisional form**, involves a set of autonomous divisions led by a corporate headquarters office. The headquarters includes a corporate staff that provides information about the internal and external business environment. Rather than organizing by function or by task, a multidivisional structure organizes by product line, related

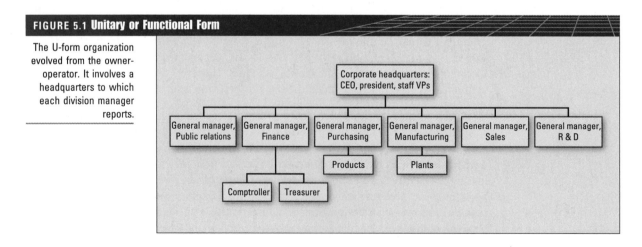

FIGURE 5.1 Unitary or Functional Form

The U-form organization evolved from the owner-operator. It involves a headquarters to which each division manager reports.

Corporate headquarters: CEO, president, staff VPs

General manager, Public relations | General manager, Finance | General manager, Purchasing | General manager, Manufacturing | General manager, Sales | General manager, R & D

Products

Plants

Comptroller   Treasurer

business units, region, or customer type (e.g., industrial, consumer, government). Divisions are groupings of interrelated subunits.

The M-form is illustrated in Figure 5.2. Each division head reports to headquarters; within each division are necessary parts of the functional departments.

Matrix   The firms turning to the M-form were temporarily able to generate more profits than comparable firms with the U-form. But as with any imitable capability, the advantage could not be sustained. Then, as the growth of markets (both downstream and upstream) raised the transactions costs of dealing with suppliers and customers for a firm with the M-form organization, new structures evolved. For example, large regional supermarket chains often operated in territories that encompassed several different regional offices within the Pepsi Bottling Group. But Pepsi's existing M-form structure gave no one region wide authority over pricing decisions. When faced with requests for promotion or special pricing deals by a large supermarket chain, executives at Pepsi Bottling Group had to obtain direction and decisions from the head of Pepsi USA, who was forced to become involved in regional-level pricing and promotion decisions. Not surprisingly, this impaired the speed with which Pepsi could respond and put it at a competitive disadvantage relative to those who could respond more quickly. Since Pepsi believed that national coordination of manufacturing helped achieve economies of scale in production—justifying organization along functional lines—but that regional coordination would increase its effectiveness in negotiating with large purchasers, the company organized in a dual-department structure, called a **matrix**.

The matrix structure, illustrated in Figure 5.3, can include product groups and functional departments or different types of divisions, such as ones focused on geographic regions and specific clients.

Network   Because some markets offer efficiencies of large size in some activities and inefficiencies of large size in others, neither small nor large firms necessarily have an advantage in all activities. In such cases, the most efficient structure may be the **network**—an affiliation of independent firms that together can exploit economies of scale but separately can avoid diseconomies of scale. The high-tech firms in Silicon Valley and along Route 128 in Massachusetts are examples of networks. Together they are able to benefit from large pools of trained labor and available supplies but separately can avoid the

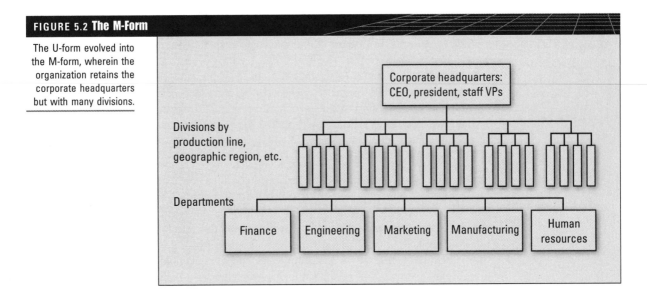

FIGURE 5.2 The M-Form

The U-form evolved into the M-form, wherein the organization retains the corporate headquarters but with many divisions.

Corporate headquarters: CEO, president, staff VPs

Divisions by production line, geographic region, etc.

Departments

Finance | Engineering | Marketing | Manufacturing | Human resources

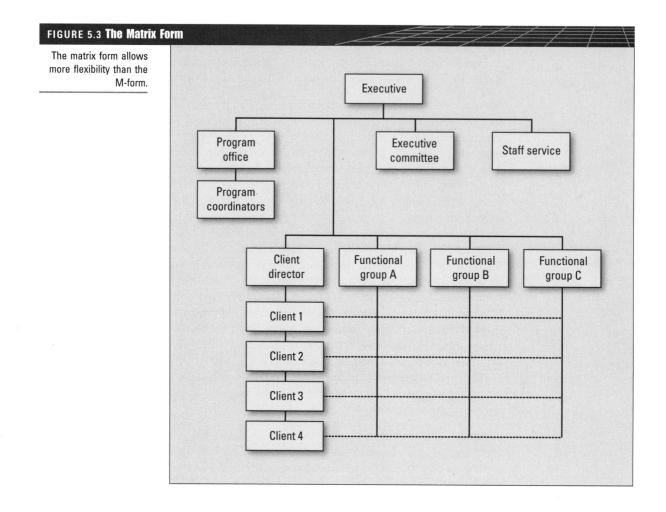

FIGURE 5.3 The Matrix Form

The matrix form allows more flexibility than the M-form.

redundancy, bureaucratic inefficiencies, and large fixed costs that would come from merging into one large firm.

Organizational Democracy

Managers are the dinosaurs of our modern organizational ecology. The Age of Management is finally coming to a close. The need for overseers, surrogate parents, scolds, monitors, functionaries, disciplinarians, bureaucrats, and long implementers is over, while the need for visionaries, leaders, coordinators, coaches, mentors, facilitators, and conflict resolvers is steadily increasing … a far reaching organizational transformation has already begun, based on the idea that management as a system fails to open the heart or free the spirit.[5]

In the past 15 years or so, many academicians have argued that the firms should be an **organizational democracy**. The idea is to eliminate the command and control structure implied by hierarchy and replace it with an organization without bosses, where employees select who is to be the monitor or leader via democracy, and where the strategy and purposes of the company are directed by democratic elections.[6] The argument is that since we are able to flourish most in a democratic form of government, that democracy should also exist in firms so that employees and all stakeholders can prosper. In addition, it is asserted that organizational hierarchies are inefficient. These hierarchies assume that high-level managers are more capable than those below them and are entitled to select or promote managers. But since political democracy was founded on the proposition that the governed have a right to determine who will govern them, why shouldn't firms be the same? The democratic organization would be a lattice structure (a structure of crossed strips arranged to form a diagonal pattern of open spaces between the strips) wherein projects to be worked on, team organization, leaders and followers, would all be selected by consensus, that is, by voting.

The assumption of those pushing the idea of a democratic organization is that democracy is efficient and successful. The problem is that throughout history, democracy has been very short-lived. It has failed as voters learn to transfer resources from the minority to the majority.

The American founders were well aware of the problems associated with democracy and attempted to minimize them by erecting a representative democracy with separation of powers and checks and balances.

As noted in Chapter 3, De Tocqueville stated the issue in his masterpiece, *Democracy in America.*

> *A democracy is always temporary in nature; it simply cannot exist as a permanent form of government. A democracy will continue to exist up until the time that voters discover that they can vote themselves generous gifts from the public treasury. From that moment on, the majority always votes for the candidates who promise the most benefits from the public treasury, with the result that every democracy will finally collapse.*[7]

It is not really a democratic organization that most people mean when they refer to the democratic enterprise. They typically mean an organization where employees participate in many but not all decisions. Enterprise Rent a Car is called a democratic enterprise. It uses "democratic" decision taking in many parts of the business. But rather than democratic it is more "participatory." In some cases, the leader makes the decision first and then persuades employees that he or she has made the right decision. In other cases, the team or employees contribute to the decision-making process, with the leader making the final decision.

In essence what the "democratic organization" refers to is the assignment of ownership or private property rights. Employees are given ownership over certain decisions and tasks. While the "leader" has final ownership over a decision, each employee has a property right over the ability to provide recommendations and inputs.

Which Form to Choose   The evolution of internal organization over the last 75 years appears to have been a move from a hierarchical to a nonhierarchical structure. This, at least, is the interpretation given by many consultants, executives, and members of the business press who attack the hierarchical structure. The late Peter Drucker, for instance, once argued that the modern organization should be an orchestra, in which a single conductor provides guidance to many players, each of whom is a highly skilled expert, not a complex hierarchy.[8] A form of the orchestra model that is often alluded to is "managing by walking around" (MBWA). The CEO is urged to manage by visiting the shop floor and front-line office and talking directly with lower-level employees.

Organizational form, like every aspect of the firm, should be the result of economizing—a result of conscientious action attempting to devise a form that is most efficient. Are the problems attributed to hierarchy valid? An orchestra is hierarchical; the director dictates everything that is going on. Research on communication does not support the idea that direct communication with the workforce is preferable to communication via the hierarchy.[9] Even in the case of MBWA, a hierarchy is implied—someone, some manager, must come down to the shop floor and mingle with floor-level employees.

The Gore Company is one of the most well-known examples of a firm without a hierarchy (a democratic enterprise). There are no bosses. All employees are associates. Decision making often involves a vote. The physical layout of the plant involves separate buildings for separate products. The objective is to keep the small feeling even as the firm grows. But this form works for only a very few firms.

In the 1990s, computing and communications technology was reputed to replace middle management. But computing and communications can replace management only if management is doing repetitive tasks or work that consists of processing data according to rules. If middle managers interpret the data and suggest strategies, then that technology won't replace the middle management; the burden on upper management will have increased which is unlikely to be efficient.

Does hierarchy create excessive overhead costs?[10] Work that can be easily specified and for which people can be trained, such as the work of telephone operators, needs little supervision. When work is less routine and when learned rules or routines can't be relied on, more involvement by supervisors is needed. When jobs are physically separated or require intricate interactions, the supervisor becomes busy very quickly. A supervisor to supervise the supervisors is needed—that is, a hierarchy.

There are always trade-offs in a firm. Increasing the hierarchy in a firm may reduce the number of interactions required and thus reduce transactions costs, but may increase free riding. There are also public goods problems inside a firm. A firm's reputation is the public good—everyone benefits from it, and one's use of it does not diminish its use for others. Employees who must choose between devoting their time and effort to a public good, such as firm reputation, or a private good—their individual output—will select the private good whenever they can free ride on the reputation of the firm. The hierarchy enables the free riding if monitoring by supervisors is limited. If all employees free ride, then none are focusing any attention on the firm's reputation—too few resources are devoted to enhancing the firm's reputation.

As with public goods in general, the assignment of private property rights will resolve the free-riding issue. Explicitly tying compensation and job requirements to time devoted to the firm's reputation will reduce the free riding. This could be done by emphasizing how each employee has a responsibility to the firm and then ensuring that employees have to interact enough to be able to monitor how much each contributes to the public good. Requiring departments or divisions or groups to take time from private tasks and devote themselves to the firm's reputation—volunteering in the community, for instance—would reduce the free riding.

Cutting costs, eliminating middle management, outsourcing, and the like, have the benefit of lowering the explicit costs of supplying and selling goods but may lead to higher costs in the form of reduced productivity or an inability to pursue growth or some other strategy. The downsizing, flattening, and cost cutting of the late 1980s and early 1990s were replaced by an emphasis on growth in the late 1990s. To enhance growth, a number of leading firms turned to a more hierarchical structure. Coca-Cola, for instance, used to sell beverages through independent bottlers and distributors, each carrying out its own pricing, promotion, and sales. But as buyers such as Wal-Mart and fast-food chains such as Pizza Hut and McDonald's became more important to Coke's sales, the company needed to control its sales and marketing more closely. So it began acquiring distributors and combining what had been thousands of small businesses operating in a flat, nonhierarchical structure into a few large, hierarchically managed organizations.[11]

The purpose of the firm's architecture is to help it be as efficient as possible. The decision is not simply a hierarchy or not, but includes the structure, compensation, and governance. These all interact to create an efficient or inefficient organization. These topics will be examined in coming chapters. In the remainder of this chapter, let's look at the way culture can help create efficiencies.

Culture

One organization could be much more efficient than another if the employees knew what to do without any interaction with superiors or with others. This is what a culture can provide an organization.

The glue that holds an organization together is referred to as corporate culture. **Corporate culture** refers to a set of collectively held values, beliefs, and norms of behavior among members of a firm that influence individual employee preferences and behaviors. Corporate culture usually encompasses the ways in which work and authority are organized, the ways in which people are rewarded and controlled, and organizational features such as customs, taboos, company slogans, heroes, and social rituals. A culture can be valuable if it reduces information-processing demands on individuals within the firm, if it reduces the costs of monitoring individuals within the firm, and if it shapes the preferences of individuals within the firm toward a common set of goals—that is, if it decreases transactions costs.

The term *culture* originally comes from social anthropology. Late-nineteenth- and early-twentieth-century studies of early societies such as Eskimo, South Seas, African, and Native American, revealed ways of life that were not only different from those in the more technologically advanced parts of America and Europe but were often very different from each other.[12] These ways of life were deemed to be the culture of the society. In each society certain behaviors and organizations were passed from one generation to the next through behavior, example, stories, and myths. Corporate culture refers to the values and practices that are shared across employees and are passed from more senior employees to new ones.

Once established, organizational cultures are perpetuated in a number of ways. Potential group members may be screened according to how well their values and behavior fit in. New members may be explicitly taught the group's style through training sessions or retreats. Stories, myths, or legends may be told again and again to remind everyone of the group's values and what they mean. Within Wal-Mart, constant allusions are made to Sam Walton's legend. The "HP [Hewlett-Packard] way" and "Houghton Mifflin casual dress" are commonly referred to in these firms. People who successfully achieve the ideals inherent in the culture may be recognized and made into heroes. The natural process of younger members identifying with older members may encourage the younger members to take on the values and styles of their mentors.[13] The company's stories or legends help employees fill in the cultural rules.

Cognitive psychologists argue that the mind naturally categorizes what people do, rather than what events transpire. If this is true, then employees trying to guess what the cultural rules mean in a new setting can learn best by generalizing from the successful actions of leaders or role models in that setting. Slogans, role models, and social rituals can be viewed as methods of communicating to workers in a low-cost fashion. Consider the following well-known vision statement from the television series *Star Trek*:

> These are the voyages of the Starship *Enterprise*. Its five-year mission: To explore strange new worlds, to seek out new life and new civilizations, to boldly go where no one has gone before.

This statement tells the employees how to behave: They are to explore new worlds and seek out new life. They are even to *go boldly* into these activities. And this mission has been passed from one generation to another (from one generation of the TV show *Star Trek* to another).

What is the purpose of corporate culture? It is a low-cost way to create and enforce contracts and to solve market failure issues. Managers could take the time to dictate exactly what employees should do by issuing a long book of rules and then monitoring employees carefully, but the firm economizes on communication and monitoring costs if employees can accurately guess what they should do.

A firm's organization is supposed to be one that increases efficiency. The firm's culture has to fit with that organization and enhance the efficiency. A firm organized in an hierarchical form would find its structure clashing with its culture if it attempted to create an informal atmosphere wherein underlings did not report to superiors. Similarly, a firm organized into teams would find a clash with a culture designed to enhance individuality or entrepreneurship.

In 1989, about a decade after the term *corporate culture* came into general use, Time, Inc. blocked a hostile bid by Paramount by arguing that its culture would be destroyed or changed by the takeover and that this would be to the detriment of its customers, shareholders, and society. The courts accepted the argument, and so the takeover was voided. Is culture important?

Corporate cultures can create additional costs for merging or combining firms. A common explanation of the failure of firms to merge successfully is that their cultures did not mesh. On May 7, 2002, the *Financial Times* noted that "JP Morgan and Chase Manhattan's banking merger is producing an intriguing culture clash. Former Chase employees, it seems, are more avant-garde than their Morgan counterparts—at least when it comes to art. As one Morgan employee says: 'We've got a pair of old grey pyjamas hanging up on our walls. … I don't get it.'"

Pharmacia was a loose patchwork of companies, whereas Upjohn had a structured, hierarchical structure. With their merger came a centralized headquarters where executives there had responsibility for the performance of the local units. This offended many Pharmacia managers, and many left the firm. The result was that the remaining company did not have sufficient numbers of people who understood some of the pharmaceuticals in Pharmacia's pipeline—transaction costs rose. Consequently, subsequent product launches were failures. The combined company's stock did not perform well, leading Pharmacia to look to additional acquisitions as a panacea. The company acquired Monsanto Co. in 1999. Since that deal closed, the company's stock has underperformed the Standard and Poor's drug industry average.

Summing Up

The firm is an extension of markets, a set of explicit and implicit contracts among suppliers, customers, resource suppliers, owners, managers, debtholders, shareholders, and so on. The firm is an individual only as a legal fiction, not an individual with its single goals and desires. The firm is the result of a market process (an arbitrage process) among the potentially conflicting objectives of various individuals. In this sense the behavior of the firm is like the behavior of a market—a sort of spontaneous result.

Incomplete contracts mean that not every contingency can be accounted for, and so when something arises that was not accounted for in the contracts, someone or some way has to define decision-making authority (assign private property rights). The incomplete contracts also create principal-agent problems and at times lead to ambiguous property rights assignments. To understand the firm, to organize it for performance, requires that these issues are understood and resolved. In this chapter we began looking at the organization of the firm. In particular, we examined whether a hierarchical structure performs better than a flat structure. We also looked at the role of corporate culture in the design of a firm's architecture.

Intelligence Failure

The information the United States gained about Iraq's weapons of mass destruction under Saddam Hussein was faulty. It has been learned that the reports on Iraq's WMD, rather than reflecting independent sources of information, probably originated from a single source, the Iraqi National Congress. Similarly, all the data corroborating reports originated from an Iraqi defector code named "Curveball," who claimed to have worked in Iraq's bioweapons program.[14] The main problem is the manner in which U.S. intelligence gathering was organized. Hierarchical organizations enable more information to be gathered. Each individual with information passes the summary up to the next level. The totality of information should then reach the top of the hierarchy. The problem is that bad information can become magnified as it moves step by step up the chain. The information could create a herd effect whereby everyone begins to build on a faulty premise or piece of information. The elimination of hierarchy will reduce the problem of the hierarchical herd effect. But the trade-off is that not all information will be collected and analyzed. The correct form of intelligence-gathering organizations depends on what their objectives are. The director's task is to design the organization that is most efficient in performing the objective.

Although the intelligence structure was redesigned, the intelligence communities in the United States, the United Kingdom, Germany, and Israel still think that faulty intelligence continues to arise. This suggests that either the structure remains incorrect or incentives are not aligned with the structure. UK intelligence outfits—led by MI-6—are "skeptical" of suggestions, most notably by U.S. intelligence agencies, that Iran stopped work on a military program to design and build a nuclear weapon in 2003.

The U.S. position is contained in a controversial National Intelligence Estimate (NIE), produced in 2007. This document reported that U.S. agencies "judge with high confidence that in fall 2003, Tehran halted its nuclear weapons program" and that "the halt lasted at least several years." The 2007 NIE also said that American agencies assessed "with moderate confidence Tehran had not restarted its nuclear weapons program as of mid-2007, but we do not know whether it currently intends to develop nuclear weapons." But in 2010 the NIE assessment was reversed.

Why was the NIE released in the first place? Was it an error of collection gathering, or was it a political document intended to deter President Bush from attacking Iran? It is possible that the American assessment is very cautious because U.S. intelligence analysts still feel burned by their mistakes in the run-up to the Iraq War, when Bush administration officials used faulty intelligence to justify military action. It is also possible that the hierarchy created in 2004 is no better at coordinating the 16 agencies than was the prior structure; it is not working as it should theoretically work.

Summary

1. The architecture of the firm refers to the firm's organization.
2. A firm will take on a specific organizational form because it is efficient. It can serve as a strategic asset if it adds value and is temporarily, at least, not able to be imitated.
3. Organizational forms have evolved from the family-owned-and-run business to the U-form, to the M-form, to the matrix and network as conditions have made one efficient and the former one inefficient.
4. Organizational democracy refers to the idea that a firm is participatory. Inputs are sought from employees, and some decisions are decided by vote.

5. Although hierarchy is often blamed for inefficiency, there are many aspects of hierarchy that increase efficiency. For instance, hierarchy can minimize the free-riding problem in a firm.
6. A firm's organization is the result of economizing. The purpose of the firm's architecture is to help it be as efficient as possible. The decision is not simply a hierarchy or not, but includes the structure, compensation, and governance. These all interact to create an efficient or inefficient organization.
7. Anthropologists define culture as a set of rules, conventions, and aspects of behavior that are passed on from generation to generation.
8. Corporate culture serves to enhance the efficiency of exchange—to enable contracts to remain general and broad without specifying every contingency.
9. A good culture can increase efficiency by enabling employees to know what to do without having to be informed by management.

Key Terms

Architecture
U-form
Unitary form
Functional form
M-form, or multidivisional form

Matrix
Network
Organizational democracy
Corporate culture

Exercises

1. Explain how singing a company song at the beginning of the workday could create a corporate culture. What would the culture be?
2. Is there a relationship between corporate culture and performance? Explain.
3. Is it possible for a firm to have several different cultures? If so, what does this imply about the relationship between culture and performance?
4. Explain why a firm might select the U-form rather than M-form of organizational structure.
5. What is the advantage of the network over the M-form?
6. If it is necessary for each employee to interact with all other employees, what organizational form makes most sense? If the employees work independently, not having to interact with one another, which organizational form makes most sense?
7. Process innovations and a firm's reputation can benefit many employees without reducing the benefits to others. What is the problem created by this type of internal product? How can it be resolved?
8. A recent *Wall Street Journal* article noted that Intel was considering following the lead of other Silicon Valley firms and doing away with cubicles. Instead of a cubicle, Intel might turn to desks on which employees share space and simply plop their computer down.

a. What could explain this change? Could it be to minimize a "hold-up" problem?
b. Might it be directed toward rent seeking?

9. Suppose that an employee has two tasks to perform—assembling machinery and evaluating quality. Suppose that the supervisor can only observe how many machines have been assembled by the worker. Is a hierarchical firm's structure necessary under this situation? Under what conditions should the principal closely tie pay to performance on the first task?
10. A shareholder in a limited-liability company is not personally liable for any of the debts of the company, other than for the value of his investment in that company. Explain why limited liability came about. Explain why it was enacted in the late nineteenth century.
11. Describe the efficiencies and the inefficiencies that occur with a top-down (hierarchical) management structure.
12. What might be a problem with democracy as a structure to run a publicly held company?
13. Would it be more efficient to enable employees to vote on decisions with majority rule or to assign the CEO full responsibility for decisions? Explain.

14. A commonly referred to management theory is Maslow's Hierarchy of Needs. It is a theory of motivation and is structured as a hierarchy.

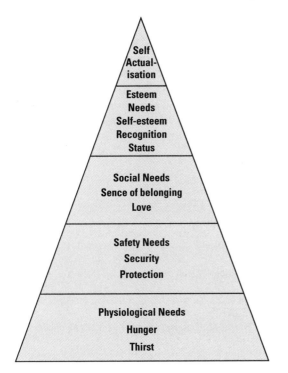

The way the hierarchy works is as follows: A person starts at the bottom of the hierarchy and initially seeks to satisfy basic needs (e.g., food, shelter). Once these physiological needs have been satisfied, they are no longer a motivator. The individual moves up to the next level. Safety needs at work could include physical safety (e.g., protective clothing) as well as protection against unemployment, loss of income through sickness, and so on. Social needs recognize that most people want to belong to a group. These would include the need for love and belonging (e.g., working with a colleague who supports you at work, teamwork, communication). Esteem needs are about being given recognition for a job well done. They reflect the fact that many people seek the esteem and respect of others. A promotion at work might achieve this. Self-actualization is about how people think about themselves—this is often measured by the extent of success and/or challenge at work

   Maslow's model has great potential appeal in the business world. The message is clear: If management can find out which level each em-ployee has reached, then they can decide on suitable rewards.
   What problems with the Maslow Model come from its hierarchy?

15. When leading business thinker Gary Hamel analyzes the central problems with the modern hierarchical organization, one problem he sees is that too few voices are heard. His suggested fix: Encourage people to write critical in-house blogs (and allow them to do it anonymously if they so wish). Track the number of responses each blog posting generates and then require senior executives to respond to those that garnered the most feedback.
   Evaluate the problem and Hamel's "fix."

16. One of the best examples of the impact structure has on operations is the transformation that began in the 1970s and is still going on today: flattening. In the early part of this century, companies had many levels between the worker in the shop or office and the president. Decisions had to pass through many levels of approval before anything got done. Now, decision makers may be found at the level of the worker in the shop. Suppose that the company is "flat" and decisions are made at the level of the worker but there is no communication channel from worker to worker. What problem might arise? How could it be resolved?

17. Why are the old, but still operational, steel mills such as US Steel and Bethlehem Steel structured using vertical hierarchies? Why are newer steel mini-mills such as Chaparral Steel structured more horizontally?

18. The following is a paraphrase of often stated comments on organizational changes.

   It was not long after the computer business got going that titles proliferated. Soon you could give yourself any title you wanted, especially in the computer business. Often, instead of a raise, employees were offered a fancy new title. The whole thing was compounded by the cultural shift in America from a blue-collar attitude to a white-collar attitude. Clerks became sales associates. Secretaries became administrative assistants. It was in the 1970s when chief this-and-that began to emerge, along with the feel-good titles—the beginnings of political correctness and an era of sensitivity. It was also in the 1970s that women seriously began to use Ms. rather than Miss or

Mrs. because of the perceived humiliation of being pigeonholed by marital status.

Do you think this explains the organizational changes that have taken place since the 1970s? Explain.

19. The fashion for flattening hierarchies has had the paradoxical effect of multiplying meaningless job titles. Workers crave important-sounding titles to give them the illusion of ascending the ranks. Everybody, from the executive suite downward, wants to fluff up their résumé as a hedge against

being sacked. Is this a good strategy to "avoid being sacked"? Explain.

20. It has been suggested that large, tall hierarchies will predominate in physical capital-intensive industries and that these will typically have seniority-based promotion policies. By contrast, flat hierarchies will be seen in human capital-intensive industries. These will have up-or-out promotion systems, where experienced managers either become owners or are fired. Can you provide a basis for or against the suggestion? Explain.

CHAPTER NOTES

1. Samuel L. Popkin, *The Rational Peasant: The Political Economy of Rural Society in Vietnam* (Berkeley: University of California Press, 1979).
2. Quoted in Frederick G. Hilmer and Lex Donaldson, *Management Redeemed* (New York: Free Press, 1996), p. 21.
3. Eileen Shapiro, *Fad Surfing in the Boardroom* (Reading, MA: Addison-Wesley, 1995), p. 39.
4. See John Roberts, *The Modern Firm* (Oxford University Press, 2004), p. 191.
5. Kenneth Cloke and Joan Goldsmith, *The End of Management and the Rise of Organizational Democracy* (San Francisco: Jossey-Bass, 2002), p. 3.
6. See Russell L. Ackoff, *The Democratic Corporation* (New York: Oxford University Press, 1994); Lynda Gratton, *The Democratic Enterprise* (London: Prentice Hall-Financial Times, 2004).
7. *Democracy in America* (original title, **De la démocratie en Amérique**) *published in two volumes, the first in 1835 and the second in 1840, by Saunders and Otley (London), now in public domain.*
8. Peter Drucker, "The Coming of the New Organization," *Harvard Business Review,* 66, no. 1 (January/February 1988): 45–53.
9. Hilmer and Donaldson, *Management Redeemed,* p. 25.
10. The hierarchy is called "too tall" when it is inefficient. John Child, "Parkinson's Progress: Accounting for the Number of Specialists in Organizations," *Administrative Science Quarterly,* 18, no. 3 (1973): 328–348; and Lex Donaldson, *For Positivist Organization Theory: Proving the Hard Core* (London: Sage, 1996).
11. Timothy J. Muris, David T. Scheffman, and Pablo T. Spiller, "Strategy and Transaction Costs: The Organization of Distribution in the Carbonated Soft Drink Industry," *Journal of Economics and Management Strategy,* 1, no. 1 (1992): 83–123.
12. John P. Kotter and James L. Heskett, *Corporate Culture and Performance* (New York: Free Press, 1992).
13. See Tom Peters and R. H. Waterman, *In Search of Excellence* (New York: Harper & Row, 1982); Vijay Sathe, *Culture and Related Corporate Realities* (Homewood, IL: Irwin, 1985); William Ouchi, *Theory Z* (Reading, MA: Addison-Wesley, 1981); and Richard T. Pascale and Anthony G. Athos, *The Art of Japanese Management* (New York: Simon & Schuster, 1981).
14. Luis Garicano and Richard A. Posner, "Intelligence Failures: An Organizational Economics Perspective," *Journal of Economic Perspectives,* 19, no. 4 (Fall 2005): 151–170.

CHAPTER 6

Market Failures and Incentive Issues Inside the Firm

Retention

Recently graduated from a top engineering program, Robert had a career on the rise with a large, international specialty-contracting firm. He had successfully completed the company's three-year project manager training program and had become one of their most reliable and promising employees. So when he suddenly resigned his position, his decision shocked his co-workers. Retaining good employees is critical to a firm's long-term success. The effect on co-workers also can be crucial. When people leave a firm, other employees may become fearful and uncertain about their status within the company. High turnover also can give a firm an unhealthy reputation in the marketplace, making recruiting future candidates especially difficult. When reduced efficiency, lower effectiveness, workforce instability, and lost productivity are added to the cost to find and train a new employee, the stakes become high. Yet, it is argued, many well-meaning companies fail to invest in retention.

1. Why does retention matter?
2. How does a firm attract and retain valuable employees?

Market Failures Inside the Firm

In some firms, praise, nonmonetary awards, and titles are emphasized. In others, nothing but money is provided as compensation. In some firms, pay is based on salary, specified prior to the employee's performance, while in others, part or all of the employee's compensation is based on his or her productivity. How a firm sets up and utilizes its personnel policies will have an important effect on the efficiency of the firm. A firm must decide how many resources to devote to retention and training and whether to promote from within or to go outside to obtain senior management. It must determine whether the morale and camaraderie of employees are important and what resources to devote to these issues. It must decide whether working in teams is better than working alone.

Public Goods

For most firms, it is difficult to measure individual contributions to the value of the firm. In such cases, the incentive of the employee is to focus attention on those activities that can be rewarded and to ignore those activities that are not rewarded. For instance, it may not be straightforward to know how well an employee does his job but very difficult to know if the employee also contributes to the firm's reputation or to the morale of the other employees. This is a public goods issue: Since no one owns the reputation, no one takes care of it. Many employee actions contribute to the reputation of the firm, but many of these actions are not attributable to an individual employee. If the employee is rewarded on the basis of the measurable contributions, there is no incentive to devote time or effort to the reputation-enhancing activities. How can management induce employees to contribute to the public good?

In a market setting, public goods can be dealt with by creating private property rights. A public good is a good to which anyone can have access (called nonexcludability), and the consumption by one person does not limit consumption by others (called nonrivalrous). For instance, a football game played out in an open park would be a public good. But building a stadium where only those who buy a ticket to the game can watch the game and there are limited seats converts the public good into a private one. National defense is a public good—no one can be excluded from protection, and consumption by one does not diminish consumption by others. But private property rights are not simple to set up; typically governments provide or subsidize protection.[1]

In the case of a firm's reputation, excludability is not likely since there is no way that some employees can be excluded from consuming the firm's reputation. Could employees be assigned property rights for the reputation of the firm? Yes, as long as monitoring is not too costly. The company might subsidize activities that enhance the firm's reputation by providing time for the employee to do the reputation-enhancing activity without subtracting from the employee's compensation. A firm could take a group of employees to a park and have them pick up litter for a few hours and have this activity in no way adversely affect those employees' compensation. The senior executives of a firm might choose to simply finance—outsource—the public good. The "adopt-a-highway" program is an example of a firm financing the provision of the public good. A firm that specializes in cleaning up highways contracts with the firm seeking a reputation enhancement; the firm that puts its name on the sign indicating that it has adopted this stretch of roadway simply pays the specialist firm.

Teams

In the 1990s, teams became a widely adopted management technique. They were instituted because of the belief that when people work together team spirit spurs individual effort and enhances the productivity of all. If output is team-oriented, compensation must be team-based. If each player on a basketball team was paid solely on the basis of points scored, rebounds, and other individual measures, each would act to increase those numbers even if the number of wins declined. Ken O'Brien was a quarterback with the New York Jets and was prone to throwing interceptions. To try to reduce the number of times the football was caught by the opposition, the Jets gave him a contract that penalized him for the number of interceptions he threw.[2] The contract resulted in fewer interceptions, but this occurred because O'Brien refused to throw the football even when he should have. The piece-rate scheme hurt team performance. If the best way to organize production is with teams, then a compensation scheme to encourage teamwork must be installed.

One benefit of teamwork that is often cited is that the whole is greater than the sum of its parts—total productivity is greater than if each individual member of the team worked alone. Teamwork also has a cost, however: When the effort of any member of the team is not easily observed, the team members have an incentive to free ride on the efforts of the others. Free riding refers to the idea of doing less work because you expect others to do the work. If everyone free rides, no work gets done.

Business Insight

Free Riding in Japanese Firms

Free riding creates problems no matter in which country it occurs. In the workplace, the people who make a substantial effort typically resent "free riders." In Japanese companies the punishment for free riding is especially important because people tend to stay with a single firm over their entire work life. Scholars have underlined peer pressure as a more distinctive aspect of life within Japanese firms than in Western firms. In Japanese firms, nondoers are penalized by peer pressure and guilt. Free riders are isolated and excluded from daily life in the firm. Western societies, by contrast, are typified by a more individualistic orientation, as shown in firms with incentives and compensation. Long-term employment, a distinctive feature of Japanese business, makes a difference in the effectiveness of punishing free riders. If an individual earns the reputation of being a free rider, he suffers far greater damages on a daily basis than what he would experience if he were given the option of leaving the firm at a low cost.[3]

So, if the benefits of teamwork are substantial, the firm must figure out ways to minimize free riding. How might an evaluation and compensation system be set up to minimize the free-riding problem? As discussed in Chapter 4, one approach to minimizing free riding in teams is to give someone in the team the private property rights to the output of the team to monitor the team's performance. But even a monitor might be unable to detect shirking if individual actions are not observable. In cases where the monitor cannot observe individual behavior but team members can, then basing part of each team member's pay on evaluations by the other team members could help minimize shirking.

Profit sharing may also reduce free riding. In a profit-sharing scheme, employees' wages or pensions are based on the profits of the entire firm. Employees have an incentive to shirk, but they also have an incentive to monitor other employees to be sure they aren't shirking. If the monitoring effect dominates the free-riding effect, then profit sharing results in increased performance.

Subjective Evaluations

Lincoln Electric is well known for its piece-rate pay system. Less well known is the fact that Lincoln Electric bases nearly half of a worker's annual compensation on the supervisor's subjective assessment of his or her innovation, dependability, and cooperation. "Subjective" means it is the supervisor's opinion, whereas "objective" refers to the use of a quantitative measure such as the number of machines the employee produces. Subjective evaluations became important when the company realized that if workers did not display cooperative behavior, total productivity declined. When employees need to share ideas and contribute to the overall environment in order for the firm to be successful, a part of the employee's compensation has to be a reward for behaving in a cooperative manner. The subjective evaluation means that a supervisor rates the employee on the dimensions the firm has found to be important, such as cooperative behavior.

While subjective evaluations may create incentives for individuals to contribute to the public good, they may also result in inefficiencies. Because the evaluations are subjective, there may be benefits to rent seeking—underlings may spend time "sucking up" to supervisors. If the supervisor responds to the rent-seeking actions of employees, then inefficient promotions, bonuses, and job assignments are likely to result. To minimize rent seeking, a firm can restrict what the supervisor can control in terms of compensation or can use a committee rather than a single supervisor to carry out evaluations. Alternatively, positions may be constrained by minimum experience requirements—that is, workers have to stay in a position for a certain amount of time before they can be promoted. Of course, any restrictions tend to reduce the efficiency of the practice. While rules such as time in position may minimize rent-seeking activities, they may distort the efficient allocation of people and jobs. For instance, a worker may be promoted because of seniority, even though there is a better candidate for the job. Determining a compensation scheme and accompanying personnel policies requires a cost-benefit calculation. The benefits of the rules must be compared to the costs to determine whether the rules will lead to appropriate actions.

Other public goods may not be as difficult to deal with as a firm's reputation. For instance, if the copy machine is available for anyone to use, employees will look upon it as a free good. Too much copying will take place. A firm could require that employees get permission from a supervisor to use the machine, but this would be a costly monitoring activity. Each user could be assigned a password so that at the end of each week or month, the use of each employee would be easily observable. Similarly, telephones, materials, and anything else considered to be a free good could be allocated through a market transaction; the employees could be allocated a budget from which each could spend as each desired. This would ensure that the allocation of materials went to the highest valued use.

Intrinsic motivation (nonmonetary) might help solve the free-riding problem. Peer pressure has been found to be an important part of the team process, as noted in the preceding Business Insight. Free riding can be reduced if senior executives constantly remind the staff how important contributions to the firm's reputation are—and if management provides rewards, trophies, praise, and the like to cases where other employees point out an employee's efforts.

Business Insight

Motivation

Is all this attention to incentives a lot of foolishness? A great deal of evidence, especially experimental evidence, indicates that people often act contrary to their material self-interest. People will forgo some income or wealth to ensure what they consider a fair outcome. People will also forgo some income or wealth to choose what they perceive as the moral or ethical direction. Some scholars, particularly social psychologists, suggest that some people possess a work ethic and choose to do good work for its own sake. These people are said to be intrinsically motivated. Some evidence has even suggested that monitoring or pay for performance incentive schemes can diminish the quality of work because the person who is intrinsically motivated perceives that he has lost control of his own work and actions. Survey evidence shows that moral and intrinsic motivations are important, and, in fact, may be more important than materialistic concerns.[4] But what people say is often not what they do. Research on whether extrinsic or intrinsic motivation interacts is entirely contradictory. The literature can be interpreted as supporting the idea that external rewards disrupt intrinsic motivation, boost intrinsic motivation, or have no effect whatsoever.[5]

Externalities

A single employee can harm the reputation of the firm, and all other employees, by acting unethically. Unethical actions impose externalities on the other stakeholders of the firm. A company has to ensure that employees know they own the property rights over their actions; they are responsible for their own actions and bear the rewards and penalties for these actions. The firm could increase monitoring to the extent that no employee could undertake unethical actions. But this would be prohibitively expensive. Some monitoring is probably necessary, but internalizing the externality has to come about through the assignment of property rights.

If employees need to work in isolation and quiet, then excessive noise can be a negative externality. The firm could create private property rights to office or cubicle locations. For instance, employees could own office locations, perhaps bidding for them in an auction. If the location turned out not to be what the employee desired, then the employee could sell his office and purchase another. Owning the rights to their locations would enable the employees to privately arrange many solutions to potential externalities. Dilbert believes his office cubicle to be much like his home; it is important to him. He isn't alone. Many employees look upon an office as an important aspect of a job.

Asymmetric Information: Principal-Agent Problems

Owners, managers, and employees typically have different objectives. Owners may want the value of the firm to increase regardless of what managers or employees want. Managers may want greater compensation, more benefits, and better perquisites, while employees may want high pay and benefits, job stability, and lots of leisure time. The problem a firm has is that many of these interests are conflicting. As a result of this conflict, decisions could lead to inefficient outcomes. An important component to a firm's success may be related to how well the interests of all parties are aligned.

When one individual acts on behalf of another individual, a principal-agent relationship is said to exist. The principal is the first individual, the one wanting some task undertaken or some result carried out. The agent is the individual who carries out the action on behalf of the first individual. We can describe the CEO of a publicly held firm as the agent of the shareholders, who are the principals. The hired manager of a private firm is the agent of the owner or owners. Employees are the agents of the CEO or manager.

The principal and agent may have different interests. How can the principal ensure that the agent acts in the best interests of the principal? The principal must create the incentives that will align the agent's interests with his or her own. If the principal and the agent had perfect information, a contract between them could be created that would ensure the correct behaviors. But seldom, if ever, is information perfect. So a contract typically leaves some wiggle room for interests to diverge. If a manager is aware of this problem and thus hires only those employees who have demonstrated high performance in the past, a different problem can arise. Knowing they cannot be observed, employees, once they have landed the new job, begin doing less work, being less productive, and devoting less effort to the job. This is a moral hazard problem.

Moral Hazard and Risk-Sharing

Firms and their employees are subject to risks. Pay may fluctuate, profits may fluctuate, people may be laid off, and firms may go bankrupt. These outcomes may be the result of actions that the individual or the firm can control, as well as actions that are out of their control. Compensation schemes and personnel policies may be based on risk-sharing. *Risk-sharing* occurs when the aggregate cost of bearing risk is lower when two or more individuals share that risk than when each bears the risk individually.

Insurance provides a good example of risk-sharing. An insurance company that has many policyholders can spread risks widely, enabling it to reduce the risks of individual policyholders. For example, the risk that you will have an automobile accident is independent of the risk that any other person will have an accident. Thus, an insurance company can ask each policyholder to pay a price for insurance equal to the expected amount of the loss plus a margin for expenses and profit and be reasonably sure that the aggregate premium will enable it to pay whatever losses may be suffered. With the insurance, the individual policyholder is avoiding the risk—in essence he or she is sharing the risk with other policyholders and with the insurance company.

If a worker is risk-averse, a firm must compensate the worker for taking on more risk. As an example, consider the situation of the shift manager at a Circle K convenience store. The shift manager has very little control over demand, pricing, and other factors that affect the profits of the store during her shift. These factors are more affected by national-level policies governing advertising and menu composition. Paying the manager on the basis of the profitability of the store during her shift would force her to bear risks that she has no control over. Similarly, farm workers cannot completely control the size of harvests because they do not control the weather. Paying them solely on the basis of the quantity of products they harvest would subject them to sizable risks over which they have no control. So the firm must provide insurance to the individual who takes on the extra risk. The problem is that once the individual has insurance, what is to stop him from altering behavior in ways that will be costly to the firm?

In insurance contracts, moral hazard is minimized with the use of co-payments and deductibles, incentivizing individuals to take ownership of their insured behavior. Having to be responsible for some payments when insurance is used reduces the likelihood that the policyholder will act in a moral hazard manner. Similarly, compensation schemes and personnel policies must take into account potential moral hazard problems. Some firms pay workers an agreed-upon contract—an assured amount independent of the firm's performance—and then provide a bonus based on the firm's overall performance. The bonus is analogous to a co-payment in an insurance contract. It creates an incentive for the employee not only to contribute to the firm above and beyond his or her job but also to monitor other employees.

Monopoly: Hold-up Problems

Problems may arise when some persons, such as managers and other insiders, know more about the current condition and future prospects of the firm than outside investors. There are various ways that managers and other insiders can exploit their information advantage at the expense of others—for example, by biasing or otherwise managing the information released to investors. This may affect the ability of investors to make good investment decisions. Financial reporting is one of the mechanisms that is used to control the problem of adverse selection by credibly converting inside information into outside information. In addition, the "analysts" employed at investment firms monitor the financial conditions of firms.

When it is difficult to acquire information held by a few employees, those employees who have the information can act as a monopolist, providing the information only at a high price. In a sense, they are *holding up* the firm. When IBM was moving toward the PC from the mainframe, those employees in the mainframe division were worried about their positions and futures. They attempted to hold the firm up, to force it to give up the work on the PC in order to maintain work on the mainframe. A firm that is vertically integrated—divisions upstream and downstream—could find that one division holds up other divisions.

Lack of outside options may be the primary reason why an agent may be subject to a hold-up. When the choices involved require investments in relationship-specific assets, then the chance of hold-up is increased. A **relationship-specific** asset is an asset that can be used in just one situation. For instance, specific learning made by scientists in pharmaceutical companies or skill acquisition that has value only in one firm are relationship-specific assets. In each case, after the action was taken, the relevant agent was tied to the relationship.

When an agent considers making a relationship-specific investment, it is important to realize that a fundamental transformation takes place with respect to his bargaining position with the other party. While an agent may be able to trade with many potential people prior to any investment taking place, after the investments have occurred, he is dealing with a monopolist.

Many actions have degrees of specificity. For some, the agent has some choice about the degree of specificity. For example, MBA students who are funded by their employer may choose subjects that would be more valuable if they were to work for another company after having completed the degree. They want to reduce the relationship-specific skills acquired.

The solution to monopoly problems, in general, is competition. The same thing applies to inside the firm. When a person or division attempts to hold up the company, there have to be substitutes available to the company for the person or the division. Although setting up the redundancies or substitutes could be costly, the firm has to trade off the cost of hold-up and the cost of substitutes.

An example is the licensing of new technology. Sometimes patent holders, in addition to producing a new product innovation themselves, may license the rights to sell the product to another manufacturer. This practice is called **second sourcing**. Second sourcing may initially seem to mean that the patent holder is giving up its monopoly rights to the new technology and thus, the monopoly profits from it. Actually, through second sourcing, the innovator induces others to commit themselves to the innovation by creating complementary investments that enhance the innovation's value. For example, a computer-chip manufacturer may second source so as to encourage the development of software for that chip. An MBA student who picked up specific skills might teach other employees those skills so that they invest in complementary skill building.

Compensation Arrangements

Compensation and personnel policies must enhance the efficiency of the firm. So why might one firm provide profit sharing and another not? Why might one firm pay employees on the basis of their job, while another firm pays employees on the basis of the employee's performance? Why might some firms utilize subjective evaluations as a significant part of determining compensation, while others compensate employees solely on the basis of their productivity? The answer is that these policies minimize some market failure or otherwise increase efficiency. Personnel policies and compensation are crucial aspects of firm behavior. They direct incentives and guide behaviors.

People possess different abilities and motives, and firms may not know which individual has which type of talent or motive. Different firms want to employ different types of individuals. One firm might want those who are best suited to working alone. Another firm might desire those able to work in teams. If firms are not likely to know which potential employee has which characteristic, then a firm that can select or attract the appropriate personnel most efficiently may have a competitive advantage.

One approach for a firm that is unable to measure a priori (ahead of time) whether an employee fits with the firm is to create a way that individuals can sort themselves into the appropriate positions. A firm's compensation and other personnel policies may induce people to choose those occupations or jobs for which they have a comparative advantage. Sometimes people sort themselves by skill. Firms such as Microsoft, Google, and Apple are known for attracting creative talent. Some of this attraction is due to idiosyncratic factors that are hard to duplicate—for example, computer hardware designers who wanted to work with the eccentric Seymour Cray or software designers who wanted to work with Bill Gates. But the reward structure of the firm can also attract specific kinds of workers. For instance, paying people solely on the basis of their performance would tend to attract those who believe they can perform very well and deter those who believe they cannot perform as well. Those who know they would not succeed in such a position would not even apply for it.

Efficiency Wage

A firm deals with asymmetric information in its employee relations. Potential employees know more about themselves than hiring officials do. Senior executives know more about the firm than outsiders. These information differences can lead to efficiency problems. Consider the hiring issue. If a firm does not know whether a potential employee has the characteristics the firm wants, it may adopt policies that induce individuals to sort themselves into the right types of jobs. For instance, paying a wage that is generally higher than the market wage, might send a signal to potential employees that this firm requires more work and success. Those who believe they can succeed in the firm's atmosphere will seek this firm out. Those who do not believe they can succeed in such an environment will avoid the firm. This is called an **efficiency wage**—one where the wage paid the employee exceeds the market wage. The objective of the efficiency wage is to attract higher-quality employees.

Once a firm has hired the type of people it wants, it has to decide whether it wants to retain those people and for how long. If an employee can switch to another job at any time and that other job is just as desirable as the current one, then the employee doesn't care if he gets dismissed. In such a case, the employee may not contribute as much to the firm as the firm would like. The firm must make the agent want to keep the job—that is, increase the agent's opportunity cost of getting fired. It can do this with the efficiency wage. Paying a premium means the costs to the employee of getting dismissed are higher.

Backloaded Compensation

Another way that firms can attract and retain the personnel they desire is to structure the pay over an employee's work life in a certain way. At many firms, compensation increases with time on the job; this is called a rising wage profile and is illustrated in Figure 6.1. Why do wages tend to increase with time on the job? A simple explanation is that the rising wage profile is just a way of paying people for the value they contribute to the firm. An employee's productivity (value to the company) rises as she gains training and experience. Medical residents, law clerks, accountants, and bank trainees, for example, earn low wages initially and then high wages as their time on the job rises.

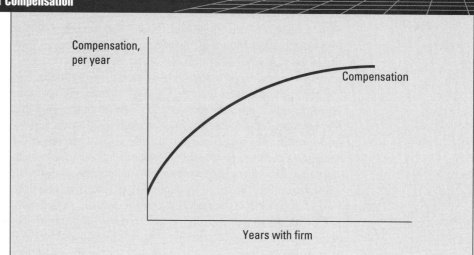

FIGURE 6.1 Backloaded Compensation

The longer a person is employed by a firm, the higher is his or her pay. Initially, pay is less than the person's value to the firm but eventually compensation exceeds the person's value to the firm.

Suppose a firm has to invest a lot of resources to train new employees but that once trained, the employee is more valuable to all firms. How can the firm offering the training retain the employee?

If, as shown in Figure 6.2, compensation is higher as the years on the job increase and the compensation eventually exceeds the contributions the employee makes to the firm, the pay structure is referred to as **backloaded** or **deferred compensation**. Backloaded pay creates an incentive for an employee to remain with a firm. It helps reduce employee turnover. Firms that spend significant amounts to train employees may find backloaded pay to be an efficient compensation structure. Training is costly, and the firm must tolerate low productivity by new workers until the employees have been fully trained. Firms that make such investments would naturally like their workers to remain with the firm at least until the firm recoups its investment.

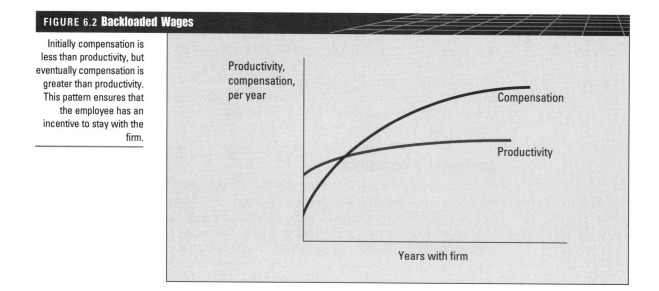

FIGURE 6.2 Backloaded Wages

Initially compensation is less than productivity, but eventually compensation is greater than productivity. This pattern ensures that the employee has an incentive to stay with the firm.

Another aspect of backloaded compensation is that it can serve as an incentive for employees to perform as they were contracted to perform. The promise of above-market wages in future years deters employees from slacking off or shirking; those who get fired lose out—they don't get to collect the "bonus" of compensation above productivity in future years.

Downsizing

If backloaded compensation serves as a carrot to reward hard work and investments in training, then increased labor-market turnover, such as occurs in corporate restructuring and downsizing, could have a pernicious effect on effort. Workers with little tenure may perceive that they are unlikely to keep their jobs long enough to climb up the wage–tenure profile. This might reduce incentives to work hard or undertake firm-specific training, and it might keep the best people from joining the firm in the first place.

What type of firm is most likely to downsize by reducing its labor force? Everything else being the same, it would be the firm that does not have backloaded compensation and a steep wage–productivity profile. A firm that has a steep wage–productivity profile and backloaded compensation may choose not to lay off workers even when demand falls. The firm would have to compare the benefits of reducing labor expenses to the costs of reducing morale and the firm's reputation. If it decided to lay off people, the firm would have to provide a separate package that would offset any losses of backloaded compensation; it would have to ensure that remaining employees and new hires were compensated for the additional risk of future layoffs. People would not want to join a firm with backloaded compensation if it was known that the firm would fire them before they could acquire the backloaded benefits. As a result, a firm offering backloaded compensation would most likely also have to maintain a reputation for retaining employees.

New Blood

Suppose a firm wants to induce turnover, to continually bring in "new blood." High-tech firms often bid for employees in other high-tech firms. This enables the companies to stay abreast of what the other companies are doing. It also enables a firm to benefit from new ideas and approaches if existing employees tend to become stale or fail to keep up with the state of the art. A relatively flat compensation profile leads to what is referred to as **wage compression**. New employees are brought in at compensation levels that nearly match or even exceed the compensation of employees who have been with the firm for a number of years. With this type of compensation scheme, the only way that an employee could receive large increases in pay would be to change companies.

Piece-Rate Compensation

Not only the level of compensation, but the way compensation and productivity are measured matter to prospective employees. A **piece-rate** pay scheme is one that compensates employees for how much each produces. Only if it is relatively easy to measure individual contributions to firm value does a piece-rate scheme make sense. In the case of Lincoln Electric, employees are paid for each machine they make and they are responsible for the quality of the products. Should a machine be defective, the employee must repair it without compensation.

Realizing the potential benefits of a piece-rate scheme, Safelite Glass Corporation of Columbus, Ohio changed from hourly to piecework pay. While guaranteed a minimum wage of about $11 an hour, glass installers were offered the alternative of receiving $20 per unit installed, giving them an incentive to earn more by working faster. To keep quality from suffering, the task of replacing defectively installed windshields at no pay was assigned to the same shop. Because the names of the initial installers were known to their co-workers, employees felt strong peer pressure to improve their performance or resign. The payoff from piecework was substantial. Average productivity per worker rose 20 percent, average earnings rose by 10 percent, and overall company output surged by 36 percent. When Canadian tree planters were paid for each tree planted, the number of trees planted increased about 35 percent. When salespeople in retail department stores were paid at piece rate, store productivity rose about 10 percent.[6]

Given these examples of productivity increases, why doesn't every firm use a piecework compensation scheme? One reason is that some firms find it difficult to measure the productivity of individual employees. Firms in which it is difficult to observe the productivity of individual employees would find it very inefficient to use a piecework system. It would be too costly to try to measure each employee's output. A second argument against the piece rate is that it can create incorrect incentives in some cases even when performance could be measured. A number of retail firms that attempted to tie sales clerks' pay to the amount they sold found that this created a situation in which clerks were undermining each other and thus negatively affecting the firm's performance. When some telemarketing firms paid according to the number of calls made, the reps reduced the quality of each contact in order to increase the quantity. Revenues from calls actually declined. In 1992 Sears abolished a system of compensating mechanics in its auto repair shops on the basis of the profit from customer-authorized repairs. The mechanics had misled customers into authorizing unnecessary repairs. When computer programmers at AT&T were paid for the number of lines of code they produced, programs became much longer than was necessary.[7]

A piece-rate compensation scheme attracts people who are productive, who work hard, and who enjoy working on their own. People who are not productive, who do not want to work hard, or who enjoy working in groups or teams would not choose to work for a firm using piece-rate compensation.

Tournaments

Hierarchy offers firms a way to reward competence and performance and to increase authority. In most corporations, promotion and pay increases go hand in hand, so we could think of promotion as the result of a large contest pitting all employees against each other. People move up the corporate hierarchy and obtain pay raises by performing better than all the others who are also trying to move up the hierarchy. Once a person is promoted, a new tournament begins, with the winner advancing to a still higher level. The final prize is the top job, the CEO position.

If job promotion within the firm is a contest, what compensation structure will elicit the most productive behavior from participants? It has been found that in golf tournaments, the more that the first prize exceeds the payoff for second and lower finishes, the better is the average performance of the contestants. Fighting for that top spot leads to a higher quality performance from everyone entered in the contest. It has also been found that in NASCAR racing, the greater the difference between the first prize and the payoff for second and lower finishes, the faster the average track speed. Carrying these findings over to the labor market inside the firm, economists have suggested that an extremely high pay package for the CEO relative to other employees might induce all employees (current and future) to exert extra effort on the job.

The tournament view also suggests that the more competent gain more authority. The authority one obtains depends on how successful one has been in the earlier tournaments. The more success one has, the more authority one is given along with compensation and a move up the corporate hierarchy. In this way, competence is allocated by the structure of the company.

Retention

Retention can be an issue for a firm if the cost of replacing an employee is greater than the cost of retaining that employee. If a company devotes resources to training and development of an employee, it wants to be sure to gain value from that employee. How can a firm provide incentives for employees to remain with a firm for a long period of time? One method is backloaded compensation—paying a premium based on length of service with the firm. This creates an increasing cost for employees to leave the firm early. Such compensation requires that other firms are not offering higher pay currently for the same services. If an employee must balance pay today with pay tomorrow, then the employee essentially carries out a comparison of net present value. The firm must have the greatest net present value for the employee.

A firm might "post a bond"—essentially providing a large sum of money the employee can keep if he remains with the firm for a period of time, but will forfeit if the employee leaves prior to the agreed upon time. One way to do this is to provide stock options that cannot be redeemed until after some period of time has passed and cannot be cashed unless the employee has been with the firm for that time period. This would be a more explicit backloaded compensation and would make clear to the employee the costs of leaving.

Summary

1. A public good results in too little being produced. Something like a firm's reputation can be a public good and thus not get the resources devoted to it that the senior executives would like. By assigning private property rights or using taxes or subsidies, the executives may be able to get the public good provided.
2. Teams are used in business because they are believed to increase productivity. The primary problem with teams is free riding. Free riding occurs because individual contributions to team output cannot be measured. As a result, each member of the team has an incentive to contribute less and to rely on the other members to carry the team.
3. One way to minimize free riding in teams is to make one team member a monitor or to have team members monitor the other team members. Intrinsic motivation may help reduce the problem if employees have additional incentives to devote efforts to the team.
4. Subjective evaluations play a role in creating the correct behavior among employees. The subjective evaluation can provide some weight in compensation to factors that are difficult to measure but that are important to firm value.
5. Subjective evaluation may lead to increased rent seeking and require some means to minimize rent seeking.
6. When an employee imposes a negative externality on other employees or stakeholders in the firm, some action to ensure the employee internalizes the externality would increase efficiency. The assignment of private property rights and the enforcement of those rights (good governance) are ways to effect the internalization of externalities.
7. When employees of a firm have different amounts of knowledge about activities in the firm, a moral hazard problem can arise.
8. Compensation schemes must create the incentives for employees to carry out actions that benefit owners. Compensation based on events over which the employee has no control would not do that. Compensation schemes often include some risk-sharing attributes in order to minimize the negative effects of uncontrollable risk.
9. The firm's organization may play a role in allocating competence; if the structure of success in a company is analogous to a tournament in sports, success means a

move up the corporate hierarchy. Thus, the more authority one has, the more successful one has been in prior engagements.

10. Firms use compensation and personnel policies to attract employees. Companies differ with respect to the type of employees desired. A firm must efficiently attract the right people for what it does.

11. Potential employees know more about themselves than the hiring officials of a firm know about them. As a result, a firm can make costly hiring mistakes. It wants to design policies that minimize such mistakes.

12. Efficiency wages and backloaded compensation are ways to increase efficiency. Efficiency wages is the name given to a pay scheme in which employees are paid a premium over the market in an effort to attract the best employees.

13. Backloaded wages are deferred wages—that is, wages that are earned today but received later. A backloaded compensation scheme is one in which employees are paid less than their value to the firm in the early years of their employment and then paid more than their value in later years. This serves to keep the employee with the firm for a period long enough to acquire the extra compensation. It also serves to minimize shirking, since employees would lose the extra compensation if they were fired.

14. Piece-rate compensation pays people for how much they produce. For piece-rate schemes to be efficient, individual output must be easily measured. A piece-rate scheme may attract people who enjoy working on their own and getting rewarded for their work.

15. It is often difficult to determine how much an individual contributes to the value of the firm. When there are public goods aspects to the firm, employees may free ride on the public good and devote resources to the private good—the one for which their efforts can be determined.

Key Terms

Relationship-specific
Second sourcing
Efficiency wage

Backloaded or deferred compensation
Wage compression
Piece-rate

Exercises

1. Personal injury lawyers may be paid a contingency fee equal to a percentage of the amount awarded. The lawyer receives payment only if his or her client wins the case and is awarded a sum of money. Lawyers in other types of cases are often paid on an hourly basis. Use the principal-agent relationship to assess the merits and drawbacks of each type of fee arrangement from the client's (i.e., the principal's) perspective. Be sure to discuss incentive effects.

2. Suppose that an employee has two tasks to perform—assembling machinery and evaluating quality. Suppose that the supervisor can only observe how many machines have been assembled by the worker. Under what conditions should the principal closely tie pay to performance on the first task?

3. It is said that the current generation of workers will have a very small probability of being employed by the same firm throughout their work life. In previous generations it was common for people to have just one employer. Is a more rapid turnover among employees beneficial to the firm? To the employee? Explain.

4. Many firms who use operators to assist customers evaluate the operators on the basis of how many customers they service. Explain the results of such an evaluation system. What would you do differently? Consider the benefits and costs of any change you recommend.

5. A recent study found that workers who were laid off generally received lower wages once they found new jobs. The study noted that white-collar workers suffered relatively large declines compared to blue-collar workers. How would you explain this development?

6. The same study of laid-off workers and their new, lower-paid jobs mentioned in Exercise 5 found that workers who had been with a firm a longer period of time suffered larger declines than those who had been with a firm for a relatively short period of time. How would you explain this development?

7. Prior to about 1990, several firms instituted explicit policies never to lay off employees; that is, to create lifetime employment. What are the costs and benefits of such a policy? What types of firms might find such a policy beneficial?

8. What type of compensation policy would you expect to observe in an industry with rapidly changing technology? Explain.

9. What type of compensation policy would you expect to observe in an industry where technology changes are few and far between?

10. When Ben and Jerry decided to step down as managers of their own company, they announced that the new CEO would not earn more than 10 times the lowest-paid employee. What do you think was the result of their policy?

11. The probability of a worker's being fired from or quitting a particular job in any unit of time is represented by

$$Q = a - bT - cT^2$$

where Q is the probability of leaving a job and T is the length of time the worker has held that job. Explain what this says and why it occurs.

12. An investment has returns of zero with probability one-half, $3,000 with probability one-third, and $6,000 with probability one-sixth. What is the expected value of the return?

13. If the investment described in Exercise 12 is an individual's possible weekly compensation and the individual has no control over the outcome, what effort will a risk-averse individual put in? What about a risk-seeking individual?

14. In Exercise 13, if the employee is risk-averse, what compensation scheme would elicit the greatest effort?

15. What is a market failure? Explain how externalities, public goods, and asymmetric information are all problems with private property rights.

16. Explain why you tend to find more shirking, more corruption, and more inefficiency in large firms than you do in small firms. Explain why you tend to find more shirking, more corruption, and more inefficiency in government than you do in large firms.

17. Could rent seeking on the part of the CEO influence the CEO's compensation? Evaluate the following argument. *Pay arrangements are set by a Board of Directors that aims to maximize shareholder value by designing an optimal principal-agent contract. But the Board does not operate at arm's length; rather, executives have power to influence their own compensation, and they use their power to extract rents. As a result, executives are paid more than is optimal for shareholders.*

18. The oil well Maconda exploded in the Gulf of Mexico in 2010, killing 11 people and creating a huge oil spill. BP did not own the *Deepwater Horizon* platform, but leased it from a company called Transocean. In what sense is this a principal-agent problem? What incentives are created by the problem?

19. The oil well Maconda exploded in the Gulf of Mexico in 2010, killing 11 people and creating a huge oil spill. BP did not own the *Deepwater Horizon* platform, but leased it from a company called Transocean. Would BP have paid more attention to safety if it owned, rather than leased, the platform? Explain

20. In an advertisement for a professional employment organization it was stated: "Outsourcing can be a cost-effective alternative to the expense and administrative burden of a traditional employer–employee relationship." Evaluate the costs and benefits of outsourcing employees. What market-failure problems could be created or eliminated by outsourcing?

CHAPTER NOTES

1. Some economists argue that national defense could be privatized. See Hans Hermann Hoppe, *The Myth of National Defense* (Auburn: Ludwig Von Mises Institute, 2003).

2. G. Baker, R. Gibbons, and K. Murphy, "Subjective Performance Measures in Optimal Incentive Contracts," *Quarterly Journal of Economics*, 109 (1994): 1125–1156.

3. G. Staffiero, "Peer pressure and inequity aversion in the Japanese firm," Public-Private Sector Research Center, 09/2006.

4. Lanse Minkler, "Shirking and Motivations in Firms: Survey Evidence on Worker Attitudes," University of Connecticut Working Paper 2002-40, September 2002.

5. Judy Cameron, Katherine M. Banko, and W. D. Pierce, "Pervasive Negative Effects of Rewards on Intrinsic Motivation: The Myth Continues," *The Behavior Analyst*, 24 (2001): 1–44; E. L. Deci, R. Koestner, and R. M. Ryan, "A Meta-analytic Review of Experiments Examining the Effects of Extrinsic Rewards on Intrinsic Motivation," *Psychological Bulletin*, 125 (1999): 627–668.

6. Canice Prendergast, "The Provision of Incentives in Firms," *Journal of Economic Literature*, 37, no. 1 (1999): 7–63.

7. Ibid., p. 21.

Sustaining
Competitive Advantage

CHAPTER 7
When Other Firms Don't Respond

CASE

Wal-Mart Predatory Pricing Case

At issue was whether Wal-Mart, which had built the nation's largest retail chain with its everyday-low-price strategy, went beyond the legally recognized retail practice of promotional pricing and intended to destroy its competition. A 1993 lawsuit filed against Wal-Mart by a group of independent pharmacies argued that Wal-Mart used predatory pricing. The Arkansas statutes, which were being tested for the first time since passage in 1937, generally forbade businesses from selling or advertising "any article or product ... at less than the cost to the vendor ... for the purpose of injuring competitors and destroying competition."

Wal-Mart's attorneys argued in a pretrial brief that what the law described as a "product" shouldn't be considered to apply to individual items, but rather to Wal-Mart's "market basket" or full line of products. If the entire line isn't priced below cost, they contended it wasn't a violation of the statute.

It is obvious that in order to determine a state violation on "predatory pricing," the court must determine what principle it would accept as "nonpredatory" in pricing below cost. This is indeed a gray area. The second element to be considered under state laws is whether there was an "intent" to injure competition and whether in fact the result of such malice was to injure the competition. The third element was "recoupment." Were the prices ultimately raised, once the competition was put out of business?

1. What is predatory pricing?
2. Why would it matter if prices were ultimately raised once the competition was out of business?

Choices

In the landscape of nations, there are clearly successful and unsuccessful nations. Standards of living and economic growth rates are measures used to evaluate the performance of nations. Figure 7.1 presents a map showing standards of living in nations around the world. The poorest nations are principally in Africa, and the wealthiest in North America and western Europe, as well as Australia, New Zealand, Japan, and a few others.

The poorest nations are poor because they have carried out the wrong strategies. They have wasted resources on conflicts, corruption, and bad governments. Similarly, in the landscape of firms there are successful ones and unsuccessful ones. The unsuccessful are in that state because they have carried out the wrong strategies, wasting resources. In this chapter, we take an introductory look at strategy.

In very general terms, strategy, whether for a nation, an organization, or an individual, is all about making choices. If no choices had to be made, then there would be no need to worry about a strategy. But, with limited resources, how those resources are utilized will determine the level of success of a nation or an organization or individual.

The choices among two resource allocations are illustrated using the trade-off curve, or what is called a **production possibilities curve (PPC) or frontier** as shown in Figure 7.2. This curve shows those combinations of outputs that can be produced/created when existing resources and technology are *fully and efficiently* utilized. Along the horizontal axis is one resource allocation (e.g., the production of military weapons) and along the vertical axis is a different resource allocation (such as the production of domestic goods and services). The curve illustrates limitations—more weapons can be obtained only by giving up some domestic goods and services. The diagram is also called a trade-off curve because it shows that in order to have more of one item one must give up some of the other item. Producing more weapons means taking some of the resources currently employed in

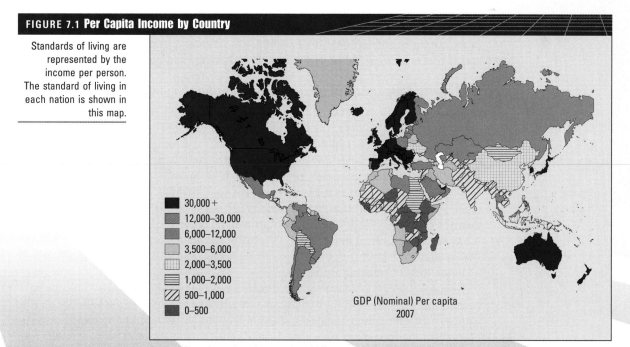

FIGURE 7.1 Per Capita Income by Country

Standards of living are represented by the income per person. The standard of living in each nation is shown in this map.

30,000 +
12,000–30,000
6,000–12,000
3,500–6,000
2,000–3,500
1,000–2,000
500–1,000
0–500

GDP (Nominal) Per capita
2007

Source: Data based on International Monetary Fund, as of April 2008.

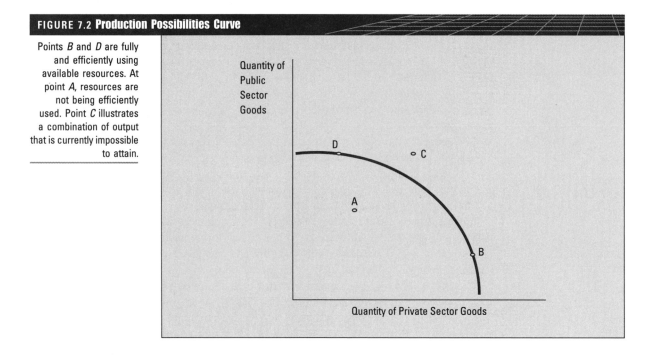

FIGURE 7.2 Production Possibilities Curve

Points *B* and *D* are fully and efficiently using available resources. At point *A*, resources are not being efficiently used. Point *C* illustrates a combination of output that is currently impossible to attain.

Quantity of Public Sector Goods

Quantity of Private Sector Goods

producing domestic goods and services and employing them in the production of weapons.

A combination that lies inside the curve represents an inefficient use of resources while a point outside the curve represents an impossible situation given current technologies and resources. In Figure 7.2, points *B* and *D* are on the production possibility frontier, point *A* is inside the frontier, and point *C* is beyond the frontier. Point *A* means that resources are not being employed efficiently or fully; better use would enable an increase in the output of both types of resource allocations. Point *C* represents a resource combination that is not possible given the current technology and quantities of resources.

Short-term, Long-term, Internal, and External Strategic Choice

National strategy involves two time frames—short term and long term. In the short term, the choice is which point on the PPC to select. In other words, the choice involves using resources fully and efficiently—being on the PPC—or using resources inefficiently—being inside the PPC. Point *C* is not possible in the short term.

The long-term strategy choice focuses on economic growth, illustrated by an outward-shifting PPC. If one combination of resources (one point on the PPC) leads to more rapid economic growth through innovation, technological change, or some other event, then the PPC would shift out further than if some other combination of resources was used. As the PPC shifts out, point *C* eventually becomes feasible. At some stage, if the PPC continues to shift out, point *C* could even represent inefficiency because it would lie inside the PPC existing at that stage.

National strategy also involves two dimensions: internal and external. Point *A* represents an output level where resources are not allocated to their highest valued uses; the nation could gain greater standards of living without acquiring more resources or technology. For instance, a bad government could cause a nation to be at point *A* rather than on the PPC because firms and businesses are allocating resources to deal with the inefficient or corrupt government rather than producing income and outputs. This would be a bad internal strategy. How to deal with other nations would be the nation's external strategy.

Strategy for individuals and firms is analogous to that for nations. Individuals must choose what to put into their bodies—chocolate chip cookies, broccoli, and millions of other things. This is part of their internal strategy. To be efficient, one must provide the body with appropriate fuel. But individuals must also choose how to interact with others, to socialize, work, and so on. This is part of their external strategy. An individual located at point *A* is operating inefficiently—eating poorly or in ill health or managing time poorly.

Similarly, a firm must choose how to allocate resources internally, how to organize, how to structure compensation, and so on. This is the internal part of a firm's strategy. The firm must also choose how to interact with other firms. Does it focus on low price or high quality, where does it locate, how big does it get, what does it do? These are parts of the external strategy.

Consider the PPC in Figure 7.3 where along the axes are measures of two generic strategies for firms—low cost and high quality. With given resources, technology, leadership, and so on, the best that can be done is given by the PPC frontier or what is called the **best practice frontier**.

The best practice frontier is the best that can be done with existing resources and technology. Strategic choice involves deciding where to locate on the best practice frontier. If a firm locates at one point, it is giving up all other points—it is making a choice. Several firms could be operating efficiently, but some could choose a high-quality strategy and others, a low-cost strategy. A firm selecting a low-cost strategy must give up high quality and vice versa. But no matter the external strategy: The firm cannot compete unless its internal strategy is efficient. A firm that persists in not using best practices will not last.

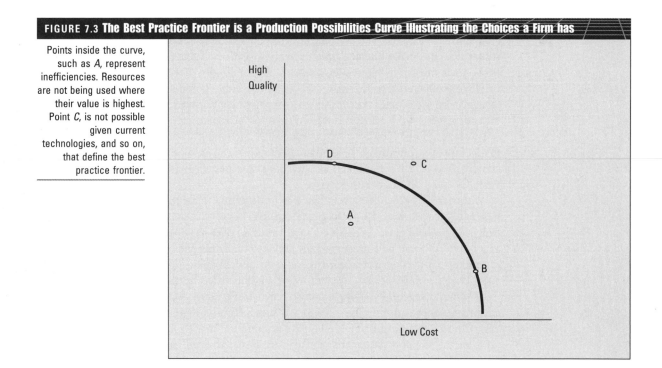

FIGURE 7.3 The Best Practice Frontier is a Production Possibilities Curve Illustrating the Choices a Firm has

Points inside the curve, such as *A*, represent inefficiencies. Resources are not being used where their value is highest. Point *C*, is not possible given current technologies, and so on, that define the best practice frontier.

Business Insight

Best Practice Might Include Contesting Frivolous Lawsuits[1]

A firm must choose how to allocate its resources, and that choice can involve nonproductive activities such as lawsuits. In 2005, Merck had to decide whether to allocate additional resources to discovering medications or to allocate those resources to defending itself against what it thought were frivolous lawsuits. Merck faced lawsuits over Vioxx, the painkiller it was forced to withdraw from the market in October 2005 after studies linked it to heart attacks and strokes. Restoring Merck's reputation as a scientific partner depended on proving that the company had not misled investors and patients. The company had to choose whether to settle the lawsuits, for a bill of more than $20 billion, or to fight them. It chose to contest the cases, not settle them. The strategy appeared to have been the correct one when Merck began winning those cases. The victories enabled the company to compensate those people who seemed to suffer from taking Vioxx and to settle the bulk of its lawsuits in 2007 for $4.85 billion rather than more than $20 billion.

You are thinking about opening a business. The first question you have to answer is "What should my business do?" For an individual or nation, specialization according to comparative advantage and then trading leads to the greatest benefits. So a good strategy is to specialize according to comparative advantage and then trade. What leads to comparative advantage? For a country, the stock of natural or human resources, the technology, infrastructure, education, and leadership may be the basis of comparative advantage, but so might a nation's economic, political, and legal institutions. Similarly for a firm, the stock of assets and/or the structure, governance, and other elements may be the basis of comparative advantage. When speaking about firms the term **competitive advantage** is typically used rather than comparative advantage. They mean essentially the same thing—what you do relatively better than others.

So for your proposed business, you must define those things that give the business a competitive advantage. For instance, a firm's current stock of assets and capabilities—its strategic assets—will influence which activities the firm is able to best perform. For many firms, their most valuable strategic asset is its employees. The intellectual property each employee contributes to the firm can create the firm's competitive advantage. Why has Google been successful? According to company reports, its success can be ascribed to the employees who work for Google. The internal aspects of the firm—the culture and institutions, compensation systems, leadership, technology, and other things—may lead to a competitive advantage. Google provides gourmet foods, flexible hours, and generous benefits, and as a result, Google is often rated the best firm to work for. This enhances Google's competitive advantage.

Wal-Mart's competitive advantage was initially due to its point-of-purchase data collection, which allowed it to respond to changes in consumer tastes quickly and flexibly. This competence gave Wal-Mart an advantage over competitors during the 1980s. Wal-Mart used that advantage to grow and eventually become so important that it could dictate to suppliers what it wanted them to do in delivering supplies and in pricing those supplies. This buyer power gave Wal-Mart a competitive advantage.

Defining direction or strategy comes down to defining competitive advantage—what advantages does a specific firm have? Strategy has to be driven by facts. Too often it is wish driven. "We want to be the best" is nothing but a wish. If you read the annual reports or the mission statements provided by firms, you will see that many are not fact based and often make quite meaningless claims.

For example, the executives of Wilkinson-Match, the unsuccessful product of a merger between British Match and razor-blade manufacturer Wilkinson Sword, claimed that their merger would "give both companies substance." What does this tell us? Similarly, we hear that a merger is going "to create critical mass" or "to become a global player." These statements are nothing more than wishes—wish-driven strategies. Much like Lake Wobegone's children all being above the average, the statements often are statistical impossibilities. They make no sense because they forget that allocating resources to one use means that these resources cannot be used elsewhere. *There is no free lunch.* Executives must evaluate each feasible option by comparing its value and its cost, and that cost is what must be sacrificed in order to attain something. Trade-offs—giving up something in order to get something else—lie at the heart of the executive's job.

Consider the following list of companies:

The Body Shop
Dell
Enterprise Rent-A-Car
E-Trade
Federal Express
Home Depot
MTV
Southwest Airlines
Starbucks
Swatch
USA Today

These companies did not offer a wish-driven strategy. They offered something new and something they saw as their competitive advantage. What distinguishes the companies on this list from many other firms is the relatively short time in which they achieved success. Most new entrants in a business fail within five years, and even those few that do not fail manage to capture only a small share of the market—perhaps 5 percent in five years.

Does every firm innovate rather than imitate? Should they? Most companies that innovate are small players or new market entrants. It is rare to find a large firm that changes the game in the industry in which it is established. There are several reasons for this, but in general the costs of strategic change are too high for established firms. Having established a competitive advantage and devoted resources to it, it is simply too costly to throw that away and do something totally different.

Xerox initially responded to Canon by ignoring it. Xerox's vice president at the time said, "We had been late to recognize market opportunities for low and mid range copiers and Japanese competitors like Canon were cutting into our market share."[2] Recognizing that it had failed to respond appropriately, Xerox decided to go directly after Canon. Xerox introduced new products and restructured sales operations to create dedicated organizations for large system customers as well as small businesses, and it opened retail stores that sold small copiers. The outcome was a situation in which both competitors occupied the same two strategic positions simultaneously, their own and each other's. As a result, the only way for either to gain an advantage was to become better than the other—through cost or differentiation or pricing strategies. As would be predicted in this situation, profit margins in the business declined sharply.

The choice of whether to imitate or innovate is an important strategic decision but having made it does not end the choices that still have to be made. Having entered a market, started a business, and gained success, what is left to do? Lots. The manager has to work for continued success and make strategic decisions on allocating resources and devising strategy vis-à-vis rivals, suppliers, customers, and others. Remember that profit attracts firms like blood in the ocean attracts sharks. Someone is always attempting to imitate or innovate such that they take your business away. Strategy, then, is an ongoing process.

Porter's Five Forces Representation of External Strategy

What accounts for a firm's success? Does it depend solely on what the firm does, or is it related to the setting in which the firm does business or to the structure of the industry in which the firm operates? The profit rate in the pharmaceutical industry greatly exceeds the profit rate in the grocery store industry. Why? And why don't the grocery store managers undertake strategies that would lead to the structure exemplified by the pharmaceutical industry?

Michael Porter, an economist trained in the field of industrial organization, argued that these are the crucial questions of business strategy. In industrial organization, it was believed that the structure of an industry determined the conduct and performance of firms in that industry. This was called the SCM or structure–conduct–performance model. Porter took that model and reworked it into what he called the **five forces model**. He argued that the ability to earn positive economic profit over long periods of time is related to industry structure—specifically, whether the industry has "market power" with respect to customers and suppliers and whether there are barriers to entry that keep the economic profits from being competed away.

Figure 7.4 illustrates the five forces model. In the center is *Competition*. This involves how competition occurs—such as through price or through factors such as quality, service, innovation and technological change, or other nonprice attributes. It also refers to

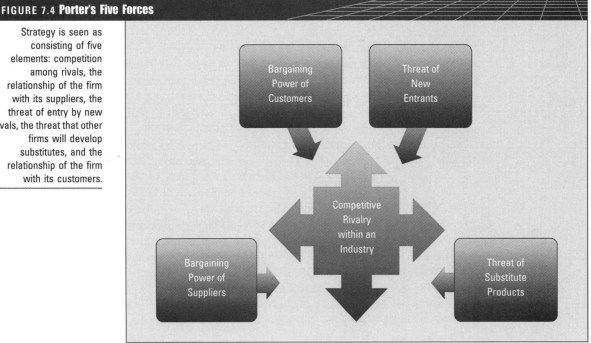

FIGURE 7.4 Porter's Five Forces

Strategy is seen as consisting of five elements: competition among rivals, the relationship of the firm with its suppliers, the threat of entry by new rivals, the threat that other firms will develop substitutes, and the relationship of the firm with its customers.

Bargaining Power of Customers

Threat of New Entrants

Competitive Rivalry within an Industry

Bargaining Power of Suppliers

Threat of Substitute Products

the number of rivals. The argument is the greater the number of rivals, the more quickly economic profits will be driven to zero.

Supplier Power refers to the ability of a firm to force suppliers to bear costs, that is, to pass along cost increases to the suppliers. If a firm is dominant over its suppliers, then those suppliers must respond to what the firm wants. They cannot simply raise prices whenever they feel it is appropriate. Wal-Mart and Tesco are in this situation. They dictate to suppliers the conditions under which each (that is, Wal-Mart or Tesco) will purchase.

Buyer Power refers to the firm's ability to pass cost increases along to the customers. If a supplier is dominant over its customers, then it can pass cost increases along to those buyers; that is, it can increase the buyer's costs whenever it deems it appropriate. For instance, a pharmaceutical firm is able to raise the price on one of its patented drugs without losing substantial customers. Safeway, on the other hand, cannot increase the price of groceries without chasing customers to other grocery stores.

The *Threat of Substitutes* refers to the possibilities that substitutes to your firm's products might be introduced. While Apple's iPod achieved remarkable success, from the time of its introduction, Apple was aware of the likelihood of substitutes. Other MP3 systems were introduced, and Apple's prices declined. Starbucks is threatened by McDonald's in terms of coffee. Yet, McDonald's coffee, even though rated as tasting better than Starbucks coffee, is not forcing Starbucks to set a lower price. The two have not been considered to be close substitutes because people go to Starbucks for the ambience, the other drinks, and the service, not just the coffee. As a result, a few cents or even a 50-cent difference in the price of a cup of coffee is not likely to cause many Starbucks customers to switch to McDonald's. Yet, the situation may be changing. Starbucks has added drive-thru and for a brief time offered breakfast sandwiches while McDonalds has added full coffee bars and baristas. E-mail servers such as Yahoo.com have become commoditized. Thanks to the advent of open-source tools like SendMail and QMail, it's hard to see why anyone would pay for e-mail server software. Essentially, any e-mail server is the same as any other. This is what commoditization means—a large, very large, number of virtually identical substitutes.

The *Threat of Entry* refers to whether a positive economic profit will attract competitors and how difficult it would be for them to open up a business. It is not difficult for someone to open a coffee shop. Yet, it is more difficult for someone to create a brand name that can take business away from Starbucks. Conversely, if Merck introduces a new cancer-fighting drug, it could be many years before another firm could enter the pharmaceutical business.

Market Structures   The selling environment in which a firm produces and sells its product is called a *market structure*. The 5-forces approach generally classifies four market structures in which firms compete, defined by number of firms, ease of entry and exit, and the degree to which products are differentiated.

- The number of firms that make up the market. In some industries, such as agriculture, there are hundreds of individual firms. In others, such as the photofinishing supplies industry, there are very few firms.
- The ease with which new firms may enter the market and begin producing the good or service. It is relatively easy and inexpensive to enter the desktop publishing business, but it is much more costly and difficult to start a new airline.
- The degree to which the products produced by the firms are different. Firms may sell identical products—wheat is wheat no matter which farm it comes from—or differentiated products—McDonald's Big Mac is not identical to Jack-in-the-Box's Ciabatta burger.

Table 7.1 summarizes the characteristics of the four market structures.

Perfect Competition   Perfect competition is a market structure characterized by the following:

- A very large number of firms, so large that whatever any *one* firm does has no effect on the market
- Firms that produce an identical product (perfect substitutes)
- Easy entry

In perfect competition, a very large number of firms in the market means that consumers have many options when they are deciding where to purchase the good or service, and there is no cost to the consumer of going to a different seller. In this market structure, the product is identical, so consumers do not prefer one seller to another or one brand to another. In fact, there are no brands—only identical, generic products. The large number of sellers also means that any one seller is a very small part of the market, and so its actions will not affect the others. A single firm can sell everything it wants to at the market price, but it cannot try to increase price, and it won't lower price. If a single small firm tried to raise the price even a very small amount, consumers would simply switch to another seller. Consumers have a perfectly elastic demand —why pay even a penny more if you can simply turn around and get the identical item for a penny less? This situation is illustrated with a single firm's demand curve that is a horizontal line, as shown in Figure 7.5(a). Notice that when a firm's price goes above the existing market price, demand for that firm's product disappears—there is no demand except at that one price. Perfect competition is often referred to as a commodity market because commodities are identical products.

Monopoly   Monopoly is a market structure in which:

- There is just one firm.
- Entry by other firms is not possible.

In a monopoly, because there is only one firm, consumers have only one place to buy the good, and there are no close substitutes. The monopolist can do anything it wants, since consumers cannot go to another seller—anything, that is, as long as it earns a profit.

The demand curve facing the single firm in a monopoly is the market demand because the firm is the only supplier in the market. This is shown in Figure 7.5(b). Being the only producer, the monopolist must carefully consider what price to charge. Unlike a price increase in a perfectly competitive market, a price increase in a monopoly will not drive every customer to another producer. But if the price is too high, consumers will not buy the product. Even if a monopolist had something that was needed—say insulin or gasoline or electricity—consumers would quit buying it if the price got too high.

Table 7.1

Characteristics of Market Structures

MARKET STRUCTURE	NUMBER OF FIRMS	ENTRY CONDITION	PRODUCT TYPE
Perfect competition	Very large number	Easy	Standardized
Monopoly	One	No entry possible	Only one product
Monopolistic competition	Large number	Easy	Differentiated
Oligopoly	Few	Impeded	Standardized or differentiated

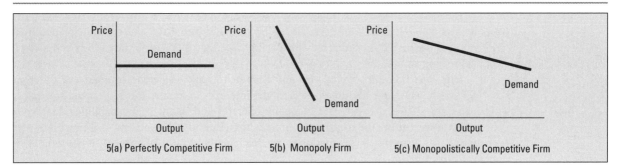

FIGURE 7.5 The Demand Curve Facing an Individual Firm

The demand curve for an individual firm in perfect competition is a horizontal line as shown in Figure 7.5(a). Figure 7.5(b) shows the market demand, which is the demand curve faced by a monopoly firm. The firm is the only supplier and thus faces the entire market demand. Figure 7.5(c) shows the downward-sloping demand curve faced by a firm in monopolistic competition. The curve slopes downward because of the differentiated nature of the products in the industry.

Monopolistic Competition   A monopolistically competitive market structure is characterized by the following:

- A large number of firms
- Easy entry
- Differentiated products

Product differentiation distinguishes a perfectly competitive market from a monopolistically competitive market. (In both, entry is easy and there are a large number of firms.) Even though there are many firms in a monopolistically competitive market structure, the demand curve faced by *any one firm* slopes downward, as in Figure 7.5(c). Because each product is slightly different from all other products, each firm is like a mini-monopoly—the only producer of that specific product. The greater the differentiation among products, the less price-elastic the demand.

Oligopoly   In an oligopoly,

- There are few firms—more than one, but few enough so that each firm alone can affect the market.
- Product can be either differentiated or identical. Automobile producers constitute one oligopoly, steelmakers another.
- Entry is more difficult than entry into a perfectly competitive or monopolistically competitive market, but in contrast to monopoly, entry can occur.
- Firms are *interdependent,* and this interdependence distinguishes oligopoly from the other selling environments.

The oligopolist faces a downward-sloping demand curve, but the shape of the curve depends on the behavior of competitors. Oligopoly is the most complicated of the market structure models to examine because there are so many behaviors that firms might display. As we discuss in the next chapter, oligopoly is often represented using Game Theory.

The five forces model is built on the equilibrium approach to markets and the structure-conduct-performance paradigm. For instance, if an industry or market is perfectly competitive – the firm has no market power—there is no room for profits. What must happen is that the firm must somehow acquire some market power. It must figure out a way to restrict entry, differentiate products, or limit competition.

Resource-Based Model

Since the 1980s, economists have argued that there is not necessarily a link between the structure of industry, the conduct of firms in that industry, and the performance of firms in that industry. The structure–conduct–performance paradigm was not supported by the evidence. Instead, it was found that company performance varies widely among firms in the same industry; this suggests that strategy may reside at the level of the company and its management, not just at the level of the industry. The focus on strategy identified not just the market structure in which a firm operated but on whether a firm had a competitive advantage.

The five forces approach does not attempt to look inside the company. A different approach called the **resource-based model** attempts to look at the fit between the external market context in which a company operates and its internal capabilities. This view holds that a firm's internal environment, in terms of its resources and capabilities, is more critical to the determination of strategic action than is its external environment. It is a firm's unique resources and capabilities that are the basis of strategy, not the industry in which the firm is doing business.

In the field of strategy, a lot of terminology is used, but most terms come down to what we have already discussed. For instance, it is said that strategy should be designed to allow the firm to best exploit its competitive advantage or **core competency**. The core competencies are the things your company can do relatively better than your competitors— essentially your firm's competitive advantage. If a core competency yields a long-term advantage to the company, it is said to be a **sustainable competitive advantage**. Strategy, then, involves making those choices that enable it to create sustainable competitive advantage—in other words, that allow the firm to earn positive economic profit and to continue doing that for a significant period of time.

Given that positive economic profit attracts those rivals that attempt to take away from the successful business, a firm must never rest on its past success. Sustainable competitive advantage is achieved by creating something of value that others cannot easily copy and for which there are few close substitutes. The opportunity for a company to sustain its competitive advantage is determined by two kinds of capabilities—distinctive capabilities and reproducible capabilities. **Distinctive capabilities** are the characteristics that cannot be replicated by competitors, or can only be replicated with great difficulty. Distinctive capabilities can be of many kinds: patents, exclusive licenses, strong brands, effective leadership, teamwork, knowledge, and employees for instance. **Reproducible capabilities** are those that can be bought or created by competitors and thus by themselves cannot be a source of competitive advantage. The structure of the firm and its culture can be distinctive or reproducible capabilities. Often, competitors can copy products and structures. Can the same be said for the firm's employees? Sometimes yes and sometimes no. It is said time and again that "People are our firm's most important asset." That may or may not be true. Typically when it is, it is the employees' knowledge that creates the competitive advantage.

The resource-based view states that firms can earn positive economic profits if and only if they have superior resources and those resources provide distinctive capabilities. Positive economic profits can be earned from resources only to the extent that they are valuable, rare, imperfectly imitable, and nonsubstitutable. This is called the **VRIN** framework. Often "N" is replaced with "O" (representing organization). and the framework is called **VRIO**:

- *Valuable*—A resource must enable a firm to employ a value-creating strategy, by either outperforming its competitors or reducing its own weaknesses
- *Rare* —To be of value, a resource must be rare.

■ *Inimitable*—If a valuable resource is controlled by only one firm, it could be a source of a competitive advantage. This advantage can be sustainable if competitors are not able to duplicate this strategic asset perfectly. If the resource in question is knowledge-based or socially complex, it is less likely to be duplicated.

■ *Nonsubstitutable*—Even if a resource is rare, potentially value-creating, and imperfectly imitable, an equally important aspect is lack of substitutes. If competitors are able to counter the firm's value-creating strategy with a substitute, prices are driven down to the point where economic profits are zero.

■ *Organization*—The firm is structured in such a way as to exploit the valuable resources.

A crucial part of the VRIN/VRIO framework is to identify important barriers to entry. Barriers to entry are circumstances particular to a given business that create disadvantages for new competitors attempting to enter the market. Anything that deters competitors from entering the market is a barrier to entry. These may include internal capabilities, government regulations, intellectual property rights, economic and market conditions, difficulties related to new product development, high start-up costs, the firm's culture, market share, strategic alliances market leadership, consumer loyalty, branded products, large expenditures on research and development, and on and on. In the following chapters these potential barriers will be examined. For instance, one of the important aspects of success for a firm is to limit competition—to limit the entry of rivals to a firm's market. Let's now consider a few strategies that focus on deterring entry.

Restricting Entry

A firm wants to distinguish its goods or services from those of rivals. The more the consumer considers the products different, the more ability the firm has to set prices and earn positive economic profits. Think about what Starbucks has been able to do. It is able to sell a cup of coffee for $1.60 when its costs are much less than that because it is selling more than just the commodity, coffee. People go to Starbucks because of the ambience and its full register of different drinks, not just its coffee. To date, no other firm has been able to do exactly what Starbucks does. Because other firms can enter the business, however, the coffee price has been bid down until the differential between the cost of all resources used in providing the coffee and Starbucks' selling price is the value consumers put on the Starbucks special attribute.

Firms earning economic profits must attempt to sustain the profit—to keep others from entering and eroding the profit. Firms looking to enter must figure out how best to do that—by lowering price, offering better quality, mimicry, or innovation. Strategy is the process of making decisions—choosing what to do and what to forgo.

Time after time, in industry after industry, companies rise to fame and fortune only to see their once-formidable positions become susceptible to attack as new players enter the field from newly created strategic positions. A company cannot settle for what it has. It must be on the lookout for new positions; otherwise others will find those new positions and exploit them at the expense of the incumbent firms.

Brand Name

The objective of creating a brand name is to increase consumer loyalty and thus reduce the likelihood that customers will purchase a different product if the price of the branded product rises. The customer's response to a price change is called the **price elasticity of demand**. The greater the price elasticity of demand, the more likely that customers will change products when the price of their current product rises. The greater the consumer's reluctance to shift brands, the lower the price elasticity of demand. (We discuss price elasticity in detail in Chapter 13.) Consumers loyal to a brand or to a firm will purchase that brand or purchase from that firm even if the prices are above those of competing brands.

The value of reputation depends on the likelihood of repeat purchase. In the long run, reputation can only be based on providing high quality in repeated trials. Because it takes a long time to establish such a reputation, some firms attempt to rent an established reputation in one market to use in a new market. Endorsement by famous personalities is a clear example. Everyone knows that celebrities give their endorsement not because they have scoured the market for the best product but because they have canvassed potential sponsors for the highest fee. So why are consumers influenced by the endorsement? The endorser is, to some degree, putting his or her reputation at risk. If the product is of low quality, the celebrity's reputation and value to other sponsors can be damaged. For the manufacturer, payment of the endorsement fee is a demonstration of its commitment to the market. Willingness to pay the endorsement fee is therefore actually a measure of product quality. Tiger Woods was the number one endorser until his private life became public. Then sponsors dropped him; they feared their products' reputations would be damaged by being associated with Woods.

Firms will sometimes use their established reputation in one market to enter a new market, although this strategy has significant risks. BMW's reputation for producing cars reinforces its reputation for producing motor bikes and vice versa. BMW also endorses a range of "Active Line" sportswear. Caterpillar has a line of clothing—"CAT"—that provides the image of tough, no-nonsense fashions. There is small reason to believe that the capabilities that distinguish BMW cars or Caterpillar equipment are applicable to the manufacture of clothes. But it would clearly be foolish for the companies to attach their name to poor-quality clothes.

Typically, brand names are costly to create and take a long time to establish. Incumbent firms are therefore often reluctant to alter products or enter new markets for fear of damaging their brand name. The liquid soap market is a good illustration. In the late 1970s, a little niche company, Minnetonka, introduced Softsoap. Softsoap sales reached $40 million in just 4 years, which then attracted the large established companies—Armour-Dial, Procter & Gamble, Lever Brothers, and Colgate-Palmolive. Although Procter & Gamble had the long-established name of Ivory soap, its entry was with a soft soap it named Rejoice. It wasn't until 1983 that P&G finally introduced its Ivory-brand liquid soap. Following that, Jergens entered and became third in the market. Two years later Colgate-Palmolive played catch-up by buying Softsoap for $60 million.

Why the delay by the big companies? The reason was to protect their brand names. P&G tried the name Rejoice simply to keep any failures from tarnishing the name of Ivory. Once the product looked to be a success, the extension of brand name from Ivory bar soap to Ivory soft soap made sense. Ivory soft soap moved almost immediately to a 36 percent market share.

Warranties and Guarantees

Guarantees and warranties can serve as barriers to entry. When Japanese automobile companies first entered the U.S. market in the 1960s, they faced the difficulty of convincing consumers of the quality of the cars. Although the manufacturers knew that their products were of high quality, their potential customers did not. In fact, many believed that Japanese goods were shoddy imitations of Western products. "Made in Japan" had become synonymous with cheap and crummy. Accordingly, Japanese manufacturers offered more extensive warranties than had been usual in the market.

Guarantees are difficult to fake. A low-quality product would break down frequently, making the guarantee quite costly for the firm. Thus, the higher the quality of the product, the better the guarantee offered by the firm. If a firm establishes a warranty policy, then other firms either have to follow or must admit to having a lower-quality product. If a potential rival is unable to imitate the warranties of existing firms, it may decide not to enter the market in the first place. If the firm can match the warranty and beat it, then when the firm enters the market it will offer a *better* warranty. This is what the Japanese auto producers did to the U.S. auto producers in the 1970s. U.S. auto producers did not offer warranties as extensive as those now offered by the Japanese. As a result, customers soon came to see that "Made in Japan" meant quality. A similar event occurred in the late 1990s and early 2000s with respect to the Korean-manufactured Hyundai. Hyundai offered a 100,000-mile full warranty at a time when other manufacturers were offering 36,000-mile warranties.

Economies of Scale

The size of the firm relative to the market can be an important barrier to entry. If a firm must be large in order to enter an industry and begin offering a good or service, then entry might be very difficult, if not impossible. In this case, the incumbent firm may be able to earn and sustain positive economic profits. The idea that a firm's cost per unit of output declines as the size of the firm grows is called economies of scale. If economies of scale exist, a larger firm can produce a product at a lower per-unit cost than can a smaller firm. Thus, a new entrant would have to enter as a large firm in order to compete with existing firms. The larger the firm, the lower cost per unit the firm can operate at. This means it can set a price that is below the costs of smaller firms. Knowing this, potential rivals may stay out of the market unless they can enter at the very large size necessary to gain the economies of scale. However, not every firm has economies of scale. For some firms, small size is more efficient than large size.

Sunk Costs

Suppose a market contains one national firm and several regional ones. Suppose further that, when one of the regional firms announces plans to expand to a national firm, the incumbent national firm responds by announcing that it is going to substantially increase its advertising and its production facilities. These expenditures would raise the costs to the regional firm to become a national firm because it would have to at least match the expenditures of the existing national firm. Potential entrants have to consider undertaking expenditures that are even more than those made by existing firms. If those expenditures are sunk, then the barrier to entry is even higher. A sunk cost is an expenditure on an asset that has no liquidation value. For instance, expenditures on advertising by one firm can't be sold to another firm. A firm that purchases a sign advertising the firm's name or product cannot then sell that sign to another firm. Sunk costs can serve as effective barriers to entry since they tell a potential new firm that it has to throw just as much money away on similar sunk expenditures if it is going to compete.

Advertising expenditures may be the most significant sunk costs of competition. When a firm advertises, it is saying, "We have just spent millions of dollars drawing your attention to our product. If we intended to disappoint your expectations, to withdraw from the market, or to produce a poor-quality product, spending that money would be a foolish thing for us to have done." The advertisement assures the reader that the product is good, but not because it says that the product is good. Rather, the assurance that the product is good comes from the mere fact that the firm has incurred the sunk costs of advertising.

Consider the case of sidewalk vendors who sell neckties on the streets of a large city. If such a "firm" tells customers that it will guarantee the quality of its ties, customers will certainly question the validity of the guarantee since if the "firm" decides to go out of business, it can do so instantaneously. It has no headquarters, no brand name, no costly capital equipment, no loyal customers to worry about—indeed, no sunk, or unrecoverable, costs of any kind. It could come or go at a moment's notice.

The incentives are different for a firm that has devoted significant resources to items that have no liquidation value. These firms are not likely to pick up and leave at a moment's notice. Buyers, knowing that, can place greater trust in the promise of a high-quality product. And potential entrants know that they, too, must devote resources to these activities, and that once the expenditures are undertaken, there is no way to recoup them. These sunk costs could deter entry.

Microsoft was accused of carrying out this strategy by refusing to release its operating system code to firms that compete in other software markets. This increased the cost to rivals of creating and updating their own software; moreover, these costs were sunk.

Unique Resources

A firm with an established distribution channel that is not easily replicable has an advantage over potential rivals. The auto industry is a good example. The dealer network is extensive and very costly to establish. Many new companies have purchased dealer arrangements with existing dealers so that one dealer now represents several different companies.[3] Kodak's distribution network was well established by the time Fuji attempted to enter the film market in the 1970s. Fuji attempted to use Kodak's suppliers, offering to sell them Fuji materials at a fraction of the cost of Kodak products. Kodak responded with ultimatums to distributors that they sell only Kodak or they would not get Kodak products.[4]

If all firms in a market have the same resources and capabilities, no strategy for earning economic profit is available to one firm that would not also be available to all other firms. Any strategy that confers advantage could be immediately imitated by any other firm. However, if a firm has a unique resource, that resource may serve as a barrier to entry. A single family owned the only mine producing desiccant clay, an important ingredient in inhibiting humidity in packaging. For years, this clay was the only material that could meet certain necessary standards for inhibiting the accumulation of humidity in packaging. A synthetic clay was eventually introduced, and the value of the desiccant clay dropped.

Limiting supply can enhance the value one brings to a game. A supplier must have a distinct capability—a product or a supply network that is not easily imitated, for example. A firm must distinguish itself from rivals in order to increase the value the firm brings to a game (by reducing the price elasticity and the cross-price elasticity of demand). DeBeers controlled about 80 percent of the non-Russian diamonds offered for sale in the world at the time the Soviet economy was tightly controlled by the government. Russia has about 40 percent of all diamond deposits in the world but had kept those diamonds from being sold and distributed outside the country. DeBeers therefore had a unique resource—acquisition and distribution of the non-Russian diamonds. With the collapse of the Soviet Union in 1991, DeBeers had to fear a flood of diamonds. It attempted to extend its uniqueness by stamping each of its diamonds with a certificate of quality and authenticity, hoping that customers would demand that such a stamp of approval was necessary to sell diamonds.

Pricing to Deter Entry

A firm may be able to use prices to deter market entry by potential rivals. A price that discourages or prevents entry is called a **limit price**. A limit price is one that will keep potential entrants from entering the market and yet allow the incumbent firm some profits. If the incumbent firm is able to charge a monopoly price but the resulting profits would attract entry, perhaps the incumbent would be better off charging a lower price. To see the potential merits of this strategy, suppose for the moment that the entrant's costs are identical to those of the incumbent and that the entrant has complete information about the incumbent's costs as well as the demand for the product. In other words, imagine that the potential entrant knows all the information enjoyed by the incumbent.

While limit pricing would seem to be a potential deterrent to entry, it could be very costly for a firm to employ the strategy. The revenue lost during the period the firm charges the low price may never be recouped, or the low price may become the company's standard—it may not be able to increase prices in the future without losing customers. But suppose the incumbent simply threatens to lower price if anyone tries to enter, would this prevent entry? If the threat is believed or credible, the incumbent will earn the higher profits and won't have to lower price.

Consider a situation in which the potential entrant does not know for certain the incumbent's costs. If the potential entrant knows that the incumbent has high costs, it will find it profitable to enter the market. If the potential entrant knows the incumbent's costs are low, on the other hand, it will find the market unprofitable to enter. If the entrant does not know the incumbent's costs, it has an incentive to use whatever information is available to infer the incumbent's costs, but the incumbent has an incentive to provide information that indicates it is a low-cost provider even if it is a high-cost provider.

Business Insight

Sunk Costs and Ancient Societies

The collapse of ancient societies such as the Mesa Verde-region pre-Hispanic Pueblos has puzzled generations of scientists. Many explanations for particular cases have been suggested, from combinations of social, political, and economic to climatic factors, such as drought. But it may have been merely the sunk cost effect that led to the decline of many ancient societies. The ancient societies had a tendency to hold on to previous investments even if this was a rationally bad choice. They tended not to abandon settlements once they had invested time and resources to establishing them, even if resources become scarce.[5]

Predatory Pricing

Limit pricing is sometimes referred to as **predatory pricing** and in global or international situations as dumping. Predatory pricing is setting a very low price (a price that is below average variable cost) in order to drive competitors out of business and then increasing price to recoup the lost revenue. Could a business do such a thing? Could it set prices below its costs in order to drive competitors out of business and then increase prices once the competitors have left the market? Wouldn't the higher price just entice new start-ups and force the dominant incumbent to lower price again, and then again, and basically forever?

According to one study, airlines that have near-monopoly status at hub airports can use their size to drive low-cost carriers from their markets.[6] For instance, in 1995 Spirit Airlines entered the Detroit–Philadelphia market, which was dominated by Northwest Airlines. Spirit started by offering one round-trip flight daily, with fares ranging from

$49 to $139. Northwest struck back by matching Spirit's fare. The result: Northwest's revenue plunged, but it regained its entire market. In late 1996, Spirit gave up. A few months later, Northwest eliminated virtually all low-cost fares on the route, and its revenue returned to precompetition levels. This same study cited 12 cases in which the upstart carrier offered initial fares at half the price of the market's dominant incumbent—and the threatened major airline responded with price cuts. Within two years, half the new carriers had exited the market because they were unable to make a profit. and most of the incumbent firms had recouped their losses.

So why didn't other start-up airlines enter once Northwest increased fares, or why didn't the fear of new entries keep the incumbent from raising fares? One reason cited was the dismal performance of the start-ups; investors would not provide funds for an airline to get started. Knowing the incumbent has deep pockets and can afford losses for a while if they can be recouped later, investors decline to get embroiled in a battle with the incumbent. But the real problem is that access to airports is tightly controlled by the federal government and airport officials; the incumbent firms have near-monopolies. Few if any start-ups can gain access to a landing gate in order to enter the business.[7] Notice where Southwest Airlines' gates are located in most airports—the furthest from the central location.

A strategy of predatory pricing is typically more costly for the predator than for the prey. It is unlikely to be a profitable way of eliminating competition in general, even if it can drive a firm with "shallow or empty pockets" out of the market. To recoup the losses the predator sustained, the predator must be able to raise prices substantially once the rival is gone. Unless entry is extremely difficult, this will not happen. The incumbent firm can not recoup losses because once the incumbent firm increases price, new rivals will enter.[8]

Suppose firms are involved in a business with very high fixed costs and very low marginal costs. Competition will drive price to marginal cost and cause the departure of the weakest firms. The surviving firm may be able to raise its price because the high fixed cost will deter entry. This is not predatory pricing even though on the surface it might look like it.

A firm with a new product may sell the product at a low price or even give it away for free initially, raising the price once consumers become aware of the product. This is not predatory pricing but instead market penetration—an attempt to enter a market. Yet, it appears to be similar to predatory pricing.

Summing Up

In this chapter we have discussed a few strategies used to deter entry. You might have noticed that in this discussion we took the viewpoint of one firm acting in isolation: Once the one firm acts, other firms don't react. This is not a very realistic scenario. In the next chapter we consider the situation when there are interdependencies among firms.

Wal-Mart Predatory Pricing Case

The case dealt with claims that Wal-Mart used predatory pricing in its pharmacy department to drive other pharmacies out of business. In order to prove "predatory pricing" the court must determine what principle it would accept as "nonpredatory" in pricing below cost and whether there was an "intent" to injure competition. The most important element is "recoupment." Were the prices ultimately raised, once the competition was put out of business?

The decision initially was in favor of the independent pharmacies. That decision was overturned in Wal-Mart's favor in the Arkansas Supreme Court. Wal-Mart did admit selling below cost, but denied the predatory charge. David Glass, Wal-Mart's CEO, said that the Bentonville, Arkansas retailer regularly sells a variety of items below cost, including such standards as Crest® toothpaste and Listerine® mouthwash. But he maintained that selling below cost doesn't violate the law or destroy competition.

Predatory pricing is the lowering of price below costs in an attempt to force a rival out of business. Then once the rival leaves, the incumbent firm raises its price to gain back all losses and more profit. If the incumbent firm does raise the price after the rival is driven from the market, is that prime facie case of predatory pricing? No. If the rival has been driven out and the incumbent increases the price, what is to keep new rivals from entering the market? So predatory pricing has to at least include both significant barriers to entry and pricing below cost, followed by the raising of the price once rivals have left the market. But even in this case, pricing below cost may not be predatory. As Wal-Mart claimed, they often use several items as loss-leaders—selling them below cost to bring in customers who purchase items with a sold profit margin on them.

Summary

1. Successful performance for a nation is measured in terms of standards of living—per capita income.
2. Successful performance for a firm is measured in terms of economic profits.
3. Strategy is making choices. Each action of a nation and a firm requires trade-offs—something is gained only by forgoing something else. Trade-offs—the recognition of opportunity costs—are involved.
4. The production possibilities curve (PPC) or best practice frontier illustrates the trade-offs involved in strategy.
5. The best practice frontier represents the efficient use of resources regardless of what a firm's strategy may be.
6. Short-term strategy involves where on or inside the frontier to locate. The long-term strategy involves a shifting out of the frontier.
7. Strategy involves making choices. The five forces model indicates some of the areas to which managers must look when designing their strategy, but is not the ideal strategy formulation model. It focuses mainly on the external environment in which a business operates. The resource-based view focuses on the internal resources and capabilities of the firm in designing strategy. The VRIN/VRIO framework states that strategy must involve finding those resources and capabilities that are valuable, rare, inimitable, and nonsubstitutable and having the organization to exploit these.
8. The most common strategy by incumbents is to raise barriers to entry. Barriers may be brand name or reputation, warranties and guarantees, and sunk costs.
9. Acquiring unique resources acts as a barrier to entry.
10. Pricing may be a deterrence to entry. Predatory pricing is the attempt to sell a good or service for less than that good or service cost to produce in order to drive rivals out of business. The strategy requires that the predatory firm then raise price to recoup all losses and deters entry while doing this. Limit pricing is an attempt to set a low enough price that others are deterred from entering.

Key Terms

Production possibilities curve (PPC)
Best practice frontier
Competitive advantage
Five forces model
Resource-based model
Core competency
Sustainable competitive advantage

Distinctive capabilities
Reproducible capabilities
Price elasticity of demand
VRIN/VRIO
Limit price
Predatory pricing

Exercises

1. Does a firm make use of comparative advantage in allocating its resources? What factors give a firm a comparative advantage?

2. Under what conditions are the two strategies of low cost and high quality a trade-off? Under what conditions would the efficient frontier not be an appropriate picture of the two strategies?

3. What is the best practices frontier? How does this relate to competitive advantage?

4. Why is growth a primary strategy of almost every firm? Would it ever make sense to "stand pat." Use the economic profit equation to provide an answer.

5. Jack Welch is heralded as a great leader of General Electric (GE). His strategy to acquire companies in different lines of business based on the requirement that each business in GE was to become the #1 or #2 competitor in the industry is touted as being particularly brilliant. While very successful, could there have been a fundamental flaw in Welch's strategy?

6. Here are some examples of strategies selected by different firms:

   a. Grow larger—AHERF
   b. Downsize—Avon, Sara Lee
   c. Diversify—Wal-Mart, PepsiCo
   d. Dominate a niche—Starbucks, Jiffy Lube
   e. Outsource production—Nike, IKEA
   f. Integrate production—Armani, Tiffany
   g. Become cost leader—Kia, Motel 6
   h. Become quality leader—BMW, Four Seasons
   i. Drive rivals from market—Philip Morris, Microsoft
   j. Innovator—Wal-Mart, Southwest Airlines, Enterprise
   k. Imitate—Acer Computer, Xerox
   l. Explain where on the best practice frontier each would lie.

7. How is national strategy different from firm strategy? How are the two the same?

8. Use what you know about Starbucks and apply the VRIO/VRIN approach to evaluate Starbucks, as you know it. Use the five forces model to evaluate Starbucks. Is the five forces model different from the VRIO model? Explain

9. Suppose that two firms, A and B, compete. They can choose different strategies—a combination of low price or high quality. The accompanying tables show the best practice frontiers for each firm.

   A's Possibilities

Price	Quality
0	12
1	8
2	4
3	0

   B's Possibilities

Price	Quality
0	6
2	4
4	2
6	0

   What is the cost to A of 1 unit of high quality? What is the cost to B of 1 unit of high quality? What is the cost to A of 1 unit of price? What is the cost to B of 1 unit of price? Which firm should focus on high quality? Which on low price? Explain.

10. Texas Instruments once announced a price for random-access memories that wouldn't be available until two years after the announcement. A few days later, Bowmar announced that it would produce this product and sell it at a lower price than Texas Instruments. A few weeks later, Motorola said it, too, would produce this product

and sell it below the Bowmar price. A few weeks after this, Texas Instruments announced a price that was one-half of Motorola's. The other two firms announced that, after reconsidering their decision, they would not produce the product. What do you think was Texas Instruments' reason for announcing the price of a product two years before it was actually for sale?

11. Explain how a strategy of increasing expenditures on advertising could deter market entry.

12. Coke and Pepsi have sustained their market dominance for nearly a century. General Motors and Ford have lost their dominance. What is the difference between the two cases.

13. Currently, a fast-food firm has a monopoly in the university student union. The monopoly pays the university $75,000 a year in order to maintain it. The firm earns an economic profit of $290,000 per year. Another fast-food firm wants to enter the market and offer its fare to students. The manager of the first firm calls the university president asking her to maintain the first firm's monopoly. How much would the first firm be willing to pay to keep the monopoly?

14. A first mover is dominating a market, with revenues of $40 million annually. The average total cost for the firm is $20 million, of which $19 million is fixed. How can the first mover keep others from entering the market?

15. When would limit pricing make sense? What price should serve as the limit?

16. The following data represent a firm serving a specific transportation market.

Total Output	Total Revenue	Total Cost
0	$0	$1,000
1	$1,700	$2,000
2	$3,300	$2,800
3	$4,800	$3,500
4	$6,200	$4,000
5	$7,500	$4,500
6	$8,700	$5,200
7	$9,800	$6,000
8	$10,800	$7,000
9	$11,700	$9,000

a. What price maximizes revenue?
b. What price maximizes profit?
c. What is fixed cost?
d. This firm faces a rival that cuts its revenue significantly. The firm has decided to undertake predatory pricing to drive the other firm out of business. The other firm has a cost structure that looks like the following:

Total Cost	$2,000	$3,000	$4,000	$5,000	$6,000	$7,000	$8,000
Total Output	0	1	2	3	4	5	6

What price would drive the firm out of business? How much would it cost the incumbent firm to drive the rival out of the market? Could the firm raise the price to recoup the losses?

17. Explain the differences between perfect competition, monopoly, monopolistic competition, and oligopoly.

18. Why would a firm want to deter entry? How much would a monopolist spend to keep other firms out of its market?

19. Explain why predatory pricing hardly works in the real world.

CHAPTER NOTES

1. Based on "How Merck Healed Itself" by John Simons, *Fortune*, February 7, 2008.
2. Quoted in John Seely Brown, "Research That Reinvents the Corporation," *Harvard Business Review* (January/February 1991): 102–111.
3. If the dealer network is a competitive advantage, why would the government force GM and Chrysler to eliminate a significant part of their dealer networks when the government took over the companies in 2009?
4. These are called exclusive dealing arrangements. The courts have ruled that unless exclusive dealing can be proven to lessen competition or close the market, it is not illegal.
5. Marco A. Janssen, Marten Scheffer, and Timothy A. Kohler, Sunk-Cost Effects Made Ancient Societies Vulnerable to Collapse, Santa Fe Institute Working Paper February 2, 2007.
6. Clinton V. Oster Jr. and John S. Strong, "Predatory Practices in the U.S. Airline Industry" (January 2010 (ostpxweb.dot.gov/aviation/domestic-competition/predpractices.pdf), and U.S. Department of Transportation, Domestic Competition Series, "Dominated Hub Fares" (Washington, DC: U.S. Government Printing Office, January 2001) (ostpxweb.dot.gov/aviation/domestic-competition/hubpaper.pdf).
7. Predatory pricing has been the basis for antitrust action. In 1999, the Department of Justice's antitrust division filed suit against American Airlines for predatory pricing at its Dallas–Fort Worth

hub, where it carried 77 percent of all nonstop passengers at the time the suit was filed. During the 1990s, new airlines such as Vanguard, Sun Jet, and Western Pacific occasionally offered stiff competition on flights to second-tier cities such as Wichita, Kansas City, and Colorado Springs. In each case, American responded by drastically cutting its fares until the fledgling was driven from the route. Then American raised fares and reduced service to accommodate the declining number of passengers. The suit was dismissed by the judge because it was not proven that American was selling below-average variable cost.

8. Price discrimination often looks like a policy of dumping or predatory pricing. A firm offers a different price in different markets for the same item. This could merely be the result of reacting to consumer desires, that is, price elasticities of demand rather than strategies directed to drive rivals from the market.

CHAPTER **8**

When Other Firms React

NutraSweet

Aspartame is a low-calorie, high-intensity sweetener known by Monsanto's brand name, NutraSweet.[1] It was the key to the success of Diet Coke and Diet Pepsi in the 1980s. NutraSweet made billions of dollars, yielding very high profits. Such profits usually attract entry, but in this case entry was barred by a patent on the sweetener and because the process of creating the sweetener was expensive and difficult. Monsanto had a distinct capability—its monopoly. It had also created another strategic asset—the NutraSweet brand name as represented by its trademark "swirl." The problem was that Monsanto's patent was about to expire. As a result, the Holland Sweetener Company began building an aspartame plant in Geleen, the Netherlands, to challenge Monsanto's hold on the aspartame market. Holland Sweetener was a joint venture between the Japanese Tosoh Corporation and DSM (Dutch State Mines).

1. What will Monsanto do?
2. What will Holland Sweetener do?

Strategy as Game Theory

If one firm chooses to do something, what is to prevent others from doing the same or countering the direction of the first firm? Wal-Mart created a competitive advantage with its inventory system. The choice to focus on low prices followed from that competitive advantage. The strategy was dependent on what Wal-Mart thought other firms could do. If Wal-Mart executives had anticipated that a rival could immediately do the same thing, they might have selected a different strategy. But they expected to be able to enjoy economic profit for a few years before other firms caught up.

Managers must make decisions in the context of existing rivals and take into account the possible actions of potential rivals. The market structure that focuses on this interdependence is called oligopoly. But interdependence must concern firms operating in other market structures as well, if not to the extent of the case of relatively few competitors. All managers are absorbed in their own firm's situations, but putting themselves in the shoes of competitors and focusing on the competitors' probable responses to actions they might undertake can be a useful exercise. This exercise has been developed through a line of economic analysis known as **game theory**.

Game theory defines strategic behavior as the interdependence of actions; what one does affects and is affected by what others do.[2] It can be relatively simple and intuitive, or it can be mathematically complex and difficult. As a result, although expressions such as game theory, zero-sum game, and prisoner's dilemma have become part of everyday language, game theory remains primarily an academic exercise.[3] Game theory can help managers to understand that the world of business is one of interdependence, that strategic decisions cannot be made in isolation. Game theory has been used in war or defense planning for nations, in planning economic or national policy, in dealings between government and business, by businesses in their interactions with other businesses, with employees, suppliers and customers, and by individuals interacting with others.

It is useful in business today to have some understanding of game theory.

Consider an example that illustrates how game theory can clarify a situation that seems confusing on the surface. People often believe news magazines collude because their covers are similar almost every week. Let's see if we can understand the strategy involved. Suppose that each week, *Newsweek* and *Time* have to select a cover story that will catch the attention of possible readers. Consider a week in which there are two major new stories, one about global warming (call it GW) and another about a scandal in the Senate (call it S). *Time* and *Newsweek* must decide between these two covers without knowledge of the other magazine's choice. Suppose that each magazine has estimated that its profits will be:

$10 million if both choose story S.
$15 million if it chooses story S, while the other magazine chooses GW
$10 million if it selects GW while the other chooses S
$10 million if both choose GW

Neither magazine has the benefit of observing the other's completed move before making its own. If one of the executives of *Newsweek* says, "Let's put ourselves in the shoes of Time" what will happen? They would find out *Time* is doing the same thing. It is often not enough simply to put yourself in your opponent's shoes because if you did you'd only discover that your opponent is doing the same thing. Each person has to place himself simultaneously in both his own and the other person's shoes and then figure out the best moves for both sides. So each firm selects S, and each week the two have the same cover.

The interaction of the news magazines is called a game. The editors making the cover decisions are the **players**. The planned decisions of the players are called moves or **strategies**.

The **payoffs** to the players are the profits or losses that result from the strategies. Due to interdependence, the pay-off to a player depends not only on that player's strategy but also on the strategies employed by other players.

One-Period Games

In the analysis of games, the order in which players make decisions is important. In a **simultaneous-move** game, each player makes decisions without knowledge of the other players' decisions. In a **sequential-move** game, one player makes a move after observing the other player's move. Chess and checkers are examples of sequential-move games, and rock-paper-scissors is an example of a simultaneous-move game.

Games can be interactions that occur just once or interactions that are repeated a number of times. For example, if you play high card draw with others just once, you are playing a **one-period game**. If you agree to play best out of three, you are playing a **repeated game**.

The **normal form representation** of a game indicates the players in the game, the possible strategies of the players, and the payoffs to the players that will result from alternative strategies. The normal form representation of the simultaneous-move game involving the magazines is presented in Table 8.1. There are two players, *Newsweek* and *Time*. The payoff matrix shows the results of the strategies. The first entry in each cell is *Time*'s payoff; the second is *Newsweek*'s.

Time has two possible strategies: It can choose S story or GW story. Similarly, the feasible strategies for *Newsweek* are S story or GW story. Finally, the payoffs to the two players are given by the entries in each cell of the matrix. The first entry refers to the payoff to *Time,* and the second entry denotes the payoff to *Newsweek.* An important thing to notice about the description of the game is that the payoff to *Time* crucially depends on the strategy *Newsweek* chooses. For example, if *Time* chooses S and *Newsweek* chooses S, the resulting payoffs are 10 for *Time* and 20 for *Newsweek.* Similarly, if *Time*'s strategy is S while *Newsweek*'s strategy is GW, *Time*'s payoff is 15 while *Newsweek*'s is 8.

Since the game in Table 8.1 is a simultaneous-move, one-shot game, the players get to make one, and only one, decision and must make their decision at the same time. Moreover, the players cannot make conditional decisions; for example, *Time* can't choose GW if *Newsweek* chooses S and S if *Newsweek* chooses GW. The players make decisions at the same time that preclude each player from basing his or her decisions on what the other player does.

What is the optimal strategy for a player in a simultaneous-move, one-period game? The answer can be quite complicated. There is one instance, however, in which it is easy to characterize the optimal decision—a situation that involves a **dominant strategy**. A strategy is dominant if it results in the highest payoff regardless of the action of the opponent.

In Table 8.1, the dominant strategy for *Time* is S. To see this, note that if *Newsweek* chooses S, the best choice by *Time* is S since 10 units of profits are better than the −10

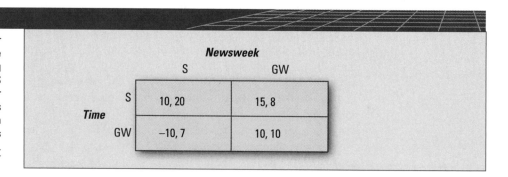

Table 8.1

Magazine Cover Selections. The payoffs for selecting one of two stories, S or GW, for each player are shown. *Time*'s payoffs are shown first and *Newsweek*'s second in each cell.

		Newsweek	
		S	GW
Time	S	10, 20	15, 8
	GW	−10, 7	10, 10

that *Time* would earn by choosing GW. If *Newsweek* chose GW, the best choice by *Time* would be S since 15 units of profits are better than the 10 *Time* would earn by choosing GW. In short, regardless of whether *Newsweek*'s strategy is S or GW, the best choice by *Time* is S; S is a dominant strategy for Time.

Newsweek in Table 8.1 should recognize that a dominant strategy for *Time* is to play S. Thus, *Newsweek* should reason as follows: *Time* will surely select the S story. Therefore, *Newsweek* should select the story that will give it the best outcome given that *Time* will select S. Assuming *Time* chooses the dominant strategy, *Newsweek* will earn 20 by choosing the S story as well.

Nash Equilibrium

The end result of a thought process where you put yourself in your rival's shoes as well as your own is captured in the definition of the **Nash equilibrium**. A set of strategies constitutes a Nash equilibrium if, given the strategies of the other players, no player can improve his payoff by unilaterally changing his own strategy. The Nash equilibrium represents a situation in which every player is doing the best he or she can given what other players are doing.

In the game presented in Table 8.1, the Nash equilibrium strategies for the two players are as follows: for *Time* it is S and for *Newsweek* it is S. Would either player have an incentive to change the strategy? The answer "no" means that the equilibrium is a Nash equilibrium.

There can be more than one Nash equilibrium in a game. In fact, some games have many equilibria, and others, none. Suppose you are talking on the telephone with a business associate and the connection is broken. Do you call your associate or do you wait for her to call you? If you call, you might get only a busy signal because she is also calling. If you wait, neither of you might call. What is best for you depends on what your associate does, and vice versa. There are two Nash equilibria to this problem. In one, you call and she does not; in the other, she calls and you do not. Even though there are two Nash equilibria, the problem is that without some rule of behavior, you may end up with a busy signal or no call. You could prevent this problem by announcing at the beginning of each phone conversation who will call if the connection is broken. Of course, this is very inefficient. No one wants to make such an announcement at the beginning of each call. What arises then, is an efficient way to move toward the Nash equilibrium, the so-called **convention**. A typical convention is that the person who called originally calls again.[4]

The Prisoner's Dilemma

The prisoner's dilemma illustrates situations in which interaction can cause the players to select an inferior strategy. Suppose two firms must decide whether to devote more resources to advertising. When a firm in any given industry advertises its product, its demand increases for two reasons. First, people who had not used that type of product before learn about it, and some will buy it. Second, other people who already consume a different brand of the same product may switch brands. The first effect boosts sales for the industry as a whole; the second redistributes existing sales within the industry.

Let's consider the cigarette industry as an example. Assume that the payoffs in Table 8.2 illustrate the possible actions that two firms might undertake and the results of those actions. The top left rectangle represents the payoffs, or results, if both A and B advertise; the bottom left shows the payoffs when A advertises but B does not; the top right shows the payoffs when B advertises but A does not; and the bottom right shows the payoffs when neither advertises.

If firm A can earn higher profits by advertising than by not advertising, whether or not firm B advertises, then firm A will surely advertise. Firm A compares the left side of

Table 8.2

Prisoner's Dilemma. The options available to each firm are to advertise or not advertise. In this case, both firms advertise even though both would be better off not advertising.

	Firm A	
	Advertise	Not Advertise
Firm B Advertise	Firm A 70 Firm B 80	Firm A 40 Firm B 100
Not Advertise	Firm A 100 Firm B 50	Firm A 80 Firm B 90

the matrix to the right side and sees that it earns more by advertising no matter what firm B does. If A advertises, then A earns 70 if B also advertises and only 40 if A does not advertise but B does. If B does not advertise, then A earns 100 by advertising and only 80 by not advertising. The dominant strategy for firm A is to advertise. The dominant strategy for firm B also is to advertise. Firm B will earn 80 by advertising and 50 by not advertising if A advertises. Firm B will earn 100 by advertising but only 90 by not advertising if A does not advertise. Notice that both firms would be better off if neither advertised; firm A would earn 80 instead of 70, and firm B would earn 90 instead of 80. Yet the firms cannot afford to not advertise because they would lose more if the other firm advertised and they didn't. This is the dilemma part of the prisoner's dilemma.

The choice to advertise is not the best for either firm in isolation. But the game theory shows that the firms have to take into account the actions of others and in so doing actually do not select the best option. They are in a dilemma.

Consider another dilemma, a price war. Two competing firms must decide whether to charge a higher price or a lower price, as shown in Table 8.3.

If both firms charge high prices, they earn more than if they both choose low prices. On the other hand, if one firm charges a high price and the other firm undercuts that price, the lower-priced firm will gain all the other firm's customers and thus earn higher profits at the expense of the competitor. In a one-period play of the game, the Nash equilibrium strategies are for each firm to charge the low price. The reason is as follows: If firm B charges a high price, firm A's best choice is to charge a low price, since 30 units of profits are better than the 10 units it would earn if A charged the high price. Similarly, if firm B charges the low price, firm A's best choice is to charge the low price, since

Table 8.3

Pricing Strategies. Each firm is better off charging a low price if the other chooses a high price. The dilemma is that they each select the low price which is the worst outcome.

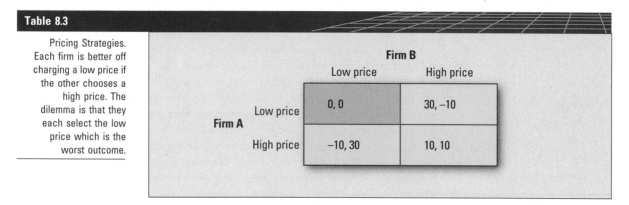

	Firm B	
	Low price	High price
Firm A Low price	0, 0	30, −10
High price	−10, 30	10, 10

0 units of profits are preferred to the 10 units of losses that would result if A charged the high price. Similar arguments hold from firm B's perspective. Firm A is always better off charging the low price regardless of what firm B does, and B is always better off charging the low price regardless of what A does.

The outcome of the game is that both firms charge low prices and earn profits of zero. Clearly, profits are less than the firms would get if they charged high prices. The Nash equilibrium outcome is inferior for the firms.

Standards: Cooperation Game

Many households are holding off buying high definition televisions and associated equipment because they are not sure which standard will occur. Similarly, until February 2008, many manufacturers were debating whether to use HD or Blue-Ray technology. Toshiba, the maker of HD, conceded defeat and left the market to Blue-Ray. Suppose there are two firms considering whether to introduce new equipment but do not know which technology to use. This is represented in the following normal representation of Table 8.4:

Table 8.4

The Cooperation Game. The two players are better off agreeing to a standard or a similar technology. Without that, the solution is the possibility of selecting a result that is not a Nash equilibrium.

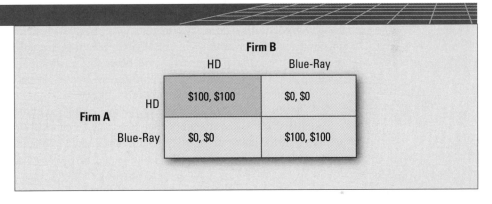

If each firm produces equipment using HD, each firm will earn profits of $100. Similarly, if each firm produces equipment using Blue-Ray, each firm will earn $100. However, if the two firms produce equipment using different technologies, each firm will earn zero. What will each firm do? If firm A thinks firm B will use HD, it should use HD as well. If firm A thinks firm B will use Blue-Ray, firm A should do the same thing.

This game has two Nash equilibria; the firms do the same thing—both use HD or both use Blue-Ray. How do they get to a Nash equilibrium without colluding? The firms might lobby the government to create a standard for the protection of the consumer: Everyone must use HD or everyone must use Blue-Ray. What actually occurred is that Sony (Blue-Ray) was able to enlist more market than Toshiba (HD). You can see here why firms call for standards—not necessarily to benefit the consumer but as a means for them to reach the profit-maximizing equilibrium and to avoid being driven out of the market.

Repeated Games: Cheating and Punishment

When a game is played again and again, players receive payoffs during each repetition of the game. Suppose the firms play the game in Table 8.4 day after day, week after week, forever. Thus, we are considering a situation in which the firms compete every period, not just once. When firms repeatedly face a normal form representation as in Table 8.4, it is possible for them to "collude" without fear of being cheated on. They do this by using automatic penalties or **trigger strategies**, strategies that are contingent on the past plays of players in a game. A player who adopts a trigger strategy continues to choose the same action until some other player takes an action that "triggers" a different action by the first player.

Collusion occurs when two or more firms agree to fix prices or otherwise reduce competition. Punishment can be used to support collusion and prevent cheating. Suppose firm A and firm B agree to charge the high price. They also agree that if either one cheats and charges the low price, the other player will "punish" the cheater by charging the low price from then on. Thus, if firm A cheats, firm B charges the low price from that point on. If neither firm cheats on the collusive agreement, each firm will earn $10 each period forever. But if one firm selects the high price and the other firm cheats by charging the low price, the cheating firm will earn a one-period profit of $30 but earn $0 from then on.

The benefit of cheating today on the collusive agreement is earning $30 instead of $10 today, while the cost is getting $0 rather than $10 every period from then on. If the present value of the cost of cheating exceeds the one-time benefit of cheating, it does not pay for a firm to cheat, and high prices can be sustained.

Another trigger strategy is called **tit-for-tat**, a variation of the eye-for-an-eye rule of behavior: Do to others as they have done to you. The strategy has the participants cooperate in the first period and from then on mimic the rival's action from the previous period. Tit-for-tat is as clear and simple as you can get. It never initiates cheating, but it never lets cheating go unpunished. The problem with tit-for-tat is that the slightest possibility of misperception can result in a complete breakdown. Any mistake echoes back and forth. One side punishes the other for a defection, and this sets off a chain reaction. The rival responds to the punishment by hitting back. This response calls for a second punishment. At no point does the strategy accept a punishment without hitting back. What tit-for-tat lacks is a way of saying "enough is enough."

Suppose that two competitors, Big Roy and Crazy Bob, are matching each other's price in a tit-for-tat strategy. They start out peacefully, matching the prices.

Round	Big Roy	Crazy Bob
1	$100	$100
2	$100	$100
3	$100	$100

Suppose that in round 4 Big Roy misinterprets Crazy Bob's actions as a price cut.

Round	Big Roy	Crazy Bob
3	$100	$100
4	$100	$100M misperceived as $95
5	$90	$100
6	$100	$85
7	$80	$100
8	$100	$75

The single misunderstanding, $95M for $100M, echoes back and forth. In round 5 the misperception of a $90 price is punished with an $85 price in round 6. The tit-for-tat strategy indicates **commitment**, but its dynamic characteristic creates problems for misperceptions.

Another trigger strategy is the **scorched-earth policy**. When Western Pacific attempted to acquire the publishing company Houghton Mifflin, the publishing house responded by threatening to empty its stable of authors. John Kenneth Galbraith, Archibald MacLeish, Arthur Schlesinger Jr., and others threatened to find new publishers if Houghton Mifflin were acquired. Western Pacific withdrew its bid, and Houghton Mifflin remained independent. The scorched-earth policy is one where an action, say cheating on a collusive agreement, brings forth actions that destroy everything of value.

The scorched-earth policy is one example of devices game theorists call commitments. A strategic move is designed to alter the beliefs and actions of others in a direction

Business Insight

Game Theory and Weight Loss

Game theory is being used for many strategic situations these days. ABC's newsmagazine *Primetime* attempted to see if game theory could help where famous diet programs had failed. Barry Nalebuff was enlisted to develop a game that would effectively induce people to lose weight. He designed a game in which one team received positive reinforcement to lose weight. The other team was told they would have their plump forms broadcast on a Jumbotron at a major league baseball game if they didn't lose 15 pounds in two months. In game theory, this is applying a credible threat: The risk of humiliation is thought to be more of an incentive to lose weight than long-term worries about health. When the results came in, all but two of the threatened team members had lost 15 pounds.

While the game did work, so did the positive reinforcement approach. In fact, the positive reinforcement worked better than the credible threat because all members met the target weight loss. Perhaps the publicity of being on *Primetime* was sufficient motivation and thus messed up the comparison of the credible threat of the game to the reinforcement approach, but there did not seem to be a strong conclusion that the game theory approach was better.

Perhaps a more appropriate game structure would have been to create a credible commitment, a loss that would have to be paid if the goal was not met. Professor Richard McKenzie used this approach by contracting with a friend to pay the friend $500 if he had not lost 9 pounds at the end of 10 weeks. He was successful and found it so useful that he has employed the approach to "force" him to do other things he really did not have a taste to accomplish.

Source: Richard B. McKenzie, "Dieting for Dollars: An Economist Explains His Weight-loss Plan." Friday, January 4, 2008.

favorable to yourself. The distinguishing feature is that the move purposefully limits your freedom of action. The lack of freedom can have strategic value. It changes other players' expectations about your future responses, and you can turn this to your advantage.

Credible Threats

Collusion is easier when few firms rather than many are involved. If there are n firms in the industry, each firm must monitor the others so that the total amount of monitoring that must go on is $n (n - 1)$. As the number of firms increases (as n increases), the total number of monitors required grows very rapidly. If there are 2 firms, then only 2 monitors are needed; if there are 10 firms, 90 monitors are required. It does not take many firms before the cost of monitoring exceeds the gains to colluding. Under these circumstances, the monitoring threat used to sustain the collusive outcome is not credible, and the collusion fails. This is why collusion often occurs when there is a single enforcer—one player who is able to essentially monitor everyone. For the oil cartel—the Organization of Oil Exporting Countries (OPEC or (OAPEC)—Saudi Arabia acts as the enforcer because of its huge supplies of oil. If one nation cheats by producing more than its quota, Saudi Arabia can open the floodgates and drive oil prices down. For organized crime it was the "families" in specific geographic areas that were the enforcers. For the drug cartels it is one family or one individual who acts as the enforcer. The enforcers make the credible threat that if cheating occurs, penalties will be severe.

Brand Name and Other Sunk Cost Investments

An economist was working for a bank in Los Angeles and had flown to Seattle to attend a 7:00 A.M. meeting with a private equity company regarding some mutual financial investments. The economist arrived the night before. The next morning he got up and dressed realizing only then that he had forgotten a tie. He had his dark suit, white shirts, but no tie. What to do? Only one thing, go to the meeting with shirt buttoned up but without a tie (think Hollywood and Don Johnson of *Miami Vice*).[5] Walking to the meeting, he ran across a street vendor just outside the Nordstrom building, with a table of ties. To make a long story short, all the economist wanted was for the tie to last a few hours without bleeding colors onto the shirt. He purchased a tie for $20 and had a successful meeting.

Could the vendor have sold the economist a terrible product? Yes, of course. The economist would have come storming back after the meeting to get his money back and get compensated for the ruined shirt and the vendor would have been gone. Had the economist been able to purchase the tie at Nordstrom for $75 rather than the $20 he paid, would he have done it? Probably because he would not have been concerned that Nordstrom would sell a shoddy product. Nordstrom would have been there when the meeting ended. The lesson is that if your firm desires to be a going concern, that is, infinitely lived, it does not pay to cheat customers if the one-time gain is more than offset by lost future sales. Is it possible that a bad product could be sold by Nordstrom? Yes, there is always a small chance of flaws or other problems with merchandise. So Nordstrom has solved that problem by guaranteeing satisfaction. If you don't like their product, you bring it back with no questions asked. Expenditures that ensure the seller will be around to back up quality promises change the game from one of a one-period game to an infinitely repeated game.

Sequential Games

A game in which players make decisions in sequence rather than simultaneously is typically represented in **extensive form** as in Figure 8.1. The circles are called *decision nodes,* and each circle indicates that at that stage of the game the particular player must choose a strategy. The single point (denoted A) at which all of the lines originate is the beginning of the game, and the numbers at the ends of the branches represent the payoffs at the end of the game. As in simultaneous-move games, each player's payoff depends not only on his or her action but on the action of the other player as well. There is a difference, however, as can be illustrated by comparing the extensive form of Figure 8.1 and Table 8.5.

Two firms face a choice as to investing in a new technology. The outcome of choices is shown in Table 8.5. What is A's best choice? A will make the most by undertaking a new investment no matter what B does. Firm B looks at the payoffs and knows what A will do. B then says not undertaking a new investment earns me $25, which is better than $10 from making the new investment. So, A ends up with $20 and B with $25.

Now, assume that A goes first, selecting either to invest in the new technology or not. That choice is followed by B who can select yes or no. The extensive form representation is shown in Figure 8.1. If A selects yes, then B can select yes, which yields him a payoff of $10, or select no, which yields a payoff $25. B would select no if A selects yes and A's payoff would be $20. If A selects no, then B says yes is better than no, $15 compared to $8. In this case A's payoff would be $30. So, if A goes first and B second, then A selects not to invest. Notice that A has a first mover advantage—going first the payoff is $30, whereas going simultaneously the payoff for A is $20.

Converting Simultaneous to Sequential

In the example of the street vendor and Nordstrom, it was noted that a firm wants the customer to think of the interaction with the firm as an infinitely repeated game. Expenditures

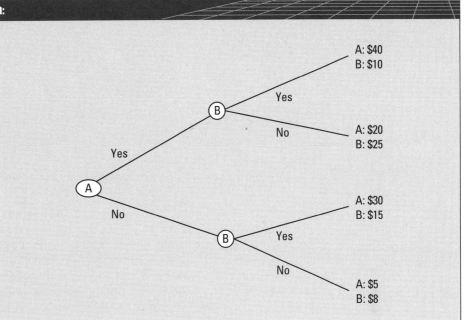

FIGURE 8.1 Extensive Form:

When one player makes a decision before the other has to make a decision, the game is called a sequential game. The circles with letters are decision nodes, indicating who has to make a decision. The lines show the possible decisions. The payoffs are indicated at the end of the lines.

that ensure the seller will be around to back up quality promises change the game from that of a one-period game to an infinitely repeated game.

Picture a rivalry between two microchip manufacturers, Intel and Advanced Micro Devices (AMD). In the absence of any unconditional moves, the two companies simultaneously choose their strategies. Each company must decide between a low or high level of marketing and advertising (see Table 8.6). Each side has two strategies, so there are four possible outcomes. Both sides regard a high-advertising race as the worst scenario. This is payoff 1 for each firm. Each side's second-worst outcome is pursuing low advertising while the other goes all out. AMD likes best the situation in which it pursues high advertising and Intel follows with a low effort. For Intel, the best situation is when both sides make low effort. Low effort is the dominant strategy for Intel. Because AMD can anticipate Intel's action, the best response for AMD is high advertising. The equilibrium of the game is the top right cell where Intel gets its second-worst payoff.

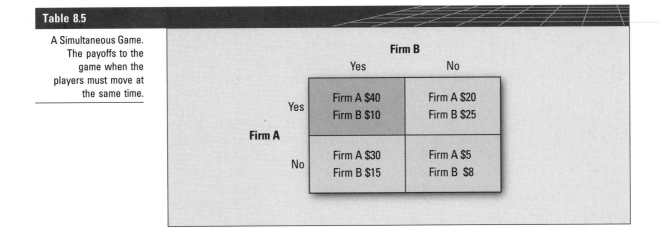

Table 8.5

A Simultaneous Game. The payoffs to the game when the players must move at the same time.

Table 8.6
Sequential Game

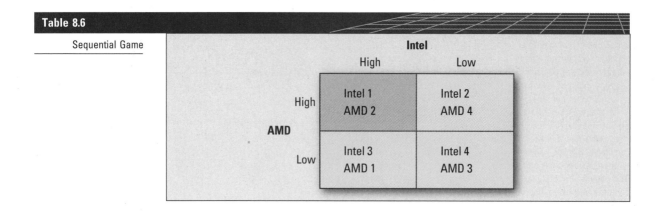

To improve the situation, Intel needs to make a strategic move. Suppose that Intel *preempts*. It announces it will pursue an extensive amount of advertising and marketing (the high choice) before AMD reaches its decision. This turns the simultaneous game into a sequential game. If Intel pursues low advertising, AMD responds with high and Intel's payoff is 2. If Intel pursues high advertising, AMD responds with low and Intel's payoff is 3. Therefore, Intel should announce high and expect AMD to respond low. This is the equilibrium of the sequential game. It gives Intel a payoff of 3, more than the 2 it got in the simultaneous game. Commitment to an action or a response rule transforms an otherwise simultaneous game into a sequential game. Although the payoffs remain unchanged, a game played with simultaneous moves in one case and sequential moves in another can have dramatically different outcomes.

The Ultimatum Game

You are an economist who has been out of town arriving back on Christmas Eve.[6] Your children are upset that the house is not decorated, so you run out to buy a tree. You come to a tree lot where the owner is tossing trees into a big bonfire. You figure you can get a great tree at a very low price. You find a 12-foot spruce with a price tag of $100 on it. You say to the proprietor, "I want this 12-foot spruce and I will give you $5 for it." You figure the owner is better off selling it for $5 than burning it. Does the proprietor accept or reject the offer? The proprietor responds, "give me $50 and you can have the tree. If not, I will burn it." What should you do? If you believe the proprietor, then the lower amount will be rejected and you will get nothing. Given the proprietor's strategy, your best choice is to give him $50, since that action gives you a tree. And given that you offer the proprietor $50, his best choice is to accept the offer. Thus, one Nash equilibrium outcome of this sequential bargaining process yields a tree for you and $50 for the proprietor. But since you are an economist, you might figure $5 is better than nothing, so you stick with your guns and offer just $5. The proprietor picks up the tree and tosses it on the bonfire. What was wrong with your strategy?

You thought the proprietor's threat to be an empty or a noncredible one. The problem was that this threat was credible. The only way you might have known this threat was credible was to remember that people tend to look at bargaining situations as requiring a "fair" solution, and fair in most cases means something where each party gets about the same amount. The ultimatum game indicates that in bargaining situations people have in mind a division that is "fair" to them. If the share they are offered is not fair, they reject the offer even though they end up with zero.

Consider the typical purchase of a car. The consumer has done research and has learned that the dealer's costs for the car the consumer wants is $20,000. The consumer values this car at $25,000. The dealer and the consumer are, therefore, bargaining over the $5,000 differential between the dealer's costs and the consumer's valuation. Suppose the consumer makes the following take-it-or-leave-it offer to the dealer: "I'll pay you $20,001 for the car. If you don't accept it, I will go elsewhere." If the dealer believes the consumer's threat, he will accept the offer figuring that a marginal gain of $1 is better than nothing.

Suppose the order of the bargaining is reversed, so that the dealer tells the consumer: "Another buyer wants the car. Pay me $24,999, or I'll sell it to the other customer." If the buyer believes the dealer's threat, then buying the car means that the consumer is gaining $1 since it costs $1 less than the consumer's valuation.

But if there is no reason for either party to know the threat is credible, the likely result is that the parties will split the $5,000 about equally. It is a "fair" split.

Risk

Game theory can become quite complex. Many of these complexities are beyond what might be useful to managers and to us, but one additional topic we should discuss is risk. Most business decisions have to be made without perfect knowledge; managers and entrepreneurs take risks. There is a risk that some level of profits won't occur or some risk regarding what a rival will do in response to an action. A seller does not know how a potential buyer values a good or service and so does not know how high a price can be driven without losing the sale. An employer does not know the ability of a new employee at the time of hiring. A supplier might not know the costs of providing a manufacturing firm with certain inputs before agreeing to supply them. How is it possible to make a decision without knowing exactly what consequences will follow?

The first component of a decision in the face of uncertainty is knowledge of the relative likelihood of the alternative possible outcomes. The process begins by listing all the possible outcomes that could follow a decision and assigning probabilities to them. Then, the **expected value** of the outcome can be calculated. Suppose, for example, a coin is flipped. If it comes up heads, you win $100; if tails, nothing. The probability of each outcome is one-half. What is the expected value of this event? The average payoff would be approximately $50 because the toss would come up heads about half the time. The expected value from the single coin toss is the probability that the event occurs weighted by the payoff if it occurs plus the probability that the event does not occur weighted by the payoff if it does not occur. In the example, the expected value is

$$(\$100 \times 0.5) + (\$0 \times 0.5) = \$50$$

Consider the situation experienced by the small upstart Sun Country Airlines. Sun Country's transformation from a charter airline to a regularly scheduled carrier became official June 1. Six days later, a Northwest executive distributed an electronic memo to Northwest personnel stating, "Effective immediately, all parts support to Sun Country is terminated until further notice." Sun Country stated that the move was a competitive attack against the airline, a slap against a tradition that is meant to help all carriers by keeping air travel an attractive mode of transportation. The executive maintained that the industry would be rife with long flight delays if carriers didn't help each other obtain parts on short notice. Officials at two other major U.S. airlines also said that collaboration on parts and tools was widespread, intended for the good of the entire industry. The cost of keeping sufficient hardware inventories in every city would be enormous. Within a few days, at least seven Sun Country flights experienced multi-hour delays in Minneapolis-St. Paul and Detroit because the airline had to scramble for parts or tools from sources in other cities. Sun Country executives dejectedly exclaimed that if Northwest could disadvantage them and their customers were inconvenienced, they saw that as a win for Northwest.

What did Sun Country do wrong? Suppose the situation facing Northwest and Sun Country is as illustrated in Figure 8.2. Sun Country must decide whether to enter the airline market. If Sun Country enters and Northwest does not respond, Sun Country will experience a substantial gain, say $60 million. But is it likely that Northwest will not respond? To make its entry decision, Sun Country must look ahead and reason back. It knows that if it converts from the commuter to the full-fledged airline Northwest will experience a substantial reduction in business, say $50 million. Northwest loses less business, only about $20 million, if it refuses to provide equipment on loan. Sun Country can reason that Northwest will respond to Sun Country's entry by breaking with tradition and not loaning the equipment.

Of course, the answer provided here depends on the assumptions made about the end of the game and future effects. For instance, if the cost to Northwest is larger than depicted here because in response still other airlines refuse to deal with Northwest, then that factor would have to be accounted for. The point is, however, that in a sequential-game situation the players must look ahead and reason back to the present. Sun Country did not do this, assuming that what had occurred in the past would continue.

Notice also that the sequential game provides an opportunity to consider the decisions as real options. Perhaps Sun Country could have made a series of steps leading to its conversion to a mainstream airline, thereby testing Northwest's response prior to investing the entire amount without having a full understanding of the response.

Suppose Sun Country is not certain what Northwest will do but believes there is a 50–50 chance that Northwest will retaliate. Sun Country then figures an expected profit from entering of

0.5(−$50 million) + 0.5($60 million) = −$25 million + $30 million = $5 million

In this case, Sun Country enters the market, since the expected profit of $5 million exceeds the expected profit of $0 from not entering. A change in beliefs can change that outcome. Suppose that Sun Country believes there is a 75 percent probability that Northwest will retaliate and only a 25 percent probability that it will not retaliate. Then the expected value or profit for Sun Country from entering is

0.75($−50 million) + 0.25($60 million) = −$37.5 million + $15 million = −$22.5 million

Entry does not occur.

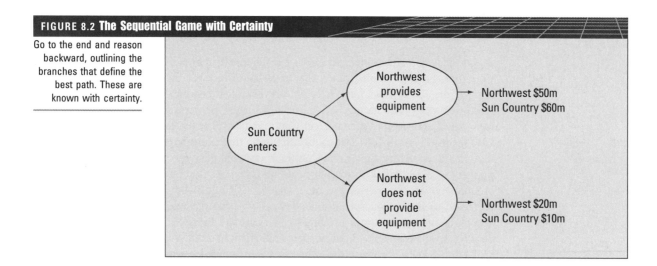

FIGURE 8.2 The Sequential Game with Certainty

Go to the end and reason backward, outlining the branches that define the best path. These are known with certainty.

Sun Country enters

Northwest provides equipment → Northwest $50m / Sun Country $60m

Northwest does not provide equipment → Northwest $20m / Sun Country $10m

Obviously, the application of the probabilities of Northwest's response is extremely important. Where does Sun Country get them? They come from a careful analysis of the position of the opponent. Sun Country might know that Northwest's reputation has value in other markets and that the airline has relations with suppliers, the government, and customers. In this case the probability of 0.75 that Northwest would retaliate would be reasonable. Or Sun Country might know that the new manager of Northwest is unlikely to devote funds to retaliating against Sun Country. In this case the probability of retaliation would be very low. One thing that Sun Country might have gained by pursuing the entry in stages is knowledge of the probabilities of certain actions by Northwest Airlines.

How people respond to risk depends on how risk-averse they are. If you were offered the choice of receiving $50 for sure and having a 50 percent chance of receiving $100 and a 50 percent chance of receiving nothing, which would you pick? The expected value is $50, but either $100 or $0 could occur. Most people would take the sure bet, $50, because it is a certain outcome. People tend to prefer a certain outcome to a gamble with the same expected return. In economics terminology, people who prefer the sure thing over the bet when the expected return is the same are risk-averse. Suppose the amount of money offered "for sure" declines. How low would this sum have to go before you preferred the gamble to the certain outcome? The more risk-averse you are, the further the amount would have to be lowered.

The difference between $50 and the amount at which you would take the gamble is called the **risk premium**. If, for example, you switch from taking the sure thing to taking the gamble at $40, you have a $10 risk premium. Your risk premium is a measure of how cautious you are toward this particular gamble. In any situation, the risk premium is defined to be the difference between the expected return of the gamble and the amount of money that, if received for sure, the individual regards as equivalent to the gamble. The risk premium is the answer to the question: How much money would you be prepared to give up to rid yourself of this risk? The size of the risk premium depends on the psychology of the individual—how cautious or adventurous the person is. It also depends on the likelihood of the event's occurring and on the size of the potential loss. A given individual has different risk premiums toward different risks, and different individuals facing the same risk can have different risk premiums.

Risk aversion and risk premiums have been measured by observing people's behavior: the amount of insurance people purchase, the types of crops farmers plant, the types of cars people purchase, the occupations people choose, and so on. Psychologists find that women, older people, married people, and firstborns tend more than others to avoid risks. Commission salespeople have been found to be less risk-averse than average, while public-sector employees and bankers are more risk-averse than average. Studies have found that CEOs are more willing to take risks than lower-level managers, that managers in small firms are more willing to take risks than managers in large firms, and that managers with a graduate degree are more willing to take risks than managers with just a bachelor's degree or high school education.[7] The rich and successful are consistently found to be less risk-averse than those who are less rich and successful.

Suppose a consumer regularly purchases a particular brand of detergent and a new detergent is being introduced. A risk-averse consumer prefers a sure thing to an uncertain prospect of equal expected value. Thus, if the consumer expects the new detergent to work just as well as the one regularly chosen, then the new one will not be purchased. There is risk associated with using a new product. The consumer prefers the sure thing—the current brand—to the risky prospect of a new product.

Firms recognize the risk aversion of consumers and attempt to overcome it, say by offering a free trial or by a lower price. A new detergent may have a lower price than the existing brand. The firm may offer free samples to induce the consumer to try the new brand. Advertisements may attempt to acquaint the consumer with the new product so that it won't seem so new and unknown.

Risk aversion can also explain why well-known chains often do better than local stores. A consumer driving through the town, knowing nothing about the local stores, sees a brand with which she is familiar. Even if the local store offered a better-quality product than the national chain, the chain has the advantage of being better known—of providing less risk.

Summing Up

Game theory is a way of thinking about strategic situations. Sometimes in situations where choices depend on what others might do, intuition leads to the wrong strategy. Game theory might provide an offset to the misplaced intuition by forcing strategists to put themselves in the shoes of others at the same time they walk in theirs. This brief chapter on game theory has barely touched the surface of what is now a large field of study. But, it does provide some insights into often encountered types of games. Prisoner's dilemmas, credible commitments, credible threats, and sunk costs are situations and terms with which everyone should be familiar.

CASE *review*

NutraSweet

Holland Sweetener failed to anticipate Monsanto's reaction. With the expiration of NutraSweet's European patent in 1987, Holland attacked the European market, but Monsanto fought back with aggressive pricing. Before Holland's entry, aspartame prices had been $70 per pound. After Holland's entry, the prices fell to about $22 per pound. At this low price, Holland was losing money. The only reason Holland Sweetener survived was that it convinced the European courts to impose antidumping duties on Monsanto.

Holland Sweetener was being courted by Coke and Pepsi to enter the U.S. market, but it failed to look at the game in terms of how Coke and Pepsi saw it. Neither Coke nor Pepsi had any real desire to switch over to generic aspartame, since neither company wanted to be the first to take the NutraSweet logo off its products. If only one switched, the other would most certainly gain market share. What Coke and Pepsi wanted was a lower price. This they received; new contracts with Monsanto led to savings for the two companies of $200 million a year. Holland Sweetener's added value in the game was zero. It had no distinct capability. But its entry into the game was worth a lot to Coke and Pepsi.[8] Holland Sweetener could have used that value to create value for itself. Before entering a game, assess the value you add to the game. In other words, define your distinctive capability and consider the imitability of that capability. If you have a high added value, you'll do well in the game. But if you don't have much added value, you won't do well unless you can figure out whether anyone stands to gain from your entry. Those players may be willing to pay you to play. If none of these conditions hold, you should ask whether it makes sense to play the game.

Summary

1. A game is defined to be a situation of strategic interdependence. Its components are players, the players' perceptions, the rules to be followed, and the limits or boundaries of the game.
2. The rules of a game may be defined by laws or government definitions, by societal convention, or by the actors themselves.

3. The boundaries of a game define where the game is played—locally, nationally, globally, and so on. A sequential game is one in which players take turns. Each player must look ahead and reason back.

4. A simultaneous game is one in which all players make their moves at the same time. Each player will begin by asking whether there are dominant strategies or dominated strategies.

5. A dominant strategy is a strategy that is best for player A no matter what player B does.

6. A dominated strategy is a strategy that is not best for a player.

7. A Nash equilibrium strategy is one in which players have no incentive to change.

8. Nash equilibrium in one-shot, simultaneous-move games often shows that resulting payoffs are sometimes lower than would arise if players colluded.

9. In games that are infinitely repeated, the use of penalties or trigger strategies enables players to enter and enforce collusive agreements.

10. When the interaction among parties is for a known time period, problems with cheating in the last period can unravel cooperative agreements that would have been supported by trigger strategies in infinitely repeated games.

11. In sequential-move games, one must determine whether the threats to induce a particular outcome in the game are credible.

12. A prisoner's dilemma is a game in which both players have a dominant strategy and end up in an inefficient equilibrium. The only ways to avoid a prisoner's dilemma result are commitment and repeated transactions.

13. Commitment includes sunk costs—actions such as guarantees, warranties, and expenditures on advertising. Commitments also include credible actions, such as the willingness to enter into a price war.

14. Cooperation may be a result of repeated transactions.

15. There is often an incentive to cheat on a cooperative agreement. Enforcement mechanisms such as triggers are used to restrict cheating. Tit-for-tat is an enforcement mechanism whereby what one does to you, you return. The scorched-earth policy is an enforcement policy whereby all other options are made untenable.

16. Uncertainty is introduced into game theory by placing probabilities on the various potential actions and deriving the expected actions or expected value of actions.

Key Terms

Game theory	Nash equilibrium
Players	Convention
Strategies	Trigger strategies
Payoffs	Tit-for-tat
Simultaneous-move	Commitment
Sequential-move	Scorched-earth policy
One-period game	Extensive form
Repeated game	Expected value
Normal form representation	Risk premium
Dominant strategy	

Exercises

1. Suppose you are the owner-operator of a gas station in a small town. Over the past 20 years, you and your rival have successfully kept prices at a very high level. You recently learned that your rival is retiring and closing his station in two weeks. What should you do today?

2. Which of the following might create first mover advantages?

a. Maxwell House introduces the first freeze-dried coffee.
b. A consortium of U.S. firms introduces the first high definition television.
c. Wal-Mart opens a store in Nome, Alaska.
d. Merck introduces Arogout, the first effective medical treatment for ulcers.

3. In a situation that occurs only once, if you advertise and your rival advertises, you will each earn $5 million in profits. If neither of you advertises, your rival will make $4 million and you will make $2 million. If you advertise and your rival does not, you will make $10 million and your rival will make $3 million. If your rival advertises and you do not, you will make $1 million and your rival will make $3 million.

   a. Set up the situation in a normal form.
   b. Do you have a strategy that you will choose no matter what your rival does?
   c. Is there a strategy your rival will choose no matter what you do?
   d. What is the solution or equilibrium?
   e. How much would you be willing to pay your rival not to advertise?

4. You and your rival must simultaneously decide what price to advertise in the weekly newspaper. If you each charge a low price, you each earn zero profits. If you each charge a high price, you each earn profits of $3. If you charge different prices, the one charging the higher price loses $5 and the one charging the lower price makes $5.

   a. Find the equilibrium when there are no repeated transactions.
   b. Now suppose there are repeated transactions. If the interest rate is 10 percent, what will be the outcome?

5. You are considering entering a market serviced by a monopolist. You currently earn $0 economic profits, while the monopolist earns $5. If you enter the market and the monopolist engages in a price war, you will lose $5 and the monopolist will earn $1. If the monopolist doesn't engage in a price war, you will each earn profits of $2.
   There are two possible solutions or equilibria. What are they?

6. Firm 1 and Firm 2 are the only ones that produce and sell good X. Each of them is trying to decide (independently and simultaneously) how much to spend on advertising. Sales and profits of each firm depend on its own advertising strategy, and also on its competitor's. Each firm can either choose a low level of expenditures on advertising or a high one; if both choose low, profits for each firm will be 60 (millions), and if both choose high, each of them will make 20 (millions). However, if one chooses low and the other chooses high, the one that chooses low makes 40 (millions) and the other one 95 (millions). Using the Nash equilibrium concept, determine how many and what are the Nash equilibria.

7. Consider the following game between player 1, who chooses among strategies U, M, and D, and player 2, who chooses among strategies A, B, and C. Why is this normal form representation different from others in the chapter? The most reasonable prediction in this game is what?

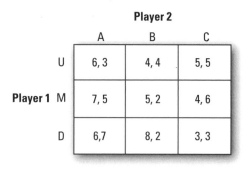

		Player 2		
		A	B	C
	U	6, 3	4, 4	5, 5
Player 1	M	7, 5	5, 2	4, 6
	D	6,7	8, 2	3, 3

8. Convert the following simultaneous-move game to a sequential-move game letting firm A go first. Demonstrate the value of a first mover. Demonstrate the value of a second mover.

	Strategy	**Firm B**	
		Yes	No
Firm A	Yes	Firm A $20 / Firm B $10	Firm A $20 / Firm B $15
	No	Firm A $20 / Firm B $15	Firm A $5 / Firm B $8

9. Convert the normal form in Exercise 8 to a sequential-move game letting firm B go first. What is the value of going first? What is the value of going second?

10. What is the equilibrium/equilibria of the following games?

Player 1

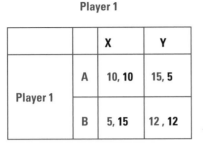

		X	Y
Player 1	A	10, 10	15, 5
	B	5, 15	12, 12

Player 2

		X	Y
Player 1	A	0, 0	0, 1
	B	2, 0	0, 0

elects not to enter, it earns profits of $0 and the monopolist maintains its profit of $10M. If the competitor enters, the monopolist must either accommodate the entry or fight. If the monopolist accommodates, both firms earn $5M. If the monopolist fights, both firms lose $5M. The game is represented by an extensive representation. What is the equilibrium?

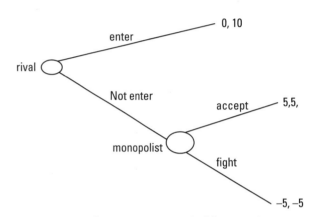

11. Two firms are involved in developing a new technology that will allow consumers to provide the most incredibly clear picture yet devised on all video sources. Given the risks, compatibility of the technologies is very important. Firm Digi-View is far advanced in developing its *RemoteHD* technology. WebView has been expanding into the Internet arena with its incompatible product, *WebHD*. The two companies agree that if they both adopt the same technology, they each may gross $200M from the developing industry. If they adopt different technologies, consumers will purchase neither product, leading to a gross of $0. Retooling one's factory to make the competing (nonproprietary) technology would cost WebView $100M and DigiView $250M. Their production decisions must be made simultaneously. Set up the above scenario as a normal form (simultaneous) game.
What is the equilibrium outcome?

12. A firm is quite happy monopolizing its industry with profits of $10M. A potential competitor considers entering the industry. If the competitor

13. Have you ever been in a prisoner's dilemma situation? Explain. Did you get out of it? Explain

14. In Table 8.1 the prisoner's dilemma of two cigarette producers with respect to increased advertising is discussed. Explain how the two firms could emerge from the dilemma?

15. What is a Nash equilibrium? How might it apply to business strategy?

16. Ludwig von Mises had this to say about game theory in 1949. Game theory had been invented only a few years before. "*There is not the slightest analogy between playing games and the conduct of business within a market society. The card player wins money by outsmarting his antagonist. The businessman makes money by supplying customers with goods they want to acquire....He who interprets the conduct of business as trickery is on the wrong path.*"
(Ludwig von Mises, *Human Action*. (London: William Hodge, 1949), p. 116).
Explain what von Mises meant.

CHAPTER NOTES

1. Michael V. Copeland, "The Game Maven of New Haven," *Strategy + Business,* www.strategy-business.com/press/freearticle/07108?pg=3&tid=230, accessed May 5, 2008. Steve Hannaford, "Soft Drinks: Suppliers and Vendors," *Oligopoly Watch: The Latest Maneuvers of the New Oligopolies and What They Mean,* July 11, 2003, www.oligopolywatch.com/2003/07/11.html, accessed May 5, 2008.

2. When students at Princeton were playing poker in the early 1930s, they were being observed by a new member of the faculty, mathematician Johann von Neuman, who then captured their actions in mathematical models. The economist Oskar Morgenstern convinced Neuman that his mathematical structure would help explain economic behavior. The result of their observations was the book *Theory of Games and Economic Behavior* (Princeton, NJ: Princeton University Press, 1947).

3. "I use game theoretic equations in business and in life, not with the expectation that all outcomes will be optimal, but rather that bad decisions will be minimized." See William B. Hakes, "Readers Report, Game Theory Wasn't Meant to Be a Forecasting Tool," *Business Week,* July 13, 1998, p. 9. The chief financial officer of Merck responded to an interviewer's question about Merck's acquisition of Medco and its effects on the attitudes of Merck's competitors by stating that game theory forces you to see a business situation from two perspectives: yours and your competitor's. Nancy A. Nichols, "Scientific Management at Merck," *Harvard Business Review,* 72 (January/February 1994): 97.

4. For more on conventions, see H. Peyton Young, "The Economics of Convention," *Journal of Economic Perspectives,* 10, no. 2 (Spring 1996): 105–122.

5. Yes, I, the author, was that economist.

6. This happened to my (the author's) first economics professor in college.

7. Kenneth R. MacCrimmon and Donald A. Wehrung, *Taking Risks: The Management of Uncertainty* (New York: Free Press, 1986).

8. Think about how Holland Sweetener might have created options and thus created value rather than simply jumping in with both feet.

CHAPTER **9**

The Entrepreneur and the Market Process

Entrepreneurs and Economic Freedom

Every country in the world has entrepreneurs—people who are creative and willing to take risks. But not all economies encourage their entrepreneurs to succeed in developing new products, ideas, or services and getting them to consumers. An economic system must provide incentives that encourage entrepreneurs to risk trying something new. The dashed line in the accompanying figure shows the relationship between economic freedom and entrepreneurial activity. Why would entrepreneurial activity pick up as economic freedom increases?

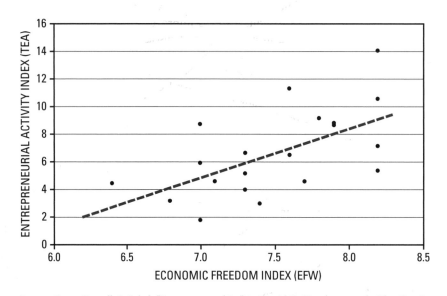

SOURCE: From Russell S. Sobel, "Entrepreneurship," in David R. Henderson, ed., *The Concise Encyclopedia of Economics*, Liberty Fund, 2008.

Markets

The market system determines a price for each traded good so that the quantities that people are willing and able to sell are equal to the quantities that people are willing and able to buy. This price informs buyers and sellers as to what they must give up to acquire a unit of the good (that is, their opportunity costs) and thereby lets them know whether their activities have value and in which activities they should specialize. Day in and day out, without any conscious central direction, the market system induces people to employ their talents and resources where these resources and talents have the highest value. People do not have to be fooled, cajoled, or forced to do their parts in a market system, but instead they pursue their own objectives as they see fit. Workers, attempting to maximize their own individual happiness and well-being, select the training, careers, and jobs where their talents and energy are most valuable. Producers, pursuing only private profits, develop the goods and services on which consumers put the highest value and produce these goods and services at the lowest possible costs. Owners of resources, seeking only to increase their own wealth, deploy these assets in socially desirable ways. Recall the discussion in Chapter 2 of how beef makes its way from Iowa to New York; it is not because of benevolence and goodwill but instead because of self interest. And, the self interest requires that sellers serve buyers – provide them what they want and are willing to pay for.

We have the things we desire when we desire them because of the market. We can purchase nearly anything 24 hours a day from the comfort of our own homes. What we purchase is not only much better than the same type of thing was just a few years ago but we are able to purchase more of it. We see this in constantly rising standards of living, which means improvement in every aspect of life: Life expectancy has nearly doubled in a century, and diseases such as polio, tuberculosis, typhoid, and whooping cough have been wiped out.

This result occurs because the market encourages people to do what they do best and to improve themselves. And everyone acting to improve and increase their own living standards leads to a thriving and ever-improving standard of living for society. This is the result of the free or unfettered market. A market is free or unfettered if nothing interferes with people entering into voluntary transactions. In an unfettered market you can purchase what you want and are able to pay for from anyone you want. Neither the government nor anyone else tells you who you have to purchase from or what price you will pay.

Specialization according to comparative advantage can generate more output than being self-sufficient. Of course, specialization means you are not producing all the things you need to survive, let alone to prosper. So to get what you want, you must exchange what you produce for those things you actually want, and this requires some form of coordination. In a market system, that coordination is carried out not by some centralized bureaucrat but by individuals pursuing their self-interests. The farmer raises cattle in order to sell the cattle and be able then to purchase whatever else the farmer wants. The butcher packages and sells the beef in order that he can have money to purchase a car, house, and so on. The truck driver delivers the beef in order that he can earn the money necessary to purchase whatever he desires. The supermarket sells the beef to customers. The beef makes its way from Iowa to New York via hundreds, if not hundreds of thousands, of transactions wherein individuals are seeking not beef, but something else.

The Market Process

In Chapter 2 we talked about how in 1990, the Mazda Miata was an especially desired product in Southern California and not so desired in Detroit. People purchased the car in Detroit and sold it in Los Angeles. The increased sales in Detroit drove the price there up, and the Miatas brought to Los Angeles increased the supply of Miatas in L.A. The price differential between Detroit and L.A. declined as the price in Detroit rose and the price in L.A. fell. The price in Detroit and the price in L.A. got closer and closer as demand continued to rise in Detroit and supply continued to rise in L.A. The prices and quantities of the cars in the two cities stopped changing once there was no chance to make a profit buying a car in Detroit and selling it in Los Angeles.

As noted in Chapter 2, this arbitrage process is the market in operation. It ensures that resources are allocated to their highest valued uses—that inefficient transactions, inefficient organizations, and inefficiency of any sort wither away.

Why does the free market work this way? It stems from the basic assumption that individuals want to make themselves as well off as possible. So, people will try to sell the use of their resources for the highest value possible. If an opportunity exists for earning more, will the resources remain where they are? No. Because people want to make themselves as well off as possible, they are always looking for ways to create greater returns—higher pay, better investments, higher rents. This is why the Miatas were moved from Detroit to Los Angeles.

The market process is dynamic because knowledge is not fixed or static. Individuals make selections on the basis of what information they have at their disposal at the time of the decision. People make the choice that they expect will make them the happiest or best off. In hindsight, after learning the outcome of their choice and acquiring new information, the individual's prior selection may not have been the best for that individual. The individual changes due to his learning. Learning continually occurs so that the market system is never in a stationary, static, continuous equilibrium. Each time new information enters an entrepreneur's thought process, a new or different search for profit begins.

The Dynamics of the Market and the Entrepreneur

According to the prisoner's dilemma game firms (players) choose strategies that are not best for them. Better options exist and are recognized, but yet, the players select poorer strategies. Why would a firm that is in a situation it knows is not the best remain where it is and do as it has always done? Consider, for instance, the advertising dilemma we discussed in the previous chapter regarding cigarette makers. The makers wanted to get out of the dilemma, but they could not call each other up and say—hey, let's not advertise—because to do so would be collusion. which is illegal. So what they did is support consumer groups who were lobbying for a ban on cigarette advertising on television. With the enactment of a ban, the cigarette makers were out of the dilemma.

The static equilibrium used in economic analysis can be misleading if it is not recognized that equilibria are, at best, temporary resting points. A firm might implement a strategy to deter entry, but that strategy is likely to have just temporary effectiveness, if that. The market process is dynamic—it occurs over time. An entrepreneur seeks profits by innovating, making decisions under uncertainty, and combining assets in new ways, and does this over time. The entrepreneur rents resources and creates organizations such as firms, learns new things, changes direction, alters organizations and moves on.

The idea of the firm as presented in intermediate microeconomics textbooks provides no role for the entrepreneur. If any firm can do what any other firm does, if all firms are always on their production possibility frontiers (best practice frontiers), and if firms always make optimal choices of input combinations and output levels, then there is no room for entrepreneurship. In other words, if the firm is thought of as a "black box" into which inputs go and out of which comes the final output (as illustrated in Figure 9.1), then there is no room for the entrepreneur.

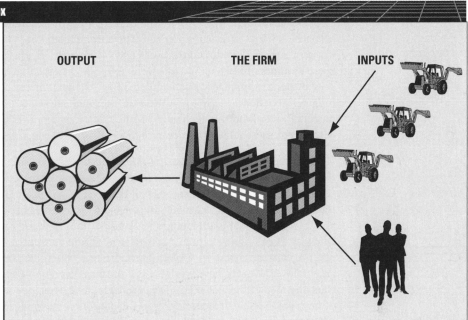

The firm is traditionally treated as a black box into which inputs go and out of which output comes.

OUTPUT   **THE FIRM**   **INPUTS**

In a world of efficient and unfettered markets, the black box firm has no reason to exist. Everything could be done by contracts without creating firms. But firms do exist, so there must be a reason. Nobel Prize laureate Ronald Coase observed that there is a "cost to using the price mechanism"[1] that the firm minimizes. Market exchange entails certain costs—discovering the relevant prices, negotiating and enforcing contracts, and so on—and these costs are lower with the presence of firms than without them. In Coase's approach, there is a role for the entrepreneur—to reduce these "transaction costs" through organization, structure, compensation arrangements, assignments of private property rights, and so on. As we discussed in Chapter 6, the entrepreneur must solve other kinds of issues inside the firm, such as the flow of information, incentives, monitoring, and performance evaluation. Also as discussed in Chapter 6, the boundary of the firm is determined by the trade-off, at the margin, between the relative transaction costs of external and internal exchange.

The Definition of an Entrepreneur   The entrepreneur is at the center of the dynamic economy, seeking profits wherever they exist. What is an entrepreneur? Probably the best-known concept of entrepreneurship in economics is Joseph Schumpeter's idea of the entrepreneur as innovator. Schumpeter's entrepreneur introduces "new combinations"—new products, production methods, markets, sources of supply, or industrial combinations—shaking the economy out of its previous equilibrium through the process Schumpeter termed *creative destruction* (see Chapter 2). According to Schumpeter, it is not price competition that counts but the competition from innovation—the new commodity, the new technology, the new source of supply, the new type of organization. The entrepreneur is not the manager, running the day-to-day business, but instead the innovator. Entrepreneurship can be exercised within the firm when new products, processes, or strategies are introduced, but day-to-day operations of the firm need not involve entrepreneurship at all.

Entrepreneurship can also be conceived of as "alertness" to profit opportunities. Since competition is a discovery process, the source of entrepreneurial profit is superior foresight—the discovery of something (new products, cost-saving technology) unknown to other market participants. One example is arbitrage. The arbitrageur who discovers a discrepancy in present prices that can be exploited for financial gain (recall the Mazda Miata discussion) is an entrepreneur. The entrepreneur may also be alert to a new product or a superior production process and steps in to fill this market gap before others. Success comes from having some knowledge or insight that no one else has. Another view of the entrepreneur is someone making decisions under conditions of uncertainty.[2] Judgment refers primarily to business decision making when the range of possible future outcomes, let alone the likelihood of individual outcomes, is generally unknown. Thus, bearing risk is the role of the entrepreneur.

Where Does the Entrepreneur Come From?   Individuals may realize income from their human capital through three means: (1) selling labor services on the open market, (2) entering into employment contracts, or (3) starting a firm. Entrepreneurs know themselves to be good risks but are unable to communicate this to the market. When an individual is unable to communicate his "vision" of a commercial experiment—a specific way of combining capital assets to serve future consumer wants—in such a way that other agents can assess its economic implications, then he cannot gain by simply being an employee. He will have to start his own firm. Entrepreneurship reveals to the market what the market did not realize was available, or indeed, needed at all. Thus the essence of entrepreneurship is being different—being different because one has a different perception of the situation. The entrepreneur does this in order to earn profits.

The Search for Profit

An entrepreneur purchases or rents resources to organize a firm and through the firm creates and sells goods and services. If the value of the goods and services created and sold exceeds the value of the resources used to create them, then the entrepreneur has added value, and the reward for that is profit. Profit is the total revenue (value of the firm's output) less the total cost of doing business (total cost of resources used by the firm).

$$\text{Profit} = \text{Total Revenue} - \text{Total Cost of Resources}$$

Total Revenue is pretty simple to measure; it is the total number of goods and services sold multiplied by the price at which they are sold, P x Q, or the dollar value of sales. Total costs are the payments to resources for creating, producing, and selling the goods and services.

Economists classify resources into three general groups: land, labor, and capital. These are the inputs used to produce and sell goods and services. **Land** refers to all natural resources as well as land and sea; **labor** refers all types of labor services—skilled and unskilled labor; and **capital** refers to structures, equipment, and inventories. So total costs are the payments that have to be made to the providers of the land, labor and capital if the firm is to use the resource services.

The cost of land is the rent that must be paid to use the land. It is not the acquisition price should a firm buy some land, but instead, the value of the services provided by that land. Rent is the payment to use the services provided by "land." The cost of labor is the wages, salaries, and benefits that must be paid to use labor services. And the cost of capital is the payments that must be made to use the capital. Think of it this way. A firm uses resources to create output. Thus, the costs are the payment the firm has to make to be able to use the services of the resources. A business does not purchase a worker but purchases the services of that person. It is similar in all resources: It is not the acquisition of the resource itself, but the services of that resource that are inputs.

The cost of anything or any activity is what you give up to acquire that item or perform that activity. When you purchase a carton of milk for $1.60, the cost of the milk

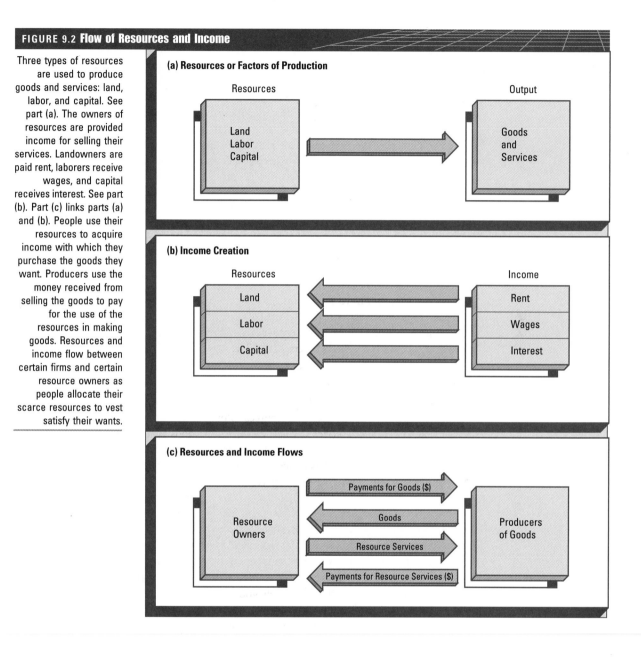

FIGURE 9.2 Flow of Resources and Income

Three types of resources are used to produce goods and services: land, labor, and capital. See part (a). The owners of resources are provided income for selling their services. Landowners are paid rent, laborers receive wages, and capital receives interest. See part (b). Part (c) links parts (a) and (b). People use their resources to acquire income with which they purchase the goods they want. Producers use the money received from selling the goods to pay for the use of the resources in making goods. Resources and income flow between certain firms and certain resource owners as people allocate their scarce resources to vest satisfy their wants.

is indeed $1.60 but more importantly, it is whatever else you could have spent that $1.60 on. Recall from Chapter 2 that this is called opportunity costs, the cost of the next most favored alternative or opportunity. *All costs are simply the cost of the next most favored thing on which the money would have been spent.* So when we talk about the costs of doing business, we are measuring the opportunity costs of running the business.

The market process results in resources being used where they have the highest value. So if a landowner accepts $5,000 per month from someone to use his land, the market has said this $5,000 is the value of the use of that land. It is the value society has placed on the use of that land. Similarly, if an accountant accepts a salary of $60,000 to work for a firm, then the market has said the value of that employee's labor services is $60,000.

Measuring the cost of capital works the same way; the only complicating factor is that there are two aspects to capital, one explicit and one implicit.

An entrepreneur must obtain funds with which he can purchase capital services—the buildings and machines whose services are used by the firm to provide its output. If someone is willing to loan the firm $1 million for an annual rate of 5 percent, then the cost to the firm of that million dollars is 5 percent or $50,000 a year. This 5 percent interest rate would be the cost of obtaining capital with debt. If the owner of a business used $1 million of his own money to start the business along with the $1 million of debt, then the owner has $2 million with which to get started. The cost of the debt is the interest or $50,000 per year. The cost of the entrepreneur's money is what that money could have earned in another use; in fact, it is the best return the entrepreneur could have expected to receive using that money in another way. The third way the entrepreneur could raise funds is to sell part of his ownership to others. This is what shares of stock represent in a publicly traded firm—shares of ownership. The ownership share of the business is called **equity** and the borrowing share is called **debt**. The cost of debt is the interest rate on the debt. This is the explicit part of capital costs. The implicit part is the cost of equity. The cost of equity is the opportunity cost to investors—the next best alternative for which investors might use their funds.

Suppose that you have a business and someone offers you $50,000 for a 10 percent ownership share. What is the cost of that $50,000 to you? You do not have to guarantee 5 percent interest. In fact, you didn't have to promise anything. So is the cost of that $50,000 zero? No—as is often said, there is no free lunch. You must implicitly promise to pay that investor an amount equal to what he could expect to earn in his next best alternative, or he will not provide you the $50,000. You sold a 10 percent equity share in your firm on the implicit promise that the person would get the $50,000 back plus what he could have expected to earn in his next best alternative. The investor may get nothing or may get something other than what was expected, so in hindsight it might look like a bad investment. But it is the expectation that matters; to make the investment in your company, he has to expect to earn at least his opportunity cost.

If we simply ignored the implicit cost of capital, we would have a measure of profit that would be relatively easy to calculate: Revenue – rent – wages – interest. This measure of profit is what is presented in financial statements and is typically called operating profit or net operating profit. This is the value of output less the cost of inputs but not including the opportunity cost of the owner's capital. Economists refer to it as **accounting profit** to distinguish it from the measure of profit that includes all opportunity costs, **economic profit**. Economic profit is the difference between the value of output and the opportunity cost of all inputs—land costs, labor costs, and debt and equity costs. In other words, economic profit takes into account all costs including *the opportunity cost of the owner's or shareholders' capital.*

$$\text{Economic Profit} = \text{Accounting Profit} - \text{Cost of Capital}$$

Economic profit is a measure—in other words, whether a firm is adding value to the resources the firm uses. Economic profit can be negative, zero, or positive.

Economic Profit Is the Entrepreneur's Signal

Economic profit is a signal to the entrepreneur; it indicates whether the entrepreneur will allocate additional resources to an activity or whether existing resources in an activity will be allocated to another use. Suppose it costs me $0.70 to produce a cup of coffee and I sell that cup of coffee for $1.50. I am earning a **positive economic profit**. That means I am earning more than my opportunity costs. Others, seeing that I am earning more than my opportunity costs, think they might do better switching over from what they currently are doing and also sell coffee. Conversely, if I can't sell the coffee for anymore than $0.65 a cup, I will eventually have to give up the business and find something else to do. In this case I would be earning a **negative economic profit** because the selling price is less than the cost of the resources used in creating the cup of coffee.

Positive economic profit attracts rivals and increases supplies. Negative economic profit means entrepreneurs must look to other markets and activities reallocate resources—and supply is reduced. In the coffee shop example, since the cost of producing and selling that great cup of coffee is $0.70 and I am selling it for $1.50, someone is going to come along and sell it for $1. Since that is still a positive economic profit, someone else will sell it for $0.90, and then $0.80, and so on. Once the price is $0.70, no one has the incentive to offer it for less. Eventually, the price of that cup of coffee is equal to the total cost of the resources used to produce it, $0.70. Competition requires that resources be used as efficiently as possible. Anyone who is not as efficient as possible will not last long in the market. If you can produce the coffee for no less than a cost of $0.90, you will not be in business when the price drops below $0.90. The resources you used in your business will flow to where they have a higher value.

A firm with negative economic profit is using resources that, if used elsewhere, would generate more value. Any firm can earn negative economic profit for a short period of time, but a firm that continually subtracts value will not exist in the long run.[3] Even during boom times you will find some well-known companies earning negative economic profit. But if the situation persists, the company will leave the business. General Motors and Ford failed to generate revenues that were sufficient to pay all opportunity costs for years. In other words, their economic profit has been negative for several years. Suppose you are an investor in General Motors. Having experienced lower returns than you had anticipated, you look at your alternatives. You realize that you could have earned much more by selling your stock in GM and purchasing shares in another firm. If many GM shareholders did this, GM could no longer acquire the use of resources. It would have to go out of business, and its resources would be reallocated to more productive uses.

GM has been destroying value for many years, so why hasn't it gone out of business? They have stayed in business simply because not enough investors have decided they could do better investing in another firm. They either thought that GM might get the business turned around or believed that the government would not let GM go out of business. In fact, in 2009 they indeed found out that the government would not let the company fail. The government took over GM in 2009, thereby eliminating any value to GM bondholders and transferring ownership to the UAW and the government.

Zero Economic Profit or Normal Profit   Competition drives revenue to the point where it is equal to the cost of doing business—to the point where total revenue equals total costs. A firm that neither adds value nor subtracts it is a firm whose revenue is sufficient to pay the cost of all of the inputs it uses—but with nothing left over. It is important to realize that this is the competitive norm—shareholders of a company with zero economic profits could not have done better in alternatives—they are earning their opportunity costs. Economists refer to **zero economic profit** as **normal profit**. The reason for the term *normal* is not that it normally occurs but that the market (the entrepreneur's search for profit) exerts pressure for it to occur.[4] Consider the illustration of the entrepreneur selling bottles of water on top of a hiking hill discussed in Chapter 2. Once he begins to earn positive economic profit, what occurs? He brings more water to the hill each morning and others also bring bottles to sell. The increased supply drives price down, and supplies increase until the sellers are just covering their opportunity cost. Consider what has occurred with Apple's iPod. When introduced in 2001, the price was about $500 while the total cost of inputs—the cost of the hard drive, screen, video processor, and so forth, was about $145. By the beginning of 2007, the product sold for $300. Late in 2007, iPod had introduced a model with a cost of just $149 and in 2010 it was below $100. This is the competitive process in action.

Business Insight

Creative Destruction—Not Always

After Starbucks began placing stores on every corner, the one criticism it faced was the effect on mom and pop coffee houses. But the presumption that introducing a Starbucks shop hurts the independent shop is usually wrong. In fact, the best way to boost sales at your independently owned coffee house may just be to have Starbucks move in next-door. The founder of the coffee trade magazine *Fresh Cup*, argued that local coffee shops want a Starbucks put in next to you. According to the Specialty Coffee Association of America, 57 percent of the nation's coffee houses are still mom and pops. During the five-year period from 2000 to 2005—long after Starbucks supposedly obliterated independent cafes—the number of mom and pops grew 40 percent, from 9,800 to nearly 14,000 coffee houses. It seems that each new Starbucks store drew new coffee drinkers who often turned to the independent shops. When the lines at Starbucks were too long, customers went to the coffee house right next-door. Often Starbucks is more expensive than the local coffee house, and it offers a more limited menu.[5]

Negative economic profit leads to exit and positive economic profit leads to entry. Undertaking a strategy that generates positive economic profit is terrific, but having been successful for awhile is no guarantee of future success. Everyone wants to get in on a good deal, and thus positive economic profit always attracts rivals. The competitive process involves an entrepreneur innovating—a new product, a new service, a new way of doing business or organizing a business—leading to a positive economic profit. The positive profit attracts entry—some mimic the successful entrepreneur, while others attempt to innovate around the first. The competition drives price down until no new entry occurs—until the normal profit level is reached. Whether that equilibrium is ever reached, and if reached how long it exists, depends on the speed with which new products are introduced and other innovations creatively destroy the first market.

In the free market every established business position is open to challenge. Any market can be entered. If incumbents do create onerous, artificial barriers to entry, it is more difficult for new entry. But even with barriers, there will usually be some compensating entrepreneurial advantage in product design and quality, method of production, or scheme for distribution to customers that puts the incumbent at a disadvantage relative to a new source of competition and that helps circumvent entry barriers. A firm never quite knows where the threats to its existence will come from; frequently, they come from such unanticipated directions that their significance is discounted until it is too late.

The Manager Compared to the Entrepreneur

If, in anticipation of an increase in the price of copper, makers of electrical cables purchase options and futures on copper or stockpile copper, we would not normally consider this to be entrepreneurial, but rather merely good management of existing economic resources. Similarly, the founding of a new business is not necessarily entrepreneurial. A business venture that merely copies existing businesses based on well-known information and thus brings nothing new to the economy is not necessarily entrepreneurial. While they require resources to be allocated appropriately, and while they inevitably carry the risks associated with the newness of the venture, their founding is not entrepreneurial.

Management makes routine decisions within known constraints to meet established objectives. It involves the stewardship of the resources owned or contractually controlled by the firm, and the managers are rewarded according to the value of the productive services they provide, just like any other form of labor. The managerial function is primarily to calculate and implement the course of action that meets the objectives of the owners of the firm. Management searches for incremental improvements in economic efficiency in response to changes in the economic environment. The manager carries out the day-to-day activities that could be considered routine or at least known.

The day-to-day flow of economic activity leads to new information. Those influenced by this information who conjecture new economic arrangements are entrepreneurs. Innovations are introduced in the context of a prevailing price structure, and it alters that price structure and generates still more new information. Those that earn economic profits then stimulate a process of competitive entry. This expands supply, changes price, and destroys the profits as the economy adapts to a new price structure.

Entrepreneurial Strategy

As discussed in Chapter 7, the aim of the five forces type of strategy is to reap superior profitability by limiting competition. In game theory, strategy involves the interaction with other players in the game. The game may be to limit competition or to cooperate or to be a first mover or a second mover, depending on the structure of the game. The aim of entrepreneurial-based strategies is to reap profits by coming up with some new processes or products or some other innovation. The entrepreneur is an innovator, a bearer of risk, and is alert to profitable opportunities.

First Mover   It might appear that the obvious strategy for an entrepreneur is to be the first mover—the first to enter a market or to create a new market. But this is not always the case. Often, being first—rushing to market prior to being prepared—is a mistake.

JVC's VHS recording technology came to the market almost two years after Sony's Betamax. Nonetheless, by licensing out the technology to other producers, creating alliances with content creators and adapting the features to address the needs of customers and rental stores, JVC managed to establish the VHS as the standard for video recording, driving Betamax out of the market.

Often, being able to understand customers, manage innovation, and adapt quickly to market changes are more important than entering a market first. The most evident example is the Internet. Google was not the first search engine. Amazon was not the first online bookstore. Ebay was not the first online auction site. All these companies were focused on understanding their customers, innovating and adapting their strategies to reflect market changes. They gained from later-mover rather than first mover strategies.

Recall in Chapter 8 where we discussed a game where two firms face a choice as to investing in a new technology. It was assumed that the two firms acted simultaneously. Comparing a sequential game to this simultaneous game provided a measure of the value of being a first mover. In the payoffs provided, A had a first mover advantage relative to moving simultaneously. But, interestingly, A's advantage was not to invest in the technology. Being the first mover actually meant not being the first to enter the market.

First movers often make some mistakes or leave parts of the market unexplored. Entrepreneurs can take advantage of those mistakes by learning from the mistakes of a first mover. But is being second really an entrepreneurial strategy? Yes, if the so-called second mover actually provides an innovation. Wal-Mart might not have been the first low-priced retailer, but it was the first with its inventory control system. Amazon and Google were not first, but each offered some new idea. These strategies are entrepreneurial strategies.

Remember that the entrepreneur is not only the mover and shaker of creative destruction, but also the equilibrator, the agent who enters existing markets with small innovations or who innovates around existing entry barriers to drive profit to the "normal" level. Despite annual sales of $35 million, first mover Pets.com shut its doors on November 2000. Why? Because purchasing pet food and accessories over the Internet did not offer customers more value than the local pet store. Being first isn't enough. What the entrepreneur does has to be valued. Simply racing out ahead of the pack does not necessarily generate success.

A large number of studies on first mover advantages and disadvantages have been undertaken, and the results are not definitive. There are cases where being first matters—such as when a firm can establish a standard or can develop customer loyalty before late movers enter. But there are also drawbacks to being the first mover. The two largest drawbacks are cost and risk. Not only is it expensive to be a pioneer—often investing in both R&D and market education—but it is risky, as the first company in a particular market cannot benefit from knowledge of successes and mistakes of others. So while the entrepreneurial strategy is to innovate, it is not always to be first to market.

The Rent Seeker as Entrepreneur

Entrepreneurial search for profits takes place in unproductive ways as well as productive ways. For much of economic history, pirates and predators innovated ways to steal from others. Seeking transfers of profits from others or seeking profits without producing anything is called **rent seeking**. These "rent seekers" who found it easier to pillage and plunder the work of others than to engage in economically productive activities were often entrepreneurs. Whether they were the King's tax collectors, highwaymen, or guilds that tightly controlled entry, the rent seeking often led to the end of the economic activity that created growth. For instance, Milan, Antwerp, and Magdeburg raised the envy and greed of strong neighbors who besieged, sacked, and taxed them.[6] Rent seeking remains an important strategy for businesses in the United States as well as in other nations. The larger the role of government in an economy, the more opportunities for rent seeking. In the next chapter rent-seeking entrepreneurship is discussed with respect to the government.

Entrepreneurs and Economic Freedom

It has been argued that capitalism is significantly more productive than alternative forms of economic organization because, under capitalism, entrepreneurial effort is channeled into activities that produce wealth rather than into activities that forcibly take other people's wealth.[7] Entrepreneurs are present in all societies. In government-controlled societies, entrepreneurial people go into government or lobby government, and much of the government action that results—tariffs, subsidies, and regulations, for example—destroys wealth. In economies with limited governments and rule of law, entrepreneurs produce wealth. It is argued that government interventions—in the form of subsidies, taxes, and regulations—can enhance market entrepreneurship. Perhaps the government could induce more funding to go toward entrepreneurship. Economists have found that infusions of funding along the lines of venture capital funding do not necessarily foster entrepreneurship. Capital is mobile, and funding naturally flows to those areas where creative and potentially profitable ideas are being generated. This means that promoting individual entrepreneurs is more important for economic development policy than is attracting venture capital. While funding can increase the odds of new business survival, it does not create new ideas. The recent academic research on entrepreneurship shows that, to promote entrepreneurship, government policy should focus on reforming basic institutions to create an environment in which creative individuals can flourish. That environment is one of well-defined and enforced property rights, low taxes and regulations, sound legal and monetary systems, proper contract enforcement, and limited government intervention.

Summary

1. An entrepreneur is an individual who innovates, who is alert to opportunities, and who bears risk.
2. The role of the entrepreneur in the economy is to foster change and to enhance the move to conformity. In other words, the entrepreneur innovates and thereby creatively destroys existing markets but also enters markets to offer slightly different or better goods and services that decreases price and abnormal profit.
3. The entrepreneur may be forced to open his own firm because of an incomplete market for entrepreneurial talent. The entrepreneur is unable to communicate his vision, and so on, without significant costs.
4. Accounting Profit is defined as: Revenue – cost of land – cost of labor – cost of debt.
5. Economic profit is defined as: Revenue – cost of land – cost of labor – cost of debt – cost of equity. It is also accounting profit – cost of capital.
6. The entrepreneur seeks profits. This seeking is the key aspect of the market process, driving resources to where they have the highest value and driving prices down to where revenue just equals the total costs of production.
7. Positive economic profit means that revenue exceeds all costs, including the opportunity costs of investors.
8. When economic profit is positive, others want to get in on the good deal and entry occurs.
9. Eventually economic profits will be competed to zero. This is called normal profit.
10. Entrepreneurship may occur in government through the process of transferring wealth from one sector to another rather than creating new products and wealth. This is a rent-seeking entrepreneur.

Key Terms

Land	Economic profit.
Labor	Positive economic profit
Capital	Negative economic profit
Equity	Zero economic profit
Debt	Normal profit
Accounting profit	Rent seeking

Exercises

1. Define entrepreneurship. How does it differ from management? Would you consider each of the following entrepreneurial or managerial?

   a. Bill Gates's creation of the Microsoft operating system.
   b. Steve Jobs's development of the iPhone
   c. Warren Buffet's investment success
   d. Wal-Mart's strategy to locate in small towns
   e. The use of teams and a flat company rather than a hierarchy
   f. Newt Gringrich's 1994 "Contract for America"

2. What is "the market process"? Describe the role of the entrepreneur in the market process.

3. What does it mean to say "Profit opportunities attract firms like sharks to blood?

4. What is the economist's interpretation of costs? "… the concept of cost is far richer (pardon the

pun) than the dollars and cents you hand over at the cash register."

5. In the book, *Naked Economics,* the author says, "Prices are like giant neon billboards that flash important information" (p. 12). Describe the types of information that market prices provide. What role does the entrepreneur play in this billboard?

6. Creative destruction—means what? Is it true that capitalism works not because it rewards winners but crushes losers? How is this reconciled with golf tournaments and professional team sports?

7. What is an asymmetrical information problem? How does an entrepreneur deal with asymmetric information?

8. List three reasons that firms exist. Do any of the reasons imply that the command and control of centrally planned economies is the appropriate form? What are the similarities and differences between firms and centrally planned economies?

9. Is rent seeking the same as corruption? Why does corruption negatively affect economic growth and standards of living? In what way might corruption be like a tax on doing business? What institutions exist to minimize corruption?

10. In the chapter rent seeking was associated with entrepreneurs dealing with or in government. Can rent seeking occur inside a firm? Explain and give an example.

11. Explain why the black rhino has become increasingly endangered. If you substituted "entrepreneur "for "black rhino" in the previous sentence, what would your answer be?

12. Explain whether the first mover strategy makes sense for an entrepreneur.

13. What does the following statement mean? "Indeed, every decision we make involves some kind of trade-off." Under what condition would the statement not be true? Does the entrepreneur face a trade-off before choosing to be an entrepreneur? Explain.

14. Compare "equilibrium" strategy (described in Chapters 7 and 8) to entrepreneurial strategy. Is there a difference? Explain

15. "Entrepreneurial profit is made possible by Schumpeterian entrepreneurs and Austrian entrepreneurs nibble away at it." What is a Schumpeterian entrepreneur? What must the "Austrian entrepreneur" be if he simply "nibbles away at profit"?

16. It has been said that the concept of opportunity cost is central to economics and economic thinking. Understanding opportunity cost will help an entrepreneur determine the true value of decisions. What does mean? What is the opportunity cost of going to play A in the following problem?

    You won a free ticket to see play A. Play B is performing at the same time and is your next-best alternative. Tickets to see play B cost $40 but on any given day you are willing to pay up to $50 to see play B. $0

    ■ $10
    ■ $40
    ■ $50

17. The chapter discussed the role of entrepreneurs as "equilibrators." What does "equilibrators" mean?

18. What is the difference between homogeneous capital and heterogeneous capital? Why would a theory of the entrepreneur make more sense if capital is heterogeneous rather than homogeneous?

19. If capital is heterogeneous and has attributes that are not changeable, how might creative destruction take place?

20. Explain why first mover is or is not a good strategy for an entrepreneur.

CHAPTER NOTES

1. Ronald Coase first raised the question about why firms exist in a market system in his paper "The Nature of the Firm," *Economica,* 4, no. 16 (1937): 386–405.

2. "Uncertainty" is a situation where the probabilities of possible events cannot be assigned. Risk is a situation where those probabilities can be assigned. This distinction came from Frank Knight in 1921.

3. Unless the firm is supported by government.

4. Managerial accountants refer to zero economic profit as normal profit and positive economic profit as abnormal profit.

5. Taylor Clark, "Don't Fear Starbucks: Why the Franchise Actually Helps Mom and Pop Coffee-houses," www.slate.com/id/2180301/fr/rs, December 28, 2007.

6. Joel Mokyr, *The Enlightened Economy* (New Haven, CT: Yale University Press, 2009), p. 5.

7. William J. Baumol, "Entrepreneurship: Productive, Unproductive and Destructive," *Journal of Political Economy,* 98, no. 5 (1990): 893–921.

CHAPTER **10**

Strategies with Respect to Government

CASE

Rent Seeking

Rent seeking comes in several forms but is generally defined as a private entity pursuing favorable treatment from the government. Corporate welfare is a good example; ADM is practically the poster child for rent seeking at the federal level. Large corporations including Boeing, Xerox, Motorola, Dow Chemical, and General Electric have received millions in taxpayer dollars.

Recipients of subsidies have a substantial interest in protecting the flow of money to them. That leads to a great deal of lobbying by special interests. It has been estimated that at least $50 billion each year is transferred from taxpayers to business as a result of lobbying. The deals are typically sold as benefiting the local community. Virginia Governor Tim Kaine gave Dollar Tree $200,000 to enable it to expand its Chesapeake headquarters. The press release about the Dollar Tree deal went something like this: Governor Kaine Announces 100 New Jobs for Chesapeake. Similarly, Governor George Pataki of New York, a Republican, approved a $1.2 billion package of grants and tax reductions for AMD to build a microchip factory in Saratoga County. The project is supposed to create 1,200 jobs, and these jobs were touted in the press releases. Of course, not much mention was made of the fact that this implies a cost per job of $1 million apiece for New York taxpayers.[1]

1. Can governments pick winners and losers in business better than the market?
2. What is the real purpose of government giveaways to business?

Government Intervention in Business

Unfettered markets result in resources being allocated to their highest valued uses and consumers getting what they want and are willing to pay for. Yet, many people argue that markets do not restrain the greed of big business. The typical argument in support of government restrictions on business are to corral the animal spirits of business and serve as bulwarks of a freely functioning market economy. Without such controls, it is often argued, harm would be done to individuals by some unscrupulous profit-seeking firms, and some firms would acquire market power and exploit it by restricting output and raising price, benefiting themselves at consumers' expense. From this point of view, government policies are imposed on unwilling producers in order to channel and redirect their behavior away from privately rational but socially harmful ends. Business decisions motivated solely by the quest for profit are displaced by those of government policymakers who pursue broader, socially beneficial, objectives.

Many economists consider this view of government actions to be pretty naïve. Humans, in or out of government, are self-interested and compare the costs and benefits of actions to determine whether their personal benefit will increase or decrease with the action. The people responsible for formulating and executing public policies toward business have incentives to enhance their own well-being by catering to the demands of politically well-organized special interest groups. In this view, interventions in markets come about not to increase economic efficiency but instead to benefit special interest groups.

Perhaps a manager doesn't really care which view of markets and government intervention is theoretically correct. But he definitely cares whether the intervention harms or benefits his firm. He also cares if the firm has to devote resources to grabbing benefits from government actions or resisting the efforts of others to take away your revenues and resources.

Government actions affect firms in many ways. Taxes alter incentives and reduce "the bottom line." Compliance and paperwork raise selling, general, and administrative costs (SG&A), while new requirements on capital and workplace affect how resources are used. Since the government is such a big player in the economy, a firm's strategy must be concerned with government actions.

Rent-Seeking Competition

If, as a manager, you believe that government actions are those of a benevolent official concerned only with increasing economic efficiency, then you need only concern yourself with actions by your firm that might reduce efficiency or impose costs on others. But what if your rivals use government regulations or the courts to restrict what you can do, to take away your market? Then they are rent seeking. Or perhaps you hire lobbyists to protect your interests. Then you are rent seeking. Who gains and who loses in the rent-seeking market? In a sense, it pays to be small when it comes to rent seeking. All else equal, small well-organized groups are the most successful in the political process because the costs of whatever favors a small group wrangles out of the system are spread over a large, unorganized segment of the population.

Consider the policy in the United States that gasoline must include a certain percentage of ethanol.[2] The benefits of that multibillion dollar subsidy go to a small population group—corn producers and ethanol manufacturers and distributors—making it lucrative for each one of them. Meanwhile, the costs are spread over the remaining population and populations in other countries. This puts ethanol below many other issues in the general public's everyday concerns.

Suppose a bill was introduced so that all economists were required to pay subsidies to noneconomists. There are roughly 13,000 economists in the U.S. labor force, or 1,000 noneconomists for every economist, so if every noneconomist were to get some government benefit worth $100, then every economist would have to pay $130,000 to finance it. The economists would be upset enough about their tax bill to make it a political concern, while the noneconomists would find the $100 subsidy not really worth fighting over.

The optimal size of lobbying groups is determined by a cost-benefit calculation. Each additional member adds a little additional influence to the lobbying effort, but less additional influence than the prior member. Moreover, payments to the members from lobbying decline as more members belong to the group and must divide a fixed pie. Thus, a single firm might be a very effective lobbyist and might obtain many government benefits, including subsidies and tariffs.

All of the government subsidy programs—subsidies for ethanol, sugar, and other agricultural products, and tax breaks for certain companies, allocation of highway funds, and on and on—are relatively small. Each is enacted into law by the government because a few voters organize and work for their passage, while the general taxpayer does not bemoan each individual program. This creates an opportunity for firms to allocate resources so as to obtain favors from government. This is referred to as the "grabbing hand."[3]

If small groups can get what they want out of the legislative process, they can also stop what they don't want. Creative destruction describes the market process as one that destroys the old, inefficient, structure while creating a new, more efficient one. While this is good for society, it is bad for those whose jobs and activities are in the old structure. Groups under siege from competition often seek protection. Federal regulation of food and drugs began in the early twentieth century when Congress enacted the Pure Food and Drugs Act of 1906. The regulatory agency spawned by this law—the U.S. Food and Drug Administration (FDA)—now directly regulates between one-fifth to one-quarter of the U.S. gross domestic product (GDP) and possesses significant power over product entry, the ways in which food and drugs are marketed to consumers, and the manufacturing practices of food and drug firms. Most people think the FDA's regulations are necessary for the health of the U.S. population, and economists rationalize the regulations as being justified by asymmetric information—producers know more about product quality than consumers. To the extent that regulators are better informed about quality than consumers, regulation that punishes firms who cheat on quality or the regulation that requires firms to disclose information about product quality can improve efficiency. But efficiency can be harmed if specific industry groups use the regulations to make it more difficult for new firms to enter the industry or begin producing competing

Business Insight

Lobbying Expenditures

How much lobbying will take place when two entities are seeking a monopoly? AT&T, which pushed legislation that would have allowed the company to obtain a statewide franchise to operate cable television, spent about $5 million on its campaign in Tennessee. The winning company, the Tennessee Cable Telecommunications Association, spent about $6 million to defeat the measure. There is a significant profit from the monopoly associated with cable tv. If the amount was $20 million, how much would the lobbyists be willing to spend to maintain their monopoly? Any amount up to $20 million. How much would AT&T spend to try to get into the market? That depends on the profits AT&T expects to earn once it enters into the market.[4]

products. Regulations that require producers to meet certain minimum standards or that ban the use of certain additives may benefit incumbent producers at the expense of producers of cheaper substitutes. State and federal oleomargarine restrictions benefited dairy-producing interests that wanted to limit the availability of oleomargarine. Meat inspection laws were introduced to placate local butchers and local slaughterhouses in eastern markets who wanted to reduce the competitive threat posed by the large midwestern meatpackers. The 1906 Pure Food and Drugs Act benefited national food manufacturers and disadvantaged smaller, local firms.[5]

Antitrust

Antitrust is the attempt by government to enhance "fair" competition. Antitrust in the United States is based on the Sherman, Clayton, and Federal Trade acts. The Sherman Act of 1890 makes illegal "every contract, combination, or conspiracy in restraint of trade" and declares that "every person who shall monopolize, or attempt to monopolize, or conspire to monopolize shall be deemed guilty of a felony." The 1914 Clayton Act built on the Sherman Act with a list of practices that could entail anticompetitive effects in certain situations, including tying arrangements, exclusive dealing, mergers, and interlocking boards of directors. Antitrust policy in the United States is the responsibility of two federal government agencies—the Antitrust Division of the Department of Justice and the Federal Trade Commission—and each state's attorney general. When the Federal Trade Commission was created in 1914, it was given authority to stop unfair methods of competition. In 1931, it was given the power to protect consumers from unfair or deceptive acts.

The conventional view of antitrust laws is that with the rise of large-scale enterprises, the trusts, businesses had power over consumers in being able to dominate markets. Responding to a public need, Congress passed the Sherman Antitrust Act. This is one view. Another is that the origins of the antitrust laws lie in politically influential businesses getting a national law passed to use the power of the state against their business rivals—in other words, rent seeking. One of the most famous antitrust cases illustrates this point. The 1911 Standard Oil Case divided the company into 33 separate organizations. Standard Oil had been buying smaller firms and increasing the efficiency of oil refining and distribution through economies of scale. Although Standard Oil had reduced prices and increased output throughout its entire history, it was found guilty of monopolization. Smaller rivals, unable to compete against Standard Oil, joined forces against Standard Oil. Also, Senator John Sherman introduced the act to damage a rival. Senator Sherman had his heart set on being president of the United States and appeared destined for the Republican nomination in 1888. His life's ambition was thwarted when Russell Alger—of the Diamond Match Company—threw his support to Benjamin Harrison, the eventual president. In an effort to hurt Alger, Sherman sponsored the antitrust law specifically to go against the Diamond Match Company.[6]

The point of this discussion is that a law may be enacted not because an entrepreneur has created or exploited some inefficiency in the market, but instead because the entrepreneur was successful and others want to take his market away through rent seeking. Thus, a manager must be aware of the laws and of when his company might be accused of violating one. For instance, a firm is contemplating a merger with a former competitor. It carries out due diligence of the merger, at considerable expense, and then makes an offer for the company. The Justice Department and/or Federal Trade Commission then intercede, disallowing the merger. Had the firm known what the government would do, it may have saved itself considerable money. This occurred in 1996 to Rite Aid, the nation's largest drugstore chain, when it decided to acquire Revco, the second-largest drugstore company. Rite Aid operated 2,760 stores nationwide and Revco 2,100, which would have made the combination more than twice the size of its closest competitor, Walgreen Co. The Federal Trade Commission (FTC) disallowed the merger on the basis of possible anticompetitive effects that might occur after the merger.

The CEO of Staples, who had faced a similar situation when the company's attempt to merge with Office Max was denied by the FTC, was asked: "During a merger attempt, a company not only has to run its own business, but it must plan for the combined company once the merger is accomplished. And, it must fight the FTC or Justice Department. How can it all be done?" The CEO responded that it was indeed very expensive: "You have to identify individuals who are accountable only for dealing with the merger. We had about 20 people working full time who were pulled off their normal jobs, letting the majority continue to focus on the business at hand. And, a kazillion outsiders: lawyers, accountants, and economists."[7]

A firm may file a suit in an attempt to change a rival's market behavior. For example, Intel filed a suit against Advanced Micro Devices (AMD) for its use of Intel's microcode. AMD then had to decide whether to copy Intel's microcode or create its own. If it continued to copy Intel's microcode and then lost the lawsuit, the court might prevent the sale of the relevant AMD microprocessors. AMD changed its behavior.

Mechanics of Antitrust   The government bases much of its antitrust policy on a measure of the market power or control a firm has over its market. The **Herfindahl–Hirschman index (HHI)** is a measure of concentration—how dominant one or a few firms are in a market. The index is calculated as

$$\text{HHI} = (\text{size})^2 + (\text{size})^2 + \ldots + (\text{size})^2$$

where $(\text{size})^2$ is the size of a firm squared.

An industry in which each of five firms has 20 percent of the market would have an HHI of 2,000. If the largest firm had 88 percent of the market and each of the others 3 percent, the HHI would be 7,780. The higher the HHI, the more dominated the market is by a single firm.

In a merger case, the government will calculate the HHI index that would result following the merger to see whether it is too high or whether it increases too much. In 1992 (revised 1997), the Department of Justice and Federal Trade Commission issued horizontal merger guidelines that antitrust enforcers have since used to judge the competitive effects of proposed mergers. The guidelines stipulate that where the postmerger HHI exceeds 1,800, it will be presumed that mergers producing an increase in the HHI of more than 100 points are likely to create or enhance market power or facilitate its exercise. But the guidelines also provide a process for overcoming an anticompetitive presumption. This involves showing that a "merger is not likely to create or enhance market power or to facilitate its exercise if entry into the market is so easy that market participants, after the merger, either collectively or unilaterally could not profitably maintain a price increase above premerger levels." In other words, not only must the market be concentrated, it must also be possible for the dominant firm(s) to maintain price increases without facing significant pressure from lower-priced rivals.

The degree to which these guidelines are followed by the FTC varies. In 2001, the Commission approved the $3 billion merger of AmeriSource Health Corp. and Bergen Brunswick Corp. The deal brought the HHI to 2,700, with an increase of 450 points. Nevertheless, the commissioners supported the companies' claim that combining the nation's third- and fourth-largest prescription drug wholesalers would result in efficiencies not possible without the merger. FTC rulings have not been consistent, however. Boeing was allowed to merge with McDonnell Douglas, even though it meant a virtual monopoly

Business Insight

The Wireless Market and the HHI

The government's latest annual report on the state of mobile wireless competition states that concentration in the industry has gone up—way up, in fact. The Federal Communications Commission (FCC) says that the two dominant providers, AT&T and Verizon, now enjoy a 60 percent chunk of revenue and subscribers and continue to gain share. Their nearest rivals, T-Mobile and Sprint, serve most of that remaining 40 percent. As a consequence, the Herfindahl-Hirschman Index, has jumped by almost 700 points since the agency first began using it in 2003. That's a 32 percent increase. Some of this newer concentration is a consequence of mergers over the last few years: AT&T/Aloha, T-Mobile/Suncom, Verizon Wireless/Rural Cellular, and Verizon Wireless/Alltel. So the wireless sector HHI is now at 2,848. The Department of Justice regards a market to be "highly concentrated" if, following a merger, the HHI in a given industry exceeds 1,800. According to the FCC, that 2,848 HHI number sticks out like a sore thumb and flashes a bright caution light as the Commission goes about the business of advancing competition and consumer well-being in the Broadband Age.

The big four providers unveiled almost 70 new smart phones between 2008 and 2009 over a variety of platforms (e.g., Apple iPhone, BlackBerry, Android, Palm, Windows Mobile). By December of 2009, consumers could choose from over 100,000 applications on the Apple Store and 15,000 via the Android Market.

Source: Government report: 4 cos. control wireless market, August 26, 2010 By Joelle Tessler www.physorg.com/news202053465.html.

in the domestic commercial-airplane manufacturing market. The acquisition of MCI Communications by WorldCom was put into serious doubt while the FTC examined its effects on the market because the combined company might control 50 percent of the Internet "backbone." Southern Pacific was allowed to merge with Union Pacific and thus to control a major share of the rail lines, but other mergers were disallowed. What are the criteria for blocking some deals and not others? The reality is that the interpretation of the statutes by the courts and government authorities changes from administration to administration. Thus, a manager must be aware of what the current administration is expecting from its antitrust officials.

In the 1980s, the only legitimate subject of antitrust enforcement was price fixing. For a decade, this translated into virtually no antitrust action by the government. Since then, the antitrust regulators have argued that there are justifications above and beyond price fixing that require antitrust enforcement. These tactics include tying, forcing customers to buy one product to get another (the Microsoft case); exclusive dealing, pressuring distributors to dump competitors' wares (this was the main issue in suits against Anheuser-Busch and against Kodak); and standard setting wherein a standard becomes the dominant or only one in use (again, the Microsoft case).

Action against alleged violators of the antitrust statutes may be initiated by the U.S. Department of Justice, by the Federal Trade Commission, by state attorneys general, or by private plaintiffs. Since 1941, the FTC and the Justice Department together have filed nearly 2,800 cases; since 1970, however, private suits have outnumbered those filed by the Justice Department and the FTC combined by about ten to one.

The public justification of antitrust laws is that they create a level playing field by restricting the anticompetitive actions of large firms. Nearly 80 countries now have such laws, although the degree of restrictiveness varies. Each country's antitrust laws are directed primarily toward its domestic firms, but the laws can also affect a foreign company's ability to enter the domestic market or even spill over into other countries' markets. For instance, a merger or an alliance between two companies from the same country could affect competition in other countries. Boeing, a manufacturer of civil aircraft, acquired McDonnell Douglas, an ailing smaller firm. This merger was applauded by U.S. antitrust authorities (FTC, Justice) but decried by the European Union's competition commission, which feared that the merger would reduce competition in Europe to the detriment of Boeing's European rival, Airbus. A merger or an alliance between two companies from different countries could also affect competition in the two markets in different ways. For example, the alliance between British Airways and American Airlines was seen in the United States as an increase in competition, while in the United Kingdom it was viewed as a reduction in competition.

Compared to other countries, the United States is restrictive in terms of allowing certain types of business behavior. When the idea that price fixing was anathema to competition and was therefore illegal was emerging in the United States during the 1920s and 1930s, most European nations had no antitrust laws at all and cartels and thus price fixing flourished. Today, many nations continue to support cartels and cooperative behavior that is illegal in the United States.

At least part of the explanation for the differences among nations lies in the growth and development of the various countries following World War II. Europe and Japan were severely damaged by the war. As the losers, Germany and Japan were occupied and their laws rewritten by the occupying forces. Thus, their antitrust laws resemble those of the United States. However, because Europe and Japan were not concerned with large business but instead with businesses that were too small to compete in world markets, the antitrust laws were never enforced. Businesses had to be large enough to achieve economies of scale, and for several decades it seemed that only U.S. firms were of sufficient size. Hence, while the United States was worrying about large businesses becoming too powerful, other countries were attempting to increase the sizes of their businesses. Only since the 1970s have the European countries begun to institute and enforce antitrust laws along the lines the United States has followed since the 1940s. With the emergence of the European Union (EU) and a convergence of member countries' antitrust laws, the EU has become much more aggressive on antitrust. The 2007 ruling on the antitrust law suit against Microsoft required the firm to pay a $613 million fine, share communications code with rivals, and sell a copy of Windows without Media Player. The EU Court agreed that Microsoft abused its monopoly in trying to muscle into server software. The Microsoft ruling showed that the EU antitrust authorities allow greater government intervention in the market than the U.S. authorities.

Competitive strategy means that a firm must develop a distinctive capability that has value in the marketplace. To increase its value, the firm often must differentiate itself, increase its size to benefit from economies of scale, or form alliances. Yet these same competitive strategies may be perceived as anticompetitive by the government antitrust agencies. In recent years, strategic alliances and other forms of cooperation have become an increasingly important part of business strategy, but collaborative arrangements often attract scrutiny by antitrust authorities. Problems can arise out of innocent actions that the government might view as having anticompetitive effects. For example, in the past 10 years or so, antitrust enforcement has targeted or forbidden each of the following: the use by airlines of a clearinghouse that listed fares; licensing agreements and renegotiations involving patented products in the chemical and pharmaceutical industries; information sharing among competing hospitals; the exchange of advertising and marketing plans by infant-formula manufacturers through an industry trade association; and certain joint ventures in the online bond trading industry and foreign-exchange trading industry.

A firm might think that it should be able to resist the use of its own equipment and supplies by rivals. But printer manufacturers such as Hewlett-Packard, Lexmark, Canon, and Epson were investigated by European regulators in 2002 regarding anticompetitive practices in the sale of ink cartridges. The market shares of these firms had been eroding due to a rise in the number of companies that refill original cartridges and sell them at a fraction of the price of a new one. The large manufacturers fought back by inserting a "killer" computer chip that makes it difficult for the cartridge to be refilled. This, the European regulatory authorities said, was anticompetitive.

The exchange of information, even in informal discussions, sometimes attracts antitrust attention. This can happen when businesspeople get together to talk about other things and inadvertently exchange information that they should not. For example, in one case, the court upheld the criminal price-fixing conviction of several realtors after one realtor discussed a commission-rate change at a dinner party with other realtors. Within months, each realtor present at the dinner party had adopted similar rates.[8] In another case, the FTC alleged that a respondent's representative met with officers of a competing firm and invited them to fix prices on certain products that both companies produced. The managers' defense was that they only went to their competitor's plant to see their competitor's low-cost production processes. It was not their intent to discuss prices. However, the complaint alleged that these discussions quickly turned to discussions about price.[9] In another case, airlines were forbidden to use a common clearinghouse to report fares. Although the clearinghouse enabled travel agents easy access to fares, the Department of Justice alleged that the eight airlines using the computerized fare-exchange system had unreasonably restrained price competition in the domestic air travel industry.

Discussions between or among competitors will often occur in the normal course of business through existing interfirm relationships such as joint ventures involving the competitors or because competitors are considering a merger or other formal relationship. Managers need to consider how antitrust laws and policies may require them to create certain internal structures or organizational designs to ensure that the flow of information is not interpreted as being anticompetitive. Also, managers attempting to negotiate a relationship with a competitor must be careful about what information is released, when it is released, and to whom it is released.

Pre-deal discussions with potential partners and suitors are settings where antitrust considerations can be important. The potential problem arises when such discussions take place between horizontal competitors and don't result in consummation of a deal.

There are limitations on which competitors can be licensed, which licenses can be exchanged, and which provisions can be written into license contracts. According to government guidelines, enabling your major competitor to sell your product through a licensing arrangement could be viewed as a reduction of competition.

The use of patents to dominate a market may also be viewed as anticompetitive. Patent policy allows the patent holder exclusive use, but this is not viewed as a problem as long as there are products that compete with the patented product. In the absence of such substitutes, managers have to be careful about their use of patents. Major pharmaceutical companies were investigated in 2001 regarding their use of patents to restrict the introduction of generic drugs.

Being aware of what actions the antitrust authorities might scrutinize or disallow is important. But being defensive is not the only way antitrust is used as strategy. Outcomes that cannot be achieved through market action can sometimes be achieved through legal action. Firms use the antitrust laws strategically by filing private antitrust suits.[10] There are approximately 10 times as many private antitrust suits filed each year as government suits.[11] Refusals to deal are the most common type of case, followed by horizontal price fixing, tying or exclusive dealing, and price discrimination.

The filing of a suit can change behavior even if the suit is not litigated. CIBA Vision Corporation agreed to a settlement with private plaintiffs not because it thought the suit was justified but because the cost and disruption to the business that would be required to litigate outweighed the cost of settlement. Even the threat of private antitrust action can change behavior.

International Regulation

Managers must also be aware of the international antitrust and regulatory authorities. The international authority dealing with trade disputes and unfair competition among global companies is the World Trade Organization (WTO). The WTO was created by the General Agreement on Trades and Tariffs (GATT) in 1995 to deal with international trade disputes. As of 2007, the WTO had 150 members. The WTO implements and enforces agreements in such areas as customs regulations, environmental restrictions, intellectual property rights, and dumping.

Dumping

Typically, a firm or an industry with complaints against foreign firms will appeal to domestic authorities and then either the plaintiff or the government agency will present a case to the World Trade Organization. **Dumping**, according to the World Trade Organization, occurs when a foreign firm sells a product at a price that is lower than the firm sells it in its home country. Dumping cases are handled by two agencies of the U.S. government: the Commerce Department, which is charged with determining whether a company is a foreign producer, whether it is selling for less than fair value, and, if so, by how much; and the International Trade Commission (ITC), which decides whether U.S. industry has been injured by the dumping. A case begins when a U.S. company files a complaint with the Commerce Department's Import Administration Office, which reviews it to decide whether to launch a formal investigation. If the petition is accepted, the case moves on to the ITC, which makes a preliminary determination of whether the affected U.S. company is injured by the dumped imports. If the ITC decides there is an injury, the case moves back to the Commerce Department for a full-scale investigation.

The United States is the largest user of antidumping taxes, essentially applying a tax on the foreign goods that are being dumped. The second largest user is the European Union. Antidumping duties are a popular strategy for domestic firms to use against rival foreign firms. From 1916 to 1970, there were about 15 dumping cases a year in the United States. In the 1980s and 1990s the pace rose to 60 per year. From the late 1990s to the early 2000s, the number was about 50 per year. Worldwide filings have followed that trend. About 1,600 cases were filed worldwide in the 1980s, which was twice the level of the 1970s. The number of cases filed has continued to increase since then.[12] Whether the claims are valid is, in most instances, irrelevant. If the businesses can get the domestic authorities to impose sanctions against foreign firms or to file actions in the World Trade Organization, the domestic businesses can benefit.

Under WTO rules, countries are allowed to impose antidumping duties on imports sold at below "normal value," which can mean the price in their home market or the cost of production. Dumping in a pure economic-theory sense occurs when a firm sells its products in a foreign market at a price that is below its average variable costs; in other words, the price per unit sold is less than the cost per unit supplied. In reality, dumping cases are filed whenever a foreign firm sells at a price that is below a domestic firm's price, not just the firm's average cost. But, this situation occurs regularly when firms sell in more than one country and the demand differs in the two.

If a firm sells in two markets—one where customers are quite sensitive to price (elastic demand) and one where customers are less sensitive to price (inelastic demand)—the firm will set two different prices. The market with an elastic demand will have a lower price, and the market with an inelastic demand will have a higher price. Lowering the price in the price-elastic demand market attracts more customers and increases revenue. Raising the price in the price-inelastic market reduces the number of customers but by less than the price per unit sold—thus the revenue increases.

Suppose the demand for a firm's product is price-inelastic in Europe and price-elastic in the United States. A European firm selling this product would maximize profit by setting a higher price in Europe than it does in the United States because the European customers are less sensitive to a price increase than are U.S. customers. But this profit-maximizing strategy would be subject to a dumping claim by the domestic U.S. firms selling that same product.

Dumping cases can be filed or begun by individual firms. For instance, the Asian economic crisis of the 1990s hurt U.S. textile businesses because the depreciations of the Asian nations' currencies reduced the prices of Asian textiles. Imports of synthetic fiber fabric from Asia increased 51 percent, and all fabric imports from Asia were up 35 percent during the late 1990s. The U.S. textile industry pursued antidumping action against Asian suppliers as a means of slowing down the competition. The financial crisis in 2008 induced a record number of dumping cases in 2009 as countries tried to protect their domestic industries. Developing countries accounted for the majority of initiations, though developed countries accounted for the greatest number of duty impositions. India was the most active, accounting for 29 percent of total initiations. In December alone, India initiated antidumping investigations involving both hot- and cold-rolled stainless steel products, affecting 19 countries. In addition to Japan, three developing countries—China, South Africa, and Thailand—were the target in both investigations. The United States and the EU were the two countries that most frequently imposed duties. For example, the EU in December 2008 imposed duties on preserved fruits from China as well as on imports of welded tubes and pipes of iron or nonalloy steel from Belarus, China and Russia. Governments often file counterclaim suits on behalf of businesses. The growing trade deficit in the United States has prompted the U.S. government to file charges against the European Union and other nations for discriminating against American products. The United States claimed that the European Union unfairly subsidizes Airbus Industrie through government support of a new flight-management system. The United States also accused the European Union of treating American cheese and wine products unfairly through European copyright and trademark practices. India was charged with imposing unfair requirements on American automakers seeking to set up operations there. South Korea was accused of unfairly restricting the ability of American construction companies to bid on airport work and restricting the import of American beef. The list goes on and on.

Trade and Tariffs

International competition is a great worry to many businesses. Thus, it often pays to rent-seek for protectionism in the form of import restrictions or tariffs. Recent developments in the shrimping industry illustrate how small interest groups seek benefits that cost large groups. American shrimpers recently petitioned the U.S. government to expand its H-2B visa program. These visas allow foreign laborers and their families to enter the United States for temporary work. The job must last less than a year and be a one-time occurrence. Southern shrimping outfits have used the program to bring in foreign workers during the peak of the shrimp harvest. The problem is that the government limits the program to 66,000 visas per year, a quota filled in the first three months of the year or earlier. If the shrimpers have to employ U.S. workers, they have to bear higher employment costs. So the shrimp industry is lobbying for some type of guest worker program. At the same time, the industry seeks protection from foreign competitors. The U.S. government slapped a 93 percent tariff on imported shrimp from Vietnam, and a 113 percent tariff on shrimp from China because, according to the shrimping industry, those countries produce shrimp from subsidized farms, enabling them to sell shrimp at deflated prices. The Commerce Department later added India, Thailand, Ecuador, and Brazil to the list of shrimp-producers covered by the tariff. The increased shrimp prices are spread out among U.S. consumers, while the benefits go to the relatively small shrimp industry.[13]

The competitors point out that tropical climates and shrimp farms enable these foreign producers to harvest shrimp more efficiently than U.S. shrimpers, allowing the foreign firms to sell at a lower price. But in rent seeking, it is not the most efficient producer who wins; rather, it is the most effective rent seeker.

Sometimes small groups seeking government benefits run up against other small groups who will have to bear the costs from those government benefits. Then it becomes a battle between rent seekers. Manufacturers who use steel (car and appliance makers, for example) oppose tariffs on imported steel, while steel producers support them. Car makers might oppose steel tariffs but will support tariffs on foreign-made cars. And steel manufacturers would likely oppose tariffs on cars, as they make it more difficult to sell U.S. steel overseas. In the case where rent seeking is competitive and entry into the rent seeking is not limited, the rents should be competed to zero. Though engaging in rent seeking, firms will gain only enough rents to cover all costs of rent seeking. There are no "above-normal" rents. Just as in any competitive situation, if a firm can create barriers to entry or can create some special attribute that is favored by the rent providers, then some rents will be retained for as long as those barriers are effective. Of course, entrepreneurs will be looking for ways around the barriers.

Economic Regulation

There are two general types of regulations—economic and social. Economic regulation focuses on a single industry and ranges from the government's prescribing the pricing and output behavior to actually running and operating the business. Social regulation, which applies across all businesses, involves health and safety standards for products and the workplace, standards for protecting the environment, and other government restrictions on the behavior of firms and individuals.

The greatest amount of economic regulation has to do with what is called the natural monopoly. The natural monopoly is one that arises from economies of scale so that the largest firm is much more cost efficient than the smaller firms.[14] When economies of scale exist throughout the market, only one firm will end up supplying the market. That firm, because of its monopoly, will be able to charge high prices, earn huge profits, and keep other firms from entering the market. So the government authorities attempt to force the natural monopolist to price and sell as would a firm competing against many similar firms. In the United States, several different industries have been regulated, allegedly because they were natural monopolies. Railroads, airlines, utilities, and trucking, for example, have been regulated on the basis of natural monopoly. Software is often taken to be a natural monopoly, due to the high cost of making the first copy and the low cost of replication, so the more copies made, the lower the average cost. This argument has been used to justify arguments relating to Microsoft's current personal computer software market domination and to suggest the possibility of its replacement by a future natural monopoly of free software.

Rate of Return Regulation

Most economic regulation is carried out by corporation or regulatory commissions at either the state level or the federal level. The natural monopoly is told what price it can charge and the quantity it must produce. Regulatory commissions determine what price to prescribe by calculating average accounting costs and adding a markup to those costs based on a "fair rate of return on capital"—called rate of return regulation. Rate of return regulation refers to the situation in which an industry is told the prices it must charge and the quantities it must sell. Industries that have been subject to rate of return regulation include electric utilities, telecommunications, trucking, railroads, airlines, and cable television. Rate of return regulation works in the following way. Suppose an electric utility has $300 million of assets and the regulatory authority is allowing it to earn a 10 percent rate of return. The utility will then be allowed to earn accounting profits of $30 million. The utility will be allowed to set a price and sell a quantity that will yield this profit—as long as all customers are served.

One of the problems of rate of return regulation is that it can bias the regulated companies toward increasing their costs and operating inefficiently. If the firm is able to increase the assets that will be included in the rate base, then it can earn more money. Depending on the scrutiny of regulators, the regulated firms might build grandiose buildings, acquire luxury furnishings and decorative items, as well as double up on equipment, and so on, and get the regulators to allow the firm to raise price.

Network Effects

Microsoft's dominance stems largely from **network effects** or **network externalities** rather than economies of scale. For Microsoft, the costs of production are high compared to the costs of distribution, but low compared to the price the market would bear. This is why Microsoft has made such large profits. Nevertheless, there have been serious calls about regulating Microsoft or breaking it up into several separate companies.

Natural monopoly effects are due to the cost conditions of the firm, while network effects arise from the benefit to the consumers of a good from **standardization** of the good. Network effects or network externalities suggest that the larger a network, the greater the benefits another member gets from joining that network. So if there is one network, then the product is standardized—the same for each customer. Many goods have both properties, such as operating system software and telephone networks.

Network effects have two implications that some use to call for increased government control or regulation. If a business is able to gather momentum before others enter, then the lower average costs may permit it to dominate a market. It is argued that by being first, it can dominate a market no matter whether it offers the best product or is the most efficient. This suggests that markets can become dominated or even monopolized by inefficient technologies or firms.

A commonly used example of network externalities is the dominance of VHS over Betamax. It is generally agreed that the Betamax was the better technology, and yet the VHS is now not only dominant, but exclusive in the marketplace. How did this happen? The network externalities explanation of this event is that the success of VHS depended on chance as much as anything else. When VHS and Beta first hit the market, no one knew which was the better product. For some reason (or no reason), a few more people bought VHS than Beta. So when people who are considering buying VCRs ask their friends what they should get, they say VHS. Thus more people began buying VHS than Beta since a majority of their friends had VHS. As video rental stores began popping up, it made very little sense for them to stock both VHS and Betamax tapes. After doing a little market research, more rental store owners chose to invest in VHS tapes than Beta tapes. This, in turn, encouraged more buyers of VCRs to purchase VHS machines, since those were the tapes that were more readily available. Thus increasing returns turned a very small initial difference in market share into VHS's market domination and Beta's extinction.

An example widely used to illustrate the potential inefficiencies created by network externalities is the typewriter keyboard, called QWERTY for short (the first letter line on a keyboard is QWERTYUIOP). The keyboard layout became a standard after an initial flurry of different layouts. QWERTY became the standard because it was optimal given the early typewriters. Typists could not work too fast because the keys on the early typewriters tended to jam.[15] So manufacturers found that the QWERTY layout slowed typists just enough that the typewriters worked well. But several decades ago, jamming keys ceased to be a problem, and it would have made sense to shift to an alternative, more efficient design. A rival layout, called the Dvorák keyboard, was available and purportedly more efficient. But the standard keyboard was a network that had become locked in. People who had learned on the QWERTY keyboard were not about to change to a new one.

Other examples of inefficiencies due to network externalities include Windows rather than the "better" Mac system, gas-powered automobiles rather than the "better" steam-powered ones, and light-water nuclear power plants rather than the "better" inert-gas version. These examples are used to support the general view that free markets cannot be relied on to select the best technology. Market winners will be the best of the available alternatives only by the sheerest of coincidences. The first technology that attracts development, the first standard that attracts adopters, or the first product that attracts consumers will tend to have an insurmountable advantage, even over superior rivals that happen to come along later. Many economists argue that in a QWERTY world, markets cannot be trusted.[16] Moreover, it is argued that if a product has an established network, it is almost impossible for a new product to displace it.

Does this mean that as society gets more advanced technologically, luck will play a larger and larger role and markets will be less and less efficient? No, it does not. The argument and illustrations of network effects have some problems. Consider the QWERTY keyboard. Wouldn't producers of alternative keyboards be motivated to cash in on any successes that alternative systems could generate? Learning new finger placements or hand positions is not that difficult. In fact, other keyboards did compete with QWERTY; they just couldn't surpass QWERTY. In comparing DOS and the Mac operating systems, the Mac system was far more expensive than DOS. Moreover, Apple failed to allow the Mac system widespread distribution. Consumers aren't fixated on a system forever. They switched to DOS and then switched away from DOS when they moved to Windows. Was the success of the inferior VHS a case of random luck? No. Consumers selected the best value for the dollar and chose the VHS. Sony refused to license the Betamax technology, adding to the higher expense of Betamax. Consumers chose the less expensive VHS since the advantage of the BETA didn't seem important to them. Those film specialists who considered the higher quality of the Beta worth the extra expense continued to purchase it. But the market was dominated by the VHS.

Some other network experiences are worth looking at. With the telegraph, there was explosive growth: The U.S. telegraphic network expanded 600-fold between 1846 and 1852. The first lines went between large cities, and then from the large to smaller cities, and so on. But the network did not enable the telegraph to dominate the communication market. The network became increasingly expensive rather than increasingly cheaper because each additional amount of line added fewer and fewer customers. It was the innovation of the telephone that destroyed the telegraph network.

America OnLine's initial growth was astronomical. Just as the Internet was becoming popular, AOL offered people an easy way to get on board, and it offered special incentives for members who enticed their friends to sign up. As a way of keeping members, AOL allowed members access to exclusive chat rooms, the ability to view who among the other AOL users they knew were currently signed onto AOL, and the ability to retract e-mails sent to other AOL users before they were viewed. The network of users joined AOL because people they knew were also members of AOL. AOL's experience was replicated by online dating services. With just a few people subscribing, the service would not be very valuable to any potential new member because it would be very unlikely any member would find a match with any other member. Thus, demand for the service is low. But as membership increases and the probability of a match rises, the value of membership rises. The larger the network, the more valuable is membership and thus, the greater the cost for any one individual user to switch to another network (the opportunity cost of not being connected to the large network). These conditions suggest that a monopoly would result —that is, that one network would dominate. So why is AOL not the only Internet service provider (ISP), and why are there many online dating services? Part of the reason might be that people like choices. When a market is dominated and standardization has occurred, choices are obviously reduced; there is no choice. Thus, if people have strong desires for variety, network externalities are less likely to exist for the entire market.

In addition to the customer desire for differentiation, a company or network must have economies of scale to enable it to continually offer value at a lower and lower cost. AOL was the largest ISP in 2002. Yet by 2005 it was far from the largest. The problem was that while the network externalities created a momentum for AOL, its capacity was not sufficient to meet demand. The consumers became frustrated and turned toward other providers. Had economies of scale enabled AOL to lower costs, lower prices, and increase the value of membership, it is likely that MSN and others would not have been able to compete. With online dating services, consumers actually wanted more of their kind of people but fewer people altogether. So today we see a wide variety of services— some by religious affiliation, some by outside interests such as sports or music, art, or the like, some by certain age ranges, and so forth.

Social Regulation

Social regulation is typically applied across all industries. For instance, all businesses are subject to the Occupational Safety and Health Administration (OSHA) standards or Environmental Protection Agency (EPA) requirements. While economic regulation has declined in the past 50 years, social regulation has been a growth industry. New government agencies are created to deal with issues, and existing ones are constantly given more responsibility. The following are just a few of the regulatory agencies involved in social regulation in the United States:

- The Occupational Safety and Health Administration (OSHA), which is concerned with protecting workers against injuries and illnesses associated with their jobs
- The Consumer Product Safety Commission (CPSC), which specifies minimum standards for safety of products
- The Food and Drug Administration (FDA), which is concerned with the safety and effectiveness of food, drugs, and cosmetics
- The Equal Employment Opportunity Commission (EEOC), which focuses on the hiring, promotion, and discharge of workers
- The Environmental Protection Agency (EPA), which is concerned with air, water, and noise pollution

Growth of Social Regulation

The Federal Register lists, in telephone-book-sized print, the regulations of the federal government. The number of pages it takes to list these regulations is over 25,000. The annual administrative costs of federal regulatory activities exceed $15 billion. The costs of complying with the rules and regulations have been estimated to exceed $300 billion per year. Complying with environmental regulations alone costs business more than $200 billion per year.[17] Added to the direct costs of regulations are the opportunity costs. For instance, the lengthy FDA process for approving new biotechnology has stymied advances in agriculture and placed many lives in jeopardy. Regulatory restrictions on the telecommunications industry have resulted in U.S. industries lagging behind those in other nations in the development of fiber optics. The total cost imposed on the U.S. economy from federal regulations has been estimated to be more than $600 billion a year.

Why do regulations come about? One argument is that regulation is needed to correct a market failure such as externalities, public goods, or asymmetric information. Most of the arguments made in support of social regulation are based on the idea that without government intervention, the public would be harmed. More than 10,000 workers die in job-related accidents in the United States each year; air pollution is an increasing problem in many cities, leading to cancer and other diseases, which in turn means increased demands on health care agencies; hundreds of children are killed each year as a result of poorly designed toys; unfair discharges from jobs occur frequently; global warming is causing havoc to our environment. It is argued that without government regulation, these events would be much more serious and would impose tremendous costs on society.

Without the EPA, would externalities created by businesses and by automobiles ever be internalized? Without the FDA, would the asymmetric problem prevalent in pharmaceuticals lead to adverse selection and moral hazard? In general, without these regulations and regulatory agencies, would the general public be protected from profit-seeking businesses?

Rent Seeking and Social Regulation

Another view of regulation is that its purpose is to benefit small, special interest groups at the expense of the general public. A classic example of environmental policy by and for special interests is the 1977 Clean Air Act amendments that mandated the use of scrubbers on coal-fired power plants. Under the 1970 Clean Air Act, the EPA established a policy whereby all coal plants were required to meet an emission standard for sulfur dioxide. The original standard of 1.2 pounds of sulfur dioxide (SO_2) per million BTUs (British thermal units) of coal could be met in a variety of ways. Despite its apparent flexibility, the regulation had disparate regional effects. Most of the coal in the eastern United States is relatively "dirty" due to its high sulfur content. Western coal, on the other hand, is cleaner. By using western coal, utilities and other coal-burning facilities complied with the federal standard without installing costly scrubbers. Scrubbers were so expensive that many midwestern firms found that it was cheaper to haul low-sulfur coal from the West than to use closer, "dirtier" deposits. When the Clean Air Act was revised in 1977, eastern producers of high-sulfur coal sought universal scrubbing. The revisions to the act required coal plants to meet both an emission standard and a technology standard. In particular, the law contained "new-source performance standards" that forced facilities to attain a "percentage reduction in emissions." In other words, no matter how clean the coal was, any new facility would still be required to install scrubbers. This destroyed low-sulfur coal's comparative advantage.

As is the case with antitrust laws, managers must be aware of regulations—both as a defensive matter and as an option in business strategy. In the regulatory context, rent seeking typically consists of pursuing government intervention that will provide a competitive advantage to a particular firm or industry. By restricting market entry or reducing output, regulations often reduce competition, create cartels, and increase returns. Thus, tariffs and licensing restrictions are regulatory measures commonly sought by rent seekers.

Firms and industries can enhance their rent-seeking activities by joining forces with "public interest groups." In the environmental arena, for example, environmental activists may prefer a policy, such as tightening hazardous waste regulations, while hazardous waste treatment firms see such regulations as an opportunity to expand their market. The Hazardous Waste Treatment Council (HWTC), a trade association of companies that operate incinerators and other hazardous waste treatment facilities, joined with environmental groups in a series of lawsuits seeking to force the EPA to impose more stringent regulations on used-motor-oil management. This would have required the treatment of used oil before disposal, providing members of the HWTC with increased business. If used oil were regulated as hazardous waste, the costs of handling it would increase, as would insurance for potential environmental liability exposure. The primary effect would be to drive smaller firms out of the used-oil-collection business and reduce the overall percentage of oil collected for reuse, recycling, or energy recovery.

Chlorofluorocarbons (CFCs) were once the most widely used class of refrigerants. CFCs were found in virtually every air conditioner, refrigerator, and chiller throughout the world. CFCs were also used as propellants in aerosol cans, cleaning agents, and foam-blowing agents. Congress banned the use of CFCs in aerosol cans in 1978 when the United Nations sponsored negotiations with the purpose of drafting a treaty to protect the ozone layer. Interestingly, the CFC industry did not oppose regulations. DuPont, the world's largest CFC producer, called for a complete global phase-out. Foreign CFC producers were taking over DuPont's market share. Under a global phase-out, consumers would have no alternative but to replace CFCs and CFC-reliant equipment with substitutes designed and patented by DuPont and other American producers. Others got into the act as well, boosting the phase-out's overall cost.

Other examples include:[18]

- The Business Council for a Sustainable Energy Future, a coalition of gas, wind, solar, and geothermal power producers and related firms, is lobbying for deep cuts in greenhouse gas emissions.
- The Environmental Technology Council, a successor to the Hazardous Waste Treatment Council (HWTC), wants to ensure that various wastes, such as fluorescent bulbs, are covered by hazardous waste regulations.
- The Alliance for Responsible Thermal Treatment (ARTT), an HWTC spinoff of incinerator operators, wants to prevent the burning of hazardous waste in cement kilns and thereby eliminate its members' toughest competitors.
- Major utilities recently lobbied to require the sale of electric vehicles in California and the northeastern United States and have sought policies that would subsidize the purchase of electric cars at the ratepayers' expense.
- Ethanol producers attempted to secure a portion of the lucrative oxygenate market for federally mandated reformulated gasoline.
- A primary purpose of the Conservation Reserve Program is to increase farm commodity prices by taking acreage out of production, though the program does little to control agricultural runoff.

The list could go on and on. Given the current interest in environmental issues and global warming, any regulation tied to reducing warming and helping the environment can collect supporters. An example of trade protectionism disguised as environmental protection is the European Economic Community's (EEC's) 1989 ban on the importation of U.S. beef produced with bovine growth hormones. There was no credible scientific evidence linking hormones in American beef to health problems. Nevertheless, health concerns were the reason given by the EEC when they prevented U.S. beef from being imported.

The United States has used environmental measures to restrict foreign imports as well. When corporate average fuel economy (CAFE) standards for automobiles were first enacted in the 1970s, Congress rejected alternative means of reducing automobile fuel consumption because these alternatives might encourage foreign imports. The CAFE standards that were adopted discriminated against high-end foreign manufacturers such as Mercedes-Benz, BMW, and Volvo, which have a limited fleet and not a wide range of automobile sizes. The CAFE standards are average fleet standards and thus are more troubling for manufacturers that do not make small cars with high fuel economy ratings.

The use of government rules and regulations to create a competitive advantage is not new and will not disappear. It is a strategy that a manager must be aware of in a defensive sense—to protect the firm from rent seeking by rivals—and must consider in the firm's portfolio of offensive strategies.

Rent Seeking

America spends well over 2 percent of the gross domestic product on pollution control, and the figure is rising. As the cost of environmental regulation increases, seeking regulatory policies that will carve out niche markets or obstruct competition becomes an increasingly profitable investment for many firms.

In the regulatory context, rent seeking typically consists of pursuing government intervention that will provide a comparative advantage to a particular industry. By restricting entry or reducing output, regulations often reduce competition, create cartels, and increase returns. Environmental regulations are conducive to rent seeking because both regulated firms and various environmental groups stand to gain from reductions in output and the creation of barriers to entry. For instance, environmental laws put a greater burden on small than on large plants. Small firms find the fixed costs of compliance to be much more costly per unit of output than large firms. Thus, regulation helps protect larger companies from the competition of smaller companies. It also can transfer large amounts to companies. The agricultural firm Archer Daniels Midland (ADM), has become very successful at enlisting government support. It is by far the biggest beneficiary of more than $2 billion in government subsidies the ethanol industry receives each year.

Why do the state and city governments attempt to pick winners and losers—to entice companies to their locations with subsidies? Are central planners able to pick winners and losers better than the market? The Mackinac Center, a think tank in Michigan, analyzed the performance of the Michigan Economic Growth Authority (MEGA), the state's most visible corporate-subsidy program. It found that among 127 deals whose employment promises were fully measurable through 2004, only 10 had met their projections. "MEGA is another in a long line of political programs disguised as economic ones. They're great for giving politicians cover but do little to produce real job growth." The economic growth councils and authorities are special interest groups or represent special interest groups that are small and focused on the subsidies, while the general taxpayers are large and do not pay much attention to each subsidy granted.

Source: Based on "Corporate-Welfare Queens (and Kings)" by John J. Miller. *National Review*, March 19, 2007.

Summary

1. When government intervenes in the economy, economic profit is affected. Rules and regulations may increase costs of goods sold and selling and general administrative costs. Requirements for workplace or capital requirements may influence capital costs or labor costs.
2. The government may intervene in the economy in reaction to inefficiency issues or to benefit special interest groups.
3. Antitrust policy is an attempt to enhance competition by restricting certain activities that could be anticompetitive.
4. Economic regulation refers to the prescription of price and output for a particular industry. Social regulation refers to the setting of health and safety standards for products and the workplace as well as environmental and operating procedures for all industries.
5. The World Trade Organization deals with international disputes. Antidumping is the issue that appears most often in claims brought to the WTO.

Key Terms

Antitrust
Herfindahl–Hirschman index (HHI)
Dumping

Network effects or network externalities
Standardization

Exercises

1. Company X has developed an important brand name through its advertising, innovation, and product quality and service. Suppose Company X sets up a network of exclusive dealerships, and one of the dealers decides to carry rival products as well as Company X's products. If Company X terminates the dealership, is it acting in a pro- or anticompetitive manner?

2. Would auctioning broadcast licenses be more efficient than having the Federal Communications Commission (FCC) assign licenses on some basis designed by the FCC? Explain.

3. Which of the three types of government policies—antitrust, social regulation, or economic regulation—is the basis for each of the following? Who benefits from the policy?

    a. beautician education standards
    b. certified public accounting requirements
    c. liquor licensing
    d. Justice Department guidelines
    e. the Clean Air Act
    f. the Nutrition and Labeling Act

4. Some airline executives have called for "re-reregulation." Why might an executive of an airline prefer to operate in a regulated environment?

5. Discuss the claim that social regulation is unnecessary. Does the claim depend on whether the structure of an industry is primarily one of perfect competition or of oligopoly?

6. Suppose a firm is selling a product for less than a foreign country does in the home country and an antidumping suit forces an end to the practice. Is it possible that the result is a loss in efficiency? Explain.

7. In the 1990s, the Justice Department sued several universities for collectively setting the size of scholarships offered. Explain why the universities' alleged price fixing might be harmful to students.

8. Suppose a consumer hires Bekins moving company to move his possessions from California to Utah and Bekins damages $3,000 worth of furniture and refuses to compensate him. The consumer in frustration says, "There ought to be a law!" Evaluate the situation.

9. "The Japanese or Chinese or Koreans or others, are beating us at every step. We must act as they do. We must allow and encourage cooperation among firms, and we must develop partnerships between business and government." Evaluate this argument.

10. Using the following HHIs, do the following:

a. Indicate in which market a merger would be allowed under Department of Justice guidelines.

b. Provide an economic explanation for why this result would occur.

c. Provide a numerical example illustrating why the result might not make economic sense. Impact of WorldCom's Acquisition of Sprint (HHIs for Long-Distance Voice, Data, and Internet Backbone Markets)

	Total Long Distance Voice	Consumer Long Distance Voice	Business Long Distance Voice	Total Long Distance Data
Premerger	3,209	4,133	2,921	1,730
Postmerger	3,881	4,441	4,105	2,290
Increase	672	308	1,184	560

11. "Government operations are often described as inefficient. In fact, they operate exactly as we would expect given their incentives." What does this mean? The example used is the DMV—a monopoly that does not care about the customer. Is this an appropriate analogy? Would a monopoly care about its customers? Can you to draw an analogy between the firm and the DMV with respect to a firm's relationships with employees and the assets it owns?

12. "The government should not be the sole provider of a good or service unless there is a compelling reason." What compelling reason? Would you agree that issuing drivers' licenses must be left to government?

13. Explain why regulations such as licensing requirements and immigration restrictions come into being and then remain in practice.

14. The "grabbing hand" may be described as merely an essential business strategy. Explain what the strategy is and demonstrate how many resources a business *should* allocate to it.

15. What is a natural monopoly? Can you think of an example of a natural monopoly? If you can, explain why you consider it a natural monopoly.

16. What are network externalities? What is the externality part of the "network externalities"? Why don't firms with network externalities become monopolists?

17. The 2010 FCC report on the wireless market also noted that the following: "There are over 900,000 rural residents who have no mobile service at all. Another 2.5 million get coverage from only one provider.. Why would the report note the rural residents? Do the rural residents have something to do with the high HHI?

18. Explain why rent-seeking competition tends to dissipate rents—to drive them down so that there are no abnormal rents.

19. Would you expect rent seeking to be practiced more by large firms or small firms? Explain

20. Suppose internal rent seeking increases as firm size increases. What would this say for the "optimal" size of firms?

CHAPTER NOTES

1. Larry Rulison, "Waiting for AMD—AMD hasn't yet decided to build a chip plant in Malta; the reason why isn't entirely clear," December 23, 2007 www.nydailynews.com/blogs/dailypolitics/2007/12/odds-and-ends-157.html.

2. The growth of ethanol as a fuel source in the United States has resulted from tremendous subsidies at the federal, state, and local levels. The biggest single item is the Volumetric Ethanol Excise Tax Credit (VEETC), which grants a tax credit to blenders who combine ethanol with gasoline, in the amount of 51 cents per gallon of pure ethanol blended. But this is only part of the story. In addition to the direct subsidy from the VEETC, many states reduce motor fuel taxes on favored fuels, and there are numerous separate subsidies and tax breaks for investment in the infrastructure required for biofuel production. There is also a large implicit subsidy in the form of the mandate from the Energy Policy Act of 2005 that 4 billion gallons come from renewable fuels in 2006, rising to 7.5 billion in 2012. The impact of these mandates on the price of ethanol is greatly amplified by the 54-cents-per-gallon tariff currently in effect for imports of ethyl alcohol intended for use as a fuel. Finally, there are significant direct agricultural subsidies for farmers that reduce their water, fuel, and other costs below market. The subsidies currently sum to about $1.38 per gallon of ethanol.

3. Andrei Shleifer and Robert W. Vishny, *The Grabbing Hand: Government Pathologies and Their Cures* (Cambridge, MA: Harvard University Press, 1998).

4. Tom Humphrey, "Lobbying Costs Hit $11M in AT&T, Cable TV Industry Battle," KnowNews.com, Tuesday, November 20, 2007 http://www.knoxnews.com/news/2007/nov/20/lobbying-costs-hit-11m-in-att-cable-tv-industry.

5. James Harvey Young, *Pure Food: Securing the Federal Food and Drug Act of 1906* (Princeton, NJ: Princeton University Press, 1989). Gary Libecap, "The Rise of the Chicago Packers and the Origins of Meat Inspection and Antitrust," *Economic Inquiry*, 30 (1992): 241–262.

6. D. T. Armentano, *Antitrust Policy: The Case for Repeal* (Washington, DC: Cato Institute, 1986).

7. Del Jones, "Today's Issue: Some Lessons Learned in an Antitrust Fight. Guest CEO: Thomas Stemberg, CEO of Staples," *USA Today*, March 30, 1998, p. 5B.

8. *United States v. Foley*, 1979-1 Trade Cas. (CCH) 62,577 (4th Cir. 1979).

9. *Quality Trailer Products*, 57 Fed. Reg. 37004, August 17, 1992.

10. R. Preston McAfee and Nicholas V. Vakkur, "The Strategic Abuse of the Antitrust Laws," *Journal of Strategic Management Education*, 1 no. 3 (2004), www.usdoj.gov/atr/public/hearings/single_firm/docs/220039.htm, accessed May 1, 2008.

11. William F. Shughart III, Private Antitrust Enforcement, Compensation, Deterrence, or Extortion? *Regulation*, Cato Institute, www.cato.org/pubs/regulation/regv13n3/reg13n3-shughart.html.

12. World Trade Organization at: www.wto.org/english/news_e/pres07_e/pr497_e.htm

13. Carolyn Said, "Prepare for Jumbo Shrimp Prices," Wednesday, July 7, 2004 *San Francisco Chronicle/SF Gate* www.sfgate.com/cgi-bin/article.cgi?f=/c/a/2004/07/07/BUG997HET11.DTL Paul Magnusson, "Peeled and Eaten by U.S. Shrimpers," *Business Week*, July 8, 2004, www.businessweek.com/bwdaily/dnflash/jul2004/nf2004078_1187_db045.htm. "U.S. Slaps tariffs on Shrimp Imported from China, Vietnam," *USA Today*, Posted July 6, 2004 http://www.usatoday.com/news/nation/2004-07-06-shrimp-tariff_x.htm, accessed May 2, 2008.

14. Economies of scale refers to a firm producing more output at lower per unit costs as the firm gets larger.

15. This question was first asked by Paul David, "Understanding the Economics of QWERTY: The Necessity of History," in W. N. Parker, ed., *Economics History and the Modern Economist* (London: Blackwell, 1986).

16. See the list of references provided in *The Economics of Qwerty: Papers by Stan Liebowitz and Stephen Margolis,* ed. Peter Lewin, (New York: Macmillan/New York University Press, 2002), including Robert Frank and Philip Cook's *The Winner-Take-All Society* (New York: Penguin, 1996); and Paul Krugman's *Peddling Prosperity* (New York: W. W. Norton & Co., 1994), pp. 221–244.

17. Information on costs of compliance is available from www.sba.gov/advo/research/rs264.pdf and www.cato.org/researcharea.php?display=11.

18. Jonathan H. Adler, *Rent Seeking behind the Green Curtain,* CATO, www.cato.org/pubs/regulation, accessed, June 10, 2007.

CHAPTER 11

What Should the Firm Do?

Corporate Social Responsibility

Corporate social responsibility (CSR) refers to the idea that firms have a responsibility to anyone affected by the firms' actions, its stakeholders, rather than just its shareholders. CSR has become such an important political entity that may firms attempt to use their expenditures on the stakeholders as good business strategy. Many companies have chief corporate responsibility officers, and many others provide a CSR report in their annual statements. Following are CSR reports taken from the annual reports of three large U.S. companies.

Starbucks—*Doing Business in a Different Way Contributing positively to our communities and environment is so important to Starbucks that it's one of the six guiding principles of our mission statement. We work together on a daily basis with partners (employees), suppliers and farmers to help create a more sustainable approach to high-quality coffee production, to help build stronger local communities, to minimize our environmental footprint and to be responsive to our customers' health and wellness needs.*[1]

FedEx—*FedEx cares about the communities in which we live and work. We are dedicated to effective corporate citizenship, leading the way in charitable giving, corporate governance and a commitment to the environment.*[2]

Gap—*At Gap Inc., we believe we should go beyond the basics of ethical business practices and embrace our responsibility to people and to the planet. We believe this brings sustained, collective value to our shareholders, our employees, our customers and society.*[3]

The political pressure on businesses also comes about through pressure on nations. The Responsible Competitiveness Index (RCI), from the British nonprofit, AccountAbility, and Brazilian business school, Fundação Dom Cabral, looks at how countries are performing in their efforts to promote responsible business practices. The index includes 108 countries covering over 96 percent of global GDP, with geographical representation on all five continents.

1. Is Corporate Social Responsibility responsible?

Stakeholders and Shareholders

Should the firm maximize shareholder value, or should it focus on some other objective? Recently, many people have argued that a firm should care about more than just the shareholders. Focusing on just shareholders may cause the firm to ignore important social issues. For instance, it is claimed that BP's blown-out well in the Gulf of Mexico in 2010 was the result of BP focusing too much on shareholders.

Business Insight

Who Does the Company Exist for, the Shareholders or the Stakeholders?

Only 3 percent of Japanese managers say companies should maintain dividend payments to stockholders even if it means the company has to lay off workers. In other words, in Japan, the first priority is with employees. That compares with 41 percent in Germany, 40 percent in France, and 89 percent in both the United States and the United Kingdom. And in Japan, 97 percent of respondents said a company exists for all stakeholders, compared with 83 percent in Germany, 78 percent in France, 76 percent in the United States, and 71 percent in the United Kingdom.[4]

Maximizing the Power of the Firm

Value maximization states that a manager should make all decisions so as to increase the long-run market value of the firm, that is, the sum of the value of all financial claims on the firm. Adding value means that a firm produces an output or set of outputs that is valued by customers at more than the value of the inputs the firm consumes in order to supply that output or outputs. Value maximization benefits society. If a firm creates an output that consumers value more than they value the inputs that went into creating that output, then society has gained from the output.

Of course, we are talking about voluntary transactions. Forced transactions provide no clues of societal values. When transactions are voluntary, we know that the owners of inputs value them less than or equal to the price at which the firm buys them. Otherwise, the resource owners wouldn't sell the inputs. Therefore, the opportunity cost to society of those inputs is no higher than the total cost to the firm of acquiring them. Similarly, the value to society of the goods and services produced by the firm is at least as great as the price the firm receives for the sale of those goods and services. If this were not true, the individuals purchasing them would not purchase them.

Stakeholder Theory Has to Be to Maximize Profit

The idea that the firm most benefits society by focusing on maximizing shareholder value or profit is counterintuitive to many people. They argue that a firm maximizing profit will not care whether it harms employees, consumers, communities, or the environment. A firm has to maximize the value to all of its **stakeholders** —everyone connected with or affected by the firm. Former Secretary of Labor Robert Reich is one among many politicians who has called for a "new corporate citizenship" whereby firms would be responsible for the social costs and benefits of economic change. As an economic incentive to encourage corporations to be more employee-sensitive, Reich suggested a reduction, or elimination, of corporate taxes for qualifying firms. Firms would have to contribute 2 percent or more of total payrolls to upgrade general skills and pro-vide decent pension and health benefits, profit sharing, layoff training, and outplacement. Reich suggested that firms that failed in their responsibility to maintain jobs should pay extra taxes and should be listed in a "corporate hall of shame."[5]

One problem with CSR is that it might not be possible for a firm to carry it out. If a manager is supposed to do all of the following: maximize current profits, market share, future growth in profits, employee health and safety, and benefits for the local commu-nity, what is the manager going to do? He cannot maximize in all these directions at the same time. There are trade-offs.

A firm has to respond to whatever issues consumers think are important and are will-ing to allocate their resources to. It must entice consumers to purchase its goods and services. If a firm is viewed as unethical or a bad citizen, and consumers refuse to do business with the firm as a result, then the firm has to change its ways or go out of busi-ness. If consumers think an action deserves to have resources allocated to it and are will-ing to pay for that allocation, the company responds. A company's resources have to be managed in such a way as to make them worth more than they would be if managed in any other way or by any other firm. In other words, a firm must maximize the value it adds to resources. If it does not, in a free market the resources will be reallocated to other, more valuable uses. Maximizing shareholder value, maximizing profit, maximizing value added—these phrases reflect the idea that the objective of business is to create value. Profit or value maximization is not inconsistent with the idea that a firm should pay attention to its stakeholders. In fact, managers have to respond to all stakeholders in the following way: *spend an additional dollar of resources to satisfy the desires of each constituency as long as consumers value the result at more than a dollar.*

An Illustration of Profit Maximization

Economists have developed a rule for how a firm maximizes profit; it equates marginal revenue to marginal cost. The firm should supply more output or carry out more of an activity or grow or outsource or whatever, as long as the resources taken out of the econ-omy by the firm to produce output or carry out an activity is valued less than the output supplied or the activity the firm is engaged in is valued. As mentioned in Chapter 1, economists focus on the incremental unit or the margin. For instance, if selling one more unit of output increases costs less than it increases revenue, then producing (and selling) that unit of output will increase profit. Conversely, if selling one more unit of output costs more than the revenue obtained from the sale of that unit, then selling that unit of output will decrease profit. So, profit is maximized when the additional rev-enue from producing and selling an additional unit of output equals the additional cost.

Marginal cost is the additional cost of producing one more unit of output, (the value of resources needed to produce one more unit); marginal revenue is the additional revenue obtained from selling one more unit of output (the value society places on one more unit). So if marginal revenue is larger than marginal cost, producing and selling more will increase profit. Conversely, when marginal revenue is less than marginal cost, produc-ing and selling more will lower profit. Thus, profit is at a maximum when the quantity offered for sale creates a marginal revenue that is equal to the marginal cost: $MR = MC$.

That this rule results in a profit maximum is illustrated in Table 11.1, showing output, price, total revenue, marginal revenue, total cost, marginal cost and profit. Assume that all aspects of the business and all stakeholder views are taken into account in the costs. The first unit of output costs $1,000 to sell (column 5). The marginal cost (additional cost) of the first unit is $1,000, listed in column 6. When sold, the first unit of output brings in $1,700 in revenue (column 3), so the marginal revenue is $1,700 (column 4).

Since marginal revenue is greater than marginal cost, the firm is better off selling that first unit of output than not selling it.

Table 11.1						
Profit Maximization						
(1) TOTAL OUTPUT (Q)	(2) PRICE (P)	(3) TOTAL REVENUE (TR = PQ)	(4) MARGINAL REVENUE (MR)	(5) TOTAL COST (TC)	(6) MARGINAL COST (MC)	(7) TOTAL PROFIT (TR-TC)
0	0	0	0	$1,000	—	−$1,000
1	$1,700	1,700	1,700	2,000	1,000	−300
2	1,600	3,200	1,500	2,800	800	400
3	1,500	4,500	1,300	3,500	700	1,000
4	1,400	5,600	1,100	4,000	500	1,600
5	1,300	6,500	900	4,500	500	2,000
6	1,200	7,200	700	5,200	700	2,000 Profit Maximum
7	1,100	7,700	500	6,000	800	1,700
8	1,000	8,000	300	7,000	1,000	1,000
9	900	8,100	100	9,000	2,000	−900

The second unit of output costs an additional $800 to sell and brings in an additional $1,500 in revenue when sold. With the second unit of output, marginal revenue exceeds marginal cost. Thus the firm is better off producing two units than none or one.

Profit continues to rise until the sixth unit of output is sold. The marginal cost of selling the seventh unit is $800, while the marginal revenue is $500. Since marginal cost is greater than marginal revenue, profit declines if the seventh unit is sold. The firm can maximize profit by selling six units, the quantity at which marginal revenue and marginal cost are equal.

If we know marginal revenue and marginal cost, determining the quantity to offer for sale and the price to charge is straightforward. The problem is that marginal revenue and marginal cost are typically not known. Financial statements do not report them. Costs are allocated among activities or across departments, but the incremental cost of producing one more unit is not calculated. Moreover, managers do not even think of marginal costs and revenues. For a firm producing millions of units of a product, one more unit would seem to be a trivial thing to worry about.

Although accountants do not provide marginal cost information and although executives say they pay no attention to marginal cost or marginal revenue, these concepts come into play in their decision making. Consider, for instance, how an airline decides to price its services. The price of seats varies considerably depending on when one flies, whether one stays over on a Saturday night, and when one purchases a ticket. Often an airline flying with some empty seats will sell the seats at the last moment very inexpensively. In fact, the price of the seat is often below the average per-passenger cost of flying the plane. The average per-passenger cost of Southwest Airlines to fly is one of the lowest in the industry, about $0.07 to $0.09 per mile. Yet Southwest will often sell some of its seats on distances of 1,000 for $25. Why? Because $25 is significantly more than $0. In addition, the incremental cost of adding one more passenger is nearly zero. Thus, the marginal revenue of the seat, $25, is greater than the marginal cost, near zero. The executives of Southwest Airlines know that they are better off selling the seat. They know this not because they know that marginal revenue is greater than marginal cost or because they have calculated marginal cost, but because they know they make more profit by doing so. The profit-maximizing rule, *MR = MC*, may not be on executives' lips or in their manuals, but it does describe their behavior. It provides a framework for understanding business behavior. *Spend an additional dollar on any activity as long as consumers value the result at more than a dollar.*

Competition and Price

The search for profit is the market in action—it is competition. Competition drives out inefficiency and ensures that resources are allocated to their highest valued uses. If resources were not being used efficiently, or in their highest valued use, by a firm, then other firms would take business away from the inefficient firm.

Competition drives prices ever closer to the costs of production.[6] As discussed in Chapter 9, if it costs $0.70 to produce a cup of coffee and I sell it for $1.50, someone is going to come along and sell it for $1. Then someone else will sell it for $0.80 and so on until it is selling for $0.70. Competition requires that resources be used as efficiently as possible. Anyone not being as efficient as possible will not last long in the market. If you can't produce that coffee for $0.70, then you will not be in business when the price drops below your costs.

When a firm earns an economic profit and others can enter the business and compete with the incumbent firm, then the incumbent cannot sustain positive economic profit. The coffee I am selling at $1.50 a cup is offered for $1.00 a cup, then $0.80, and so on until the price of a cup of coffee is just the cost of supplying that cup of coffee, that is, until my economic profit is zero. The price of the coffee is driven to the point where it equals the cost of offering the coffee for sale.

To make and sustain profit, you not only have to build a better mousetrap, but you have to continually improve it. There is no resting on one's laurels when competition is present. This is why competition is a learning process, a striving to come up with the next great thing, the next innovation or technological change. Without that, your market or product becomes commoditized; it is not distinct from products sold by rivals. A firm selling a commodity is at the mercy of the market. Since the good or service is identical to those sold by rivals, the firm is unable to set a price that is any different from those of its rivals.

Market Power   Society benefits from competition because resources are allocated to their highest valued use and consumers can buy what they want at the lowest possible prices. Yet, as a manager, you would like to keep some more of that added value for your investors and yourself. So what you must do is find a way to separate yourself from your rivals; to move your product from being a commodity or commoditized to a product that is distinguished from others or, even better, is unique. As a manager you want to limit competition; you want to earn a profit and then not have to scurry around trying to keep others from taking business from you. You want *market power*. In fact, the best thing for you would be to be the only supplier, a monopolist. How do you become a monopolist? The most prevalent method is via the government (rent seeking). Suppose the government has given me a special license to locate a coffee shop where there are no substitutes available. I have a monopoly because of the license the government has issued. In other words, I am the only supplier in the local area where I do business. What will happen? The price of the coffee will be set where the value to the consumer of not going elsewhere is the differential between my costs and the price of the coffee. If consumers place a value of $1.00 on not having to traipse around the corner for coffee, then I can charge $1.70. The government license is a barrier to entry that enables me to charge more than the competitive price.

How much would I spend in rent seeking to maintain my monopoly? I would be willing to spend nearly all of the extra profit the monopoly gives me relative to zero economic profit I would end up with in competition.

The primary reason a monopoly exists is the government; most monopolies are created and sustained by the government. In the fifteenth through the seventeenth centuries, governments raised revenue by granting monopolies to special interest groups in return for some of their profits. Christopher Columbus was granted a monopoly from Queen Isabella of Spain; the Hudson Bay Company was granted a monopoly by the English monarchy; most of the explorers and trading ships of the time had been granted monopoly charters. Today, government-granted monopolies include the U.S. Postal Service—a monopoly supplier of first-class mail delivery; the Federal Reserve Bank—a monopoly supplier of U.S. currency; and other government agencies. In addition, patents can provide a government-created monopoly. Glaxo-Wellcome, for example, was granted a patent on AZT and thus was, by law, the only supplier of the anti-HIV/AIDS drug for a period of 17 years. In many businesses a license or permit is required from government in order to do business. Taxi service at an airport, vendor sales at ballparks, beauticians, contractors, lawyers, doctors, and so on all require government licenses to operate a business. Starbucks may have an exclusive with a university to provide coffee services; in this case the university is acting like a government in granting the monopoly.

Many businesses gain exclusivity by rent seeking. Rent seeking does not, by itself, create or add value; instead it transfers value from one party or group to another. Consumers pay more and receive less when a government monopoly provides a good or service than when it is competitively provided. Rent seeking destroys value for society as a whole but yet, for an individual firm it may be the case that a dollar allocated to rent seeking generates more than a dollar allocated to production.

Theoretically, a monopoly could arise because of cost conditions rather than because of government action. For instance, a natural monopoly could arise if cost conditions would allow it. The basic theory of natural monopoly employs sunk costs. Sunk costs are the costs of entering a market that you cannot recover if you leave it: the costs you must incur to be able to deliver the good or service even if nobody buys it. Existing suppliers have already invested in sunk costs, but new suppliers will have to invest in them to get into the market, and they may not enter the market because of the fear of losing the sunk costs. So the incumbent firm has made the sunk costs and has grown; and as it grows, its costs per unit of output it supplies declines. The larger the firm, the lower it can set prices. This limits competition; new firms would have to enter very big—bigger than the incumbent firm.

It is difficult to find cases of natural monopolies. Electric utilities used to be thought of as natural monopolies because of the economies of scale that existed in the generation of electricity, and so it was argued that governments needed to regulate these industries. But in most cases where there are large economies of scale, it has not taken long for technology to alter the benefits that large scale provides. Electricity is no different. It has been deregulated and privatized successfully in many countries—and competition does for it exactly what it typically does, driving profits down to normal levels. Telecommunications has been called a natural monopoly, but the entry of so many new providers argues against that.

Nevertheless, the objective of a manager is to differentiate the output of the firm from substitutes—to reduce the substitutability of the products. The firm wants market power, the ability to set price where it wants without losing all of its customers.

Differentiation and Market Power   A manager wants to avoid commoditization and acquire the benefits of having some exclusivity, some monopoly (market) power. If a business can create a special attribute that others cannot easily mimic, then it will have a monopoly of sorts. Competition will exist, but it will not be able to completely replicate the special attribute. As a result, profits are not driven to zero, but instead will be zero plus the value of the special attribute. Thus, one of the primary strategies of business is to find that special attribute that will enable the firm to sustain abnormal profits for at least some period of time.

A firm wants to distinguish its goods or services from those of rivals. The more the consumer considers the products different, the more ability the firm has to set prices and earn positive economic profits. Think about what Starbucks has been able to do. It is able to sell a cup of coffee for $1.60 when its costs are only about $0.70 per cup because it is selling more than just the commodity, coffee. Starbucks developed a special attribute, a brand name or reputation that others were unable to duplicate. People go to Starbucks because of the ambience and the full register of different drinks, not just coffee. To date, no other firm has been able to do exactly what Starbucks does. But because other firms can enter the business, the coffee price has been bid down until the differential between the cost of all resources used in providing the coffee and Starbucks' selling price is the value consumers put on Starbucks' special attribute. As long as this attribute has value to consumers, the company is able to earn abnormal profits.

Thus an important strategy for firms is to create a special attribute. Every firm— producer, fabricator, seller, broker, agent, merchant—tries to distinguish its offering from all others. This is true even of those who produce and deal in commodities or products that are not differentiable, such as primary metals, grains, chemicals, plastics, and money. In the case of the commodity, it is the entire firm—sales, service, personnel, and appearances of offices and personnel—that matters. The reason firms try to differentiate themselves or their products is to make it more difficult for competitors to take away business.

Successful differentiation reduces the consumer's sensitivity to price—the price elasticity of demand. What does this mean for a firm? It means the firm can raise the price without incurring the loss of revenue that would come if the elasticity was higher. For years Intel was able to charge more for its microchips than competitors could charge for essentially the same microchip. Intel was able to do that because of its successful campaign to differentiate itself —"Intel Inside."

A brand name differentiates a product from other products. It is a key factor in consumer purchase decisions.[7] On average, a brand name is responsible for 18 percent of the total purchase decision. Moreover, prices of the strongest brands (in terms of the brand's importance in the decision to buy) are, on average, 19 percent higher than those of the weakest brands.[8]

When people do not have complete and perfect information, economists say that information is costly, which means that consumers have to search for information by perusing magazines or going from store to store to compare products, try out certain types of products, or purchase the advice of experts. Each of these activities takes time and, in some cases, money. Firms, realizing that search is costly for consumers, have an opportunity to increase business and differentiate their product by providing information and increasing familiarity with their product. This can be through promotion, placement, and packaging—marketing. It can also be done by devoting resources to portraying an image or creating a brand name. For instance, a firm that wants the public to realize it is stable and likely to be around for some time may devote resources to a large building or beautiful offices or large billboards. A clothing store in a mall is more stable than a vendor on the street corner, even though the mall location is just being rented. Harrod's massive building on Knightsbridge and Kensington High Street in London is so well known that it is a tourist attraction. For some products, an important signal that the product is of high quality is a guarantee or warranty. Prudential Insurance shows "the rock," and Allstate shows the "good hands" to illustrate their reliability. While these symbols have nothing to do with the actual service, they display an aspect that consumers find valuable—that the service will be offered in the future, so that an experience now might be used to evaluate the service in the future. Lawyers and financial advisers need to present an image of success. Who wants to use an unsuccessful attorney or financial adviser? Thus, attorneys and financial advisers typically have richly appointed offices located in large central-city buildings. They dress in expensive clothes and carry expensive briefcases. Consider the effect of a senior partner in a well-known brokerage firm who appears at a New York City bank in casual clothes to solicit business in financial instrument futures. Clearly, the executive has differentiated (although demeaned the image of) his firm's product. It is unlikely that bank officials would trust the decision of someone who was not serious. No wonder that in the early years of IBM Thomas Watson insisted that his salesmen dress in what became known as the IBM uniform—white shirt, dark tie, and dark suit.

Why would consumers be willing to pay extra for a firm or product with a reputation or brand name? Because reputations and brand names reduce the consumers' costs of gathering information. If consumers had perfect information, producers would have no incentive to create brand names or to differentiate products other than by actual physical characteristics. Aspirin would simply be aspirin, not Bayer. The brand name provides information to consumers; it is a signal of quality or reliability. The objective of creating a brand name is to increase consumer loyalty and thus reduce the price elasticity of demand. The greater the consumer's reluctance to shift brands, the lower the price elasticity of demand. Consumers loyal to a brand or to a firm will purchase that brand or purchase from that firm even if the price is above the prices of substitute products.

Guarantees and warranties can be indicators of quality and enable firms to differentiate themselves from rivals. Guarantees are difficult to fake. A low-quality product would break down frequently, making the guarantee quite costly for the firm. If a firm establishes a warranty policy, then other firms either have to offer matching warranty policies or admit to having a lower-quality product. If a potential rival is unable to imitate the warranties of existing firms, it may decide not to enter the market in the first place. If the firm can match the warranty and beat it, then when the firm enters the market it will offer a better warranty. This is what the Japanese auto producers did to the U.S. auto producers in the 1970s. U.S. auto producers did not offer warranties as extensive as those now offered by the Japanese. As a result, customers soon came to see that "Made in Japan" meant quality.

We know that a firm will devote a dollar of resources to any activity if society values the resulting output more than a dollar. A firm will devote a dollar of resources to creating a brand name or otherwise providing information to consumers if consumers value that expenditure more than a dollar.

Exit

What occurs when a firm finds that society does not value its output more than it values the resources that went into generating that output? If a firm makes inefficient decisions or fails to match the efficiencies of other firms, it will earn negative economic profits. If this occurs in the short run, the firm must decide whether to continue operating until it is able to liquidate (through bankruptcy or by being acquired) or to temporarily close down. It does not matter whether the firm is a perfect competitor or a monopolist; it can earn negative economic profit. The U.S. Postal Service, for instance, has seldom earned positive economic profit. What occurs when a monopolist earns a negative economic profit? It depends: The government may step in to subsidize the monopolist, or the monopolist may shut down temporarily or go out of business entirely. In the latter instance, the monopolist is no different from any other firm. Whether a firm closes its doors temporarily or gets out of business altogether depends on a couple of factors, and these factors apply whether the firm is a perfect competitor, monopolist, or anything else.

Consider three firms that have the costs and revenues shown in Table 11.2. **Fixed costs** are costs that do not vary as output changes; examples are rent and also labor costs if long-term contracts are used. **Variable costs** are costs that vary as output varies; examples include electricity, water, fuel, and materials. Although all three firms are incurring losses of $300, they make very different decisions. Firm A decides to continue producing and selling its products. Firm B decides to discontinue operations *for a while* and see what the future holds. Firm C gets out of business as soon as it can. The difference is that the firm A is earning sufficient revenues to pay for its variable costs and some of its fixed costs. If it discontinued operations, it would still have to pay the fixed costs, and its losses would be much larger—$1,100 as opposed to $300. Firm B is in a different situation because it is not able to pay its variable costs. If it shuts down operations, its losses are only $100, the fixed costs, as opposed to its operating losses of $300. Firm C earns sufficient revenue to cover variable costs, so it is better off operating than discontinuing operations, but the firm's outlook for the future is nothing but losses. It will continue operating until it can liquidate and get out of the business. In the cases of the first two firms, the long-term outlook must be for improvements or they, too, would be looking to get out of business.

Table 11.2					
Temporary Closures	FIRM FIXED COSTS	VARIABLE COSTS	REVENUE	PROFIT (LOSS)	DECISION
	[A] $1,000	$ 100	$800	($300)	Continue
	[B] $ 100	$1,000	$800	($300)	Discontinue
	[C] $ 600	$ 500	$800	($300)	Continue/Quit

Temporary closures turn into liquidation if losses continue. To remain in business, the firm must add value in the long run. If an inefficient firm is kept in business through government subsidies or barriers to exit, then value is being subtracted. Society is worse off because resources are not allowed to be used where they have the highest value. It is such restrictions in an economy that lead to economic stagnation or economic collapse and has been the common experience of centrally planned economies.

Value over Time

To maximize profit, should the firm devote resources to attempt to restrict entry by getting larger, or should it devote resources to enhancing its brand name, or should it devote resources to defining or creating a special attribute? The simple, straightforward rule for maximizing profit is as follows: Allocate resources to an activity only if the value society places on the activity exceeds the costs. In other words, if the additional revenue that an additional dollar of spending on an activity creates is larger than a dollar, carry out the activity.

Maximizing profit means a firm should continue to expand purchases of inputs and sell the resulting outputs as long as an additional dollar of inputs generates sales of at least a dollar. This general rule applies even when cash flow or profit and cost flows are not uniform over time. Knowing whether society is benefited or harmed by an activity requires knowing whether the output that occurs in the future is valuable enough to offset the cost of having people give up their labor, capital, and material inputs in the present. Interest rates give us the answer to this. They tell us the cost of giving up a unit of a good today in order to receive it at some time in the future.

The value one year from now of a dollar today saved for use one year from now is thus

$$\text{Future value} = \$1 \times (1 + r)$$

where r is the interest rate. Alternatively, the value today of a dollar of resources to be received one year from now is its present value, or

$$\text{Present value} = \$1/(1 + r)$$

An individual is as well off as possible if his wealth measured by the present value of all future claims is maximized. It is similar with a firm. Those who guide a firm are doing the best they can if the firm is maximizing the present value of its expected profits. But to simplify, we just say that the firm's objective is to maximize profit.

Adding risk to the situation really changes nothing as long as there are financial markets in which the individual can buy and sell risk at a given price. When such financial markets exist, it is the risk adjusted interest rate that is used in calculating the present value of risky claims. So whether looking over a longer time period or when information is not perfectly known, the rule for the manager is maximize the value of the firm.

The Abnormal Net Income Model

The profit that results when economic profit is zero is referred to as normal profit because it is the profit that competition will permit—revenue equal to total opportunity costs. When economic profit is positive, the return necessary to keep resources in their current use is less than the returns being generated. This difference is referred to as abnormal, as in abnormal net income, because it exists only temporarily. The competitive process that drives profit toward "normal" does not occur instantaneously. How long it takes depends on the ease of entry and on the factors that distinguish one firm from others.

The abnormal net income model[9] is an approach used by financial accountants to value companies. It says that the market value of a firm is its book value (the current stockholder's equity) plus the present value of economic profits expected to be earned in the future. In symbols,

$$P_0 = \text{current book value} + \text{present value of expected economic profits}$$

And expected economic profits are next year's expected accounting profit in excess of the cost of capital. Next year's expected accounting profit in excess of the cost of capital is termed abnormal net income next year.

The Value of a Firm A firm's value is the amount that owners would pay to keep ownership and also the amount that new owners would pay to acquire ownership.[10] For a publicly held firm, the value of that firm is its market capitalization, the value per share that owners place on the firm multiplied by the number of shares of stock that are outstanding. For privately held companies, valuation is often difficult because there is no stock market that is providing minute-to-minute valuations. At a minimum, a firm is worth its liquidation value; the value of a firm's assets when they are dismantled and sold.[11]

The market value of a firm is society's valuation of future earnings and takes account of factors such as the productive capacity of the assets, the expertise of employees, and the value of brands. Since a firm expected to consistently earn negative economic profits would be liquidated, its value would be the value of its assets when the firm is dismantled. A firm earning positive economic profits would have a market value dependent on how long the abnormal profits are expected to last.

Economic Profit and Stock Price Performance Is there a relationship between economic profit and stock price performance?[12] The Abnormal Net Income model would say yes. A glance at stock prices would suggest not. What is the difference? In any one year, some of the top-performing firms will have stock price gains that are above the market average, and some will have stock price gains that are below the market average. The reason is that the stock market looks ahead. The value of a stock depends entirely on the economic profits that investors *expect* a company to produce in the future. Past profits matter only because they play a role in creating expectations about future performance.

As the period over which we look back grows longer, companies we recognize as excellent companies today (that is, ones that generated substantial economic profit) are increasingly likely to have outperformed stock market expectations and today's bad companies to have done worse than yesterday's stock market expectations. Economic profit is a snapshot, a one-year look at a firm's performance, and one year does not make a trend. But economic profit over several years gives a great picture of performance, and this is what the stock market looks at. The present value of all expected future economic profits is what tells us whether a company creates or destroys wealth.

If the connection between economic profit and stock price requires a long time to see, is economic profit a useful piece of information? Are investors patient enough to wait 10 or more years before making an evaluation of a firm's performance? Yes, it is, and no, they are not—and they don't have to be. Investors evaluate how well they think the firm will do tomorrow, next week, six months from now, or next year when deciding whether to purchase the stock of a company. Thus, the phrase "maximizing shareholder value" is often interpreted as a focus on short-term profits even at the expense of long-run losses.[13]

Short Termism   Although it might seem that investors demand this short-term outlook by purchasing a company's stock as it earns short-term profits and then selling, this perception is incorrect. Such behavior would create arbitrage opportunities for others. Since the long-term value of the company would be undervalued and the short-term value overvalued, an investor could buy shares of stock long term and sell them short term. This would occur through various financial means, such as futures and options, which would tend to equalize the short- and long-term market values of the company. Thus, focusing on short-term results at the expense of long-term results would drive the shareholder value down, not up, and the short-term stock performance would be low, reflecting the long-term prospects of the firm.

Suppose an investor is considering two firms, A and B, as possible investments. The investor knows that the CEO for firm A is going to carry out an activity that will increase profits next year but lead to losses in the following years. He also knows that the CEO for firm B, on the other hand, is looking to the long term and wants to increase profits each year but in the short term performance will not match that in the long term. The result of this is that firm B will not increase profits next year as much as firm A does. The investor, knowing the directions in which the two CEOs are going, thinks, "I want to own firm A's stock only next year. I don't want to be holding it after that. But I don't want to be the last to sell. In fact, I want to be the first to sell and then the first to own firm B, so that when everyone else tries to buy firm B, I will make a large appreciation. So I should sell firm A's stock before the end of the year—perhaps in month 11. But if others have the same knowledge I do, I will need to sell before they do.

The process of moving the time of sale forward would continue until the investor realizes that the only way to gain is not to buy stock in firm A at all but instead to buy stock in firm B now. If other investors have the same information and do the same thing, the stock price of firm A decreases now, not next year, and that of firm B rises now, not next year. The stock price reflects the expected long-term economic profit stream.

This illustration assumes that the investor knows with certainty how firms A and B will perform. In reality, such certainty does not exist for one person or for the market as a whole. In fact, if everyone had perfect knowledge, there would be no stock trades. For stocks to be traded, buyers and sellers must have different views about the firm's future performance. If you and I have exactly the same view about a firm's future, why would one of us want to buy the stock form the other? [14]

Investors must gather information and form expectations about future performance. Since the stock price reflects the expected economic profit stream, shareholder value will be a reflection of the current and expected future economic profits of a firm. Thus, maximizing shareholder value should mean the same as maximizing economic profit. It is not a short-term tactic but instead a focus on long-term performance. It is not just an attempt to increase earnings but instead an attempt to maximize the difference between net earnings and the cost of capital.

A stock price is determined by the demand for and supply of shares of that stock. Both demanders and suppliers base their valuation of the price of the stock on expectations of future firm performance. For them to trade, they must have different viewpoints about the movement of the stock price or different objectives for owning stock. The buyer has to expect it to improve more than alternatives, and the seller must expect it not to improve as much as alternatives. If they had exactly the same viewpoints, there would be no reason to trade.[15]

It is the market's expectations (buyers and sellers) of future firm performance that determine the price of a share of stock. Once determined, if nothing changes, share price won't change. What causes the stock price to rise or fall? The answer is revisions of expectations. The abnormal net income model indicates that the market value goes up when expectations of future net income rise (as when announced earnings exceed expectations, triggering increased net income expectations going forward) and vice versa, everything else held constant. But, it is not just expected earnings that matter; it is the excess of expected net income over the cost of capital, that is, abnormal net income. When the cost of capital, r, rises, everything else held constant, market value declines.

When expectations are revised upward, the stock price rises because more investors want to buy and fewer want to sell. When expectations are revised downward, the stock price falls because fewer investors want to buy and more want to sell. Thus, when a firm does better than it was expected to do, its stock price will rise, and when a firm does worse than it was expected to do, its stock price will fall.

From the mid-1990s through 2000, Cisco generated very substantial economic profit, a value that was reflected in the high price of its shares. Changes in the market value of Cisco in 2001, therefore, reflected its actual performance relative to its expected performance. Since expectations were high for Cisco, it would have been difficult for the company to have done better than those expectations, and, in the short term, stock price reassessments were as likely to be downward as upward, even though Cisco was earning significant profits. In fact, from March to June 2000, Cisco stock fell 40 percent, from a high of $80 per share to about $50 per share, even though Cisco earnings and profits were rising faster than the market as a whole. In August 2010 in the midst of a recession, Cisco said revenue rose 27 percent from a year ago, and net income jumped 79 percent, as business bounced back from the recession. But the stock dropped from nearly $25 per share to $22. Analysts had expected even higher revenue after a couple of strong quarters. But Cisco said it hit a weak spot in mid-June, as the European debt crisis was at its worst.

How long will a firm be able to maintain abnormal profits, if it earns any? The answer depends on how fast competitors come on line to drive economic profit to zero. The decay rate is the speed at which abnormal net income is driven to zero—the rate at which entrepreneurs are able to innovate or otherwise compete with the firm. The competitive conditions of the industry define the decay rate. Markets characterized by relatively easy entry and large numbers tend to be cases where firms cannot sustain economic profits. When a firm has a competitive advantage and can keep others from competing, it can sustain economic profit for some period of time. But all firms are expected to lose their advantages over time. Entrepreneurs always find a way around entry barriers. Thus, the calculated measure of the value of the firm depends crucially on the decay rate—that is, the horizon over which economic profit is assumed to be positive.

Corporate Social Responsibility

Over the past 10 years or so, corporate social responsibility (CSR) has come to command the attention of most executives and especially the managers of multinational companies headquartered in Europe or the United States. It would be a challenge to find a recent annual report of any big international company that justifies the firm's existence merely in terms of profit, rather than some service to other stakeholders. Such reports often talk proudly of efforts to improve society and safeguard the environment. But are these reports real? That is, do executives allocate the firm's resources to stakeholders as opposed to shareholders?

If a dollar is allocated to any activity that society values more than a dollar, then carrying out that activity adds value. If society values green activities and will express that valuation by purchasing from the firm that devotes resources to that activity, then maximizing shareholder value and being "responsible" correspond. Each dollar allocated to any activity by a firm must generate more than a dollar in return. If a manager allocates a dollar to some activity not valued by society, then the manager is actually subtracting value, making the firm and society worse off. The stakeholder theory of the firm cannot be different from the shareholder theory. Spending on corporate social responsibility is responsible only if each dollar allocated brings in more than a dollar.

Summary

1. The objective of firms is to maximize value. Value is the difference between the costs of inputs the firm consumes in producing and selling output and the value of the output.
2. Stakeholder theory maintains that the firm must appeal to all its constituents. The theory says nothing about how the trade-offs among differing objectives of these constituents are to be resolved.
3. The firm must allocate a dollar of resources to the desires of any stakeholder only if society values the resulting output more than a dollar.
4. A firm maximizes profit by operating at the point where the marginal revenue equals the marginal cost. If the last unit of output generated a marginal revenue that exceeded its marginal cost, then more profit could be earned by increasing output. Conversely, if the last unit of output generated a marginal revenue that was less than its marginal cost, then more profit could be earned by not producing that last unit of output.
5. Competition will drive prices down until equal to opportunity costs. In other words, the price of the last unit sold will equal marginal cost. Economic profit is zero. Consumers are getting what they want at the lowest possible price.
6. A manager wants to earn positive economic profit. To do that, he must limit the effects of competition. Specifically, he can enlist government to grant him a monopoly or create a special attribute that differentiates his firm or product from rivals.

7. Anything that consumers value positively can be a differentiator for a firm or product. Brand name, appearance of office or building, location may all provide that special attribute that distinguishes the firm or product from others.

8. Size can be a barrier to entry when there are economies of scale. Capital requirements can serve as a barrier to entry. Sunk costs may be a barrier to entry. Limited access to distribution channels can be a barrier to entry.

9. Considering the flow of cash and services over time does not change the objective. It merely says we consider the present value of profit rather than the one time profit. Similarly, considering uncertainty of cash and service streams changes nothing as long as risk can be sold or purchased in capital markets.

10. When revenue does not pay for variable costs, the firm should shut down. If the situation remains for the long run, the firm will liquidate and its resources will be allocated elsewhere.

Key Terms

Stakeholders

Fixed costs

Variable costs

Future value

Present value

Exercises

1. The technology exists that would enable a consumer to purchase electricity from any producer. In fact, a computer could be installed in a consumer's electrical box so that electricity would be acquired automatically from wherever it is least expensive. What does this mean for an electrical producer?

2. What types of products are phone service and electricity?

3. Services marketing is a current business buzzword. It is a branch of marketing that focuses on services. Why would it be different from the marketing of goods?

4. Why does a firm spend an enormous amount on advertising when the ads provide consumers virtually no information? For instance, what does the advertisement showing the Rock of Gilbraltar and suggesting that we should "own a piece of the rock" tell us?

5. Why do firms build enormous buildings or skyscrapers when they could rent a less pretentious structure for a lot less money?

6. Why do consumers pay twice as much for Bayer aspirin than for generic aspirin when they know that the two are chemically identical?

7. Why do firms hire celebrities to advertise their products—why care whether Shaquille O'Neal (basketball player) eats at Taco Bell or whether Tiger Woods (golfer) wears Nike shoes?

8. What does it mean to say that a firm should devote resources to an activity as long as society values that activity more than it values the resources allocated to that activity?

9. Explain the relationship between fixed costs, variable costs, and revenue for determining when a firm should temporarily shut down.

10. Using the following Marginal Revenue and Marginal Cost, determine the profit maximizing price and quantity.

Output	MC	MR
0		
1	$30	$80
2	$50	$80
3	$80	$80
4	$120	$80
5	$170	$80

11. Is it possible to earn positive economic profit in the long run?

12. What economic role do brand names play in the economy? Why do firms devote resources to developing a brand name?

13. Explain why the rule $MR = MC$ defines profit maximization.

14. What is the abnormal net income model? Where does the entrepreneur show up in this model?

15. Explain why the argument that a manager should focus on short-term performance rather than

long-term performance might be invalid. In what sense might it be valid?

16. How long has Wal-Mart made positive economic profits? How long has Starbucks earned positive economic profits? Have entrepreneurs been able to innovate and otherwise compete with Wal-Mart and Starbucks? Explain.

17. What should the firm do, maximize profit or maximize stakeholder value? Explain

18. The owner of Whole Foods Markets, John Mackay, argues that firms should maximize stakeholder value. He uses his firm as an example. Mackay takes money from the profits and allocates it to community charities and other good works, and his firm is very profitable. Explain why Mackay is wrong.

19. Milton Friedman once said that the social responsibility of a company is to earn a profit. Explain whether or not Friedman is correct.

20. Does a firm maximize profits today or the present value of the profit stream? How far out does a firm look to determine its profit stream? If a CEO could be fired at any time for poor performance, why would he focus on the long term rather than the short term?

CHAPTER NOTES

1. www.starbucks.com/aboutus/csr.asp, accessed April 29, 2008.
2. www.fedex.com/us/about/responsibility/community/index.html, accessed April 29, 2008.
3. www.gapinc.com/public/SocialResponsibility/socialres.shtml, accessed April 29, 2008
4. www.soxfirst.com/50226711/stakeholder_vs_shareholder_capitalism.php, accessed April 14, 2008.
5. Robert Reich, *Supercapitalism: The Transformation of Business, Democracy, and Everyday Life* (New York: Knopf, 2007).
6. Remember, costs refer to all opportunity costs.
7. Stephanie Coyles and Timothy C. Gokey, "Customer Retention Is Not Enough," *The McKinsey Quarterly,* No. 2 (2002) (www.mckinseyquarterly.com/search_result.asp), December 18, 2002.
8. Laura Blackwell, "Brand Name Influence for Consumer Electronics Losing Luster," *PC World,* pcworld.about.com/news/Jul112006id126377.htm. According to the Vertis Customer Focus 2006 Home Electronics study, only 29 percent of survey respondents called brand name the "most important" factor aside from price, whereas in 1998, 58 percent said it was the most important.
9. The abnormal net income model is also known as the residual net income model, the Feltham-Ohlson model, and the Edwards and Bell-Ohlson model.
10. Firms that are expected to earn positive economic profit would have a market value in excess of the accounting value of stockholders' equity called the book value. They will have market-to-book ratios greater than one. Firms that are expected to earn near zero economic profit will have market-to-book ratios close to one, and firms expected to earn negative economic profit will have market-to-book ratios that are less than one. (*Note:* The median market-to-book ratio, as of the end of 2006, of firms in the pharmaceutical industry was 4.59. In contrast, the median ratio of firms in the airline industry was 1.57.)
11. Liquidation value and book value are sometimes confused; liquidation value is not necessarily equal to book value. The book value of a corporation is the *shareholders' equity* (assets minus liabilities) divided by the number of outstanding shares. Consider a company owning a 30-year-old building. That building might have been depreciated fully and is carried on the books for 0, while it might have a resale value of millions. In this case, the book value understates the liquidation value of the company. On the other hand, consider a fast-changing industry with a three-year-old computer equipment which has a few more years to go before being fully depreciated, but that equipment couldn't be sold for even 10 percent of its book value. Here the book value overstates the liquidation value.
12. Several studies have examined the relationship between economic profit (as measured by EVA, Economic Value Added) and stock price performance. One study followed 241 firms over the period 1987–1993 and found that three accounting measures—return on assets, return on equity, and return on sales—as well as EVA are correlated with stock returns. However, it found that EVA is more highly correlated with stock prices than the other measures. Perhaps even more suggestive of the importance of economic profit is that the turnover of executives is more closely related to EVA than to the accounting measures, suggesting that managers are better served to focus on economic profit than accounting profit. See Kenneth Lehn, and Anil K. Makhija, "EVA & MVA as Performance Measures," *Strategy and Leadership,* 24, no. 3 (May 1996): 34.

13. Many executives claim that the pressure to perform each quarter forces them to ignore long-term payoffs and focus only on short-term results. The CEO of Bell & Howell noted: "When the typical institutional portfolio in the U.S. has an annual turnover rate of 50% and some smaller ones have turnover rates of more than 200%, it is no surprise that American business is hobbled compared with foreign rivals. The pressure for short-term results puts unnecessary hurdles in the way of sound management." Another CEO agreed: "The only pressure I have on me is short-term pressure. I announce that we're going to spend half a billion dollars at Courtland, Alabama, with a hell of a payout from redoing a mill and my stock goes down two points. So I finally caved in and announced I'm going to buy back some stock, which makes no sense." G. B. Stewart III, *The Quest for Value* (New York: HarperCollins, 1991), p. 56. A study by Michael Porter concluded that excessive emphasis on short-term results was stifling investment and undermining U.S. competitiveness and that the problem had worsened in the 1970s and 1980s when institutional ownership and takeovers were growing. Porter decried the impatient U.S. investors and praised the patient German and Japanese investors. Michael Porter, *Capital Choices* (Cambridge, MA: Harvard Business School Press, 1992); and "Capital Choices: Changing the Way America Invests in Industry," *Journal of Applied Corporate Finance,* 5, no. 2 (1992).
14. This is assuming everything else between investors is the same.
15. Assuming that investors are identical otherwise.

Analytic Problem-Solving Tools

CHAPTER 12

Demand and Revenue Management

CASE

Knowing the Customer[1]

The typical supermarket has 30,000 different products on sale at any given time. The manager of that supermarket must determine not only what mix of products to have on hand but where to locate those products and what price to set on each one at any specific time. Usually, the price is based on a markup on the cost of the item, and the only reason the price is altered is that costs change. When you reserve a hotel room, you find that there are several different prices offered for that same room, depending on whether you work for the government, are a member of AARP or some other organization, are staying more than one night, and so on. Why doesn't the hotel just offer a single price?

These examples illustrate just a few of the many problems confronting businesses in their relations with customers. Companies do not seem to know much about their customers. For instance, companies often base prices on the anecdotal evidence of a few vocal salespeople or product managers. Even Mercedes-Benz, when it was about to launch one of its A-class models in the German market, initially proposed a price tag of DM29,500, based on little more than the belief that DM30,000 was a psychologically important barrier. Consultants point out that price has a disproportionate effect on the bottom line, far more than greater volume or cuts in fixed and variable costs. Assuming that volumes stay constant, a 1 percent price increase produces between an 8 percent and 11 percent improvement in operating profits.

1. So does this mean that most businesses should raise their prices?
2. Are these businesses leaving money on the table—that is, not generating the greatest revenue they could by knowing the customer better?

Price, Sales, and Consumer Choice

Revenue less costs is profit; obviously, revenue is a crucial determinant of a firm's success. Revenue depends on the customer, so we have to know how the customer reacts to various aspects of business. At what price will consumers purchase the product, and how high a price will they pay? Do they have a loyalty to us or our products, or will they switch to another product at the slightest provocation? Do we have different sets of customers or niches? Are we better off seeking new customers or retaining existing ones? How important is service? Does advertising have an effect on customer actions? Answers to these and other questions define the customer.

Consumer behavior is all about making choices. Since people have limited incomes and wealth, they must choose what to purchase and how much to purchase. If they purchase one thing, the money they spend is not available to be spent on something else. An important assumption in economics is that individuals act to make themselves as well off as possible. Economists don't particularly care how individuals define well off; they simply accept that each individual has a set of preferences. Given an individual's preferences, economists know that the individual will attempt to get the most bang for the buck. In other words, each person will allocate his income so as to get the greatest enjoyment, fulfillment or happiness. If spending a dollar on coffee in the morning gives me more pleasure than spending a dollar on a bottle of soda, I will spend it on the coffee. Economists figure that if people spend money on something and not on something else, then they are displaying or revealing their preferences.

So if we assume that people are presented with all possible combinations of goods, they will choose the combinations they prefer over other combinations and indicate those among which they are indifferent. However large our income, we can spend it on an amazing array of goods and services. Each choice reveals preferences.

Suppose Alberta purchases two cups of coffee every day at the local Starbucks. The cost is $1.50 per "tall" coffee. What does Alberta do when one day she walks in and discovers the cost has risen to $1.75? She decides to purchase just one cup on Tuesdays and Thursdays. So, the higher cost has caused her to purchase two fewer cups of coffee each week. This is what happens to most people; when costs rise and incomes do not, people purchase less of the now higher priced item. A 10 percent decrease in the price of street cocaine is estimated to increase the number of users by about 10 percent. A 30 percent increase in the price of cigarettes causes about a 25 percent reduction in smoking.

This relationship between the price of something and the quantity of that item that is purchased is called the law of demand. The law of demand reads as follows: The quantity of a good or service that is purchased will decline as the price of that good or service rises, everything else unchanged. So, if the price of a good or service rises while income and people's tastes are unchanged and, in fact, if nothing changes except the price, then the quantity of that good or service that is purchased will decline. The law of demand is called a "law" because it holds for every good and service.

The money price of an item is not the total cost of that item. Cost is what must be given up in order to get something. When you purchase a treadmill from Sears, your cost is not only the purchase price but also the delivery and setup charge or your time and effort in getting the unit home and set up. When you buy a carton of milk, the cost is the price of the milk plus the cost of transportation to the store and the time you devoted to purchasing the milk. When a company hires an employee, the cost is the salary and benefits, as well as the value of resources devoted to training, supervising, and so on, for that employee. If the price of an item rose by 10 percent but the time spent purchasing the item declined by 50 percent, it is possible the cost actually declined. This is why the law of demand states that the relationship between price and quantity demanded exists, *everything else held constant.*

Elasticity

The law of demand states that when the price of an item goes up, the quantity purchased of that item goes down. If the price rises 10 percent, how much does the quantity purchased go down? It is vitally important for the manager to know whether the firm's customers are sensitive to price or whether they are willing to pay a little more to purchase the firm's product. Bayer, Coca-Cola, Kodak, Xerox, IBM, and Microsoft are well-known brand names. The products offered by these companies are typically priced above competitive products that are not as well recognized because people prefer to deal with a product or firm they know than purchase a generic one. How far can the brand-name product be priced above rival products? The answer depends on how sensitive consumers are to price.

Economists have devised measures of how consumers alter their purchases in response to changes in various attributes of a firm's goods or services. These measures are called elasticities. We have discussed the price elasticity of demand in previous chapters. There are more measures of elasticity than just the price elasticity. Elasticities are measured as the percentage change in the purchases of a good or service that results when some *attribute* is changed by a fixed percentage. The attribute could be price or income or tastes and preferences or number of customers and on and on. Elasticities are measured in percentage changes in order to put all goods and services on a common footing. For instance, to compare a $1 change in the price of a hamburger and a $1 change in the price of an automobile would not make much sense. But to compare a 10 percent change in the price of a hamburger and a 10 percent change in the price of an automobile puts matters in perspective. Let's examine several of the most often used elasticity measures.

Price Elasticity of Demand   The **price elasticity of demand** is a measure of the magnitude by which consumers alter the quantity of some product they purchase in response to a change in the price of that product. The more price-elastic demand is, the more responsive consumers are to a price change—that is, the more they will adjust their purchases of a product when the price of that product changes. Conversely, the less price-elastic demand is, the less responsive consumers are to a price change.

The price elasticity of demand is measured as the percentage change in the quantity demanded of a product divided by the percentage change in the price of that product.[2]

Consider the case of Globastar Canada, a provider of satellite-based mobile communications throughout Canada. The company found that its customers were price-sensitive; when it tried to charge rates as high as $1.50 per minute when customers were able to get rates as low as $0.80 per minute elsewhere, the customers flocked to companies offering lower rates. If the quantity of phone calls that are made falls by 3 percent whenever the price of a call rises by 1 percent, the price elasticity of demand for the telephone calls is −3.[3]

$$e^d = \frac{\%\Delta Q}{\%\Delta P} = -3$$

Demand can be **elastic**, **unit-elastic**, or **inelastic**. When the price elasticity of demand is between −1 and −∞, demand is said to be elastic. For instance, the demand for mobile phone minutes, according to the example of $e^d = -3$, is elastic. When the price elasticity of demand is −1, demand is said to be unit-elastic. For example, if the price of private education rises by 1 percent and the quantity of private education purchased falls by 1 percent, the price elasticity of demand is −1. When the price elasticity of demand is between −1 and 0, demand is said to be inelastic. In this case, a 1 percent rise in price produces a smaller than 1 percent decline in quantity demanded. For example, if the price of gasoline rises by 1 percent and the quantity of gasoline purchased falls by 0.2 percent, the price elasticity of demand is −0.2.[4]

A demand curve illustrates the quantity of an item that will be purchased at each price; it is a relationship between the price and quantity demanded of a good or service. The price is measured along the vertical axis and quantity along the horizontal axis. Since the demand curve includes just the two dimensions, price and quantity demanded, everything else that might affect demand is being held constant.

The shape of a demand curve depends on the price elasticity of demand. A perfectly elastic demand curve is a horizontal line showing that consumers can purchase any quantity they want at the single prevailing price, as shown in Figure 12.1(a). The demand for something that has been commoditized is perfectly elastic. For example, the demand for disk drives in PCs could be thought of as having been commoditized. There are many manufacturers of disk drives, and the PC manufacturers do not care which they install in their machines; most consumers have no idea which disk-drive company produced their drives. As a result, if the price of one brand of disk drives is increased, the PC manufacturers are likely to move to another brand. A perfectly elastic demand means that even the smallest price change will cause consumers to change their consumption by a huge amount; in fact, they will totally switch to the producer with the lowest price.

A perfectly inelastic demand curve is a vertical line illustrating the idea that consumers cannot or will not change the quantity of a good they purchase when the price of that good is changed. Perhaps heroin for an addict is a reasonably vivid example of a good whose demand is perfectly inelastic. The addict will pay almost any price to get the quantity that satisfies the addiction. Figure 12.1(b) shows a perfectly inelastic demand curve.

In between the two extreme shapes are the demand curves for most products. Figure 12.1(c) illustrates two demand curves. One is a relatively flat line, D_2, and the other is a relatively steep line, D_1. D_2 is more price elastic than D_1.[5]

Price Elasticity and Revenue Clearly, sales is a crucial part of economic profit—with no sales there can be no profit. The price elasticity of demand tells us what happens to

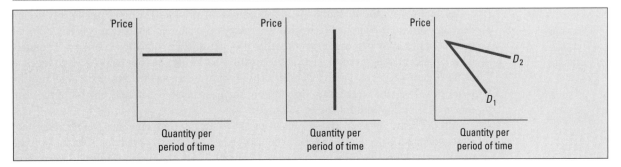

FIGURE 12.1 Demand Curves

The demand curve is a graphic relationship between quantity demanded and price. The graph is drawn with price on the vertical axis and quantity on the horizontal axis. (a) Perfectly elastic demand: Demand is so sensitive to price that even an infinitesimal change leads to a total change in quantity demanded. (b) Perfectly inelastic demand: The quantity demanded is the same no matter the price. Demand is completely insensitive to price. (c) Alternative demand curves: and D_2 represents straight downward-sloping demand curves. D_2 is said to be more elastic than D_1 because at every single price the elasticity of demand is higher at D_2 than D_1.

sales when the price is changed. Total revenue (*TR*) or dollar value of sales, equals the price of a product multiplied by the quantity sold: $TR = P \times Q$. If *P* rises by 10 percent and *Q* falls by more than 10 percent, then total revenue declines as a result of the price rise. If *P* rises by 10 percent and *Q* falls by less than 10 percent, then total revenue rises as a result of the price rise. If *P* increases by 10 percent and *Q* falls by 10 percent, then total revenue does not change as the price changes.[6]

Thus, total revenue increases as price is increased if demand is inelastic, decreases as price is increased if demand is elastic, and does not change as price is increased if demand is unit-elastic. A firm wanting to increase total revenue would lower the price as long as demand is elastic and raise the price as long as demand is inelastic.

What makes the demand for one product price-elastic and the demand for another price-inelastic? The difference depends primarily on how many substitutes there are for that product and how good of substitutes they are. For instance, the demand for the services provided by Amazon.com and BN.com are very price-elastic since consumers can switch from one to the other or to a different book seller without losing quality or some other attribute associated with the original good or service. Amadeus Petroleum NL is building a commercial biodiesel plant in Perth, Western Australia, to convert low-value tallow, a by-product of the livestock industry, into a high-quality diesel fuel, a direct substitute for traditional diesel made from fossil fuels. Once online, the price elasticity of demand for diesel will rise.

In contrast, when there are few substitutes for a product, the price elasticity of demand for that product is low. Drug addicts have few substitutes that satisfy their addiction; business travelers have few substitutes for the airline routes and times they travel. As a result, the demands for these goods are relatively inelastic. There are just two sources of salt, desert salt and sea salt. It would seem that the two are perfect substitutes. However, Chevron/Texaco found that the two did not work equally well in its refining system. As the price of sea salt rose relative to desert salt, Chevron/Texaco had to pay the higher price to maintain its supply of sea salt.

Commoditization occurs when there are a lot of perfect substitutes for a good. This means the price elasticity of demand is very large—infinite at the extreme. The price elasticity is infinite because customers would immediately purchase a substitute when the price of the item increases even a very small amount. One product does not differ from its substitutes for the consumer. Hence, even a penny increase (assuming no other costs such as travel to another store, time, etc.) will drive customers to competitors. When your product is a commodity, you don't have any control over price. You have to set the price at the price of competitors. Any higher price and you won't have any customers.

When the demand for a product is price-inelastic, the firm can increase the price without losing significant business. A price increase will actually increase revenue when demand is price-inelastic. It is for this reason that firms attempt to differentiate their goods and services. The greater the differentiation of a good or service, the fewer substitutes for that good or service.

In Figure 12.2 the demand for a commoditized product is shown as the horizontal demand curve, D_1. The seller begins a strategy of changing the price elasticity. To do that, it has to convince consumers that its product differs from those of rivals. It undertakes an advertising program that is successful. As a result, the demand curve changes to D_2 in Figure 12.2. The greater the differentiation, the steeper the demand curve and the more price inelastic is demand. In addition, the less elastic is demand, the more the firm can increase price without losing sales.

Although the number and closeness of substitutes is the principal characteristic that makes demand price-elastic or inelastic, two other elements contribute. One is the time period over which we measure the price elasticity. If we are speaking about a very short

FIGURE 12.2 Changing Price Elasticity

Demand is perfectly elastic for Demand$_1$. The firm cannot charge more without losing all of its customers because the product is a commodity—there are many perfect substitutes. The firm undertakes an advertising campaign to change the image of the product. If successful, consumers begin to think the product is not a commodity, that there are not lots of perfect substitutes. The demand curve then becomes steeper, as with Demand$_2$.

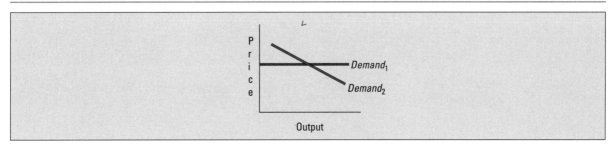

period of time, then the demand for most goods and services will be relatively price-inelastic. With a longer period of time, more substitutes are available. For instance, the demand for gasoline is very price-inelastic over a period of a month. No good substitutes are available in so brief a period. Over a 10-year period, however, the demand for gasoline is more elastic. The additional time would allow consumers to alter their behavior to make better use of gasoline and to find substitutes for gasoline. *The longer the period under consideration, the more elastic is the demand for any product.*

Business Insight

Price Elasticity of Demand for Gasoline

According to most studies, the price elasticity of demand for gasoline in the United States over a period of one year or less is −0.26. That is, a 10 percent hike in the price of gasoline lowers quantity demanded by 2.6 percent. In the long-run (defined as longer than one year), the price elasticity of demand is −0.58; a 10 percent hike in gasoline causes quantity demanded to decline by 5.8 percent in the long run. If the real price of fuel goes, and stays, up by 10 percent, the result is a process of adjustment whereby the volume of traffic will go down by about 1 percent within about a year, building up to a reduction of about 3 percent in the longer run (about five years or so), and the volume of fuel consumed will go down by about 2.5 percent within a year, building up to a reduction of over 6 percent in the longer run. In addition, the efficiency of use of fuel goes up by about 1.5 percent within a year, and around 4 percent in the longer run.[7]

Other Demand Elasticities

Since factors other than just price affect people's purchasing decisions, measures have been devised to determine how much a change in one of these factors affects demand. We can calculate an income elasticity of demand, a cross price elasticity of demand, an advertising elasticity, a promotion elasticity, and other elasticity measures.

Figure 12.3 illustrates what occurs when something other than price changes. For instance, when income rises, people tend to purchase more of some goods. How much more depends on the income elasticity of demand. Also, when the price of a substitute good rises, the demand for the first good rises—people don't buy as much of the now more expensive good (the substitute) and purchase more of the now relatively less expensive good.

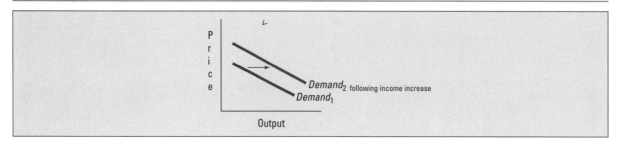

FIGURE 12.3 Changes Other than Price

The demand curve is a relation between price and quantity demanded, everything else held constant. The things held constant are income, advertising, expectations, tastes, preference, and anything else that could affect demand. When one of these changes, the demand curve shifts. For instance, Demand$_2$ represents demand following an increased income. The distance the demand curve shifts is reflective of the income elasticity of demand.

Income Elasticity of Demand The total output in the U.S. economy (real gross domestic product—RGDP) is shown in Figure 12.4 for the years 1929–2007. What do you observe in this graph? It presents two important characteristics of the U.S. economy: (1) The U.S. economy has grown over the years; and (2) the growth has not been at a steady pace. At times the economy has grown rapidly, at other times it has grown slowly, and at still other times it has declined. Economists study both of these characteristics—they want to know why economies grow and why some grow faster than others. They also study the fluctuations—they want to know what causes the downturns and upturns.

Taking out the growth and leaving just the cycles results in Figure 12.5. this figure is, in fact, a picture of business cycles in the United States. Business cycles are important to most businesses. During an upswing in business activity, incomes are growing and sales

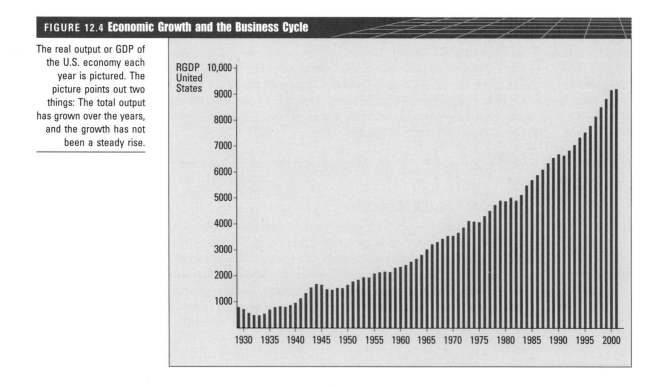

FIGURE 12.4 Economic Growth and the Business Cycle

The real output or GDP of the U.S. economy each year is pictured. The picture points out two things: The total output has grown over the years, and the growth has not been a steady rise.

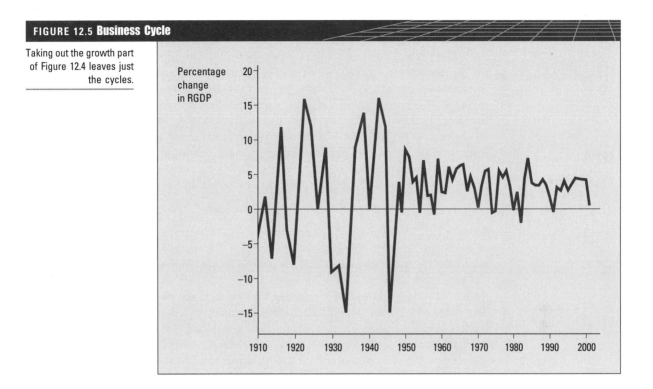

FIGURE 12.5 Business Cycle

Taking out the growth part of Figure 12.4 leaves just the cycles.

of many products are rising. During a downswing, incomes are not rising and sales of many products may be declining. But there are firms for which sales rise during downswings and decline during upswings. For other firms, sales are not dependent on the business cycle.

Consider a firm that specializes in kitchen designs, cabinets, and appliances. The demand for new kitchen cabinets and appliances increases much faster than does income growth. The problem is that when the economy falls into a recession, the company struggles. Price is a consideration, but it is not price so much as income that affects the company's business. The manager of such a company must know how much demand will change whenever incomes change. In contrast, sales of the Australian company Billabong, makers of surfer and other leisure wear, do not seem to be sensitive to income growth. The company has experienced sales growth in Japan, whose economy was in recession, and in North America during years of growth and recession. A manager would like to know whether or not the level of income or rate of growth of national income would affect the sales of his firm. A measure known as the **income elasticity of demand** informs the manager about how sensitive sales are to income changes. The income elasticity of demand is a measure of the responsiveness of consumer purchases to income changes; it is defined as the percentage change in demand divided by the percentage change in income, everything else held constant.

We do not say that demand is elastic or inelastic when referring to income elasticity. Instead, we may refer to some item as a luxury good or an inferior good, or we may call a good a cyclical good or a countercyclical good. A *luxury good* is one for which the income elasticity is very high—some value significantly greater than 1.0. A high-income elasticity value tells us that a 1 percent increase in income will lead to a greater than 1 percent rise in demand. A high-income elasticity means that as long as the economy is growing and incomes are rising, sales are rising. But if the economy slows and/or incomes decline, sales decline. A *normal good* is one for which the income elasticity is positive but probably less than 1.0 or near 1.0. Hotel rooms are a normal good—occupancy rates rise when incomes rise and fall when incomes fall. These goods are also called **cyclical goods** since their sales vary with the business cycle (levels of income). An *inferior good* is one for which the income elasticity is negative, meaning that as income rises, demand falls.[8] Bankruptcy services are an inferior good—sales of bankruptcy services rise when income falls and decline when income rises. These are also called **countercyclical goods** since as incomes rise, demand falls, and vice versa. Billabong clothing appears to be noncyclical, rising even when incomes are not. This could be due to it being in the midst of a fad where young people the world over want to join in the Billabong revolution, or it could be due to Billabong entering new markets and thus experiencing growth even though incomes in Australia or in North America were not rising in 2001.

Cross Elasticity   The latest version of the Windows operating system is more valuable on a computer that has the most powerful version of a microchip than on a less powerful machine. The operating system and the microchip are complements. A **complement** to one product or service is any other product or service that makes the first one more attractive. Hot dogs and mustard, cars and auto loans, televisions and videocassette recorders, television shows and TV Guide are examples of complementary products and services. The Canadian companies Liqui-Box, a manufacturer of packaging systems for pumpable food products for institutional applications, and DuPont Canada, a diversified science company that produces food products, generate complementary products. When the demand for the food products rises, the demand for the packaging systems rises.

Firms that produce complementary products are called **complementors.** DuPont Canada and Liqui-Box are complementors, as are Microsoft and Intel. Microsoft benefits when Intel develops a faster chip, and Intel benefits when Microsoft pushes forward in software development. Unless customers feel the need to upgrade, they won't continue buying the new Intel chip. For this reason, Intel has sought out other complementors such as ProShare and local phone companies to increase the demand for video applications that extend the limits of the microprocessor chips.

In 1913 General Motors, Hudson, Packard, and Willys-Overland, together with Goodyear tires and Prest-O-Lite headlights, set up the Lincoln Highway Association to develop America's first coast-to-coast highway.[9] The association built several miles along the proposed transcontinental route. The roads so complemented the cars that more cars were sold; this in turn increased the demand for roads. It was not until 1916 that the federal government committed its first dollars to building roads; by 1922 the first five transcontinental highways had been completed.[10]

Complements and **substitutes** are an important aspect of business. Complements are items used together, whereas substitutes are items used in place of each other. Starbucks coffee and the Coffee Bean coffee are substitutes. While businesses may seek complementors, they want to distance themselves from substitutes. A business does not want a large number of substitutes for its product. The more substitutes, the more price-elastic is demand.

The **cross elasticity of demand** measures whether goods and services are complements or substitutes. Goods that are close substitutes for each other will have high positive cross elasticities. As the price of one good—say, Trek bikes—rises, the quantity demanded of other bicycles—Specialized, for instance—rises. If the two brands of bikes are considered virtually the same by most consumers, then a small price change in one will significantly affect the demand for the other. Goods that are complements have negative cross-price elasticities. As the price of movie tickets rises, the quantity of popcorn consumed declines. Movies and popcorn are used together—they are complements. If the cross-price elasticity is near zero, the goods are not closely related—they are not really either substitutes or complements.

The cross elasticity is defined as the percentage change in the demand of one good divided by the percentage change in the price of a related good. A firm whose products have high positive cross elasticities with other products must be very conscious of what the related product's firm is doing; the products are substitutes. A move to "value pricing" or "everyday low prices" by Federated Department Stores affected close substitutes such as other department stores and specialty apparel stores. The rivals had to respond quickly or face a loss of business. A firm whose products have low positive cross elasticities with other products faces fewer or less close substitutes. For instance, should the price of Coca-Cola rise, the demand for coal, gas, or other sources of energy is unlikely to change. When the cross elasticity is negative, the products are considered to be complements; they are used together. When the price of microchips goes up, the demand for computer software goes down.

An elasticity measure could be calculated for anything that affects demand. For instance, it is not unusual for firms to want information on how advertising expenditures affect demand or on how sales forces affect demand. The calculation of these elasticities is similar to the calculation of price, income, and cross-price elasticities: percentage change in the quantity demanded divided by the percentage change in the variable under consideration.

Elasticity Estimates

Computer technology has enabled firms to get much better information about their customers and the elasticities of demand. Consider the petroleum industry, for example. Most retailers look at their sites, factor in overhead, and try to price slightly lower than their competition, with price increases or decreases being fairly uniform across all grades of fuel.[11] Usually, there is a standard difference between grades of gas, and when one is increased by a few cents the other is raised by the same amount. But the gut-feel approach typically leaves money on the table. Computer technology allows gasoline retailers to determine price elasticity relationships quite readily. Elasticity models operate through a daily evaluation of pricing factors, site by site, that are stored on a running database. The process starts by entering historical price, volume, and competitive data for use by the model, with continual fine-tuning accomplished through daily data updates. Typical elasticity estimates for a single retailer, according to the pricing company MPSI Systems Inc., are 6 for regular, 4.5 for mid-grade, and 3 for premium: A 1 percent change in price will result in a 6 percent loss in volume for regular, a 4.5 percent loss in volume for mid-grade, and a 3 percent loss in volume for premium. So when the prices on all grades of gasoline are increased the same amount, the consumers of each brand act differently.

Computer technology is enabling many "low-margin" industries to improve their margins by knowing their customers better. The supermarket business is a prime example. Companies such as SAP-KhiMetrics and Customer Analyst provide the technical means to gather detailed information at the checkout counter. This information is then fed into a central computer and analyzed. The results are then used to determine prices on the products for the next day, week, or month.

Software companies create pricing models for businesses—even for retail businesses such as supermarkets that have more than 30,000 products for sale at any one time. These software firms offer a service they call revenue management. Their results are a significant improvement in revenue. SAP-KhiMetrics has found that its clients add about 1.9 percent to sales and from 3 percent to nearly 5 percent on profit margins.[12]

Petroleum retailers, supermarkets, and many other firms are increasing profits because they better understand the customer. Computer technology enables firms to keep records of each customer—what they like and don't like, how sensitive they are to prices, and so on. A firm whose managers do not understand elasticities may be at a competitive disadvantage.

Knowing the Customer

CASE *review*

Are businesses leaving money on the table? The short answer is yes, they are. As we have seen in this chapter, how customers respond to price depends on several characteristics, and these must be known to understand consumer behavior. A price increase will result in a revenue increase only if the price elasticity of demand is less than 1 or inelastic. It is quite amazing that the majority of companies use ad hoc pricing procedures. A survey conducted in October 2001 among the members of the U.S.-based Professional Pricing Society found that about 38 percent tried to determine a price based on value, cost, and competition; 25 percent narrowed it down to value versus competition; and 18 percent relied on cost-plus or some formula based on margin or return on investment; while the remaining firms chose other methods.

With the technologies available today, these ad hoc procedures are costly. Knowing the customer requires more than guessing or relying on some feeling about psychological aspects. It requires information, and that information can be obtained and utilized. The science of knowing the customer is referred to as revenue management. For example, revenue management system (RMS) vendors are incorporating new techniques such as group rates, guest history, and application service provider (ASP) technology to provide hotels an affordable and automated way to increase revenues. Data are collected, analyzed, and then stored in an easily retrievable format.

Most revenue management systems are "real time," meaning that each transaction is immediately fed into a large database that can be called up immediately. For instance, Bell Canada's database can be used to pull not only the customer's history but also psychodemographic information and other sales flags, such as whether the customer is at high risk of switching carriers. Part of knowing the customer is knowing when customers are satisfied or are about to leave for a competitor—and what to do about it.

Revenue management systems are being offered by a growing number of companies. Satmetrix provides firms with a measure of the degree of customer loyalty and determines what needs to be done to maintain or improve that loyalty. In essence, the company measures the price elasticity of demand: Is it low enough; that is, is there a firm or product loyalty? SAP-KhiMetrics provides large retail operations with scientific real-time pricing. Scanner data are collected and analyzed, and then price elasticities, cross-price elasticities, and other measures are calculated and used to set prices. SAP-KhiMetrics has found that its customers have significantly increased profits simply by adopting the technological approach to knowing the customer.

Summary

1. Know your customer. This phrase means understand the demand curve and know the values of the elasticity measures.
2. The price elasticity of demand is a measure of the sensitivity of customers to price changes.
3. There is a relationship between price elasticity of demand and revenue. When the price elasticity of demand is less than 1 (inelastic), an increase in price increases revenue.

When the price elasticity of demand is greater than 1 (elastic), an increase in price decreases revenue.

4. The more substitutes, the more time involved, and the larger the proportion of the consumer's budget devoted to the item, the greater is the price elasticity of demand.

5. Income elasticity is a measure of the sensitivity of demand to changes in income, with the price and other factors held constant. A cyclical good is one for which the income elasticity of demand is positive. A noncyclical good is one for which the income elasticity of demand is near zero. A countercyclical good is one for which the income elasticity of demand is negative.

6. The cross-price elasticity of demand measures the relationship between two goods. A negative cross-price elasticity means that as the price of one good (or service) rises, the demand for the other good (or service) falls. These goods are complements. A positive cross-price elasticity of demand means the goods are substitutes—as the price of one rises, the demand for the other rises.

Key Terms

Price elasticity of demand
Elastic
Unit-elastic
Inelastic
Income elasticity of demand
Cyclical goods

Countercyclical goods
Complements
Complementors
Substitutes
Cross elasticity of demand

Exercises

1. For each of the following pairs of goods or services, identify the one for which the price elasticity of demand is greater and explain why.

   Coffee/Starbucks coffee
   Tuition at a public university/tuition at a private university
   Emergency room medical service/annual physical exam
   Movies in the afternoon/movies at night
   Prescription medicine/over-the-counter medicine

2. Although water is essential to life no matter where one lives, the demand for water differs across regions. In one study it was found that the price elasticity of demand for water in all regions of the United States ranged from 0.39 to 0.69.

   a. Why is the demand for water price-inelastic?
   b. In those regions where outdoor use of water makes up a relatively large portion of total use, the price elasticity is high. Why?
   c. The demand for water in the summer months is greater than in the winter months. Explain why.

3. Many proponents of public transit argue that the service should be provided free to the public in

metropolitan areas in order to reduce pollution and traffic congestion. Estimates by economists found the price elasticity of demand for public transit to be 0.17. The economists also found the cross-price elasticity of demand with the automobile to be 0.10.

   a. What will free public transit mean to the use of the public transportation service?
   b. What will free public transit mean to the use of the automobile?

4. The income elasticity of demand for automobiles in the United States was estimated by a government agency to be between 2.5 and 3.9.

   a. What does this mean?
   b. If incomes rise by 10 percent, what happens to the purchase of automobiles?

5. Explain why the demand curve is a horizontal line in the situation called perfect competition.

6. Many retailers will use short-term price cuts to attract customers. These often include "loss-leaders"—products sold at a loss for a short time. Why would a firm ever sell at a loss?

212   **Part 4:** Analytic Problem-Solving Tools

7. The demand curve slopes downward. Explain why it slopes down.
8. What would happen to the demand curve in each of the following cases:

    a. income rises
    b. the number of customers rises
    c. the number of substitutes increases
    d. people expect that the price of the good will decline in the near future
    e. people expect that the price of the good will rise in the future

9. Economists have found that cigarette smoking declines about 4 percent for every 10 percent increase in cigarette price. Several states have increased taxes by 100 percent on cigarettes to pay for improvements to education. Does the policy make sense? Explain.
10. Using the following equation for the demand for a good or service, calculate the price elasticity of demand, cross price elasticity with good x, and income elasticity.

$$Q = 8 - 2P + 0.10I + P_x$$

    where Q is quantity demanded, P is the product price, I is income, and P_x is the price of a related good. Assume that $P = \$10$, $I = 100$, and $P_x = 20$. (*Hint:* find quantity demanded. Then use the elasticity formula: percentage change divided by percentage change to calculate the elasticity. The formula for price elasticity is: $(\partial Q/\partial P)(P/Q)$ where ∂ means change. For Quantity demanded: Simply substitute the values given into the demand equation)
11. A firm has estimated the following demand function for its product:

$$Q = 10 - 2P + 0.20I + 2A$$

    where Q is quantity demanded per month in thousands, P is product price, I is an index of consumer income, and A is advertising expenditures per month in thousands. Assume that $P = \$5$, $I = 50$, and $A = 10$.
    Based on this information, select the correct values for: quantity demanded; price elasticity of demand; income elasticity of demand; and advertising elasticity. (Use the point formulas to complete the required elasticity calculations).

    Hint Quantity demanded: Substitute the values given for the variables into the demand equation. Then calculate elasticities. Price elasticity: Use the point elasticity formula: $(dQ/dP)(P/Q)$
    Income elasticity: Use the point formula: $(dQ/dI)(I/Q)$
    Advertising elasticity: Use the point formula: $(dQ/dA)(A/Q)$

12. If a firm has two sets of customers, those who want the newest version of the product immediately and those who are more patient, how should it price its product?
13. Under what condition would it make sense for a firm to offer quantity discounts?
14. The price elasticity of demand for Japanese autos is more elastic in the United States than it is in Europe. How should the Japanese firms price their autos to gain the most revenue?
15. If the price of a Big Mac is increased by $0.50 and the price of a BMW convertible is increased by $5,000, who will react more, the Big Mac customers or the BMW customers? Explain
16. Why would movie theaters offer discounts to seniors?
17. Explain why the price elasticity of demand is negative. What would the price elasticity of demand be for a "prestige good," one for which quantity purchased increases as price increases? How do you reconcile these two statements?
18. Using elasticity, explain what "market power" means.

CHAPTER NOTES

1. A simple Internet search on pricing and profit margins will bring up a multitude of companies now consulting on how to determine prices. The following is an interesting survey on pricing: *Pricing for Profit ... the Critical Success Factors,* www.policypublications.com/pricing_for_profit.htm.
2. $e_d = \partial \ln Q_d / \partial \ln P = [\partial Q_d / Q_d] / [\partial P/P]$, where e_d represents the price elasticity of demand, $\partial \ln Q_d$ is the percentage change in the quantity demanded (the derivative of the logarithm of quantity demanded, which is the change in Q_d divided by the base quantity demanded or the initial quantity demanded), and $\partial \ln P$ is the percentage change in price (the derivative of the logarithm of price, which is the change in price divided by the base price or initial price).

3. Notice that we say 3 rather than −3. According to the law of demand, whenever the price of a good rises, the quantity demanded of that good falls. Thus, the price elasticity of demand is always negative, which can be confusing when one is referring to a "very high elasticity" (a large negative number) or to a "low elasticity" (a small negative number). To avoid this confusion, economists use the absolute value of the price elasticity of demand and thus ignore the negative sign.

4. Note that the price elasticity of demand is always negative because of the law of demand.

5. Demand curves need not be straight lines. The straight line is used to illustrate demand concepts because it incorporates most of the important aspects of demand.

6. These are based on very small incremental movements. When using larger discrete amounts, the results are only approximate. For instance, if price is $1 and quantity is 100, then revenue is $100. A 10 percent rise in price to $1.10 and a 10 percent fall in quantity to 90 means that revenue is $99.

7. Molly Espey, "Explaining the Variation in Elasticity Estimates of Gasoline Demand in the United States: A Meta-analysis," *Energy Journal*, 17, no. 3 (1996): 49–60. Phil Goodwin, Joyce Dargay, and Mark Hanly, "Review of Income and Price Elasticities in the Demand for Road Traffic," *Transport Reviews*, 24, no. 3 (2004): 275–292.

8. Notice that while the price elasticity of demand is always negative, the income elasticity can be negative, zero, or positive.

9. Drake Hokanson, *The Lincoln Highway: Main Street Across America* (Iowa City: University of Iowa Press, 1988).

10. Farmers wanted all-weather, farm-to-market roads. Motorist groups and the automobile industry wanted hard-surfaced, interstate roads. The Post Office Department Appropriations Bill, enacted August 24, 1912, appropriated $500,000 for an experimental program to improve post roads. The funds would be made available to state or local governments that agreed to pay two-thirds of the cost of the projects. Continued lobbying by automobile manufacturers and their suppliers led to the interstate system in 1956.

11. Keith Reid, "The Science of Pricing," *Business and Management Practices*, 5, no. 2 (March 2000): 33–35.

12. Interview with Ken Ouimet, founder of Khi-metrics, September 2006.

CHAPTER **13**

Costs

CASE

The Problem with Size

Does corporate size necessarily confer an advantage in business? Wal-Mart is the largest corporate employer in the world. It has built its position in many markets by being operationally better than any other competitor. As it has grown larger, it has exploited its buying leverage with suppliers. On the other hand, its impact on communities, its treatment of employees, and its dealing with suppliers have all generated bad will for the company. Its top management has recently unveiled a number of actions and recommendations to make it appear to be a more responsible corporate citizen.

The CEO of British Petroleum (BP) decided that not only should the company maintain worldwide operations, but should be a model of good corporate citizenship. But BP ran into difficulties with size. An explosion at its Texas City refinery killed 15 people, and subsequent investigations found many safety lapses. Then came evidence of a big environmental problem in the company's Alaskan operations. The problems were attributed to the complexity of the organization.[1]

1. Why would size not mean continued success?
2. Why would CEOs want to grow their firms?

Output and Productivity

Costs are the costs of resource services needed to produce output. The more productive the resources, the fewer that are required to produce any given amount of output. Productivity is defined as output per unit of a resource's services. Labor productivity is the quantity of output divided by the number of hours worked by labor, everything else held constant; land productivity is the quantity of output divided by the quantity of land, everything else held constant; capital productivity is total output divided by total capital; and total factor productivity is total output divided by total inputs. In short, productivity is the efficiency with which inputs are converted into output. Figure 13.1 shows how productivity growth and GDP per capita in the United States performed between 1949 and 1999.[2]

In 1850 in the United States, it took about 1,800 hours of labor for a household of four to acquire its annual food needs. Today it takes only about 250 hours of work. Since 1900, the average work year has fallen from 3,100 hours to about 1,700 as RGDP per capita has increased from $4,800 to around $35,000. In a similar vein, if a firm is more efficient at converting inputs into output, that is, if it is more productive, it would probably be more successful as well. And if one brick layer is twice as productive as another, everything else held constant, then the more productive one ought to earn more income.

Where do increases in productivity come from? They come from improvements in the quality of resources—technological change and human capital in particular. New technology enables resources to be more efficient. Computers embedded in automobiles enable problems to be discerned more easily and more accurately. Computers have allowed medical diagnoses to be made more quickly and with more accuracy. But it is not just computers—technological change includes not only the efficiency of capital but

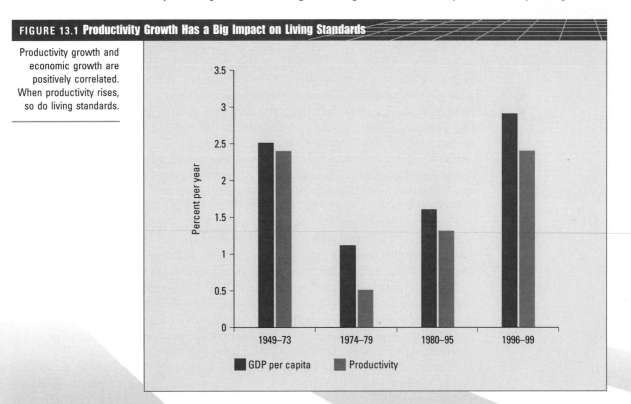

FIGURE 13.1 Productivity Growth Has a Big Impact on Living Standards

Productivity growth and economic growth are positively correlated. When productivity rises, so do living standards.

Percent per year

GDP per capita   Productivity

1949–73   1974–79   1980–95   1996–99

Source: Evan Koenig, "Productivity Growth," Federal Reserve Bank of Dallas, *Expand Your Insight*, March 1, 2000, www.dallasfed.org/eyi/usecon/0003growth.html, Chart 1.

also the efficiency of management, communication, information, financial markets, and on and on. Wal-Mart's inventory control system that made it so successful has been copied by almost every firm. The SKUs are read when purchases are made, fed back into computers that restock inventories, catalogue buyer purchases and tendencies, and provide feedback to everyone along the supply chain.

From Production to Costs

Typically, when productivity is rising, costs are declining because the same amount of output can be produced using fewer resources. Conversely, when productivity is falling, costs are rising because the same amount of output requires more resources. We can speak of total factor productivity, which is a measure of the change in output resulting from a change in all resources, or marginal productivity, which is the change in output that results from a change in just one resource, everything else held constant. In most cases, it makes most sense to speak about marginal productivity since firms are not able to vary all resource services at the same time; they have fixed capacity or are unable to open new outlets or factories for several months or years or to change labor contracts rapidly. When a firm increases its output without being able to increase all resources, the firm runs up against a law of physics known as the law of **diminishing marginal returns**. The law of diminishing marginal returns states that as a variable resource is increased and combined with a fixed quantity of other resources, marginal productivity will initially rise but eventually will decline. You can't keep adding more and more labor to a fixed amount of capital and land and expect that the labor will continue to be more productive.

Suppose you place a flower bulb in a small container and cover it with good soil. As the plant is watered, it begins to grow. So more water must mean more growth, right? Obviously not; everyone knows that the plant will eventually die if more and more water is added. Productivity will eventually decline. Consider the effort to improve passenger safety during collisions by installing air bags in cars. The air bags open on impact to keep the passengers from contact with the car. The first air bag added to a car increases protection considerably. The second adds an element of safety, particularly for an adult front-seat passenger. Additional bags also add some safety—for instance, the side-impact bags protect the passengers from injuries due to collisions on the doors. Each additional air bag adds less additional safety than did the previous one. Eventually another air bag would actually lessen protection because the bags would interfere with each other. As successive units of the variable resource, air bags, are placed on the fixed resource, the car, the additional amount of protection provided by the air bags—the output—declines.

Table 13.1 captures production possibilities for a hypothetical airline. The resources are mechanics and planes, and the output is passenger miles. With one mechanic servicing the planes, the company can generate 30,000 passenger-miles if the airline has 5 airplanes, 100,000 passenger-miles if it has 10 airplanes, 250,000 passenger-miles if it has 15 airplanes, and so on. With a second mechanic working on the planes, output is increased with each quantity of airplanes; five airplanes now generate 60,000 passenger-miles, and so on. The airline could produce about the same amount, say 340,000 to 360,000 passenger-miles with several different combinations of mechanics and airplanes—three mechanics with 10 airplanes, two mechanics with 15 airplanes, or one mechanic with 20 airplanes. And several other output levels can be produced with a number of different combinations of mechanics and airplanes.

What combination or combinations does the airline use? It depends on the airline's current situation. Suppose that the airline had previously leased or purchased 10 airplanes and could not change the number of planes for at least a year. The airline can alter the number of mechanics it uses but not the number of airplanes during that one year period. Thus, the options open to the airline are only those under the column label

Table 13.1

Production and
Diminishing Marginal
Returns

The combinations of total output (thousands of daily passenger miles) that can be produced by an airline using different combinations of mechanics and airplanes. If one resource is fixed, such as number of airplanes fixed at 10, then increasing the number of mechanics increases output but by decreasing amounts. This is diminishing marginal returns.

NUMBER OF MECHANICS	NUMBER OF AIRPLANES							
	5	10	15	20	25	30	35	40
0	0	0	0	0	0	0	0	0
1	30	100	250	340	410	400	400	390
2	60	250	360	450	520	530	520	500
3	100	360	480	570	610	620	620	610
4	130	440	580	640	690	700	700	690
5	130	500	650	710	760	770	780	770
6	110	540	700	760	800	820	830	840
7	100	550	720	790	820	850	870	890
8	80	540	680	800	830	860	880	900

"10" airplanes in Table 13.1. In the short run, the firm can increase some resources but not all. This means the firm becomes less and less efficient as it turns inputs into outputs because it has to combine an increasing amount of the resources it can acquire with a fixed amount of the resources it cannot acquire. A constraint facing many businesses is their space or building. As the firm expands, it hires more employees, obtains more machines or more inventory, and must find room for these additional resources.

Diminishing marginal returns show up in Table 13.1 whenever one of the resources is fixed and the other is variable. For instance, when the number of airplanes is fixed at 10, then the first mechanic increases total output from 0 to 100,000 passenger-miles. Increasing the number of mechanics from one to two increases total output to 250,000 passenger-miles, an increase of 150,000 passenger-miles. The third mechanic raises total output to 360,000, an increase of 110,000. The fourth mechanic increases output to 440,000 passenger-miles, an increase of 80,000 passenger-miles. The additional output produced by an additional unit of the variable resource diminishes.

The law of diminishing marginal returns defines the relationship between costs and output, when at least one resource is fixed. Suppose in our airline example, the cost per mechanic is $1,000 and that this is the only cost the airline has. Then, as we increase output, notice what occurs to total costs. As output rises, total costs rise, but the two do not rise proportionately. Initially, total output rises more rapidly than costs, and then costs rise more rapidly than output.

Two pieces of information about costs are particularly useful in economic analysis, per unit cost and marginal cost. The **average total cost (ATC)**, or cost per unit of output, is derived by dividing total cost by the quantity of output. Average total cost is shown in column 3 of Table 13.2: Average total costs fall initially and then rise as output rises. **Marginal cost (MC)** is the change in cost caused by a change in output and is derived by dividing the change in total cost by the change in the quantity of output. It is, essentially, the additional cost that comes from producing an additional unit of output. If labor is variable while capital is fixed, then marginal cost is the cost of the additional labor used to provide one more unit of output. The additional quantity that comes from an additional unit of labor services is the marginal product of labor, MP. So, if the additional cost of labor is represented by W, the wage rate, and MP represents the marginal product of labor, then the marginal cost of output is:

$$MC = W/MP$$

Marginal cost is shown in the last column of Table 13.2; it, too, falls initially and then rises as output rises. The reason that average and marginal costs initially fall and then rise is the law of diminishing marginal returns. The link between marginal cost and marginal productivity should make sense. Marginal product tells us how much additional output an additional resource will generate for the firm. Marginal cost tells us how much the additional output will cost—that is, how much additional resources are required to generate that additional output. When marginal productivity (MP) is rising, it says that fewer additional resources are used to produce a certain amount of additional output—so marginal cost is falling. Conversely, when marginal productivity is falling, then marginal cost is rising.

Fixed and Variable Costs

The most common way to present costs is to distinguish between overhead (SG&A) and direct costs (COGS). Economists don't find that distinction to be as useful to their analyses as that between fixed and variable costs. As noted in Chapter 11, fixed costs are costs that do not change as the quantity of output changes. Variable costs, on the other hand, are costs that depend on the quantity of output. Insurance premiums, taxes, and managerial salaries are fixed costs. They must be paid regardless of how much is produced. Electricity used to operate the production process is a variable cost, increasing as the quantity of output produced is increased. Many resource costs include elements of both fixed and variable costs. If employees work overtime or new employees are brought on board when the firm is producing more output and then released during reductions in output, then the costs of labor are variable. But long-term labor contracts fix labor costs during the period of the contract, so that during any period shorter than the period of the contract, labor costs are fixed.

Suppose the labor, capital, and land costs have been allocated to either variable or fixed costs, as shown in the first three columns of Table 13.3. Column 1 lists the total quantity (Q) of output produced. Column 2 lists the total fixed costs (TFC)—costs that must be paid whether or not the firm produces. Fixed costs are $10—this is what must be paid regardless of whether any output is produced. Column 3 lists the total variable costs (TVC), costs that rise or fall as production rises or falls. Total costs (TC), the sum of total variable and total fixed costs, are listed in column 4.

Table 13.2				
Total, Average, and Marginal costs	**TOTAL COST**	**OUTPUT**	**AVERAGE TOTAL COST**	**MARGINAL COST**[a]
	$ 0	0	—	—
	$1,000	100	$10	$ 10
	$2,000	250	$ 8	$ 6.67
	$3,000	360	$ 8.33	$ 9.09
	$4,000	440	$ 9.09	$ 12.50
	$5,000	500	$10	$ 16.67
	$6,000	540	$11.11	$ 25
	$7,000	550	$12.73	$100
	$8,000	540	$14.81	—

[a]This is the average of the individual unit marginal cost. The marginal cost of $10 for the first 99 units indicates that the average marginal cost of units 1 through 100 is $101, and so on for units 101–250, units 251–360, etc.

Table 13.3

Cost Schedules

This table shows the calculation of the various cost measures. Average costs (average fixed, average variable, average total) are derived by dividing total costs (fixed, variable, total) by output. Marginal cost is the change in total cost divided by the change in output.

OUTPUT (Q)	TOTAL FIXED COSTS (TFC)	TOTAL VARIABLE COSTS (TVC)	TOTAL COSTS (TC)	AVERAGE FIXED COSTS (AFC)	AVERAGE VARIABLE COSTS (AVC)	AVERAGE TOTAL COSTS (ATC)	MARGINAL COSTS (MC)
0	$10	0	10				
1	10	10	20	10	10	20	10
2	10	18	28	5	9	14	8
3	10	25	35	3.33	8.33	11.6	7
4	10	30	40	2.5	7.5	10	5
5	10	35	45	2	7	9	5
6	10	42	52	1.66	7	8.66	7
7	10	50.6	60.6	1.44	7.2	8.6	8.6
8	10	60	70	1.25	7.5	8.75	9.4
9	10	80	90	1.1	8.8	10	20

The law of diminishing marginal returns defines the relationship between costs and output in the short run for every firm, no matter whether that firm is a billion dollar a year corporation or a small proprietorship. Obviously, the size or scale of the companies will differ, but the general nature of the relationship between short-run costs and output will not.

The Cost Curves Plotting the Average Total Cost and Marginal Cost columns of Table 13.3, we derive Figure 13.2.

The curves for both average and marginal costs are described as U-shaped; as output rises, per-unit and incremental costs initially fall but eventually rise. The shape of these

FIGURE 13.2 Average Total Cost (ATC) and Marginal Cost (MC) are U-shaped Due to The Law of Diminishing Marginal Returns

The figures in Table 13.3 are plotted. MC, AVC, and ATC all fall initially and then rise. AFC continually falls. MC intersects AVC and ATC at their minimum points.

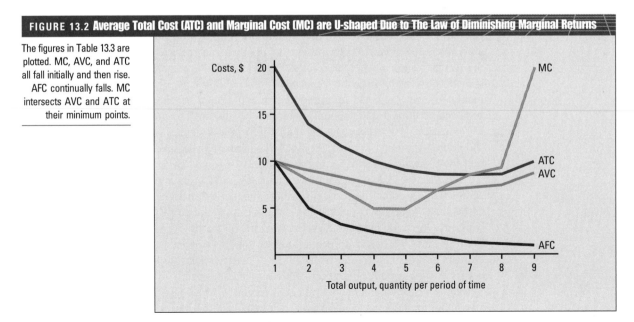

curves is quite important because every firm, no matter what it does and no matter what its size, has cost curves that are U-shaped in the short run. This U-shape is due to the law of diminishing marginal returns. When successive equal amounts of a variable resource are combined with a fixed amount of another resource, output will initially increase rapidly, then increase more slowly, and eventually decline. This means that equal increments of output will initially not require many additional resources, but eventually, equal increments of output will require accelerating variable resources—thus accelerating costs. In every instance in which increasing amounts of one resource are combined with fixed amounts of other resources, the additional output initially increases but eventually decreases. In other words, since the firm has to pay for each employee or each unit of a variable resource, its costs rise slowly at first as output increases, but then they rise more and more rapidly as output rises. This fact gives us the U-shape of the average-total- and marginal-cost curves.

Operating Leverage, Sunk Costs

The ratio of fixed costs to variable costs, called **operating leverage**, can present strategic issues to firms. When operating leverage is high, the firm has less flexibility. It has large fixed costs that have to be paid even if sales are temporarily low. General Motors is buying out existing United Auto Workers contracts with the idea of reducing its operating leverage. With the contracts in place, GM was faced with very large fixed costs that often made it operate in the red.

New technology is enabling companies to alter their operating leverage through the scheduling of their workforce. Workers are moved from predictable shifts to schedules that are based on the number of customers in stores at any given time. Wal-Mart, Payless Shoe Source Inc., RadioShack Corp., and Mervyns LLC. are all implementing such a system. Individual store sales are tracked in 15-minute increments over a period of time, and the data are compared to previous periods or years. The idea is that more employees are at the store when customer demands are highest, and then when customer demands are low, fewer workers are at the store. Fixed costs associated with employees set to work a fixed number of hours at specific times, are moved to variable costs as number of employees and time schedules vary as output varies.[3]

Sunk costs are costs that have already been incurred and that cannot be recovered. These costs are called sunk because they are gone and not retrievable. Since they are gone and cannot be recovered, they should not influence decisions. For example, suppose a company has invested $20 million on research regarding a new anticancer drug, but the search has not yet yielded results. The $20 million is a sunk cost because the research is incomplete and no sale or recovery is possible. But suppose the research and development could be completed for an additional $40 million. At the same time, however, suppose the additional $40 million could also be allocated to a different project having a better chance of success. What should the firm do? To argue that the original project should be continued because so much has already been invested is to ignore the fact that the costs already experienced are sunk.

There are no lack of cases, however, where sunk costs are used to justify continued action. This is called the sunk cost fallacy, which is also sometimes known as the Concorde Effect. This term derives from the fact that the British and French government continued to fund the joint development of Concorde even after it became apparent that there was no longer an economic case for the aircraft. Supposedly the British government privately regarded the project as a "commercial disaster" that should never have been started, but political aspects kept the project funded.

Sunk costs often enter into strategic decisions. Developers often will get work underway, build foundations, or clear areas with the idea that once money in some significant

Business Insight

A Builder's View of Sunk Costs

Jonathan Ward, a remodeler, recently wrote about his experience with sunk costs. He noted that humans seem to be the only animals that don't understand the concept of sunk costs. If a cat destroys a bird's nest and eats the hatchlings, the birds immediately set about building a new nest and laying eggs. They don't waste time trying to find someone to blame—or for that matter, someone to sue. Nor do they go on TV talk shows to weep about their misfortune, or attempt to "seek closure." They get on with their business. It is important to know when a situation is untenable, and when to walk away from a project, Ward says. He also says that you must continually ask yourself if, knowing what you know now, you would have funded the venture in the beginning. If you answer no, then change course. [4]

amount has been spent, it would be difficult for financiers to do anything except scream and holler. If a project is terminated, the financiers would have an irretrievable loss, not only of money but of reputation. Very few partially built bridges exist, for example, because once construction has started sunk costs are too high to reverse the decision and stop again.

The Planning Horizon: The Long Run

The existence of fixed costs indicates that the firm is constrained; it cannot alter a resource for a certain period of time. This time period is referred to as the **short run**. The short run is also called the **operating period** to indicate that the firm is actually in business. Any firm that is actually operating faces some fixed costs. The **long run or planning period** is a time period just long enough that everything is variable. There are no fixed costs in the long run.

Akio Morita, the founder of Sony Corporation, came to America in 1955 to sell a small transistor radio his company had developed.[5] He received an offer that seemed irresistible: A chain store would buy nearly 100,000 radios.[6] Amazingly, Morita turned it down. Why? One possibility was that Morita knew Sony did not have the capacity to produce that many radios, and attempting to do so could be risky. Sony's capacity was less than 1,000 radios a month. An order of 100,000 would mean hiring and training new employees and expanding facilities even more. The explanation could be illustrated with a curve that looks something like the lopsided letter U, shown in Figure 13.3. The cost per unit for 5,000 units would be quite high, the beginning of the curve. For 10,000 units, the per-unit costs would be quite a bit lower than for 5,000 units. But as size continued to rise, the per-unit cost would begin to climb. At 100,000 units, the cost per unit would be exorbitant.

Morita had to decide whether to expand the size or scale of his firm, not simply add more workers or acquire more materials, but to increase all resources. A firm can choose to relocate or to build a new plant or to purchase additional planes only in the long run. A manager can choose any size of plant or building and any combination of other resources when laying out the firm's plans because all resources are variable in the long run. In essence, during the long run the manager compares all short-run situations. In the short run or operating period, a manager can decide whether to produce and how much to produce but is unable to increase the size of the manufacturing plant or to change locations or enter a new market or leave a market. In the long run, the manager can expand, contract, relocate, enter a new business, exit any line of business, or quit doing business altogether.

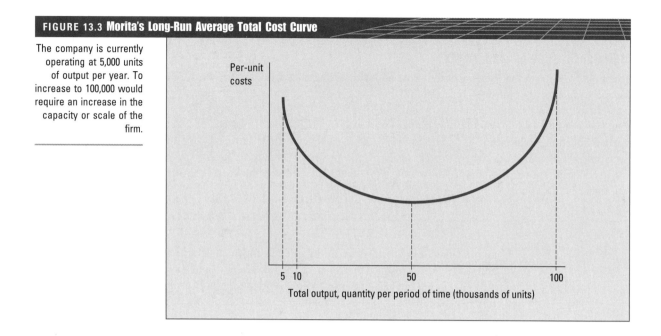

FIGURE 13.3 Morita's Long-Run Average Total Cost Curve

The company is currently operating at 5,000 units of output per year. To increase to 100,000 would require an increase in the capacity or scale of the firm.

In Figure 13.4, note that if Morita had increased capacity to SRATC$_2$ the company would have had to operate along that curve no matter what output the company decided to produce. Had the order not continued at the high level and the company was back producing 5,000 units, its cost per unit would have been exorbitant. In fact, the company would have had to go through a multiyear restructuring to get rid of the excess capacity so that the company could move from SRATC$_2$ to SRATC$_1$.

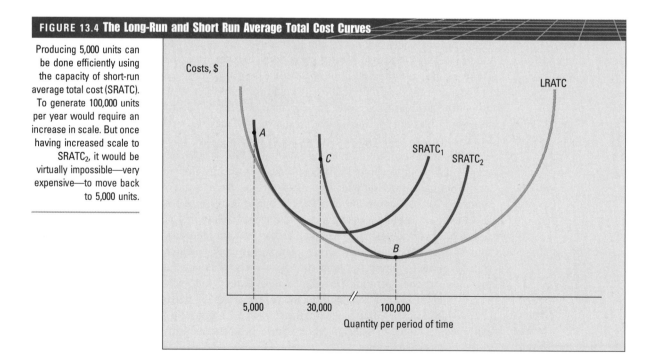

FIGURE 13.4 The Long-Run and Short Run Average Total Cost Curves

Producing 5,000 units can be done efficiently using the capacity of short-run average total cost (SRATC). To generate 100,000 units per year would require an increase in scale. But once having increased scale to SRATC$_2$, it would be virtually impossible—very expensive—to move back to 5,000 units.

Costs in the Long Run

The long run is a planning period—any combination of resources can be selected. Once a specific combination is selected—that is, once a certain size of operation is chosen—the firm must operate within that constraint. For instance, Sony had one factory with a capacity of 5,000 radios a month. It could increase the number of employees and other supplies, but it was constrained to that one factory. However, in the future it could expand its capacity either by adding on to its single factory or building additional plants. In the long run, a firm can choose to operate at any size. All it needs to do is choose the level of output it wants to produce and then select the least-cost combination of resources with which to produce the chosen output level. But once it has built that given capacity, then it is constrained to operate at that level.

Tom Lasorda, CEO of DaimlerChrysler in January 2007, stated that "Currently we have too much capacity ... the fundamental issue is how we see the market, and where its headed."[7] Lasorda was considering a restructuring—he was looking at what he thought the best size would be. Currently, he said, the company was operating inefficiently; being able to change the capacity in the long run will increase efficiency. But Lasorda noted that the capacity change was consistent with how the company "sees the market". The way DaimlerChrysler saw the market in 2007 was to get rid of the Chrysler division. Chrysler still could not make it and was bailed or taken over by the U.S. government in 2009.

Economies and Diseconomies of Scale

If the size of the firm is doubled—if all resources including capacity are doubled—and output more than doubles, then we say that there are **economies of scale**. In such a case, cost per unit of output decreases as output rises. Notice how this principle differs from the law of diminishing marginal returns. Diminishing returns applies if at least one of the resources cannot be changed; economies of scale refers to the situation where all resources are changed.

When the size of the firm is doubled and output increases by less than double, then we say there are **diseconomies of scale**. In this case, the cost per unit of output increases when the quantity of production increases. If the cost per unit of output is constant as output rises and all resources are variable, then we say there are **constant returns to scale**.

The long-run average total cost curve can be downward sloping, upward sloping, or constant. If we drew the long-run average total cost curve as U-shaped, then we would be saying that initially the firm experiences economies of scale; then as it grows it experiences constant returns to scale; and finally, as it continues growing it experiences diseconomies of scale. While this shape is probably the most common long-run cost situation for firms, there is no reason that a firm could not experience only economies of scale (a downward-sloping long-run average total cost curve), or only diseconomies of scale (an upward-sloping long-run average total cost curve), or only constant returns to scale, a straight horizontal line.

Economies of scale may result from the ability to use larger machines that are more efficient than small ones. In 1892, John D. Rockefeller's Standard Oil Company (the precursor of Exxon) dominated the production of kerosene. Kerosene was, at that time, the key product refined from crude oil and was by far America's largest nonfarm export. Standard Oil made 90 percent of all the kerosene produced in the United States. But when Russia's Caspian Sea oil fields were discovered and kerosene began to be shipped from there to the European market, Standard Oil feared that it would lose its domination in Europe. The company had to become more efficient. It did this by closing several small refineries and building three enormous new ones. The huge scale of production in these new refineries led to significant cost reductions. In 1880, plants with a 2,000-barrel-a-day capacity made kerosene for 2.5 cents a gallon. In 1885, with the new plants having a 6,000-barrel-a-day capacity, Standard Oil could make kerosene for less than half a penny per gallon. This allowed the company to price its kerosene in Europe below the Russian kerosene, even though the American product had much higher shipping costs.

Sometimes economies of scale result from specialization. Being larger enables companies to use their specially trained labor and management in specific activities rather than over a broad range of activities. Size, however, does not automatically improve efficiency. The specialization that comes with large size often requires the addition of specialized managers. A 10 percent increase in the number of employees may require an increase greater than 10 percent in the number of managers. A manager to supervise other managers may be needed. Paperwork increases. Meetings are held more often. The amounts of time and labor that are not devoted to producing output grow. Managerial inefficiencies need not be the only reason for diseconomies of scale, but they are typically the primary reason.

As the size of a firm increases, economies of scale followed by diseconomies of scale is common. The generation of electricity has traditionally experienced economies of scale. One huge plant can generate electricity at a lower cost per kilowatt-hour than can several small plants. But the transmission of electricity is a different matter. The farther the electricity has to be transmitted, the greater the loss of electricity and the higher the cost per kilowatt-hour transmitted. At some size, diseconomies of scale dominate economies of scale.

Many different types of firms face similar problems. Mrs. Fields' Cookies trained the managers of all Mrs. Fields' outlets at its headquarters in Park City, Utah. The training period was referred to as Cookie College. By spreading the cost of Cookie College over more than 700 outlets, Mrs. Fields' Cookies was surely able to achieve economies of scale. However, the company faced some diseconomies because the cookie dough was produced at one location and distributed to the outlets in premixed packages. The dough factory could be large, but the distribution of dough produces diseconomies of scale that worsen as outlets are opened farther and farther away from the factory.

The law of diminishing marginal returns applies to every resource, every firm, and every industry. Whether there are economies of scale, diseconomies of scale, constant returns to scale, or some combination of these depends on the industry under consideration. No physical law dictates that an industry will have economies of scale eventually followed by diseconomies of scale. Theoretically, it is possible for an industry to experience only diseconomies of scale, only economies of scale, or only constant returns to scale.

Large Scale Is Not Always Best

Economies of scale mean lower costs per unit of output as the quantity of output increases. It might seem, then, that a large firm would always have an advantage over smaller firms, but that isn't necessarily so. Efficiency and specialization are limited by the size of the market. A large firm would not have an advantage over a smaller firm if the larger firm produced more than what the market wanted to buy. In such a case, the large firm could not sell all the output necessary to realize its most efficient output level. If demand is not sufficient to purchase all the output produced by the larger firm, then producing that much output would not make sense.

Examples of production being limited by the size of the market often arise in small developing countries, where the domestic market for manufactured goods is quite limited. The most modern technology for an industry may involve a size whose output exceeds the reasonable market in the country. Sri Lanka, for example, sought assistance from Russia to establish a steel mill. The smallest plant the Soviets operated had a capacity of 60,000 tons of steel a year, but total demand in Sri Lanka was only 35,000 tons a year. As a result, the mill set up by the Soviets could be used only to about 58 percent of its capacity. At that rate of output, the mill operated inefficiently. The mill had been set up to benefit the local government officials, not to generate low-cost steel.[8]

Since markets in different countries may not support the most efficient size of a firm or plant, you might wonder why nations don't specialize in industries where they can achieve a scale that is competitive with the most efficient producers and buy from other countries the products for which the domestic market is too small to support competitive production. In fact, there is some evidence that scale economies help determine the pattern of trade across countries. But because governments often intervene in trade, scale economies do not always come into play. Many countries do not allow certain goods and services to be purchased from other countries. As a result, local firms are the only sources of these goods and services. When protectionism limits the size of a market, then the small size of that protected domestic market may mean the use of inefficient methods of production.

Larger size is not necessarily beneficial for individual firms. While growth is often the stated or actual strategy of a firm, it is not necessarily the best step toward success. Most firms run into the wall of diseconomies of scale, which opens the market up to smaller firms. Indeed, the very difficulties that arise as companies become larger and more complex—the diseconomies of scale associated with bureaucracy, the pressures associated with quarterly reporting, the rent seeking that takes place inside the firm—make it very probable that new kinds of private firms will proliferate. The financial sector is a case in point. Even as giants have formed, such as Citibank, new and nimbler species have arisen. Hedge funds, private equity partnerships, and sovereign wealth funds (holdings of hard currency reserves of exporters of manufactured goods and energy) have proliferated.

Economies of Scope

Firms producing more than one product may find synergies in their production while increasing productivity. For instance, petroleum companies such as Exxon and Mobil produce petroleum and chemical products; pharmaceutical companies produce many different pharmaceuticals; and many other firms produce a full line of different goods. When a firm obtains a production advantage from producing more than one product, we say there are **economies of scope**. These advantages may arise because a production facility used to make one product can also be used to make another, or because by-products of one product are useful in the production of another product, or because the people trained to produce one product can use their training in the production of another product.

In the 1890s, three large chemical companies—Bayer, Hoechst, and BASF—were building huge dye-making factories. Prior to the construction of these large factories, each different dye had been produced in a separate small factory. The new plants were able to produce hundreds of different dyes using the same basic chemical stock. The result was a substantial reduction in costs. This was a case of economies of scope.

Economies of scope occur when the cost of producing two (or more) products jointly is less than the cost of producing each one alone. For example, suppose that the chemical company Boscht produces 1,000 tons of a chemical and 500 tons of a paint per year at a cost of $15 million, whereas producing the chemical alone would cost $12 million and producing just the paint would cost $6 million. Then we would say Boscht experiences economies of scope.

It is often claimed that an advertising agency can provide many products at a lower per-unit cost than by simply focusing on a single product. In other words, they can carry out many different types of advertising—such as network television, spot television, magazines, special print media, newspapers, radio, outdoor services, and so on—or they can just supply one type of advertising. The cost reduction from joint production for advertising agencies is in the range of 5 to 70 percent.[9]

The attempt to gain "synergies" from combining different operations is another term for economies of scope. Like economies of scale, the reality is that there are serious limits to gaining these synergies. Sony Corporation, which bought out Columbia Pictures

Entertainment Inc. in the late 1980s to reinforce its image software business, did not appear to experience economies of scope. Hitachi Ltd. is finding the hard-disk drive business it purchased from IBM Corporation to be a problem as the unit has yet to turn a profit. Gaining economies of scope is more difficult than is often perceived. It seems likely that combining overlapping departments would save money. Yet, combining finance departments, legal sections, or personnel departments can be very difficult. Often attempting to integrate information systems will lead to unexpected glitches and disrupt service to customers.

The Experience Curve

Economies of scale are often confused with the **experience, or learning, curve**. In the early 1970s, a major consulting company, Boston Consulting Group, observed that costs often seem to fall as output rises; in many cases, costs fall by around 15 percent with each doubling of overall output. This observation was termed the experience curve because the declining costs were thought to be the result of learning, of gaining experience.[10] In fact, the experience curve mixes or confuses several different factors. For instance, it includes the influence of both learning that is specific to the firm and learning that is general to the industry, and it includes costs that fall with the cumulative amount of output a firm has produced over time and costs that fall with the rate of output (economies of scale) per unit of time.

Figure 13.5 shows experience curves drawn from two industries—aircraft manufacturers and broiler chickens. The apparent similarity of the curves is remarkable, but the causes and the implications are very different.[11] The falling costs of the airline are the result of learning by experience—learning that is mostly specific to Boeing and largely specific to a particular aircraft. There is no experience curve for chickens. In the case of chickens, the cost per chicken fell because of the industrywide adoption of a new technology to mass-produce chickens (as opposed to providing free-range chickens) supported by the use of antibiotics. Thus, the experience curve for chickens in Figure 13.5 is misleading. What actually occurred is that the technology allowed costs per unit to decline at each quantity of output.

Experience can be an important advantage to a firm. In Chapter 8 we discussed the case of Monsanto marching down the experience curve and driving Holland Sweetener

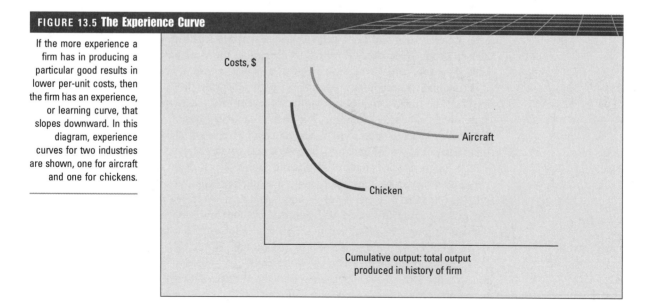

FIGURE 13.5 The Experience Curve

If the more experience a firm has in producing a particular good results in lower per-unit costs, then the firm has an experience, or learning curve, that slopes downward. In this diagram, experience curves for two industries are shown, one for aircraft and one for chickens.

Costs, $

Aircraft

Chicken

Cumulative output: total output produced in history of firm

out of the market. The problem for Holland was that Monsanto had a huge cost advantage because it had spent the previous decade learning how to cut manufacturing costs.[12] Monsanto had developed a name brand, reduced manufacturing costs until they were only 30 percent of Holland's, and developed distribution networks. These factors meant that Holland was not able to compete with Monsanto.

The value of a lower position on the learning curve can induce firms to acquire other firms—firms that have more experience in certain activities. For instance, in August 2002, Halliburton Energy Services acquired Pruett Industries, Inc., in order to "hit the ground running in regard to field service, for DTS as well as future fiber optic sensors." Halliburton executives said that "Pruett's critical mass of experience and know-how positions us way up the learning curve in the critical installation competencies."[13]

The Problem with Size

Does corporate size necessarily confer an advantage in business? The answer is not necessarily. Very large companies eventually lose their effectiveness, and performance deteriorates. The causes are clear. In most cases bureaucracy begins to interfere with performance. Overhead costs increase relative to total costs, and decision making becomes very inefficient. In management terms, decisions exceed an individual's span of control. Remedies typically are the disappearance of the firm or a reduction in the firm's size. The new CEO at Ford, Alan Mulally, is doing this now. Diseconomies of scale may not be a physical law like diminishing marginal returns, but few firms can escape the minefield of becoming too large.

Yet, most managers and the general public believe that firms should strive to grow. Recent economic research shows that it is virtually impossible to avoid diseconomies of scale; that growth is not a beneficial strategy for most firms. In fact, firms ought to focus more on profits and less on growth. Indeed, it might be that the optimal size for most firms is small. Most firms just can't grow much without sacrificing efficiency.[14]

Summary

1. The short-run is a period of time just short enough that the quantity of at least one of the resources cannot be altered. The long run is a period of time just long enough that all resources are variable.
2. According to the law of diminishing marginal returns, when successive equal amounts of a variable resource are combined with a fixed amount of another resource, there will be a point beyond which the extra or marginal product that can be attributed to each additional unit of the variable resource will decline.
3. Total costs are the sum of fixed and variable costs. Fixed costs are costs that do not change as the quantity of output changes. Variable costs are costs that do change as the quantity of output changes. Both COGS and SG&A have elements that are variable and other elements that are fixed.
4. Average total costs are the costs per unit of output—total costs divided by the quantity of output produced.
5. The relationship of costs and output in the short run is due to the law of diminishing marginal returns.
6. Economies of scale take place when a doubling of all resources (size or scale) results in more than a doubling in the quantity of output.
7. Diseconomies of scale take place when a doubling of all resources (size or scale) results in less than a doubling in the quantity of output.

8. Large scale is not always best. The best size depends on the structure of costs and the extent of the market.
9. Operating leverage is the ratio of total fixed costs to total variable costs.
10. The experience curve is a relationship between cost per unit of output and cumulative output—output produced from time zero to current time. If with experience a firm is able to lower costs, then the experience curve slopes down, with costs measured on the vertical axis and cumulative output on the horizontal axis.

Key Terms

Diminishing marginal returns
Average total cost (ATC)
Marginal cost (MC)
Operating leverage
Short run
Operating period

Long run or planning period
Economies of scale
Diseconomies of scale
Constant returns to scale
Economies of scope
Experience, or learning, curve

Exercises

1. Use the following information to list the total fixed costs, total variable costs, average fixed costs, average variable costs, average total costs, and marginal costs.

Output	TC	TFC	TVC	AFC	AVC	ATC	MC
0	$100						
1	150						
2	225						
3	230						
4	300						

2. Use the following table to answer the questions listed below.

Output	TC	TFC	TVC	AFC	AVC	ATC	MC
0	$20						
10	40						
20	60						
30	90						
40	120						
50	180						
60	280						

   a. List the total fixed costs, total variable costs, average fixed costs, average variable costs, average total costs, and marginal costs.
   b. At what quantity of output does marginal cost equal average total cost and average variable cost?

3. Describe some conditions that might cause larger firms to experience inefficiencies that small firms would not experience.
4. Why would different industries have different degrees of economies or diseconomies of scale?

5. Describe the relation between marginal and average costs. Describe the relation between marginal and average fixed costs and between marginal and average variable costs.
6. Consider a firm with a given-sized production facility.

   a. Explain what would happen to those cost curves if a mandatory health insurance program were imposed on all firms.
   b. Explain what would happen if the plan requires a firm to provide a health insurance program for each employee worth 10 percent of the employee's salary.
   c. How would that plan compare to one that requires each firm to provide a $100,000 group insurance program that would cover all employees in the firm no matter the number of employees?

7. Explain the statement "We had to increase our volume to spread the overhead."
8. Express Mail offers overnight delivery to customers. It is attempting to come to some conclusion about whether or not to expand its facilities. Currently, its fixed costs are $2 million per month, and its variable costs are $2 per package. It charges $12 per package and has a monthly volume of 2 million packages. If it expands, its fixed costs will rise by $1 million and its variable costs will fall to $1.50 per package. Should it expand?

9. Explain outsourcing and what it means for the costs of a firm.

10. "The thing a lot of people don't understand about e-commerce is the degree to which it is a scale business," says Jeff Bezos, CEO of Amazon.com. Where a conventional retailer might have to double its capital spending to double sales, Amazon's costs are largely fixed. "Once our software is written, we can handle a lot of customers with it." Explain what this paragraph means.

11. Suppose the costs (in cents) per passenger-mile of operating a jumbo jet on flights of 1,200 and 2,500 miles with 250, 300, and 350 passengers aboard are:[15]

Number of Passengers	Number of Miles	
	1,200	2,500
250	4.3	3.4
300	3.8	3.0
350	3.5	2.7

a. What is the marginal cost of one more passenger on a 1,200-mile flight if there are between 250 and 300 passengers.

b. If the number of passengers is 300 and the flight is between 1,200 and 2,500 miles, what is the marginal cost of flying an additional mile?

c. What would the fare on a 2,500-mile flight have to be for a company to cover the operating costs?

12. What is the economist's interpretation of costs? What does the following statement mean: "the concept of cost is far richer (pardon the pun) than the dollars and cents you hand over at the cash register."?

a. Costs are opportunity costs plus sunk costs.

b. **Costs are what must be given up to gain something.**

c. Costs are the value of the opportunity costs of employees.

d. Costs are direct and overhead.

e. Costs are direct, overhead, and sunk.

13. Why might a large firm be more efficient than a small firm?

a. Large firms enable more specialization and trading according to comparative advantage.

b. Large firms experience economies of scale.

c. Large firms may be less efficient than small firms if there are diseconomies of scale.

d. A large firm is able to purchase at quantity discounts.

e. All of the above are correct.

14. What best accounts for the saying "Too many cooks spoil the broth."?

a. Economies of scale

b. Diseconomies of scale.

c. Diminishing marginal returns.

d. Increasing marginal returns.

e. The law of demand

15. If average fixed costs equal $40 and average total costs equal $100 when output is 10, then total variable cost when output is 10 must be:

○ a. $40

○ b. $60

○ c. $600

○ d. $6,000

16. What would it mean if experience results in lower costs per unit but that this result eventually confronts diminishing marginal product?

17. Could a first mover gain a sustainable advantage from gaining experience? Explain.

CHAPTER NOTES

1. Martin LaMonica, "BP CEO: Today's Clean Tech not Nearly Enough," March 4, 2008, www.news.com/8301-11128_3-9885351-54.html.

2. Evan Koenig, "Productivity Growth," Federal Reserve Bank of Dallas, *Expand Your Insight,* March 1, 2000,

3. Kris Maher, "Wal-Mart Seeks New Flexibility in Worker Shifts," *Wall Street Journal,* January 2, 2007, p. A1.

4. Jonathan Ward, "Don't Be Afraid to Run from a Job That's not Right for You," *Remodeling Magazine,* January 1, 2007, www.remodeling.hw.net/industry-news.asp?sectionID=149&articleID=416777.

5. Shlomo Maital, *Executive Economics* (New York: Free Press, 1994) discusses Morita's trip to America.

6. In fact, a purchasing agent at the Bulova watch company saw the miniature radios and said he would take 100,000 of them, provided he could market them under the Bulova name. This was a huge order, far larger than Sony's total capitalization at the time. But Morita wanted to build Sony into an international brand, so he turned Bulova down. See John Nathan, "Akio Morita," Time Asia, *TIME* 100, 154, no. 7/8 (August 23–30, 1999), www .time.com/time/asia/asia/magazine/1999/990823/index.html, accessed February 24, 2008.

7. *Wall Street Journal,* January 13–14, 2007, p. A13.

8. Jayantha de Silva, "Unravelling the Mess," *Ministry of Defence,* April 12, 2008, www .defence.lk/new.asp?fname=20080220_02; "The Snags That Slow Down Soviet Steel," *Business Week,* September 19, 1977, p. 82, www.businessweek.com/index.html.

9. A. Silk and E. Berndt, "Scale and Scope Effects on Advertising Agency Costs," National Bureau of Economic Research, Cambridge, MA, Working Paper No. 3463, October 1990.

10. Boston Consulting Group, "Perspectives on Experience," Boston Consulting Group, Boston, MA, 1968.

11. As someone said, the only thing the two industries have in common is wings.

12. Adam M. Brandenburger, Barry J. Nalebuff, and Ada Brandenberger, *Co-Opetition* (New York: Doubleday, 1997), p. 70.

13. "Halliburton Advances Strategy in Reservoir Performance Monitoring," *PR Newswire,* August 15, 2002.

14. ideas.repec.org/p/esi/evopap/2007-03.html; academic.csuohio.edu/yuc/perf03/03-zipf_us_firm_size.pdf; econpapers.repec.org/paper/cwlcwldpp/1457.htm

15. S. Breyer, *Regulation and Its Reform* (Cambridge, MA: Harvard University Press, 1982). It is pointed out that these data were approximately what Boeing said its 747 would cost to operate in 1977; see Edwin Mansfield, *Applied Microeconomics* (New York: Norton, 1997).

Looking Outside
the Firm

CHAPTER 14
The Mechanics of Profit Maximization

Analytics

Who are the best customers for credit card companies? Do the companies want the customer with terrific debt and credit habits who pay the balance every month or the customer who always has a balance and never pays it off? Who are the best customers for airlines, the business traveler who uses airlines Monday through Friday and often can't make advanced plans or the tourist traveler who plans a long time in advance of the trip and has the flexibility to travel any day? The objective of a firm is to find that price and quantity combination that maximizes profit. When the firm has different niches or different sets of customers, it is typically better to treat each differently than to have a single uniform price. When different customers pay different prices for the same good or service, this is called personalized pricing or price discrimination. Suppose the economics division of a major airline company estimates that the demand functions for business and tourist travelers from Los Angeles to Beijing are as follows.

First Class	Excursion
$Q_A = 2{,}100 - 0.5P_A$	$Q_B = 8{,}800 - 4P_B$

1. What does this information provide?
2. What prices should the airline set?

Golden Rule of Profit Maximization

Entrepreneurs are always chasing profit. They innovate, perhaps organize a firm, perhaps hire a manager, or take the company public and sell shares of stock. In this chapter, the standard neoclassical approach to the firm is presented. Maximizing profit is a fairly straightforward task; it is considered primarily to be a managerial function rather than an entrepreneurial one. The manager has to determine the amount of output to offer for sale and at what price to sell the output. This is not necessarily a straightforward proposition, for it involves choices about how to allocate resources—quantity of resource services, organizational structure, culture, location, and on and on. But once these things are determined it is assumed they do not change. Thus, the simple, straightforward rule for profit maximization is: Continue expanding output until the value society places on the last unit sold just equals the amount spent on resources to produce that unit of output—equate marginal revenue and marginal cost: $MR = MC$.

Selling Environments: Market Structure

It has been said that business behavior is a matter of numbers. That is, the behavior of firms depends on the ease of entry and the resulting number of competitors a firm has. The profit-maximizing (or cost-minimizing) rule $MR = MC$ does not vary; it is the same for all firms, selling environments, and the decisions being considered. Recall that the Austrian approach focuses on the competitive process, not the decision to set $MR = MC$. The Austrian approach also does not separate selling environments into the four market structures utilized in neoclassical economics. Nevertheless, the examination of market structures can be instructive in a purely pedagogical view even for the Austrians.

Table 14.1 reviews the characteristics of the four market structure models used to illustrate business behavior. The name of the market structure is listed in column 1 of the table. The next three columns are the characteristics of the market structure—the entry conditions, the number of firms, and the product type of the firms. Differentiated products are perceived by consumers as having characteristics that products offered by other sellers do not have. Standardized products are perceived by consumers as being identical; these are often referred to as commodities.

Perfect Competition   Perfect competition is a market structure characterized by a very large number of firms—so large that whatever any one firm does has no effect on the market. In the perfectly competitive market structure, all firms sell an identical product, and anyone can begin a business or leave the business without difficulty. Because of the large number of firms, consumers have many choices of where to purchase the good or service, and there is no cost to the consumer of going to a different place to make the purchase. Since the products are identical, consumers do not prefer one store to another

Table 14.1				
Characteristics of Selling Environments	**MARKET STRUCTURE**	**ENTRY CONDITION**	**NUMBER OF FIRMS**	**PRODUCT TYPE**
	Perfect Competition	Easy	Large	Identical
	Monopoly	None	One	One
	Monopolistic Competition	Easy	Large	Differentiated
	Oligopoly	Impeded	Few	Identical or Differentiated

or one brand to another. In fact, there are no brands—only identical, generic products. The model of a perfectly competitive market is used to illustrate a commodity market.

Monopoly   A monopoly refers to a situation in which only one firm supplies a good or service. No firm can enter the business and begin competing with the monopoly.

Monopolistic Competition   A monopolistically competitive market structure is characterized by a large number of firms, easy entry, and differentiated products. Each brand is to some degree different from the others. Nature Valley Granola is not Wheaties, and Sam Adams beer differs from Budweiser, Miller, and Moosehead. Product differentiation distinguishes a perfectly competitive market from a monopolistically competitive market.

Oligopoly   Oligopoly is the name for a market in which just a few firms provide the good or service. Each firm is large enough to significantly affect the other firms. When one lowers price, it affects sales of the others; when one introduces a new product or a new technology, that affects the others. Oligopoly firms can be differentiated—automobiles, for example—or they can produce the same product—steel, for example.

The Graphics of Profit Maximization

A market is the sum of all firms and all consumers. It is represented by the downward-sloping demand curve and the upward-sloping supply curve that is so familiar to us. This is shown in the left side of Figure 14.1. When we look at one firm selling in a perfectly competitive market, we are just looking at one of the many, many participants in the market and isolating it. Remember, this is a commodity—there are no differences among firms or goods or services. As a result, the individual firm in a perfectly competitive market must sell its goods and services at the price determined in the market. The individual firm cannot charge more because no one would purchase from that firm, and it won't charge less because it could sell all it wants at the market price. This is why the firm is called a "price taker."

The horizontal demand curve means that the marginal revenue is the price—each additional unit sold brings in additional revenue equal to the price at which it is sold, and all products are sold at the same market price. The demand curve and the marginal revenue curve are the same horizontal line.

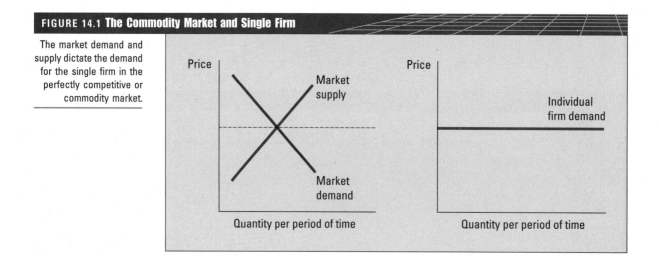

FIGURE 14.1 The Commodity Market and Single Firm

The market demand and supply dictate the demand for the single firm in the perfectly competitive or commodity market.

The individual firm in a perfectly competitive market maximizing its profit must select the quantity it will offer consumers. The price is defined by the market, P. The firm will select the quantity by finding where $MR = MC$. The marginal revenue is the price since each additional product sold by the firm is sold at the market price. So, for the individual perfectly competitive firm, demand is the same as the price, which is the same as marginal revenue.

For a firm selling in any market other than a commodity market, the demand curve slopes down because to sell more the price must be lower. A downward-sloping demand curve means the firm has some degree of "market power." Consider Figure 14.2, which shows a single firm in a market that is not perfectly competitive. The average total and marginal cost curves of producing and selling a product are drawn along with the demand and marginal revenue curves that arise from the firm's customers. The first unit of output costs $1,000 to sell; the marginal cost of the first unit is $1,000. When sold, the first unit of output brings in $1,700 in revenue, so the marginal revenue is $1,700. Since marginal revenue is greater than marginal cost, the firm is better off selling that first unit of output than not selling it.

The second unit of output costs an additional $800 (column 8) to sell and brings in an additional $1,500 (column 5) in revenue when sold. With the second unit of output, marginal revenue exceeds marginal cost. Thus the firm is better off producing two units than none or one.

Profit continues to rise until the sixth unit of output is sold. The marginal cost of selling the seventh unit is $800, while the marginal revenue is $500. Since marginal cost is greater than marginal revenue, profit declines if the seventh unit is sold. The firm can maximize profit by selling six units, the quantity at which marginal revenue and marginal cost are equal.

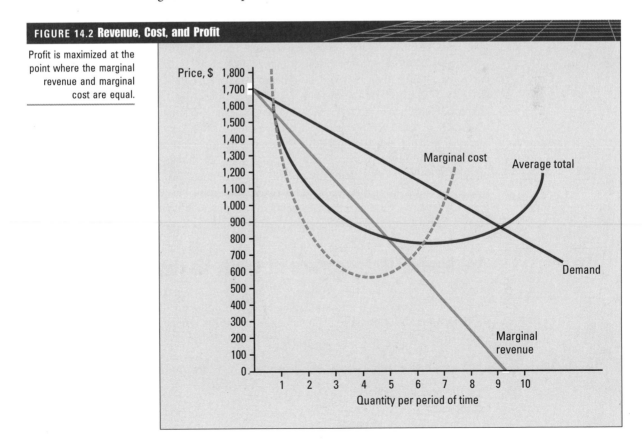

FIGURE 14.2 Revenue, Cost, and Profit

Profit is maximized at the point where the marginal revenue and marginal cost are equal.

(1) Total Output (Q)	(2) Price (P)	(3) Total Revenue (TR)	(4) Average Revenue (AR)	(5) Marginal Revenue (MR)	(6) Total Cost (TC)	(7) Average Total Cost (ATC)	(8) Marginal Cost (MC)	(9) Total Profit (TR-TC)
0	0	0	0	0	$1,000	—	—	-$1,000
1	$1,700	1,700	1,700	1,700	2,000	2,000	1,000	-300
2	1,600	3,200	1,600	1,500	2,800	1,400	800	400
3	1,500	4,500	1,500	1,300	3,500	1,167	700	1,000
4	1,400	5,600	1,400	1,100	4,000	1,000	500	1,600
5	1,300	6,500	1,300	900	4,500	900	500	2,000
6	1,200	7,200	1,200	700	5,200	867	700	2,000 Profit Maximum
7	1,100	7,700	1,100	500	6,000	857	800	1,700
8	1,000	8,000	1,000	300	7,000	875	1,000	1,000
9	900	8,100	900	100	9,000	1,000	2,000	-900

The profit-maximizing quantity of output is given by the quantity at which $MR = MC$; quantity is 6. To illustrate total costs, revenue, profit, and price, we draw a vertical line up from $Q = 6$ to the ATC curve, and then on up to the demand curve. The point at which the vertical line hits the ATC curve identifies the cost per unit of output. Total costs are shown by drawing a horizontal line from the ATC curve over to the vertical axis, tracing out rectangle 06EF. This rectangle is total cost, ATC multiplied by the quantity. [$ATC \times Q = $ (total cost/Q) $\times Q = $ total cost].

Back to $Q = 6$ and the vertical line. Continuing up to the demand curve identifies the price—the price that consumers will pay for that quantity. A horizontal line from the demand curve over to the vertical axis identifies total revenue, $PQ_1 = 06AB$. Subtracting total cost 06EF from 06AB leaves the rectangle EFAB. This is total profit.

Figure 14.2 provides a great deal of information about business behavior. The demand curve for a different firm would be different (steeper or flatter) depending on the price elasticity of demand, or the position of the cost curves might be different depending on cost conditions, but regardless, this is the general look to a single firm. Profit is maximized when $MR = MC$. Every decision a manager or owner makes comes down to comparing marginal revenue and marginal cost. Should the firm increase advertising expenditures? If the MR from doing so is greater than the MC, then yes. Should the firm hire another employee? If the MR from doing so exceeds the MC, then yes. This decision-making approach shouldn't be surprising. It is how you make decisions as well. You compare your marginal revenue (your additional benefits) of doing something to your marginal costs. If your marginal benefit exceeds your marginal cost, then you do it.

The Simple Mathematics of Profit Maximization

Profit maximization can also be illustrated using some straightforward mathematics. Demand is represented as a function of variables that influence consumer spending, called the **determinants of demand**. The demand function is represented as:

$$Q_x = f(P_x, I, P_y, T, Pe_x, N)$$

which says that quantity demanded depends on or is determined by:

P_x is the price of good x
I is income
P_y is the price of other goods

T is tastes and preferences
P_e is the expected price of good x at some point in the future
N is the number of consumers

The effect of each of these determinants of demand on the quantity demanded is shown in the accompanying box. Note that ∂ means "change." So, $\partial Q_x/\partial P_x$ means change in quantity of X demanded divided by change in price of X.

Business Insight

Effects of Determinants of Demand

$\dfrac{\partial Q_x}{\partial P_x} < 0$ the law of demand

$\dfrac{\partial Q_x}{\partial I}$ $\begin{array}{l} > 0 \text{ if normal or luxury good} \\ < 0 \text{ if inferior or countercyclical good} \end{array}$

$\dfrac{\partial Q_x}{\partial P_y}$ $\begin{array}{l} < 0 \text{ if complements} \\ > 0 \text{ if substitutes} \end{array}$

$\dfrac{\partial Q}{\partial T}$ > 0 if consumers prefer more to less

$\dfrac{\partial Q_x}{\partial Pe_x}$ $\begin{array}{l} < 0 \text{ if expectations of a future price decrease} \\ > 0 \text{ if expectations of a future price increase} \end{array}$

$\dfrac{\partial Q_x}{\partial N}$ > 0 if number of buyers rise. the quantity demanded rises and vice versa

Elasticity

There are two definitions of price elasticity:

1. Point elasticity
2. Arc elasticity

Point elasticity refers to price changes that are extremely small, whereas arc elasticity refers to price changes over some range of values that may be quite large. Which measure is used depends on the data available and the magnitude of the price changes potentially under consideration.

$$Point\ elasticity = \partial \ln Q/\partial \ln P = [\partial Q/\partial P][P/Q]$$

$$Arc\ elasticity = \left\{\frac{Q_2 - Q_1}{P_2 - P_1}\right\} * \left\{\frac{P_2 + P_1}{Q_2 + Q_1}\right\}$$

Marginal Revenue

The demand equation shows quantity demanded to be a function of price and the determinants of demand. In its simplest linear form, $Q = g - hP$, where g and h are parameters and P is the product price. Economists typically present demand as the inverse of this general form, with Price specified as the independent variable: $P = a - bQ$ where a is the vertical intercept and $-b$ is the slope of the demand curve.

Total revenue is obtained by multiplying the inverse demand function by Q: $P \times Q = TR$:

$$TR = P \times Q = (a - bQ) \times Q = aQ - bQ^2$$

Marginal revenue is the change in total revenue divided by the change in quantity:

$$\partial TR/\partial Q = MR = a - 2bQ$$

Notice that *MR* has the same vertical intercept as the demand function (= *a*), but the slope of *MR* (= −2*b*) is twice the slope of the *D* curve (= −*b*). In other words, the *MR* curve falls twice as fast as the *D* curve in this example (and for any linear *D* curve). Put slightly differently, if the firm lowers its price, the fall in *MR* will be twice as fast as the fall in *P*. This means that for any straight-line demand curve, the marginal revenue curve will intersect the quantity axis exactly halfway between the origin, 0, and the point that demand intersects the quantity axis.

Illustration 1   Consider the following linear demand function: $Q = 11 − P$. The slope of the demand curve defined by this function is −1, as each change of $1 in *P* results in a change of −$1 in *Q*. The inverse demand function is:

$$P = 11 − Q \text{ so that total revenue function is } PQ = 11Q − Q^2$$
$$\text{Marginal revenue is, then, } \partial TR/\partial Q = 11 − 2Q.$$

The price elasticity is $[\partial Q/\partial P] [P/Q]$. This tells us that price elasticity is the slope of the inverse demand function multiplied by the ratio of price to quantity. Using the simple demand function $Q = 11 − P$, the first term of the elasticity is $[\partial Q/\partial P] = −1$. Selecting a particular *P* and *Q* will then yield the point elasticity. For instance, if *P* is 1, *Q* will be 10. This means the price elasticity at a price of 1 is

$$(−1)(.1) = −.1$$

At a price of $P = 10$, quantity will be $Q = 1$. In this case, price elasticity is $(−1)(10) = −10$.

Illustration 2   Now consider a slightly more complicated demand function for product X specified as

$$Q_x = 100 − 3P_x + 4P_y − .01I + 2A$$

where *A* is advertising, *I* is income, and P_y is a related good Y. Suppose good X sells at $25 a pair, good Y sells for $35, the company utilizes 50 minutes of advertising, and consumer income is $20,000. Advertising, income, and price of Y are determinants of demand. The price elasticity is:

$$[\partial Q/\partial \mathbf{P}] [P/Q] = −3(\$25/Q_x)$$

which means we must determine Q_x, the quantity of X. We do this by substituting the values of the determinants of demand into the demand equation:

$$Q_x = 100 − 3(\$25) + 4(\$35) = .01(\$20,000) + 2(50) = 65$$

Substituting $Q_x = 65$ into the elasticity solution, we see that the elasticity is $−3(25/65) = −1.15$.

Cross-price and income elasticity measures are derived in a similar manner to the price elasticity of demand. For instance, the cross price elasticity of demand between products X and Y is:

$$[\partial Q_x/\partial P_y] [P_y/Q_x] = 4(\$35/65) = 2.15$$

Since the cross price elasticity is positive, the goods are substitutes. The income elasticity is:

$$[\partial Q_x/\partial I] [I/Q_x] = −.01(\$20,000/65) = −3.0815$$

Product X is an inferior or a countercyclical good because the income elasticity is negative; an increase in consumer incomes reduces the quantity demanded.

The Calculus of Profit Maximization

Let's find the price and quantity that maximize profit. Symbolize profit as π. Then

$$\pi = TR − TC = TR(Q) − C(Q)$$

This equation specifies both total revenue and total costs as functions of output. This includes the perfectly competitive situation where $TR = PQ$ and the other market total revenue functions where the price depends on the output the firm desires to sell, $TR = P(Q)Q$. To find the profit-maximizing quantity, we find the point where marginal revenue equals marginal cost. By setting the change in profit divided by the change in quantity equal to zero:

$$\partial\pi /\partial Q = \partial TR(Q)/\partial Q - \partial C(Q)/\partial Q = 0$$

$\partial TR(Q)/\partial Q$ is the marginal revenue and $\partial C(Q)/\partial Q$ is the marginal cost. Equation (14.1) just tells us that to maximize profit, we set marginal revenue equal to marginal cost.

If the price does not depend on the quantity (that is, if we are calculating marginal revenue for a perfectly competitive firm), then

$$\partial PQ/\partial Q - \partial C(Q)/\partial Q = P - MC = 0 \text{ or } P = MC$$

If the price does depend on the quantity ($P = P(Q)$), as is the case for all firms not in a perfectly competitive market, then marginal revenue is:

$$\partial TR/\partial Q = \partial P(Q)Q/\partial Q = P + Q(\partial P/\partial Q)$$

Business Insight

Convexity

Using math, let's illustrate economic concepts in a simple manner. Yet, the math requires some rather rigorous assumptions. One such assumption is convexity. A convex set has the property that a collection that contains two items also contains an average of these two items. If there are two goods, food and heroin, then if you like x units of food and y units of heroin, convexity would imply you like any linear combination of x food and y heroin more than you like either alone. Addiction violates convexity. Convexity also has a problem when goods are indivisible. No one wants half a car.

In a convex environment, minor adjustments, trial and error, and piecemeal improvements tend to make things better. For this reason, economists have focused on the "margin" as being the most important aspect of decision making. How reasonable is the assumption of convexity? It is reasonable but does have weaknesses. Psychologists have confirmed that humans seem to have an instinctual bias toward convexity. The collection "faces I find attractive" is convex. If you take the faces of two beautiful women and use computer technology to merge them, people like the result.[1]

Nevertheless, there are many real-world observations that do not seem consistent with convexity. For instance, convexity implies that there are no benefits from specialization. If "things that I can make" formed a convex set, then it would be desirable for everyone to be self-sufficient—to do everything. Thus convexity here is nonsensical; people specialize and they gain by specializing and then trading with others. With convexity choices aren't either or. For instance, the observation that management jumps from one strategy to another is not consistent with convexity. With convexity, management would move in increments, increasing the hierarchy just slightly from period to period rather than shifting from a flat to a hierarchical form and vice versa. But that is not what we see. We observe management shifting totally and immediately from a hierarchical structure to a flatter structure. We also often see the same management team shift back to a hierarchical form. Convexity is too limiting to assume it applies to everything. On the other hand, assuming it does apply to most things enables us to use the simple mathematics to illustrate many real-world observations and economic concepts.

Again, we set marginal revenue equal to marginal cost, but the marginal revenue of a firm that is not perfectly competitive consists of two parts: the price of the additional unit sold, P, and the effect on revenue from lowering the price on all goods sold, $Q(\partial P/\partial Q)$, which is negative. In other words, $P > MR$ and since $MR = MC$, $P > MC$. This is a principal difference between the perfectly competitive firm and the firm with market power.

When a firm is selling a perfectly competitive or commodity market, entry by rivals will occur whenever the firm earns a profit. The entry will increase supply and drive price down. Price will be driven down until it just covers opportunity costs or $P = MC$. When entry occurs but a firm can maintain the value of its special attribute, then price is driven down until opportunity costs plus the value of the special attribute is reached. Here, $P > MC$. When entry does not occur, price will not be driven down. The firm will maximize profit by finding $MR = MC$, and at that point, $P > MC$.

Operating Rules

All firms maximize profit by operating at the quantity level where $MR = MC$. But not all firms make a profit at that point; some may make a loss and in that case, $MR = MC$ identifies the loss-minimizing point. The firm illustrated in Figure 14.3 is not making a profit. It is minimizing its loss if it operates where $MR = MC$, but it has a loss of distance AC.

The loss is short run, but what the firm's actions are will depend on its outlook of the future. It is currently earning enough revenue to pay variable costs, D. Thus, the amount illustrated as DA can be used to pay some of the fixed costs. In other words, the amount by which revenue exceeds variable costs can be used to pay some of the fixed costs. The firm will continue operating at this loss if it expects business to improve in the future. If it does not expect things to improve, the firm's owners will try to get out of the business as soon as possible.

Three situations are shown in the accompanying table. Situation A shows revenue of $700, fixed costs of $1,000 and variable costs of $800. The firm has a choice of operating and sustaining losses of $1,100 or of shutting down and paying fixed costs, $1,000. Shutting down is the way to go. In Situation B, the firm shows revenue of $900, fixed costs of $1,000 and variable costs of $800. The firm has a loss of $900 if it operates and $1,000 if it shuts down and pays just the fixed costs. The better decision here is to continue operating. In Situation C, the firm shows revenue of $2,100, fixed costs of $1,000, and variable costs of $1,000. It is earning a profit of $100.

Situation	Revenue	Fixed Costs	Variable Cost	Decision
A	$ 700	$1,000	$800	Shut Down
B	$ 900	$1,000	$800	Operate
C	$1,900	$1,000	$800	Operate

Notice that the firm's decision as to whether to shut down or continue operating is whether the revenue exceeds variable costs. In Figure 14.3 notice that price exceeds average total cost, meaning that the firm is paying all variable costs and some fixed costs by operating. If the price is less than average variable costs, then the firm is better off shutting down immediately.

Breakeven   A firm will break even on an economic basis when total revenue equals total cost. So what is the firm's breakeven output level? Total Cost is given by:

$$TC = TFC + TVC$$

Since Total Variable Cost, $TVC = AVC * Q$, then

$$TC = TFC + AVC * Q$$

Since Total Revenue, $TR = P * Q$, we can find the breakeven sales level

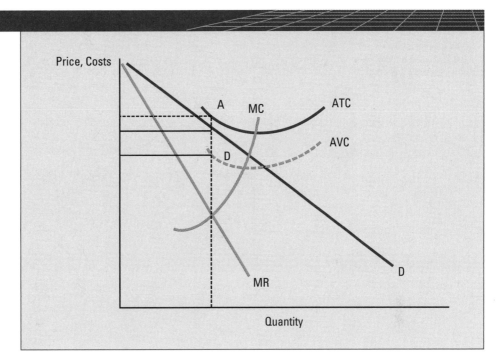

FIGURE 14.3 A Loss

Profit is maximized or loss is minimized at the point where the marginal revenue and marginal cost are equal.

$$TR = TC$$

$$P * Q = TFC + AVC * Q$$

Solving for Q yields:

$$Q = TFC/(P - AVC)$$

This is the breakeven output level; the denominator is called the **contribution margin per unit** because it represents the portion of the selling price that can be applied to cover the fixed costs of the firm and provide for profit. Remember, $P = AVC$ is the shutdown point, so if $P > AVC$, the firm will be operating, and if $P <$ **AVC**, the firm will shut down.

Sales Maximization

Many firms declare that they want to increase market share, to become bigger, rather than maximize profit. The firm maximizes total sales (total revenue) by finding the quantity and price where marginal revenue is zero. A positive marginal revenue means that additional sales could be obtained by lowering price; a negative marginal revenue means that additional sales could be obtained by raising price. Assuming a linear demand equation, the revenue maximization is shown in Figure 14.4.

A firm's market share is the percentage of the market's sales (or revenue) constituted by that firm.

$$market share = revenue/market size$$

and

$$\partial market share/\partial Q = 0 \text{ yields, } \partial TR/\partial Q = 0 \text{ assuming market size constant.}$$

So, assuming the size of the market to be constant, then if one firm increases its sales other firms lose sales. In this case, maximizing market share is equivalent to maximizing total revenue. The market share strategy is the same as the revenue maximization strategy.

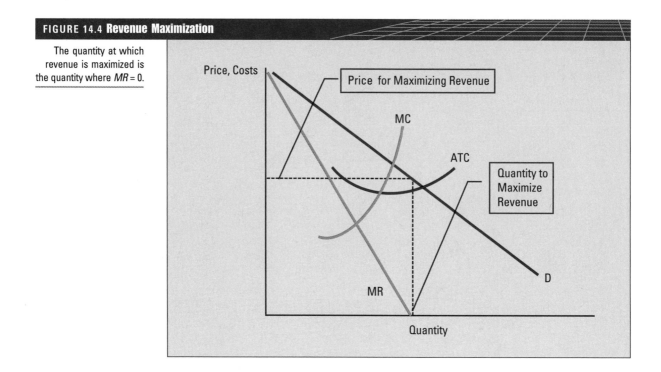

FIGURE 14.4 Revenue Maximization

The quantity at which revenue is maximized is the quantity where $MR = 0$.

Oligopoly

Oligopoly presents special problems because of the interdependence of firms. We will consider three popular presentations of oligopoly: the Cournot Model, the Kinked Demand Model, and the Cartel Model.

The Cournot Model

The Cournot model, named after the economist Augustin Cournot (1801–1877), was the first representation of oligopoly. Cournot assumed there are only two firms selling an identical good. He also assumed that marginal cost is zero. Then he assumed that each firm, while trying to maximize profits, decides that the other firm holds its output constant at the existing level. The result he came up with is that each firm moves and then countermoves until an equilibrium is reached where each supplies one-third of the market.

Let's assume the market demand is specified as $Q = a - bP$ with $b = 1$ and zero total costs. Firm A's decision to supply depends on what firm B does. So firm A says, I will supply one-half of the difference between $Q = a$ (the amount offered at price $P = \$0$) and the amount offered by firm B, QB. This means

$$Q_A = \frac{a - Q_B}{2}$$

Firm B says the same thing: I will supply one-half of what firm A supplies and a:

$$Q_B = \frac{a - Q_A}{2}$$

Using the two equations to solve for the two quantities, we have

$$Q_A = \frac{a-(a-Q_A)/2}{2} = \frac{.5a - Q_A}{2}$$
$$2Q_A = .5a - .5Q_A$$
$$2Q_A - .5Q_A = .5a$$
$$1.5Q_A = .5a$$
$$Q_A = a/3$$

Solving for Q_B yields the same result, Q_B = a/3. This Cournot solution is one in which neither firm has an incentive to change.[2]

The Kinked Demand Model

All firms know the law of demand. Thus, they know that sales will increase if price is lowered because people will purchase more of all goods (the income effect) and will substitute away from the more expensive goods to purchase more of the less expensive goods (the substitution effect). But the firms in an oligopoly may not know the shape of the demand curve for their product because the shape depends on how their rivals react to one another. They have to predict how their competitors will respond to a price change in order to know what their demand curve looks like.

Let's consider the auto industry. Suppose General Motors' costs have fallen (its marginal-cost curve has shifted down), and the company is deciding whether to lower the prices of its cars. If GM did not have to consider how the other car companies would respond, it would simply lower the price in order to be sure that the new MC curve intersected the MR curve. But GM suspects that the demand curve labeled D_1 in Figure 14.5 does not represent its true market situation. Instead, GM believes that if it lowers the prices on its cars from their current level of P_1, the other auto companies will follow suit. If the other companies also lower the price of their cars, the substitution effect for the GM cars does not occur; sales of GM cars might increase a little, but only because of the income effect. In other words, GM does not capture the market share indicated in Figure 14.5 by D_1, but finds the quantity demanded increasing along D_2 (below price P_1). Also, GM suspects that should it increase the price of its cars, none of the other auto companies would raise theirs. In this case, the price increase would mean substantially reduced sales for GM because of both the income effect and the substitution effects. The quantity demanded decreases, as indicated along D_1. Consequently, the demand curve for GM is a combination of D_1 and D_2. It is D_1 above P_1 and D_2 below P_1, a demand curve with a *kink* at point A. The kink creates a *gap* in the marginal revenue by combining the marginal revenue curve associated with D_1 and the curve associated with D_2. Thus, the MR = MC at the same quantity. If the other firms had not followed GM, GM's sales would have increased to Q_2.

What should GM do? It should price where MR = MC. But the resulting marginal-revenue curve is given by a combination of MR_1 and MR_2. The MR_1 curve slopes down gently until it reaches the quantity associated with the kink. As we move below the kink, the MR_2 curve becomes the appropriate marginal revenue curve. Notice that GM's marginal cost curves, MC_1 and MC_2, intersect the combined MR curves at the same price and quantity, P_1 and Q_1. Thus, GM's strategy is to do nothing: not to change price, even though costs have changed.

Mathematical Illustration of Kinked Demand The kinked demand curve requires two demand functions, one for price increases and one for price decreases.

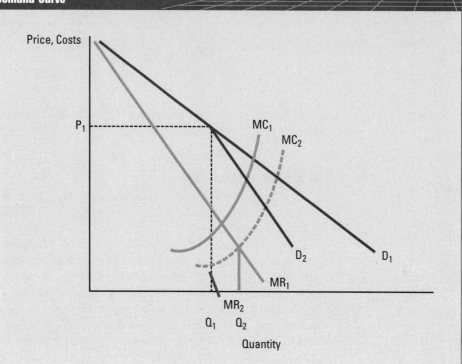

FIGURE 14.5 The Kinked Demand Curve

The price and quantity for the firm pictured is given by the point where $MR = MC$, price P_1, and quantity Q_1. The marginal cost declines, so the firm decides to lower price. Since other firms match the price decrease, sales don't increase, whereas without the other firms following the price decline, sales would increase from Q_1 to Q_2

$$\text{Price Increases: } P_I = 7 - .025Q_I$$
$$\text{Price Decreases: } P_D = 10 - .01Q_D$$

Suppose marginal cost is $MC = 2 + .05Q$. We can find total revenue and then marginal revenue associated with each demand.

$$P_I\, Q_I = 7Q_I - .025Q_I^2$$
$$P_D\, Q_D = 10Q_D - .01Q_D^2$$

So, marginal revenue is $MR = 7 - .05Q_I$ for price increases and $MR = 10 - .02Q_D$ for price decreases. Setting the two demand curves equal, we can find the quantity and price at which the kink occurs.

The kink occurs at $Q = 40$, and the price is \$6. At $Q = 40$, $MR_I = 7 - 2 = 5$. And at $Q = 40$, $MR_D = 10 - 8 = 2$. Since at $Q = 40$, $MC = 4$, then MC intersects the vertical part of the MR curves, that is, in the gap.

The Cartel Model

A **cartel** arises when rival firms agree to cooperate and determine price and quantity to maximize joint profits. Suppose a two-firm (duopoly) cartel has the following demand and marginal cost functions.

$$MC_A = 25Q_A$$
$$MC_B = 6.25Q_B$$

The market demand function is:

$$Q = 1{,}200 - 0.10P$$

Rewriting the marginal cost functions, we have:

$$Q_A = 0.04MC_A$$

$$Q_B = 0.16MC_B$$

Now we want to horizontally sum the marginal cost functions to obtain the cartel's marginal cost function:

$$Q_A + Q_B = Q = 0.20MC, \text{ so the } \textbf{cartel's MC = 5Q}$$

Next, we need to calculate *MR* by using the inverse demand function for the cartel (with *P* as a function of *Q*):

$$P = 12,000 - 10Q, \text{ so } \textbf{MR = 12,000 - 20Q}$$

Profit-maximizing output is derived by setting *MC* = MR as follows:

$$5Q = 12,000 - 20Q, \text{ so } 25Q = 12,000 \text{ or } \textbf{Q = 480}$$

By substituting $Q = 480$ into the demand equation, we find: **P = $7,200**.

We know the optimal output for the two firms together is 480, as that is the Q where their joint *MC* equals the *MR* for their market demand curve. The firms would allocate the 480 units by using the *MC* for the cartel at the profit-maximizing output to substitute into the individual *MC* schedules for each firm to determine its output level.

The Cartel's $MC = 5Q$, so the *MC* of output for the cartel at the profit-maximizing output level is $= 5 * 480 = \$2,400$. Substituting the cartel's equilibrium *MC* into the individual firm's *MC* functions yields the following allocation of the 480 units to each firm:

$$Q_A = (0.04)(2,400) = 96 \text{ and } Q_B = (0.16)(2,400) = 384$$

These three models of oligopoly—Cournot, kinked demand, and cartel—are far from the only models of oligopoly; they are presented here merely to illustrate the idea that the firms in an oligopoly are interdependent. What one does affects the others enough that they all have to take into account the actions of each other. The difficulty of arriving at solutions increases with the complexity of interaction.

Analytics

Thousands of analytical tests on credit card customer data were run over a two-year period. It was discovered that the most profitable customers were people who borrowed large amounts quickly and then paid off the balances slowly. At the time, the credit card industry treated such customers just as they treated people who made small purchases and paid their balances off in full every month. By treating the customer types differently, soliciting the profitable type, Capital One was able to increase profits considerably. This is called price discrimination.

The airline case illustrates the practice of identifying customers and their demands and using these to increase profits. The economics division of a major airline company has estimated the demand for business and travelers from Los Angeles to Beijing. Having the demand, they figure out marginal revenue.

Business	Tourist
$Q_B = 2,100 - 0.5P_B$	$Q_T = 8,800 - 4P_T$
$MR_B = 4,200 - 4Q_B$	$MRT = 2,200 - 0.5Q_T$

If the marginal cost of production is $200 per passenger, what fare and what number of passengers will maximize profit?

Profit is maximized by setting prices such that $MR_T = MR_B = MC$.

$$MRB = 4{,}200 - 4Q_B = 200$$

which implies that $QB = 1{,}000$.

$$MR_T = 2{,}200 - 0.5Q_T = 200$$

which implies that $Q_T = 4{,}000$.

Prices are obtained by substituting the profit-maximizing quantities into the demand equations. This gives $P_B = \$2{,}200$ per passenger and $P_T = \$1{,}200$ per passenger.

This is the price-discriminating result. It indicates that the airline can segment the market into the two groups and that the two customer segments cannot exchange with each other—in other words, that arbitrage cannot occur. Does price discrimination generate more profit than a single uniform price?

If a single price is to be set, the demand equations from each market segment have to be combined. Expressing the demand in terms of Q and then adding the two together yields $Q = 10{,}900 - 4.5P$. Marginal revenue is $(10{,}900/4.5) - (2/4.5)Q$. Equating marginal revenue and marginal cost gives $Q = 5{,}000$ passengers. Substituting this into the total demand function yields $P = 5{,}900/4.5 = \$1{,}311$. Thus if a single uniform price of $\$1{,}311$ is charged, profit is $\$6{,}555{,}556 - \$1{,}000{,}000 = \$5{,}555{,}556$, which is less than the $\$6$ million obtained under price discrimination.

Summary

1. The supply rule for all firms is to supply the quantity at which the firm's marginal revenue and marginal cost are equal. This is the profit-maximizing point.
2. Profit maximization can be illustrated graphically or mathematically. In either case the process is to find the quantity and price where $MR = MC$.
3. Economists look at four models of markets to illustrate possible business behaviors. These models are perfect competition, monopoly, monopolistic competition, and oligopoly.
4. Perfect competition illustrates a commodity market. There is free entry and identical goods and services. The result of competition is that price will be driven down until its revenue just equals opportunity costs.
5. With monopolistic competition, competition occurs as firms differentiate their products. If a firm successfully creates a special attribute that society values, the firm is able to earn economic profit equal to the value society places on its special attribute.
6. With oligopoly, a few large firms dominate the market. With monopoly, one firm is the only supplier in the market.
7. In oligopoly, the firms are interdependent. What one does seriously affects the others. As a result, the firms act and react to each other.

Key Terms

Determinants of demand   Cartel
Contribution margin per unit

Exercises

1. Using the following cost equation, create a table showing TC, TVC, TFC, ATC, AFC, AVC, and MC for quantities of 5, 10, 15, 20, and 30.
$C = 100 + 60(Q) - 12(Q)^2 + (Q)^3$.

2. Draw a perfectly elastic demand curve on top of a standard U-shaped average total cost curve. Now add in the marginal cost and marginal revenue curves. Find the profit-maximizing point, $MR = MC$. Indicate the firm's total revenues and total cost.

3. Describe profit maximization in terms of marginal revenue and marginal cost.
4. Use the following information to calculate total revenue, marginal revenue, and marginal cost. Indicate the profit-maximizing level of output. If the price was $3 and fixed costs were $5, what would variable costs be? At what level of output would the firm produce?

Output	Price	Total Costs	Total Revenue (P x Q)
1	$5	$10	
2	5	12	
3	5	15	
4	5	19	
5	5	24	
6	5	30	
7	5	45	

5. A firm's profits are the difference between its revenues and costs as represented by the function

$$\text{Profit} = P(Q)Q - C(Q)$$

where P is price, which depends on the output to be sold, $P(Q)$; Q is output; and C is costs, which depend on how much output is produced, $C(Q)$. Find the profit-maximizing price and quantity.

6. The demand function is $Q = 100 - .5P$. The cost function is $TC = C = 100 + 60(Q) + (Q)^2$

   a. Find MR and MC.
   b. Demonstrate that profit is maximized at the quantity where $MR = MC$.
   c. Derive the relationship between marginal revenue and the price elasticity of demand, and show that the profit-maximizing price and quantity will never be the unit-elastic point on the demand curve.
   d. Using the information in (b), demonstrate that the profit-maximizing price and quantity will never be in the inelastic portion of the demand curve.

7. Explain the competitive process when a firm earns a positive economic profit.
8. Explain what is different between firms in monopolistic competition and firms in oligopoly. What does this difference mean for prices and quantities and for economic profit?
9. A firm has estimated the following demand function for its product:

$$Q = 8 - 2P + 0.10I + A$$

where Q is quantity demanded per month in thousands, P is product price, I is an index of consumer income, and A is advertising expendi-

tures per month in thousands. Assume that $P = \$10$, $I = 100$, and $A = 20$.
Based on this information, calculate values for: quantity demanded; price elasticity of demand; income elasticity of demand; and advertising elasticity. (Use the point formulas to complete the required elasticity calculations).

10. The market demand and marginal cost functions for a product sold by a monopolist are as follows:

$$\text{Demand: } QD = 100 - 2P$$

$$\text{Marginal Cost: } MC = 1.5Q$$

Based on this information, calculate the profit-maximizing price and quantity and the revenue-maximizing price and quantity:

11. You have begun a new business of transcential learning. You have fixed costs of $1,800 a month and a variable cost of $48. You charge $16 per session. You can provide sessions at $66 each. Based on this information, calculate the breakeven level of daily output for the firm. After operating for a while, your variable cost rises to $50. What does this mean for the breakeven quantity of output.

12. The market supply and demand functions for a product traded on a perfectly competitive market are given below:

$$QD = 40 - P$$

$$QS = -5 + 4P$$

Based on this information, calculate the equilibrium price and quantity in this market.

13. Now, suppose the competitive market in Exercise 12 is monopolized. Calculate the price and quantity for the monopolist.

14. If the (profit-maximizing) level of output that a monopolist produces is such that marginal revenue, marginal cost, and average total cost are equal, then economic profits must be:

   a. negative
   b. positive.
   c. zero.
   d. indeterminate from the given information.

15. Draw a demand curve for a firm with market power. Portray the situation where that firm is earning positive economic profits. Now illustrate what occurs as entry occurs and rivals begin competing with that firm.

16. Show that it is possible for a monopolist to earn negative economic profit.

CHAPTER NOTES

1. John Kay, *Culture and Prosperity: Why Some Countries Are Rich but Most Remain Poor* (New York: HarperCollins, 2004), p. 180; J. L. Langlois, L. Roggman, and L. Musselman, "What Is Average and What Is Not Average about Attractive Faces?" *Psychological Science* (1994): 214–220.
2. A situation in which each firm's strategy is optimal, given the strategy chosen by the other player, is called a Nash equilibrium, named after Nobel Prize winner John Nash.

CHAPTER 15

Pricing

Pricing Chips

A Phoenix tortilla chip producer enjoyed a competitive advantage over a national brand. Its price was lower and its quality higher than the national brand's chip. Nevertheless, the local chip maker watched the national company very carefully because of its huge size relative to the local firm. Thus, when the national company upgraded its chip, the Phoenix firm believed it had to respond. It chose to reduce the quality so that its costs would be lower. It believed that in this way it could maintain its price advantage. A specific size of the national brand's potato chips was priced at $1.59 while a comparable size of the local brand was $1.29, a difference of 30 cents. Over time, the price of the national brand increased to $1.89. The local brand followed the lead of the national brand but maintained its 30 cent price differential by raising its price to $1.59. These changes caused the local company to go out of business.

1. How is it possible for a firm to have a lower price on its good relative to a competitive good and still lose out to the rival?
2. Why would equal price increases on two products lead consumers to purchase more of the higher-priced product and less of a relatively lower-priced product?

What Price?

The business strategies that get the most press involve cutting costs, introducing new products, and divesting or merging. But perhaps the most important strategy for a firm is its price strategy. Managers consider pricing to be extremely important, but only a small percentage of firms do any serious pricing research, and one-third of these don't know what to do with the results once they have them.[1] As a result, many firms abrogate pricing responsibility—"The market sets the price" or "We have to match our competitor" or "It is determined by our costs."

Marginal Revenue and Marginal Cost

Pricing seems easy enough, doesn't it? Just find the quantity where marginal revenue equals marginal cost and set price according to demand at that quantity. Although this is the fundamental approach to pricing, it involves many complications: The firm may offer more than one product; the firm may have different customer niches it tries to market to; the firm may have to consider what rivals will do if it raises or lowers price; the firm may have to consider what a high or low price means for the perception of the quality of the product; the firm might have to consider whether a high price will attract low-priced competitors; a firm has to determine whether a lower price will suggest that the product is low quality; and on and on. In fact, all these and other complications do come into play. It is therefore very difficult for managers to consider all the important aspects when determining the price to set. Many firms are turning to software to handle these complications for them.

For instance, petroleum retailers are using technology to help them set prices. Some retailers price higher on the strengths of their brands, whereas others aim to be known as offering the lowest prices. But in general, most retailers simply try to price slightly lower than their competition, with price increases or decreases being fairly uniform across all grades of fuel.

Computer technology now allows retailers to calculate price elasticity. The process starts by entering historical price, volume, and competitive data, with continual fine-tuning accomplished through daily data updates. The expected volume, the impact of a price change on volume, and the effect of a competitor's price change can all be calculated. The technology allows gas stations to change prices five times a day or more.

It isn't just the petroleum retailers who are adopting the technology of pricing. The job of pricing the 30,000-plus items in a typical supermarket seems virtually impossible. No one individual could keep track of each item and ensure that MR and MC are equal. But computerized software enables firms to set prices by tracking elasticities.

The managers of the gas station or the supermarket might not recognize that what the pricing technology is enabling them to do is find the profit-maximizing price level. But that is exactly what is occurring. For each product, the price is set by finding the quantity where marginal revenue is equal to marginal cost. Yet, if you ask executives how they are setting prices, very few will utter words such as marginal revenue and marginal cost. Most refer to cost plus pricing or value pricing or some other term, even if they are deploying software to determine the optimal prices.

Personalized Pricing

As just stated, technology is enabling firms to be much more precise about their pricing. In many cases, they can personalize price to each customer and according to the time of day, or the intensity of the heat, or some other variable. In Figure 15.1 the demand for and supply of some product is illustrated. The price determined

FIGURE 15.1 Consumer Surplus

The market price for a good or service is illustrated as P_1. Consumers would be willing and able to pay more for the good or service, as pointed out by the demand curve above the market price. The area ABC is the consumer surplus.

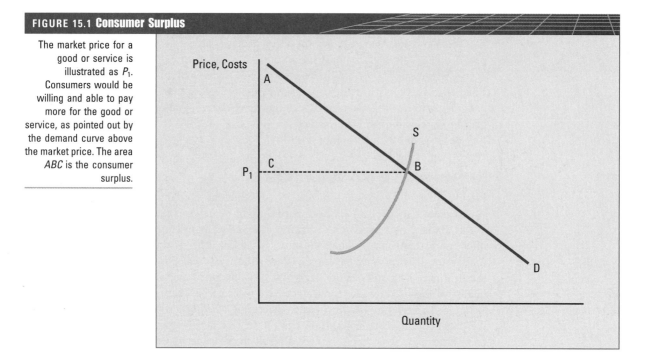

by the interaction of buyers and sellers is P_1. Notice that many consumers would be willing and able to pay more for the product—illustrated as the area under the demand curve and above the market price. But, these consumers do not have to pay that price because they pay just the market price. This area, shown as ABC, is called **consumer surplus**.

Firms would like to acquire the consumer surplus for themselves, rather than allow the consumers to get all the benefits. One approach to getting more of the consumer surplus is **personalized pricing**. Catalog retailers have been able to use personalized pricing even without the technology. They send out catalogs that sell identical goods except at different prices. The unlucky consumers who live in a more free-spending ZIP code may see only the higher prices. Victoria's Secret and Staples used these tactics for years, but now pricing has become even more precise. Websites are programmed to recognize individual consumers, remember what they paid for items in the past, and charge them a customized price based on that history. When a customer purchases at Amazon.com, the customer's tastes in books or music are filed, and suggested complementary or substitute products are offered the next time the customer logs in. For a brief period of time, over Labor Day Weekend in 2000, Amazon.com experimented with quoting each customer a different price based on that customer's price elasticity of demand. In other words, each consumer would pay a different price for the same product. In this way, Amazon was having each consumer pay what each was willing and able to pay. Amazon abandoned the practice when customers started complaining.[2]

As shown in Figure 15.2, when a firm gains some market power, say through differentiation, the demand curve slopes down. As a result, the firm sets price according to demand at the quantity where $MR = MC$, which is a higher price than if the firm is a commodity firm. As a result, consumer surplus is smaller. In Figure 15.2 the consumer surplus is reduced from ABC to ADE because the firm is able to acquire the consumer surplus of $CDEF$ for itself. But a great deal of consumer surplus remains; the consumer is still getting a benefit of paying just a market price. How can the firm collect the entire

FIGURE 15.2 Pricing with Market Power

A firm with market power charges a higher price and sells a lower quantity than the perfectly competitive or commodity firm. Consumer surplus is reduced from *ABC* to *ADE*.

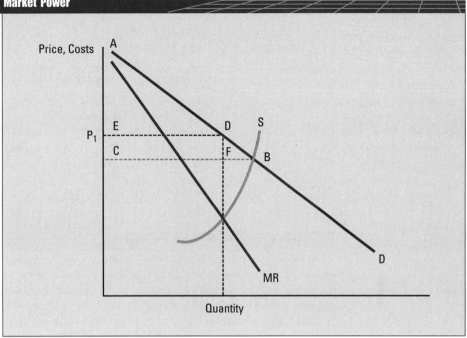

consumer surplus? It would have to charge each customer exactly what each was willing and able to pay.

At Peapod.com, customers may order groceries over the Internet; Peapod provides price per unit, ingredients, and nutritional information, thus giving customers a means of comparison shopping. As the customer clicks on and thus considers the prices, the nutritional information, or other aspects of the product and the time spent on each item are recorded. Marketers can then use the information to design ways to appeal to that customer. The customer becomes an individual entity rather than a member of a group of customers.

With each customer dealing with the firm online—"one-to-one marketing" in business jargon—the firm is able to personalize the price. In essence, what the firm does is find out how much any given customer is willing and able to pay and attempt to set the price at that point for each customer.[3] If each customer is sold the product at a different price, **perfect price discrimination** occurs. If there are groups of customers with similar price elasticities of demand and each group pays a different price for the identical product, the price discrimination is referred to as third-degree price discrimination. **Second-degree price discrimination** occurs when the firm is not able to identify the value each consumer places on each unit of the good, but instead the firm is able to group multiple units of the good and to charge different prices for the different groups. Quantity discounts fall under the category of second-degree price discrimination; a consumer pays a high price for a small number of units, a lower price for a larger number of units, and a still lower price for an even larger number of units.

A firm is able to earn an economic profit when it provides a good or service at a price that exceeds all of its costs. In order to maximize profit, a firm will set a price and sell a quantity determined by equating marginal revenue and marginal cost. When every customer pays the same price, the price strategy is referred to as a single or uniform price.

When the price elasticities of demand are different for two identifiable market segments, then charging both segments the same price would be "leaving money on the table." Profit could be increased by raising the price for the market segment with the lower price elasticity of demand relative to the price charged the segment with the higher price elasticity of demand.

If two classes are better than one for an airline, are three better than two? Are four better than three? Is a different price for each customer better than a different price for groups of customers? The answer to all these questions is yes, as long as the firm can effectively build fences to separate the market segments. In other words, the seller must be sure that the market segments cannot transact with each other and essentially skip the seller. If, for instance, Circuit City offered computers to senior citizens for half price, no one other than a senior citizen would purchase the computer since each potential customer who is not a senior citizen would enlist a senior citizen to purchase the machine.

Self-Selection: Product-Line Extension

Proctor-Silex sells its top-of-the-line iron for $54.95, while its next-best iron is priced at $49.95. The manufacturing cost difference between the two is less than $1, as the top model adds only a small light to signal that the iron is ready for use. This **product-line extension** allows the company to improve margins because there is a segment of the market that wants to "buy the best." How does Proctor-Silex find these people and separate them from the other customers? It doesn't. It allows the customers to self-select.

When Ford introduced the newly designed Taurus in two models, the basic GL and the more upscale LX, some customers complained that the price of the GL was too high for Taurus's traditional customers. Ford responded to the price-sensitive customers not by dropping the GL price but by announcing the introduction of a new lower-priced version of the car, the G.[4]

Publishers offer the first-line copy of a book in hardback, with later versions offered in paperback. These are all called product-line extensions. The product-line extension is similar to price discrimination. But since the firm is not able to easily distinguish the customers, a new product is introduced so as to induce the customers to self-select, to separate themselves, and thereby to pay different prices for essentially the same product.

You might say that product-line extension is not the process of setting price where $MR = MC$. But it is. Profit is maximized by setting the price of the product and the product-line extension so that the marginal revenue of each of the products equals the marginal cost of producing each product.

$$MR_1 = MC_1$$
$$MR_2 = MC_2$$

Peak-Load Pricing

Executives of Coca-Cola let it slip that they were considering introducing a computer chip in vending machines that would raise the price of the soda as the temperature rose.[5] Although the negative outcry that followed forced Coke to back away from the strategy, it is not uncommon for firms to use what is called a **peak-load pricing** strategy. A firm that uses the same plant or facility to supply a good or service whose demand varies at different points in time can increase profit by the use of peak-load pricing. Peak-load pricing is a form of price discrimination whereby customers purchasing the product at peak times pay a higher price than customers purchasing the product at off-peak times.

Business Insight

Peak-Load Pricing at the Movies

Peak-load pricing makes sense when there are large lines. Raise the price during popular times, cut the price during off-times, and watch those lines disappear. It also makes sense why businesses are reluctant to adopt peak-load pricing: Most of their customers feel that peak-load pricing is "unfair." Yet, movie theaters seem to have employed peak-load pricing without a problem. They have expensive evening shows and cheap matinees, and the crowds are bigger in the evenings. Strangely, however, as economist Bryan Caplan has pointed out, weekend matinees are a lot more crowded than weekday evenings. It seems more sensible to have peak pricing all day on Friday, Saturday, and Sunday, and discount pricing all day on Monday through Thursday or to have different prices for weekend and weekday matinees and for matinees and non matinees. Why do the theaters use just two prices?[6]

The pricing of electricity often provides an example of peak-load pricing. Most usage takes place in late afternoon/early evening during the workweek. The electrical company has to have the facilities to meet this demand, but this means that much of the firm's capacity sits idle during off-peak times. The company would prefer to have demand be at a more even level so that its facilities could be more uniformly used throughout the week.

If electricity could be stored at a small cost for later use, then the company could build facilities for the "average" use rather than the peak use. In such a case, the marginal cost of providing electricity would be no different whether it was a peak or off-peak time.

Cost-Plus Pricing

Consider the following two statements: (1) Products must be sold for about two and a half times what they cost to make. (2) In a restaurant, food is marked up three times direct cost, beer four times, and liquor six times. These remarks represent the approach a large proportion of businesses take to pricing. It is called **cost-plus pricing** (also called full-cost pricing or markup pricing).

There are many forms of cost-plus pricing, but all basically involve two steps. First, the firm estimates the per-unit cost of producing and selling the product. Second, the firm adds a markup to the estimated cost. The markup is meant to include certain costs that cannot be attributed to any specific product and to provide a return to the firm's investment. Intel forecasts what demand for its microchips will be and then determines costs of production and finally sets a price based on the forecasts and costs, being sensitive to what its chief rival, AMD, is doing. John Deere determines costs of production and sets a Moline price—the price provided to dealers. The dealers then have discretion to change price for their particular market situation. Petroleum companies such as Chevron/Texaco set a retail price for their gasoline based on crude oil prices, the costs of the additives in refining, and the prices charged by other retail operations.

When a firm uses a cost-plus pricing strategy, price is typically given by

$$P = (\text{average cost})(1 + \text{markup})$$

where markup is a percentage. For example, the markup might represent a predetermined profit margin or a target return on investment. Does cost-plus pricing maximize profit? In most cases it does not.

The markup must be a very specific number to have the price resulting from a cost markup equal the price determined by setting marginal revenue equal to marginal cost. The cost-plus pricing rule will be the profit-maximizing strategy only if marginal cost rather than average cost is used and if the markup equals[7]

$$[1/(1 - 1/e)] - 1$$

How likely is it that a manager of a firm would realize that it must set this particular markup? Very unlikely. Nevertheless, the end result will not be all that different if the manager is at all sensitive to customer demands. As demand becomes less elastic, the markup increases, so the price is higher. Conversely, the more elastic the demand, the lower the markup and, thus, the lower is price.

Framing

In 1987, Burroughs-Wellcome (now Glaxo-Wellcome) introduced its anti-AIDS drug AZT to a hostile market reception. As a pioneering medical breakthrough, AZT gave AIDS victims and doctors the first medical hope of extending life. The introductory price for AZT was $12,000 annually. Although Burroughs-Wellcome's marketing department developed a very substantial publicity campaign that justified the price—due to the significant research costs needed to discover and develop AZT—the intensely negative public reaction nonetheless threatened the product and even the company itself.[8] In 1991, Bristol Myers Squibb introduced a similar anti-AIDS drug, under the brand name Videx. It was not as effective as AZT and had a price tag of $150 per month, or $1,800 annually, but public reaction was overwhelmingly positive. Gay rights groups praised Bristol's actions as exemplary.

Why the difference? Videx enjoyed a significant perceptual advantage relative to AZT. People had something to compare Videx's price to, which was something they could not do with AZT when it came on the market. The context in which a choice is presented is important to the decision maker. The context will affect the price elasticity of demand. In short, perceptions matter.

For instance, when a customer calls a hotel regarding a reservation, the hotel reservationist generally quotes the highest rates charged during peak-demand periods and then discounts those rates. This is an attempt to create a high reference price for the consumer. If the initially stated high price is the buyer's reference, then the buyer looks upon the price actually paid as a gain. Similarly, airline reservationists initially note the highest fare on a route before quoting discounts and associated travel restrictions. In written advertisements or on radio and TV advertisements, both hotels and airlines provide the lowest price as well as a reference to which they want consumers to compare the stated price. "This fare is 50 percent below previous fares" and "Friends fly free," suggesting a 50 percent discount, are common advertisements.

People generally want more for less. However, in some situations how the "more" and "less" are presented makes a difference. Consider how people respond to the following situation.

> Who is happier—person A, who wins the office football pool for $100 on the same day she ruins the carpet in her apartment and must pay the landlord $75, or person B, who wins the office football pool for $25?

Most people believe person A is happier even though both A and B end up with the same $25 gain. Consider the same problem with a slight revision.

> Who is happier—person A, who ruins the carpet in her apartment and must pay the landlord $100, or person B, who wins the office football pool for $25 but also ruins the carpet in his apartment and must pay the landlord $125?

In this case, most people believe person B is happier, even though A and B must pay the same amount, $100. In these situations, the individual market baskets being compared include the presentation of the goods in the baskets. If the market basket involves a gain, people prefer to have the results of the actions presented separately so that the gain seems larger—a $100 gain and a $25 loss rather than a $75 gain. But if the market basket involves losses, people prefer to have the losses integrated or shown just once.

For a few months, hotels were imposing "energy fees" of $1.50 to $7 per night because energy costs had risen and the hotels were simply passing these along to the consumer. The hotels thought they would be able to raise the price of their rooms without having to take the blame for the price increase. Consumers did not react positively. According to the idea that people prefer getting bad news all at once, this pricing strategy is very poor. Hoteliers should be lumping the entire fees together into one amount. They mistakenly believed that consumers would blame the energy charges on something other than the hotel.

Odd pricing is the practice of specifying the rightmost digits in the price in amounts that are less than the higher even price. For instance, $2.98 as compared to $3.00 or $499 as compared to $500 are odd prices. The use of odd pricing is based on reference prices. The advertised price of $499 allows the consumer to realize there is a gain relative to $500, the reference price. Moreover, because a loss means more than an equal gain, we don't see odd prices above the even reference price.[9]

It is more painful to consumers to give up an asset that they possess than it is pleasurable to acquire an asset they don't possess. Buyers want to retain the status quo, to keep the assets they already own. This means that the price elasticity of demand can be changed—made less elastic—if consumers feel like they own the product. Thus, the purchase decision can be influenced by having the buyers assume ownership, even temporarily, prior to purchase. If buyers can be persuaded to take the product home to try it out, they will adjust their reference point to include the new asset. They will then be reluctant to return the product when payment is due, since they would be giving up something they now feel they own. A frequent tactic of home decorator and furniture stores is to encourage customers to take a piece of furniture or a carpet home to "see how it looks." This is also the approach of buy-now, pay-later plans. During holidays, for example, retailers frequently offer installment plans that delay payment for 90 days so that buyers can integrate the new purchases into their reference points. Health clubs, fitness centers, and weight-loss clinics often offer an initial trial membership either free or at nominal rates.

Publisher's Clearinghouse addresses individuals who receive their direct-mail promotion as "finalists" and warns them that they are about to lose millions of dollars if the entry form is not returned. Publisher's Clearinghouse is attempting to give consumers the impression that they possess an asset that they will have to give up if they don't submit the entry form.

More Complexities

What we have discussed to this point is the situation in which the firm has a single product to sell and a single price to determine. This is the simplest pricing situation facing managers, and as we have discussed, many fail to use the optimal strategy to determine price. What occurs as the situation gets more complicated? For instance, suppose a firm sells many products to many different segments of customers or a firm is dependent on what its rivals do and cannot determine its own prices without considering the prices the rivals are using. Let's now consider more complex situations.

Bundling

Cable television providers have a difficult pricing situation. They have several channels to sell (several products), and customers differ distinctly in the channels that are of interest to them. To illustrate, suppose that Cox Cable has just two channels, 1 and 2. Also, suppose there are just two segments among the viewer population: A and B. The A segment gets much more value out of channel 1 than does segment B, and segment B likes channel 2 more than does segment A.

Suppose that members of segment B would be willing to pay no more than $12 a month for channel 1 and no more than $12 a month for channel 2. Members of segment A would be willing to pay no more than $20 a month for channel 1 but only no more than $4 a month for channel 2.

If the channels are sold separately, the most Cox Cable could get for the channels would be the sum of the prices each segment was willing to pay. If Cox set a price of $20 for channel 1, it would sell only to segment A. To get segment B to purchase channel 1, Cox has to set a price of no more than $12. Since Cox is not able to distinguish between segments A and B, it has to set the same price for all customers. Thus, total revenue from channel 1 is

$$TR = (Q_A + Q_B)\$12$$

where Q_A is the number of people in segment A and Q_B is the number of people in segment B.

Similarly, Cox can charge only $4 to get segment A to purchase channel 2, so it cannot charge more than $4 for channel 2. The total revenue from channel 2 is

$$TR = (Q_A + Q_B)\$4$$

Now, consider what would happen if Cox sold the two channels as a package—that is, if it bundled the two channels together. Cox could set a price of $24, the lowest price that would attract the two groups to the bundle of channels 1 and 2. In the bundling case, $TR = (Q_A + \mathbf{Q_B})\$24$. This is called **pure bundling** since the only way the channels can be purchased is as a package. Pure bundling does not discriminate among the customer segments—all customers pay the same price.

Mixed Bundling

In the preceding example, the seller, Cox Cable, offered the channels only as a bundle. Often, the seller can make a larger profit by allowing buyers a choice between the bundle and the individual products. To illustrate, suppose that Cox Cable incurs a marginal cost of $5 per month per channel for each customer. The marginal cost of $5 is more than segment A would pay for channel 2. It wouldn't make sense to sell channel 2 to segment A at a price that is less than marginal cost. Since segment A is willing to purchase channel 1 at a price of $20 or less, it would make sense to offer channel 1 at a price of $20. Segment B would not pay more than $12 for channel 1 alone but would pay up to $24 for the two channels together. If the price of channel 1 alone is set at $20 and the bundle of channels 1 and 2 at $24, total revenue would be $TR = Q_A(\$20) + Q_B(\$24)$ and profit would be $Q_A(\$20 - \$5) + Q_B(\$24 - \$10)$.

Compare this to offering only the bundle at a price of $24. Total profit with pure bundling and a marginal cost of $5 for each channel is

$$TR = Q_A(\$24 - \$10) + Q_B(\$24 - \$10)$$

Cox's profit is higher by offering the **mixed bundle** than it is by offering a pure bundle.

Bundling is, in fact, a rather common pricing strategy. In the travel business, a package consisting of airline travel and rooms in a beach resort will be relatively more attractive to vacationers than to business travelers. Given a choice of airline travel and a package holiday at a somewhat higher price, business travelers are relatively more likely to choose the separate airline travel. Vacationers will prefer the package. Cable television does a great deal of bundling. It offers a "basic" package, which is a bundle of channels, then different packages at additional prices. Procter & Gamble, Gillette, Schick, and other firms bundle products quite regularly. A razor is packaged with shaving cream, laundry detergent with hand soap, and so on. Microsoft's Office bundle contains several programs—Word,

Excel, and PowerPoint—as well as an Internet browser. Each could be purchased individually. McDonald's and other fast-food outlets offer different bundles, such as food items and a beverage, for a price that is less than would be the case if the items were purchased separately.

Tying

Tying is a form of bundling. Tying is a general term referring to any requirement that products be bought or sold in some combination. The buyer of the main product (tying good) agrees to buy one or several complementary goods (tied goods) that are necessary to use the tying good. Often the tying good is a durable, such as a copier, while the tied goods are nondurables, such as toner or paper. Cellular phone companies tie their goods and services—a phone, activation, and the calling service.

Knowing which elements customers focus on can be critical in constructing the right ties among goods and pricing the tied products correctly. If the customer is more price-sensitive to one aspect of the bundle than another, then the firm will want to price accordingly. It will want to attract the buyers to the good to which they are price-sensitive by making that good appear to have a low price.

Cannibalization

When a firm produces or offers for sale more than one good or service, it must set the price and the quantity of each good or service it produces and/or offers for sale by taking into account the effects of the price and quantity on all of its goods and services. Consider the case of a firm that produces two interdependent products, A and B; sales of one affect sales of the other. The marginal revenue associated with a change in the quantity sold of product A is composed of two parts: the change in total revenue for product A associated with a marginal increase (or decrease) in the quantity sold of product A and the change in total revenue for product B associated with a marginal increase (or decrease) in the quantity sold of product A. Similarly, the marginal revenue for product B consists of two parts. The interdependency between A and B can be positive, negative, or zero. If the two products under consideration are complements, then an increase in the quantity sold of one product will result in an increase in total revenue for the other product. If the products are substitutes, then an increase in the quantity sold of one product will result in a decrease in total revenue for the other product.

As an illustration, suppose Procter & Gamble (P&G) has identified two segments in the market for its laundry detergent, single people and families. Suppose that P&G produces two different-sized packages of detergent, 5 ounce and 10 ounce. Let's also assume that the marginal cost of laundry detergent is constant at 10 cents per ounce and that there are no other costs.

If P&G did something like set the price of the 5-ounce bottle at $2.50 and the 10-ounce bottle at $6, a family would substitute the smaller bottles for the larger one. In marketing language, the small bottle would cannibalize the demand for the large bottle. **Cannibalization** occurs when sales of one product produced by a firm reduce the demand for another product produced by that same firm.

Cannibalization occurs because P&G has no way to separate the two market segments—that is, to distinguish families from singles. Accordingly, P&G must design and price the two bottles so that families voluntarily choose the large bottle. P&G sets its quantities and prices where $MR_A = MC = MR_B$. The complication is that the two products are interdependent. This means that sales of the small bottle affect the large bottle and vice versa. The marginal revenue equals marginal cost rule thus takes the form:

$$MR_A + MR_{AB} = MC = MR_B + MR_{BA}$$

where MR_{AB} represents the effect of sales of product B on the marginal revenue of product A and vice versa for MR_{BA}.

As another example, consider the Gillette Company, which sells razors, razor blades, toiletries, cosmetics, stationery products, Braun personal care appliance products, Braun household appliances, and Oral-B preventive dentistry products. Its razors and blades include Sensor, Altra, Trac II, Good News, and Daisy Plus, and each of the other divisions includes several different brands. There is probably no interdependence between pens and electric shavers, but there is between the Altra and Trac II razors. In fact, when Gillette introduced a new shaver, sales of its stick razor and razor blades declined. Gillette had to take the cannabilization effect into consideration when deciding how to price its new Trac II razors.

Multiple Products

The profit-maximizing strategy for firms with multiple products is quite straightforward—find the point where $MR_i = MC$ for all i; that is, for each product, set the price where the product's marginal revenue is equal to the firm's marginal cost. The independence of products is important because a change in price of one product could affect others if the products are complements or substitutes. Then looking at just one product in setting prices could lead to a profit level that is not the maximum. Firms selling multiple products must examine the margins on all the products to determine the marginal revenue equals marginal cost points.

Supermarkets illustrate this strategy quite well. Shelf space can be allocated among a wide variety of product categories, such as meat, dairy products, canned goods, frozen foods, and produce. The supermarket is obviously providing multiple products. It maximizes profit by setting $MR = MC$ for each product. Suppose that for one product marginal revenue is less than the marginal cost and for another marginal revenue is greater than the marginal cost. Clearly, it would make sense to increase the production of the second at the expense of the first. This is what supermarkets have done by adding higher-profit-margin categories such as delicatessens, in-store bakeries, and floral departments and reducing the shelf space assigned to lower-profit-margin items. If it is found that when the price of bakery items is increased the sales of dairy products fall, then the supermarket must determine the profit-maximizing prices of both bakery items and dairy products simultaneously. As complicated as this approach is, several independent firms now use it for retailers. SAP-Khimetrics, for instance, determines prices for the 30,000 products carried by an Albertsons.

Joint Products

Rather than producing several alternative products, firms often produce joint products—products that are interdependent in the production process instead of at the consumer level. A change in the production of one causes a change in the cost or availability of the other. Examples include the production of liquid oxygen and nitrogen from air, beef and hides from steers, and gasoline and fuel oil from crude oil.

Pricing for joint products is a little more complex than pricing for a single product. To begin with, there are two demand curves. The characteristics of each demand curve could be different. Demand for one product could be greater than for the other product. Consumers of one product could be more price-elastic than the consumers of the other product (and therefore more sensitive to changes in the product's price). To complicate things further, both products, because they are produced jointly, share a common marginal cost curve. In addition, their production could be linked in the sense that they are bi-products (referred to as complements in production), or they could be linked in the sense that they can be produced by the same inputs (referred to as substitutes in production). Also, production of the joint product could be in fixed proportions or in variable proportions.

When joint products are produced in fixed proportions (example: cow hides and cow steaks), then one of the products will not be produced at the same quantity as would occur if the products are produced in variable proportions. In fact, the profit-maximizing quantity and price of the B part of the joint product will be different from the profit-maximizing amount if that item were considered separately.

Interdependencies among Firms

Pricing strategies are used by firms that have market power.[10] In other words, they are not competing in a perfectly competitive or commodity market. Moreover, these strategies are used by firms whose behavior does not depend on the behavior of rivals. In most markets, firms can't act so independently. When one does something, rivals try to offset the move (this is the oligopoly). For instance, if one lowers price, rivals are sure to lower their prices as well. The result could be a price war where the rivals drive prices down until they are the competitive level or where a few rivals are forced out of the market. It is for this reason that firms that are interdependent don't like to compete on the basis of price. The prisoner's dilemma, discussed in Chapter 8, demonstrates the problem with price competition.

Prisoner's Dilemma

Consider the situation where firms are trying to determine whether to devote more resources to advertising. When a firm advertises its product, its demand may increase for two reasons. First, people who had not used that type of product before learn about it, and some will buy it. Second, other people who already consume a different brand of the same product may switch brands. The first effect boosts sales for the industry as a whole, while the second redistributes existing sales within the industry.

Let us consider a potential price war between two office supply superstores, Staples and Office Max. Each store has a core of loyal customers, but there is also a group that is price-sensitive. The firms are considering how to set the prices of a popular item. Through market research, the companies know how they will do if they respond to the other's pricing in a certain way. But each must set the prices now and advertise the price without knowing what the other company will do. Depending on what both firms do, they will earn more or less profit. The results are shown in Figure 15.3.

If Staples selects a lower price and so does Office Max, then Office Max earns 70 and Staples 80. If Staples selects the lower price and Office Max the higher price, then Staples earns 100 while Office Max only 40. If Staples sets the higher price while Office Max sets the lower, then Office max gains the most. If both stores select the higher price then both do well. Clearly, they would be better off if they would each select the higher price. But not knowing what the other will do, neither wants to be the higher price store while the other takes the major portion of the market. Thus, each looks at the payoffs and decides that the other is likely to select the lower price. Choosing lower yields a better result in each case than choosing higher, assuming the other store chooses low.

The solution in the upper left portion of the matrix indicates that each firm gains less revenue than if the two would each set a higher price. The firms are caught in what is called a dilemma.

The firms could get out of this dilemma and increase profits by cooperating. For instance, they might agree to set the higher prices, that is, to "fix" prices. The problem is that in the United

FIGURE 15.3 Price War

Office Max finds that a lower price is its best choice no matter what Staples does. Staples similarly finds that the lower price is its best choice as well.

		Office Max	
		Lower	Higher
Staples	Lower	Office Max 70 Staples 80	Office Max 40 Staples 100
	Higher	Office Max 100 Staples 50	Office Max 80 Staples 90

States it is illegal to fix prices. Thus, the firms must figure out a way to create the same result but not by explicitly price fixing. One way to "implicitly" fix prices is to set up a **meet the competition clause,** a situation whereby the company has the option to meet any offer the customer receives from a rival firm. This reduces the incentive for one firm to attempt to steal customers from another. The Meet the Competition Clause is seen in phrases such as "We can't be undersold" and "Low price guarantee." The firm tells the customers that if they find a price that is lower at any other store, the firm will match the price in some cases and refund a percentage in addition.

Another method to avoid price fixing and end up with a fixed price is called a **most favored customer clause**. This ensures the customer that he or she will get the best price the company gives to anyone. If another customer receives a lower price, then all most favored customers will get the lower price as well. When the firm has a most favored customer policy, it is better able to withstand pressure to lower price. The firm informs the customer "I'd really like to give you a lower price, but I can't. If I do, I have to give everyone the lower price." Sometimes firm rivalry evolves to a point that one firm becomes the price leader. What that firm does is then followed by others in the industry. In the Staples and Office Max example, if Office Max was the price leader, it would set the higher price, which would then be followed and matched by Staples. Each would be better off by cooperating in this way than indulging in a price war.

Competing on Other Than Price

Few firms actually compete solely on the basis of price. Most attempt to differentiate their product or themselves in some manner. Why? Because price competition typically leads to commoditization, and the result is zero economic profits. Unless a firm is able to acquire a favorable cost situation relative to competitors, price competition leads all firms to pricing at marginal cost and earning zero economic profit. A firm is better off if it is able to differentiate itself or its products.

For instance, Linear has built one of the world's enviable market niches.[11] It makes 7,500 products that solve problems for a long list of customers. Instead of digital chips that power the brains of the world's computers, Linear makes analog chips that serve small roles. Many of Linear's chips cost less than 50 cents to build, and they sell for $1.50 to $2.00. How could Linear set price so far above marginal cost? Linear earned nearly 40 percent profit on its $1.1 billion in sales in calendar 2006, more than five times the average for U.S. industrial companies. It outpaced Microsoft Corporation and Google Inc., which earned profits of 26 percent and 24 percent of sales, respectively. And its success in 2007 was even better. How was it able to do that? It created a niche market without substitutes. Its price elasticity of demand was very low.

What is likely to occur now that Linear is doing so well? Rivals will enter the business and compete profits down. In fact, Texas Instruments is moving strongly into analog production. Richtek Technology of Taiwan and Freescale Semiconductor of Austin Texas are also targeting Linear. If entry does occur, then Linear's profit rates will decline. The CEO of Linear argues that his is not an easily copied company because of its wide product line. If it had just one product, then companies would be able to compete for that product. Because it has many chips, however, each designed for a different customer, Linear executives think it will be more difficult for new firms to compete. But if economic profits exist, firms will find ways to seek those profits. If Linear was attempting to compete solely on the basis of price, it probably wouldn't match up against the larger companies which could acquire resources and a lower price.

For 89 years, Parker Hannifin Corporation, a big industrial parts maker, has set the prices of its 800,000 parts in a simple manner.[12] Company managers would calculate how much it cost to make and deliver each product and add a flat percentage on top, usually about 35 percent. In 2002 the company began determining prices by finding the profit-maximizing point for each product. The company claims that simply pricing according to what customers are willing and able to pay increased net income $500 million and increased the return on invested capital from 7 percent to 21 percent. Many companies are learning the role of pricing in economic profit. Pricing incorrectly is, in essence, leaving money on the table.

Pricing Chips

How is it possible for a lower price to be a problem for a firm and even to be the cause of the firm's failure? Why did the consultants determine that the problem with the local tortilla chip firm was its low price? The Phoenix tortilla chip maker altered its product, lowering quality. In essence, this act had the effect of actually increasing the cost to the consumer. Even though the price did not change, the quality of the chip did. A constant price for a lower-quality product is, in essence, a higher price. If consumer demand is price-elastic, the higher real price means lower sales and lower revenue. Had the Phoenix chip maker been able to maintain both its quality and its price, it would not have had the problem competing with the national brand that it did. One strategy the Phoenix chip maker might have taken would have been to separate the market into different price elasticities of demand by positioning its chips as the high-quality chip. This less elastic niche might have enabled the Phoenix firm to maintain profitability. Another strategy might have been to offer two chips, one a lower-quality chip and one a high-quality chip, thereby appealing to both sets of customers.

Why would equal price increases on two products lead consumers to purchase more of the higher-priced product and less of the relatively lower-priced product? The national brand increased its price 30 cents, from $1.59 to $1.89, while the local company also increased its price 30 cents, from $1.29 to $1.59. The difference is that the price increase from $1.59 to $1.89 is a 19 percent increase whereas from $1.29 to $1.59 it is a 23 percent increase. The larger percentage increase means a larger percentage change in quantity demanded. The higher-priced firm increased prices relatively less than the lower-priced firm and thereby took market share from the lower-priced firm.

Summary

1. When a firm sells just one product, it will maximize profit by setting a single or uniform price where marginal revenue equals marginal cost as long as customers cannot be separated according to price sensitivity.

2. When customers or customer segments can be separated by price elasticity of demand and when resale between and among customers can be avoided, the firm can increase profit by price discrimination, which is often called personalized pricing.

3. The Internet has made personalized pricing much more prevalent because firms are able to learn more about customers and their likes and dislikes.

4. There are various forms of price discrimination. Third-degree price discrimination essentially separates customers into two groups. Perfect price discrimination personalizes price to the extent that each customer pays a different price. Second-degree price discrimination sets different prices on different quantities of a good or service.

5. The profit-maximizing rule for price discrimination is to set a price at which the marginal revenues for the market segments are equal and are also equal to marginal cost.

6. Product-line extension is a form of discrimination—providing a slightly different version of the same product at a different price. The profit-maximizing rule is to set the price where the marginal revenue of each product equals the marginal cost of each.

7. Peak-load pricing is a form of price discrimination whereby different prices exist for different times of the day or different periods of time. The profit-maximizing rule for peak-load pricing is to set the price where the marginal revenue of each time period equals the marginal cost of each time period.

8. Cost-plus pricing is the practice of setting a price based on a markup above costs. The cost-plus pricing strategy is a profit-maximizing strategy only if the markup is equal to $[1/(1 - 1/e)] - 1$ and is based on the marginal cost.

9. Bundling is the practice of offering more than one good or service in a package for a single price.

10. Pure bundling is the practice of offering only the package of bundled goods for purchase. Mixed bundling is the practice of offering both of the bundled products in one package and at least some of the products in the bundle individually.

11. Tying is a general term referring to the practice of pricing and selling combinations of complementary products.

12. Cannibalization occurs when sales of one product offered by a firm reduce the sales of another product offered by that same firm.

13. Pricing strategies become more complex when there are interdependencies among firms.

14. Pricing interdependencies can be illustrated quite well by the prisoner's dilemma. In a prisoner's dilemma, players become trapped in a second-best solution. The only way to get out of the dilemma is to have repeated interactions and/or to change the payoff.

15. A price war may result if the cooperative arrangements arrived at in order to get out of a dilemma break down as one party attempts to cheat on the others.

16. Joint products refer to the production process: Production of one product also results in production of other products.

17. In every case, the profit-maximizing strategy is to set marginal revenue equal to marginal cost. The trick is to appropriately define the marginal revenue and marginal costs of different products, combinations of products, or production processes.

Key Terms

Consumer surplus
Personalized pricing
Perfect price discrimination
Second-degree price discrimination
Product-line extension
Peak-load pricing
Cost-plus pricing

Odd pricing
Pure bundling
Mixed bundle
Tying
Cannibalization
Meet the competition clause
Most favored customer clause

Exercises

1. Explain why marginal revenue is less than or equal to price. How does the difference between price and marginal revenue depend on the price elasticity of demand?

2. Why would a firm not want to price at the point where marginal revenue is greater than marginal cost?

3. Many supermarkets sell both branded and private-label goods. Suppose that a supermarket estimates that the demand for its private-label cola is less elastic than the demand for Coca-Cola. How should it price its private-label cola?

4. An engineer has discovered a way to improve the production of a microchip to reduce its marginal cost from $1 to $0.80. Should the firm reduce the selling price of the microchip by $0.20?

5. Magazines are sold both on newsstands and by subscription. Advertising accounts for up to one-half of the revenues of magazines such as *Time* and *Sports Illustrated,* and advertising depends on the number of subscriptions. How should a publisher determine the subscription price relative to newsstand price?

6. Some personal computer software is sold at special discounts to students. Other software is provided in a less powerful version for students. Why do publishers offer discounts to students? What is the purpose of developing less powerful editions?

7. Using the kinked demand model, explain why a decrease in costs might not lead to a change in price or output (see Chapter 10).

8. At one time a major U.S. airline proposed that all airlines adopt a uniform fare schedule based on mileage. Doing so would have eliminated the many different fares that were available at the time. Most major airlines applauded the suggestion and began to adopt the plan. Soon, however, various airlines began cutting fares. Explain this occurrence using the prisoner's dilemma.

9. When one airline announced a substantial reduction in domestic airfares, within a day, other airlines announced similar price cuts. What would you expect the outcome of this price war to be?

10. Stargazer Recordings sells compact discs in two markets. The marginal cost of each disc is $2. Demand in each market is given by $Q_1 = 40 - 10P_1$ and $Q_2 = 40 - 2P_2$ where Q is thousands of compact discs.

   a. If the firm uses price discrimination, how much output should it produce and what price should it charge? What is its profit? What type of price discrimination is it using?

   b. If the firm cannot prevent resale of compact discs, what will its profit be?

11. A major airline estimates that the demand and marginal revenue functions for first-class and excursion fares from New York to Paris are:

   First class : $P = 4,200 - 2Q$ $MR = 4,200 - 4Q$
   Excursion : $P = 2,200 - 0.25Q$ $MR = 2,200 - 0.5Q$

   If the marginal cost of flying is $200 per passenger, what fare and what number of passengers will maximize profit? Show that profit is greater than if the airline used a single or uniform price.

12. Explain what peak-load pricing is. What is its intended purpose?

13. Explain and demonstrate why cost-plus pricing is probably not the same as profit-maximizing pricing.

14. What is framing? How could you alter the price elasticity of demand by framing?

15. Two pizza shops have just opened on campus: Giuseppe's Pizza, and Capri's Pizza. The "pricing game" these competitors face can be described in simple terms as follows. Each of them has to choose a price (high, medium, or low) for its

"double cheese pizza," and the profitability of each choice depends on the price that the rival chooses. The situation is depicted in the accompanying table, where Giuseppe's Pizza is the row player and Capri's Pizza the column player. Profits are expressed in hundreds of dollars.

Capri's Pizza

		high	medium	low
Giuseppe's Pizza	high	60, 60	36, 70	36, 35
	medium	70, 36	50, 50	30, 35
	low	35, 36	35, 30	25, 25

a. What is the Nash equilibrium (or equilibria) of the game? Is (high, high) a Nash equilibrium? Explain.

b. If these players play this game twice, what would be your prediction? What if they play it over and over again? Explain.

16. A firm offers two products for sale. The marginal cost of one product is near zero once the first unit has been produced. The marginal cost of the other product rises as output rises. What would be the effect of bundling the two products? What price would the firm charge for the bundle?

17. A car dealership typically determines a distinct price for a car for each customer. This is an example of what type of price discrimination? Why is the dealership able to carry out this type of price discrimination?

18. Amazon.com and Apple have recently agreed to sell ebooks for $9.99. Do you think this price reflects marginal cost? Is it too high or too low? Explain.

CHAPTER NOTES

1. Nancy Feig, "The Silent Buzz; Price optimization promises increased profits. But banks remain quiet about their price optimization strategies and technologies," *Bank Systems & Technology*, May 1, 2007, p. 35. Garret Van Ryzin, "Survey-Mastering Management: The Brave New World of Pricing," *Financial Times* (London), October 16, 2000, Monday Surveys MMC1, p. 6. K. Clancy and R. Shulman, *Marketing Myths That Are Killing Businesses: The Cure for Death Wish Marketing* (New York: McGraw-Hill, 1994). Shiv Prasad, "Pricing Element in Marketing, *New Straits Times* (Malaysia), May 26, 2007, p. 37.

2. Amazon.com, www.ocf.berkeley.edu/~elram/competitive-edge.html, accessed May 1, 2008.

3. The firm is attempting to collect the consumer surplus.

4. Jeff Karr, "Balance of Power: America's Most Popular Car Is All New. How Does It Stack Up?" *Motor Trend* (August 1995): 51–60. www.motortrend.com/, accessed February 6, 2008.

5. Coke's New Pricing, *New York Times*, October 29, 1999 topics.nytimes.com/top/news/business/companies/coca_cola_company/index.html?query=VENDING%20MACHINES&field=des&match=exact, accessed April 29, 2008.

6. Bryan Caplan, "Peak Load Pricing at the Movies," September 17, 2006. econlog.econlib.org/archives/2006/09/peak_load_prici_1.html. For more pricing puzzles, see Richard b. McKenzie, *Why Popcorn Costs So Much at the Movies* (New York: Springer, 2008).

7. Profit is maximized by setting marginal revenue equal to marginal cost. Marginal revenue is given by $MR = P(1 - 1/e)$, where e is the price elasticity of demand [if the absolute value of e is used, then the term in parentheses is $(1+1/e)$]. So, $MR = MC$ is $P(1 - 1/e) = MC$ Solving for P gives us a cost-plus pricing rule that is in fact based on profit maximization:

$$P = MC[1/(1 - 1/e)]$$

The cost-plus markup pricing rule is

$$P = MC(1 + \text{markup})$$

8. Jeanne Liedtka, "Burroughs Wellcome and the Pricing of AZT (B)," UVA-E-0075, available at SSRN: ssrn.com/abstract=908128.

9. Interestingly, odd pricing is often thought to be not an application of framing but rather an attempt to trick consumers or to control employee theft. A best-selling marketing textbook, *Marketing: Concepts and Strategies* by William M. Pride and O. C. Ferrell (Boston: Houghton Mifflin, 1995),

p. 649, notes that "Odd pricing assumes that more of a product will be sold at $99.99 than at $100. Supposedly, customers will think, or at least tell friends, that the product is a bargain—not $100 but $99, plus a few insignificant pennies." Odd pricing is also explained as an attempt to exploit a psychological bias in T. T. Nagle and R. K. Holden, *The Strategy and Tactics of Pricing* (New York: Prentice Hall, 1995), p. 300: "The belief is that buyers perceive the odd-numbers as significantly lower than the slightly higher round numbers that they approximate." While this rationale seems appealing, it assumes that consumers are pretty dense—that they do not learn from mistakes. Perhaps seeing an odd price once might induce consumers to think that the price was actually a lower number, but wouldn't they eventually learn?

The second rationale of odd pricing—which is more folktale than academic explanation—is that odd pricing is used to minimize employee thefts. The origination of odd pricing is attributed to Macy's around 1862. Early corporate historians stated that the reason Macy's used odd pricing was to control theft by clerks. When a customer gave a clerk an even amount of currency in payment for an item with an odd price, the clerk would have to make change at the cashier's desk, thus reducing the opportunity of pocketing funds.

10. Also called monopoly or market power. The idea is that the firm can raise or lower price as it wishes; quantity demanded will fall or rise, respectively.

11. Linear Home Page, www.linearcorp.com/about_linear.html, accessed May 2, 2008.

12. Timothy Aapell, "Seeking Perfect Prices, CEO Tears Up the Rules," *Wall Street Journal*, March 27, 2007, online.wsj.com/article/SB117496231213149938-search.html?KEYWORDS=pricing &COLLECTION=wsjie/6month.

Putting It All Together

CHAPTER **16**

The Knowledge Economy

Industrial or Innovation Policy[1]

Industrial policy refers to the government essentially picking winners and losers in business and subsidizing or developing winners and not helping losers. It is currently being argued that the government must invest in new industries because it is prohibitively expensive for firms to do it. They point to the Defense Advanced Research Projects Agency (DARPA), which supported creation of ARPANET, the predecessor of the Internet. If the government had not created ARPANET, we would not have the Internet today. Companies were reticent to invest in the new field of computer networking because the sums required were enormous and the technology was so far from potential commercialization that companies were unable to foresee how to monetize potential investments. And they point out that this situation pertains today to a range of emerging infrastructure technologies such as biotechnology, nanotechnology, and robotics. The levels of investment required to research and develop emerging technologies is so great that the private sector cannot support it alone. Thus, government must increasingly assume the role of partner with industry in managing technology research projects.

Companies such as IBM, Google, Oracle, Akamai, Hewlett-Packard, and many others may not have even come into existence—and certainly would not have prospered to the extent they have—if the U.S. government had not either been an early funder of R&D for the technologies they were developing or a leading procurer of the products they were producing. The government has a role to play in thoughtfully, strategically, and intentionally placing strategic bets on nascent and emerging technologies that have the potential to turn into the industries, companies, and jobs that drive an economy two to three decades hence. This requires policies and investments in industries such as robotics, nanotechnology, clean energy, biotechnology, synthetic biology, high-performance computing, and digital platforms such as the smart grid, intelligent transportation systems, broadband, and Health IT.

1. Is there a need for government to pick winners and losers?
2. What objections to the industrial policy suggested in the essay do you have? If no objections, how do you support a government selecting losers and winners when the free market does that type of thing so well?

Everything Has Changed

In the 1990s, business gurus told us that nothing we are used to would remain in the future. A headline in the *Wall Street Journal* on January 1, 2000, announced: so long supply and demand. In that same issue of the *Wall Street Journal,* others declared that "conventional economics is dead." The novelist Saul Bellow observed that "There does seem to be some possibility that the war with scarcity is tapering off. There will be enough for everyone." This is what people meant when they referred to the *New Economy.* But the term *New Economy* has fallen by the wayside, most likely because of the dot.com bust.

The claim made today is that we live in a knowledge or learning economy, but again, the argument is that *everything has changed.*[2] By knowledge economy, it is meant that knowledge and information are the crucial elements in the economy. Most discussions of the knowledge economy refer to recent information and communication technologies—particularly digital—as the primary characteristic. The technological changes in information processing have altered the business landscape in four ways. First, the supply chains of many businesses were destroyed or decomposed. Second, private property rights have been altered. Third increasing rather than diminishing marginal returns may occur. And fourth, networks have become important.

Supply Chain Decomposition

The *Encyclopaedia Britannica* went from a peak of $650 million in revenue and a sales force of 2,300 in 1989 to a point where today it won't release financial figures and has only about 300 employees. What happened? The content of encyclopedias is now provided online, making the door-to-door sales force obsolete. This same phenomenon has occurred to virtually every supply chain.

Consider Figure 16.1, which shows part of the supply chain of a newspaper. Before the Internet, journalists and advertisers sent their articles and advertisements to copyeditors and then to the editors, to the printing press, to delivery, and finally to the customer. But in the wake of the Internet, newspapers and magazines offer online versions so that readers can forego the hard copy of the material. Moreover, specific parts of the newspaper or magazine, such as columnists and want ads, can be obtained separately.

Prior to the 1990s, a sales force, a system of branches, a printing press, a chain of stores, or a delivery fleet could serve as strategic assets in creating barriers to entry. By the 1990s, these often became liabilities. For example, in banking, people used to have to go to the bank building to conduct business. With the advent of automated teller machines (ATMs), people were provided the opportunity not to have to wait in line for a teller to provide service. Now ATMs are also located independently of bank buildings so that consumers can do banking business without even visiting the bank building. Most banking can be done from home via the Internet.

The result of the technological changes is that the information content of a good can be distinguished from the physical product. When the information content of a product can be separated from the physical product, the business is fundamentally different than when they are inseparable. The information content of a newspaper no longer has to be tied to the actual physical newspaper; the information content of an automobile purchase does not have to be tied to an auto dealership; the information content of banking does not have to be tied to the physical presence of a bank.

Music is no longer tied to a physical product such as a CD. Napster was one of the first to recognize the possibility of profiting on the phenomenon of P2P sharing (peer to peer). Napster specialized exclusively in music in the form of MP3 files and created a system whose popularity generated an enormous selection of music to download. Prior to the downloading of music, the music was tied to the physical product; you couldn't listen to music without the physical device.[3]

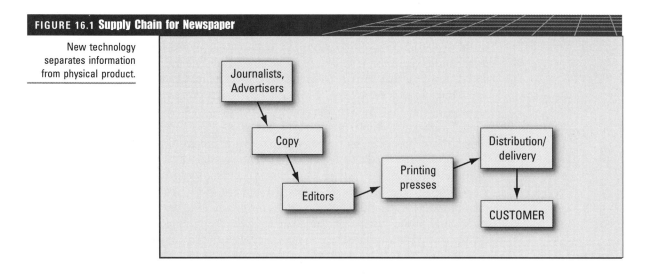

FIGURE 16.1 Supply Chain for Newspaper

New technology separates information from physical product.

Intellectual Property Rights and Knowledge Businesses

The separation of physical product and information changes the allocation of private property rights. It is more difficult to "own" information and almost impossible to enforce the ownership. Suppose you order a pizza to be delivered to your home. When it comes, all your neighbors come over and eat it. You are unlikely to order another pizza if this situation doesn't change. Suppose you come up with a great idea, something like $E = MC^2$. Once the idea is presented, it is a public good. Anyone can use the idea and no one's use will diminish it for someone else to use.

There is a lack of private property rights, a lack of what is called **intellectual property rights**. As soon as an innovation is made public, others can duplicate the process and sell a comparable product, without having to bear the costs of the research that allowed for the innovation. In the case of recorded music or movies, copies can be made at minimal cost, which means that in a free market, the original producers could not sell the products at a high enough price to allow the creative workers to be compensated for their work.

When it is the information that has value and the information can be separated from the physical product, it is more difficult to erect barriers to entry or to create monopolies and maintain property rights. Typically, information is costly to create but then is virtually free to distribute. Once the information is provided, it is a public good because of the difficulty of maintaining the private property rights. Metallica created CDs that its recording company sold through retail outlets. The creation of the initial songs was expensive. Once the first CD was completed, the marginal cost of each additional copy was just pennies. So, if facing a competitive situation, the price of the music would be driven to marginal cost and the start-up costs could not be covered.

This is a problem for any business that has high start-up costs and very small marginal costs. A pharmaceutical company invests billions of dollars in research and development for a single drug. The information and knowledge that go into the drug has great cost and great value. But once the drug is brought to market, the cost of an additional pill (the marginal cost) is virtually zero. If the company faces competition, the price of a pill would be driven to the marginal cost of providing the pill and the large start-up costs would never be paid for.

You can see in Figure 16.2 how the marginal cost declines very rapidly. The cost of research and testing is high. But once the work is completed, the cost of each pill is very, very small. The marginal cost declines rapidly to where it is near zero. The

FIGURE 16.2 **Start-up costs are high and marginal costs very low**

MR = *MC* near zero. The firm is unable to charge a high enough price to earn a profit because rivals drive price to *MC*.

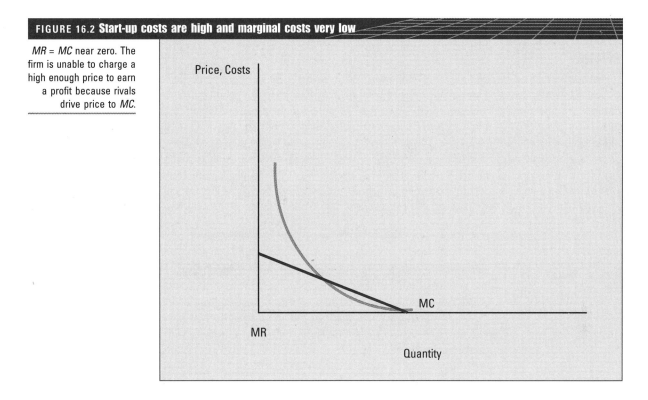

firm has a difficult time setting the price high enough to cover the initial costs; notice that *MR* and *MC* will be equal at about zero, and the resulting price will be lower than initial costs.

Would a company be willing to carry out the R&D and develop pharmaceuticals if once a drug was introduced anyone could produce and sell it? Many people answer no to this question, and this forms the basis of patents, copyrights, and other government-granted monopolies.

The basic argument for patents and copyrights is that in a free market, without protections for intellectual property, there will be underinvestment in research and in creative activity such as writing or recorded music or movies. How can this problem be resolved? Private property rights have to be created and enforced. This has been the argument for patents and copyrights; they confer a property right—a right to the exclusive ownership of the patented product or process or copyright on the creative endeavor.[4]

If perfectly enforced, the government monopoly would create the private property rights and ensure the holders of those rights a return on their investment. But the digital technology means the government monopoly is not enforceable. Music is downloaded and passed among friends and music is pirated and sold for minimal amounts without the artists getting any returns. Movies are similarly downloaded or pirated. Although such sharing is illegal, enforcing the law is so difficult that such downloading and sharing has become common practice. While most people believe shoplifting from a store is stealing and not only illegal but unethical, most people do not believe downloading music without paying is unethical.[5] In the first case, the shoplifters are carrying the physical product out. But, in the second, the information is separated from physical product, and it is the information being carried out.

The Economics of Free If the initial unit of output is very costly to produce and the marginal cost of each additional unit is near zero, and patents and copyrights cannot be

Business Insight

Gillette[6]

Businessman King C. Gillette thought of the disposable razor blade one day while he was shaving with a straight razor that was so worn it could no longer be sharpened. Rather than spending time maintaining the blades, he thought, men could simply discard them when they became dull. The sales of Gillette's first razors were not strong. In its first year, 1903, he sold a total of 51 razors and 168 blades. Over the next two decades, he tried every marketing gimmick he could think of. He sold millions of razors to the Army at a steep discount, hoping the habits soldiers developed at war would carry over to peacetime. He sold razors in bulk to banks so they could give them away with new deposits. Razors were bundled with everything from Wrigley's gum to packets of coffee, tea, spices, and marshmallows. The freebies helped to sell those products, but the tactic helped Gillette even more. By giving away the razors, which were useless by themselves, he was creating demand for disposable blades.

---

enforced, the entrepreneur can not recoup the initial costs. Doesn't this mean that no one will enter an industry characterized by large initial costs and very small marginal costs? Doesn't this also mean that no new drugs will be produced, no music will be recorded, no books will be written, and in general no creative activity will be generated? The answer to these questions is no. Some entrepreneur will figure out a way to profit from the situation.

Business models have emerged to deal with the problem. For instance, give away those items for which private property rights cannot be enforced. Musical groups have found that by giving away their CDs, they earn much more at live concerts. The bands have increased their market size by using the CDs as a free promotional resource; rather than playing small shows in tiny clubs that don't pay very well, they get to play large venues that pay well. A band that sticks to the old way is limited in the audience that will hear them—especially as more and more bands give their music away for free. Fewer people will be interested in going to their concerts or buying their merchandise or joining their fan clubs—when the benefits are so much greater for following other artists who actually give their music away for free.

Websites and search engines have relied on the same business model since inception. They give away their services and earn money on advertising. So the more use they have, the more they can charge advertisers. The fastest-growing parts of the gaming industry are ad-supported casual games online and free-to-try massively multiplayer online games. Virtually everything Google does is free to consumers. In a competitive market, price falls to the marginal cost so if the marginal cost of digital information is near zero, it is logical that digital information will be priced at or near zero.

What about inventors? Won't they lose any incentive to invent if they can't gain a government monopoly—a patent? The business model they must create is one that pays up front. Being "first on the market" is its own reward. The various spinoffs and short-term advantages that accrue to innovators who develop new products provide incentive and profit to innovate. Bundling of products where two or more products are sold as one is a viable option, as are Tie-Ins that wed a product to a service. Television broadcasts are already "tied" to advertising, as are Web pages, e-books, and movies.

Increasing Returns and Networks

When a firm has a building and equipment and alters short-run supplies by increasing the number of employees, the first few employees each generate increasing amounts of additional output. Eventually, however, another employee adds to output but less than previous employees did. As more employees continue to be added, the additional output added continues declining. As we have discussed previously, this is called diminishing marginal returns. The law of diminishing marginal returns states that as a variable resource is increased in combination with fixed quantities of other resources, marginal productivity will initially rise but eventually will decline. You can't keep adding more and more labor to a fixed amount of capital and land and expect that the labor will continue to be more productive.

Now suppose we look at the diminishing marginal returns in terms of a simple equation:

$$Q = f(K^*L)$$

where K^* means that the capital is fixed for a period of time. For instance, a managerial consulting company has an office with equipment and hires additional consultants in order to generate more results. As more and more consultants are added, the law of diminishing marginal returns applies. The capital is the buildings and equipment, and it is fixed for as long as the consulting company is constrained to that office. Suppose, however, that new technology enables more consultants to work out of the office without any loss in productivity. Then, the equation becomes something like

$$Q = f[(1 + a)K^*L]$$

In essence, the fixed capital is expanded by the new technology. The new knowledge alters the fixity of capital, which in turn alters diminishing marginal returns. Now if a doesn't change, diminishing returns still applies, but at a different level than it occurred when $a = 0$. If a changes each period, then each additional worker is adding increasing amounts of additional output rather than decreasing amounts. This is called **increasing returns**.

The comparison of increasing returns and diminishing returns is illustrated in Figure 16.3. Combining additional resources with a fixed amount of capital eventually leads to a decline in the productivity of the resources. This is diminishing returns. If that capital is increased as well, then adding more resources with that capital need not cause diminishing returns. It could cause productivity to rise. This is increasing returns. The point at which diminishing returns would set in if capital remains fixed doesn't occur when capital is embellished by new knowledge. The implication of increasing returns is that the bigger a firm becomes, the larger it is still likely to become. The more of something there is, the more valuable each

FIGURE 16.3 Increasing and Diminishing Returns.

In Figure 16.3(a), the average product curves are drawn. These indicate how adding more workers to a fixed quantity of capital leads to diminishing returns—the downward-sloping curves. But as the quantity of capital is increased, the product curve shifts out. This reflects increasing returns. In Figure 16.3(b), the average cost curves are shown. These also show diminishing returns in their U-shape, but as capital is increased, the curves shift out, showing that more output leads to lower average costs—increasing returns.

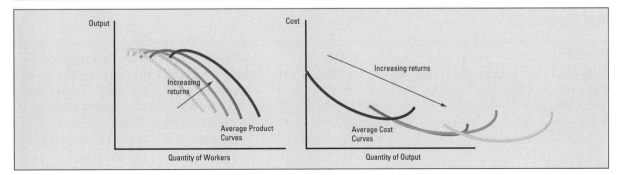

additional one becomes. So if the world is one of increasing returns, a monopoly is likely to control each market since the larger firm can drive smaller ones out of business.

A related aspect of the knowledge economy often discussed is **network effects or network externalities**. The idea of a network can be illustrated by comparing fax machines to refrigerators. The first fax machine ever produced was worth little because there was no one to send a fax to. Each additional fax machine sold added value to every fax machine sold before it because it adds to the network of fax machines. The externality is the value imposed on all other machines when someone purchases a machine. Therefore, like a snowball rolling down a snow-covered hill, the bigger the snowball is, the bigger it gets. As more of us bought fax machines, more of us wanted fax machines—to talk to those who already had them. This is not the case with refrigerators; there is no network of refrigerators.

Network externalities refers to the idea that the benefits to an individual of joining a network go to every member of the network, not just the member joining. Suppose that the value of a network to each individual member rises as the number of members rises. Specifically, suppose that value is proportional to the number of users who can interconnect, so that if there are n users, the value of the membership is proportional to $n(n - 1) = n^2 - n$. If the value of a network to a single user is \$1 for each other user on the network, then a network of size 20 has a value of $(20 \times \$20) - \$20 = \$380$, whereas a network of size 200 has a value of $(200 \times \$200) - \$200 = \$40,000 - \$200 = \$39,800$.

Thus, if an innovator can package his innovation in the form of a network and experience increasing returns, a substantial profit potential can exist. Moreover, with increasing returns, once out in front, the network can gain market share faster than can rivals at least until another innovator changes the network or alters the cost of switching to a different network. WordPerfect was originally the leading software typing program. Initially, few people wanted to switch from WordPerfect to Word. But as Microsoft reduced the costs of changing, more and more people jumped ship.

Internal Organization and Knowledge

The organization of a business is often thought of in terms of a production facility where capital equipment, workers, and raw materials are combined into manufacturing some physical entity. Employees are either production or nonproduction workers. Production workers do the actual work in the factory, while nonproduction workers are the managers and others who make up overhead. But production workers do other tasks that are more important than just monitoring, tasks that have become crucial in the knowledge economy. In the early 1960s, these nonproduction workers began to be called **knowledge workers**.[7] Now, this term is universally used to describe people who deal with information and knowledge.

Business Insight

The Water Cooler

It used to be that management considered conversations by the water cooler to be time-wasters. Now, many see this as valuable time being used to share experiences. In addition to valuing informal communication, Intel takes a deliberate approach to knowledge worker productivity by studying social networking and improving work processes based on the results. In 2003, Tom Davenport was a key contributor to Intel's Information Work Productivity Council study. The study identified what companies are doing to improve knowledge work productivity and concluded, among other things, that a company's best performers were proficient at building effective knowledge networks on the job. Would this council consider smoking breaks as equally productive? Probably not because it excludes the nonsmokers.[8]

Markets versus Authority with Knowledge Workers

While information is continuously becoming less expensive to process, store, and transmit, the knowledge needed to create value is becoming increasingly distributed. Distributed knowledge is knowledge that is not possessed by any single mind. Single pieces of information belong to individuals, and these pieces of information have to be aggregated to form something of value. The information emerges from the aggregation of individuals and can be mobilized for productive purposes. Back in the 1940s, this is what the economist Friedrich Hayek argued markets could do and central planning could not.[9] Hayek criticized socialism and central planning as being inefficient in that it could not bring forth the information necessary for production. Only free markets could do that.

Is this the case with firms in the knowledge economy? The growth of knowledge workers and the increasingly distributed knowledge would seem to challenge traditional authority relations. The knowledge worker may be the only one able to make decisions regarding his specific knowledge, and so knowledge workers have more bargaining power and can create hold-up problems. Moreover, the specialist nature of knowledge work implies that employers know little or nothing of the actions of specialist employees, thus making the exercise of authority through direction inefficient. Authority means that a superior owns the property rights to decisions; the authority can restrict the decisions of a subordinate, overrule him, and even fire him. Thus, although decisions may be delegated, the ownership of those decisions belong to an authority in a firm. If decision rights are granted to the employees, what is the role of authority? Is the role of the manager obsolete and is the use of hierarchy and authority inefficient in the knowledge economy?

Hierarchy can be justified as an efficient way to deal with free rider and moral hazard problems inherent in teams. It may also be an efficient method of allocating competence (tournaments, for example). But in a firm based on the knowledge of employees, does hierarchy make sense? Does ownership of decision rights in the knowledge firm differ from ownership rights in a factory firm?

The individual worker owns his knowledge but contracts to rent the use of this knowledge to the firm; it is the task of the manager to elicit that information efficiently so that it can be aggregated with the rest of the distributed knowledge. In the free market the distributed knowledge accumulates in the price. But in a firm where there is no price and no free market interaction among knowledge workers, how is the distributed knowledge accumulated? This could be the primary role of a manager in a knowledge firm.[10] The manager may be the elicitor of knowledge.

Monitoring is less important, or at least more costly, to do in the knowledge economy. If a worker knows more than the manager, it is pointless for the manager to monitor the work. In the extreme case the agent's behavior may be observable, but the monitor does not know what the agent is doing. In this situation, the decision rights and residual income may be given to the agent rather than the principal. Managing the so-called knowledge worker is essentially no different than any other management. The idea is to incentivize the employee to produce what is desired. But if knowledge-based companies, such as Google, perform nearly every task with teams, then they have to deal with free riding, and hierarchy is one way of dealing with free riding.

When managing in what seems to be a new situation, think of what makes nations successful. Well-defined and enforced private property rights and economic freedom are what leads to successful nations. Similarly for successful firms—whether factory-type firms or knowledge-based firms—well-defined and enforced private property rights and economic freedom are necessary. Ownership of responsibilities, tasks assignments, and the like must be clear. Who makes what decisions must be well defined. And once the property rights are well defined, let the owners improve the value of their assets. Provide economic freedom by not interfering with decisions or by micromanaging situations

Innovators   Where do we find most innovators: in new, upstart firms or in large, dominant firms? Business history is primarily a replay of a company with a wealth of assets, innovative products, strong reputation, financial resources, and powerful distribution channels whose market position is eroded or overtaken by companies whose resource bases are seemingly much smaller. Small firms are often the result of an innovation. Canon, for example, entered as a small firm and took market share of copiers from Xerox; Sony followed RCA in television; and CNN was the upstart as compared to the networks in news programming. A frequent explanation for this ability is that small firms are more nimble and less bureaucratic than large ones. It is often said that large companies become fat and happy and fall asleep, while small companies are hungry or lean and mean. An additional explanation lies in the conspiracy theories about how dominant firms keep innovations hidden away and even buy up and hide the innovations of small upstart firms (This argument is examined in Chapter 21.)

Though superficially appealing, these arguments fail to answer a fundamental question: Why are established firms systematically less able to innovate or break with established practice than new entrants or marginal firms? Part of the reason is the likelihood that entrepreneurs start new firms rather than provide innovations to the large firms.

In many situations it may be appropriate for the established firm to delay entering a new venture until some upstart has shown there is a market. By virtue of well-established reputation, distribution channels, and other attributes, dominant firms may not be afraid of losing market share. Suppose that the dominant firm, firm A, would win 80 percent of the new product's sales and the upstart firm B only 20 percent if each rolled out the fruits of their R&D on the same day. Moreover, suppose the dominant firm expects to lose very little market share by delaying introduction but that the new firm would gain nothing if it introduced the product later than the dominant firm. In this situation, it would be a surprise for the dominant firm to be the first mover.

Another explanation of why dominant firms tend to lag with the introduction of innovations is called the sunk cost effect. Sunk costs, as noted earlier, are expenditures that cannot be recouped. You purchase tickets to a play for $50 and there is no reselling of the tickets. Whether or not you go to the play, the $50 has been spent. Suppose you are invited to dinner at a friend's house the same night as the play. If you would rather go to dinner but don't because you purchased the tickets, then you are failing to ignore sunk costs. This is the sunk cost effect. The sunk-cost effect arises because a firm that has already committed to a particular technology has made investments in resources and organizational capabilities that are likely to be specific to that technology. If the firm fails to switch technologies because of these prior expenditures, then it is experiencing the sunk cost effect. This is why marginal costs and marginal benefits have been stressed throughout this text—they do not include sunk costs. Suppose research and development (R&D) requires an up-front investment of $1 million and then annual expenditures of $2 million until the product is finally brought to market. Once spent, the firm must decide whether to continue the R&D. Its decision depends on whether the additional expected benefits are larger or smaller than the additional costs. But note: Once an expenditure has been made, it does not enter in to the decision to continue spending. The expenditures is a sunk cost.

In the early 1950s, steelmaking was changed by the oxygen furnace. The furnace reduced milling time to 40 minutes as compared with the 6 to 8 hours needed with the open-hearth (OH) furnace that had been the industry standard since World War I. Despite the apparent superiority of the oxygen furnace, few American steelmakers adopted it. Throughout the 1950s, U.S. steelmakers added nearly 50 million additional tons of the old furnace (OH) capacity; they did not begin to replace their OH furnaces with the new furnaces until the late 1960s. Meanwhile, steelmakers in the rest of the world were building new plants incorporating state-of-the-art technology. The cost advantage afforded by this new technology was a key reason why Japanese and Korean steelmakers were able to penetrate the American domestic market. Why did American steelmakers continue to invest in a seemingly inefficient technology? American steel firms had developed a considerable amount of specific know-how related to the old technology, but the investment in this know-how was sunk. It should have made no difference to the decision to switch to new technology. Was the reluctance to change due to managerial ignorance—the mistake of not ignoring sunk costs? According to one study it was.[11]

Actually, what is a sunk cost for the firm might not be a sunk cost for individuals involved with the firm. The CEO may have to justify costs to shareholders or the Board of Directors. Underlings may have vested interests in maintaining the current technology—their jobs may be based on it. Suppliers may realize that a technological change by the firm would mean a loss of business for them. In such cases, there is a reluctance to adopt the newest technology not because of the failure to ignore sunk costs but because of the costs to individuals within the firm.

In the case of the steel companies, because the new technology used relatively more pig iron than the old technology, a steel plant that was located closer to sources of pig iron would gain large operating cost reductions by adopting the new technology. A change to the new technology might require new plants to be built at different locations. This could cause a considerable loss of income for many individuals within the firm, suppliers working with the firm, and communities in which the plants were located. Thus, a great deal of pressure (rent seeking) was placed on U.S. steel companies not to change technologies.[12] The Japanese and Korean steelmakers could adopt the newest technology because they started from scratch. There were no special interest groups tied into the old technology. IBM failed to develop personal computers profitably after having invented them because the "mainframe people" within IBM opposed the growth of the PC group. The mainframe group saw the PC group as a potential threat to their internal power.[13]

This discussion is not meant to imply that the large, incumbent firms don't innovate or introduce new technology first. Microsoft, Hewlett-Packard, and Intel, for example, have been innovators in their respective markets. The point of this discussion, rather, is to look more carefully into the reasons that it is not always the large, dominant firm that is the innovator. On the surface, it might seem that with large market share, deep pockets, and experience, the incumbent firm would always be the innovator and would, therefore, be able to sustain its economic profit seemingly forever. But such a situation is exactly what draws entrepreneurs—a profit opportunity. The entrepreneur figures out a new way of doing what the large firm is doing. In many cases, new firms are created because of an innovation that an entrepreneur believes will enable that firm to wrest profits from the incumbent firm. Positive economic profit creates an incentive for innovation; the more successful a firm is, the more likely the competition for that firm will increase.

Industrial or Innovation Policy?

1. Is there a need for government to pick winners and losers?
2. What objections to the industrial policy suggested in the essay do you have? If you have none, how do you support a government selecting losers and winners when the free market does that type of thing so well?

A government picking winners and losers is essentially a central planning model. It does not work. The government cannot know in advance which technologies will succeed and which will not. The only way that can be determined is for the free market to judge. Let the free market work without government intervention, and all of the distributed knowledge that exists will be captured in prices. That will determine success and failure. When government chooses, there are seen effects and unseen effects. The unseen effects are the technological innovations that would have occurred had the government not intervened in the system. Some amazing breakthrough might not take place because the government was directing resources elsewhere.

But what about ARPANET? Without having the free market take over, the Internet would have ended up like France's Minitaur system. It is defunct. No one used it to expand innovations or create new and different technologies. Perhaps government can finance the start-up and then step away as in the case of the Internet. This still suggests that government can pick winners and losers.

How, without the financing of government, can these highly expensive projects ever get off the ground? Just as in the music world where P2P sharing essentially destroyed private property rights on digitized music, the firm or band will have to provide a different business model. With huge start-up and very small marginal costs, a firm cannot earn a profit competing on marginal cost. The firm must earn money on a different stage or up front. The bands use the digital music as advertising and make their money from concerts. A pharmaceutical makes its money from patents. But without patents, could the pharmaceutical make a return by branding its product and earning its profits up front?

Summary

1. The knowledge economy refers to the innovations and technologies that enable the collection, dissemination, and use of information.
2. A winner-takes-all means that one firm or one technology dominates the market.
3. First mover advantages refer to being able to dominate a market by being the first firm to enter the market. The first firm to obtain a patent might be able to restrict others from entering the business and might be able to dominate the market for a long time. The first network to experience positive feedback might be able to achieve economies of scale and restrict entry.
4. The advantages of being first or even being the winner in a winner-takes-all situation is not necessarily a long-lived event. The incentives for others to take some of the economic profit from the dominant firm or network increase over time. Technological change enables new entrants to leapfrog the incumbents or to compete with the incumbents.
5. Often the incumbent dominant firms are slower to innovate or introduce new technology than are new or upstart firms. One reason is called the sunk cost effect. This means that existing, dominant firms have invested heavily in the status quo and do not want to alter it. In addition, in many cases a subset of employees within the firm will be harmed by the adoption of new technology and thus will work to impede its adoption.

Key Terms

Intellectual property rights
Increasing returns

Network effects or externalities
Knowledge workers

Exercises

1. If the downsizing trend of the late 1980s and early 1990s was due to technological change, what should it mean for individual firm costs? If the downsizing trend was a mistake—firms cutting employees and increasing productivity in the short term only to suffer long-term reductions in productivity—what should it mean for individual firm costs?

2. Several cities are associated with specific industries: Akron with tires, Sunnyvale with computer chips, Orlando with tourism, Hollywood with movies. Why do such centers emerge?

3. Two networks are vying for dominance in the HDTV network, the United States and Europe. It has been said that the winner is likely to be determined by economies of scale in manufacturing televisions. Explain.

4. Amazon.com was the first mover in online book sales. It patented the one-click purchasing system. Barnes and Noble was a later entrant with BN.com. Is this a battle with a "winner-takes-all" outcome? Why or why not?

5. In early 1998, S3 was a small microchip-design firm with a big problem. The company knew that Intel's patent wall would eventually stall its high-performance graphic-microchip business. S3 hatched a plan to fix the problem. It outbid Intel to acquire the patents of bankrupt microchip maker Exponential Technologies. In doing so, S3 acquired a patent that predated Intel's. Explain why S3 spent $10 million to purchase a bankrupt firm. What is the implication for the dominance of Intel?

6. In 1994, the $3.5 billion Avery Dennison Corporation developed a new film for use in product labeling. The film unit won a contract to provide the labels for Procter & Gamble shampoo bottles and appeared to have huge growth potential. But an analysis of patent activity indicated that Dow Chemical was beginning to move into this business. Should Avery commit the huge resources needed to exploit the market opportunity for the film unit?

7. Consider the following payoffs in a situation where the two firms have to choose simultaneously.

		Firm B	
	Strategy	**Yes**	**No**
Firm A	Yes	Firm A: $30 Firm B: $10	Firm A: $20 Firm B: $15
	No	Firm A: $20 Firm B: $15	Firm A: $2 Firm B: $4

a. How much would firm A pay to go first?
b. How much would firm B pay to go first?
c. Can you set up the payoff so that there is no first mover advantage?

8. How is the competition between Blu-ray and HD similar to the competition between VHS and Beta?

9. Explain why an organizational structure other than hierarchy might make sense in the knowledge economy. Can you justify a hierarchical organization?

10. What are intellectual property rights? How are they different from property rights to physical assets? Why has digitization been a hazard to intellectual property rights?

11. How would you encourage innovation when whatever is invented or created is expensive to invent or create and has a very low cost of copying and distribution?

12. Why do economists tend to disagree with protectionist measures that interfere with trade and also support patents and copyrights?

13. What does it mean to say that information can be separated from its physical product? What does this imply for pricing the information?

14. Why are so many digital items given away for free?

15. Haven't there always been "knowledge" workers, people who do more than what a robot could do? Why then is such a big deal made of the "knowledge economy" and the "knowledge worker" in recent years?

16. What leads to a patent race? Is such a race productive or unproductive? Explain.

17. "The beauty of markets is that, over time, they tend to ensure that both people and money end up employed in the highest-value enterprises. In corporations, decisions about allocating resources are made by people with a vested interest in the status quo." Alan Murray, *Wall Street Journal,*

August 21, 2010, Weekend. Evaluate this statement. Is it true? Explain.

18. It is often said that in today's world, gale-like market forces—rapid globalization, accelerating innovation, relentless competition—have intensified what economist Joseph Schumpeter called the forces of "creative destruction," so that even the best-managed companies aren't protected from this destructive clash between whirlwind change and corporate inertia. What does this mean? Would you agree that even the best managed companies are not protected?

19. British economist Ronald Coase laid out the basic logic of the managed corporation in his 1937 work, *The Nature of the Firm*. He argued that corporations were necessary because of what he called "transaction costs." It was simply too complicated and too costly to search for and find the right worker at the right moment for any given task, or to search for supplies, or to renegotiate prices, police performance, and protect trade secrets in an open marketplace. The corporation might not be as good at allocating labor and capital as the marketplace; it made up for those weaknesses by reducing transaction costs. What implications does Wikipedia have for this view of the firm?

20. According to some management gurus, mechanisms will have to be created for harnessing the wisdom of crowds. Feedback loops will need to be built that allow products and services to constantly evolve in response to new information. Change, innovation, adaptability—all have to become orders of the day. Explain how markets inside the firm might be the solution to these challenges.

CHAPTER NOTES

1. This case is based on Stephen Ezell, "The Economist's Strange Attack on Industrial Policy," August 25, 2010, Progressive Fix, www.progressivefix.com/the-economist%E2%80%99s-strange-attack-on-industrial-policy, accessed September 4, 2010.
2. As an example, notice the subtitle in Don Tapscott and Anthony D. Williams, *Wikinomics: How Mass Collaboration Changes Everything* (New York: Penguin, 2006).
3. Lawsuits by the rock band Metallica and other artists eventually put Napster out of business. Roxio purchased the Napster name and currently operates a pay for selection downloading company. Since the original Napster was driven from the market, personal computer (PC) makers—Gateway, Dell, HP/Compaq, and others—have packed their machines with software to download music and movies and, of course, iTunes found a way to provide the service at a very low cost and make a large profit.
4. It is interesting that while economists generally agree that protectionism or barriers to trade is inefficient, they support patents and copyrights. While tariffs and quotas rarely raise the price of goods by more than 30 or 40 percent, patents on prescription drugs typically raise the price of protected products by 300 to 400 percent, or more, above the marginal cost. In some cases, patent protected drugs sell for hundreds or thousands of times as much as the marginal cost. In the case of copyrighted material, recorded music and video material that could be transferred at zero cost over the Internet instead command a substantial price when sold as CDs, DVDs, or licensed downloads. Copyrighted software commands even higher prices.
5. Diane Smiroldo, "Shoplifting vs. Downloading," *NewYorkMetroParents*, September 26, 2007, www.nymetroparents.com/newarticle.cfm?colid=8984, accessed May 1, 2008.
6. Chris Anderson, "Free! Why $0.00 Is the Future of Business," *Wired Magazine*, February 25, 2008, www.wired.com/techbiz/it/magazine/16-03/ff_free.
7. Peter Drucker, *Landmarks of Tomorrow* (New York: Harper, 1959).
8. Doug Cooper and Thomas Davenport, "Are Your Workers Hanging out at the Water Cooler? Relax, It's a Good Thing," *The Globe and Mail* (Canada), December 10, 2007, p. B9.
9. Friedrich Hayek, "The Use of Knowledge in Societies," *American Economic Review*, 35, no. 4 (September 1945): 519–530.
10. Some firms are using internal markets to accumulate the distributed knowledge. See Chapter 18.
11. W. Adams and H. Mueller, "The Steel Industry," in W. Adams, ed., *The Structure of American Industry*, 7th ed. (New York: Macmillan, 1986), p. 102.
12. Sharon Oster, "The Diffusion of Innovation Among Steel Firms: The Basic Oxygen Furnace," *Bell Journal of Economics*, 13 (Spring 1982): 45–68.
13. P. Carrol, *Big Blue: The Unmaking of IBM* (New York: Crown, 1993).

CHAPTER 17

The Corporate Form and the Cost of Capital

Free Capital

The following statements were taken from annual reports listed on the Internet.

Flynt Fabrics, Inc. was losing money due to its high inventory levels and long lead times. An internal analysis found that Flynt Fabrics' actual production time was about two days but the company carried 19 days worth of inventories. The executives knew that if the company could deliver products very rapidly with lower inventories, the company's competitive position would improve.[1]

By integrating edge routing, ethernet aggregation, and subscriber management into a single, scalable platform, the SmartEdge Multi-Service Edge Router (MSER) allows service providers to deliver video, voice, and data services on a single, converged broadband network. The innovative, purpose-built SmartEdge platform also reduces capital and operational expenses by reducing the number of network elements and simplifying the network architecture.[2] Yankee Group analyzed the total cost of ownership of building a multi-play network and uncovered that integrating edge routing, ethernet aggregation, and subscriber management yields measurable TCO advantages. The highlights of the study are[3]:

> Total TCO Advantage: 22%
> Capital Expenditure: 20.9%
> Operational Expenditure: 52.6%

Level 5 Networks invented EtherFabric, a complete solution of software, specialized silicon and high performance NIC hardware that allows Ethernet Networks to be used as high-performance server interconnects that are future-proof even as performance requirements continue to increase. According to the company, EtherFabric is the only Ethernet-based, performance-enhanced interconnect that maintains 100% binary compatibility with existing standards, while providing easy scalability to 10Gb/sec and beyond. One of the important characteristics of EtherFabric, according to the following is the reduced capital expenditures.

continues

CONTINUED

Reduced Capital and Operational Expense—Along with full backward compatibility with existing standards, which dramatically decreases deployment costs, EtherFabric reduces the number of servers required by up to 50 percent. This reduction is a direct result of EtherFabric requiring less computing resources from the host server CPU to transfer network data, while also enabling the communication between servers to occur both more quickly and at higher speeds.[4]

1. Why are these firms focused on reducing capital?
2. Isn't capital necessary for carrying out business?

Economic Profit and the Capital Markets

It takes money to operate a business. An entrepreneur has to lease or buy buildings and purchase materials as well as hire employees. Where does the entrepreneur get the money? He can use his own money and he can entice others—investors and lenders— to supply it. The money raised is called financial capital or just capital, and the cost of the money to the firm is called the cost of capital. The cost of capital is determined in the capital market, just as the price of any item is determined in the market for that item.

Consider a simple illustration of the capital market—the demand for and supply of capital. The demand for capital is the quantity of capital the firm demands at each price. Suppose the firm has five potential projects for which it must raise capital. The expected returns on each project as well as the amount of funds required for each are listed in Table 17.1.

According to Table 17.1, if the cost of capital is 14 percent, then only $2 million capital is demanded. If the cost of capital is 12 percent, then another $3 million is demanded or a total of $5 million is demanded. If the cost of funds is 10 percent, then a total of $6 million is demanded; at 8 percent, a total of $10 million is demanded.

Suppose the firm can raise funds from four different sources in the amounts and at the costs given in Table 17.2. No one will provide any funds at 6 percent; a source will provide $3 million at 8 percent; $3 million more at 10 percent; and so on.

So the firm can get enough at 8 percent to fund project 1. If it is willing to pay 10 percent, it can then get enough to also fund project 2. Beyond that, the projects would not be profitable. The firm will purchase a total of $6 million of capital. It will purchase $3 million of capital from source 1 at 8 percent. It will also purchase $3 million from source 2 at 10 percent.

The cost of capital is a combination of its payment to the different sources. This combination is called the **weighted average cost of capital (WACC)**.

Table 17.1		
PROJECT	**RETURN EXPECTED**	**FUNDS NEEDED**
1	12%	$3 million
2	6%	$3 million
3	14%	$2 million
4	10%	$1 million
5	8%	$4 million

Table 17.2		
CAPITAL SOURCE	**COST**	**FUNDS OFFERED**
none	6%	0
1	8%	$3 million
2	10%	$3 million
3	12%	$1 million
4	16%	$5 million

WACC = 8%(share of total funds raised provided by source 1) + 10%(share of total funds raised provided by source 2)

$$.08(1/2) + .10(1/2) = .09$$

The cost of capital to this firm is 9 percent. In general, the cost of capital to a firm is the weighted average cost of its debt and its equity. The cost of debt is the interest paid on the debt, and that interest may differ according to the type and length of the debt. The cost of ownership is the amount of expected profits the firm must return to investors to entice them to invest in the company. Thus,

WACC = [cost of debt](debt/total capital) + [cost of equity](equity/total capital)

The cost of capital is determined in the capital markets by the interaction of buyers and sellers. Capital markets do what other markets do—ensure that resources are allocated to their highest valued use. When the market is allowed to work, when private property rights exist, and when people can voluntary trade, capital flows to where it will earn the highest return.

Stocks

Whether you say shares, equity, or stock doesn't matter; these terms all mean the same thing—ownership of a piece of a company. Technically, owning a share of stock means that you own a share of everything the firm owns—every item of furniture, every piece of equipment, every building. In actuality, you are entitled only to a share of the company's earnings; you can't walk into the company's headquarters and walk out with a chair. There are two main types of stock: common and preferred stock. When people talk about stocks, typically they are referring to common stock. Preferred shares usually guarantee a fixed annual payment, or **dividend**. Common stock may or may not provide such a payment; that choice is at the discretion of the company. The firm's executives may choose to keep the profit and use it for other projects, or it can distribute the profits to the owners of common shares. Its decision should depend on which use provides the greatest marginal benefits. A firm sells or issues shares of stock, and the dollars raised is the firm's capital. Once the shares are owned by investors, they can be bought and sold, in what is called the secondary market. Transactions in the secondary market do not provide capital to the firm; yet, the price of stocks determined in the secondary market is vitally important to the firm since if the stock price is high, it is less expensive for the firm to raise a given amount of new capital. Yet, the price of stocks determined in the secondary market is vitally important to the firm; it makes it less expensive to raise new capital if the stock price is high.

Demand for and Supply of Stocks   The prices of stocks vary from day to day and even minute to minute due to changes in demand and supply. The demand for stocks

Business Insight

Stocks

Most newspapers report stock prices. The reports look something like the following:

| | | | | Yield | | | | | | | Net |
52W high	52W low	Stock	Ticker	Div	%	P/E	Vol 00s	High	Low	Close	chg
45.39	19.75	ResMed	RMD			52.5	3831	42.00	39.51	41.50	−1.90
11.63	3.55	RevlonA	REV				162	6.09	5.90	6.09	+0.12
77.25	55.13	RioTinlo	RTP	2.30	3.2		168	72.75	71.84	72.74	+0.03
31.31	16.63	RitchieBr	RBA			20.9	15	24.49	24.29	24.29	−0.01
8.44	1.75	RiteAid	RAD				31028	4.50	4.20	4.31	+0.21
38.63	18.81	RobtHalf	RHI			26.5	6517	27.15	26.50	26.50	+0.14
51.25	27.69	Rockwell	ROK	1.02	2.1	14.5	6412	47.99	47.08	47.54	+0.24
Column 1	Column 2	Column 3	Column 4	Column 5	Column 6	Column 7	Column 8	Column 9	Column 10	Column 11	Column 12

- Columns 1 and 2: 52-week high and low. These are the highest and lowest prices at which the stock has traded over the previous 52 weeks (one year).
- Column 3: Company name and type of stock. This column gives the name of the company. If there are no special symbols or letters following the name, the stock is common stock. Different symbols imply different classes of shares. For example, "pf" means that the shares are preferred stock.
- Column 4: Ticker symbol. This is the unique alphabetic name that identifies the stock. If you are looking for stock quotes online, you use the ticker symbol.
- Column 5: Dividend per share. This indicates the annual dividend payment per share. If this space is blank, the company does not currently pay out dividends.
- Column 6: Dividend yield. This gives the percentage return provided by the dividend. It is calculated as annual dividends per share divided by price per share.
- Column 7: Price/earnings ratio. This is calculated by dividing the current stock price by the earnings per share for the last four quarters.
- Column 8: Trading volume. This figure gives the total number of shares traded for the day, in hundreds. To get the actual number traded, add "00" to the end of the number listed.
- Columns 9 and 10: High and low for the day. This indicates the price range within which the stock has traded that day.
- Column 11: Close. The close is the last trading price recorded when the market closed for the day. If the closing price is up or down more than 5 percent from the previous day's close, the entire listing for that stock is given in bold type.
- Column 12: Net change. This is the dollar value change in the stock price from the previous day's closing price.

Stock indexes are also reported in newspapers and other sources. A stock index is a measure of the price movements of a group of stocks. The most commonly referenced indexes are the Dow Jones Industrial Average (DJIA), the Standard & Poor's 500 (S&P 500), and the Nasdaq Composite Index. The DJIA contains 30 companies, the S&P 500 includes 500 companies, and the Nasdaq Composite includes all companies listed on the Nasdaq stock exchange. The S&P 500 tries to represent all major areas of the U.S. economy. It does not use the 500 largest companies, but rather includes 500 companies that are widely owned and represent all sectors of the economy. The stocks in the index are chosen by the S&P Index Committee, which typically makes between 25 and 50 changes every year. The Nasdaq Composite Index represents all the stocks that are traded on the Nasdaq stock market. Most are technology and Internet-stocks (small-cap stocks), which are often excluded from the big indexes.

comes from investors—individuals, mutual funds, and other institutions like insurance companies—who are looking for the highest return on their funds. The return to a shareholder is the dividend the stock pays plus the appreciation in the price of the stock. Suppose, for instance, you purchased Microsoft at $5 per share in 1997 and then sold it for $100 per share in 2007. Your appreciation would have been $95 per share over the 10-year period. Since Microsoft paid no dividends during this period, your total return would have been the appreciation. If it had paid dividends as well, then the return would have been higher than $95.

The supply of a stock comes from current shareholders who want to sell their shares of stock (called the secondary market) and the new issues of stock (called the primary market). For one investor to sell a share of a particular company's stock to another investor, the buyer has to expect that the purchase of this stock will return more than any other comparable purchase, and the seller has to expect that the purchase of other financial assets, goods, or services with the money obtained from the sale of this stock will generate more satisfaction than holding onto the shares of this stock. An important point here is that buyers and sellers are comparing all possible investments and seeking the one that they think will give them the best return. Buyers and sellers evaluate the firm's stock on the basis of a comparison with comparable investments. A comparable investment is an investment that has the same features, such as risk and ease of selling (called liquidity), as the one being considered.

What causes the demand for and supply of a stock to change? It is primarily the expected performance of the company. When investors change their expectations so that they now expect the price of the stock to rise more than they previously did, more investors will want to buy. At the same time, fewer will want to sell, and the price will rise.

Firms are required to report earnings (accounting profit) each quarter (for most companies, the end of March, June, September, and December). Stock market analysts and investors use these quarterly reports to evaluate how well their previous forecasts of the firm's performance match what has actually been happening. When the quarterly results are not consistent with the investors' forecasts or expectations, the investors will revise their expectations of future performance up or down. If the earnings reports indicate lower earnings than had been expected, the forecasts will be revised downward and the stock price will most likely decline. When a firm does better than it had been expected to do, the forecasts will be revised upward and the stock price will most likely rise.

As an illustration, consider what a report such as the following would indicate: *Google stock soared Friday, continuing Wall Street's love affair with the company after its earnings easily topped estimates.* The report states that investors realized that the revenues they had expected Google to earn were less than what Google actually earned, and so they began to think that the value of the company was higher than they expected—they wanted to own more of it as a result. In addition, fewer owners of Google stock wanted to sell the stock than before the report. As a result, the supply of Google stock on the secondary market declined.

Market prices incorporate all the information that buyers and sellers use to make their buying and selling decisions. Stock prices reflect or incorporate all relevant information about the companies, expectations of the company's performance, the economy's performance, and any other event that could affect the firm.

Bonds

A bond (sometimes called a fixed-income security or debt security) is an IOU issued by a borrower to a lender. When you buy a newly issued bond, you are lending money to the borrower. When you purchase a bond that is not a new issue, you are not buying that bond from the issuing firm. You are choosing to own a portion of the debt obligation of a company because you think the return on that bond will exceed what else you might have done with the money used to purchase the bond. There is a specified time at which the borrower will repay your loan; this is the maturity date. In most cases the bond's face or par value is $1,000; this is the amount that the lender will be repaid once the bond matures. The borrower pays the lender a fixed amount, called a coupon, each year. These interest payments are usually made every six months until the bond matures.

The rate of interest that must be paid—that is, the coupon rate—depends on how risky the borrower is. U.S. government bonds are considered no-risk investments because it is so unlikely that the United States will default on its obligations. Corporations must offer a higher yield than the government in order to entice lenders to purchase corporate bonds because corporate bonds are more risky. On average, a bond carries less risk than a share of stock because in the event of the firm's collapse, the shareholders cannot get anything until all debtholders have been paid.

Business Insight

Bonds

In every financial newspaper there are bond tables similar to the one shown here.

Corporate	Coupon	Mat.Date	Bid $	Yld%
GTE Florida Inc	6.860	Feb 01/28	102.562	6.635
General Motors Corp	8.375	Jul 15/33	76.000	11.205
General Mtrs Acep Corp	8.000	Nov 01/31	98.358	8.152
General Elec Co	5.000	Feb 01/13	100.112	4.979
Ford Mtr Co Del	7.450	Jul 16/31	74.437	10.306
Column 1	Column 2	Column 3	Column 4	Column 5

The columns in the bond table provide the following information:

- Column 1: Issuer. This is the company, state (or province), or country that issued the bond.
- Column 2: Coupon. The coupon refers to the fixed interest rate that the issuer pays to the lender. The coupon rate varies by bond.
- Column 3: Maturity date. This is the date when the borrower will pay the lenders (investors) their principal back. Typically, only the last two digits of the year are quoted: 25 means 2025, 04 is 2004, and so on.
- Column 4: Bid price. This is the price that someone is willing to pay for the bond. It is quoted in relation to 100, no matter what the par value is. Think of the bond price as a percentage: A bid of $93 means that the bond is trading at 93 percent of its par value.
- Column 5: Yield. The yield indicates the annual return until the bond matures. Yield is calculated as the amount of interest paid on a bond divided by the price; it is a measure of the income generated by a bond. If the bond is callable, the yield will be given as "c—," which indicates the year in which the bond can be called. For example c10 means that the bond can be called as early as 2010.

Demand for and Supply of Bonds   The market for bonds is not very different from the stock market, and the two are closely linked. Bond demanders are investors who are looking for the best return on their savings. They will purchase a bond when the return on the bond is expected to be greater than the return on other comparable investments—for instance, better than the return on stocks adjusted for risk. Consider a $100 bond maturing in one year that pays a 5 percent rate of interest, or coupon rate. The bondholder receives $5 per year in interest until the bond matures. If the price of the bond is $100, the same as the face value, then the yield is 5 percent ($5/$100). But if the price of the bond is lower than the face value, say $95, the yield is $10/$95 or 10.52 percent.

The suppliers of bonds are the companies, governments, and other institutions offering new issues of IOUs (primary market) and investors owning previously issued bonds who want to sell (secondary market). If interest rates on other investments rise, the quantity of bonds offering a 5 percent coupon that suppliers are willing and able to sell will rise—the increased supply means the bond price will fall. Bond prices and interest rates are inversely related. Everything else the same, when interest rates rise, bond prices fall. Also, if the expectations of a firm's performance decline, the bond price falls.

Capital Structure

The cost of capital is the cost to a firm of obtaining funds with which it can purchase resources, equipment, buildings, inventories, and so on. As stated above, it is a combination of the debt costs and the cost of equity. **Capital structure** refers to the ratio of debt to equity. Optimal capital structure refers to the specific ratio that minimizes the cost of capital while maximizing the stock price.[5]

The more debt a firm has relative to its equity, the lower is the chance of not being able to make the debt payments and thus failure or bankruptcy becomes more likely. For a firm with 100 percent debt financing, the firm's net revenues (net operating profits after tax [NOPAT] without interest deducted) would have to be larger than interest payments in every period. A firm with a very large percentage of financing that is debt would have a difficult time convincing anyone to purchase shares of ownership. Owners would demand a higher return in order to hold equity, and the cost of equity capital would rise. The smaller the debt, the lower is the burden of such debt payments and the lower the cost of equity capital. It would seem then that there is a trade-off between debt and equity capital—that, in fact, there is some ratio of debt to equity that will minimize the cost of capital.

Since corporations can deduct interest payments from tax payments, a higher debt to equity ratio lowers tax payments. Dividends, on the other hand, are nondeductible. Thus, it makes sense for the firm to increase the debt on the basis of the tax advantages. But, as noted before, increased debt to equity reduces flexibility and thus increases risks. The optimal ratio of debt to equity will be where the marginal revenue of adding more equity equals the marginal cost.

CAPM

A firm's cost of equity capital depends on how risky an investment in the firm is perceived to be. One formulation of the cost of capital is that the cost of capital for a firm, A, is equal to the cost of a risk-free investment plus an equity premium. The typical presentation of this formulation is the capital asset pricing model or CAPM. CAPM states that the expected return on firm A's stock, $E(R_A)$, is equal to the risk-free return, R_f, plus the equity premium. The equity premium is beta, β, times the difference between the expected return on all investment opportunities, $E(R_m)$ and the risk-free return R_f. The idea here is that beta will measure the volatility of the firm's stock relative to the market as a whole—an attempt to measure the opportunity cost of investing in A.

$$E(R_A) = R_f + \beta[E(R_m) - R_f]$$

What goes into the riskiness of a firm? One aspect is how well the stock behaves relative to other stocks. Does it fluctuate a lot or just a very little. In the CAPM equation, is beta smaller or larger than unity? If larger, it fluctuates more than the market as a whole; if smaller, it fluctuates less than the market as a whole.

Another factor is the countries in which the firm does business. Are these countries stable or risky? Country risk refers to the likelihood that changes in the business environment adversely affect operating profits or the value of assets in a specific country. For example, financial factors such as controls on exchange rates, devaluation or regulatory changes, or social upheaval such as mass riots, civil war, and other potential events contribute to companies' operational risks. (Exchange rate risk is discussed in Chapter 20.)

Doing business in different countries exposes a firm to the quality of the governance of each country. The legal system can make it easy to do business or can increase costs and increase risk. In Venezuela it might take months or even years to start a new business, while in Singapore it might take an hour. In the latest report on the *Ease of Doing Business*, Venezuela ranked 164th, the United States third, and Singapore first in ease of doing business.[6] Thus, doing business in Venezuela was significantly more costly and riskier than doing business in the United States or Singapore.

Rules and regulations imposed on businesses by governments can affect the cost and risk of doing business as well. In July 2002, the U.S. Congress passed the Sarbanes-Oxley Act (SOX), which increased the reporting and accounting requirements for firms listed on U.S. stock exchanges. The result was increased compliance costs and an increased cost of capital for smaller firms, relative to what they would pay if they raised the capital in a country other than the United States. The idea behind SOX was that the U.S. companies did not have good enough governance systems; SOX was a government reaction to Enron, Tyco, and other failed companies. There is no doubt that good governance reduces the capital costs of a firm. However, if regulations impose more costs than they benefit consumers, the regulations will lead to higher costs of doing business and raising capital.

Internal Use of Capital

The use of the capital is often what defines whether a firm is successful. Firms have to choose where to put their capital to use. They have many investment projects but can't fund them all. In all companies, someone or some committee determines which projects to fund, which to put off until another time, and which to forget altogether. This means it is important to have some way to compare the proposals. When Enron was considering the purchase of the Brazilian power company, it was also considering spending $2.25 billion for a water business and similar expenditures for other businesses. Andrew Fastow, Enron's chief financial officer said: "Capital is not an issue for Enron."[7] But he was totally wrong. Capital is an issue for every firm. If one project is funded, another might not be. How does a firm determine which investments to pursue?

Net Present Value

The typical rule of operation for a firm is to accept an investment proposal if the present value of the expected future cash flows from the investment is greater than the present value of the cost of the investment. The net present value (NPV) of a project is the present value of revenues less the present value of costs. Suppose that an investment costs $100 today and that it is expected to result in revenues of $60 a year for two years. The net present value equals

$$NPV = \$60 + \frac{\$60}{(1+r)} - \frac{\$60}{(1+r)^2}$$

At a 10 percent discount rate, $r = 0.10$,

$$NPV = \$60(0.90909) + \$60(0.82645) - \$100$$
$$= \$94 - \$100$$
$$= -\$6$$

The net present value of this project is negative using the 10 percent rate of discount, which means that in today's dollars, the project would cost more than the revenue it would generate. However, suppose the cash flow projection is $70 per year for two years rather than the $60 per year. Increasing the cash flow projection would increase the net present value to $21; in which case the project probably would be undertaken.

The net present value approach is fine in principle but can be troublesome in practice if not used appropriately. When capital is allocated according to the NPV calculations, division managers have an incentive to fiddle with cash flow projections until the NPV of the project they support is positive. A common problem is that the managers' forecasts of future revenues often depend on advertising and sales promotions, but the costs of these promotions are not considered to be costs associated with the capital requests. This creates an upward bias in the calculation and thus presents a greater likelihood that a project will be undertaken. This type of decision making is ignoring the cost of capital.

If capital costs are not taken into account in the capital budgeting process, then management is treating capital as if it were free. Whenever some item with value is free, much more is wanted than is available. In most corporations, every division head wants to get the division's projects funded, but there is not enough capital to fund every project. Management has to allocate that scarce capital. If the capital is allocated at a price—the cost of capital—then only the most profitable projects will be funded. In October 2000, questions were being asked internally about Enron's investments. One person asked whether the company was comparing alternatives. Does the company care whether a particular use of funds is the best option? The response from executives was that the company typically did not compare one use of funds with other uses of the funds.[8] In other words, there were no trade-offs—capital was free.

The Corporate Form

The cost of capital has both explicit and implicit aspects. We have discussed the explicit factors in terms of the risks of the investments and the projected or expected performance of the firm. Other aspects of the firm's risk and performance stem from how efficiently the firm converts resources to output.

The corporate form is a remarkable institution. Literally millions of individuals voluntarily entrust billions of dollars of personal wealth to the care of managers on the basis of a complex set of contracting relationships that define the rights of the parties involved. Stockholders take on the risk of ownership without having any role in the control of the firm because the corporate form enables this risk to be diversified in the capital markets. The holders of common stock can create their own individual portfolios to minimize their individual risk by holding stocks or bonds from any other corporation as well as government bonds. Thus, the common stock of corporations allows more efficient risk sharing among individuals than proprietorships and partnerships where the primary decision makers are also the risk bearers.[9]

But there are always trade-offs, and there are always costs. The fact that the owners have no control of the company leads to the problem of separation of ownership from control. This principal-agent problem requires that the behavior of managers be aligned with what owners want. The structure of the corporation, with hierarchies, boards of directors, and governance at least partly stems from the attempt to align the interests of the owners and the managers. When the governance breaks down or the architecture becomes inefficient, the cost of capital rises and the firm has to either change or exit the business. Contributing greatly to this is the ease with which the common shareholders can dispose of their shares and purchase shares of other companies. The corporate form enhances the movement of resources to uses where they are most highly valued.

Debtholders versus Equityholders

The corporate form often pits debtholders against equityholders. Some corporate decisions increase the wealth of stockholders while reducing the wealth of bondholders, and other decisions increase the wealth of bondholders at the expense of stockholders.

If the price of a bond is determined with the assumption that the firm will maintain its dividend policy, the value of the bond would be reduced by unexpected dividend increases. Essentially the stockholders would be taking money out of the firm and away from bondholders. Similarly, if bonds are priced assuming that additional debt of the same or higher priority will not be issued, then if the firm issues more such debt, the value of the bondholders' claims is reduced. Stockholders are better off and bondholders are worse off when the firm substitutes high-risk-high-return for low-risk-low-return projects.

Conversely, giving the bondholders control of the firm does not solve the stockholder-creditor conflict. Bondholders would have incentives to pay too few dividends, issue too little debt, and choose projects with too little risk. So a balance must be struck. Bondholders need to monitor the behavior of stockholders to ensure that the wealth of bondholders is not transferred to the stockholders and stockholders need to ensure that the optimal amount of risky projects is undertaken. The existence of both bondholders and stockholders provides some checks and balances on the use of capital. In addition, restrictions written in contracts, so-called **bond covenants**, provide some control of the bondholder–stockholder conflict. For instance, a convertible bond gives the holder the right to exchange the bond for the firm's common stock. This limits stockholder action such as risk-increasing activities. Secured debt gives the bondholders title to pledged assets until the bonds are paid in full. This limits the possibility of stockholders substituting low quality assets for high quality assets. In addition, secured debt allows stockholders to sell claims to the payoffs of a new project that otherwise would prove a windfall to holders of previously issued debt. Thus, some new positive net present value projects can increase the value of equity if financed with secured debt but not with unsecured debt. The standard bond covenant restricting the payment of dividends specifies that the maximum allowable dividend payment is a positive function of both accounting earnings and the proceeds from the sale of new equity. The specification of a maximum on dividends imposes a minimum on the fraction of earnings retained in the firm.

Summing Up

In summing up, it is important to note the role of the prime directive in determining the cost of capital. The corporate form is not imposed from outside. It is endogenously determined—a reflection of the market process. It evolves in order to be the most efficient means of converting resources to output. The organizational structure, the creditor–debtor division, the separation of ownership and control, the internal allocation of capital—all contribute to the efficiency of the firm. The cost of capital depends on the efficiency of the firm. Interest expenses and the opportunity costs of investors depend on how well the firm is expected to perform. When the corporate form is not efficient or when government imposes additional costs on it, changes will occur. In recent years, many publicly traded firms have been privatized, and private equity firms have acquired formerly publicly traded firms. Some of these changes have occurred due to increased regulations on public companies including SOX. The additional compliance and reporting requirements impose substantial costs of public corporations.[10]

Free Capital

Why are these firms focused on reducing capital? Isn't capital necessary for carrying out business?

The cost of capital is a cost, just as is the cost of labor or the cost of material. Many firms fail to account for the cost of capital. They may not realize that inventories sitting on shelves or backrooms constitute capital tied up and not earning anything. John Deere found that it had lots of very expensive farm equipment sitting at the dealers. The executives did not seem to realize that capital was tied up in these machines. Coca-Cola shipped its syrup in expensive containers and let the containers sit unused for days. The company did not account for the capital tied up in these containers. All these actions increase costs, specifically the cost of capital.

If costs can be reduced without altering revenues, then profit will increase. A firm has to use its capital efficiently. It has to ensure that capital is allocated to its highest valued use inside the firm, and it has to ensure that the cost of capital is minimized. Holding more inventories than needed is costly. Having a capacity that is not used is costly. Allocating capital to nonperforming projects is costly. Inappropriately applied capital budgeting is costly. In fact, capital budgeting is an attempt to compare the expected return on a project to the cost of capital necessary to undertake that project. It is costly if the firm allocates capital to a project that is not expected to earn more than the cost of that capital. Capital is not free.

Summary

1. The supply of funds with which firms acquire capital comes from selling stocks and bonds and taking out loans from financial institutions.
2. Stocks are bought and sold on a stock exchange.
3. The demand for stocks comes from investors who are seeking the greatest return on their savings—individuals, mutual funds, and institutions like insurance companies. The supply of equities comes from stock owners who want to sell their stock and purchase something else. This is known as the secondary market. The primary market is the market for new issues—stocks that had not previously been sold by the firms.
4. Bonds are IOUs provided by a lender or issuer of the bond to the purchaser of the bond. The demanders of bonds are individuals and mutual funds that are seeking the highest return given a certain amount of risk. The suppliers of bonds are corporations and governments attempting to borrow money and the owners of previously issued bonds who choose to sell their bonds.
5. The market for a bond consists of the demand for and supply of that bond. As with the stock market, demand depends on the prices of and expected returns on other investments and investor expectations; supply depends on the prices of and expected returns on other investments and supplier (bond issuer) expectations.
6. There is an inverse relationship between bond prices and interest rates. As the interest rate rises, bond prices fall, and vice versa.
7. Capital budgeting is the process of allocating capital internally. The present value of income streams generated by alternative investment projects is compared to the cost of the capital.

8. Net present value is the present value of the income stream generated by an investment project minus the present value of the cost of that project.
9. Projects expected to generate cash flows with a positive net present value should be undertaken; those with a negative net present value should be forgone.
10. Foreign-exchange exposure can increase the risks of doing business and thus increase the cost of capital.
11. Increased risk increases the cost of capital. A faulty governance system, instability in the countries in which a firm does business, and rules and regulations in different countries that lead to differential costs of doing business can increase the cost of capital.
12. The corporate form—diverse ownership without control, managers, creditors, hierarchy—exists because it is efficient. The existence of diverse ownership enables the risk of ownership to be minimized. The creditor–owner division ensures that the appropriate risks are undertaken and the performance of the firm is maximized.

Key Terms

Weighted average cost of capital (WACC)   Capital structure
Dividend   Bond covenants

Exercises

1. The Benly Company needs to raise funds for a major expansion. The company is debating whether to issue stock or to issue bonds. If the company issues bonds, then its debts will increase and it will be under additional stress to ensure that its revenues can cover the costs of its debt. If it issues stock, the current owners will lose power and influence. What should the company do? Explain your answer.

2. Explain how the corporate form is more efficient than a form in which the owner is also the manager.

3. What is the creditor–owner conflict? Explain why 100 percent equity might be inefficient. Explain why 100 percent debt might be inefficient.

4. Middleton Steel Company is considering whether to temporarily close one of its manufacturing plants. If it does close the plant, it faces the costs of shutting down and then starting back up, the costs of criticism from the city in which the plant is located, and the costs of customer abandonment as some customers purchase products elsewhere. If it does not close the plant, it will experience substantial losses because revenues will not cover variable costs.

    a. What would a net present value analysis say about the decision?
    b. What other strategies might be used?

5. The marketing director of National Midland Mortgage has been arguing with senior management about building a $50 million publishing facility. Other managers worried about the assumptions in the analysis that support the investment—an increase in the number of mortgages processed and a reduction in processing costs. What if the mortgage market did not grow as expected?

    a. Should National Midland invest in the publishing facility?
    b. What assumptions might the marketing director have made to make the investment look worthwhile?

6. Bob Davies must decide whether to invest $100,000 in his own business or in another local business. Both investment projects have an expected life of five years. The cash flow of each is as follows:

Year	Davies	Other
1	$20,000	$10,000
2	30,000	10,000
3	40,000	30,000
4	10,000	40,000
5	5,000	50,000

Suppose the risk of the projects is the same and is accounted for by a risk premium of 6 percent per year. Would either investment make sense? Which would be better?

7. An oil company recently evaluated a proposed investment for improvements in a particular type of refining equipment. According to the analysis, such improvements would require an investment of $15 million and would result in an incremental after-tax cash flow of $2 million per year for nine years following the year of the investment.

   a. If the discount rate is 10 percent, what is the net present value of this project?
   b. If the discount rate is 15 percent, what is the net present value of this project?
   c. What discount rate would you argue makes most sense in evaluating this project?

8. What discount rate is most appropriate for net present value calculations of large-scale projects? Of small projects? Of the quantity of inventories to hold?

9. What would the effect be of a law that makes shareholders personally liable for debt the firm acquires?

10. In 2009, the U.S. government took over Chrysler. It gave about 25 percent of the equity to the UAW and kept the rest. It eliminated the claims of the bondholders. The corporate form provides bondholders first claim on assets if the firm goes under; stockholders receive what is left after everyone else is paid off. What does the government's actions mean? What effect is the action likely to have on other firms that might be struggling?

11. Explain what the incentives of bondholders and stockholders are. Are they the same? How do they differ? Will a firm with no debt act differently than a firm with a significant amount of debt?

12. Unlike equity, debt is unforgiving if the firm performs poorly. If a firm goes bankrupt, debtholders have the right to repossess funds and exercise their residual control rights about how the funds will be spent. Thus, under debt financing, debtholders possess a larger set of control rights than managers. Does this mean that a manager that wants to maintain control should finance more with equity?

13. What is the effect on a firm's cost of capital when a CEO is found to have engaged in unethical behavior? Explain.

14. How would country risk affect a firm's cost of capital?

15. Use the CAPM to explain whether a firm that is diversified to perform exactly as the stock market performs would be a better investment for an individual than a firm that is not diversified.

16. In 2010 few firms were investing in new projects or expanding. Yet, interest rates were extremely low. Why, with this very low cost of capital would firms not be investing in new projects?

17. What happens to the cost of capital when inflationary expectations are high? Explain. (Inflationary expectations are high when expectations that inflation in coming months and years will increase.)

18. What happens to the cost of capital when expectations of deflation are high? Explain. (Deflation occurs when prices decline.)

CHAPTER NOTES

1. www.i2.com/assets/pdf/705DFA04-7A09-4FF9-A1D636E8AD51E1DD.pdf
2. www.redback.com/Redback/Home/Products/SmartEdge.html
3. www.crm2day.com/news/crm/114696.php
4. www.level5networks.com/prod_features.htm
5. Under certain assumptions there is no optimal capital structure. This is referred to as the M and M result after the economists who defined it, Modigliani and Miller; see F. Modigliani and M. Miller, "The Cost of Capital, Corporation Finance and the Theory of Investment," *American Economic Review* (June 1958). [The primary assumptions that are necessary for the M&M result are that there are no tax consequence differences between debt and equity and that an investor can borrow money at the same cost as the firm. Neither of these assumptions is generally valid—debt cost can be written off against taxes while dividends (equity costs) can not and, typically, firms can borrow at a lower rate than individual investors.
6. *Ease of Doing Business,* 2008, http://www.nationmaster.com/graph/eco_eas_of_doi_bus_ind-economy-ease-doing-business-index.
7. Kurt Eichenwald, *Conspiracy of Fools* (New York: Basic Books, 2005), p. 194.
8. Ibid., *Conspiracy of Fools*, p. 388.
9. Michael C. Jensen, *A Theory of the Firm* (Cambridge, MA: Harvard University Press, 2000).
10. Liz Peek, "Why Private Equity Is through the Roof," December 5, 2006; Business, *New York Sun,* March 8, 2008, www.nysun.com/article/44594?page_no=1, accessed January 15, 2008.

CHAPTER 18

Internal Markets

CASE

Terrorist Markets

It is vitally important for the United States to anticipate and possibly offset future terrorist attacks. Similarly, it is necessary to know whether certain government leaders might be overthrown or what developments in other parts of the world might occur such as Russia invading Georgia or Poland. How can such information be obtained? Could markets be used? A few people thought the best method would be to create a market whereby people could speculate on certain events and could profit from correct predictions. The Defense Advanced Research Projects Agency (DARPA), a research think tank within the Department of Defense, decided to create a market through which traders could buy and sell contracts that specified various events. For example, contracts could be based on questions such as "How fast will the non oil output of Egypt grow next year?" or "Will the U.S. military withdraw from country A in two years or less?" The concept was to discover whether trading in such contracts could help to predict future events and how connections between events were perceived.

Critics tore into DARPA for creating a way to bet on terrorism. It was argued that a terrorist could bet on some act of terrorism and then carry it out, thereby profiting on tragedy. Once people started to hear about the DARPA project, funding was cut and all research related to it was terminated.

1. What information can markets provide that spies, informants and others might not?
2. How could a market provide information about terrorism?

The Market as a Collector of Information

The market process—countless individuals pursuing their own interests by trading with one another—is a path of discovery. Through the price system and free competition, the trade-offs of scarce resources are clarified, the lowest-cost solutions are reached, and feedback about success and failure are provided through profit and loss. When people buy something, they are showing that they value the item they purchase more than anything else a comparable amount of money could buy. Similarly, when people sell something, they are showing they would rather have the money price of that item than they would the item. They value something else more than what they are selling. So when buyers and sellers agree to exchange some item, the price of the item is the result of the buyer saying that the item has more value to him than the money price, while the seller simultaneously says the item has less value than the money price. The resulting price is the result of the tastes and preferences as well as beliefs and expectations of the buyers and sellers. The price, therefore, incorporates all the information buyers and sellers use to determine tastes, preferences, beliefs and expectations.

Once the market price is determined, a change in that price will come about when the information that buyers and/or sellers have changes. For instance, if the buyer learns something new about the item, say that it has more uses than was previously known, the buyer will immediately be willing to pay a higher price. The new price incorporates the buyer's newfound information. Similarly, if the seller learns that the costs of an important resource are going to increase, the seller will cut supply or require a higher price to supply the same amount. The market price rises to reflect the increased costs of resources. The market does this without anyone dictating what buyers and sellers do or defining the price at which trade will occur.

Central planning didn't and doesn't work for nations. The central planners could not know what price to set on items to be traded. They don't have all of the information the anonymous buyers and sellers in a market have. They couldn't know the tastes, preferences, beliefs, and expectations of buyers and sellers. As a result, the price set by the planners was either too high or too low, resulting in shortages of some items and surpluses of others. Resources were misallocated.

The long and short of it is that markets work and central planning does not. As discussed previously, this raises the curious observation that allocation within a firm appears to be more like central planning than it does free markets. Typically, the manager or CEO makes the decisions, determining how many employees to hire, how much capital to acquire, and how to allocate that capital. In addition, someone defines how resources are allocated within the firm. How can this be efficient in a firm when central planning is so inefficient when carried out at national or state levels? As we discussed in previous chapters, while the firm appears to be a centrally planned system it is not. The firm evolves to be efficient; its structure arises due to efficiency. But there is no doubt that elements of central planning exist in firms. Could the firm be more efficient by mimicking the market even more, using prices determined by **internal markets** to allocate internal resources[1]?

Transfer Prices

Many firms do use prices to allocate a few goods or resources internally. When firms are large enough that one division provides goods or services to another, then the question arises whether the upstream division should charge the downstream division. Senior managers usually negotiate the prices and other conditions for large-scale transfers. Theoretically, the managers would determine a **transfer price** at which the overall firm would maximize profit. But what is this price?

Consider a situation in which an upstream division (production) ships the product to the downstream division (distribution), where the product is assembled and shipped to retailers. The divisions could be in different countries so that a translation from the currency of the country in which the production division exists to the currency of the country in which the distribution division exists has to occur. Let's assume that the divisions are in the same country and that the divisions have been set up as profit centers. This means that each division wants to maximize the profits of the division.

The manager of the production division wants to maximize the profit of the production division, and the manager of the distribution division wants to maximize the profit of the distribution division. These two objectives could easily be in conflict. If the only source of the transferred product is the production division, then the manager of the production division doesn't have to worry about competitors entering and driving price down to marginal cost. The manager will act as a monopolist, reducing the quantity so that the price can be increased. As a result, the production division's price is higher than its marginal cost. The distribution division has to purchase the product at the monopoly price. The monopoly price becomes the distribution division's marginal cost. Since the distribution division has a higher marginal cost than would be the case if the production division were pricing at the competitive level, the distribution division will supply a smaller quantity of output. The overall firm does not maximize profit.

Only if the transfer price is set at a level that maximizes the overall value of the firm rather than the profits of the production division will the problem be resolved. The overall profit of the firm is maximized when the production division produces where its marginal cost equals the firm's marginal revenue minus the marginal cost of the distribution division, called the firm's **net marginal product**.

If the product being transferred can be bought and sold to and from other firms—in other words, if there is an external market for the product—then the external market would discipline the managers of the production division. If the production division charges more than the external market price, then the distribution division would purchase product from the external market. If the production division was competing in a perfectly competitive market where price is competed down until it equals marginal cost, then the transfer price would be the production division's marginal cost. If the production division were competing in a market where different firms are able to establish some differentiation, then the transfer price could be above marginal cost.

For years large multidivisional organizations have used transfer prices to help coordinate at least some of the internal activities. In the early twentieth century, the rise of multidivisional companies necessarily meant that operating divisions had a great deal of autonomy from the central office. Companies such as Sears, DuPont, General Motors, and Standard Oil of New Jersey quickly realized that the central office was not able to make all of the decisions for business divisions located in diverse regions or involved in different product lines. Thus, the firms restructured from the U-form to the M-form. Decentralization (the M-form) was a managerial invention in 1920, but by 1970s it was a universal practice. Transfer pricing, therefore, was a common development in the M-form organization.

Asset Allocation within the Firm

In the 1990s, a few firms began experimenting more widely with internal markets. British Petroleum (BP) relied on an internal market to meet CO_2 target levels levied on the firm. In 1998 the CEO of British Petroleum committed to reducing the company's greenhouse gas emissions 10 percent below 1990 levels by 2010. BP set up an internal market to coordinate the business units' efforts. Senior managers assigned targets to the business units by issuing each unit a certain number of "permits." Each permit gave the holder the right to generate one ton of carbon dioxide–equivalent emissions per year. Together, these targets would meet the companywide goal for reduced emissions. BP's business units were allowed to buy and sell permits among themselves. If one manager saw that the reduction target could be met at a cost that was less than the price at which the permits were trading, then the manager could sell the permits to other units and make a profit on them. Some other unit, facing the costs of meeting its target reductions that exceeded the permit price, could buy additional permits. In 2001, BP business units traded more than 4.5 million tons of emissions rights among themselves, at an average price of about $40 per ton. And that year, BP met its original goal, nine years ahead of schedule.

The BP exercise successfully allowed an internal market to determine the most efficient allocation of resources to reach the goal of reducing emissions. The CEO could have simply specified how much each department had to reduce emissions and left it at that. But he figured that the individual division heads would have better ideas how to solve the problems in their divisions than he would. By allowing the price of permits to signal to the division managers the most efficient way to meet targets, BP met its targets efficiently and quickly. During trading, the price of permits would rise until some division found ways to reallocate resources or use resources differently so that it could meet targets at a lower cost than the price of the permits. Then that division would offer to sell its permits. As additional divisions met targets efficiently, they too offered permits. Those divisions that could not meet targets at a cost that would be less than the cost of permits would purchase the permits.[2]

Prediction Markets

In the BP case, the price of permits was the result of the divisions buying and selling permits. The price resulted from each division head using all the information each had available to determine whether to be a buyer or a seller of the permits. Thus, the "market" price ought to be the best information one can get about the good or service being traded in a market.

The Iowa Electronic Markets website[3] uses this idea to create what are called **prediction markets**. Markets have been developed to forecast the outcome of all U.S. presidential elections since the 1988 George H.W. Bush–Michael Dukakis contest. Anyone with access to the Internet can participate with up to $500 of real money. In these markets, people purchase contracts that say who will win the election. If you hold contracts for the winner once the election is over, then you receive a share of total money in the market.

The Iowa electronic prediction market has been more accurate at predicting actual vote proportions than the opinion polls. On the eve of the 1988 election, for example, the Iowa market forecast a vote share for Bush of 53.2 percent, which was exactly right, and a share for Dukakis of 45.2 percent, which was only 0.2 percent less than the share he actually received. This was substantially more accurate than any of the opinion polls that year. Why? Most traders based their bets not on their desires or other ulterior motives but on a cold assessment of what they really thought would happen. And those with the most money at stake—and thus the most influence over the market—had the greatest incentive to rely on their information. The prediction markets work because they create incentives for widely dispersed people to reveal information about which they feel confident.

Figure 18.1 shows a comparison between the predictions of the electronic market and various polls for the 2008 presidential election. The Iowa Election Market clearly bested the polls.

A few companies have begun to use prediction markets to solicit information about events that are important to the firm. Eli Lilly, for example, tested a prediction market in which employees forecast which drug candidates were likely to be approved and

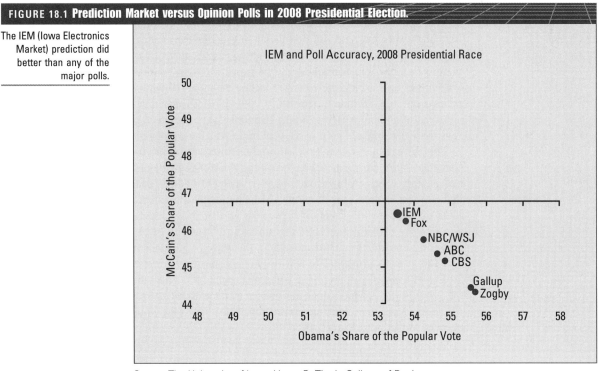

FIGURE 18.1 **Prediction Market versus Opinion Polls in 2008 Presidential Election.**

The IEM (Iowa Electronics Market) prediction did better than any of the major polls.

Source: The University of Iowa, Henry B. Tipple College of Business.

which rejected by the FDA. The market rapidly zeroed in on the winners, pushing up their prices while the prices of the losers plummeted. Yahoo created a prediction market called the Tech Buzz Game. A small number of rival technologies are matched against one another, and traders buy contracts specifying which technology consumers will use the most. Google created internal predictive markets to forecast product launch dates, new office openings, and other strategic issues. All three companies stated that the market performed better than alternative approaches.

HP Labs created its own internal market system to help predict certain critical business issues such as the quarterly sales forecast or the price of DRAM memory chips in one, three, or six months. The importance of being right about a forecast can have a major impact. If a chip price forecast is off by just a couple of pennies, a significant impact on HP's hardware profit margin can result. HP has found that its internal market predictions were more accurate than the company's official forecasts (for instance, six out of eight times the market was better at predicting computer sales than the company forecast).[4]

The first internal market in Hewlett-Packard was set up to determine what computer sales would be in a month. A few dozen employees, mostly product and finance managers, were each given $50 in a trading account to bet on what they thought computer sales would be at the end of the month. If a salesman thought the company would sell between $201 million and $210 million worth, he could buy a security for that prediction, signaling to the rest of the market that someone thought that was a probable scenario. If his opinion changed, he could buy again or sell. When trading stopped, the highest priced stock was the one the market had said was most likely. The traders got to keep their profits and won an additional dollar for every share of stock they owned that turned out to be the right sales range. The result was that the stock market forecast was twice as good as the company's official forecast. HP now uses an internal market to determine the group's monthly sales and profit.

GE's computing and decision sciences group created a stock market for 150 lab scientists to enter and rank product ideas. The grand prize was $50,000 in research funding. Of the 150 people in the lab, 85 participated, including managers, researchers, and interns. The managers seeded the market with 10 ideas, and the staff added their own. Two weeks later, 62 stocks were trading—each with its own description page where anyone could blog about it, anonymously building a case for it or building a case against it. The winning idea came from a researcher, not a lab manager.

Many other companies are experimenting with or creating different types of internal prediction markets: Microsoft for predicting product ship dates; GE for discovering new ideas; Intel for allocating computer chip production; Siemens AG for improving the accuracy of product developments; and others.

Using Markets to Collect Dispersed Information

In principle, a firm ought to be able to use the efficiency, flexibility, and motivation of a free market to make decisions and allocate resources internally. If people can buy and sell to one another based on their self-interests and the overall result is a continuous reallocation of resources to the places where the resources are most valued, the firm ought to benefit just as societies with free markets excel over societies with centrally planned markets. Central planners don't have all the information that the dispersed individuals collectively have. In a firm, the CEO doesn't have all the information that the sales force has. Even if the central staff were to poll the sales force continuously, the answers would not be as useful as the market results. With central planning and polls, individuals do not have much of an incentive to provide accurate information. A salesperson may want to look as if he is doing better than he is. A manager may want to provide a number that argues for a bigger staff. Interests within the firm may be able to hide or delay information that could end up costing the firm. A free market in which individuals have an incentive to provide the best and most accurate information should excel over central planning.

Hundreds of people are involved in allocating resources in a large firm. Product-line managers compete for factory capacity. Sales representatives lobby to get products for their customers. Strategic-planning groups, factory schedulers, and logistics managers try to coordinate everyone else's conflicting plans and desires. But it is difficult, if not impossible, for anyone to really see the whole picture. By contrast, in the market, salespeople are motivated to trade based on what they actually think will happen—not what they want to happen or what they want others to think will happen. Even more important, the traders can see the current consensus of all their colleagues reflected in prices. Then they can use whatever other data they have (even if it's just their instincts) to judge whether or not a given prediction at a given price is a good buy. With an internal market, all prices for all products in all future time periods are visible to everyone.

In an unfettered free market, the market price is the best predictor of an event. Thus, it seems that prediction markets could allow corporations to estimate the effect on stock price of different major decisions, such as whether to acquire a target, whether to adopt a governance reform, or whether to dismiss a CEO. Suppose that a corporation is considering building a new plant. It might launch markets predicting the corporation's stock price several months in the future. One market would predict the stock price if the corporation committed to building the plant, and the other, the stock price if the corporation committed to not building the plant. After about a month, the corporation would check which prediction was higher and make its decision accordingly.

Prediction markets could also serve as a check on the accuracy of information a CEO is receiving. According to the Sarbanes-Oxley Act, a CEO has to sign a statement that the reports of the company are true. A penalty of up to 25 years in prison can be imposed on the CEO who falsifies the report. The CEO gets information on what the firm's situation is through the normal hierarchical channels—from line salespersons to sales managers to sales executives to finance and then finally to the COO or CFO. Instead of relying on command-and-control mechanisms or computerized "internal controls," the CEO could create a prediction market in which the firm's employees, auditors, and anyone else that the CEO wishes could trade on whether the firm will be required to restate its earnings over some period of time.

Creating a Market

Markets arise spontaneously whenever private property rights are well defined and enforced and people believe there are gains from trade. No one has to create a market. But in the case of markets inside the firm, the necessary conditions for the emergence of a market have to be specified and a market has to be created. What is required for a market to exist and work?

A market requires a well-defined good or service. In prediction markets, the question is the well-defined part. For instance, "Weapons of Mass Destruction are not in Iraq" is not a well-defined question primarily because there is no time limit. Compare that to "WMD will be found by September 2003." This latter question is one on which a market can be created.

In addition to a well-defined good or service, a market requires private property rights that are well defined and enforced. In the predictive markets, the private property is the contract or share representing an answer to the question being posed. For instance, the proposition, "WMD will be found by September 2003 in Iraq," will have shares with the response true or false. When you purchase a share, you own it. You can sell it or you can hold onto it as you desire. Holding a share is holding ownership of the answer specified on that share; moreover, it is a guarantee that if the answer is correct, you receive a share of the profits generated by the market.

A market arises when people own something and expect to gain from trading that item for a different item someone else owns. So with private property rights, there is a basis for a market to exist. But in order for individuals to have an incentive to get involved with a market, they must expect to gain from trade. Specialization according to comparative advantage and trade provides gains to all traders. In predictive markets, the comparative advantage one has depends on the information one has—the belief that a buy or sell will result in gains.

Internal Market Failure

For a market to function, issues such as externalities, public goods, free riding, asymmetric information, and monopolization have to be minimal. If these problems arise in internal markets, they may render the markets not very useful. For instance, asymmetric information can doom a market. When it is expected that someone might have much better information than others, it might be difficult to get people to trade or participate in the market. For instance, the Tradesports contracts on the next Supreme Court retirement or the future of the papacy have generated very little trade because people suspected insiders had much better information.

No one should be able to corner or manipulate the market. If it is expected that someone will monopolize the market, then price won't reveal all information because not all potential traders will participate. To keep a market efficient, people need to be allowed to speculate whenever they believe current prices don't accurately reflect actual

Business Insight

Internal Markets in Academia, an Aside

The typical academic institution, including business schools, is very much a command-and-control hierarchy. Budgets come from the legislature (in public institutions) or Board of Directors and are distributed to the university central administration, which then allocates shares to the various colleges. The leaders of the colleges then take their share and allocate to individual departments. The faculty may use telephones, printers, copiers, and secretarial services and have access to as much paper, pens, and other supplies as they wish, but they must gain permission from the department head or dean to travel to conferences or otherwise gain support for academic activities. Offices are assigned by the department head, as are teaching assignments—classes and times. It is ironic that economists and business teachers find themselves presenting the costs and benefits of markets in allocating resources, never thinking about using markets in their own jobs.

In addition to the centrally planned approach to allocating resources, the institutions have annual budgets. This means that any funds remaining or not committed by fiscal year end revert to the central administration and/or the initial granting agency. Typically, a mad rush at fiscal year end occurs as employees, departments, colleges, and divisions seek to eliminate any excess. The inefficiencies are widespread. Yet again, even in economics departments and business schools where market allocation is well understood, there is no design to implement market allocation.

In the late 1980s, the head of the Economics Department at Arizona State University attempted to create internal markets. Individual faculty were given budgets to use as they wanted—pens, papers, printers, travel, telephones, and so on. Offices were allocated via an auction. Teaching assignments were also allocated via a market. A price was established for each course, and the relative prices among courses. For instance, a huge principles of economics course (350 to 500 students) was equal to 1.5 upper division undergraduate courses and 1.7 graduate courses other than MBA courses. MBA courses were worth just slightly less than the huge principles courses. So a faculty member could teach two extremely large principles courses in place of three upper division courses.

Due to constraints at the university, class times were set outside the department. So instructors could bid for different times and could execute trades. The results were fascinating. First, the allocation of faculty budgets among supplies, services, and travel were totally changed. Instead of huge telephone bills, because telephone service had been free, and little travel, because travel was the purview of the department head, faculty chose to trade off telephone usage for additional travel. Instructors were much happier with teaching assignments than had been the case prior to market-determined assignments. Some faculty made intertemporal trades—getting a colleague to teach an additional class one semester in exchange for no teaching another semester. [5] All in all, the market experiment was a success. Yet, some preferred not to use the market system. Significant rent seeking occurred, with the result that the dean and provost interfered with market allocation and terminated most of it. "How can one sell state property?" "Students are getting cheated as faculty buy teaching assignments" were some of the headlines in university papers.

Louisiana State University reached the point where departments could allocate their budgets as desired and could even increase the size of their budgets by attracting more students.[6] Under the model, each department was allocated a budget from the university and had total control over that budget. The department could raise salaries or carpet offices or purchase equipment. Several departments saved money by firing the custodial staff provided by Physical Facilities and hiring a private contractor to keep bathrooms clean. The budgets were determined by student credit hours, which led departments to compete with each other for students.

The critics of the approach argued that the departments with the lowest academic standards were pulling in larger numbers of students and the more difficult departments were losing students. Were these critics correct? Would students flock to "easy" fields if there were no jobs in those fields after graduation?

---

values. For instance, if a product-line manager is tempted to exaggerate the probable demand for her products, she has to back up her claims by actually buying futures contracts for the demand she projects. But if others in the market believe her estimate is unrealistic, they can sell her contract now with the expectation of buying it back more cheaply in the future. If this cannot happen, the market will not be useful.

In addition to creating markets on subjects where one or a few people have significantly better information than everyone else, some activities within the firm require careful handling if markets are to be useful. When one employee uses goods or services used by others and when no employee has exclusive control over a good or service, then the public goods problem arises. For example, innovations in processing are nonrivalrous in that many employees can benefit from them without reducing the benefits of others. The problem is that no one has an incentive to provide the innovation, and thus the innovation does not occur. Or the firm's reputation is a public good and without compensation specifically directed toward activities that can enhance that reputation, no employee has an incentive to devote resources to the activity. If the good is centrally provided, then each employee has an incentive to free ride, to overuse the good.

Most employees produce both internal private goods and internal public goods. They have an incentive to substitute away from the provision of public goods toward the provision of private goods. As noted in the chapter on personnel, it is necessary to implement reward systems that induce employee effort toward public goods.

Internal negative externalities lead to the oversupply of the externality-creating activity. If a specialized employee is the sole supplier of a service, then the employee can act as a monopolist. These internal market issues exist even when internal allocations are not price-mediated exchanges. In fact, rent seeking and corruption are more likely in nonmarket allocations than in market allocations. As was discussed in Chapter 6, the compensation and personnel policies must take into account public-type goods and externalities; otherwise the incentives in the firm will lead to inefficient solutions.

Internal markets may do more than predict events. An internal market is faster and more flexible than many hierarchical decision-making approaches. Salespeople, planners, and plant managers can immediately start trading based on new information. In fact, everyone has an incentive to trade as soon as possible to gain an advantage. Instead of one group of senior managers sequentially working through a single set of options, many people can simultaneously explore a variety of possibilities. If a natural disaster disrupts work at a critical factory, for instance, the value of factory capacity will immediately shoot up, and all the other factory managers will be highly motivated to see how they can reconfigure their own schedules to take over some of the extra work. They may have to postpone other scheduled projects, but if the prices in the internal market are more or less accurate, they will know exactly which jobs to do and which should be postponed. These adjustments can occur simultaneously, all over the company, without any single person or group trying to figure them out. The invisible hand of the market coordinates all the separate actions into a single coherent plan.

Market-Based Management[7]

A firm's internal exchange has both public goods and private goods aspects. Centrally provided services such as human resources, education and training, and legal aid have public goods characteristics such as nonexcludability. They are accessible to anyone in the firm. It is standard accounting practice to charge business units for centrally provided services through arbitrary allocations of overhead expenses. Under this system, executives at the top decide how much will be spent on various activities, and then the departments can use the funding to give internal customers what the experts think they need. Internal service providers have weak incentives to listen to their customers because the budget comes from top management. In addition, business units using internal services have few incentives to compare the value they receive with the costs to the company. As a result, these services have more requests for work than they can fill.

Similarly, capital costs are typically allocated as a central cost or charged to business units as a percentage of total capital costs. There are no incentives for divisions to economize on the use of capital. If a division knows it will be charged a percentage of total capital, it wants to be sure it gets more than its fair share of capital. It is like the dinner where the bill is going to be equally divided among diners, no matter what each diner orders. The incentive is to order far more than a diner would order if alone and to attempt to order more than the average. Internal services and capital thus become public goods, and each division attempts to free ride.

If each division is able to handle personnel issues and hiring and firing, each could contract out for its human resources needs. Similarly, a division could be responsible for legal and accounting that apply only to the division. Then the division could decide whether human resource, legal, and accounting are purchased internally or externally. The services that the CEO deems necessary for the firm's reputation and efficiency could be provided via a tax on the divisions. Reputation building and other items of a public goods nature would have to be dealt with through compensation and personnel issues. For instance, a portion of compensation would have to be determined by the central headquarters and not just the division. Otherwise, there would be an incentive to not invest in activities that benefit the overall firm but not necessarily the division. Compensation systems would also have to be defined in such a way that one division would not "hold up" another division. If a firm relies on internal markets, creates profit centers, and enables divisions to utilize external or internal resources, then we will call the firm market-based.

Is a Firm with Internal Markets a Firm?

Is a market-based firm actually a firm? Yes it is. It has a headquarters and a boss or CEO who must make some decisions regarding resources. For instance, the CEO often allocates capital costs. Since capital costs apply to the firm as a whole, each profit center has to pay some proportion of those costs. In Koch Industries, for example, each division is responsible for a portion of these costs. Similarly, other costs that apply to the firm as a whole have to be apportioned to each division by someone, typically the CEO. The public goods aspects of the firm have to be dealt with as well. If the firm was the same as a market, there would be no public goods aspects such as reputation to deal with.

Oticon is an example of a firm that attempted to be a market.[8] The company was a traditional industrial company with administrative systems organized into functional departments. The company began to experience problems in the late 1980s. The CEO decided to radically change the company. Departments were eliminated, and competence centers such as audiology and engineering were created. Employees could voluntarily sign up to work on any project, and project managers were free to manage projects as they wanted. Wage negotiations were decentralized, and project managers were given the right to negotiate salaries. The structure was called "spaghetti," illustrating the idea that while things were tied together it was done so only loosely. Employees were given many decision-making rights. Most hierarchical levels were eliminated, and formal titles were done away with.

By 1996, Oticon had returned to a more traditional matrix structure because the spaghetti structure had not worked. The spaghetti structure eliminated what hierarchy can do in terms of allocating competence, enabling specialization, and reducing the costs of coordination and knowledge sharing. Oticon eliminated hierarchy, but perhaps its greatest problem was that it did not assign property rights very well either. The people given ownership of decision rights knew these were temporary and that they were more of a loaning of decision rights. As a result, they were afraid to invest in the assets by making decisions and being entrepreneurial.

The idea of making firms more marketlike may ignore factors that brought these transactions inside firms in the first place. Transaction costs may be less for a traditional firm than one that relies on internal markets, or proprietary information may require internal transactions as opposed to using the external market. But relying on internal markets as much as possible makes sense. In particular, it enables the invisible hand of the market to replace the visible hand of a central planner for many decisions. It enables the collection of distributed knowledge in the most efficient manner.

Headquarters and Management   What is the role of the headquarters and managers in the market-based firm? The headquarters is much like the government in a free market economy. It enforces private property rights. Different from a government, the headquarters assigns property rights within the firm. The decision rights in a firm have to be assigned by someone, and those rights have to be owned—not rented as in the Oticon case. It is up to headquarters to ensure that the decision rights are owned by the right people and are not abridged by others. The headquarters is also responsible for ensuring that governance is not violated and for handling financial reporting and reporting to government and other relevant agencies. The manager monitors the team aspects of the firm, and together the manager and headquarters create incentives and provide approaches to minimizing standard market failures. Headquarters likely creates the culture of the firm or at least sets up the initial institutions that generate a culture. Then the managers and employees ensure that the culture is communicated to future employees.

Summing Up

In the 1950s and 1960s economists proposed that the transfer-pricing problem should be solved by charging market prices for internal transactions. Similarly, in the 1980s, financial economists suggested that the capital allocation problem should be solved by charging the external cost of capital for internal investments. Wave after wave of organizational restructuring has advocated flattening the hierarchy, decentralization, empowerment, intrapreneurship, and, in short, making employees feel like the owners not just of their decisions but of the firm itself. Proponents of making transactions within firms more marketlike often seem to ignore the factors that brought these transactions inside firms in the first place. Remember that the firm exists because it is more efficient than contractible relationships in the market. There are trade-offs—there is no free lunch. As discussed in prior chapters, in some cases integration and hierarchy are efficient precisely because market incentives are eliminated; for instance, often firms need employees to share information when if they were independent contractors these employees would have an incentive not to share. In such cases, bringing the market inside the firm would be undesirable. And in some cases, bringing the market inside the firm is not feasible, even if it would be desirable.

Yet, the value of a market in collecting distributed information must be recognized. If that value can be realized inside the firm without imposing a cost that exceeds the value, then the market should be relied on inside the firm.

Terrorist Markets

The Policy Analysis Market (PAM) was designed by a host of people, including Net Exchange and the Intelligence Unit of the economist for DARPA. While the original announcement on July 28 by U.S. senators Ron Wyden of Oregon and Byron L. Dorgan of North Dakota claim that this was a terror market that traded in assassinations and terrorist attacks, the truth was that this market did not trade on those kind of events. What apparently occurred was that the company, Net Exchange, had a couple of ill-advised examples. The examples included the possibility of betting on the assassination of Palestinian leader Yasser Arafat or the overthrow of Jordan's monarchy.

The PAM system would have been the first time that markets were attempted as a way of accumulating information in the intelligence community. There are strong reasons to think that PAM would have worked. The key is that markets are the best way discovered so far for aggregating the knowledge of participants. The market would have been a betting market that traded in the outcomes of events like one would trade stocks. The market would have been open to more than just government employees. Even extreme views such as radically destructive elements like terrorists and assassins could have traded in this market. All trading would be anonymous, so that government employees who were forced to slant their reports the "right way" could still accurately report their views via the market. The insiders would trade, again improving the accuracy of the markets.

The potential problem that worried the senators was the moral hazard problem wherein a buyer engages in risky or dangerous activity after a purchase of a security might arise, so terrorists could profit off of their own acts. But it would be very unlikely to occur. The same potential of insiders profiting off of their actions exists in the stock markets, insurance markets, gambling markets, and many other areas every day. Yet, these problems do not occur.

Summary

1. An unfettered or free market results in an efficient allocation of resources.
2. The market price incorporates all information that traders bring to the market.
3. Transfer prices are the prices at which one division in a firm sells product to another division in the firm.
4. The optimal transfer price is one set to maximize overall firm profits, not just the profits of the transferring divisions.
5. Internal markets are markets that exist within a firm to allocate resources.
6. Prediction markets are created to elicit the information that a diverse and anonymous set of traders have about an event. The market price yields the best valuation of an event occurring.
7. Internal markets can be used to allocate scarce resources as well as to form forecasts or predictions about events.
8. The creation of an internal market requires a well-defined good or service, private property rights, incentives for traders to participate, and minimization of issues such as externalities, public goods, asymmetric information, and monopolization.
9. Will a firm continue to evolve into one where internal markets make all decisions inside the firm? Although markets have a comparative advantage over command and control, the markets have to be created and developed and the rules and regulations defined.
10. While the firm may use markets to allocate resources inside the firm, there are reasons that the firm exists in the first place. Individuals voluntarily agree to join a firm, trading services for a salary.
11. Relational contracts do not try to contract for every possible contingency but recognize that situations will change and evolve and relations will develop. So, one reason the firm exists is to enable relations to thrive. The firm has to enlist the distributed information that individuals in the firm have, and it would be extremely costly, if even possible, to set up fixed contracts for every contingency.
12. The role of headquarters and managers is much like the role of government in a free market economy—to enforce and secure private property rights.

Key Terms

Internal market
Transfer price

Net marginal product
Prediction market

Exercises

1. You have been hired as a consultant to create a market-based economy in a nation that has never before experienced markets. Explain how you would do that.

2. A large firm has two divisions: an upstream division that is a monopoly supplier of a resource, whose only market is the downstream division that produces the final output. Would the firm's profit be maximized by paying upstream and downstream divisional managers a percentage of its divisional profits? Explain.

3. A large firm has two divisions: an upstream division that produces an output that is used by the downstream division. The downstream division could obtain that output from external firms as well as the upstream division. Should the firm allow the downstream division to purchase the product externally, or should it require that the firm use only the upstream division's product? Explain

4. Define the term *principal-agent problem*. What principal-agent problems exist in a market? What principal-agent problems exist in a firm? What are possible solutions to principal-agent issues within the firm?

5. What is moral hazard? How does the firm deal with moral hazard in its relationships with suppliers or customers? How does the firm deal with moral hazard internally?

6. Capital markets enable us to spend large sums of money that don't belong to us. Would it be necessary to create an internal capital market if a firm was to be led by market-based management? Explain.

7. What would be the CEO's role in a company led by market-based management?

8. If market-based management is more efficient than the command and control of a hierarchy, why have firms not employed the strategy?

9. How would internal markets adjust for or take the cost of capital into account?

10. Suppose economic profit was used to evaluate each division in a company. Describe how it would serve to foster the correct incentives inside the firm.

11. The following demand and marginal cost equations represent the demand for some service inside the firm. At what price should the service be sold? Would it matter whether there was an external market for this service?
The demand function

$$P = 30 - 2Q$$

The marginal cost function: $MC = 20$.

12. A firm has estimated the following demand function for its product:

$$Q = 8 - 2P + 0.10I + E$$

where Q is quantity demanded per month in thousands, P is product price, I is an index of consumer income, and E is expectations of economic conditions in the future. Assume that $P = 10, $I = 100$, and $E = 20$ when conditions are expected to be good and -10 when conditions are expected to be bad. Explain and/or demonstrate what it means to say that price takes into account all information available.

13. Explain why firms exist. Explain why there is not just one huge firm.

14. Using markets to gather information is quite different than market-based management. Explain how they are different.

15. What steps are necessary to create an internal market?

16. BP relies on internal markets to collect information and help make decisions. Would the use of a predictive market related to oil well blowouts have predicted the 2010 Gulf of Mexico disaster? Explain your answer.

17. What is the role of headquarters and the CEO in a factory-type firm? What is their role in a market-based firm?

18. A recent book was titled *The End of Management*. Suppose the technology evolves in such a way that a high percentage of employees do not work in the company office. They telecommute or work offline. What then is the role of management? Is there one, or is the book title correct?

CHAPTER NOTES

1. Ajit Kambil, "Leading with an Invisible Hand," Accenture, *Outlook Journal*, July 2002 www .accenture.com/Global/Research_and_Insights/Outlook/By_Alphabet/LeadingInvisibleHand.htm, accessed May 4, 2008; David McAdams and Thomas Malone, "Internal Markets for Supply Chain Capacity Allocation," MIT Sloan School Working Paper 4546-05, June 2005; Alix Stuart, "Magic Markets: Internal Markets Can Solve Thorny Allocation Problems and Predict the Future," *CFO Magazine*, November 1, 2005 www.cfo.com/printable/article.cfm/5077917?f=options, accessed May 4, 2008.

2. The approach BP took was similar to the emissions trading program used by the EPA and by the signers of the Kyoto Protocol. By signing the Kyoto Protocol in 2005, more than 160 countries committed themselves to reduce CO_2 emissions and the emissions of five other greenhouse gasses. At the same time the countries also committed to engage in emission certificate trading. This type of system, also known as cap-and-trade, enables a source with a high cost of reducing an additional unit of emissions to purchase a permit from a source with a lower marginal abatement cost. Sources will trade permits until the price for the permits equals the marginal abatement cost. The level of emissions permitted, the cap, is established by some authority. Then the permits are sold via auction or given away. Once initially allocated, the divisions can begin trading the permits. As the permit price rises, the incentive to purchase emission-reducing equipment rises. If enough such investment occurs, the demand for permits rises, the supply rises, and the price falls.

3. www.biz.uiowa.edu/iem

4. Kathleen Melymuka, "Bringing the Market Inside: IT-enabled Internal Markets Can Speed Up and Improve Decision-making," *Computer World Management*, April 12, 2004 www.computerworld.com/managementtopics/management/story/0,10801,92084,00.html, accessed May 4, 2008.

5. William J. Boyes and Stephen Happel, "Managing in an Academic Environment," *Journal of Economic Perspectives*, 3, no. 3 (Summer 1989): 32–40. Reprinted in Don Cole, ed., *Annual Editions Economics 91/92* (Guilford CT: Dushkin Publishing Group, 1991–1992), pp. 43–46.

6. Marginal Revolution Bog. Market Failure? Academic Departments, www.marginalrevolution.com/marginalrevolution/2006/08/market_failure_.html.

7. Charles Koch developed this term to describe how he manages his firm, Koch Industries. See, Charles Koch, *The Science of Success* (New York: John Wiley, 2007).

8. Nicolai J. Foss, *Strategy, Economic Organization, and the Knowledge Economy* (New York: Oxford University Press, 2005), Chapter 7, pp. 157–186.

CHAPTER 19

Measuring Economic Profit

Considering the Cost of Capital

When Roberto Goizueta became Coke's CEO in 1981, he took over a poorly performing company that had diversified into unrelated businesses ranging from water purification to shrimp farming. One of his first initiatives was to analyze Coke's various businesses using *economic* profit. The analysis concluded that only Coke's core carbonated beverage business was creating shareholder value. The other businesses, while generating revenue, were actually consuming value. Consequently, they were divested or shut down. Goizueta then focused on Coke's core beverage business using its substantial competitive advantages: global brand, worldwide distribution system, and sales and marketing expertise. The result was 18 years of success.

Similarly, when Bob Lane took over a poorly performing John Deere in August 2000, he quickly identified Deere's biggest problem: spending too much money to make money. Factories tended to overproduce, leading to a large number of very expensive, large farming machines simply sitting on dealer floors. Lane began looking at economic profit. He decided managers were treating capital as a free resource. He charged each division manager 1 percent each month of the cost of the assets they used and required that at the end of the year their financial results exceed the charges. Deere has done well in the succeeding years.[1]

1. What is the appropriate measure of a firm's performance?
2. What does a focus on economic profit as opposed to a focus on accounting profit mean for a firm and its investors?

Calculation of Economic Profit

The performance of a nation might be judged on the basis of how much people's lives improve each year—in other words, how much value is added to society in general. If incomes are growing and standards of living are rising, then perhaps the nation is doing well. The performance of a firm can be described in somewhat the same way; the value the firm is able to add to society rises each year. If the value of output the firm provides exceeds the value of the resources the firm uses, then the firm is adding value.

Adding value is the purpose of business activity in a market system. An organization that adds no value—whose output is worth less than the value of its inputs in alternative uses—has no long-term rationale for its existence. In the long run, organizations that fail to add value will not survive. Inefficient decisions and allocations will eventually be replaced or overturned by more efficient ones.

The measure of added value on which "for-profit" firms focus is profit. How is profit measured? If we ignore the implicit cost of capital, we would have a measure of profit that would be relatively easy to calculate: Revenue – rent – wages – interest. This measure of profit is what is presented in financial statements and is typically called operating profit or net operating profit. This is the value of output less the cost of inputs but not including the opportunity cost of the owner's (shareholders') capital.

$$\text{Economic profit} = \text{Accounting profit} - \text{Cost of capital}$$

The objective of the owners of a firm is to maximize profit. Since economic profit is total revenue minus total cost, strategy seems rather straightforward—raise revenue and lower cost. But this is often easier said than done. Let us look more closely at profit. Economic profit is:

(1) Economic Profit = Total Revenue – Cost of land – Cost of labor – Cost of capital

Or writing economic profit in accounting terms, where **NOPAT** is **net operating profit after taxes** and NOPAT = (1 – tax rate) [revenue – cost of land – cost of labor]: and WACC is the weighted average cost of capital:

$$\text{Economic profit} = \text{NOPAT} - (\text{WACC} * \text{Invested capital})$$

Economic profit is obtained by subtracting the cost of capital from net operating profit after tax (NOPAT). NOPAT is the income derived from the company's operations, after income taxes, but before all financing costs and noncash bookkeeping entries except depreciation.

We can rewrite NOPAT as revenue less cost of goods sold (COGS) and selling, general, and administrative costs (SG&A).

$$\text{NOPAT} = (\text{Revenue} - \text{COGS} - \text{SG\&A})(1 - \text{Tax rate})$$

The accounting measurements of labor and land costs are **cost of goods sold (COGS)** and the **selling and general and administrative costs (SG&A)**. Cost of goods sold is essentially the cost of land and labor used to produce a good, the expenses a company incurred in order to manufacture, create, and sell a product. It includes the purchase price of the raw material as well as the expenses of turning it into a product. SG&A expenses consist of the combined payroll costs (salaries, commissions, and travel expenses of executives, salespeople, and employees) and advertising expenses a company incurs. General and administrative expenses (G & A) represent expenses to manage the business (officer salaries, legal and professional fees, utilities, insurance, depreciation of office building and equipment, stationery, supplies), while selling expenses (S) represent expenses needed to sell products (e.g., sales salaries and commissions, advertising, freight, shipping, depreciation of sales equipment).

So the second way that economic profit can be written is:

$$(2) \text{ Economic profit} = \{(1 - \text{Tax rate}) * (\text{Revenue} - \text{COGS} - \text{SG\&A})\} \\ - (\text{WACC} * \text{Invested capital})$$

Table 19.1 illustrates how a firm can calculate economic profit. The firm earns $16,741 million, and its costs are as given in the table.

Economic profit equals NOPAT less capital charges. Capital charges equal the company's invested capital multiplied by the weighted average cost of capital (WACC). The WACC equals the sum of the cost of each component of capital—short-term debt, long-term debt, and shareholders' equity—weighted for its relative proportion of the company's capital structure. Invested capital is the sum of all the firm's financing, apart from short-term, non-interest-bearing liabilities, such as accounts payable, accrued wages, and accrued taxes. It equals the sum of shareholders' equity, interest-bearing debt (both short and long term), and other long-term liabilities.[2]

Table 19.1

Economic Profit

LINE ITEMS	DOLLARS (MILLIONS)	WHAT THE ITEM MEANS
Total revenues	$16,741	The total revenue of the company for the fiscal year
Accounting net income from the financial statements	$1,101	The net income to common shareholders as reported in the income statement of the company. Calculations for NOPAT and economic profit start here
Interest expense Tax adjustment Unusual income	$889 + 87 – 32	Adjustments made to the accounting financial statements to reflect the accounts of the company on a cash and operating basis. Only cash expenses are retained. The only noncash expense remaining is the depreciation for fixed assets. Paper gains or losses are adjusted to a cash basis. For example, the sale of a building for $1 million when its value in the books of the company are recorded at $400,000 account for a $600,000 paper gain, which gain provides no additional cash to the company. The interest expense is added back as an adjustment because it will be deducted later on with the cost of capital.
NOPAT	$2,044	NOPAT is the profit of the company net of all paper losses or gains, on a cash basis, and net of income taxes.
Cost of capital	$1,294	The cost of capital is the charge to the company for providing it with all of the capital it needs to operate the business. The charge is dependent on the level of risk that investors and lenders take for investing in the company. In this example, the weighted average cost of capital is 7.3 percent on total capital of $17,726,220
Economic profit	$750	When the capital charges have been subtracted from NOPAT, the remainder is economic profit.

Step-by-Step Calculation of Economic Profit

The calculation of economic profit starts with the income statement. The **income statement** is a financial statement that indicates how revenue is transformed into net income (called the bottom line).[3] We are interested in **earnings before interest and taxes (EBIT)**. EBIT is revenues less land and labor costs. Accounting profit is later obtained by subtracting interest and taxes from the result. This is called net operating profits after taxes (NOPAT). So, to move to economic profit we need to a capital charge. We obtain the EBIT from the firm's income statement.

The Walt Disney Co. income statement is shown in Figure 19.1. To calculate NOPAT, we must add interest expense back to ensure we measure the profits that accrue to all capital holders, including lenders. We begin with accounting profit or net operating profit after taxes (NOPAT).

NOPAT is net income without interest expenses; it tells us whether the firm is paying its costs, but not whether it is meeting its debt obligations or rewarding its owners. Without knowing whether owners are being paid, we cannot answer questions such as: Should the resources be deployed elsewhere? Are there incentives for other firms to enter this industry and begin competing? We need to know whether NOPAT is sufficient to pay the cost of capital.

$$\text{Economic profit} = \text{NOPAT} - \text{Cost of debt} - \text{Cost of equity capital}$$

To calculate the cost of capital, it is necessary to determine how much capital the firm is using. The invested capital, the total investment debtholders and shareholders have made in a company, is the measure of capital in use. There is more than one way to

FIGURE 19.1 Income Statement of Walt Disney Company

Income Statement	(all numbers in thousands)
Period ending	September 30, 2006
Total revenue	34,1285,000
Cost of revenue	28,807,000
Gross profit	5,478,000
Operating expenses	
Research and development	
Selling general and administrative	
Nonrecurring	(18,000)
Operating income or loss	5,496,000
Total other incomes/expenses net	114,000
Earnings before iinterest and ttaxes	6,153,000
Interest expense	706,000
Income before tax	1,890,000
Minority interest	(183,000)
Net income from continuing ops	3,374,000
Net income	3,374,000

Source: Yahoo Finance.

FIGURE 19.2 Net Operating Profit after Taxes

Earnings before interest and taxes	6,153,000
Add interest expense	706,000
Cash operating taxes	(2,400,000)
NOPAT	3,753,000

get to invested capital, but the most common approach is to get total assets and subtract accounts payable and current liabilities. These are reported in the firm's balance sheet, which is a financial statement showing Assets – Liabilities = Stockholders' Equity.

In measuring economic profit, we want to include only the company's funds or financing provided by shareholders and debtholders. Short-term loans and accounts payable are not associated with investing in the company. This is why accounts payable and current liabilities are subtracted out.

The Disney balance sheet is summarized in Figure 19.3. For Disney, we use total assets listed on the balance sheet and subtract accounts payable and other current liabilities.

Using total assets of $59,667,000 and subtracting accounts payable and current liabilities the invested capital is $52,609,000.

Cost of Capital   The cost of debt is the interest expense on debt (short- and long-term debt). The cost of debt can be found on the 10-K footnotes recognizing different forms of debt often listed there.[4] It is also important to recognize that debt expenses can be deducted from the firm's tax bill so the cost of debt must be adjusted to reflect this. For instance, suppose the cost of debt is 6 percent. This is the pretax cost of debt. The

FIGURE 19.3 Figure A: Balance Sheet for Disney

Assets	
Current Assets	
Cash and Cash Equivalents	3,464,000
Net Receivables	5,727,000
Inventory	608,000
Other Current Assets	1,019,000
Total Current Assets	10,818,000
Long-term Investments	934,000
Property Plant and Equipment	17,065,000
Goodwill	22,015,000
Intangible Assets	7,405,000
Other Assets	1,430,000
Total Assets	59,667,000
Liabilities	
Current Liabilities	
Accounts Payable	5,137,000
Other Current Liabilities	2,461,000

after-tax cost of debt is therefore lower. To obtain this number we multiple the pretax cost of debt by (1 – tax rate). If the company's effective tax rate is 34 percent, the after-tax cost of debt would equal 6 percent multiplied by 66 percent, or 3.96 percent.

Unlike the cost of debt, which is explicit and can be referenced, the cost of equity is implicit: Shareholders expect returns on their investment. The cost of equity capital is the opportunity cost to investors of leaving their money with a particular firm. There are several approaches to estimating the opportunity cost to investors, but the most commonly used is referred to as the capital asset pricing model or CAPM.[5]

As discussed in Chapter 17, the CAPM formula is as follows:

$$\text{Cost of equity} = \text{Risk-free rate} + \text{Equity premium}$$

The equity premium is the overall average return that investors in the stock market expect above that of a risk-free investment. The typical risk-free rate is the rate on U.S. Treasury bonds. There is always a debate about the size of the equity premium, but most people agree that a reasonable value is 4 to 5 percent. So if the risk-free rate is 5 percent, the equity premium is 4 percent, and the beta is 1.1, the cost of equity would be estimated to be

$$\text{Cost of equity:} \quad 5\% + (4\% \times 1.1) = 9.4\%$$

Once we have a measure of the cost of equity capital, we combine it with the cost of debt to determine the total cost of capital. We cannot simply add the two costs together because a firm may not use half debt and half equity. We average the costs by adding the cost of equity capital multiplied by the percent of total capital that is equity to the cost of debt capital multiplied by the percent of total capital that is debt. This is referred to as the WACC or weighted average cost of capital. This is illustrated in Figure 19.4.

$$\text{WACC} = (\text{cost of equity}) \times (\% \text{ of total capital that is equity}) + (\text{cost of debt}) \times (\% \text{ of total capital that is debt})$$

Now we can calculate the WACC. To do this, we simply multiply the cost of debt and equity by their respective proportions of invested capital, and then add the two resulting numbers together. The proportion of debt and equity depends on the total dollar amount of each, and we can find this information on the balance sheet. If we add up the debt (i.e., long-term debt plus short-term debt plus other liabilities), we get $17.36 billion. The market value of the equity (market capitalization) is $59.98 billion. Debt is therefore 22 percent of invested capital and equity is 78 percent. This means

$$\text{WACC} = (.22 \times 4.6) + (.78 \times 8.6) = 7.72$$

Final Step   The final step is to determine economic profit. Economic profit = NOPAT – capital charge.

NOPAT		$3,753,000
Invested capital	$52,609,000	
× WACC	7.72%	
= Capital charge	$4,061,415	
Economic profit	(308,415)	

FIGURE 19.4 Calculating the Cost of Capital Using Disney, 2006

Pretax cost of debt 6.5 × (1 – tax rate) (1 – .347)		= After tax Cost of debt 4.6
Risk-free rate 4% + (Equity premium × beta) (4% × 1.1)		= Cost of equity 8.4%

According to the calculations, Disney had a negative economic profit in 2006.

The calculation of economic profit seems to be extremely difficult, but it is not. You can think of economic profit as being similar to the concept of net worth to an individual. You begin with revenue and then deduct costs.

Individual	Business
Salary	Revenue
Less	Less
Nonfinancial expenses (food, clothing, utilities, insurance, misc)	Operating expenses (cost of goods sold, SGA, etc.)
Taxes	Taxes
Income before interest	NOPAT
Less	Less
Interest loans	Capital charge
Equals	Equals
Change in net worth	Economic profit

Economists' Definition of Profit

A third way to represent economic profit is more familiar to economists, and that is to consider fixed and variable costs. Variable costs are all expenses that vary with or depend on the quantity of output a firm provides for sale. Fixed costs are expenses that do not vary with the quantity of output.

$$(3) \text{ Economic profit} = \text{Revenue} - \text{Variable costs} - \text{Fixed costs}$$

Each of these representations of economic profit can provide useful insights into the firm's performance. Equation (2) is more of an accounting representation of economic profit, while equation (3) uses traditional economic terms to represent economic profit. Cost terms do not directly translate. COGS is not necessarily only variable costs and SG&A fixed costs. They each contain elements of variable and fixed costs.

Abnormal Net Income and Discounted Cash Flow Models

The profit that results when economic profit is zero is referred to as normal profit because it is the profit that competition will permit—revenue equal to total opportunity costs. When economic profit is positive, the return necessary to keep resources in their current use is less than the returns being generated. This difference is referred to as abnormal as in abnormal net income.

The abnormal net income model[6] is an approach used by financial accountants to value companies. It says that the market value of a firm is its book value (the current stockholders' equity) plus the present value of economic profits expected to be earned in the future. In symbols,

$$P_o = bv_o + [(X_1 - rbv_o)/(1 + r)^1] + [(X_2 - rbv_1)/(1 + r)^2] + [(X_3 - rbv_2)/(1 + r)^3] + \ldots$$

where P_o is the predicted market value of the company; X is NOPAT less debt costs, bv_o is current stockholders' equity, r is the cost of capital, and thus rbv_o is the total cost of capital and represents what next year's net income would be if return on beginning stockholders' equity (ROE) equals the cost of capital. Stated another way, rbv_o is next year's cost of capital measured in dollars instead of a percentage. Thus $X_1 - rbv_o$ is next year's expected net income in excess of the cost of capital. That number is termed abnormal net income and is an accounting based measure of economic profit. The entire second term is the *present value* of next year's expected economic profit. The entire third term is the *present value* of the third year's expected economic profit, and so on.

The market value of the firm's equity is the accounting value of current stockholders' equity (bv_o) plus the present value of a sequence of expected economic profits. Present value refers to the value today of streams of earnings in the future. The future values are put into today's values by discounting each term using the cost of capital as the discount rate.

Firms that are expected to earn positive economic profit would have a market value in excess of the accounting value of stockholders' equity or book value. They will have *market-to-book ratios* greater than one. Firms that are expected to earn near zero economic profit will have market-to-book ratios close to one, and firms expected to earn negative economic profit will have market-to-book ratios that are less than one. (*Note:* The median market-to-book ratio of firms in the pharmaceutical industry, as of the end of 2006, was 4.59. In contrast, the median ratio of firms in the airline industry was 1.57.)

Another way to look at performance is to compare the return on invested capital to the cost of capital. Invested capital is the amount of capital that has been put into the firm. The return on invested capital (ROIC) is the profit per dollar of invested capital. Since ROIC is NOPAT/Invested capital, and

$$\text{Economic profit} = \text{NOPAT} - (\text{WACC} * \text{Invested capital})$$

we can write economic profit as:

$$\text{Economic profit} = [\text{ROIC} - \text{WACC}] * \text{Invested capital}$$

This formulation of economic profit states that if the return on invested capital equals the cost of capital, economic profit is zero. Economic profit is positive if the return on invested capital exceeds the cost of capital.[7]

Stock Price and Abnormal Net Income

A stock price is determined by the demand for and supply of shares of that stock. Both demanders and suppliers base their valuation of the price of the stock on expectations of future firm performance. For them to trade, they must have different viewpoints about the movement of the stock price. The buyer has to expect it to improve more than alternatives, and the seller must expect it not to improve as much as alternatives. If they had exactly the same viewpoints, there would be no reason to trade.

It is the market's expectations (buyers and sellers) of future firm performance that determine the price of a share of stock. Once determined, if nothing changes, share price won't change. What causes the stock price to rise or fall? The answer is revisions of expectations. The abnormal net income model indicates that the market value goes up when expectations of future net income rise (as when announced earnings exceed expectations, triggering increased net income expectations going forward) and vice versa, everything else held constant.[8]

$$\frac{\eth P_o}{\eth X_1} > 0$$

But it is not just expected earnings that matter: It is the excess of expected net income over the cost of capital, that is, abnormal net income. When the cost of capital rises, everything else held constant, market value declines:

$$\frac{\eth P_o}{Dr} < 0$$

When expectations are revised upward, the stock price rises because more investors want to buy and fewer want to sell. When expectations are revised downward, the stock price falls because fewer investors want to buy and more want to sell. Thus, when a firm does better than expectations, its stock price will rise, and when a firm does worse than expectations, its stock price will fall.

From the mid-1990s through 2000, Cisco generated very substantial economic profit, a value that was reflected in the high price of its shares. Changes in the market value of Cisco in 2001, therefore, reflected its actual performance relative to its expected performance. Since expectations were high for Cisco, it would have been difficult for the company to have done better than those expectations, and, in the short term, stock price reassessments were as likely to be downward as upward, even though Cisco was earning significant profits. In fact, from March to June 2000, Cisco stock fell 40 percent, from a high of $80 per share to about $50 per share, even though Cisco earnings and profits were rising faster than the market as a whole.

Decay Rate   How long will a firm be able to maintain abnormal profits, if it earns any? The answer depends on how fast competitors come online to drive economic profit to zero. The **decay rate** is the speed at which abnormal net income is driven to zero. The competitive conditions of the industry define the decay rate. Markets characterized by relatively easy entry and large numbers tend to be cases where firms cannot sustain economic profits at all. When a firm has a competitive advantage and/or there are barriers to entry, it can sustain economic profit for some period of time. All firms are expected to lose their advantages over time. This is part of what entrepreneurs do—drive economic profits to zero. Thus, the calculated measure of the value of the firm depends crucially on the decay rate—that is, the horizon over which economic profit is assumed to be positive.

Strategic Formulation of Economic Profit

Part of strategy is to determine how much output to provide for sale. That depends on what occurs to economic profit as sales increase or decrease. So we make a few simple manipulations to put the economic profit equation into a form that allows us to examine strategic factors more readily. Let's begin with formulation (2).

$$(2)\ \text{Economic profit} = \{(1 - \text{Tax rate}) * (\text{Revenue} - \text{COGS} - \text{SG\&A})\} \\ - (\text{WACC} * \text{Invested capital})$$

First, multiply the equation by revenue/revenue. Then multiply it by market size/market size. Since each of these manipulations is just multiplying by the number 1, the equation is not changed.

Now, since market share is just the firm's revenue divided by market size, economic profit can be written as:

$$2(s)\ \text{ECONOMIC PROFIT} = \left\{(1 - \text{tax rate}) * \frac{\text{Revenue} - \text{COGS} - \text{SG\&A}}{\text{Revenue}}\right\} \\ - \text{WACC} * \frac{\text{Capital}}{\text{Revenue}} * \left\{\frac{\text{Revenue}}{\text{market size}} * \text{market size}\right\}$$

Let's call this formulation of economic profit the *strategic formulation of economic profit*. It enables us to look at strategic actions that a firm can undertake to affect economic profit. For instance, equation (2s) informs us that we need to focus on each of the following:

1. *Revenue.* Will increasing revenue increase or reduce economic profit? It depends on how an increase in revenue affects costs. If more goods are sold and costs rise less

than revenue, then profits rise. Thus, we need to know the relationship between goods sold, revenue, and costs.

Also, since Revenue = *PQ*, we need to know if revenue would be increased by increasing price—that is, will an increase in price increase or decrease revenue? The answer is that it depends on customer reactions to changes in price – price elasticity of demand.

2. *COGS to Revenue Ratio.* In accounting, the cost of goods sold (also, cost of sales) describes the *direct* expenses incurred in producing a particular good for sale, including the actual cost of materials that comprise the good, and direct labor expense in putting the good in salable condition. Cost of goods sold does not include indirect expenses such as office expenses, accounting, shipping department, advertising, and other expenses that cannot be attributed to a particular item for sale. Will reducing direct costs increase profit? It depends on whether reductions in direct costs lead to revenue reductions. We need to understand the relationship between price, output and direct costs.

3. *SG&A to Revenue Ratio.* Will an increase in revenue lead to a smaller ratio of SG&A to sales? It depends on the efficiencies in marketing or administration and whether the efficiency depends on the amount of sales. This item represents all commercial expenses of operation (i.e., expenses not directly related to product production) incurred in the regular course of business pertaining to the securing of operating income. These are costs not linked to the production of specific goods, but including all selling, general company expense, and administrative expenses. These include such things as salespersons salaries, advertising, and salaries for executives. Superior relationships with and knowledge of channels and customers lead to lower sales and service costs.

4. *WACC.* Will a change in revenue affect the cost of capital, or vice versa? We need to understand the components of WACC.

5. *Capital to Revenue Ratio.* Will an increase in capital increase or decrease economic profit? That depends on the relationship between capital and revenue and the effect of increased capital on COGS and SG&A.

6. *Market Share,* What is the effect of a higher or lower market share on economic profit?

The strategic formulation of economic profit using the traditional economic terms is derived with the same manipulations as those used to get Equation (2s):

$$(3s)\ \text{ECONOMIC PROFIT} = \frac{\text{Revenue} - \text{variable costs}}{\text{Revenue}} - \frac{\text{fixed costs}}{\text{Revenue}}$$
$$* \left\{ \frac{\text{Revenue}}{\text{market size}} * \text{market size} \right\}$$

Formulation (3s) changes the focus on costs by classifying them as fixed and variable. It requires that we understand the relationship between revenue and fixed and variable costs.

The Practical Effect of a Focus on Economic Profit

If firms focus on an accounting measure of performance, they are essentially ignoring the cost of capital or at least the equity cost of capital. Introducing economic profit as the focal point can change a firm's behavior.[9] Before Quaker Oats adopted economic profit as its measure of performance, the manager of Quaker's granola bar plant in Danville, Illinois, used long production runs to turn out the various sizes of bars in order to minimize downtime and setup costs. This bolstered operating profits but also resulted in huge inventories of bars that sat in a warehouse until gradually they were shipped to customers. Inventory is not free, however. Capital is tied up in that inventory. Thus, when the company charged the manager for the inventory—that is, the capital tied up in inventory—he switched to short production runs, which reduced net operating profits but increased economic profit.

Prior to focusing on economic profit, Coca-Cola shipped its soft-drink syrup to bottlers in stainless-steel cans, which could be used over and over. The problem was that the steel cans were expensive; they required significant amounts of capital. When the company began focusing on economic profit, it sold off the stainless-steel cans and switched to cardboard containers. The cardboard increased operating costs—but by less than the cost of capital declined.[10] As a result, economic profit rose.

Diageo PLC owns United Distillers and Vintners, Unlimited, which sells both scotch and vodka. Diageo analyzed its production costs and found that even though both the scotch and the vodka were making accounting profit, the vodka production was making more economic profit. Scotch is aged, whereas vodka does not have to be aged to the same degree before imbibing. The result is that a lot of scotch sits around being aged, which of course uses a significant amount of capital for storage. When the cost of this capital was taken into account, the vodka production was vamped up and the scotch production was decreased. After assessing economic profit, Diageo moved its resources to the place where they have the highest value.[11]

Considering the Cost of Capital

Measuring economic profit requires that capital be allocated to where it is used and that the opportunity cost of capital be measured.

$$\text{Economic profit} = \text{Revenue} - \text{Cost of land} - \text{Cost of labor} - \text{cost of capital}$$

The main point of economic profit as compared to accounting profit is the cost of capital. Measures such as accounting profit fail to account for the cost to capital. And if capital is treated as if it is "free," then it does not matter whether or not it is allocated efficiently. This is what Deere and Coke managers were doing—treating capital as if it was free. Using economic profit forces managers to recognize the cost of both debt and equity capital used to generate revenues.

Economic profit is a snapshot, a one-year look at a firm's performance, and one year does not make a trend. But economic profit over several years gives a great picture of performance, and this is what the stock market looks at. The present value of all expected future economic profits is what tells us whether a company is expected to create or destroy wealth. When CEOs such as Goizueta and Lane tie annual manager bonuses to economic profit, what happens? Managers are incentivized to recognize that all resources have costs. According to the results of Coke and John Deere, the result improved performance. Even with a rather simplistic 1 percent charge on assets used by each division, the managers began to pay attention to how much capital they were using. Large pieces of equipment did not sit idle on dealer floors.

Summary

1. Economic profit is defined as: Revenue – Cost of land – Cost of labor – Cost of debt – Cost of equity. It is also Accounting profit – Cost of capital.
2. Economic profit is defined as: NOPAT – Cost of debt – Cost of equity.
3. The measurement of economic profit is difficult only because the cost of equity capital is difficult to measure. The standard estimate of the cost of capital is based on the capital asset pricing model (CAPM).
4. The value of a company depends on the expected stream of future economic profits. The abnormal net income model illustrates how market value depends on current stockholders' equity and on expectations of future economic profits.
5. Eventually economic profits will be competed to zero. An important question is how long does it take. This is the decay rate in the abnormal net income model.

6. (2s) $\text{ECONOMIC PROFIT} = \left\{ (1 - \text{tax rate}) * \dfrac{\text{Revenue} - \text{COGS} - \text{SG\&A}}{\text{Revenue}} \right\}$
$$- \text{WACC} * \frac{\text{Capital}}{\text{Revenue}} * \left\{ \frac{\text{Revenue}}{\text{market size}} * \text{market size} \right\}$$

Formulation (2s) of economic profit is called the *strategic formulation of economic profit*. It enables us to look at strategic actions that the firm can undertake to affect economic profit.

7. (3s) $\text{ECONOMIC PROFIT} = \dfrac{\text{Revenue} - \text{variable costs}}{\text{Revenue}} - \dfrac{\text{fixed costs}}{\text{Revenue}}$
$$* \left\{ \frac{\text{Revenue}}{\text{market size}} * \text{market size} \right\}$$

Formulation (3s) changes the focus on costs by classifying them as fixed and variable. It requires that we understand the relationship between revenue and fixed and variable costs.

Key Terms

Net operating profit after taxes (NOPAT)

Cost of goods sold (COGS)

Selling and general and administrative costs (SG&A)

Income statement

Earnings before interest and taxes (EBIT)

Decay rate

Exercises

1. Calculate the added value for each of the following firms.

    Microsoft:
Value of output	$2,750
Wages and salaries	400
Cost of capital	40
Cost of materials	1,650

    Barclays Bank:
Value of output	$5,730
Wages and salaries	3,953
Cost of capital	916
Cost of material	556

    General Motors:
Value of output	$50,091
Wages and salaries	29,052
Cost of capital	15,528
Cost of materials	7,507

2. Following is some standard accounting information for each of the firms shown. Can you tell which firm is the most successful? Explain.

	Boeing	Good year	Liz Claiborne	Circuit City
Sales	5601	423	622	1767
Profits	254	26.9	56.2	31.6
Return on sales	4.5%	5.2%	9%	1.8%
Return on equity	10.2	13.9	15	14.5

3. A cost of capital figure for each of the firms is listed below. Explain what this figure means.

Motorola	11.6
Hershey Foods	12.8
Home Depot	12.2
Dillard Department Stores	10.5
Coca-Cola	12.0

4. Listed below are financial figures for Abbott Labs. How well is Abbott doing? Explain your answer.

	89	90	91	92	93	94	95	96
Sales ($mil)	5,380	6,159	6,877	7,852	8,408	9,156	10,012	11,014
Net income	860	966	1,089	1,239	1,399	1,517	1,689	1,882
Capital per share (book value/share)	3.08	3.30	3.77	4.00	4.48	5.04	5.58	6.15

5. Explain why economic profit provides a better measure of profit than accounting profit.

6. The manager of Global X is contemplating the purchase of a new machine that will cost $300,000 and has a useful life of five years. The machine is expected to yield cost reductions to Global X of $50,000 in year 1, $60,000 in year 2, $70,000 in year 3, and $80,000 in each year in years 4 and 5. Will the acquisition of the machine add value?

7. Using the following balance sheet and income statement information, calculate accounting profit and economic profit:

Balance Sheet	Jan 01
Cash	57
Net receivables	547
Inventories	3,364
Other current assets	332
Total current assets	4,300
Net fixed assets	9,622
Other noncurrent assets	2,156
Total assets	16,078
Accounts payable	2,163
Short-term debt	82
Other current liabilities	1,150
Total current liabilities	3,395
Long-term debt	5,942
Other noncurrent liabilities	931
Total liabilities	10,384
Total equity	5,694
Shares outstanding (mil)	405
Income Statement	
Revenue	36,762
Cost of goods sold	25,335
Gross profit	11,427
Gross profit margin	31.1%
SG&A expense	8,740
Depreciation & amortization	1,001
Operating income	1,686
Nonoperating expenses	385
Income before taxes	1,274
Income taxes	509
Net income after taxes	765

8. Explain what occurs when a new technology makes another one obsolete in terms of economic profit. Consider firm A to be an existing firm using the old technology. Firm B is the new firm with the new technology. Firm A earned positive profits for years, but with the entrance of Firm B, Firm A's goods and services are no longer desired.

9. In measuring economic profit:
   a. How do you deal with a one-time event?
   b. How do you deal with money provided by relatives to get the business started?
   c. How do you handle off-balance-sheet expenses—that is, expenses that are incurred by the firm but are not measured as part of the firm's balance sheet?

10. The following type of report occurs each quarter as firms announce their earnings:
   Weaker-than-expected results last week from Exxon Mobil have set a gloomy backcloth for results on Thursday from Royal Dutch/Shell. A consensus of Wall Street analysts polled by Thomson Financial/ First Call had projected ChevronTexaco would report earnings of 70 cents per share. However, the company said that after excluding special items and merger-related expenses in both periods, operating earnings were $931 million (88 cents). Using that math, the company beat the analysts' figure by 18 cents. The company said it lost $154 million in the first quarter, compared with the year-ago quarter, in refining, marketing, and transportation operations. The company said its profit margins in that sector were at their lowest levels since the mid-1990s. Chevron stock closed up 90 cents, to $85.90, yesterday on the New York Stock Exchange.
   a. Why does the stock market react to earnings reports?
   b. What do the earnings reports mean?

11. The manager of Global X is contemplating the purchase of a new machine that will cost $300,000 and has a useful life of five years. The machine is expected to yield cost reductions to Global X of $50,000 in year 1, $60,000 in year 2, $70,000 in year 3, and $80,000 in each year in years 4 and 5. Will the acquisition of the machine add value?

12. You have just been hired as a consultant to help a firm determine which of three options to take to increase shareholder wealth. The following table shows year-end profits for each option. Assume that the risk-free cost of capital is 5 percent and the risk premium is 8 percent.

Option	Profit in Year 1	Profit in Year 2	Profit in Year 3
A	$70,000	$80,000	$90,000
B	$50,000	$90,000	$100,000
C	$30,000	$100,000	$115,000

   a. Calculate the economic profit for each option.
   b. Suppose that the profit figures are based on earnings figures of 10 times profits and that there are 100,000 shares of stock outstanding. What are the earnings per share for each option?

13. It is often stated that free cash flow is the same as economic profit. Define *free cash flow*. Demonstrate whether it is or is not the same as economic profit.

14. Using the formula given in the text for stock price determination, explain why stock prices move up or down in response to quarterly earnings reports.

15. Use the following data to calculate economic profit in year 1.

Year	0	1
Sales		1,000
Expenses other than interest		500
Depreciation		200
Earnings before interest and taxes (EBIT)		300
Taxes on EBIT @40%		120
Earnings before interest and after taxes (EBIAT)		180
Current assets less excess cash and securities	300	340
Non-interest-bearing current liabilities	100	120
Adjusted net working capital	200	220
Gross property, plant and equipment	2,000	2,300
Accumulated depreciation	1,000	1,200
Net property, plant and equipment	1,000	1,100
Invested capital	1,200	1,320
Return on invested capital (EBIAT/ invested capital)		15%

Based on previous year's invested capital

16. Calculate the WACC—the weighted average cost of capital—using the following data:

Market value of debt = $30 million
Market value of equity = $50 million
Cost of debt = 9 percent
Tax rate = 40 percent
Cost of equity = 15 percent

17. You have the following betas for firms. Calculate the cost of capital for each.

Intel	1.0
GE	1.26
IBM	1.2
Merck	1.4
GM	1.1

18. You are analyzing the beta for Hewlett-Packard and have broken the company into four business groups with equity value and betas for each group. Calculate the beta for HP as a company. If the Treasury bond rate is 7.5 percent, calculate the cost of capital.

Business Group	Equity
Mainframes	$2 billion
Personal computers	$2 billion
Software	$1 billion
Printers	$3 billion

19. Would it make a difference in the calculation of the cost of capital whether you looked at the short-term U.S. government rate rather than the long-term U.S. government rate as your risk-free rate? Under what conditions would you choose long term? Short term?

20. Evaluate the following statements:
   a. The price of a firm's stock is a function of the expected earnings of that firm.
   b. Changes in the stock price result from surprises rather than realized expectations.
   c. If everyone had the same expectations, no stocks would be traded.

CHAPTER NOTES

1. *Sources: Business Week,* Readers Report, September 4, 2006, www.businessweek.com/magazine/content/ 06_36/c3999022.htm Jia Lang, "Reviving John Deere," Fortune Report, October 10, 2007, money.cnn .com/2007/10/09/news/companies/john_deere.fortune/index.htm

2. Many analysts argue that the focus of attention ought to be on free cash flow since free cash is what companies have available to make interest payments, pay off the principal on loans, pay dividends, and buy back shares, in other words, to return cash to their capital providers. Free cash flow is calculated as follows:

   NOPAT
   + depreciation and amortization
   − capital expenditures
   − changes in working capital required
   = free cash flow

You can see from this calculation that free cash flow is really no different than economic profit. It is simply another way to calculate economic profit. Capital expenditures plus changes in working capital required in the free cash flow calculation is the same as the capital costs that are subtracted from NOPAT to yield economic profit.

Invested capital = excess cash + working capital required + fixed investment
Working capital required = the amount of money that must be used to finance inventories and receivables + the amount of operating cash − accounts payable, accrued expenses, and advances from customers

Thus, invested capital = total assets − short-term non-interesting-bearing liabilities. Which is the same as: short-term debt + long-term debt + other long-term liabilities + shareholders' equity.

3. In reference to charitable organizations, an income statement is called a Statement of Activities and Changes in Net Assets.

4. The 10-K is a comprehensive summary report of a company's performance that must be submitted annually to the Securities and Exchange Commission. Typically, the 10-K contains much more detail than the annual report. It includes information such as company history, organizational structure, equity, and holdings.

5. CAPM relates the price volatility of an asset and the return on that asset. The expected return is a function of only the presumed risk of the stock as implied by the beta. A higher beta implies greater risk but actually just measures the volatility of the share price relative to a bundle of other stocks. Nevertheless, the higher is beta, the higher is the expected return—and the expected return is the same as the cost of equity. Let R^i denote the return on an asset, R^f the return on a risk-free asset (interest rate on U.S. Treasury bonds), and R^m the return on the entire market of assets (S&P 500 Index, for example). CAPM states that the expected return on the asset is equal to the risk-free rate plus beta (β) multiplied by the difference between the expected market return and the risk free return:

$$E[R^i] = R^f + \beta^i(E[R^m] - R^f)$$

where E represents expectation.

The beta of the security, denoted by β^i, is the sensitivity of a particular stock to changes that affect all stock. Beta is the covariance between the security's return and the market's return, divided by the variance of the market's return. In other words, beta measures the volatility of a company's stock price relative to the entire market. Beta is scaled so that on average it equals 1.0. To use the CAPM to measure a company's cost of equity, an estimate of the company's beta must be obtained. There are several ways to find an estimate of a company's beta. The easiest is simply to look it up on one of the many published sources. Sources include the Value Line Investment Survey, Yahoo! Finance, and Hoovers. An alternative is to estimate beta yourself. The most commonly used method is the simple ordinary least squares regression, with the return on the company as the dependent variable and the return on the market as the independent variable. The slope of the regression is an estimate of beta.

If a company has a beta exactly equal to 1, the company has the same volatility as the market itself. If a company has a beta that is greater than 1, its stock will probably go up higher than the market if the market is going up; it also will go down farther than the market if the market is falling. The reverse is true for a company with a beta that is less than 1. If the market is going up, the firm's stock will probably go up but by less than the market; if the market is going down, the firm's stock will probably go down but by less than the market. A low-beta firm is less sensitive to swings in the market. Intel's beta is about 1, which means that, during the time this beta is measured from, the market and the Intel stock essentially moved up and down together at the same rate. Studies have shown that CAPM underpredicts the returns to low beta stocks and overstates the returns to high beta stocks. Over the long run there has been essentially no relationship between beta and return. If beta is a measure of risk, then the studies show no relationship between risk and return. The problems in the CAPM lie in its assumptions, such as that that all investors can borrow or lend funds on equal terms, that there are no transaction costs, that all investors have the same expectations and risk appetites, that investors can take any market exposure without affecting prices, and that there are no tax differences between dividends and capital gains. Recognizing the weaknesses of the CAPM does provide useful information about the cost of capital.

6. The abnormal net income model is also known as the residual net income model, the Feltham-Ohlson model, and the Edwards and Bell-Ohlson model.

7. See Nancy L. Beneda, "Valuing Operating Assets in Place and Computing Economic Value Added," www.nysscpa.org/cpajournal/2004/1104/essentials/p56.htm, for an example of calculating economic value added.

8. These partial derivatives are comparative statics—looking at the change in one variable that results when one other variable is changed, everything else held constant.

9. The recognition that it is the economic profit that matters has led to a brisk business in management consulting. Spurred by lucrative fees, consultants are scrambling to help companies install new value-based performance metrics to replace the old standbys of per-share earnings (EPS), return on equity (ROE), and others. The dominant firm in this business is Stern-Stewart, promoting its *economic value added* (EVA). Another major firm in the business is the Boston Consulting Group, whose experts combine cash flow return on investment (CFROI) with a concept they call *total business return*. McKinsey uses the term *economic profit*, while the LEK/Alcar Group push for *shareholder value added* (SVA). These are far from the only consulting firms in the business. The field has become quite crowded, with each firm trying to offer a slightly different measurement tool or metric. While differing somewhat, all of the metrics attempt to provide a measure of economic profit.

10. Al Ehrbar, *EVA: The Real Key to Creating Wealth* (New York: John Wiley, 1999), p. 141.

11. Paul R. Niven, *Balanced Scorecard: Step by Step* (Hoboken, NJ: John Wiley, 2006), p. 118.

CHAPTER 20

The Firm in a National and a Global Setting

The Foreign-Exchange Curiosity

In late 2009, Oracle's earnings were reduced by 0.05/share due to foreign exchange effects. This was the third quarter in a row this happened. SAP had its total 2007 earnings wiped out by foreign-exchange effects. In 2007, Airbus estimated that every euro appreciation of 10 cents against the U.S. dollar cost his company €1B, due to the fact that Airbus costs are denominated in euros, whereas the bulk of its revenues are in dollars. In the 1990s, Procter & Gamble lost $157 million in a currency bet involving dollars and German marks, Gibson Greetings lost $20 million, and Long-Term Capital Management, a hedge fund, lost $4 billion with currency and interest rate derivatives. In 2009, Fortune 100 companies lost between $15 billion and $20 billion due to currency moves.

The 2008 crisis also affected China and Russia as multinational companies reduced or terminated their expenditures in these nations. Although both China and Russia experienced a decline in the investment by foreign companies, it does not mean that all multinational corporations are reducing investment in these two large emerging markets. Indeed, some of these corporations are actually increasing their investments to capture the opportunities created by the global financial crisis and the responses of the Chinese and Russian governments.

1. How can firms lose money due to foreign-exchange effects?
2. What causes a company to locate or not locate in a certain locale?

The National Setting

The economy does not simply grow constantly and smoothly. It fluctuates, sometimes rising slowly, sometimes quickly, sometimes declining. The movement from a trough to a peak and back to a trough is referred to as a **business cycle**. Table 20.1 lists U.S. business cycles since 1854.

Many managers fail to recognize the importance of the business cycle to the firm's business partly because they don't understand either the business cycle or the government policies designed to control the cycle. In other words, they are not business cycle literate.

Most companies do well during growth times, and most don't do so well during recessions. But a few companies are able to do better than others in both situations. When Johnson & Johnson anticipates an approaching recession, the executive team begins to cut production and trim inventories. For instance, in anticipation of the 2001 recession, J&J cut capital expenditures by more than $100 million at the height of the economic boom in 2000—its first decrease in seven years. J&J significantly built up its cash reserves and prepared for the downturn. In contrast, Cisco failed to read signs that the March 2001 recession was on its way and was eventually forced to write off more than $2 billion in excess inventory and lay off more than 8,000 people.

In the depths of a recession, it seems illogical to hire more people. But for some companies, it is exactly the time to hire. The labor pool may be at its deepest and highest quality, and wage pressures will have subsided. Then when the new expansion begins, a company may be able to deploy a more highly skilled workforce with lower labor costs than its rivals.

Many companies don't anticipate downturns and thus get caught with bloated inventories that often must be written down. Growing inventories as a recession approaches is a common problem, but so is a failure to increase production and build inventories in anticipation of an economic recovery.

Managers must have some literacy of business cycles, including a literacy of international developments and exchange rates. In the world today, international developments affect virtually every company—some very directly and some more implicitly. Companies that are multinational or acquire supplies from other nations can be dramatically affected by changes in exchange rates. Royal Caribbean Cruise lines hedges the company's exchange rate risk with currency futures when purchasing billion-dollar ships in euros from Europe. Good Humor-Breyers hedges the costs of its most important ingredients—from premium vanilla cultivated in Madagascar to premium-quality New Zealand butterfat. Southwest Airlines hedges the cost of fuel.

The Institution of U.S. Economic Policies

Monetary policy in the United States is determined and implemented by the Federal Reserve System, established in 1913 as the Central Bank of the United States. The Congress gives the Federal Reserve the responsibility of using monetary policy to move the economy toward full employment with low inflation. The Federal Reserve (the Fed) attempts to do this through its control of the money supply and interest rates. The Fed has three main mechanisms for manipulating the money supply: **open market operations**, the **discount rate**, and **reserve requirements**. In practice, the Fed almost exclusively uses open market operations to influence short-term interest rates. An open market operation occurs when the Fed buys or sells securities in the financial market.

The typical steps of monetary policy are as follows: The Federal Open Market Committee (policy directors of the Fed) announces a target for the **federal funds rate**. The fed funds rate is the rate banks borrow from and loan to each other. Open market

Table 20.1

U.S. Business Cycle Expansions and Contractions, 1854–2001

BUSINESS CYCLE REFERENCE DATES		DURATION IN MONTHS			
PEAK	TROUGH	CONTRACTION	EXPANSION	CYCLE	
Quarterly dates are in parentheses		Peak to Trough	Previous Trough to This Peak	Trough from Previous Trough	Peak from Previous Peak
	December 1854 (IV)	–	–	–	–
June 1857 (II)	December 1858 (IV)	18	30	48	–
October 1860 (III)	June 1861 (III)	8	22	30	40
April 1865 (I)	December 1867 (I)	32	46	78	54
June 1869 (II)	December 1870 (IV)	18	18	36	50
October 1873 (III)	March 1879 (I)	65	34	99	52
March 1882 (I)	May 1885 (II)	38	36	74	101
March 1887 (II)	April 1888 (I)	13	22	35	60
July 1890 (III)	May 1891 (II)	10	27	37	40
January 1893 (I)	June 1894 (II)	17	20	37	30
December 1895 (IV)	June 1897 (II)	18	18	36	35
June 1899 (III)	December 1900 (IV)	18	24	42	42
September 1902 (IV)	August 1904 (III)	23	21	44	39
May 1907 (II)	June 1908 (II)	13	33	46	56
January 1910 (I)	January 1912 (IV)	24	19	43	32
January 1913 (I)	December 1914 (IV)	23	12	35	36
August 1918 (III)	March 1919 (I)	7	44	51	67
January 1920 (I)	July 1921 (III)	18	10	28	17
May 1923 (II)	July 1924 (III)	14	22	36	40
October 1926 (III)	November 1927 (IV)	13	27	40	41
August 1929 (III)	March 1933 (I)	43	21	64	34
May 1937 (II)	June 1938 (II)	13	50	63	93
February 1945 (I)	October 1945 (IV)	8	80	88	93
November 1948 (IV)	October 1949 (IV)	11	37	48	45
July 1953 (II)	May 1954 (II)	10	45	55	56
August 1957 (III)	April 1958 (II)	8	39	47	49
April 1960 (II)	February 1961 (I)	10	24	34	32
December 1969 (IV)	November 1970 (IV)	11	106	117	116
November 1973 (IV)	March 1975 (I)	16	36	52	47
January 1980 (I)	July 1980 (III)	6	58	64	74
July 1981 (III)	November 1982 (IV)	16	12	28	18
July 1990 (III)	March 1991 (I)	8	92	100	108
March 2001 (I)	November 2001 (IV)	8	120	128	128
December 2007 (IV)			73		81
Average, all cycles:					
1854–2001 (32 cycles)		17	38	55	56*
1854–1919 (16 cycles)		22	27	48	49**
1919–1945 (6 cycles)		18	35	53	53
1945–2001 (10 cycles)		10	57	67	67

*31 cycles

**15 cycles

Source: NBER.

operations change the supply of reserve balances banks have, and thus banks will either lend or borrow to each other to meet these reserve balances. A higher demand for funds, given the amount of funds available, raises the fed funds rate, and less demand lowers the fed funds rate. So if the Fed wants to raise the fed funds rate, it will reduce the amount of money in circulation, causing banks to demand funds to meet their reserve requirements.

The Federal Reserve System engages in open market operations daily. If the Federal Reserve wants to increase the money supply, it will buy securities (such as U.S. Treasury bonds) from banks in exchange for dollars. If the Federal Reserve wants to decrease the money supply, it will sell securities to the banks in exchange for dollars, taking those dollars out of circulation. When the Federal Reserve makes a purchase, it credits the seller's reserve account (with the Federal Reserve). The money that it deposits into the seller's account is not transferred from any existing funds; it is simply money created by the Federal Reserve.

The Department of the Treasury was established by Congress in 1789 to manage government revenue. The department is administered by the secretary of the Treasury. The Treasury prints all paper currency and mints coins in circulation, collects all federal taxes through the Internal Revenue Service, and manages U.S. government debt instruments. Currency wears out and coins get lost. When the Federal Reserve determines that more actual currency is required, it places an order for printed money with the U.S. Treasury Department. The Treasury Department sends these requests to the Bureau of Engraving and Printing (to make paper currency) and the Bureau of the Mint (to stamp the coins). The U.S. Treasury sells this newly printed money to the Federal Reserve for the cost of printing, about 6 cents per bill for any denomination. The Federal Reserve provides collateral, which consists of government securities such as Treasury bonds to put new money into circulation. This printed cash can then be distributed to banks, as needed.

Although the Federal Reserve authorizes and distributes the currency printed by the Treasury, it is the lending process of commercial banks that is the big factor in determining the total money supply. Commercial banks are required to hold only a percentage of their deposits on hand or in the vaults of the Fed. This percentage is called the reserve requirement. The rest of the funds can be lent out. This is called a fractional reserve banking system. Each time the banks lend money, they create more money. A loan is money, and then when the loan is spent and a seller deposits in another bank, that bank can then lend more. This loan is also money, so lending by commercial banks expands the money supply by a multiple of the money the Fed had put into the banks. Thus, the Fed controls the money supply in the United States by controlling the amount of loans made by commercial banks.

The relationship between the Fed and the Treasury is straightforward. The Treasury finances the government's spending with taxes or by borrowing—issuing debt. The government need not have the money in hand when it spends; it does not have to raise taxes each time it spends but instead can issue debt. It issues or sells its debt through Treasury auctions. If the Federal Reserve purchases some of the debt, it provides new money to the Treasury, which spends it and adds it to the amount of money in circulation. When the Fed purchases debt, it increases the money supply. The Fed can also sell the debt it holds, and when it does sell, it reduces the money supply.

When the Fed purchases Treasury debt, it is called "monetizing the debt." The Fed does not purchase all of the Treasury's debt. Some of the debt is purchased and held by other government agencies, some by individuals and investors, and some by other governments. The Treasury must eventually pay off its debt.[1] It can do this by raising taxes or issuing new debt. If the Fed purchases this new debt, then the money supply increases.

We can illustrate the relationship between the Treasury and the Fed with a simple equation: $G = T + \Delta B$, where G represents government spending, T represents tax revenues, and

B represents Treasury bonds or debt. So whenever the government runs a deficit, $G - T > 0$, it must issue new debt, ΔB. Since the new debt must be paid for with increases in the money supply (or taxes and money supply increases in the future), we simplify and write $\Delta B = \Delta M$. So, we have $G - T = \Delta M$; deficits mean increases in the money supply.

When spending exceeds revenues, a deficit is created. The deficit means more debt and thus an increase in the national debt. As of July 28, 2010, the total public debt outstanding was approximately 93 percent of annual gross domestic product, GDP ($13.258 trillion).[2] The gross debt increases or decreases as a result of this budget deficit or surplus. The total debt has increased over $500 billion each year since fiscal year (FY) 2003, with increases of $1 trillion in FY2008 and $1.9 trillion in FY2009.

Table 20.2 lists the foreign nations holding U.S. debt. China owns the most U.S. debt.

Some growth in the money supply is necessary to support a growing economy. For instance, if the economy is to grow by 3 percent, perhaps 4 percent growth in the money supply is necessary. Typically there is a relationship between the rate of growth of money and the rate of growth of GDP, $\Delta M = \Delta Q + \Delta P$, where ΔM is the growth of the money supply, ΔQ is the growth of real GDP or output, and ΔP is the growth of the price level or inflation.

So what happens if the money supply grows by 10 percent? Eventually that excess growth in the money supply will mean increases in inflation; 10 percent $= \Delta Q + \Delta P$ and if ΔQ is 3 percent, inflation (ΔP) will be 7 percent. There will be increasing amounts of money chasing a limited amount of goods around. If instead of 10 percent, the money supply growth was 1 percent, what would occur? 1 percent $= \Delta Q + \Delta P$, which would mean lower $\Delta Q + \Delta P$. The reason is that too little money would mean that interest rates go up and the higher interest rates then dampen $\Delta Q + \Delta P$.

Keynesian vs. Free Markets

Theoretically, the government uses its spending and taxing, and the Federal Reserve changes the money supply to control the business cycle. This idea that the government (and the Fed) are responsible for the condition of the economy began in 1946 with the Employment Act. This Act mandated that the federal government had the responsibility to ensure full employment. The Act required the president to submit an annual economic report in addition to the national budget. The report, designated the Economic Report of the President, must estimate the projected employment rate for the next fiscal year, and if not commensurate with the full employment rate, to mandate policies to attain full employment.

The Employment Act of 1946 grew out of the philosophy of the Keynesian school of economics. The Keynesians argue that when the economy enters a downturn, the government

Table 20.2			
Leading Foreign Owners of U.S. Treasury Securities, May 2010	NATION/TERRITORY	BILLIONS OF DOLLARS	PERCENTAGE
	People's Republic of China	867.7	21.9
	Japan	786.7	19.8
	United Kingdom	350.0	8.8
	Brazil	161.4	4.1
	Hong Kong (Special Administrative Region)	145.7	3.7
	Russia	126.8	3.2
	Republic of China (Taiwan)	126.2	3.2
	Grand total	3963.6	100

needs to increase its deficits (and the Federal Reserve should support this by increasing the money supply). Then, when the economy begins recovering, the government should reduce the deficit and move toward a balanced budget or even a surplus. The argument is that a reliance on free markets to self-adjust and solve unemployment problems is faulty. The Keynesians assert that markets often fail and get stuck in unemployment situations.

This argument is contested by the Austrian school of economists and other free market economists who argue that the best course is to just leave things alone and the free markets will adjust – just give it some time. This school of thought maintains that the actions proposed by Keynesians are what lead to booms and busts. Instead of using government spending and taxing and changing the money supply, the government should stay out of the economy, run balanced budgets, and the money supply should be fixed to a commodity like gold, or should be determined by free markets and competition among private issuers of money.

The debate between Keynesians and Austrians rose strongly as the 2008 crisis played out. Let us look at that period and what each of these schools of thought has to say about it.

The 2008 Crisis   In 2008, a series of bank and insurance company failures triggered a financial crisis that effectively halted global credit markets and led to unprecedented government intervention. Fannie Mae and Freddie Mac, government-sponsored (but ostensibly private) enterprises (GSEs), were both taken over by the government. Lehman Brothers declared bankruptcy on September 14. Bank of America agreed to purchase Merrill Lynch, and American International Group (AIG) was saved by an $85 billion capital injection by the federal government. Shortly afterward, on September 25, J.P. Morgan Chase agreed to purchase the assets of Washington Mutual.

It was argued that these institutions were "too big to fail" because failure would collapse the entire financial system. Following the Lehman collapse, $150 billion was withdrawn from U.S. money funds in just two days. The average two-day outflow had been $5 billion. In effect, the money market experienced a bank run. The money market had been a key source of credit for banks and nonfinancial firms. The response of the Fed, the European Central Bank, and other central banks was immediate and dramatic. During the last quarter of 2008, these central banks purchased $2.5 trillion of government debt and troubled private assets from banks. This was the largest liquidity injection into the credit market, and the largest monetary policy action, in world history. The governments of European nations and the United States also raised the capital of their national banking systems by $1.5 trillion by purchasing newly issued preferred stock in their major banks.

The crisis had its roots in real estate and subprime lending, which in turn was instigated by government policies. In the 1990s Congress pressured Fannie and Freddie to lower the requirements for borrowers to get a loan. The objective was to increase home ownership in the United States from 66 percent of the populace to 70 percent. Fannie and Freddie's impact on the financial market was huge. By the end of 2008 Fannie and Freddie held or guaranteed $5 trillion or about half the U.S. mortgage market. In 1995, they had begun receiving government tax incentives for purchasing mortgage-backed securities, which included loans to low-income borrowers. In 1996, the Housing and Urban Development agency set a goal for Fannie Mae and Freddie Mac that at least 42 percent of the mortgages they purchase be issued to borrowers whose household income was below the median in their area. This target was increased to 50 percent in 2000 and 52 percent in 2005.

The foundation for a real estate boom had been constructed. It was pushed into frenzied activity by the Federal Reserve holding interest rates very low; in fact, real interest rates (interest rates less inflation) were negative. This means that the Fed is paying individuals, institutions, and the government to borrow. And borrow they did. Everyone jumped into the market, purchasing ever more expensive real estate, only to turn it over and sell it at even higher prices. A real estate bubble had taken shape.

The mortgage market had changed as well. Prior to 2006, the traditional mortgage model involved a bank originating a loan to a borrower/homeowner and holding on to the mortgage—in essence, retaining the credit (default) risk. Entrepreneurs had discovered that they could purchase these mortgages, then slice and dice and bundle bunches of them together and call it a **mortgage-backed security (MBS)**. Selling these mortgages allowed the banks to offload the risk and to acquire more money for additional lending. The profit potential was significant.

The market for debt securitization was massive, reaching $14 trillion by 2008. European banks entered the market in varying degrees, with some firms such as UBS, Deutsche Bank, and Credit Suisse originating and selling loans in the United States through their American banking arms while others focused on regional markets, which catered to a more localized investor base.

As securitization of mortgages increased, the investment banks urged the mortgage lending industry (Countrywide, Washington Mutual, New Century Financial, Wells Fargo, Household Finance, and many others), to increase their loan volumes. Since the government had been and was continuing to pressure lenders to provide loans to the subprime borrowers, the mortgage lending industry was not reluctant to embrace these high-risk borrowers. "Subprime" mortgages are loans given to individuals without the credit or income to meet the loan requirements. The share of MBSs backed by subprime loans increased dramatically.

In sum, government pressure to increase home ownership created the subprime loans. The Federal Reserve interest rate policy induced a great deal of borrowing and lending, including more and more subprime loans. These loans were combined with other loans and sold as a single security, the MBS. These were then sliced and diced and bundled again into still other securities, the collateralized debt obligations (CDOs). Then to provide some insurance against default, companies bought credit default swaps (CDS) on the CDOs. A CDS is an insurance policy that pays off if a CDO or a part of a CDO defaults. These securities were bundled, folded, combined, sliced, and diced to an extent that few, if any, knew what was in a security.

Amazingly, even though 71 percent of all mortgages issued by the private mortgage industry in 2006 were subprime or risky loans, nearly all of the MBSs received AAA ratings. Subprime mortgages are questionable assets. Each one alone would deserve a "junk" rating. But Moody's, Standard & Poor's, and Fitch, the rating agencies, deemed 85 percent of the securities to be AAA. There are three reasons this occurred. First, there is an inherent conflict of interest between bond issuers (which pay to get their issues rated) and the ratings agencies (which receive fees from the issuer to rate the issuers bonds). Second, the securitization process had become so opaque that the ratings agency simply relied on what the issuers told them. Third, the three rating agencies are the only ones sanctioned by the government. They are in essence a cartel acting as a monopoly; competitors cannot arise and offer better or different results.

The problem started when the Federal Reserve drove interest rates up. Most of the subprime loans had been issued as adjustable rate mortgages, or as teaser rates, so that payments rose automatically over time and rose as interest rates rose. As these defaults rose, the MBS market began to topple. Since no one knew what was in each MBS, no one knew which contained defaults on mortgages and no one knew the value of any of the MBSs. Thus, no one would buy or sell them, and their values dropped dramatically. The global credit market followed the U.S. market and nearly closed up. Institutions holding the MBSs, CDOs, and CDSs were failing. The bubble had burst.

The boom had been created by the Federal Reserve keeping interest rates too low for too long and the government pressuring the GSEs and others to increase loans to the subprime borrowers. Similarly, the bust was created by the Federal Reserve raising interest rates and the subprime and other borrowers being unable to make mortgage payments.

With the collapse of the MBS market, higher interest rates, and falling real estate prices, many more borrowers defaulted, consumer spending declined, and businesses started cutting back and laying people off. Hundreds of banks collapsed, as did many nonfinancial companies. GM and Chrysler were bankrupt, as were Fannie Mae and Freddie Mac. The Treasury Department and the Federal Reserve, fearing a total collapse of the financial system, went into overdrive offering bailouts, taking over companies, increasing the money supply by incredible amounts, driving interest rates down, and creating government deficits and public debt at record levels.

The Fed lowered the target for federal funds and discount rates to near zero and, along with other central banks, undertook massive open market operations to ensure member banks remained liquid. The Fed also lent directly to banks and nonbank institutions. In November 2008, the Fed announced a $600 billion program to purchase the MBSs of Fannie and Freddie, to help lower mortgage rates. In March 2009, the Fed decided to increase the size of its balance sheet further by purchasing up to an additional $750 billion of Fannie and Freddie mortgage-backed securities. Moreover, to help improve conditions in private credit markets, the Fed decided to purchase up to $300 billion of longer-term Treasury securities during 2009.

On February 13, 2008, President Bush signed into law a $168 billion economic stimulus package, mainly taking the form of income tax rebate checks mailed directly to taxpayers. The Emergency Economic Stabilization Act (EESA or TARP) was enacted during October 2008. This law included $700 billion in funding for the Troubled Assets Relief Program (TARP), which was used to lend funds to banks in exchange for dividend-paying preferred stock. In addition to U.S. action, nearly every government in Asia, Europe, and North America pursued some vigorous form of Keynesian spending policy, defined generally as debt-financed increases in government spending to push up aggregate demand in the hope that economic output, jobs, and incomes would follow.

In 2010 when it became clear that these policies were not putting people back to work and increasing growth in the economy, many Keynesians argued for doubling down—further increasing deficits and debt. If this was not done, the Keynesians feared, another Great Depression might occur.

The Austrian school and other free market economists were saying enough already: The debt that was currently out there was a burden on the economy that was threatening the future and the present. This debt would have to be paid at some point, and that could mean only extremely high taxes or a rapid inflation at some point in the near future. What needed to be done immediately, they maintained, was to cut government spending, eliminate bailouts and government takeovers, and allow the markets to adjust.

The Keynesians point to the 1930s and argue that what FDR did to get the United States out of the Great Depression needed to be duplicated but at much higher rates of spending. The world could not hope for a war to solve things, as World War II for the Great Depression.

The Austrians also point to the Great Depression, but they argue that FDR's policies did not get the United States out of the Great Depression; FDR's policies created the Depression. His antibusiness stance and restrictions of markets and takeovers of enterprises led to a fear that investing funds and expanding businesses was a foolish thing to do. Business did not begin investing until it was more certain that private property rights were secure; that what was created would not be confiscated. Confidence did not return to business until after World War II.

The Keynesians argue that a more massive stimulus is necessary in 2010 and 2011 to get the economy growing again. The Austrians counter that President Obama's policies have created the same kind of regime uncertainty that FDR's did. They say that until that changes, taxes are reduced, government debt is reined in, and businesses and investors are confident in their private property rights, the economy will not be able to recover and return to growth.

At the end of 2010 with the U.S. economy very anemic, the Keynesians affirm that the actions taken since 2008 were necessary to stop the economy from falling off a cliff. And now, they argue, additional spending and continued expansionary monetary policies are necessary.

The Austrians warn of another bubble and rapid inflation. When businesses begin to borrow and banks lend, and spending increases, there is so much money sitting in commercial banks that there will surely be "too much money chasing too few goods." The Austrians urge that the government stop the huge deficits and begin cutting spending so as to reduce debt, and that the Fed draw the money out of the system; they see a time bomb waiting to explode.

Globalization

Whether we are driving to work in a Japanese car, wearing clothes manufactured in China, or having a French wine before dinner, we are using products originally purchased with currencies traded through the foreign-exchange market. An understanding of this market is essential to firms that operate internationally because they are exposed to foreign currency fluctuations. But it is not just the multinational companies that are affected by changes in the exchange rate. In fact, changes in exchange rates can often affect the operating profit of companies that have no foreign operations or exports. Today, every executive must have some understanding of international trade, exchange rates, and exchange rate risk.

Foreign Exchange

In most instances, when consumers in the United States buy a foreign product they see only the U.S. dollar price. They don't see the price denominated in yen, pounds, or other currency. Usually it is the business that must trade dollars for yen or dollars for pounds in order to purchase the Mitsubishi TV or the Nestle chocolate. The business must carry out a transaction in the foreign-exchange market in order to acquire the foreign products they sell or use in their production.

Foreign exchange is foreign money, including paper money and bank deposits like checking accounts. When someone with U.S. dollars wants to trade those dollars for Japanese yen, the trade takes place in the foreign-exchange market, a global market in which people trade one currency for another. The foreign-exchange market involves participants buying and selling currencies all over the world. Trading takes place throughout most of each day, starting in Tokyo; moving west to Singapore and Hong Kong; continuing to Zurich, Frankfurt, and London; and then ending in New York, Chicago, and San Francisco. Participants in the market include individuals, corporations, commercial banks, and central banks.

An **exchange rate** is the price of one country's money in terms of another country's money. A shirt manufactured in Tijuana, Mexico sells for 30 U.S. dollars in San Diego and for 250 pesos in Mexico. Where would you get the better buy, Tijuana or San Diego? Unless you know the exchange rate between U.S. and Mexican currencies, you can't tell. The exchange rate allows you to convert a foreign currency price into its domestic currency equivalent, which can then be compared to the domestic price. For example, on August 13, 2010, the exchange rate between the Mexican peso and the U.S. dollar was

$1 = 12.733Ps. This means that 250Ps is equivalent to $19.63 Thus, the shirt was less expensive in San Diego than in Tijuana.

Several nations, their currencies and the symbols for those currencies, are noted in the following table.

Country	Currency	Symbol
Australia	Dollar	A$
Canada	Dollar	C$
China	Yuan (RMB)	¥
Denmark	Krone	DKr
India	Rupee	Rs
Iran	Rial	RI
Japan	Yen	¥
Kuwait	Dinar	KD
Mexico	Peso	Ps
Norway	Krone	NKr
Russia	Ruble	Rub
Saudi Arabia	Riyal	SR
Singapore	Dollar	S$
South Africa	Rand	R
Sweden	Krona	SKr
Switzerland	Franc	SF
United Kingdom	Pound	£
Venezuela	Bolivar	B
European Economic Community	Euro	€

An exchange rate is determined by the demand for and supply of a currency. A country's currency is demanded by businesses wanting to purchase the goods and services of that nation and by investors wanting to purchase the financial assets of that nation. The supply of a country's currency is provided by businesses of that nation wanting to purchase the products of other nations and investors of that nation wanting to purchase financial assets of other nations.

If Micron in Boise, Idaho, sells $1 million worth of chips to a manufacturer in France, the exchange of the chips requires an exchange of currencies. The manufacturer in France must offer the equivalent of $1 million in euros. A banker in France might arrange for the exchange with a banker in San Francisco, offering to buy 1 million U.S. dollars for some amount of euros. This is a demand for dollars and a supply of euros. Similarly, if a U.S. bank wants to purchase a Mexican bond in order to reap higher interest rates, the bank must purchase Mexican pesos with dollars. This creates a demand for pesos and a supply of dollars. Thus, both real transactions (the sale and purchase of goods and services) and financial transactions (the sale and purchase of financial assets) affect the demand for and supply of currencies. The relative amounts of currencies offered in the foreign-exchange market determines the exchange rate between currencies.

The foreign-exchange market for dollars and euros is illustrated in Figure 20.1. The price measured on the vertical axis is the exchange rate, dollars per euro; the quantity measured along the horizontal axis is the quantity of euros. The demand for euros represents the U.S. demand for European goods and financial assets. To purchase these items, euros are needed. The U.S. consumers must buy euros. The higher the price, that is, the higher is $/€, the lower is the quantity of euros demanded. The supply of euros represents the European demand for U.S products and financial assets. To buy these U.S. items, European buyers must offer euros in exchange for dollars. The higher is the price, that is, the higher is $/€, the higher is the quantity of euros offered.

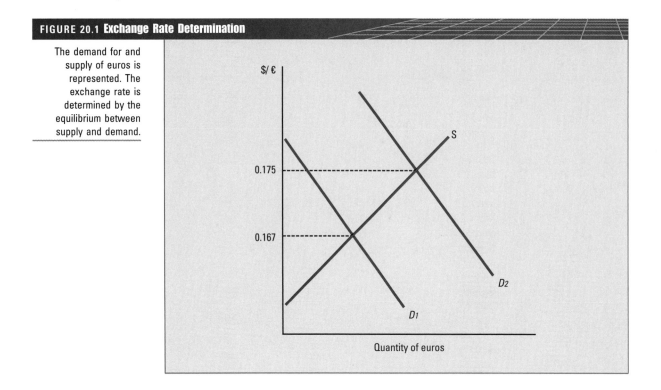

FIGURE 20.1 Exchange Rate Determination

The demand for and supply of euros is represented. The exchange rate is determined by the equilibrium between supply and demand.

An increase in the demand for European goods and services means an increase in the demand for euros, illustrated as an outward shift of the demand curve in Figure 20.1. This leads to a higher price—higher exchange rate. The dollar depreciates (the euro appreciates).

Exchange Rate Regimes

Except for wars, until 1973 most nations defined their currency in terms of gold and/or silver. This was a system of fixed exchange rates. During World War II, the Bretton Woods Agreement established a system similar to a Gold Standard. Under this system, many countries fixed their exchange rates relative to the U.S. dollar and the United States promised to fix the price of gold at $35 per ounce. Implicitly, then, all currencies pegged to the dollar also had a fixed value in terms of gold. The United States ended convertibility of the dollar for gold in 1971, and the major industrial nations abandoned fixed exchange rates in March 1973.

The world did not move to purely free-market-determined floating exchange rates. The major industrial countries have allowed their central banks to intervene to keep their currencies within certain ranges, and many smaller countries have fixed or pegged their rates to a major currency such as the dollar or the pound. In fact, only 48 nations allow their exchange rates to be determined in the free market. The European Union nations fixed their own currency rate to the euro in 1999 and prices were listed both in the domestic currency value and the euro until January 1, 2002. The euro began circulating on January 1, 2002 and the national currencies like the lira, German mark, and French franc, were no long considered legal tender on July 1, 2002. China fixes its yuan to the dollar at a rate of about 6.8Y/$.

Flexible versus *Fixed Exchange Rates*   In a flexible exchange rate system, demand and supply determine the exchange rate. In Figure 20.2 the initial equilibrium in the foreign-exchange market for U.S. dollars and Mexican pesos is located at point *A,* where the

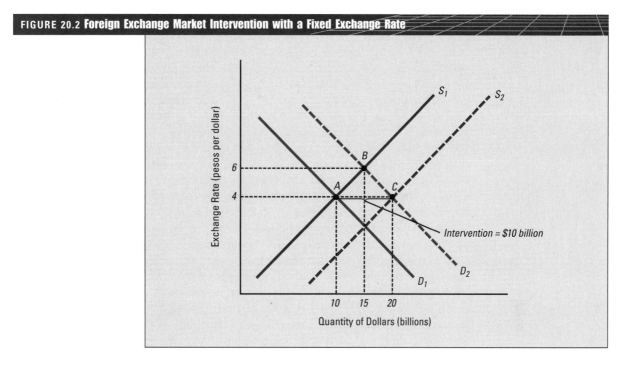

FIGURE 20.2 Foreign Exchange Market Intervention with a Fixed Exchange Rate

exchange rate is 4 pesos per dollar, and $10 billion are traded for pesos each day. If there is concern that Mexican financial assets will fall in value, then investors will start to sell peso-denominated assets and will sell their pesos for dollars in order to buy dollar-denominated assets. This shifts the demand curve for dollars from D_1 to D_2. The new equilibrium would then be at point B, with a depreciated peso exchange rate of 6 pesos per dollar and $15 billion per day being traded. This would be the result with a flexible exchange rate system.

Under a fixed exchange rate system, Mexico would have to define the rate and take action to maintain it. To maintain a fixed exchange rate of 4 pesos per dollar and avoid private traders from shifting the equilibrium to point B, the central bank (Banco de Mexico) must intervene in the foreign-exchange market, selling dollars equal to the private market demand for dollars in excess of the amount that would yield an equilibrium at point A. In the figure, we see that the new equilibrium with central bank intervention is at point C, where the central bank is selling $10 billion per day ($20 billion − $10 billion) in order to maintain the exchange rate at 4 pesos per dollar.

If the shift in private investors' demand from D_1 to D_2 is not a temporary phenomenon, then there is a problem for the Banco de Mexico: It has a limited supply of international reserves, including U.S. dollars. The intervention to support the fixed exchange rate involves selling dollars and buying pesos. Eventually the central bank will exhaust its supply of dollars, and it will then be forced to devalue the currency, letting the exchange rate adjust to the free market equilibrium of 6 pesos per dollar.

Once speculators realize that the central bank is losing a substantial fraction of its international reserves, a speculative attack occurs as private speculators start selling even more pesos for dollars, expecting that the central bank will be forced to devalue the currency. If a speculator sells pesos and buys dollars for a price of 4 pesos per dollar, and then the peso is devalued to 6 pesos per dollar, that speculator can turn around and sell the dollars for pesos, receiving 6 − 4 = 2 pesos in profit for each dollar invested in the speculative activity. Of course, once the speculative attack occurs, the demand for dollars shifts out even further, and the central bank will have to spend even more of its international reserves to defend the fixed exchange rate.

An unanticipated currency devaluation hurts local business. In Thailand, for instance, prior to the crisis of 1997, the Thai government had repeatedly stated that there was no way it would ever change the fixed exchange rate. Business firms, believing that the exchange rate between the Thai baht and the U.S. dollar would not change, borrowed in U.S. dollars, expecting that the dollars they borrowed and the dollars they would have to repay would be worth the same amount of baht. Imagine a firm that had a debt of $1 million. Prior to the financial crisis that started in the summer of 1997, the exchange rate was about 25 baht to 1 U.S. dollar. At this exchange rate, it would cost 25 million baht to repay $1 million. By January 1998, the exchange rate was about 52 baht per dollar. So the firm would find that the baht price of repaying $1 million had risen to 52 million baht. The cost of repaying the dollar loan had more than doubled as a result of the currency devaluation. Because of such exchange rate changes, the financial crises of the 1990s had devastating effects on local businesses in each country. As business firms in these countries lost value, foreign investors who had invested in these firms also suffered large losses. The 1990s financial crises imposed huge costs on the global economy.

Countries involved in recent crises, including Mexico in 1993–1994, the Southeast Asian countries in 1997, and Argentina in 2002, utilized fixed exchange rates prior to the onset of the crisis. The fixed exchange rates meant that if one country expanded the money supply and increased inflation above the inflation of trading partners, that currency would flow from the inflating country and drive inflation up in those other countries. That would put pressure on the inflating country to devalue its currency. When large devaluations ultimately occurred, domestic residents holding loans denominated in foreign currency suffered huge losses.

In a pure fixed exchange rate regime, economic activity adjusts to the exchange rate. In a purely floating regime, the exchange rate is a reflection of economic activity. A country cannot maintain a fixed exchange rate, open capital market, and monetary policy independence at the same time. If a country wants to manage its own domestic economy through monetary policy, it must have flexible exchange rates. Flexible exchange rates allow a country to pursue an independent monetary policy, rather than have its own monetary policy set by an anchor currency country. But this also means that countries can run inflationary policies without a correction by other countries. A fixed exchange rate restricts the ability of a country to run an inflation.

The major currencies—the dollar, the euro, and the yen—float against one another. The economies represented by these currencies account for 42 percent of global economic activity. Nearly all global trade and capital flow transactions are denominated in one of these three currencies, as are nearly 95 percent of official foreign exchange reserves. Other large economies with well-developed financial sectors, such the United Kingdom, Canada, and Australia have floating exchange rates as well. With China's huge trade account surplus, world pressure has been on China to allow the yuan (RMB) to float. While China has made some noise about doing this, in reality it has maintained a relatively fixed rate relative to the dollar. This ensures that the prices of Chinese goods are low relative to other countries' goods.

Exchange Rate Exposure

A firm may be exposed to exchange rate changes if items on the balance sheet, such as debt, payables, and receivables are denominated in a foreign currency. Since these items have to be converted or translated, at the end of the fiscal year, to the currency of the country in which the headquarters is located, an exchange rate change can affect their value. For example, Laker Airways, a UK-based company, figured it did not have to worry about exchange rate changes between the pound and the dollar because any changes would just create offsetting behaviors by British and American tourists. Although fewer British tourists would visit the United States when the dollar was strong, more Americans would travel to Britain. The two effects seemed to offset each other. When the dollar was declining in 1980, Laker financed new aircraft purchases in dollars, increasing its debt, debt that was denominated in dollars. When the pound weakened relative to the dollar, the airline couldn't pay its interest costs and was forced into bankruptcy. It had not considered the effects of exchange rate changes on its balance sheet.

Exchange risk is simple in concept: a potential gain or loss that occurs as a result of an exchange rate change. But who loses and who gains? If an individual owns a share in Daimler AG, the German company, he or she will lose if the value of the euro drops relative to the U.S. dollar. But what about a company based in the United States and doing business in Germany? The firm's subsidiary in Germany may lose, but the firm may not if the loss has been offset by positions taken elsewhere in the firm. The shareholder value of the company may be affected by exchange rate changes because anticipated future cash flows may be altered.

In the fall of 2009, the Board of Directors of General Motors learned that GM had lost $1 billion betting on Korean currency earlier in the year. It turned out that neither the CEO nor senior management knew about this speculative venture. This example brings up two points. First, GM's governance was faulty in that important information about currency strategies had not been communicated to management. Companies have to know how exposed they are to exchange rate changes. Second, people have to know the difference between betting on a currency move and hedging currency risk.

The task of gauging the impact of exchange rate changes on an enterprise begins with measuring its *exposure*, that is, the amount, or value, at risk. The most common problem arises when an enterprise has foreign affiliates keeping books in the respective local currency. For purposes of consolidation, these accounts must somehow be translated into the reporting currency of the parent company. In doing so, a decision must be made as to the exchange rate that is to be used for the translation of the various accounts. This is called **balance sheet exposure**.

A company can reduce balance sheet exposure by refusing to do business in any other country but its domestic one. But this doesn't guarantee solving the problem of exchange rate exposure. Consider a company that does not do any business across national borders. For instance, Lincoln Electric is a U.S. small motor manufacturer that, until the 1990s, sourced domestically, sold exclusively in the home market, and had no foreign debt. It would seem that the company had no exposure to changes in exchange rates. However, its operating profit was exposed to changes in the yen–dollar rate because the company competed in the United States with Japanese manufacturers. When setting a dollar price in the United States, the Japanese companies considered their yen costs. In a year when the yen and the dollar were at purchasing power parity, Lincoln Electric's dollar costs would equal the dollar equivalent costs of its Japanese competitors and Lincoln Electric would earn a normal operating profit margin. But if Japan experienced a higher inflation rate than the United States, then Lincoln Electric's position would depend on whether purchasing power parity held. If the yen weakened in line with purchasing power parity, the competitive position of Lincoln Electric would not change. If, however, the yen weakened relative to the dollar, the dollar equivalent costs of the Japanese companies would be less than the costs of Lincoln Electric and the competitive position of Lincoln Electric would weaken. This is called **market-based exposure**.

How much market-based exposure a company has depends on whether it does business globally, whether it competes domestically with foreign competitors if it does not export or import, and the selling environment in which the firm operates. Consider a domestic firm that sources domestically but competes with foreign firms in the domestic market. When the value of the foreign firms' home currencies falls, then the costs of those firms fall. If the demand in the domestic market is highly price-elastic, then the foreign firms' lower costs will likely lead to lower prices. The domestic firm must follow suit or lose substantial business. Yet, because the domestic firm's costs did not decline, its profits will decline.

Now consider a domestic firm that sources domestically and competes with foreign firms but has a demand that is very price-inelastic. In this case, when the exchange rate changes the competitive position of the foreign firms, the domestic firm does not have to worry about matching lower prices.

How does a firm reduce its exchange rate exposure? If it has balance sheet exposure, it has to reduce those aspects of its business that have to be translated from one currency to another. Perhaps the most straightforward way to do this is to locate in the country where the firm does most of its business. In this way, most of the balance sheet will be defined in the same currency. However, this may not be the profit-maximizing strategy.

What factors are important in deciding where to locate facilities? The size of the local market plays an important role because the firm can utilize those facilities to sell in that market. This is why China has been so enticing for firms to locate in. The potential of the local market is huge. However, a country's political climate is important, and this is where China creates problems for firms. A country that might confiscate property at any time is a high-risk proposition for a firm thinking about spending millions of dollars in building facilities. Google has been hampered from offering full services in China because China's government wants searches to be censored. The constant fear in China is that private property will be confiscated.

If a firm decides to establish a facility in another country, it has to determine whether to build from scratch or to acquire existing facilities and whether to do the project alone or in an alliance or joint venture with a domestic firm in that nation. Each decision involves trade-offs and cost-benefit calculations.

The location of a manufacturing facility is a long-term commitment. Exchange rate risk is more a short-term problem. Locating a facility simply to minimize exchange rate exposure may be a costly decision. Events could cause the firm to be subject to even greater exchange rate risk in future years. Seldom does a firm select a location for its facilities based on reducing exchange rate risk. Most such decisions are based on resource costs—a firm wants a lower cost source of labor or materials—or distribution costs—a firm wants to be close to the final market—and the quality of government.

Once a firm has established facilities in more than one country, it is subject to balance sheet exposure. A firm must select the currency in which it invoices. It may select the invoicing currency so that its cash flows and assets are primarily defined in one currency. Its choice could benefit customers but put it at greater exchange rate risk, or it could reduce its exchange rate risk by placing the burden of that risk on customers. For example, suppose Jabil is choosing to invoice in either U.S. dollars or Czech koruna. If it selects the koruna, then its Czech customer has no worry about exchange rate changes, but Jabil does. It has to translate the koruna back to the dollar. If Jabil invoices in dollars, then it is the Czech customer who must translate back to the domestic currency. Jabil will select the invoicing currency that maximizes profit and that depends on the price elasticity of demand. If the Czech customer has no other sources of the equipment, then the demand for Jabil hardware is very inelastic; Jabil can shift the exchange rate risk to the customer. However, if Jabil is just one among a few or several sources of equipment, and the price elasticity of demand is high, then Jabil will not be able to shift the risk to the customer.

A firm may turn to the foreign exchange market and arrange forward contracts to reduce exchange rate exposure. The forward market allows corporations to establish the exchange rate between two currencies for settlement at a fixed future date. The rate is fixed at the time the contract is made, but payment and delivery are not made until the value date. Whether the exchange rate changes in a direction expected by the firm or in the opposite direction does not matter. The firm is obligated to buy or sell the currency at the agreed upon rate.

Another hedging practice is to use currency futures. Currency futures are similar to foreign exchange forwards in that they are contracts for delivery of a certain amount of a foreign currency at some future date and at a known price. In practice, they differ from forward contracts in important ways. One difference between forwards and futures is standardization. Forwards are for any amount, as long as it's big enough to be worth the dealer's time, while futures are for standard amounts, each contract being far smaller than the average forward transaction. Futures are also standardized in terms of delivery date. The normal currency futures delivery dates are March, June, September, and December, while forwards are private agreements that can specify any delivery date that the parties choose. Both of these features allow the futures contract to be tradable. Another difference is that forwards are traded by phone and telex and are completely independent of location or time. Futures, on the other hand, are traded in organized exchanges such the LIFFE in London, SIMEX in Singapore, and the IMM in Chicago. In a forward contract, whether it involves full delivery of the two currencies or just compensation of the net value, the transfer of funds takes place once: at maturity. With futures, cash changes hands every day during the life of the contract, or at least every day that has seen a change in the price of the contract. This daily cash compensation feature reduces the possibility of one party failing to deliver on the contract. Forwards and futures serve similar purposes, and tend to have identical rates, but differ in their applicability. Most big companies use forwards; futures tend to be used whenever credit risk may be a problem.

With a forward contract one can lock in an exchange rate for the future. In a number of circumstances, however, it may be desirable to have more flexibility than a forward provides. For example a computer manufacturer in California may have sales priced in U.S. dollars as well as in euros in Germany. Depending on the relative strength of the two currencies, revenues may be realized in either euros or dollars. In such a situation, the use of forwards or futures would be inappropriate: There's no point in hedging something you might not have. What is called for is a foreign exchange option: the right, but not the obligation, to exchange currency at a predetermined rate.

A foreign-exchange option is a contract for future delivery of a currency in exchange for another, where the holder of the option has the right to buy (or sell) the currency at an agreed upon price, the strike or exercise price, but is not required to do so. The option seller is obliged to make (or take) delivery at the agreed-upon price if the buyer exercises his or her option.

Consider the situation faced by a major U.S.-based potato chip company. It agreed to purchase 15 million punt worth of potatoes from a supplier in County Cork, Ireland.[3] Payment of 5 million punt was to be made in 245 days' time. The dollar had recently declined against the euro, increasing the cost of the potatoes to the U.S. firm. How could it avoid any further rise in the cost of imports? The CFO of the potato chip company decided to hedge the payment. He had obtained dollar/punt quotes of $2.25 spot ($2.25 for each punt) and $2.19 for 245 days forward delivery. In other words, the foreign-exchange market was anticipating that the dollar would fall relative to the punt. But what if the dollar rose in the next few months? This would make the $2.19 price much too high. The CFO decided to buy a call option. With this action, he was paying for downside protection while not limiting the possible savings that could be obtained if the dollar did rise. If the dollar rose to $2.35, the CFO would not exercise the option and would purchase the punt at the spot rate of $2.35. But if the dollar fell to $2.15, the CFO could exercise the option and purchase the punt at $2.19.

This simple example illustrates the lopsided character of options. Futures and forwards are contracts in which two parties exchange something in the future. They are thus useful to hedge or convert known currency or interest rate exposures. An option, in contrast, gives one party the right but not the obligation to buy or sell an asset under specified conditions while the other party assumes an obligation to sell or buy that asset if that option is exercised. The option enables one to offset the risk of movements in exchange rates in one direction only.

If a firm believes the exchange rate is more volatile than the market says it is, then purchasing an option makes sense. In other words, the firm believes the option should have a higher price than what the market says. When a firm believes the likely change in exchange rates is in a specific direction, then purchasing an option to protect against unexpected changes in the other direction makes sense.

The Global Capital Market

Capital markets are global—capital flows in and out of countries at the touch of a button. Understanding the global capital market is becoming extremely important to all managers. Interestingly, the world's economies were almost as globalized 100 years ago as they are now. Capital mobility (the flow of capital across national borders) reached a peak at the beginning of World War I and then declined until about 1960. It took until 2000 to reach the 1918 level again. From 1945 until the 1980s, the world consisted of a series of closed national economies, each with its own unique set of factors of production. These economies competed with each other on the basis of manufactured goods. What determined the standard of living of any one of them was the effectiveness with which it produced the goods that it exported. Savings were channeled within these national economies by a capital market that interacted with other countries only at the margin.

When the major economies gave up fixed exchange rate regimes in the 1970s, the capital market began changing. Large multinational banks discovered that they could borrow for a short period, such as 90 days, in one currency at one rate, and lend in another currency at a higher rate, while protecting themselves from foreign-exchange movements with a forward exchange contract. These institutions began profiting from arbitrage opportunities. But arbitrage was just one of the ways financial institutions made money in the foreign-exchange markets. Many also bet or speculated on price movements. For example, if you believed that the U.S. dollar was going to decline against the Japanese yen, you could simply borrow dollars and convert them into yen. If the yen appreciated as you expected, you could sell the yen after it rose in value, convert it back into dollars, pay off the U.S. dollar loan, and pocket the amount by which the dollar had depreciated relative to the yen less the interest on the loan. Or if you didn't want to borrow, you could buy a foreign-exchange call or a forward exchange contract. Of course, if you take a position and you are wrong about the price movement, you lose money. And many institutions did indeed lose money from speculative activities.

The Asian Crisis

In the late 1990s, Asia nearly melted down. Japan's economy declined 10.7 percent, Korea 43 percent, Malaysia 31 percent, Thailand 40 percent, and Indonesia 72 percent from their highs in the early 1990s. For comparison, the U.S. economy declined 34 percent during the Great Depression. These Asian economies had such great difficulties primarily because Japan, which is two-thirds of the Asian economy, did not have the financial structure to handle the huge capital outflow that occurred.

The initial result of the Japanese structure (copied by Korea and other Asian nations) was to jump-start development and lead to rapid rates of growth. But, when the foreign exchange market was liberalized and the global capital market began moving capital quickly from one investment to another no matter the country, Japan's industrial structure proved too rigid. It could not prevent neither outflows of capital nor depreciation of equity values.

Asia was not the only area in which markets were not allowed to function freely. Prior to 1990, a major share of most economies was protected from competition by government regulations, including capital controls, product market restrictions, and labor restrictions. Most governments limited the entry of certain products, declaring the inconvertibility of local currency, imposing onerous approval processes for acquisitions of companies by foreigners, dictating very high labor costs through minimum wages and benefits, and even setting constraints on the hours stores were allowed to remain open. Governments influenced the allocation of capital in the economy and had a primary role in setting interest rates with their monopoly on printing money and the ability to raise taxes.

These barriers restricted the mobility of capital and the adoption of best practices. The agricultural industry in France illustrates these conditions. Despite low levels of productivity and the resulting high costs of agricultural products, farmers in France were protected from competition for decades. By protecting that industry for so long, the government was able to avoid the disruption of displacing large numbers of people who had been in farming families for centuries. But the French public paid much more for their domestic produce than was necessary. In Japan restrictions have kept competition to a minimum in most industries. The low level of competition, in turn, has resulted in many highly unproductive sectors. Only in some export-based industries such as the steel or auto assembly are Japanese productivity levels high by global standards. Most of the Japanese labor force works in industries with productivity levels only one-third of U.S. levels. To compete abroad, Japanese industries are heavily subsidized by the Japanese government, and to compete domestically, imports are severely limited, if not totally disallowed.

While the movement toward openness and global markets moves forward, groups threatened by these developments turn to the government for help. As local producers and local labor are faced with external competition, they lobby the government for protection. In some cases, restrictions are imposed—such as on foreign steel producers by the U.S. government; in others, subsidies are provided—such as with U.S. agriculture.

Free trade based on comparative advantage maximizes world output and allows consumers access to higher quality products at lower prices than would be available in the domestic market alone. If trade is restricted, consumers pay higher prices for lower quality goods and world output declines. Protection from foreign competition imposes costs on the domestic economy as well as on foreign producers. When production does not proceed on the basis of comparative advantage, resources are not expended in their most efficient uses. Why then are restrictions placed on trade? The primary reason is due to politics: Some group or groups would be hurt by free trade, so they lobby the government for protection. The most common arguments used to rationalize protection are to save jobs, to support national defense, and to protect new industries until they are old enough to compete.

If foreign goods are kept out of the domestic economy, it is often argued, jobs will be created at home. This argument is based on the idea that domestic firms will produce the goods that otherwise would have been produced abroad, thus employing domestic workers instead of foreign workers. The problem with this argument is that only the protected industry would benefit. Since domestic consumers will pay higher prices to buy the output of the protected industry, they will have less to spend on other goods and services, which could cause employment in other industries to drop. If other countries retaliate by restricting entry of U.S. exports, the output of U.S. firms that produce for export will fall as well.

The Foreign Exchange Curiosity

When firms speculate or bet on currency changes, they are susceptible to losing money if the currency changes in the opposite direction from which they were betting. For that reason, most businesses hedge, not speculate. They offset their exposure to a currency change with the use of financial instruments such as options or forward contracts.

Firms can also lose money because their exposure to exchange rate changes was not hedged. For instance, where they locate, what currency they define their invoicing in, what currency they define their financial statements in—all put firms into some risk for currency changes.

Currency changes can occur rapidly, especially under flexible exchange rate systems. A firm should not make long-term commitments on the basis of short-term events. Thus, selecting a country in which to locate a business should not be made because of expectations of exchange rate changes.

Summary

1. The economy does not simply grow constantly and smoothly. It fluctuates, and these fluctuations are called business cycles.
2. Managers must have some literacy of business cycles and this includes a literacy of international developments and exchange rates.
3. Monetary policy is the policy of controlling the nation's money supply. In the United States monetary policy is the responsibility of the Federal Reserve System.
4. Government spending and taxing, often called fiscal policy, is the responsibility of Congress and the president and is handled by the Treasury.
5. Monetary policy consists primarily of open market operations, the buying and selling of Treasury bonds by the Federal Reserve. An increase in Fed purchases represents an increase in the money supply, and an increase in Fed sales, a reduction of the money supply.
6. When government spending exceeds revenue, a deficit occurs. The deficit can be paid for by borrowing or by future tax increases.
7. Keynesians are economists who believe that the government has the responsibility for employment and must use government spending and taxing to control the economy. Keynesians do not think that free markets function well and thus need to be controlled by government.
8. Austrians are economists who believe that free markets should be allowed to function and that the government should not intervene.
9. An exchange rate is the rate or price at which one currency trades for another.
10. The law of one price says that price (or interest rate) differences of identical goods in different markets will only be large enough that a profit cannot be made by simultaneously buying and selling the good in the different markets.
11. Purchasing power parity, PPP, states that identical goods should have the same price in different countries once adjusted by the exchange rate. Interest rate parity,

IRP, says that identical financial assets should have the same rates of return once adjusted by the exchange rate.

12. Foreign exchange risk is the risk that a change in the exchange rate will adversely affect profits.

13. Forward and futures contracts are agreements to buy or sell foreign exchange at a specified time in the future at a specific rate.

14. An option to buy foreign exchange is a contract that allows but does not require the purchaser of the option to purchase foreign exchange in the future at a specified rate.

15. Foreign exchange exposure consists of two types: balance sheet or contractual and market based. Market-based exposure depends on whether rivals are foreign or domestic and on whether the demand is price-elastic or price-inelastic.

Key Terms

Business cycle	Mortgage-backed security (MBS)
Open market operations	Foreign exchange
Discount rate	Exchange rate
Reserve requirements	Balance sheet exposure
Federal funds rate	Market-based exposure

Exercises

1. What is monetary policy? How does the Fed increase the money supply? What is the effect of an increase in the money supply?

2. Explain how government deficits lead to increases in the money supply.

3. An overvalued currency is one that is expected to decline in value relative to other currencies. What is the effect on your firm when the currency it uses is overvalued? Suppose you are managing a firm that produces in each of the countries listed below and sells according to the description. How would you protect the firm from exchange rate changes? How would you expect downturns in the United States to affect your business?

   a. A small country that conducts all of its trade with the United States.
   b. A country that has no international trade.
   c. A country whose policies have led to a 300 percent annual rate of inflation.
   d. A country that wants to offer exporters cheap access to the imported inputs they need but to discourage other domestic residents from importing goods.
   e. A large country like the United States or Japan.

4. What does it mean to say that a currency appreciates or depreciates in value? Give an example of each and briefly mention what might cause such a change. Explain how each change could affect your firm's sales when your firm produces in one nation and sells to others.

5. Illustrate the exchange rate effect of a change in tastes prompting German residents to buy more goods from the United States. How would this affect the sales of your firm that produces in the United States but sells to German residents.

6. Your firm needs to raise $10 million for an expansion. How would you propose the money be raised?

   a. If your firm sells only domestically.
   b. If your firm sells in several nations.
   c. If your firm is privately owned and has issued no shares of stock.

7. Explain the effects of an increase in the value of the domestic currency on your firm's revenues under each of the following conditions:?

   a. Your firm sells only domestically.
   b. Your firm purchases supplies from other countries.
   c. Your firm sells products domestically and in other countries.
   d. Your firm has manufacturing plants located in other countries.

8. Your firm has manufacturing facilities in an emerging market. That country decides to impose trade restrictions requiring that all companies be majority owned by local firms. How would you deal with this change?

9. You are being clobbered by exchange rate changes. You decided to minimize the exchange rate risk. How would you proceed? Describe the trade-offs of minimizing exposure via the financial markets and establishing manufacturing sites in countries in which you do business.

10. Mexico and the United States are the only producers and consumers of a certain type of electronic switch. The demand for and supply of the electronic switch in each country is as shown in the following table.

United States

Price (dollars)	Quantity Demanded (millions)	Quantity Supplied (millions)
20	10	4
40	8	6
60	6	8
80	4	10

Mexico

Price (Pesos)	Quantity Demanded (millions)	Quantity Supplied (millions)
190	5	2
380	4	6
570	3	10
760	2	14

a. Suppose that there is free trade and that the exchange rate is 9.5 pesos to the dollar. What is the equilibrium price?

b. Which country will export the switches to the other country?

c. Suppose the United States imposes a tariff of $100 per switch. What will happen to imports and exports?

d. Suppose the exchange rate changes to 10 pesos to the dollar. How does that change the answers to the previous questions?

11. Explain why flexible exchange rates allow a country to have independence for its monetary policy and fixed exchange rates do not.

12. What would be the likely effect of the Fed allowing the money supply to grow at a rate of 10 percent a year? 5 percent? Zero percent?

13. What does it mean to say that China is going to dump U.S. dollars? What if China decides not to purchase any more U.S. debt?

14. The Federal Reserve increased its balance sheet by purchasing so-called toxic assets from large banks that were holding them. This was an attempt to capitalize the banks. What does it mean for the Fed? What happens if the assets end up having no value?

15. You are managing a multinational enterprise that does business in the EU, the United States, and Latin America. What would you do if you expected Latin America's inflation rate on average to be double that of the United States and the EU?

16. If inflation is a rise in prices throughout the economy, what is deflation? Explain why inflation reduces the cost of debt over time and why inflation increases it.

17. What type of monetary policy would you anticipate to occur over the next several years in the United States given the huge increase in debt that occurred in 2009 and 2010? Explain.

18. An overvalued currency is one that is expected to decline in value relative to other currencies. What is the effect on a firm that produces in the country whose currency is overvalued and sells to other nations?

19. Explain the effects of an increase in the value of the domestic currency on a firm's revenues under each of the following conditions:

a. The firm sells only domestically

b. The firm purchases supplies from other countries

c. The firm sells products domestically and in other countries

d. The firm has manufacturing plants located in other countries

CHAPTER NOTES

1. The country could refuse to pay off the debt and thus declare bankruptcy.
2. State and local government securities, issued by state and local governments, are not part of the U.S. government debt, nor is debt of households.
3. The Irish punt was fixed against the euro in 1999. This case took place prior to that date.

CHAPTER 21

Strategy Myths

CASE

Conspiracy

Driving home one evening listening to talk radio, I heard somebody claim that a solar-powered car had been developed that was ready to go and was as cheap and as safe as an average family car. The car would need only a few dollars worth of fuel per year to get it started. The talk host asked when were we likely to see it in the marketplace, and the engineer coolly replied "probably never. The oil companies will buy us out and throw the blueprint for the car away." The next time I heard about special energy saving innovations that were mysteriously not available to the general public was a car that ran on water. The story went that the inventor ended up committing suicide and no one knows where the plans for the car ended up.

1. Does this story make sense?
2. Why are such myths so enduring?

A Firm Has to Grow to Be Successful

Pets.com's first annual report announced that it expected to lose money until it had garnered the dominant market share in the online pet product category. Amazon.com is the largest online book seller, moving more volumes than almost all of its bricks and mortar rivals. But despite seven years of market share growth, it didn't report a net profit until January 2002, and then that profit was tiny, $5 million on $1.12 billion in sales. DEC once had a large share of the minicomputer business, but profits slipped as market share remained firm. DEC was rescued by Compaq, and then Compaq was acquired by HP. Wal-Mart is profitable, but the company is focused on expanding into new markets whether they are fully profitable or not, and in recent years many were not. 3M is gargantuan, a $15 billion business that towers over its competitors in nearly every product category. Yet others earn more profit in many of these same categories.

Why do so many believe that market share leads to profitability? Part of the blame has to be placed on economic theory and the comparison of monopoly and perfect competition. Economists looked at the varying performance of firms and noted that it should depend on whether or not the firms have market power. The way an industry is organized—that is, whether it is perfectly competitive or more monopolistic—is assumed to affect the way firms in the industry behave and pursue profits. This became known as the structure–conduct–performance (SCP) paradigm (discussed in Chapter 7). The structure of an industry determines the conduct of firms in the industry, and this, in turn, affects industry performance or profitability. For instance, the firms in a perfectly competitive market are unable to raise price above the market price. Price is competed down until it just equals marginal cost and economic profits are zero. The way a firm gains some market power is to reduce the number of substitutes. It has to differentiate itself or its goods and services in some manner. If successful, the differentiation enables the firm to increase price and earn positive economic profit. In the extreme, the firm is a monopoly. The monopolist will increase price, and no competition will arise to drive the price to marginal cost and economic profit to zero. So the idea is, the closer to a monopoly the market is, the greater the profitability of the firm(s) in that market.

As discussed in Chapter 10, the concentration of the market is defined as how dominant one or a few firms are—how market share is divided. The fewer firms dividing market share, the more concentrated the market; the larger the market share held by one or a few firms, the greater is concentration. The more concentrated the market, the more market power each firm has.[1] As a result, each firm in a concentrated market should be able to earn more profit. This view is characterized as the following statement: "Capturing a dominant share of a market is likely to mean enjoying the highest profits of any companies serving that market." This sentiment appears over and over again in major business journal articles.[2]

The problem is that being dominant is not as important as being profitable and does not necessarily yield profits. Years ago, the video-game industry was ruled by one player, Nintendo. The company had machines in a third of American homes, and it was Japan's most profitable electronics company. The title of a 1994 book summed up the situation: *Game Over: How Nintendo Conquered the World.*[3] Then the Sony PlayStation arrived, and everything changed. Today, Sony is the dominant force, and its chief rival is not Nintendo but Microsoft, which makes the Xbox. Sony's PlayStation 3 was greeted by crowds of hysterical consumers lining up to buy the new console. But then, surprisingly, Nintendo's new console, Wii, appeared a few days later and muted the hysteria. As the third party in the market, Nintendo has been like the ugly stepsister struggling to be recognized. After all, the prevailing wisdom is that companies need to be market leaders, or face disaster. Nintendo, though, has not just survived out of the spotlight; it has thrived.

It has years of solid profits. Sony's game division, by contrast, did not cover its cost of capital and Microsoft's division lost money.

The way to gain market share is to increase sales or maximize revenue, but revenue maximizing is not the same as profit maximizing. Economic profit is: Equation (3s) from Chapter 19:

$$(3s)\text{ECONOMIC PROFIT} = \frac{\text{Revenue} - \text{variable costs}}{\text{Revenue}} - \frac{\text{fixed costs}}{\text{Revenue}}$$

$$* \left\{ \frac{\text{Revenue}}{\text{market size}} * \text{market size} \right\}$$

This can be written as (where π is economic profit):

$$\pi = [\pi/ \text{ Revenue}][\text{Market share}][\text{Market size}]$$

Then, solving for market share we have:

$$\text{Market share} = TR/\text{Market size}$$

Market share is maximized by setting marginal revenue equal to zero:

$$\frac{\partial \text{market share}}{\partial Q} = 0 \text{ yields, } \frac{\partial TR}{\partial Q} = 0 \text{ assuming market size constant.}$$

Assuming the size of the market to be constant, then if one firm increases its sales other firms lose sales. In this case, maximizing market share is equivalent to maximizing total revenue. Since marginal revenue is not set equal to marginal cost, a market share strategy is not a profit-maximizing strategy. It might generate profits, but these are not the greatest profits that might be earned. The only way it might be is if, in the long term, the increased size enabled the firm to erect strict barriers to entry and thereby acquire and sustain profits that were lost while obtaining the market share. Suppose the market and the firm's place in it after the firm has created its barriers to entry is shown in Figure 21.1. The firm acts like a monopolist, setting a high price and earning substantial profits. Compare the revenue-maximizing strategy of producing where marginal revenue is zero and setting the price to sell that much and the profit-maximizing strategy of setting the price and producing where marginal revenue equals marginal cost. Profit is positive in this case for revenue maximizing but is significantly smaller than for the profit-maximizing strategy, AGHD versus BEFC.

Sony and Microsoft have faced off in their attempts to "control the living room"; they have invested billions of dollars in an attempt to surpass each other technologically. Nintendo has dropped out of this race. The Wii has few bells and whistles and much less processing power than its "competitors," and it features less impressive graphics. It's really well suited for just one thing: playing games. But this turns out to be an asset. The Wii's simplicity means that Nintendo can make money selling consoles, while Sony is reportedly losing more than $240 on each PlayStation 3 it sells. Nintendo is not trying to rule the entire industry, so it has been able to focus on its core competency, which is making entertaining, innovative games. And because Nintendo sells many more of its own games than Sony and Microsoft do, its profit margins are higher, too.[4]

Nintendo's success is not an anomaly either; it is not the "exception that proves the rule." The business landscape is full of situations in which companies have flourished as third or fourth wheels and also with companies that have struggled to make money despite being No. 1 in their industries. And while it's true that in many industries there is a correlation between market share and profitability, market share does not necessarily

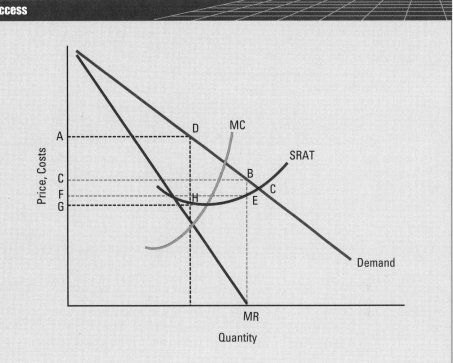

FIGURE 21.1 Growth and Success

If the firm can achieve economies of scale and create barriers to entry, then the firm can charge a high price and earn substantial profits. Revenue maximizing occurs where marginal revenue is zero. Profit would be BEFC, whereas the profit maximizing profit would be AGHD.

lead to profitability.[5] Firms with better offerings and higher profits tend to achieve higher market shares, not the other way around. Nevertheless, growth is more often a business's strategy than not.

Acquiring Growth

A quick way to build market share is to buy your competitor. Theoretically, an acquisition leads to synergies, as is illustrated in Figure 21.2. The synergies anticipated by combining several functions that are separate in the two firms would lead to a reduction in average total costs—a resulting economy of scale. The problem is that such synergies often are not experienced, and so the combined firms' costs are higher than they were separately. International Paper (IP) decided that the way to improve performance was market share. IP acquired Federal Paperboard, Union Camp, and Champion Paper Corp, making IP the biggest firm in the industry. But IP experienced only one year in the past decade in which returns exceeded the company's cost of capital.

Economies of scale are not an automatic result of combining two large firms. When Ford bought Jaguar in 1989, Ford planned to share platforms between Jaguar and Lincoln. This prompted years of retooling and harmonization that cost Ford hundreds of millions of dollars. The Jaguar unit didn't start to show profits until 1996 but then was losing money again by 2000. The alleged economies of scale never did occur. Ford sold Jaguar to India's Tata Motors in 2008.

The big problem with acquisition-based growth strategies is generating value for the acquiring company's shareholders through the process. In general, it seems very hard for owners of a firm to gain from an acquisition of another firm. A consistent finding from a number of studies is that when measured by stock market reactions, mergers and acquisitions on average do create value, but most or all of it accrues to the target firms'

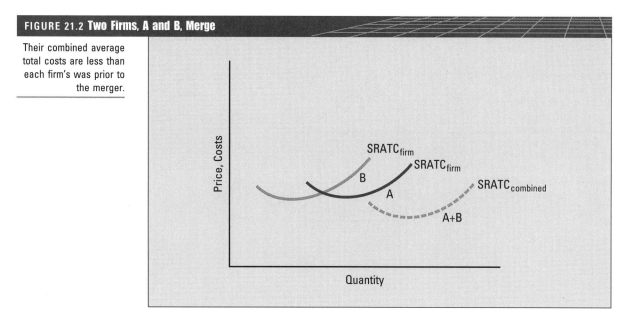

FIGURE 21.2 Two Firms, A and B, Merge

Their combined average total costs are less than each firm's was prior to the merger.

owners. The general pattern is that the stock price of the acquired firm shows positive abnormal returns, while the stock price of the acquiring firm tends to be unaffected or to decline.

What could account for the differences? If there are more suitors than potential acquisition targets, then the prices of the targets would be expected to rise. Are there always more potential suitors than targets? Perhaps so, if more firms are trying to acquire growth and market share than firms attempting not to do that. Another possible reason could be a **winner's curse**. A winner's curse arises when buyers pay more for something than it is worth because they are afraid others are bidding for the same object.

Since the different stock price effects are widely known, why do so few buyer-side shareholders attempt to block mergers even in the face of such losses, particularly when millions or billions of dollars are at stake? According to one study, the reason is that the major shareholders of large companies own about equal shares of both the acquiring firm and the target firm. In general, those who only owned stock in acquiring companies lost up to 1.5 percent of the value of their holdings. Those who owned stock in both acquiring and target firms, on the other hand, made a decent net gain of about 2.5 percent. In the largest 100 mergers, acquiring shareholders of acquiring firms lost up to 4.5 percent of the value of their holdings, while those owning both acquiring and acquired firms enjoyed a modest net gain of 1 percent. If you owned shares in both companies, would you vote to approve what might seem like a bad merger?[6]

The bulk of corporate mergers taking place in 2003–2006 were transacted in cash, whereas those done in earlier periods were mainly transactions in stock. In the cash mergers, an acquirer pays cash for the shares of the acquiree and in the stock mergers the acquirer simply issues newly created shares. When Company X buys Company Y for cash, it exchanges the cash for Company Y's shares and then simply destroys those shares. This means that after the deal there are the same number of X's shares as before the deal and no shares for Y. The new Company X consists of both its and the former Company Y's earnings, so the new Company X's earnings per share should rise. In addition, the supply of equity outstanding has been reduced since Company Y's stock no longer exists. With a smaller supply, as long as the demand for equities does not change, prices will rise.

Takeovers transacted wholly in stock are different. Usually the acquirer's earnings per share fall because more shares are supplied to the market, diluting value. Firm A is worth X and Firm B is worth Y. To acquire Firm B, Firm A must bid up B's price. The extra price is paid for by increasing the supply of stock of Firm A—newly created, never before existing shares. Firm A issues enough new shares to cover all of the prior value of firm B, plus enough newly created shares to cover the 25 percent markup. So there are more real share equivalents after the deal than before. With no more earnings, the new firm A's earnings per share fall when the deal is done. This is how most of the mergers and acquisitions in the 1920s, 1960s, and 1990s were carried out. These increase the supply of equity and make earnings per share fall.

The only way value can be created by a merger is if there are so-called synergies or economies of scale. So investors are betting on whether the synergies will yield value. In cash acquisitions, the acquiring shareholders assume the entire synergy risk, while in stock transactions the selling shareholders share it. A stock deal sends two potential signals to investors. One is that management lacks confidence in the acquisition. If they didn't lack confidence, they would do a cash deal because they would be much more certain of gaining synergies. The second is that the acquiring company's shares are overvalued. In both of these cases it would be logical for the acquiring company's shares to be revalued downward due to an acquisition.

In addition to buying market share, firms might look to market niches or attempt to leverage the brand name into new markets. The evidence suggests that neither of these strategies is usually successful. Chasing market share by offering supply in every niche and at every price in the market is usually unsuccessful. It is much the same as chasing market share by extending the brand. In most cases it results in dilution of brand rather than increased profitability.

Chasing market share is typically an illusion, a strategy that does not generate synergies, economies of scale, and most importantly, profits. Instead, profitability is the desired goal, and being profitable typically brings with it some increase in market share. When would market share lead to increased profitability? If the market has significant economies of scale, then the larger a firm is, the more efficient it can produce. Or, if a market has significant network externalities or increasing returns, then the larger a network is, the more efficient it is. The problem is, that neither of these events occurs often and when one does occur, it typically is quickly overcome by entrepreneurial action and technological change.

Business Insight

Most Businesspeople Are Unethical

TV dramas are overwhelmingly negative toward business. According to TV dramas, you were 21 times more likely to be kidnapped or murdered at the hands of a businessman than by any criminal elements. The Business and Media Institute (BMI) looked at 129 episodes from 12 top-rated dramas on the four networks: ABC, CBS, FOX and NBC. These broadcasts were picked from two "sweeps" months in 2005—May and November—when networks try to attract the largest audiences to maximize ad dollars. In this look at primetime, BMI found that negative plots about business and businessmen outnumbered positive ones by almost 4 to 1. Of the 39 episodes that included business-related plots or characters, 30 (77 percent) cast businessmen and commerce in a negative light. When businessmen appeared on TV, they were up to no good. Only NBC's "Medium" and "Las Vegas" featured businessmen in a consistently positive light. Businessmen committed crimes five times more often than terrorists and four times more often than gangs. Businessmen turned up as kidnappers or murderers almost as often (21 times) as hardened criminals like drug dealers, child molesters, and serial killers put together (23 times).

When looking at movies, businessmen come off even worse. Half of the movies earning top Oscar nominations (8 of 16) portrayed businessmen in either primary or secondary roles committing crimes ranging from petty drug offenses to murder, mass murder, and an international conspiracy to overthrow a nation's government. Only one major character out of more than 70 across all 16 movies was depicted as successful and ethical while actively engaged in business. Of the movies that included businessmen, 79 percent (11 out of 14) portrayed business in a negative way. Three (21 percent) were direct assaults on industry—oil, mining, and pharmaceuticals.[7]

Why are businesspeople depicted so negatively? Are they less ethical than others—say politicians, police, ministers, athletes, or professors? By most measures they are not. Businessmen are no more virtuous than preachers, politicians, and professors. But who might be more likely to profit from dishonesty? Businessmen are more honest than preachers, politicians, and professors because they have the least to gain from dishonest claims about the benefits their products provide.[8] Remember that in the market you gain by serving people, providing them what they want at prices they want. This does not occur for government employees, athletes, or even ministers.

A Firm Must Be Diversified to Minimize Risk

There is a continuing belief that a firm should be diversified to minimize risk. Consider the lesson given by the author of a best-selling management book. A firm should consider *business unit diversification* to hedge business cycle risk. That is, a firm should have two business units whose revenue streams move in opposite directions. For instance, Countrywide Financial created a hedge by having one business unit that focuses on mortgage loan originations and another that focuses on mortgage loan servicing. Because the revenues from these two businesses move in opposite directions with movements in interest rates, Countrywide is able to achieve more stable revenues over the course of the business cycle and related interest rate cycle. Another way to diversify, the author says, is geographically. Such geographical diversification works, it is argued, because the business cycles and political conditions of various countries are not perfectly correlated. In lay terms, this means that while Europe or Japan might be experiencing a recession, China or the United States might be in the midst of a robust expansion.[9]

Beginning around 1960, many firms expanded (horizontally) beyond the boundaries of a particular business area. General Electric produced toasters and turbine generators; Morton Thiokol produced salt and aerospace equipment; Martin Marietta produced electronics and cement; TRW produced seat belts, air bags, and credit rating services, and so on. These firms are called conglomerates—firms diversified into apparently unrelated lines of business. Why would a firm enter a business that is unrelated to its core expertise?

Rationales for diversification include offsetting "dogs" with "cash cows." The cash cow rationale argues that the long-term success of a growing firm requires it to develop a portfolio of businesses that assures an adequate and stable cash flow with which to finance its activities. In addition to boosting and stabilizing cash flows, the parent firm can use profits from one business to subsidize another. Some say that this is what General Electric has done. GE Capital has provided the growth and revenue to support GE industry.[10] While portfolio strategies may smooth cash flows and may help the parent firm save troubled business lines, they do not necessarily create value for the owners of the firms. It is easier and less costly for shareholders to diversify their personal portfolios than for a firm to do so.[11] What advantage could a firm have by diversifying?

If a combined firm could allocate resources between businesses more efficiently than the market could, then the diversified firm would make sense. For instance, if the diversified firm offered a way to give managers valuable and varied experiences more efficiently than if the managers acquire the experiences on their own, then this development of human capital would provide a rationale for combining firms. This argument has been made in the case of General Electric. Jack Welch in his autobiography[12] provides detailed descriptions of the value he obtained from the diversified experiences within GE.

Virtually every merger is greeted with the claim that there are unexploited synergies that the combined entity will be able to exploit.[13] Bank One's CEO said that with the merger with J.P. Morgan Chase in 2004 "We will have the resources to develop and deploy compelling, differentiated services by unleashing the combined strengths of the two companies." And Nextel's CEO argued in 2004 that with a merger with Sprint "Our combined company will have the size, scale, product mix, customer base, distribution channels, and earnings stability to achieve outstanding result"

If mergers created firms that were more efficient than prior to a merger, then the merged entity would have a higher valuation than would the separate companies. But studies show that only shareholders of the acquired firm gain from the merger and that once the firms are merged, the market actually reduces its valuation of the combined company. These results tell us that the merger did not occur for efficiency reasons. If not efficiency, then what? It would seem that the reason might stem from rent seeking or from nonproductive activities.[14]

If diversification does not occur owing to a market inefficiency, then is it due to the self-interest of executives? If executives enjoy heading bigger companies and if the opportunities for growth in existing lines of business are limited, then the obvious choice is to grow by increasing scope. Some scholars have argued that diversification for growth is pursued not because it benefits shareholders but because it benefits managers. Growth may provide increased career development opportunities for managers and employees. Unrelated acquisitions may also enhance job security.[15] The argument rests on the idea that shareholders are unlikely to replace top management unless the firm performs poorly relative to the overall economy. To reduce the risk of job loss, managers must therefore reduce the risk of poor performance. One way to do this is through unrelated acquisitions—diversification. The performance of a highly diversified firm is likely to mirror the performance of the overall economy and, therefore, is less likely to lead shareholders to get rid of current management.

The problem with the diversification argument is that if other firms are focused narrowly and do better as a result, shareholders of the diversified firms lose. Then the diversified firm will be forced to change as shareholders sell their stock. Those executives attempting to build themselves a safe haven may have been behaving quite rationally from a personal point of view. But if they are not adding value, why would the stock market reward them?

Leadership and CEO Compensation

It has been said, *"If CEOs deserve what they get, they must be getting more important and more deserving all the time."* In 1980, the average CEO in America made 42 times as much as the average blue-collar worker, a ratio that rose to 85 times in 1990 and to 531 times in 2000. The average CEO of a company with at least $1 billion in annual revenue made about $400 more in one day in 2005 than the average worker made in a year. The average worker earned $41,861, while the average CEO made $10.9 million, or 262 times the salary of the average worker. From 1992 to 2005, the average CEO saw his or her pay rise by 186.2 percent, while the median worker saw wages rise by 7.2 percent.

In the 1970s and 1980s, executive pay was largely a matter of salaries and bonuses that were paid out only if financial targets were met. As studies began casting doubt on the relationship between bonuses, financial targets, and stock prices, corporate Boards of Directors turned their attention to shareholder value.[16] They became convinced that the surest way to align the interests of managers with those of shareholders was to make stock options a large component of executive compensation. By 2000, stock options accounted for more than half of total CEO compensation in the largest U.S. companies and about 30 percent of senior operating managers' pay.

The typical way stock options are structured is that the exercise price (the price at which the stock can be purchased) is established at the market price on the day the options are granted and stays fixed over the entire option period, usually 10 years. If the share price rises above the exercise price, the option holder can cash in on the gains. The idea was that this would give the CEO an incentive to increase stock price and shareholder value. The problem firms ran into in the 1990s is that almost all stock prices rose. When the market is rising, stock options reward both superior and subpar performance because any increase in a company's share price will reward the holder of a stock option. In the 1990s, stock options gave many managers huge compensation increases. Many managers whose firms had not performed even as well as the market average received large option-based compensation increases.

The huge pay increases have received enough publicity that politicians began focusing on the issue. Some have argued that the government should limit executive pay.[17] A limit on pay, if effective, would be a price ceiling located below the market or equilibrium price, where quantity demanded would exceed quantity supplied. In other words, there would be a shortage of qualified CEOs. The best-performing CEOs would leave the CEO market. They would quit being hired managers and seek fame and fortune elsewhere. The remaining people in the CEO market would be the less competent managers, those for whom the price ceiling is not lower than their opportunity cost.

Many Boards of Directors have considered placing ceilings on CEO bonuses. But such ceilings could lead to perverse behavior. For instance, when the CEO's bonus is at its upper limit, the CEO might have the incentive to manipulate earnings downward—perhaps as a means of deferring the earnings to a later period when the bonus ceiling is not binding. When near the upper limit, a CEO could choose not to pursue a project that appears to be potentially profitable but is risky for fear that the risky venture could reduce his or her rewards.[18]

Limiting pay might be a media-created issue that has little substance. How big a problem is CEO pay? There are probably fewer than 500 CEOs subject to the huge pay referenced in the media. Moreover, the highest CEO pay might cost shareholders two cents per share. If the CEO generates more than two cents per share of additional benefits, then the cost is a good investment.

Is it possible the CEO compensation is efficient? Many people would argue that it is, that the high compensation elicits more and higher quality work by others in a company.

Tournaments and Superstars

Why is CEO pay so much greater than that of other employees in the firm? One answer could be that the market for CEOs has failed—that CEOs have been able to pursue their own interests at the expense of the shareholders. Another explanation could be that this structure is efficient—that it elicits the most productivity from the CEO and from other employees in the firm. There are two versions of the efficiency argument—the tournament rationale and the superstar rationale.

The tournament rationale is presented as an analogy to sporting contests. The argument notes that in most corporations, promotion and pay increases go hand in hand, so we could think of promotion as the result of a large contest pitting all employees against each other. People move up the corporate hierarchy and obtain pay raises by performing better than all the others who are also trying to move up the hierarchy. Once a person is promoted, a new tournament begins, with the winner advancing to a still higher level. The final prize is the top job, the CEO position.

If job promotion within the firm is a contest, what compensation structure will elicit the most productive behavior from participants? As noted earlier, in golf tournaments, the more that the first prize exceeds the payoff for second and lower finishes, the better is the average performance of the contestants. Fighting for that top spot leads to a higher quality performance from everyone entered in the contest. It has also been found that in NASCAR racing, the greater the difference between the first prize and the payoff for second and lower finishes, the faster the average track speed. Carrying these findings over to the labor market inside the firm, economists have suggested that an extremely high pay package for the CEO relative to other employees might induce all employees (current and future) to exert extra effort on the job.

The second argument that CEO compensation might be efficient is also explained with an analogy to sports. It is called the **superstar effect**. Consider the fact that the playing ability of the top 10 tennis players or golfers is not much better than the playing ability of the players ranked between 40 and 50. Nonetheless, the compensation differences are incredibly large. The average income of the top 10 tennis players and golfers is in the tens of millions, while that of the lower-ranked 10 players is in the hundreds of thousands. If their performances are not that much different, why is their compensation so different? The explanation provided is that since consumers have limited time, they choose to follow the top players. A tennis match between the fortieth- and forty-first-ranked players might be nearly as good as that between the first- and second-ranked players. Yet nearly everyone would choose to watch the first- and second-ranked players. At golf tournaments, huge throngs surround the top players, while lesser-known contenders play the game without many onlookers. These differences mean that the demand for the top players is huge relative to the demand for the lesser-ranked players.

The superstar effect also occurs outside of sports. Two lawyers of relatively equal ability might earn significantly different fees because the one who is just slightly better has a huge demand for his services relative to the one just slightly worse. Suppose one lawyer wins cases just slightly more often or wins just slightly more money than the second lawyer. A huge firm dealing with billions of dollars in a lawsuit would demand the services of the first attorney. As a result, the fees earned by the first attorney would be significantly greater than the second, even though their quality is only slightly different. Consider two people who could direct the firm according to various strategies. If the choice could mean billions of dollars in firm value, even if there are very small differences between the two people, the one with the better chance of making the wealth-enhancing decision will receive a huge compensation relative to the other.

The principle to keep in mind in the area of personnel and compensation is that incentives matter. To observe some feature of personnel or compensation and automatically claim it is unfair or incorrect is probably to miss the point. There probably is an efficiency reason the situation exists. Remember that competition and entry drive inefficiency out. If a compensation scheme was inefficient, it would not last long if competition and entry could occur. But suppose the CEO could control the Board of Directors and thus could garner a huge compensation package. Then we could argue that the market was not working, that it was being manipulated fraudulently or illegally. But how would that occur? Would the Board of Directors subject themselves to the bad publicity or even legal difficulties of overpaying a CEO? Is there no way to control the CEO?

Market for Corporate Control

Suppose you, as a shareholder, believe a certain CEO is running your firm into the ground. What can you do? You can sell your shares and purchase shares of companies whose CEOs are running their firms in such a way as to increase shareholder value. This action imposes some discipline on CEOs. But the CEO has some room between running the firm into the ground and running the firm so as not to drive all shareholders away but still create benefits for him- or herself.

Financial innovations in the 1980s, such as junk bond financing, allowed leveraged buyouts (LBOs) and management buyouts (MBOs), which increased the ease with which an investor could take over a company. Certain investors became known as raiders or takeover experts. T. Boone Pickens and Carl Icahn, two of the best-known raiders, would purchase the majority of shares using leveraged buyouts and then often sell or dismantle the assets of the firm. To the takeover experts, the firm was worth less than the sum of its parts. Since even the largest of the Fortune 500 companies is potentially subject to takeover, CEOs have to maintain the value of the company. Getting taken over typically means that the CEO is out of a job. In fact, more than 50 percent of the top-level managers of target firms are gone within three years of acquisition. In general, CEO positions have become very precarious; between 1995 and 2000, the average tenure of 450 CEOs was less than three years.[19] Since then, the private equity takeovers have increased. This shortened tenure for CEOs means additional risk for them. Taking a position with a very short expected tenure would require some extra compensation as compared to taking a job with a longer expected tenure. Moreover, if you were on the Board of Directors of a company that was not performing well, would you want potential candidates to expect to be treated well? If you refuse to provide termination payments or benefits to the former CEO, would that send a signal to the potential successors?

The possibility of being a takeover target can discipline managers. The market value of companies cannot fall below the value that takeover experts believe that the firm can be dismantled for, or else the CEO is out of a job. The CEO is not immune to market forces; he or she cannot manipulate Boards of Directors or shareholders to grant excessive compensation packages at the detriment to the firm's value.

Suppressed Technologies

One of the most common and enduring myths in business regards the suppression of technology by big business. An invention that will destroy a major industry is stolen, purchased, or otherwise acquired by a big firm which immediately hides it. In early years it was the automobile companies buying all the rail track and destroying it. Today, it is new energy producing methodologies that oil companies and other energy-related companies keep off the market. You hear about a solar-powered car as cheap and as safe as an average family car—except that you would only need about 5 dollars worth of fuel per year—that was in production until the oil companies bought the car and destroyed its plans. Or perhaps you have heard about Stanley Meyers. Stanley supposedly developed a method of extracting hydrogen from water and utilizing it as a car fuel. The story goes that he and a friend drove the water-powered car from California to New York using about 28 gallons of water. But the plans disappeared when Stanley was poisoned.

The list of suppressed technologies and dastardly deeds to keep the inventions secret goes on and on. Do large businesses suppress technologies? Consider a large firm looking at an invention that would surely change the firm's market. Assume the invention is true and it works as advertised. The firm has a choice. It could ignore the invention, thinking it might never become reality. It could buy the rights to the invention and market and sell the invention itself, or it could put the invention on the shelves not to see the light of day. Which choice makes sense?

If the company ignores the invention, then the firm is likely to be the next buggy manufacturer facing the automobile as others introduce the product. If it purchases the invention, it then must decide to profit from the invention itself or to keep it off the market. But can it actually expect to keep the invention off the market? If a major innovation with a huge potential market was developed once, can it be kept secret? Will all the employees involved in purchasing the invention remain silent? Think of all the people with an incentive to attempt to create a market for the invention and to profit from that market. The firm would really have no choice. The only profitable decision would be to bring the invention to market.

What if the profit the existing firm earned from its current product looked to be greater than what it could get from the new invention? Would the firm still choose to bring the good to market, or would it conspire to keep it hidden? It might want to conspire, but the likelihood of keeping the invention hidden is not very good. Conspiracies, like cartels, are very difficult to maintain. A cartel is an organization of independent firms that have agreed to limit supplies in order to raise prices. In essence, a cartel is a group attempting to act as a monopolist. To do that, each cartel member must agree to reduce supply to an amount defined by the cartel. The problem for the cartel is that once the price of the product is raised because quantities have been limited, cartel members have an incentive to cheat on the agreement. Just think: If a firm makes $100 million on a volume of 3 billion, what would another billion mean? So several firms begin surreptitiously supplying more. But, of course, as firms begin supplying more, the price drops. The cartel falls apart. This is exactly what occurs with conspiracies—there are incentives to cheat on agreements.

"That's the exception that proves the rule." This statement implies that nonconforming cases, by the mere fact of their existence, somehow confirm or support a generalization. Obviously, they do nothing of the kind. In conspiracy theories it usually takes just a semblance of truth to prove that conspiracies exist. Lending some credence to the suppressed technology conspiracy theories by big business is the case of the Great American Streetcar Scandal, also known as the General Motors streetcar conspiracy. General Motors, Firestone Tire, Standard Oil of California, and Phillips Petroleum formed the National City Lines (NCL) holding company, which acquired most streetcar systems throughout the United States, dismantled them, and replaced them with buses in the early twentieth century. Between 1936 and 1950, National City Lines bought out more than 100 electric surface-traction systems in 45 cities, including Detroit, New York, Oakland, Philadelphia, St. Louis, Salt Lake City, Tulsa, Baltimore, Minneapolis, and Los Angeles, and replaced them with GM buses.

Was the NCL a huge conspiracy foisted on an unwary public at a huge loss to their welfare? If the electric cars were more desirable and less expensive for the consumer, wouldn't someone have been able to stop NCL and offer the products and services? In fact, the trolley industry was in financial difficulty. Its ancient equipment and poor service had devastated the market. Streetcar ridership had been steadily declining through this period.[20]

Globalization: Harms Developing Nations, Homogenizes Cultures, and Ensures Business Practices Are the Same

Globalization has set off a series of claims against business. People riot when a group of nations is to meet about creating free trade areas or reducing subsidies and import restrictions. The following is a common theme: The increase of free trade and globalization is benefiting multinationals and monopolies, and destroying small businesses who can't compete. Free trade reduces production of quality products and destroys a country's industries, lowering the standard of living in the area. Or consider the arguments against the outsourcing of jobs from wealthier countries to poorer countries. For instance, it is claimed that unemployment increases further when multinationals change to automation and slave labor, particularly in Third World countries. In sum, the common complaint is that free trade is not free, and it brings with it injustice, environmental ruin, economic chaos and the dislocation of American jobs.

The world's largest company measured by sales, Wal-Mart, calls itself a global retailer. However, it only has direct sales operations in around 5 percent of the countries that make up the United Nations; around 80 percent of its sales come from the United States, and approximately 90 percent of all sales come from North America. Is Wal-Mart a "global" company then? The answer would have to depend on the definition of "global." Wal-Mart sells products produced in a number of countries, but directly operates in only a select few markets. The vast majority of the citizens on the planet have never been inside a Wal-Mart store. BMW considers itself a "global" company; however, the majority of its customers come from two markets, Western Europe and the United States. Moreover, BMW, as is true in most "global" companies, has a top management team made up almost exclusively of individuals from the country of origin, in this case Germany. While BMW does have sales throughout the world, the products are aimed at those people with incomes in the top 1 percent of the citizens on the planet. Can a company be global when it manufactures products that are priced out of reach of over 99 percent of the planet's citizens and is directed by a top management team from a single country? Once again, it depends on the definition of global. In actuality, all human activities, whether business, political or social, have a limited reach and rarely directly affect everyone on the planet.

When the government of Haiti was planning to lower duties on imported cooking oil, public cries of protest were loud.[21] It would put the country's only oil plant out of business—and its 300 employees out of work. The media ran an intensive campaign against liberalization, focusing on the 300 workers. Yet, cooking oil represented 5 percent of the entire budget of Haitian households—and a much larger proportion for poorer families. Since imports would cut the price in half, this meant that liberalization would raise the real income of the average Haitian household by at least 2 percent in one fell swoop. In other words, it would have the impact of a year's worth of GDP growth. The positive impact on poorer households was even greater. But the media ignored the positive impacts. Because they tend to be unorganized and because the impact of price reductions on each individual is small, consumers in developing countries do not have a voice. The special interests such as producers and organized labor are better organized and care more about the specific legislation. As a result, they typically carry the day. The same thing happens in the industrial countries. Increased trade has not driven unemployment in the industrial countries up. While some workers lost jobs due to trade, many more found new ones.

Who benefits from the free movement of ideas, goods, people and capital? The vast majority of the world's population. Necessities such as food and clothing are much cheaper today than they were 10 or 20 years ago. In large part, this is a direct consequence of liberalization and trade expansion. Such gains benefit literally billions of people, while workers who lost their jobs number in the millions, a quantum difference.

Many U.S. retailers have ties to facilities known as sweatshops, which are usually foreign owned and operated. Nike moved production out of the United States to Taiwan and South Korea when U.S. workers demanded better wages. Nike moved production to Indonesia, Vietnam, and China when Taiwanese and South Korean wages rose. Facilities in China that produce clothing for Wal-Mart pay their workers as little as $0.13 an hour. The Gap produces clothing in six factories in Saipan. In Russia, Gap factory workers are paid as little as $0.11 per hour. Wages are low, and overtime is required in these factories. *Sweatshops exist because of corporate greed, international trade policies (that push indebted nations to exploit their own people), and the market's demand for quick production, low costs, and high profits.*[22]

The companies that outsource to less developed nations because of cheap labor are claimed to be exploiting labor in sweatshop factories. As the previous paragraph notes, major U.S. companies have been linked to these sweatshops. But conditions in the sweatshop factories should be compared to the job choices available to the women and men of each respective developing country, not to labor conditions in the United States, Canada, or Europe. To the workers in the sweatshops, their job with Nike beats working in the fields or working for a local firm.

If you want to improve the lives of poor workers in developing countries, should you refuse to do business with any company associated with sweatshops? Just the opposite: You should seek to do business with these companies. When economists looked at reams of economic data on wages and workers' rights in developing countries, they found that multinationals generally paid more—often a lot more—than the wages offered by locally owned companies. Affiliates of U.S. multinationals pay a wage premium that ranges from 40 percent in high-income countries to 100 percent, or double the local average wage, in low-income countries.[23]

Vietnamese workers in foreign-owned apparel and footwear factories rank in the top 20 percent of the Vietnamese population by household expenditure. Indonesian workers in Nike subcontractor factories earned $670 per year, compared to the average minimum wage of $134. In Mexico firms that exported more than 80 percent of their output paid wages that were 58 percent to 67 percent higher than wages paid by domestic firms. So why would workers be willing to accept a dollar or two a day to work in hot conditions for long hours? Because it is better than any other option they have. According to the Institute for International Economics, the average wage paid by foreign companies in low-income countries is twice the average domestic manufacturing wage.[24] These workers are not more productive than American workers; they are not better educated; they do not have access to better technology. The are paid very little by Western standards because they accomplish very little by Western standards. If foreign companies are forced to raise wages significantly, then there is no longer any advantage to having plants in the developing world. In fact, many firms that shipped engineering work to India because their trained engineers earn about 10 percent of U.S. engineers have now found the cost of the Indians has risen so much that it is more profitable to close factories and shops and produce in the United States. If sweatshops paid decent wages by Western standards, they would not exist.

Globalization sets in motion a process that can make poor countries richer; restricting trade makes these countries poorer. When child workers in Bangladesh were found to be producing clothing for Wal-Mart, Senator Tom Harkin proposed legislation banning imports from countries employing underage workers. The direct result was that Bangladeshi textile factories stopped employing children. Did the children go to school or return to happy homes? No. The child workers ended up in worse jobs or on the streets.[25]

Do the large multinational firms exploit the environment, destroying it in the developing nations while selling the goods and services back in the home country? While there are exceptions to the rule, foreign firms tend to behave better environmentally (and socially) than do local firms in the developing countries. Why? Foreign firms value their global reputations, while local firms do not place much value on their reputations in areas such as the environment.

The impact of globalization on income and inequality is a subject that has spawned whole libraries of studies. It is an area where not only is there little or no consensus among disciplines, but also economists themselves have widely differing views. So, what can one say with a fair degree of certainty about growth and inequality in developing countries? Life expectancy at birth has increased considerably around the world. And the gap in life expectancy between the old industrial and the developing countries has narrowed. Everywhere, except in some countries of the former Soviet Union, people live longer than did their grandparents and great-grandparents. Child mortality has declined in every developing region of the world. In South Asia, one of the world's largest concentrations of poor people, average life expectancy at birth more than doubled from only 30 years just before World War II to 63 years today. In Latin America, life expectancy increased from 40 years prior to the war to 70 years today. Even in sub-Saharan Africa, the least developed region, life expectancy increased from 30 years before World War II to about a peak of about 50 years before the AIDS pandemic and other diseases started to force it down to the current level of 47 years. In comparison, life expectancy in the old industrial countries increased from 56 years prior to World War II to 78 today.

Individuals do things that make themselves better off. This point is often lost in the globalization debate. Starbucks does not build a coffee shop in Beijing and then force people at gunpoint to purchase drinks there. People buy the drinks there because they want to. If no one frequented the shops, Starbucks would lose money and close. Do Starbucks, McDonald's, Coca-Cola, and many other major companies change local cultures? Yes. The threat of "cultural homogenization," the worst of it coming from America, is a common complaint against globalization. But, the homogenization occurs only if the consumers want it. The Starbucks in the Forbidden City in Beijing just closed. The reason was that many people were offended by it being located there and wouldn't purchase the drinks there. It was not the fact that the company was Starbucks. Consumers went to other Starbucks located throughout Beijing. They just did not like a company located in the Forbidden City.

Conspiracy

The Prime Directive tells us to look to the market. If we observe or hear about things that we want to understand, we should first ask, do they make sense? Are they created by the market or are they efficient? If not, then we need to ask why not? Is the market not being allowed to work or is it failing for some reason? In the case of suppressed technologies, what is being alleged doesn't fit with the market. The behavior required would mean lost profits or huge opportunity costs. The reason innovation occurs is to seek profits. The reason economic freedom has led to the most rapid standards of living among nations is that the incentive to innovate, to improve living conditions, is greatest when innovators can reap the returns of that innovation. There simply is no incentive for inventions to be hidden, to be kept off the market. The profit potential is too large.

Summary

1. A myth is something that is widely believed but false.
2. Market share translates into profitability is a myth.
3. Profits may lead to an increase in market share as more consumers seek the high quality, low price, or unique goods and services offered by the profitable firm.
4. Growth may be obtained by growing the market, acquiring other firms, extending the brand, or moving into new markets.
5. Growth makes no sense unless it is profitable. In fact, one of the big problems of acquisitions is creating value for the shareholders. Studies show that shareholders of acquired firms tend to do well, while shareholders of acquiring firms lose value.
6. The CEO is often looked upon as having much more influence on the performance of a company than is actually the case.

7. CEO compensation has risen rapidly since the mid-1990s, primarily as the result of stock options.

8. CEO compensation creates incentives for others in a firm or others who are entertaining the idea of becoming a CEO. The compensation structure of executives in a firm may be like a golf tournament or sporting event where huge pay differences may result in the greatest average performance. This is called the tournament effect.

9. If differences among leaders are very small but the results of these difference very large, then compensation differences may be huge. This is called the superstar effect.

10. When CEOs run their companies in the ground, then others may take over the firm and get rid of the CEO. This is called the market for corporate control.

11. There is no incentive for companies to suppress technologies. The profit potential is simply too large.

12. Globalization and free trade are good for societies. Restrictions and limits to trade are bad for societies. This does not mean that free trade is good for individual firms or that restrictions and limits to trade are bad for individual firms.

13. Outsourcing is the process of taking transactions mediated within the firm and having them occur outside the firm. Outsourcing occurs because it increases the efficiency of firms.

14. Outsourcing is good for the firm and for the countries to which the firm outsources. It is not necessarily good for those individuals whose jobs were outsourced.

Key Terms

Winner's curse   Superstar effect

Exercises

1. What are "gains from trade"? What is the primary benefit of trade? Why is the idea that trade is beneficial counterintuitive?

2. What is the difference between "absolute advantage" and "comparative advantage"? How can a less developed country like Mexico have a comparative advantage relative to the United States?

3. Mark Twain, who said, "I'm all for progress; it's change I don't like." What does this mean?

4. Describe the costs and benefits of protectionism. Who gains and who loses? Why are the costs so much more subtle/difficult to see than the benefits?

5. Explain how trade barriers can act as a hidden tax.

6. Can a country have free trade and limited immigration? Can a country engage in free trade in capital and restricted trade in other resources?

7. Are businessmen more likely to be honest than professors? Explain.

8. Explain the following statement: "Environmental quality is a luxury good."

9. According to a recent study, "In the late 19th century, it was popular for executives to strive for revenue maximization" (see J. Scott Armstrong and Kesten C. Green, "Competitor-oriented Objectives: The Myth of Market Share," *International Journal of Business,* 12, no. 1 (2007): 116.) Explain and demonstrate how market share and revenue maximization are related.

10. Explain why suppressed technologies is unlikely to occur in competitive markets. Use the idea of cartels to demonstrate why a conspiracy is unlikely to exist or to last.

11. Look up "planned obsolescence" online and then make a case for and against planned obsolescence in competitive markets.

12. Is there an economic reason that CEOs are given huge compensation packages when they are fired? Could the reason be corruption on the part of Boards of Directors and CEOs?

13. Explain the tournament view of compensation. Would a tournament be more effective if CEOs were hired from people working at the firm or were hired from anyone, those working at the firm or at any other firm?

14. Would you expect to find more corruption in private businesses or in government? Explain

15. It has been proposed that executive pay should not exceed the average non-CEO pay by more than 20 times. Is this a good proposal? Explain

16. What does the following statement mean? The problem with sweatshops is that there are not enough of them.

17. What does homogenization of cultures mean? Is it a necessary consequence of free trade? Explain.

18. Kenyan economics expert James Shikwati says that aid to Africa does more harm than good. He is an avid proponent of globalization and argues that Western development policy in Africa is disastrous. Why would Shikwati be opposed to foreign aid and in support of free trade?

CHAPTER NOTES

1. Market power refers to the inelasticity of demand. The greater the inelasticity, the more market power a firm has. The firm can raise price without losing revenue.

2. Richard Mintner, *The Myth of Market Share* (New York: Crown Business, 2002), p. 25 summarizes these arguments.

3. David Sheff, *Game Over: How Nintendo Conquered the World* (New York: Vintage Press, March 29, 1994).

4. Christopher Megerian, "Console Makers: Move It or Lose It," *Business Week,* August 13, 2007, www.businessweek.com/innovate/content/aug2007/id20070813_409882.htm, accessed May 5, 2008.

5. J. Scott Armstrong and Kesten C. Green, "Competitor-oriented Objectives: The Myth of Market Share," *International Journal of Business*, 12, no. 1 (2007): 115–134, summarizes the studies.

6. Michael Ostrovsky and Gregor Matvos, "Cross Ownership, Returns, and Voting in Mergers," March 2006, Stanford Graduate School of Business Working Papers.

7. Business and Media Institute http://www.businessandmedia.org/specialreports/2006/badcompanyII/badcompanyII_execsum.aspNational Association of Manufacturers http://blog.nam.org/archives/2006/08/are_businessmen.php, accessed, May 5, 2008.

8. Dwight Lee, "Why Businessmen Are More Honest than Preachers, Politicians, and Professors," *The Independent Review*, 14, no. 3 (Winter 2010), pp. 435–444.

9. Peter Navarro, *Well Timed Strategy* (Philadelphia:Wharton School Publishing, 2010), Chapter 1.

10. "The Jack and Jeff Show Loses Its Luster," *The Economist* (U.S. edition), May 4, 2002 (www.economist.com).

11. V. Ramanujam and P. Varadarajan, "Research on Corporate Diversification: A Synthesis," *Strategic Management Journal,* 10 (November/December 1989): 523–553.

12. *Jack: Straight from the Gut* (New York: Warner Business Books, 2001).

13. The rhetoric surrounding mergers is interesting. In most cases, it is claimed that the merger will exploit synergies. However, Dennis K. Berman, "Mergers Horrror II: The Rhetoric," *The Wall Street Journal,* May 24, 2005, p. C1, reports that the common rhetoric of "synergies" has become taboo, and now the argument is in terms of cost cutting.

14. This has been referred to as "the grabbing hand," which seems to make more sense than the term *rent seeking*. Both refer to the idea that a firm or an individual is devoting resources to obtaining a wealth transfer from another sector of the economy rather than producing or generating income. See Andrei Schleiffer and Robert W. Vishny, *The Grabbing Hand* (Cambridge, MA: Harvard University Press, 1998).

15. Y. Amihud and B. Lev, "Risk Reduction as a Managerial Mode for Conglomerate Mergers," *Bell Journal of Economics,* 12 (1981): 605–617.

16. See K. Murphy and K. Hallock, eds., *The Economics of Executive Compensation* (Boston: Edward Elgar Publishing, 1999), for several articles on the issue.

17. For a historical perspective on this issue, see Mark J. Roe, *Strong Managers, Weak Owners* (Princeton, NJ: Princeton University Press, 1994).

18. John M. Abowd and David S. Kaplan, "Executive Compensation: Six Questions That Need Answering," *Journal of Economic Perspectives,* 13, no. 4 (Fall 1999): 145–168; and Brian J. Hall and Jeffrey Liebman, "Are CEOs Really Paid Like Bureaucrats?" *Quarterly Journal of Economics* (August 1998): 653–691. An interesting view of the CEO market is provided in Rakesh Khurana, *Searching for a Corporate Savior* (Princeton, NJ: Princeton University Press, 2002).

19. Roberto Newell and Gregory Wilson, "A Premium for Good Governance," *The McKinsey Quarterly,* no. 3 (2002). Retrieved September 15, 2002 at www.mckinsey.com/practices/CorporateGovernance/articles/index.asp.

20. See among other articles, Robert C. Post, "The Myth behind the Streetcar Revival," *American Heritage Magazine*, 49, no. 3 (May/June 1998), www.americanheritage.com/articles/magazine/ah/1998/3/1998_3_95.shtml.

21. Guy Pfeffermann, "The Eight Losers of Globalization," *The Globalist,* April 19, 2002, www.theglobalist.com/DBWeb/printStoryId.aspx?StoryId=2429, accessed May 8, 2008.

22. Sweatshops: What you need to know. www.mtholyoke.edu/org/action/catalyst/sweat.html; www.webster.edu/woolflm/sweatshops.html.

23. Benjamin Powell and David Skarbek, "Sweatshops and Third World Living Standards: Are the Jobs Worth the Sweat?" September 27, 2004, Working Paper 53. www.independent.org/publications/working_papers/article.asp?id=1369.

24. Edward Graham, *Fighting the Wrong Enemy: Antiglobal Activists and Multinational Enterprises,* Institute for International Economics, September 2000, Table 4.2, p. 92.

25. Paul Krugman, "Hearts and Heads," *New York Times,* April 22, 2001.

CHAPTER **22**

Cases

This chapter presents a set of applications or cases taken from current events. They are of the length and type used as "opening cases" in each chapter. In other words, they are relatively short. Each case is presented and followed by a few questions.

Is Management Necessary?[1]

Once called the most important innovation of the twentieth century, many argue that management does not carry over into the twenty-first. The corporation grew out of the industrial revolution. It has evolved through various organizational forms—the U form, the M form, and so on until today's corporation is seeking ways to deal with the rapid changes occurring in the twenty-first century. Corporations are experiencing an intensified process of creative destruction based on globalization, accelerating innovation, and relentless competition. It took radio 38 years and television 13 years to reach audiences of 50 million people, while it took the Internet only four years, the iPod three years, and Facebook two years to do the same (www.youtube.com/watch?v=GVwWE_WOY0Q).

Clayton Christensen's *The Innovator's Dilemma* argues that leading companies have missed game-changing transformations in industry after industry not because of "bad" management, but because they followed the dictates of "good" management.[2] They listened to their customers, allocated capital to the innovations that promised the largest returns, and in general did what the business schools have told them to do. And in the process, they missed disruptive innovations that opened up new customers and markets for lower-margin, blockbuster products.

Some wonder if, rather than just the manager, it is the corporation that is obsolete. Economist Ronald Coase, in his 1937 work, *The Nature of the Firm,* argued that firms were necessary because they minimized the costs of transacting in the market. Has this defense of the corporation dissolved with the technology that allows mass cooperation? When complicated enterprises, like maintaining Wikipedia or building a Linux operating system, require no corporate management structure, then is one required for anything but a factory? In the book *Wikinomics,* the authors predict the end of corporate hierarchies,[3] as individuals work together in creating "a new era, perhaps even a golden one, on par with the Italian renaissance or the rise of Athenian democracy."

Markets tend to ensure that both people and resources end up employed in the highest valued uses. In corporations, decisions about allocating resources are made by people. They likely have some type of vested interest in the status quo. Change is disruptive—creative destruction is disruptive. The big companies Mr. Christensen studied failed, not necessarily because they didn't see the coming innovations, but because they failed to adequately invest in those innovations. They did not recognize the value of the innovations. As a result, information gathering is a crucial aspect of business in the twenty-first century. Those creatively destructive innovations must be recognized before the company is destroyed. But how will the "wisdom of crowds" be captured; in other words, how can that distributed knowledge be centralized?[4] Can the twentieth-century corporation evolve into this new, twenty-first-century organization?

Exercises

1. What was the role of the manager in the factory-type firm? What does the manager do in the firms that require cooperation from large numbers of diverse people?
2. Is the corporate form becoming inefficient? Are transaction costs being reduced to the point the firm won't be more efficient than the market?
3. What is the twentieth century firm; the twenty-first century?

Passing along Costs

In 2010, the costs of powdered milk, cocoa, coffee, and wheat rose at double-digit rates.

Wildfires in Russia had caused wheat and other crop prices to shoot up. Cocoa prices reached a 33-year high in July, helped along by speculative activities, including the London-based commodity trading house Armajaro Holdings Ltd.'s move to store 240,000 metric tons of cocoa, worth roughly $1 billion. Tea prices went up significantly on account of higher fuel costs and poor harvests in India.

Big consumer-goods companies often find ways to offset the commodity price increases, sometimes through cost-cutting and sometimes by passing along higher prices to retailers and consumers. J.M. Smucker Co. raised prices about 9 percent on products in its coffee lineup, which includes Folgers, Dunkin' Donuts, and Millstone brands. In response to rising milk prices, Danone, which makes yogurt products, increased prices in markets including Mexico and Poland. Unilever's chief financial officer noted that tea costs have gone up, and Unilever has already sent that higher cost down the chain on its consumer tea products.

Exercises

1. Suppose the price of coffee beans increases by $0.20 per pound. What is the effect of this raw material price increase on the demand for roasted coffee? If one pound produces 50 cups of coffee, would the price of a cup of coffee rise by $0.01? Explain.
2. The article reports that J.M. Smucker Co. plans to increase its coffee prices by 9 percent. If Smucker has a lot of rivals but has a brand name that has value, will this 9 percent increase in retail prices imply that profit will rise by 9 percent?
3. Is it optimal for a firm to slash prices to retain market share? Is cutting prices during a recession and then raising them in a recovery a good strategy?

Competition in the Information Economy

Google's stock price had fallen nearly $150 from January 1, 2010 to August 20, 2010, driven by competition from Apple. Apple's iPhone launched a new wave of Web growth on a platform that largely bypassed the browser and Google's search box. The "app" revolution seemed to spell an end to Google's dominance of Web advertising. The declining stock price led many critics to wonder why Google doesn't give more cash back to shareholders in dividends. They argue that all that cash has led the executives running the company to waste money on gimmicky ideas that never pay off.

But Google's CEO does not sound as if he is running a company in trouble. Google estimated that 200,000 Android smartphones were being activated daily by cell carriers on behalf of customers. That's a doubling in just three months. Since the beginning of 2010,

Android phones have been outselling iPhones by an increasing clip and appear destined to outstrip Apple in global market share. This result is primarily because Google gives away Android to handset makers, while Apple sells its phones for large profit margins.

Google is obliged to share with Apple search revenue generated by iPhone users. On Android, Google gets to keep 100 percent. That difference alone is more than enough to pay for Android's continued development. And coming soon is Chrome OS, which Google hopes will do in tablets and netbooks what Android is doing in smartphones.

Google executives say that the real challenge is how to preserve Google's franchise in Web advertising, the source of almost all its profits, when "search" is outmoded. The day is coming when the Google search box and the activity known as Googling will no longer be of much interest. Then what? Google thinks it is not just search but actually knowing people so well that they can answer questions before people even ask them. Let's say you're walking down the street. Google knows what you like and use, and Google knows, to within a foot, where you are. So if you need milk and there's a place nearby to get milk, Google will remind you to get milk. It will tell you a store ahead has a sale on a pair of shoes you like. But before Google gets to that point, it faces ever-growing legal, political, and regulatory obstacles. The net neutrality debate, which Google has led, the brouhaha with China, and growing antitrust, privacy, and patent scrutiny, pushed by rivals such as Oracle and even Microsoft, are troubles remaining with Google.

Exercises

1. Why does Google give away its Android operating system to handset manufacturers?
2. What is the effect of a well-established gmail and calendar account on a Google user's willingness to switch to another provider's services? How does Google benefit from these services?
3. When Google is telling customers where products are located or reminding them that they should pick up some milk, will brand names be more or less valuable?
4. Should the federal government regulate how Google can use the personal information that the company acquires about its users?
5. Will Google's network externalities lead it to be a monopoly?
6. What will net neutrality, relations with China, and antitrust scrutiny mean for Google?

The Yen and the Dollar

The value of foreign deals struck by Japanese buyers in 2010 has nearly doubled to $21.77 billion. This has been induced by a strengthening yen. The yen has strengthened even though the Japanese economy remains very lackluster. The strong yen is good for Japanese companies looking to acquire foreign companies but bad for companies trying to export to other nations. With the higher yen, Japanese companies flush with cash can acquire local foreign businesses to fuel growth more quickly than building their own businesses abroad. Acquisitions of companies with strong domestic demand, such as retail and food sectors, have been particularly attractive. Nippon Telegraph & Telephone Corp. reached a deal to buy Dimension Data Holdings PLC of South Africa for $3.1 billion, making it Japan's biggest deal yet in Africa. Kirin Holdings Co. in July agreed to acquire a stake in Singaporean brewer Fraser & Neave Ltd. for nearly $1 billion, and JFE Holdings Inc. agreed to acquire a minority stake in India's JSW Steel Ltd. for more than $1 billion. In March, Japan's Astellas Pharma Inc. purchased OSI Pharmaceuticals Inc. of Melville, New York for about $4 billion in the biggest deal of this year to date.

A strong yen makes Japan's exports—a cornerstone of the domestic economy—less competitive overseas. That puts pressure on policymakers to take immediate and extensive action to rein in the yen's strength. But the ability of Japanese companies to acquire foreign companies puts pressure on policymakers not to take action. In addition, the same factors pushing the yen up also are pushing Japanese interest rates down, reducing the government's borrowing costs at a time when its massive public debt is under scrutiny.

Exercises

1. What does a strong yen mean?
2. What could cause the yen to strengthen?
3. Why might Japan not want a strong yen?
4. With the various sectors fighting each other in order to influence Japanese policy-makers, what is likely to happen to the yen?
5. Why has the yen strengthened even though the Japanese economy has been in a very sluggish growth pattern for a decade?

New Retail Strategy

September 2010: American retailers are cutting expenses to maintain stable profits through what is increasingly looking like another challenging holiday season. Approaching the 2010 holiday season, stores are looking for ways to maintain profit margins.

Wal-Mart Stores Inc. reported a 3.6 percent gain in second-quarter earnings on August 17, 2010 and raised its annual profit forecast, despite notching negative sales at U.S. stores open at least a year for the fifth consecutive quarter. Home Depot Inc. reported a 6.8 percent quarterly profit jump despite a moderate same-store sales boost of 1.7 percent, and also raised its full-year profit forecast, even as it lowered annual revenue projections. How can you increase earnings with tighter revenue? By reducing costs. Wal-Mart is cutting advertising budgets and resuming its traditional "every day low prices" strategy after aggressive temporary "rollback" price cuts failed to stimulate new sales.

The top retail chains are adapting to the prolonged economic slowdown by reducing employee work hours, maintaining thin inventories, and squeezing costs out of supply chains. Although retail executives have been planning conservatively for months, many had expected the economy to show signs of improvement by this point. Abercrombie & Fitch Co. plans to close 60 of its 1,098 stores this year and 50 next year. The teen retailer reported a 5 percent jump in quarterly same-store sales, but noted that average prices fell 15 percent as stores wage price wars to wrest a bigger share of back-to-school budgets. Urban Outfitters Inc., the apparel company for twenty-somethings that also operates Anthropologie and Free People, voiced similar cautions. Saks Inc. said Tuesday it was closing luxury department stores in Plano, Texas, and Mission Viejo, California, after reporting a quarterly loss of $32.2 million.

Exercises

1. Why don't the stores raise prices to increase revenue?
2. What costs is Abercrombie cutting?
3. Why would stores wage price wars in a declining economy?
4. Is cost cutting in a recession a good strategy? What does it mean when a recovery takes place?

The Black Swan

The Black Swan Theory was developed by Nassim Nicholas Taleb[5] to explain (1) the disproportionate role of high-impact, hard-to-predict, and rare events that are beyond the realm of normal expectations in history, science, finance, and technology; (2) the noncomputability of the probability of the consequential rare events using scientific methods (owing to their very nature of small probabilities); and (3) the psychological biases that make people individually and collectively blind to uncertainty and unaware of the massive role of the rare event in historical affairs.

Is the explosion and resulting oil spill of the BP Macondo well in the Gulf of Mexico a black swan?

An e-mail from a manager at BP said, "WHO cares, it's done, end of story, will probably be fine." This was in regard to the decision to use fewer centralizers when cementing into place the pipe that ran from an oil reservoir 13,000 feet below the sea floor to *Deepwater Horizon,* the drilling rig floating 5,000 feet above it. The cement failed four days after the e-mail was sent, on April 20. Oil and gas rushed up the well, dooming the rig and 11 of her crew.

Was the blowout due to corruption or to bad management? According to BP's partner in the well, Anadarko Petroleum: "The mounting evidence clearly demonstrates that this tragedy was preventable and the direct result of BP's reckless decisions and actions. Some in the American oil industry think this reflects a poor corporate culture at BP, in which personal advancement has depended more on cutting costs than on technical proficiency. When Mr. Hayward, with a background in exploration, replaced John Browne, who was much more associated with finance, in 2007, he emphasized a commitment to safety, with ambitious companywide schemes meant to deliver these results. But chief executives cannot renew cultures without years of protracted and increasingly disseminated effort to that end.

Additional spending of $7 million to $12 million on a safer wellhead piping structure might have prevented natural gas from seeping to the surface and blowing up the rig. So, saving several million has cost BP $20 billion and its shareholders initially $87 billion in stock market value. In 2003, the Interior Department agreed with oil companies that installing a $500,000 acoustic shutoff switch on every offshore rig would be unreasonably expensive (even though such a switch would likely have prevented all that oil from spewing out). Of course, now that BP is staring at billions of dollars in cleanup costs and the prospect of bankruptcy, that $500,000 switch looks like a bargain. A single well out of the thousands drilled and developed by BP across the globe is responsible for wiping out $87 billion in shareholder wealth and causing a cash dividend that was providing a 6 percent yield to evaporate. Severe damage has been done to the shares of Anadarko and Mitsui, BP's partners and Trans-ocean the rig owner. By comparison, Exxon's market cap fell only less than 6 percent in 1989 after the spill in Alaskan waters from a single tanker, the *Exxon Valdez.*

How should black swans be dealt with? Some argue that the *Precautionary Principle* should be followed for every decision. The precautionary principle says that if we are embarking on something new, we should not go ahead until we are convinced it is safe. But this means that many innovations will never see the light of day.

Taleb argues that there should be a redundancy for everything to protect against the results of a black swan event. He points out that Mother Nature has created redundancy—two eyes, two kidneys, and so on. This is what risk management should be about, creating redundancies, and isolating the effects of black swan events.

Taleb also argues that the financial crisis of 2008 was *not* a Black Swan, only the result of fragility in systems built upon ignorance—and denial—of the notion of Black Swan events. He provides an analogy, "You know with near certainty that a plane flown by an incompetent pilot will eventually crash."

Was the well blowout a Black Swan event? Accidents of this type are unusual but not rare. During the last decade, there were 72 offshore blowouts that caused significant spills, compared to 15 the previous decade. Naturally, the more wells that are drilled, and the farther underwater that equipment must operate, the more likely an accident will happen. Despite these facts, BP was so confident that industry risks were overblown that they canceled their accident insurance three years ago. BP clearly decided to save time and money at the expense of safety precautions.

Is preventing a Black Swan event or containing its effects to be examined like any other event? Does the action involve trade-offs? If so, and because it is a low probability event, are the costs of preventing the event or containing the results, simply not worth it. If the odds of an event occurring are .00000000001 and the cost is $100 billion, the expected value is relatively small. In the BP case the odds of a blowout were considerably higher. In fact, investigations and hearings suggest that human errors caused the blowout; it was to be expected.

Exercises

1. What is a Black Swan event?
2. Does it ever make sense a priori to devote resources to preventing a black swan event? Explain.
3. Does it ever make sense a priori to devote resources to containing a black swan event should one occur? Explain.
4. Is human error different than a Black Swan event? Can human error lead to a Black Swan event?
5. If you were BP's executive and you were looking at the cost of a blowout loss of 87 percent market value, possible bankruptcy, and so on, and you were determining whether to spend several million dollars providing redundancies—relief wells drilled at the same time as the main well—how would you decide whether to spend the money?

Privatizing Public Activities

California is looking to shed state office buildings. Milwaukee has proposed selling its water supply; in Chicago and New Haven, Connecticut, it's parking meters. In Louisiana and Georgia, airports are up for grabs. Many communities are using asset sales to balance current budgets. In many cases, the private takeover of government-controlled industry or services can result in more efficient and profitable operations.

The most popular deals in the works are metered municipal street and garage parking spaces. One of the first was in Chicago where the city received $1.16 billion in 2008 to allow a consortium led by Morgan Stanley to run more than 36,000 metered parking spaces for 75 years. Around the country, at least a dozen public parking systems are up for bid, including in San Francisco and Las Vegas. In Pittsburgh, the mayor is proposing to lease out the parking system for an up-front sum of about $300 million over 50 years and funnel the money into the pension system. Among assets being sold all over the country are state and city office buildings. Arizona received national attention in late 2009 when it announced plans to raise more than $1 billion turning over control of public buildings and leasing them back. Much of the money is being used to plug the state's budget hole. Airports also are being privatized under a limited federal program. Deals under consideration for lease include airports in New Orleans and Puerto Rico. Dallas is selling prized outdoor spaces. After turning over operation of the zoo to a private firm, the city is now selling the Farmers' Market and Fair Park.

Why do governments do more than the Constitution stated they should do? Protecting private property rights and a few other minor items were the responsibility of government. Governments typically do not do as good a job as private companies in any activity. Many municipalities have long done a poor job of running their roads, parking spaces, and bridges. Maintenance contracts, for example, are highly political, and with revenues shrinking, infrastructure is increasingly deteriorating. Moreover, private businesses are better at balancing parkers with spaces, advertising, and matching prices with demand.

Critics say buyers are taking advantage of municipalities at a vulnerable time and lack the incentive that governments have to maintain quality. Moreover, some properties are being sold at fire-sale prices into a weak market and will lead to higher costs later.

Municipalities argue that the money they raise could help build more long-term assets, boost efficiency, and avoid raising taxes. Moreover, some wonder why cities should be in all the businesses they are? Why, for instance, should the City of Los Angeles be in the parking business, Milwaukee in the water business, Dallas in the zoo business, and so on?

It is often stated that private for-profit interests will not serve the public. A private water company will not provide the quality the government provides. Besides, water users cannot vote private managers or state-appointed regulators out of office. The experience with private water companies is that they raise prices and provide better service.

Exercises

1. What are the incentives of government bureaucrats who run the water services, the parking services, and airports? Do these incentives differ from those of private companies in running these services?
2. If a business has terrible cash flow but has assets of value, how does the business avoid bankruptcy?
3. Why would the general public want government to provide water rather than a private for-profit company?
4. Why does government do so much more than protecting private property rights?

Job Sharing

Americans work more hours per year than most advanced countries in the world. The table below gives the average hours worked in 2006 for 12 countries, and only South Korea exceeds the United States. But even in South Korea time worked is decreasing: Since 1980, South Korea has had a drop of nearly 20 percent in average hours worked. The United States has hardly changed, however.

Country	Average annual hours worked in 2006	Percentage decrease since 1980
United States	1804	0.8
Canada	1766	2.3
Japan	1784	15.9
South Korea	2305	19.9
Belgium	1571	9.2
Denmark	1577	4.2
France	1564	15.1
Germany	1436	18
Norway	1407	10.9
Spain	1764	11.9
Sweden	1583	−4.4
United Kingdom	1669	5.9
Average of other countries	1675	9.9

With this in mind, a proposal to reduce unemployment, one that has been adopted in several European countries, is to **share jobs.** In July 2010 there were 139 in the United States. If they work an average of 1,800 hours per year, that would be 250.8 billion hours. Now, if workers averaged 1,675 hours a year (lower than current U.S. hours worked but higher than hours worked in Europe), it would take 149.7 million workers, or 10.7 million more than we employ today, to equal 250.8 billion hours. There are 15 million unemployed in the United States in July 2010. So by working the number of hours that western Europe works, all the unemployment problems would be solved.

Exercises

1.   What do you think of this proposal to share jobs? Explain whether it would work.
2.   What would a firm do if law was enacted restricting each employee to 35 hours per week?
3.   Would it make sense to require people to retire at age 50 in order to let younger people have their jobs? Would that reduce unemployment?

How to Nurture the Entrepreneur

In 2010, there were quite a few verbal skirmishes between the Obama Administration and critics over how to promote more entrepreneurship. President Barack Obama held a conference in 2010 called Presidential Summit on Entrepreneurship.[6] Interestingly, the entrepreneurs present remained in the back of the room, while senior government officials led the proceedings. An Administration spokesman had said that "entrepreneurship is a fundamental American value, and it's also a force that has the ability to unlock opportunity for people around the world .... We're hosting no government officials as a part of this. This is a summit that is going to bring together entrepreneurs—social entrepreneurs ... around this question of how we can galvanize entrepreneurship on behalf of economic growth." But the program was led, not by entrepreneurs, but by the secretary of commerce, the administrator of the Small Business Administration, the director of the White House Office of Social Innovation and Civic Participation, and a senior director for global engagement of the White House national security staff. Secretary of State Hillary Clinton provided closing remarks.

Previously, President Obama had described free private enterprise as "a corporate culture rife with inside dealing; questionable accounting practices and short-term greed ... the real problem is not that someone who doesn't look like you might take your job; it's that the corporation you work for will ship it overseas for nothing more than a profit."[7] It is the Obama Administration's belief that government direction of business and civil institutions is absolutely necessary to combat most economic and social problems. It is up to the government to foster and direct entrepreneurship.

There is a serious problem with this view. Entrepreneurship is neither created nor nurtured by government. Without the freedom to learn, discover, and act, the process of entrepreneurship is stymied, and economic progress is not possible. Entrepreneurship is essential to all manner of economic and social improvement. Market-based, proprietary development and voluntary, community-based entrepreneurship, not government command and control, are what makes progress in human well-being possible.

Exercises

1.   Do you agree with the viewpoint expressed here? Explain why or why not.
2.   Can the government increase entrepreneurship by providing subsidies and other benefits for entrepreneurs?

3. Do you agree with President Obama that free enterprise is a corporate culture rife with inside dealing; questionable accounting practices, and short-term greed? Explain.
4. Which would create more entrepreneurship, central planning or freedom, free markets, and competition? Explain.

Private Equity Firms

In 2010 there were many critics of private equity firms. These critics claimed that private equity firms are shaping corporate policy, intensifying the attacks on workers' living standards. Private equity firms are organizations made up of shareholders who band together to seek to influence, and in some cases take over, the boards of publicly traded companies. The critics argue that these groups are, in contrast to the stated focus of a corporate board, uninterested in the long-term viability of a company, instead focusing on the short-term gains to be made by increasing efficiency and shedding less profitable divisions. Once these gains are realized, these large investors often sell their shares and move on to a new target.

One private equity firm to make news in the last year is Trian Group, controlled by billionaire Nelson Peltz. In mid-2005, Trian used a threat to take over the board of Wendy's International, Inc., to force the closure of many stores of its Baja Fresh chain, which had lost money the two previous years. The short-term cost reduction to Wendy's brought with it a more than 25 percent increase in share price. In 2006, Peltz and the Trian Group set their sites on Heinz Foods. Trian is the second-largest shareholder and wants to force Heinz to sell off some of its less profitable operations and lay off several thousand employees.

In the media, spokesmen for private equity funds and corporate executives regularly justify job cuts and plant closures by claiming these measures will "raise shareholder value." According to critics, this is nothing but a euphemism for increasing their control over corporate decision making and focusing on the most short-term profit goals to the detriment of both workers and the long-term viability of a company. The hedge fund and private equity investors are looking for fundamentally sound companies that have taken on too much debt, so they can restructure them and sell them to another buyer for a profit. This prospect spells disaster for workers.

Exercises

1. Do you agree with the viewpoint expressed in this piece? Explain why or why not.
2. Is the private equity firm doing something wrong by cutting expenses, increasing efficiency, and driving up stock prices? Is there a trade-off between the short-run policy of increasing profit and a long-run policy of increasing profit?
3. What is a fundamentally sound company? If it has taken on too much debt is it fundamentally sound? Explain.
4. What do the critics of the private equity firms actually want?

Corporate Governance[8]

Corporate governance structures vary in significant ways around the world. In many countries employees have an important role in running the firm. In Germany, the employees of some firms are allocated some control rights by law, although they have no residual financial claims. The idea is to ensure that capital owners do not control the firm. Capital owners and labor are to "cooperatively" run the firm. Moreover, employees are legally immunized from the wishes of shareholders and management.

The German codetermination system provides an alternative model of corporate governance to the Anglo-American shareholder system. Under the German system of codetermination, firms may be required by law to appoint employees to the supervisory board of the firm. Codetermination laws apply to all German private corporations with more than 500 employees and to all stock corporations. Depending on the size of the firm, employees may constitute either one-half or one-third of the firm's supervisory board. These two codetermination regimes are called parity codetermination and nonparity codetermination, respectively. The board system in Germany is two-tiered: the supervisory board and the management board. The management board runs the day-to-day operations, and its chairman is the firm's CEO. The supervisory board oversees the management board, appoints its members, sets their salaries, and approves major decisions. The management board determines the strategic direction of the firm.

It has been argued that the effect of codetermination is that employees use the firm to resist restructuring, layoffs, and wage reductions. The wage structure in Germany displays relatively little dispersion compared to other developed economies. In addition, wages don't vary over the business cycle as they do in other countries.

Exercises

1. If contracts are incomplete, would allocating some control rights to employees be an efficient way to induce employees to develop firm-specific human capital? Explain.
2. Since the government introduced codetermination by law and shareholders did not voluntarily choose it, is codetermination beneficial to shareholders?
3. How might shareholders attempt to allocate capital to minimize the influence of employees?
4. What are the incentives of the employees on the board? What are the incentives of outside directors? Are they in conflict?
5. Would you argue that less wage dispersion and more stable wages over the business cycle is good or harmful to the company, to the employees, to society in general?

The Regulatory Origins of the Flash Crash[9]

On May 6, 2010, the stock market suddenly swung a thousand points. Nobody really knows why. But Dennis Berman, in the *Wall Street Journal*, has a clue: Maybe the regulators did it. He notes that it results from 1975 market reforms aimed at eliminating market makers who were increasing trading costs by increasing spreads:

> [B]y the time the last big market reforms were issued in 2005, the intent was to "give investors, particularly retail investors, greater confidence that they will be treated fairly," the SEC said at the time.

But now those *greedy* market makers have been replaced by machines, leaving nobody with the responsibility to step in at a time of distress like the flash crash. So according to Berman, we have traded cheaper up-front costs for unknown back-end ones. That is exactly what is spooking the same investors the SEC vowed to protect in 2005.

Congress is now thinking of fixing this system, apparently suggesting that maybe investors are not, in the words of Delaware's Senator Kaufman, "best served by narrow spreads." And we'll undoubtedly get a regulatory fix, perhaps in the form of the Dodd–Frank bill enacted in 2010. But will additional regulations solve matters? Berman quotes Vanderbilt's William Christie: "It's kind of like a balloon—you squish one side and it pops out the other."

Exercises

1. Could it be possible that a government regulation led to the flash crash? Explain.
2. What does it mean "it's like a balloon"? What is like a balloon? Why is it like a balloon?
3. Explain why government regulations to restrict some activity occurring in a free market typically end up making matters worse.
4. Who supported the Dodd–Frank bill? Who opposed it?

DeadHeads[10]

The uninitiated wouldn't associate the Grateful Dead with finance or commerce or business practices of any sort. But this band is, in its various iterations, the most successful touring band of all time.

The band built its success on an approach to the music business that was pure entrepreneurial. While other bands posted signs at the entrances to concert venues saying, "Recording and photography of tonight's performance is strictly prohibited," the Grateful Dead encouraged fans to record their concerts and shoot pictures of the show.

People used to drive around from concert to concert—the Deadheads—with suitcases full of tapes from Dead concerts. Did this taping hurt album sales? No. It served as free marketing for the band.

Scott and Halligan[11] point out that for the Dead, the concerts are the experience they are selling. The scarce good is that particular night's performance, and the band makes each performance radically different. The band in its various forms has done over 2,300 shows, and no two are alike. Not only have the song lists been different each night, but the band plays different versions of all the songs. Instead of only touring periodically in support of a new album, the Dead has toured constantly.

Committed Deadheads have followed the band around to see hundreds of shows. In some cases these fans support their Dead habit by selling merchandise or food items in the parking lot, and this activity is endorsed by the band.

Early on, the band took control of selling tickets to their shows. They cut out the middlemen (such as Ticketmaster) and were able to ensure that their most dedicated fans purchased the best.

Give away what isn't scarce, and make what *is* scarce—live performance—truly scarce and unique. Sell service and upgrades, and always foster loyalty. That is the marketing lesson the Grateful Dead have offered.

Exercises

1. If the Grateful Dead were protected by copyright laws, why did they tend to give away their concerts?
2. Under what conditions does the "economics of free" seem to apply most readily?
3. Under what conditions does it make sense to cut out the middlemen in a transaction?
4. The band has had 19 gold albums, 6 platinum albums, and 4 albums that have gone multiplatinum. How could this occur if the band was giving its music away free?
5. Explain why the Dead supports anyone who sells band merchandise. How does it resemble Amazon's affiliate program?
6. What is the likely cost structure faced by the band in producing its albums and CDs?

The Coffin Cartel

A recent *Wall Street Journal*[12] article discussed the cartel of mortuaries and how it attempts to use the government to restrict entry. Benedictine monks at St. Joseph Abbey near New Orleans decided they would hand-craft and sell caskets. But local funeral directors decided to put a stop to the monks' activities. A Louisiana law makes it a crime for anyone but a licensed parlor to sell "funeral merchandise." Violators can land in jail for up to 180 days.

In the past, funeral homes were monopoly suppliers of caskets. But this monopoly is dissipating. Costco Wholesale Corp. and Wal-Mart Stores Inc. jumped into the casket trade last fall. Some states actively restrict third-party casket sales, but federal law prohibits funeral homes from refusing caskets brought in from elsewhere. So these other suppliers are cutting into funeral home profits.

The monks continued to peddle the caskets while lobbying for the official right to sell them. Their state representatives tried twice, unsuccessfully, to pass legislation broadening casket distribution. But the state board argued that only licensed directors have the training to sell caskets; after all, these are very complicated transactions.

Exercises

1. What rationale might the funeral homes have used to get the legislature to pass a law providing them a monopoly in selling caskets?
2. How much money would the funeral homes devote to fighting the monks?
3. Why would the funeral homes attack the monks but not go after CostCo and Wal-Mart?
4. Most crematories require that the body at least be enclosed and in an acceptably rigid container. The container or casket must be strong enough to assure the protection of the health and safety of the operator. It should provide a proper covering for the body and meet reasonable standards of respect and dignity. Why would crematories require the body be enclosed in "an acceptably rigid container"?
5. Explain how a small group like the funeral home directors can get government to provide them monopoly rights to various transactions.

Business Myths[13]

Several blogs have pointed out what they called "business myths." Some of these are:

1. **To be successful you have to be first.** This is also sometimes reworded as "the first in, wins" or "first mover advantage.".
2. **To be successful, you have to be cheaper.** Take an SBA (Small Business Administration) course, and they will tell you that if your only competitive point is to be cheaper, don't bother starting your business.
3. **I'm a good cook so I should start a restaurant.** "Hey, this meal is fantastic! You should start a restaurant!"
4. **The customer is always right.** You should never tell a customer that you don't want them as a customer any more.
5. **I'll just open my store, and people will stream in off the sidewalks and buy from me.** This is also known as the "If you build it, they will come" approach to business.
6. **It's a cool idea. Everyone will love this.** Often focus groups provide such input to marketers—we love the idea.

7. **Ours is better so we'll be successful.** Quality always wins.

8. **Adding more people to the project will make it go faster.** This is a very common view in the software world.

9. **Failure is bad. Failure is the opposite of success.** This is why dodge ball has been banned in schools and soccer teams are penalized if they get more than five goals ahead of their competitors.

10. **Knowledge is Power.** In the knowledge economy, knowledge is the distinct capability that is necessary for success.

11. **Cash flow is what really matters in business.** Profit can just be a trick of accounting whereas cash flow controls whether you can stay in business. Many companies go out of business due to cash flow challenges, even though they were profitable on paper.

12. **Having more customers is better than having fewer customers.** Would you believe that some companies go out of business because they have too many customers or too much demand for their product?

Exercises

1. Are these myths? Explain why each is either true or a myth.

2. Is it true that: YOU CAN WIN CUSTOMERS JUST by LOWERING YOUR PRICES? Explain.

3. Would you say that you should never form a partnership or a new business with close friends? Explain.

Creative Destruction

Foster and Kaplan,[14] drawing on research they've conducted at McKinsey & Company on more than 1,000 companies over 36 years show that even the best-run and most widely admired companies are unable to sustain market-beating levels of performance for more than 10 to 15 years. They write: "Corporations are built on the assumption of continuity; their focus is on operations. Capital markets are built on the assumption of discontinuity; their focus is on creation and destruction."

They argue that corporations do not change or create value at the pace and scale of markets or entrepreneurs who drive the markets. The philosophy of continuity means that their governance, their control processes, and other aspects that have enabled them to survive over the long haul, deaden them to the vital and constant need for change. Corporations, they argue, must learn to be as dynamic and responsive as the market itself if they are to sustain superior returns and thrive over the long term.

Exercises

1. How can corporations be as dynamic and responsive as the market itself if they are not markets?

2. Does the argument of the book make any sense? How can corporations learn to be as dynamic as markets without experiencing creative destruction as well as creatively destroying?

3. Can a company be an entrepreneur? Explain.

4. What does the following mean? *Corporations are built on the assumption of continuity; their focus is on operations. Capital markets are built on the assumption of discontinuity; their focus is on creation and destruction.*

5. Can any firm "sustain superior returns and thrive over the long term"?

Does Management Theory Offer Anything New?[15]

In an article in the *Atlantic,* Matthew Stewart criticizes business schools, MBA programs, and management theory in general. He makes some interesting remarks and raises questions about management theory. The following is the gist of what he had to say about management theory.

Management theory began with Frederick Winslow Taylor's *The Principles of Scientific Management* in 1911. There was not much science in Taylor's work. Rather, it was some simple measurement. In 1899 he observed men lifting pig iron bars onto a rail car and wondered, "How many tons of pig iron bars can a worker load onto a rail car in the course of a working day?" He measured how much pig iron the best workers could lift, and then he tried to get all workers to be as productive.

Even though Taylor's successors developed statistical methods and analytical approaches to business problems, can it be called science? Many people argue that new solutions are not forthcoming from these approaches to management. In fact, rather than solutions, what is proposed is a fad—first it's efficiency, then quality, next it's customer satisfaction, then supplier satisfaction, then self-satisfaction, and then efficiency again.

In the 1990s, the gurus were unanimous in their conviction that the world was about to bring forth an entirely new mode of human cooperation, which they identified variously as the "information-based organization," the "intellectual holding company," the "learning organization," and the "perpetually creative organization." Tom Peters, in *In Search of Excellence,* called on businesses to "mutilate, destroy that hierarchy." The "end of bureaucracy" is here is a common refrain from management gurus.

But these are not new ideas. According to Matthew Stewart, "The "flat" organization was first explicitly celebrated by James C. Worthy, in his study of Sears in the 1940s, and W.B. Given coined the term *bottom-up management* in 1949. And then there was Mary Parker Follett, who in the 1920s attacked "departmentalized" thinking, praised change-oriented and informal structures, and advocated the "integrative" organization. Then came the "cooperative corporation." And now we hear of the "democratic enterprise."

Where do these ideas come from, and why do they keep appearing? According to Stewart, "Simply because all economic organizations involve at least some degree of power, and power always pisses people off."

Exercises

1. Is management a science?
2. Would you say that management theories come from management scholars or gurus? If so why would they rechannel proposals over and over again?
3. Would you say that management theories are the result of competition in the marketplace—the result of success? If so why would the same theories keep coming back, then being replaced only to appear again?
4. What does Stewart mean when he says "all economic organizations involve at least some degree of power"? Why would this irritate people?

Capitalism and Morality

Business Ethics and Capitalism

In the following essay it is claimed that free market capitalism is consistent with morality. It is also argued that the teaching of business ethics should simply be the teaching of the foundations of the free market.

Every time an economic crisis occurs, there is a thunderous call for teaching more "business ethics" at the university level. This is particularly the case when it is widely thought that a lapse of ethical behavior led to the crisis. What does it mean "to teach ethics"? Is ethics just a branch of philosophy so that spending time with Aristotle and Locke is satisfactory? A few courses are taught as a branch of philosophy. Or is ethics a branch of religion and spending time in the new or old testaments what is desired? Very few courses delve into the "book." Or is ethics a list of what shouldn't be done?

The latter seems to be the most common approach to teaching ethics. Isolated examples of unethical behavior in the business world are used to illustrate actions that should not be undertaken. Many of these illustrations demarcate legal and illegal behavior as if what is legal is moral and what is illegal is immoral. Some courses are based on some aspect of social justice. For instance, many devote considerable time arguing that companies need to take a stakeholder view rather than a shareholder view. The implicit assumption is that a moral company does more than simply earn profit for its shareholders. It takes care of all of its stakeholders—employees, suppliers, local community, larger community, the environment, shareholders, and anyone else affected by actions of the firm. A common statement from professors of business ethics is: We *object to the all too common tendency for business managers to focus on very short-term profits for a very limited constituency (typically stockholders).*

A moral system defines right and wrong and ethic is based on the moral system. Ethics seeks to address questions such as how a moral outcome can be achieved in a specific situation, how moral values should be determined, and what morals people actually abide by. Morality is conduct that enables the human to flourish. Morality can only occur if people are free to reason and act on their reason without coercion.

Morality is consistent only with free market capitalism, what we will call capitalism. Morality requires that people can do what they want with what they own as long as it does not harm others. In other words, a moral system is a system of private property rights and nonaggression. Yet, few are willing to say that capitalism is moral. With the fall of communism, many commentators and politicians grudgingly acknowledged the practical value of capitalism, that the free market is the best system for producing wealth and promoting prosperity. But this has not led to an acceptance that capitalism is moral. Quite the opposite: coercion and the state have only grown.

If capitalism is recognized as the only *practical* economic system—then why is it losing out to state control? The reason is that most people consider capitalism to be immoral. It leads to inequality, companies that exploit workers and consumers and despoil the environment. Consider George Soros's *Atlantic Monthly* article: "The Capitalist Threat," *Atlantic Monthly,* 279, no. 2 (February 1997).

> Popper showed that fascism and communism had much in common, even though one constituted the extreme right and the other the extreme left, because both relied on the power of the state to repress the freedom of the individual. I want to extend his argument. I contend that an open society may also be threatened from the opposite direction—from excessive individualism. Too much competition and too little co-operation can cause intolerable inequities and instability.
>
> Insofar as there is a dominant belief in our society today, it is a belief in the magic of the marketplace. The doctrine of laissez-faire capitalism holds that the common good is best served by the uninhibited pursuit of self-interest. Unless it is tempered by the recognition of a common interest that ought to take precedence over particular interests, our present system—which, however imperfect, qualifies as an open society—is liable to break down.

Soros's view is not a minority view. Many argue that capitalism has to be constrained if it is to be moral. The firm must be forced to take a stakeholder view of its business—*the recognition of a common interest*—rather than just a shareholder view. A corporate stakeholder is commonly defined as any identifiable group or individual who can affect or is affected by the firm. The stockholder approach assumes that the interactions between business organizations and those affected by their operations are most effectively structured as marketplace activities. So, if what is central to capitalism and the stockholder concept is that business relations should proceed along market lines, then the stakeholder view says the market has to be replaced with something else.

This view is wrong. It is coercive and counter to human reasoning. Human flourishing requires reasoned self-interested action. Capitalism is based on this fact. It requires individual or private property rights and nonaggression. All individuals have a right to act on their own judgment for their own sake, as long as they do not violate the same rights of others. This is why capitalism is moral. It enables human flourishing. Acting in one's rational self-interest while respecting the rights of others to do the same is the *basic* requirement of human life. The essence of capitalism is that it bans the use of physical force and fraud in people's economic relationships. All decisions are to be left to the "free market"—that is, to the uncoerced decisions of buyers and sellers, manufacturers and distributors, employers and employees. Capitalism also recognizes the necessity of responsibility. Thus, it seeks to match the liberty of making a decision with the responsibility for the consequences of making said decision. Hence, creators get to own whatever they create, whether it's good or bad. Destroyers are responsible for what they destroy, whether it's good or bad.

But Soros and many others tell us that capitalism fails to promote social justice, that instead it leads to inequality. Capitalism does not lead to egalitarianism, but it does require that everyone have equal rights to life, liberty, and the pursuit of happiness, and this is moral. It is social justice or egalitarianism that is immoral. By definition social justice does not treat everyone equally. It penalizes hard work and skills and rewards the opposite. Most importantly, it is coercive, taking from some to give to others.

We are also told that capitalism leads to bad dealing by businesses. The fact is that free markets lead to just the opposite. It is coercion and control that leads to bad dealing and corruption. Under free markets when a business does engage in bad dealing, the market penalizes it. Customers refuse to do business with the company and/or the company is sued, and the firm's stock price plummets. Capitalism does not guarantee ethical behavior, but it does reward it with profits. Under capitalism businesses cannot gain unless they *serve* the public, not cheat it.

We are told that capitalism means exploitation of employees, not treating employees "fairly." The result of the free market is just the opposite. Capitalism demands that workers be treated fairly in the sense that they are not exploited. A business that does not treat employees in what the employees deem to be fair will lose those employees and have to work harder to attract new ones.

In a free market economy, everyone is driven by his own ambitions for wealth and success. That's what free trade means: that no one may demand the work, effort, or money of another without offering to trade something of value in return. If both partners to the trade don't expect to gain, they are free to go elsewhere. All parties to a voluntary transaction must gain.

A system that sacrifices the self to society is a system of slavery—and a system that sacrifices thinking to coercion—is a system of brutality. This is the essence of any anticapitalist system, whether communist or fascist. And "mixed" systems, such as today's regulatory and welfare state, merely unleash the same evils on a smaller scale. Only capitalism renounces these evils *entirely*. Only capitalism is moral. Only capitalism protects the individual's freedom of thought and his right to his own life.

So much of what goes on in existing economies is immoral because behavior is coerced. Consider the 2008 financial crisis and aftermath. Under capitalism, if an individual or a corporation chooses to create a bank, he or it is free to establish the policy that the bank will offer loans only to individuals and businesses the bank regards as creditworthy. The government may not force the bank to lend money to those it regards as unable to repay a loan or as too risky for business. Nor may the government dictate or limit the interest rates or other terms or conditions that the bank chooses to offer. The bank owner or owners are free to decide how they will run their business at every step and turn; free to open new branches, to purchase other banks, to purchase insurance companies, and to expand or diversify their bank in countless other ways. They are free to maximize their profits and to grow and thrive and prosper to the best of their ability. The only thing they are not free to do is to use physical force or fraud (indirect force) against people. If the bank's policies lead to success, its success is good for the bank, good for its owners, and good for its customers. Remember, the bank can only succeed if it serves customers, that is, gives them what they want and value. If the bank's policies lead the bank to failure, it may not seek a bailout from the government; nor may the government offer to bail out the bank. Under capitalism, bankers and banks, like all individuals and businesses, are responsible for the consequences of their decisions, whether good or bad, profitable or not. Consequently, under capitalism, if a bank fails, it files bankruptcy or offers itself for sale on the cheap or goes out of business; its owners suffer losses; and its customers find other means through which to save or borrow money.

But none of this occurred in 2008; government forced banks to behave as government demanded, and government bailed out and took over banks.

Under capitalism, an automaker is free to manufacture and market cars and the company is free to succeed or to fail accordingly. The government may not force the company to sell a particular kind of car, nor force it to pay its employees a particular minimum or maximum wage, nor force it to contract with a particular vendor, nor a union, nor anyone else. The automaker is free to make all such decisions according to the judgment of its owners. If the automaker uses good judgment and succeeds, it is free to keep, use, and dispose of its profits. If it uses poor judgment and fails—or if its competitors outperform it such that it cannot remain profitable—the automaker may file for bankruptcy or offer itself for sale or close its doors. But it may not seek a bailout from the government. Under capitalism, individuals and corporations legally own not only their profits but also their problems, and the government is prohibited from intervening in the marketplace. But the government has dictated what kinds of autos, their sizes and performances, and the wages that they had to pay employees.

In a system such as the mixed economy, when actions occur because of coercion from government, the system is immoral. Under capitalism, the initiation of physical force is barred from human relationships. Citizens may delegate the use of retaliatory force to their government, which may use force only in retaliation and only against those who initiate its use. Those who initiate force against others are met with force by the law. Government regulation, by contrast, coerces behavior. It subordinates the businessperson's judgment to the decrees of government officials, who impose their will, not by reason, but by physical force.

So why teach business ethics as if morality was anything other than free market capitalism? Just teach what is required for free markets and capitalism to exist and endure and you have taught ethics.

Exercises

1. Define a moral action. Define an immoral action.
2. How can capitalism be a moral system if some people have a great deal of wealth and others very little wealth?
3. What does it mean to act morally? To act immorally?
4. How could capitalism be moral when it leaves some people with so much and others with so little?
5. How can capitalism be moral when greed prevails, individuals stab other individuals in the back, businessmen alter books, embezzle, and otherwise take advantage of others?
6. Is the BP oil well blowup moral or immoral? Is the government's taking of $20 billion from BP to redistribute to the Gulf moral or immoral?

CHAPTER NOTES

1. Alan Murry, "The End of Management," *Wall Street Journal*, August 21, 2010, Weekend Section. Jason Fried, "Getting Real: The Smarter, Faster, Easier Way to Build a Successful Web Application Heinemeier David Hansson, Matthew Linderman, "37signals," *Wall Street Journal,* November 18, 2009 Blogs, July 6, 2010, Gary Hamel, "HCL: Extreme Management Makeover," blogs.wsj .com/management/2010/07/06/hcl-extreme-management-makeover/
2. Clayton M. Christensen, *The Innovator's Dilemma: The Revolutionary Book that Will Change the Way You Do Business* (New York: Harper Paperbacks, 2003).
3. Anthony D. Williams and Dan Tapscott, *Wikinomics* (Portfolio Hardcover, expanded ed., 2008).
4. James Surowiecki, *The Wisdom of Crowds,* (Garden City, NY: Anchor, 2005).
5. *The Black Swan Theory* (New York: Random House Trade Paperbacks; 2nd ed., May 11, 2010).
6. www.america.gov/entrepreneurship_summit.html; April 22, 2010.
7. A speech given on March 3, 2008 at the Constitution Center in Philadelphia.
8. Gary Gorton and Frank Schmid, "Class Struggle inside the Firm: A Study of German Codetermination," Working Paper 2000-025B, research.stlouisfed.org/wp/2000/2000-025.pdf; September 2000, Revised April 2002, Federal Reserve Bank of St. Louis.
9. Posted by Larry Ribstein on August 24, 2010 truthonthemarket.com/2010/08/24/the-regulatory-origins-of-the-flash-crash.
10. Doug French, Secrets of the Most Successful Touring Band of All Time, posted August 23, 2010, Mises.org.
11. David Meerman Scott and Brian Halligan, *Marketing Lessons from the Grateful Dead: What Every Business Can Learn from the Most Iconic Band in History* (Hoboken, NJ: John Wiley, 2010).
12. Jennifer Levitz, "Coffins Made with Brotherly Love Have Undertakers Throwing Dirt," *Wall Street Journal,* August 25, 2010, p. 1.
13. weblogs.sqlteam.com/markc/articles/4280.aspx; rondam.blogspot.com/2006/10/top-ten-geek-business-myths.html; www.morebusiness.com/6-business-myths
14. Richard Foster and Sarah Kaplan, *Creative Destruction: Why Companies that Are Built to Last Underperform the Market—and How to Successfully Transform Them* (New York: Doubleday/ Currency, 2001).
15. This is based on an article appearing in 2006. See Matthew Stewart, "The Management Myth," *The Atlantic,* June 2006.

Glossary

A

absolute advantage   When a country (or individual) can produce a good using fewer resources than another country (or individual).

accounting profit   Revenue less costs not including capital costs.

adverse selection   The lower quality item drives the higher quality out of the market.

antitrust   Against trusts or large firms.

arbitrage   Simultaneously buying an identical item where it is less valued and selling it where it is more highly valued.

architecture   The structure or organization of the firm.

average total cost (ATC)   Cost per unit of output.

B

backloaded or deferred compensation   Compensation increases as time with firm increases—pay exceeds value later in one's work life.

balance sheet exposure   A firm's balance sheet is affected by changes in exchange rates.

best practice frontier   Illustrates given resources and technology, the best use of resources.

bond covenants   Requirements of behavior contained in the bond.

boundaries   The point at which it is more efficient to carry out a transaction outside the firm than inside.

brand name   Characteristic differentiating an item from competitive items.

business cycle   Movement of national output from a trough to a peak and back to a trough.

C

cannibalization   Firm introduces a product that takes sales away from another of its products.

capital structure   The ratio of debt to equity.

capital   Structures, equipment and inventories.

cartel   Individual firms combine to act as a monopolist.

commitment   An expenditure or action that limits choices.

comparative advantage   When a country (individual) produces some good at a lower opportunity cost than its trading partners.

competitive advantage   What a firm does relatively better than others.

complement   Good used together.

complementors   Firms that produce complementary products.

complete contracts.   Agreements accounting for every possible contingency.

constant returns to scale   The relationship between per unit costs are the size or scale of the firm.

consumer surplus   The difference between what consumers are willing and able to pay and what they actually pay.

contribution margin per unit   Ratio of total fixed costs to difference between price and average variable cost.

convention   An institution or procedure that increases efficiency.

core competency   What a firm does best.

corporate culture   Set of collectively held values of behavior.

cost of goods sold (COGS)   Selling general and administrative expenses.

cost-plus pricing   Average cost plus markup.

countercyclical goods   Good for which sales vary inversely with income.

cross elasticity of demand   Percentage change in quantity demanded of one item divided by percentage change in price of a different item.

cyclical goods   Good for which sales vary with income.

D

debt   Capital raised by borrowing.

decay rate   The time it takes for abnormal profit to become zero.

determinants of demand   Factors that affect demand other than own price.

diminishing marginal returns   Combining increasing quantities of variable resources with fixed resource causes marginal output to rise at diminishing rates.

discount rate   Rate at which banks can borrow from the Federal Reserve.

diseconomies of scale   The relationship between per unit costs and the size or scale of the firm.

distinctive capabilities   Unique ability to carry out some activity.

dividend   The amount of profit distributed to each owner of a share of stock.

dominant strategy   The best choice for one player no matter what others do.

dumping   Firm charges less in foreign country than it does in home country for same product.

E

EBIT   Earnings before interest and taxes.

economic profit.   Revenue less all costs.

economies of scale   Cost per unit of output declines as output increases.

economies of scope   Cost per unit of output declines as more different products are produced.

efficiency wage   Pay that is more than market pay to select among the best workers.

efficient   Carrying out an activity at the lowest possible cost.

Elastic   Percentage change in quantity exceeds percentage change in price.

equity   Capital raised by selling ownership.

exchange rate   The price of one currency in terms of another.

expected value   The average amount one expects from a random event.

experience curve   Declining costs resulting from learning and gaining experience.

extensive form   Representation of the decisions and payoffs of a sequential game.

externalities   Not all costs and benefits of a transaction are included in the transaction.

F

federal funds rate   Rate at which banks can borrow and lend from and to each other.

five forces model   Theory that strategy is defined by industry characteristics.

fixed costs   Costs that do not vary as output changes.

foreign exchange   Foreign monies.

free rider   Consuming something without paying for it.

future value   Value in the future of dollar received today.

G

gains from trade   The additional income/output created by trading; amount greater than created by self sufficiency.

game theory   Theory of strategic interaction.

H

Herfindahl–Hirschman index (HHI)   A measure of how a market is divided among firms.

hold-up problems   A necessary resource without substitutes demands extra payment.

I

income elasticity of demand   Percentage change in quantity demanded divided by percentage change income.

income statement   A financial report on the transformation of revenue into net income.

incomplete contracts   Some contingencies are not accounted for in contracts.

increasing returns   Each additional resource adds increasing additional output.

inelastic   Percentage change in quantity is less than percentage change in price.

intellectual property rights   The right to ownership of an idea or the creation from an idea.

internal markets   Using prices to allocate resources inside the firm.

K

knowledge workers   Nonproduction workers.

L

labor   Labor services.

land   Natural resources, land and sea.

limit price   Price set to bar entry.

long run or planning period   Period of time just long enough that everything is variable.

M

M-form, or multidivisional form   Organized by product line or customer type.

make-or-buy   Carry out transaction inside the firm or outside the firm.

Marginal Cost (MC)   Change in cost divided by change in output.

marginal   Incremental.

market failures   Market does not allocate resources efficiently.

market share   The total sales by one firm divided by the total sales of all firms in that market.

market-based exposure   A firm is affected by exchange rate changes because it competes or deals with foreign companies.

matrix   Departments responsible for many activities.

meet the competition clause   Guarantees a firm will match other firms' prices.

mixed bundle   Products purchased individually or as a bundle.

monopoly   The only seller.

moral hazard   Changing behavior after agreeing to a different behavior.

mortgage-backed security   Security created by combining mortgages.

most favored customer clause   Guarantees customers will receive lowest price offered by the firm.

N

nash equilibrium   When no player has an incentive to change.

negative economic profit   Revenue is less than all costs.

net marginal product   Marginal revenue less marginal cost of transferring division.

NOPAT   Net operating profit after taxes.

network effects or network externalities   Each additional user increases value of entire network; the larger a network, the greater the benefits a new member would get from joining that network.

network   Affiliation of independent firms.

normal form representation   Payoffs for a simultaneous game.

O

odd pricing   Price ends in odd number.

one-period game   Players choose strategies only once.

open market operations   Sales and purchases of government bonds by the Federal Reserve.

operating leverage   Ratio of fixed costs to variable costs.

opportunity costs   What must be given up to gain something else.

organizational democracy   Organization without bosses, where employees select who is to be the leader or monitor via democracy.

P

payoffs   The results of each strategy.

peak-load pricing   Price differences dependent on demand.

perfect price discrimination   Each customer pays a different price.

personalized pricing   Prices set according to individual customer price elasticities.

piece-rate   Pay for each unit of output produced.

players   Participants in a case of strategic interaction.

positive economic profit   Revenue exceeds all costs.

predatory pricing   Price set below cost of producing.

prediction markets   Use of markets to forecast events.

present value   Value today of a dollar to be received in the future.

price elasticity of demand   Percentage change in quantity demanded divided by percentage change in price.

principal-agent problem   The agent acts on behalf of the principal but does not have same interests and information as the principal.

private property rights   The right of individuals to do what they want with what they own as long as they don't infringe on the private property rights of others.

product-line extension   Adding features to a product to enable price discrimination.

production possibilities curve (PPC) or frontier   Shows combinations of outputs possible when resources are fully and efficiently used.

public goods   Common ownership; a good that is nonrivalrous and nonexcludable.

pure bundling   Combining products into a single package.

R

rational self-interest   Individuals compare personal costs and benefits.

relationship-specific asset   An asset that can be used in just one situation.

rent seeking   Allocating resources to transfer wealth, not create wealth.

repeated game   Players choose strategies more than once.

reproducible capabilities   Capability of one firm that can be copied by others.

reserve requirements   The percent of deposits that a bank must keep available.

residual income   Income remaining for owners once all expenses are paid.

resource-based model   Theory that strategy is defined by a firm's resources.

risk premium   Extra payment for bearing risk.

S

scarce   Limited; not enough to meet everyone's desires.

scope   The variety of goods and services offered by a single firm.

scorched-earth policy   Punishment strategy—leave nothing behind.

second-degree price discrimination   Quantity discounts.

second sourcing   Licensing brand technology so that the innovator induces others to commit themselves to the innovation.

SG&A   Selling, general and administrative costs.

sequential-move   One player selects strategy before another.

short run or operating period Period of time just short enough that at least one resource is fixed.

simultaneous-move Players select strategies at same time.

stakeholders Anyone affected by a firm's activities.

standardization Products or services are the same for each customer.

strategies The choices players may make.

substitutes Items that can be used in place of each other.

superstar effect Huge compensation differential for very small productivity differentials between the best and second best.

supply chain. The steps of transforming raw materials to final customer product.

sustainable competitive advantage The ability of a firm to retain positive economic profit.

T

tit-for-tat A form of trigger strategy.

trade-offs What must be given up to gain something else.

transfer price The price one division in a firm charges another.

trigger strategies An automatic response to a rival cheating on an agreement.

tying Products must be bought or sold in combination.

U

unit-elastic Percentage change in quantity equals percentage change in price.

U-form or unitary form Single department assigned single business function.

V

variable costs Costs that vary as output varies.

vertically integrated Elements of the supply chain exist inside the firm.

VRIN and VRIO Aspects of the resource-based theory of strategy determining whether resource provides distinctive capabilities.

W

wage compression New employees earn as much or more than long time employees.

weighted average cost of capital (WACC) [cost of debt](debt/total capital) + [cost of equity](equity/total capital).

winner's curse When the winner pays far more for an item than would have been necessary to purchase it.

Z

zero economic profit as normal profit Revenue equals all costs.

Company Index

General Electric (GE), 3, 5–6, 65, 162, 303, 356–358
General Motors (GM), 63, 68, 76, 155, 208, 220, 243, 300, 335–336, 341, 361
Gibson Greetings, 328
Gillette Company, 258, 260, 274
Given, W. B., 381
Glaxo-Wellcome, 187, 256–257
Globastar Canada, 202
Goldman Sachs, 15, 69
Good Humor-Breyers, 329
Goodyear Tire, 208
Google, 110, 157, 270, 277, 288, 302, 342, 369–370
Gore Company. *See* W.T. Gore

H

Halliburton Energy Services, 227
Harros, 188
Heinz Foods, 376
Hewlett-Packard, 6, 83, 168–169, 270, 279, 302, 351
Hires Root Beer, 3
Hitachi Ltd., 226
Hoechst, 225
Holland Sweetener Company, 128, 142, 226–227
Home Depot, 111, 371
Houghton Mifflin, 77, 83, 134
Household Finance, 334
HP Labs, 302
Hudson Automobile Company, 208
Hudson Bay Company, 187
Hyundai, 119

I

IBM Corporation, 4, 7, 63, 96, 189, 202, 226, 270, 279
Intel Corporation, 4, 7, 63, 137, 188, 208, 276, 279, 303
International Harvester, 78
International Paper, 354–356
International Telephone and Telegraph (ITT), 5
Iowa Electronic Markets, 301–303
iPod, 15–156

J

Jabil hardware, 342
Jaguar Motors, 354–355
JFE Holdings Inc., 370
J. M. Smucker, 369
John Deere, 255, 312, 322
Johnson & Johnson, 76–77, 329
J. P. Morgan Chase, 69, 333, 357
JSW STeel Ltd, 370
JVC VHS systems, 157, 173–174

K

Kellogg Company, 3
Kirin Holdings Co., 370

Kodak. *See* Eastman Kodak
Kohlberg, Kravis, and Roberts (KKR), 68
Kornitzer Capital Management LLC, 73n.9

L

Laker Airways, 341
Lands' End, 63
Lehman Brothers, 69, 333
Lever Brothers, 118
Lexmark, 168–169
Lincoln Electric, 92–93, 99, 341
Linear Company, 262–263
Lions Gate Entertainment, Inc., 73n.9
Liqui-Box, 209–210
Long-Term Capital Management, 328

M

Marks and Spencer, 5, 7
Marlboro, 6
Martin Marietta, 356
Matsushita, 4
Mazda Miata, 30–31, 149–150, 152
McDonald's, 5–7, 40, 113, 364
McDonnell Douglas, 166–168
McGraw Hill, 77
MCI Communications, 167
Merck Corporation, 110, 113, 146n.3
Merrill Lynch, 69, 336
Mervyns LLC, 220
Micron Corporation, 337
Microsoft, 4, 7, 64, 120, 167–168, 173, 202, 208, 263, 279, 288, 303, 351–352, 370
Miller Brewery, 5
Monsanto, 84, 128, 226–227
Moody's rating agency, 334
Morton Thiokol, 356
Motorola, 162
MPSI Systems, Inc., 209
Mrs. Fields' Cookies, 224
MTV, 111

N

Napster, 271–272, 282n.3
Nasdaq Composite Index, 287–288
National City Lines, 361
Nestlé, 6
New Century Financial, 334
Newsweek, 129–131
Nike, 5, 77, 362–363
Nintendo, 351–352
Nippo Telegraph & Telephone, 370–371
Nordstrom, 136
Northwest Airlines, 121–122, 139–142
NutraSweet, 128, 142

O

Office Max, 166, 261–262
Oracle Software, 328, 370
OSI Pharmaceuticals Inc, 370
Oticon, 307–308

P

Packard Company, 208
Paramount, 84
Parker Hannifin Corporation, 263
Payless Shoe Source, Inc., 220
Peapod.com, 253
Pepsi-Co, 76–79, 128, 142
Pets.com, 158, 351
Pharmacia, 84
Philip Morris, 5
Phillips Petroleum, 361
Prest-O-Lite, 208
Price Club, 6
Procter & Gamble, 4, 63, 78, 118, 259–260, 328
ProShare, 208
Prudential Insurance, 188
Pruett Industries, Inc., 227
Publisher's Clearinghouse, 257

Q

Quaker Oats, 6, 64, 321–322

R

RadioShack Corp., 220
RCA Corporation, 278
Revco, 165–166
Richtek Technology, 263
Rite Aid, 165–166
RJR Nabisco, 68
Rowntree, 6
Royal Caribbean Cruise Line, 329

S

Safelite Glass Corporation, 99–100
Saks Inc., 371
SAP-KhiMetrics, 209–210, 260
SAS Airways, 3–4
Satmetrix, 210
Schick Company, 258
Sears Company, 63, 300
Siemens AG, 303
Singer, 78
SmartEdge platform, 284
Snapple, 6
Softsoap, 118
Solectron, 77
Sony Corporation, 4, 6, 157, 221–223, 225–226, 230n.6, 351–352
Southern Pacific, 167
Southwest Airlines, 7, 111, 185–186, 329
Spirit Airlines, 121–122
Sprint, 167
Standard Oil Company, 165, 223, 300, 361
Standard & Poor's 500, 287–288, 334
Staples, 166, 261–262
Starbucks, 5, 111, 113, 117, 156, 182, 188, 364
Stern-Stewart, 327n.9
Sun Country Airlines, 139–142
Swatch, 111

Subject Index